Using
Assembly Language

Allen L. Wyatt

 Que™ Corporation
Carmel, Indiana

Library of Congress Catalog No.: 87-060813
ISBN 0-88022-297-2

90 89 88   5 4 3 2

Interpretation of the printing code: the rightmost number of the first series of
numbers is the year of the book's printing; the rightmost number of the second
series of numbers is the number of the book's printing. For example, a printing
code of 85-1 shows that the first printing of the book occurred in 1985.

This book was written for DOS version 3.30. The examples in this book should
work with the following versions of LINK.EXE, MASM.EXE, and LIB.EXE:

LINK.EXE versions 3.51 through 3.60
MASM.EXE versions 4.00 through 5.00
LIB.EXE versions 3.02 through 3.07

Dedication

Dedicated to my God,
who gives me talents to develop and the ability to work,
and to my wife, Debbie,
who gives me the freedom and latitude to do so.

Product Director
David Solomon

Editorial Director
David F. Noble, Ph.D.

Acquisitions Editor
Pegg Kennedy

Editors
Gail S. Burlakoff
Jeannine Freudenberger, M.A.
Rebecca Whitney
Steven L. Wiggins

Technical Editor
V. Mitra Gopaul

Book Design and Production
Dan Armstrong
Sharon Hilgenberg
Jennifer Matthews
Joe Ramon
Dennis Sheehan
Carrie L. Torres

About the Author

Allen Wyatt has been working with small computers for more than ten years, and has worked in virtually all facets of programming. He has published several books related to programming and programming languages. He is the president of Discovery Computing, Inc., a microcomputer consulting and services corporation based in Zionsville, Indiana. In his spare time, Allen likes to spend time with his wife and children doing the things that families do together.

Contents at a Glance

Table of Contents

Part I
Interfacing Assembly Language with Other Programming Languages

Part II
Assembly Language Tools

Part III
Advanced Assembly Language Tools

13 Accessing DOS Services 329

Part IV
Intel Processor Instruction Sets

Instruction Set for the Intel 8088 447

Instruction Set for the Intel 80286 497

Instruction Set for the Intel 80386 557

Instruction Set for the Intel 8087 Numeric Coprocessor 639

Instruction Set for the Intel 80287 Numeric Coprocessor

A ASCII Character Set

B The Disk Base Table

Trademark Acknowledgments

Que Corporation has made every attempt to supply trademark information about company names, products, and services mentioned in this book. Trademarks indicated below were derived from various sources. Que Corporation cannot attest to the accuracy of this information.

Advanced Trace86 is a trademark of Morgan Computing Co., Inc.

AT Probe, PC Probe, Software Source Probe, and Mini Probe I, II, and III are trademarks of Atron Division of Northwest Instrument Systems.

CodeSmith–86 is a trademark of Visual Age.

COMPAQ 386 is a registered trademark of COMPAQ Computer Corporation.

ICD286, PDT-AT, PDT-PC, and RBUG86 are trademarks of Answer Software Corp.

IBM is a registered trademark of International Business Machines Corporation. OS/2, PCjr, PC XT, and Personal System/2 are trademarks of International Business Machines Corporation.

Intel is a registered trademark of Intel Corporation. I^2ICE is a trademark of Intel Corporation.

LATTICE C COMPILER is a registered trademark of Lattice, Inc.

Microcosm is a trademark of Microcosm, Inc.

Microsoft, MS-DOS, and XENIX are registered trademarks of Microsoft Corporation. CodeView is a trademark of Microsoft Corporation.

Motorola is a registered trademark of Motorola, Inc.

Periscope I, Periscope II, Periscope III, and Periscope II-X are trademarks of The Periscope Co., Inc.

Pfix86+ is a trademark of Phoenix Technologies Ltd.

ProKey is a trademark of Rosesoft, Inc.

SideKick and Turbo Pascal are registered trademarks of Borland International, Inc.

Introduction

Welcome to *Using Assembly Language*, a book written to help you learn how to use assembly language subroutines to increase the performance of your programs.

If you write programs in BASIC, Pascal, or C on the IBM® family of microcomputers and you want to "make the most" of your programming, you'll find *Using Assembly Language* a helpful learning aid and reference guide. Each carefully designed chapter is packed with detailed information about the use of assembly language subroutines in high-level language programs.

I've written from a programmer's perspective, trying to teach by precept and by example, and have included detailed reference materials. I've done my best to convey information as clearly as possible.

So that you (as a programmer) can understand *why* what happens happens, I've emphasized the effects of assembly language instructions, commands, and functions—how they are used and what they produce. With any luck, there should be no "black boxes" here—nothing mysterious or questionable. You should simply learn how to make better use of your particular IBM environment through assembly language.

The computer field changes quickly, seeming to go from simple to complex almost overnight. *Using Assembly Language* lays a firm foundation of the precepts and underlying concepts on which complex ideas are built. I've tried to simplify many of the concepts that the assembly language programmer must understand, without going so deep that all interest in and focus on the guiding precepts is lost.

I've included many examples that you can try out on your computer. Working through these examples on the computer (or even in your mind) should help you to retain key ideas. I recommend that you use the computer.

Clearly, *Using Assembly Language* is not intended as light, after-dinner reading. It is meant to provide a sound basis in the principles of developing assembly language subroutines, tapping the internal power of BIOS and DOS functions, and interfacing assembly language subroutines to high-level language programs. You can use many sections of the book as reference.

Why Use Assembly Language?

You may ask, "Why should I use assembly language?" There's no easy answer. The reasons for using assembly language vary, depending on the application in which you use it and the high-level language you use as the controlling program. A brief look at the development of high-level languages may help you better understand the value of assembly language.

Assembly language once was the only language available for microcomputers. But with the advent of such powerful high-level languages as BASIC, Pascal, and C, many programmers learned only these languages. Compared to assembly language, they were easy to learn and provided most of the functions ordinarily needed to program. Assembly language was often relegated to programmers in research labs (and padded cells).

Over time, as applications became increasingly complex, the limits of various high-level languages were tested and pushed about as far as they could go. Surely you have experienced the frustration of knowing that there must be a faster, slicker, more efficient way to do something than what you can do with the high-level language you're using. This frustration has led some programmers either to change languages (in hopes of finding one that addressed most, if not all, of their needs) or to accept the limitations of their current high-level language.

No language is perfect. High-level languages are no exception—they all have strong points and corresponding weak points. And that's where assembly language subroutines come in: we can use them to augment the capabilities of the high-level languages in which we program.

The benefits of programming well-defined tasks in assembly language fall into four general areas: *speed, versatility, flexibility,* and *compact code.*

Assembly language is *fast*. To paraphrase an old saying, "It don't get any faster." During the assembly process, assembly language mnemonics translate directly into machine language—the native language for computers. No language is faster than machine language—its execution speed is the fastest possible on any given computer. Because assembly language is the root of all high-level programming languages, assembly language runs faster than any of these languages.

High-level languages can be *interpretive, compiled,* or *pseudocode*. Interpretive and pseudocode (a cross between interpretive and compiled code) languages require some translation into machine language at the time of execution. It is true that, depending on the implementation of the language, some high-level languages, once compiled, require no such translation at run-time. But assembly language source code files, once assembled, never require translation; they have no overhead penalty of greater execution time.

Assembly language is *versatile*. Anything that can possibly be done with a computer can be done with assembly language. The only limiting factor is the capacity of the computer system you're using.

Many high-level languages are designed to execute on a wide variety of computers, each of which has different capabilities and peripherals. These languages are designed for the "lowest common denominator" so that they cover the capabilities and peripherals likely to be on virtually every machine on which they may run. Assembly language has no such artificial limitation. Because the capabilities of your specific machine are the only limiting factor, assembly language allows great versatility in program development.

Although specifically suited to a particular type of CPU, assembly language is *flexible*. Assembly language gives you a multitude of ways to accomplish one task.

Some languages have rigid coding restraints that restrict the number of approaches to coding a particular task. Assembly language has no coding restraints. If your coding style is undisciplined, this degree of freedom may present drawbacks—you can easily end up with "spaghetti code." But if you are a disciplined, structured person (or at least write disciplined, structured code), you'll find the flexibility of assembly language refreshing. Mastering the language can be both challenging and rewarding.

Assembly language produces *compact code*. Because assembly language routines are written for a specific purpose in a language that translates directly into machine language, these routines will include only code that you, the programmer, want included.

High-level languages, on the other hand, are written for a general audience and include extraneous code. For instance, many high-level languages include intrinsic graphics functions or file-handling functions that can be used only by a limited number of applications. Needed or not, this irrelevant coding is included in every application.

Because assembly language mnemonic instructions translate directly into one (or, at most, several) bytes of data, there is no overhead, unless you specifically choose to include it in your executable file.

What You Should Know

In any book, assumptions are made about what the reader knows. Those assumptions may be stated up front or may become clear after you've read the book. Before you read this book, you need to know what the assumptions are.

First, I assume that you know at least one of the high-level languages—BASIC, Pascal, or C—used throughout this book. (If you know more than one of these languages, you will benefit even more from *Using Assembly Language*.)

You should be familiar with ASCII, the native coding scheme used for character representation on the IBM PC family of microcomputers. Many assembly language subroutines in this book (and elsewhere) use and manipulate ASCII characters. You don't need to memorize the entire code, but you may want to keep an ASCII table within reach while you work through this book.

Because you're reading this book, I assume also that, at one time or another, you have had experience programming and that you are familiar with the different numbering systems commonly used with microcomputers: binary (base 2), decimal (base 10), and hexadecimal (base 16). If you're familiar with octal (base 8), so much the better—but you don't have to be. *Using Assembly Language* doesn't delve into the differences between numbering systems or the reasons for using binary and hexadecimal. If you have trouble working with any of these systems, writing assembly language code should quickly provide all the familiarity you could ever want.

Depending on your programming background, you may be familiar with many differing notations for numbering systems. Because of the inherent possibilities for confusion when you work with decimal, hexadecimal, and binary numbers, some sort of notation is needed to differentiate between the systems.

This book's approach to notation is simple but straightforward: I append a lowercase *b* to *b*inary numbers and a lowercase *h* to *h*exadecimal numbers; decimal numbers have no appendage (see table I.1).

As you can see from this table, binary and hexadecimal numbers occupy an even number of digits. Every digit within a binary number represents a *bit*. Every two digits of a hexadecimal number represent a *byte*, or eight bits, and every four digits represent a *word*, or two bytes. As an assembly language programmer, you must learn to think in groupings—bits, bytes, and words.

Speaking of words—the other kind—you should be familiar with certain rudimentary terms. You'll find a glossary at the end of this book, but the following definitions should prove helpful at this point and throughout this book:

Table I.1
Number Representation

Binary	Decimal	Hexadecimal
00001110b	14	0Eh
01101011b	107	6Bh
10111011b	187	BBh
11010101b	213	D5h
0000000110110000b	432	01B0h
0000001001010101b	597	0255h
0000001101100111b	871	0367h
0000101111111111b	3071	0BFFh
0101111111111000b	24568	5FF8h

Assembler: The software program that translates (assembles) assembly language mnemonics into machine language for direct execution by the computer.

Assembly: A process of code conversion, done by an assembler, that translates assembly language source code into machine language.

Assembly Language: The English-style language (also called *source code*) that is understandable to humans. Assembly language is not directly executable by computers.

Linking: The process of resolving external references and address references in object code. The resulting machine language instructions are directly executable by a computer.

Machine Language: The series of binary digits executed by a microprocessor to accomplish individual tasks. People seldom (if ever) program in machine language. Instead, they program in assembly language and use an assembler to translate their instructions into machine language.

Object Code: A half-way step between source code and executable machine language. Object code, which is not directly executable by a computer, must go through a *linking* process that resolves external references and address references.

Source Code: The assembly-language instructions written by a programmer and then translated into object code by an assembler.

What Is in This Book

Whenever I pick up a book, the first thing I want to know is whether the book will help me. Will it teach what I need to know?

You can see from the table of contents that *Using Assembly Language* covers many technical areas related to assembly language programming. For easy reference, the book is divided into four parts. The following is a quick outline of the contents of each chapter.

Part I, "Interfacing Assembly Language with Other Programming Languages." Chapter 1, "An Overview of Assembly Language," introduces you to the basics of programming in assembly language. This chapter touches on the structure, main commands, and operations needed to use assembly language.

Chapter 2, "Interfacing Subroutines," covers general information about interfacing assembly language subroutines with high-level language programs.

Chapter 3, "Interfacing with BASIC," provides specific information and examples on using assembly language subroutines from both interpretive and compiled BASIC. In Chapter 4, "Interfacing with Pascal," you will find specific interfacing information for programs written in Pascal. And Chapter 5, "Interfacing with C," details how to interface assembly language subroutines with the popular C language.

Part II, "Assembly Language Tools." Chapter 6, "Using MASM," explains how to use Microsoft®'s Macro Assembler (MASM) to translate assembly language instructions into machine code.

Chapter 7, "Using the Linker," covers how to link successfully assembled programs. LINK parameters and file types are included in this chapter.

Chapter 8, "Debugging Assembly Language Subroutines," shows how to use the DEBUG command set to locate, isolate, and correct errors and problems in assembly language subroutines. This chapter includes a variety of software and hardware debuggers available to aid in program development.

Chapter 9, "Developing Libraries," covers the creation, use, and management of object file libraries of assembly language subroutines.

Part III, "Advanced Assembly Language Topics." Chapter 10, "Video Memory," provides extremely detailed information on how to manipulate (from assembly language) the memory areas that control the display of information on a computer monitor.

Chapter 11, "Accessing Hardware Ports," covers working at the hardware level from assembly language. Examples include accessing the keyboard and speaker controllers.

Chapter 12, "Accessing BIOS Services," details the different BIOS interrupts and services and the various tasks they perform. Corresponding information for the different DOS interrupts and services is included in Chapter 13, "Accessing DOS Services."

Part IV, "Intel Processor Instruction Sets." Five sections provide detailed reference information for the Intel 8086/8088, 80286, 80386, 8087, and 80287.

Using Assembly Language contains three useful appendixes. Appendix A presents the standard ASCII character codes. Appendix B lists the disk base table, a set of parameters that controls the operation of a disk drive. The BIOS keyboard codes and keyboard controller codes are included in Appendix C.

Finally, *Using Assembly Language* contains a brief glossary.

What Is Not Covered in This Book

Using Assembly Language is packed with information—but cannot possibly cover all related subjects. This book has limits.

First, this book does not teach *high-level languages*. In fact, it does not purport to teach any language. Its purpose is to show how to make two languages—assembly language and either BASIC, Pascal, or C—work together for the benefit of both the program and programmer.

As you read and work through this book, you probably will learn something about each of these languages. You'll undoubtedly learn a great deal about assembly language, but please don't feel that you've learned it all. Learning how to do things well takes *years*—and by then the rules have all changed. And don't be surprised if someday you learn from another source a quicker, easier way to do a task than what you learn here. Part of the fun of living is that people keep developing new ideas and methods.

Programming style is a big deal for many authors. Style is fine, and promotes logical thinking, but I believe that coding must meet only a few criteria:

- *Is the code intelligible?* Adequate remarks (perhaps for every line) and appropriate line formatting help.

- *Will others understand the code?* Because you may not be the one hired to make changes to the code a year from now, you *must* write for those who follow.

- *Does it work?* In my opinion, this is the most important criterion of all.

This book does not adhere to any published or unpublished set of programming conventions or techniques. My goal is for this book to provide clear, concise, intelligent, working code to help you become more productive. You can organize and optimize your software by simply applying to assembly language programming the same logical structures and common sense encouraged by high-level languages.

Graphics programming, because of its specialized nature, is beyond the scope of this book. Entire volumes can be written about true graphics and graphic manipulation. Indeed, graphics routines are well suited for being written in assembly language. For example, the sheer volume of data that must be processed to perform animation demands a level of speed available only through assembly language.

Writers, programmers, and others often misuse the word *graphics*. Text screens are frequently referred to as "graphics" screens. This confusion arises because, on the IBM, certain ASCII codes correspond to special characters that are neither textual nor numeric, but clearly graphic. Although these characters permit you to enhance an otherwise bland text screen, the screen is not a true graphics screen. Text screens deal with data on a character level; graphics screens manipulate data on a pixel level.

Using Assembly Language **does** cover the use of textual graphics and color. Library routines that allow all sorts of snazzy screen creations (using text characters) with assembly language drivers from high-level languages are discussed and developed.

Summary

I hope that you now have a sense of what this book is, as well as what it isn't. Because I've felt the need for this type of book, writing it has been important to me. Ideally, you also have felt that need and will benefit from reading and working with *Using Assembly Language*.

Now, if you are ready, let's begin the process.

Part I

Interfacing Assembly Language with Other Programs

Includes

An Overview of Assembly Language
Interfacing Subroutines
Interfacing with BASIC
Interfacing with Pascal
Interfacing with C

1

An Overview of
Assembly Language

Before examining how assembly language routines are combined with high-level languages, let's take a look at assembly language.

This is a *quick* introduction to assembly language, not an exhaustive discussion on the development of assembly language programs. It is meant to give a flavor of the language, touching on its structure, and the main commands and operations that you must know to use the language effectively from BASIC, Pascal, or C.

Conceptual Guide to Assembly Language

Assembly language is similar to many other computer languages. At their root, computer languages provide a set of building blocks that the programmer can arrange in a specific manner to create programs. It just so happens that the building blocks in assembly language are smaller (and less singularly powerful) than those in high-level languages.

The concept of building blocks should already be familiar to you. As you program, you use commands, variables, and words that are almost like English words to instruct the computer what to do. These words eventually are translated into machine code, a series of numbers that the computer understands. But as far as the programmer is concerned, the work is done with the building blocks, not with the numbers used by the computer.

As I've already stated, the building blocks in assembly language are smaller and less singularly powerful than those in high-level languages. Let's take a moment to examine this statement.

Programmers who work with high-level languages do not have to concern themselves directly with many operations that occur "behind the scenes." For instance, you generally do not need to be concerned with *where* and *how* your data will reside in the computer's memory. These matters are arranged either by the compiler or by the *run-time system* used by your language. A run-time system is a system manager that oversees the proper operation of the language during program execution.

Another example of these "behind the scenes" operations is the use of what I will call *compound commands*. For instance, consider the BASIC statement

```
PRINT "This is a test"
```

Pascal uses this syntax to accomplish the same task:

```
writeln('This is a test');
```

C uses this syntax:

```
printf("This is a test\n");
```

All three of these statements accomplish basically the same task. They print to the current output device (usually assumed to be the display monitor) a string of characters followed by a carriage return and line feed. Inherent within the PRINT, writeln( ), and printf( ) commands, however, are several smaller commands that do other tasks related to displaying the information. These smaller commands locate the information to display, determine where to display it, handle how the information is to be displayed, and handle the carriage return and line feed at the end of the string.

In assembly language, little happens "behind the scenes." You must specify virtually everything related to the composition, storage, and execution of your program or subroutine. For example, if you want to perform the equivalent of printing a string (as previously done) in assembly language, the following lines will accomplish the task:

```
MSG             DB          'This is a test',13,10,'$'
                MOV         DX,OFFSET MSG
                MOV         AH,09h
                INT         21h
```

Although many other elements (which are covered later in this book) must be added to make this an executable statement, this example should help to clarify the point that the programmer must be extremely specific when working in assembly language. This need for specificity requires that, to perform even relatively simple tasks, you use much more source code than you would with a high-level language.

Another point may not be quite as obvious in this example: data must be declared explicitly. If you are accustomed to working in Pascal or C, you will not have to change your programming habits much. BASIC programmers, however, will need to get used to declaring data elements explicitly. Later in this chapter I will discuss how assembly language data is defined and how it is manipulated.

You already should be able to see that, *conceptually*, assembly language is the same as any other computer language—it allows you to instruct the computer to perform specific tasks. Depending on your background, however, you may find the *application of the concepts* radically different.

The assembly language development process is similar to that for many high-level languages. There are several distinct phases:

- Source code generation or editing
- Assembly
- Linking
- Execution

If your high-level language uses a compiler and linker, you will notice that this process seems familiar. The second step (assembly) is analogous to the compilation step of high-level language development. The third step (linking) generally uses the same linker that you are already familiar with. The point is that the development process is no different from the steps most high-level language programmers currently perform.

The 25-Cent Tour of Memory

Because assembly language inherently involves working at a level that is much closer to the computer than other languages, you need to understand how your computer uses memory. (Memory and memory management are generally handled automatically and "behind the scenes" by other languages.)

The IBM PC, running under PC DOS or MS-DOS®, has up to a total of 640K of memory available (655,360 bytes of storage). However, the entire 640K is not available to the assembly language programmer. Certain areas are reserved for BIOS (the Basic Input/Output System) and DOS. Other areas are considered as system areas that hold information which allows BIOS and DOS to function properly. Still other areas may have user-installed resident programs such as SideKick® or ProKey™. A typical memory map is shown in figure 1.1.

If it weren't for some of the memory management functions built into DOS, the average programmer would have difficulty not running into memory conflicts with other programs. Later in this book, you will see how to use DOS functions to request blocks of memory for your program.

BIOS/DOS Interrupt Vector Tables
DOS Work/System Area
Device Drivers
COMMAND.COM (resident portion)
KBFIX2.COM (resident keyboard program)
MSPOOL2.COM (resident print spooler)
SMARTKEY.COM (resident program)
SK.COM (SideKick resident program)
Free memory
Video Buffers
ROM Area

Fig. 1.1.
Sample memory map.

Microprocessors use an address register to keep track of where in memory operations should be occurring. The size of the address register generally dictates the maximum amount of memory that can be used in a computer. You can determine the number of directly addressable memory locations by raising 2 to a power represented by the number of bits in the address register. Table 1.1 shows the amount of memory that is addressable by various address register capacities.

Each addressable memory location requires its own unique address. Two memory locations cannot have the same address; if they did, operations affecting the locations would become jumbled. Imagine what would happen if your house and your neighbor's house had the same address—without additional information, the mailman wouldn't know what mail went to which house.

Table 1.1
Addressable Memory by Address Register Size

Address Register Bits	Addressable Memory (bytes)	Memory Size
8	256	
9	512	
10	1,024	1K
11	2,048	2K
12	4,096	4K
13	8,192	8K
14	16,384	16K
15	32,768	32K
16	65,536	64K
17	131,072	128K
18	262,144	256K
19	524,288	512K
20	1,048,576	1M
21	2,097,152	2M
22	4,194,304	4M
23	8,388,608	8M
24	16,777,216	16M
25	33,554,432	32M
26	67,108,864	64M
27	134,217,728	128M
28	268,435,456	256M
29	536,870,912	512M
30	1,073,741,824	1G
31	2,147,483,648	2G
32	4,294,967,296	4G

The IBM's processor uses an instruction pointer (IP) to keep track of the machine-language instructions that are currently being executed. This pointer is simply a 16-bit address register specialized for this purpose. From table 1.1, you can determine that 16 bits can hold unsigned integers in the range of 0 to 65,535.

As you know, the IBM (running under PC DOS or MS-DOS) can have up to 640K of memory. If the IP can hold only up to 65,536 values, how can each of 655,360 possible memory locations be addressed? Holding the 655,360 values necessary for 640K of memory would require an address register of at least 20 bits. The obvious solution would have been to use a larger register size. But

Intel® (the developers of the CPUs used in IBM microcomputers) used a more indirect, and potentially confusing, solution.

Intel used a *segment register* to control the general area of memory being pointed to, with the IP as an offset pointer into that segment—each segment of memory can be up to 65,536 bytes (64K) in size. This scheme was a radical departure not only from the memory addressing schemes used in earlier microprocessors but also from that used by other microprocessors such as the Motorola® 68000 family. Suddenly, the program could address directly a maximum of only 64K of memory.

Through segment notation, each memory location can be addressed individually in the format

   SSSS:OOOO

where SSSS is the segment and OOOO is the offset. Memory locations given in this format are always in hexadecimal notation. The segment portion of the address can range from 0 to FFFFh and, depending on the segment, the offset portion also can range from 0 to FFFFh.

The absolute address of any memory location can be determined by multiplying the segment value by 10h (which is the same as 16 decimal) and then adding the offset value. Thus, the absolute location of 1871:321F is determined by 18710h plus 321Fh, or 1B92Fh. Based on this addressing notation, it would seem logical that the total addressable memory could range from 0000:0000 (0) to FFFF:FFFF (1,114,095)—slightly over 1 megabyte of memory. Remember, however, that the limit for PC DOS or MS-DOS is 640K; therefore, the calculated absolute memory between the segment and the offset cannot exceed 655,360.

Clearly, memory segments can overlap, and one memory location can be addressed in many ways. Table 1.2 shows the notation of several memory addresses, all of which refer to the same absolute memory location.

To create figure 1.2, addresses were attached to the memory map shown in figure 1.1. The address in your system may vary (sometimes greatly) depending on your memory configuration, DOS version, program use, and other factors.

When you program in assembly language, you generally do not need to be concerned about where your program or subroutine will physically reside. The linking process, and subsequent DOS loaders, will take care of positioning your program and getting it ready to execute. If you want more information concerning where the program will reside, a number of technical manuals deal with how programs are loaded and how they begin execution. If you find this topic interesting, you may want to note the differences between .COM and .EXE files as outlined in those manuals.

Table 1.2
Segment/Offset Pairs Address Absolute Memory Location 027920h

2792:0000	2515:27D0
2791:0010	2292:5000
2790:0020	1F93:7FF0
278F:0030	1D90:A020
2777:01B0	1AFF:C930
26D0:0C20	1A74:D1E0
2654:13E0	17A5:FED0

00000h	BIOS/DOS Interrupt Vector Tables
00500h	DOS Work/System Area
04C00h	Device Drivers
05400h	COMMAND.COM (resident portion)
0E0A0h	KBFIX2.COM (resident keyboard program)
0E8E0h	MSPOOL2.COM (resident print spooler)
1E720h	SMARTKEY.COM (resident program)
26F70h	SK.COM (SideKick resident program)
37A80h	Free memory
A0000h	Video Buffers
C0000h	ROM Area

Fig. 1.2.
Sample memory map with addresses.

Although you don't need to worry about where the program or subroutine will reside, you do need to worry about segment and offset notation for addressing specific data in memory, such as system parameters or vector addresses. That specific topic is covered shortly.

The Stack

A special segment of memory, called the *stack*, is reserved for the temporary storage of data. To program effectively and efficiently in assembly language, you must understand the stack. Even though you may already be familiar with the concepts behind a stack, let's take just a moment to cover them again. Later sections of this book present assembly language instructions and routines that rely on the stack; thus, the basics must be covered now.

If you have never worked with one, a stack can be a little confusing at first. The stack is simply a last-in, first-out (LIFO) queue. It may sound strange, but the stack operates in a fashion similar to the spring-loaded plate servers in a cafeteria line. Each plate that is placed on the server makes the previous plates inaccessible by conventional means. Conversely, removing a plate makes the one under it immediately accessible. Plates can be removed only in the reverse order of their placement on the server. The last plate added is always the first to be removed.

In the conceptual representation of the stack shown in figure 1.3, notice that each box contains one word (16 bits) of data. The boxes can be removed in the reverse order of their placement on the stack. Only data at the top of the stack is accessible by conventional means. Data is shown as individual bytes, even though it can be deposited or extracted from the stack only one word (two bytes) at a time.

On the IBM PC, data is always stored on and removed from the stack one word (16 bits) at a time. Even if you need to store only one byte of data, you must deposit (and later remove) a full word.

Throughout this book, you will see references to the stack. Some specific assembly language commands cause information to be deposited in the stack; others cause the information to be removed. This depositing and removing frequently results from another action that you want to perform. As I discuss the assembly language mnemonic commands, I will touch on these specific operations that affect the stack.

The stack is integral to passing information from the high-level language to assembly language. Generally, information to be passed is pushed on the stack and then removed as needed by the assembly language routine. The process is

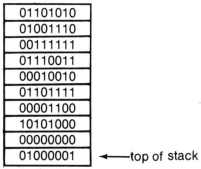

Fig. 1.3.
Conceptual representation of the stack.

covered in detail in Chapters 2 through 5, which discuss parameter passing to assembly language subroutines.

If you are a little confused about how the stack operates and why it is important in assembly language programming, don't despair—it's normal. As you work through the examples in this book, pay particular attention to how operations affect the stack. Doing so should help to clarify the concepts introduced here.

If you are quite confused about the stack, reread this section until you begin to grasp the concepts. Understanding the stack is crucial to concept development.

Segments and Classes

As you know, the IBM family of microcomputers uses processors that address memory by using segment and offset addresses. When you program in assembly language, segments are set either explicitly, by loading the segment registers, or implicitly, through assembler directives to the linker.

But there are segments—and then there are segments. So far, I have talked about segment addresses and how they are used. This is the logical use of the word *segment* for the Intel 8086/8088/80286/80386 microprocessors. To program effectively in assembly language, you need to understand these segments and their use.

Another type of segment, however, is used by the macro assembler and linker developed by Microsoft®. Because many different assemblers and linkers are based on standards developed by Microsoft, and because MASM is the assumed assembler for those reading this book, we need to look at this alternate (and potentially confusing) use of the word *segment*.

When you write assembly language source code, a segment is simply a group of instructions that all operate relative to the same segment address. It is difficult not to confuse assembly language segments with memory segments. But they are not directly related. Assembly language segments are simply a block of coding delineated by an explicit starting and ending point. To avoid potential confusion, in certain other assemblers these coding sections are called PSECTs (for program sections) rather than SEGMENTs.

At the beginning of any group of instructions (usually at the beginning of the code in the file), the assembler directive SEGMENT is used to signify the start of a segment. At the close of the group of instructions, the ENDS directive is used. The assembler and linker then use these directives to delineate the explicit start and end of groups of assembly language code.

The following example shows how the SEGMENT and ENDS directives might be used in an assembly language file:

```
CODE            SEGMENT BYTE PUBLIC 'CODE'

        assembly language coding goes in this area

CODE            ENDS
```

Let's take a look at each portion of this SEGMENT directive. The first occurence of the word CODE is the name of the segment (I've used CODE arbitrarily). Notice also the corresponding use of CODE with the ENDS directive.

The word BYTE directs the assembler to place this segment at the next available byte in the object file. In the example, BYTE is the *align type* of the segment. A segment can be aligned to a byte, word, paragraph, or page. BYTE starts the segment at the byte following the end of the preceding segment. WORD begins the segment at the next even address. PARAgraph begins the segment at the next hexadecimal address that ends in a 0. PAGE begins the segment at the next hexadecimal address that ends in 00. Table 1.3 summarizes these align types.

The word PUBLIC is a declaration of the segment's *combine type*. The combine type, which is optional, denotes how a segment will be combined with other segments that have the same name. Several different combine types are possible (see table 1.4). For the vast majority of purposes that involve writing subroutines which will be incorporated into high-level language programs, the combine type will be PUBLIC.

The word 'CODE' is the segment's *class type*. This name, which must be enclosed in single quotation marks, signifies the groupings to be used when the different segments are linked. All segments of a given class type are loaded

Table 1.3
Align Types Possible with the Microsoft Assembler

Type	Description
BYTE	Segment is placed at the next available byte in the object file
WORD	Segment is placed at the next available even byte in the object file
PARAGRAPH	Segment is placed at the next available paragraph boundary in the object file. Address of the segment will end in a 0.
PAGE	Segment is placed at the next available page boundary in the object file. Address of the segment will end in a 00.

Table 1.4
Combine Types Possible with the Microsoft Assembler and Linker

Type	Description
PUBLIC	Results in all segments with the same name being joined into one segment when linked. All addresses and offsets in the resulting segment are relative to a single segment register.
STACK	All segments with this combine type are joined to form one segment when linked. All addresses and offsets in the resulting segment are relative to the stack segment register. The SP register is initialized to the ending address of the segment. This combine type normally is used to define the stack area for a program. The Linker requires that one stack segment be defined.
COMMON	Same as PUBLIC, except that the segments are not joined to form a new, large segment. All COMMON segments with the same name begin at the same point; the resulting segment is equal in length to the longest individual segment.
MEMORY	Works exactly like the PUBLIC combine type

Table 1.4—cont.

Type	Description
AT	Used to prepare a template that will be used for accessing fixed location data. In the format AT XXXX (where XXXX is a memory address), AT signifies that addresses and offsets are to be calculated relative to the specified memory address.

contiguously in memory before another class type is begun. In the directives example, the segment belongs to the 'CODE' class type. It will be grouped with other segments of the same class type.

Normally, you will use only one class type when you prepare assembly language subroutines for use from high-level languages. Sometimes this class type is specified by the high-level language you are using. (This topic is covered in Chapters 3, 4, and 5.)

Registers and Flags

The 8086/8088 and subsequent generations of microprocessors use *registers* to operate on data and to perform tasks. Registers are special storage areas built into the microprocessor. All registers are 16 bits (one word) wide, but some operations can be performed on only one byte (eight bits) of specific registers. Table 1.5 shows the 8086/8088 register set.

The four general-purpose registers (AX, BX, CX, and DX) can be addressed also by their component bytes. For instance, AH and AL are the individual bytes that make up the word register, AX. The H and L indicate, respectively, either the high byte or low byte. Similarly, BH and BL comprise BX, CH and CL make up CX, and DH and DL comprise DX.

The stack, segment, and instruction pointer registers are discussed in the following section. Understanding the flag register will help you understand the 8086/8088 instruction set introduced in the next section of this chapter.

The flag register is the same size as the other registers (16 bits) but uses only nine bits to signify status flags. These flags, shown in table 1.6, are set or cleared based on the results of individual operations.

Notice from table 1.6 that only nine flags are represented in the flag register. Bits 1, 3, 5, and 12 through 15 of this register are not used. Each of the other bits can, of course, be set to either 0 or 1. A 0 indicates that the flag is clear; a 1 indicates that the flag is set.

Table 1.5
The 8086/8088 Register Set

Name	Category	Purpose
AX	General Purpose	Accumulator
BX	General Purpose	Base
CX	General Purpose	Counter
DX	General Purpose	Data
SI	Index	Source index
DI	Index	Destination index
SP	Stack	Stack pointer
BP	Stack	Base pointer
CS	Segment	Code segment
DS	Segment	Data segment
SS	Segment	Stack segment
ES	Segment	Extra segment
IP		Instruction pointer
FLAGS		Operation flags

Table 1.6
Usage of the 8086/8088 Flag Register

Bit	Use
0	Carry flag (CF)
1	
2	Parity flag (PF)
3	
4	Auxiliary carry flag (AF)
5	
6	Zero flag (ZF)
7	Sign flag (SF)
8	Trap flag (TF)
9	Interrupt flag (IF)
10	Direction flag (DF)
11	Overflow flag (OF)
12	
13	
14	
15	

Certain assembly language instructions are used to set or clear individual flags. These instructions, which generally are referred to as *Flag and Processor Control* instructions, will be detailed shortly. Other instructions set or clear individual flags to indicate the result of a previous operation. For instance, the zero flag (ZF) is set if the result of an arithmetic operation is zero, and cleared if the result is not zero.

A group of instructions referred to as *Control Transfer* instructions are used to test the value of the flags and then, based on the result, to conditionally transfer program control. To program effectively in assembly language, you need to understand what the flags are and how they are used.

The Segment Registers

The processors used in the IBM family of microcomputers have four different segment registers that are used for addressing: the code, data, extra, and stack segments.

The code segment register (CS) contains the segment used with the instruction pointer register (IP). Thus, CS:IP contains the segment and offset of the next instruction to be executed by the processor.

The data segment register (DS) contains the segment used by general-purpose data operations. It is used also as the source segment for string operations.

The extra segment register (ES) is used as the target segment for string operations. It can be used also as a secondary segment register for general-purpose data operations.

The stack segment register (SS) is used as the reference segment for the stack, and is used with the stack pointer (SP). Thus, SS:SP points to the top of the stack, the last place where information was stored in the stack segment.

When you write small routines for use from high-level languages, most segment registers are set to the same addresses. In most instances, the code and data segments can be set to the same values so that the data used by the subroutines is actually part of the coding. This approach simplifies subroutine development. Exceptions to this approach occur when you want to set up or use a specialized data area, in which case the DS or ES registers would be changed. The most common such occurrence is when these registers are changed to point into the data areas used by the high-level language. Many of the sample programs in this book use this technique.

When you are writing subroutines, don't change the stack segment. This register generally is set by the controlling program. You don't need to change it within your routines. Changing it without knowing the full use of the stack, or changing it without restoring its value, can result in undesirable side effects.

The Assembly Language Instruction Set

The actual mnemonic instructions used by the assembler and subsequently translated into machine language depend on the type of microprocessor being used in the computer. The IBM PC and PC XT™ (and their clones) use the Intel 8088; the IBM Personal Computer AT uses the Intel 80286. Newer computers use the Intel 80386. The new generation of MS-DOS or OS/2™ computers, including the IBM Personal System/2™ line, all use one of these three microprocessors.

All of these microprocessor chips are *upward compatible*, which means that anything programmed for the 8086/8088 will run on the 80286 and 80386, and anything programmed for the 80286 will run on the 80386. These processors are not *downward compatible*, however. Software written for the 80386 will not necessarily run on the 80286, and that written for the 80286 may not run on the 8086/8088.

Each generation of microprocessor has added different instructions and operating modes to the basic set used in the 8086/8088. These improvements have prevented the processors from being downward compatible. In addition, you might have a numeric coprocessor in your computer that will make it possible to add even more assembly language instructions. These chips are usually called the 8087, 80287, or 80387 numeric coprocessors.

Because of the diversity of possible assembly language instructions, and because of the installed base of computers using the 8086/8088 and the upwards compatibility of 8086/8088 code, the discussions of specific assembly language instructions will focus on that instruction set. All assembly language examples in this book are written to work on the 8086/8088; they will work also on computers that use the 80286 and 80386 microprocessors.

Approximately 116 different assembly language mnemonics for the 8086/8088 can translate to 180 different machine language codes, depending on their context usage. The assembler takes care of the actual translation into machine language (see Chapter 6).

What may seem a formidable number of assembly language instructions is not as bad as it seems. Most of the time, only a handful of these instructions are used. Other instructions are used less often but are still available as you need them. Other microcomputer chips include even more instructions and provide correspondingly greater power to the programmer.

Because of the sheer number of assembly language instructions, only those for the 8086/8088 are listed in this chapter. They are listed also, with detailed instruction information, in Part IV, as are the corresponding instruction sets for the 80286, 80386, 8087, and 80287.

Table 1.7 shows the different classes of assembly language mnemonics for the 8086/8088. Notice that the instructions are divided into six different groups, depending on the type of operation that they perform. Also listed are the individual assembly language instructions that comprise each group.

Table 1.7
The 8086/8088 Microprocessor Instruction Set

Data Transfer Instructions

IN	Input from port
LAHF	Load AH register with flags
LDS	Load DS register
LEA	Load effective address
LES	Load ES register
MOV	Move
OUT	Output to port
POP	Remove data from stack
POPF	Remove flags from stack
PUSH	Place data on stack
PUSHF	Place flags on stack
SAHF	Store AH into flag register
XCHG	Exchange
XLAT	Translate

Arithmetic Instructions

AAA	ASCII adjust for addition
AAD	ASCII adjust for division
AAM	ASCII adjust for multiplication
AAS	ASCII adjust for subtraction
ADC	Add with carry
ADD	Add
CBW	Convert byte to word
CMP	Compare
CWD	Convert word to doubleword
DAA	Decimal adjust for addition
DAS	Decimal adjust for subtraction
DEC	Decrement by 1

Table 1.7—cont.

Arithmetic Instructions

DIV	Divide, unsigned
IDIV	Integer divide
IMUL	Integer multiply
INC	Increment by 1
MUL	Multiply
NEG	Negate
SBB	Subtract with carry
SUB	Subtract

Bit Manipulation Instructions

AND	Logical AND on bits
NOT	Logical NOT on bits
OR	Logical OR on bits
RCL	Rotate left through carry
RCR	Rotate right through carry
ROL	Rotate left
ROR	Rotate right
SAL	Arithmetic shift left
SAR	Arithmetic shift right
SHL	Shift left
SHR	Shift right
TEST	Test bits
XOR	Logical exclusive-or on bits

String Manipulation Instructions

CMPSB	Compare strings, byte for byte
CMPSW	Compare strings, word for word
LODSB	Load a byte from string into AL
LODSW	Load a word from string into AX
MOVSB	Move string, byte by byte
MOVSW	Move string, word by word
REP	Repeat
REPE	Repeat if equal
REPNE	Repeat if not equal
REPNZ	Repeat if not zero
REPZ	Repeat if zero
SCASB	Scan string for byte
SCASW	Scan string for word
STOSB	Store byte in AL at string
STOSW	Store word in AX at string

Table 1.7—cont.

Control Transfer Instructions

CALL	Perform subroutine
INT	Software interrupt
INTO	Interrupt on overflow
IRET	Return from interrupt
JA	Jump if above
JAE	Jump if above or equal
JB	Jump if below
JBE	Jump if below or equal
JC	Jump on carry
JCXZ	Jump if CX=0
JE	Jump if equal
JG	Jump if greater
JGE	Jump if greater or equal
JL	Jump if less than
JLE	Jump if less than or equal
JMP	Jump
JNA	Jump if not above
JNAE	Jump if not above or equal
JNB	Jump if not below
JNBE	Jump if not below or equal
JNC	Jump on no carry
JNE	Jump if not equal
JNG	Jump if not greater than
JNGE	Jump if not greater than or equal
JNL	Jump if not less than
JNLE	Jump if not less than or equal
JNO	Jump on no overflow
JNP	Jump on no parity
JNS	Jump on not sign
JNZ	Jump on not zero
JO	Jump on overflow
JP	Jump on parity
JPE	Jump on parity even
JPO	Jump on parity odd
JS	Jump on sign
JZ	Jump on zero
LOOP	Loop
LOOPE	Loop while equal
LOOPNE	Loop while not equal
LOOPNZ	Loop while not zero
LOOPZ	Loop while zero
RET	Return from subroutine

Table 1.7—cont.

Flag and Processor Control Instructions

CLC	Clear carry flag
CLD	Clear direction flag
CLI	Clear interrupt flag
CMC	Complement carry flag
ESC	Escape
HLT	Halt
LOCK	Lock bus
NOP	No operation
STC	Set carry flag
STD	Set direction flag
STI	Set interrupt flag
WAIT	Wait

As you can tell from table 1.7, there are quite a few assembly language mnemonics. Don't be overly concerned, however. Some mnemonics, although they appear to be different in this table, translate to the same machine-language value. For instance, JZ and JE perform the same task and translate to the same value. Even though the instructions test the same flags and make branching decisions based on the condition of those flags, more than one mnemonic is provided so that the programmer can write code that is easier to understand in the context of the task being performed.

Although this chapter does not discuss each of these instructions in any depth, you need to understand what each instruction does and how the instructions affect the flags and registers. Each of these instructions is outlined in detail in Part IV.

Data Storage in Memory

Data is stored in the computer's memory as a series of bytes. In the discussion of addressing, I stated that the IBM PC, operating under PC DOS or MS-DOS, could normally address up to 640K of memory. Special hardware or software makes expanded memory above the 640K boundary accessible, but the use of such expanded memory is beyond the scope of this book. The normal 640K work area has 655,360 individual bytes, each of which can store a specific, individual value. Because each byte is made up of 8 bits, and each bit can have a value of 0 or 1, each byte can store a value in the range of 0 through 255.

As you program in assembly language and then assemble and link the programs you create, your instructions (if syntactically correct) will be translated into individual bytes of information that the microprocessor later uses to perform tasks. To the computer, no physical difference exists between *machine language program instruction bytes* and *data bytes*. To the programmer, a distinction is vital to ensure that data bytes do not overwrite coding bytes while the program is executing.

Several methods are available for setting aside data areas in an assembly language program. The usual method involves the use of data definition *pseudo-ops*. Another related, but distinctly different, method of defining data is through the use of equates. Let's take a look at each of these areas, focusing on equates first.

Equates

Equates do not set aside memory area for data. Instead, the assembler uses them as substitute values later in the program. For instance, the following set of equates can be used to define the IBM color set.

```
; ------------------------------------------------------------
BLACK           EQU       Ø
BLUE            EQU       1
GREEN           EQU       2
CYAN            EQU       3
RED             EQU       4
MAGENTA         EQU       5
BROWN           EQU       6
WHITE           EQU       7
GRAY            EQU       8
LT_BLUE         EQU       9
LT_GREEN        EQU       1Ø
LT_CYAN         EQU       11
Lt_RED          EQU       12
LT_MAGENTA      EQU       13
YELLOW          EQU       14
BR_WHITE        EQU       15
; ------------------------------------------------------------
```

This usage is helpful because remembering RED is much easier than remembering that 4 is equal to the color red. In this fashion, the following commands are functionally the same, although the first one is considerably more understandable to humans:

```
MOV       AH,LT_BLUE
MOV       AH,9
```

Both commands result in the value 9 being placed in the AH register. In the following section, other uses for the EQU directive will become apparent.

Data Definition Pseudo-ops

A pseudo-op is simply an assembly language mnemonic that the assembler interprets and uses. No corresponding machine language instruction is generated. Pseudo-ops differ, depending on the assembler being used.

In assembly language programs, data is defined through the use of several different pseudo-ops that instruct the assembler to set aside specific amounts of memory for the program to use at a later time. Optionally, you can direct the memory to be filled with specific values. Table 1.8 shows the different assembly language data definition pseudo-ops.

Table 1.8
Data Definition Pseudo-Ops and Their Meanings

DB	Define Byte (1 byte)
DW	Define Word (2 bytes)
DD	Define Doubleword (4 bytes)
DQ	Define Quadword (8 bytes)
DT	Define ten bytes (10 bytes)

Each of the data definition pseudo-ops sets aside memory for subsequent use by your program. They can be further modified and made more powerful through the use of the DUP and OFFSET operators. Understanding how all these pseudo-ops function may be easier if you see how they are used in a program. Look at the following selected data declarations in a program:

```
; -------------------------------------------------------------------
ORIG_DRIVE      DB      ØØ
ORIG_PATH       DB      64 DUP(Ø)
PRE_PATH        DB      '\'
PATH            DB      64 DUP(Ø)

ANY_FILE        DB      '*.*',Ø

DIR_TABLE       DB      256 DUP(19 DUP(Ø))

BREAK_INT_SEG   DW      ØØ
BREAK_INT_OFF   DW      ØØ
```

```
CMD_TABLE        EQU     THIS BYTE
                 DW      OFFSET ACTION_CMD
                 DW      OFFSET DOIT_CMD
                 DW      OFFSET DRIVE_CMD
                 DW      OFFSET PATH_CMD
                 DW      OFFSET EXIT_CMD

ACTION_CMD       DB      'SELECT',Ø
DOIT_CMD         DB      'DELETE',Ø
DRIVE_CMD        DB      'DRIVE',Ø
PATH_CMD         DB      'PATH',Ø
EXIT_CMD         DB      'EXIT',Ø

ONE_MOMENT       DB      'Examining diskette ... One moment please!',Ø

; ------------------------------------------------------------------
```

These few lines set aside and define a data area 5,084 bytes long. Further, they provide a structure in which data can later be referenced in the program. Referring to each line by its name, let's look at what the different usages of data definition pseudo-ops accomplish in this example.

ORIG_DRIVE is defined as a variable one byte long, initially set to 0. Also, ORIG_PATH is set to an initial value of 0 but, through use of the DUP function, ORIG_PATH is defined as 64 consecutive zeros. Notice that ORIG_PATH can only be referenced directly as a byte value. For instance, the command

    MOV   AH,ORIG_PATH

would work, because a byte value (the first of the 64 bytes of ORIG_PATH) is being loaded into a byte register. However, the line

    MOV   AX,ORIG_PATH

would not work, because the assembler will not allow 8 bits to be loaded directly into 16.

The following example shows how to override this declared reference to ORIG_PATH as byte values only:

    MOV   AX,WORD PTR ORIG_PATH

The use of WORD PTR tells the assembler that even though the label ORIG_PATH is a reference to a byte value, you want to reference the word that begins at the address associated with ORIG_PATH.

PRE_PATH is similar to ORIG_DRIVE, except that here the byte is being set to 92, the ASCII value of the backslash character. ANY_FILE translates directly to the following four individual bytes:

```
 42      46      42      ØØ
  *       .       *
```

DIR_TABLE becomes an area of zeros 256 * 19, or 4,864 bytes long. Notice that you can use DUP multiple times in the same declaration, thereby improving readability.

BREAK_INT_SEG and BREAK_INT_OFF set aside one word each, and initially set the contents of those memory locations to zero. Later, the contents of this named memory location can be loaded directly into a register by a line similar to

    MOV   AX,BREAK_INT_SEG

CMD_TABLE is set up, through the use of EQU and THIS BYTE, to reference the first byte of an area that will later be used as an offset table to other values. In this case, the five words beginning at CMD_TABLE are set equal to the offset addresses of other variables. In this way, the messages ACTION_CMD, DOIT_CMD, DRIVE_CMD, PATH_CMD, and EXIT_CMD can all be accessed by address, even though each message is of a different length.

Finally, ONE_MOMENT is a series of bytes that spells the message Examining diskette . . . One moment please!, followed by a zero, or null byte.

Addressing

The 8086/8088 offers a multitude of ways to address data: register-to-register, immediate addressing, direct addressing, and several different types of indirect addressing. Because you will use each of these methods as you program, you need to understand them now.

Each addressing mode always has a source and a destination. The destination is always to the left of the comma; the source is always to the right. In addition, both direct and indirect addressing assume an implied addressing segment. Let's take a look at each type of addressing and any applicable segment addressing assumptions.

Register Addressing

Register addressing is the fastest type of data addressing. These instructions take fewer physical bytes, and the entire execution of the instructions is performed in the CPU. If your data needs are small within certain subroutines, always perform manipulations within registers. Some examples of this type of addressing are

MOV	AX,BX
MOV	DX,CX
MOV	DI,SI

These instructions result in the contents of the register to the right of the comma being copied into the register to the left of the comma. Thus the contents of BX, CX, and SI are copied into AX, DX, and DI, respectively. Notice that the contents are *copied*, not simply *moved*. On completing the first instruction, then, AX and BX contain the same values.

Immediate Addressing

Immediate addressing causes a constant numeric value to be placed into a register or a memory location. Consider the following instructions:

RED	EQU	4
LOC_1	DB	ØØ
LOC_2	DW	ØØØØ
	MOV	AX,5
	MOV	BL,RED
	MOV	LOC_1,RED
	MOV	LOC_2,5

In all instances, a constant value (right of the comma) is being placed at the specified destination (left of the comma). The specified destination is either a register or a memory location. Notice that several of these instructions use equates instead of specific numbers. Remember, however, that when the coding is assembled, the correct numbers will be substituted for the equates. Thus, all occurrences of RED will be replaced by 4, making the statement of the immediate-addressing type.

Direct Addressing

Direct addressing differs from immediate addressing in that direct addressing moves data from a memory location to a register, or from a register to a memory location. The following instructions illustrate this type of addressing:

```
LOC_1           DB          ØØ
LOC_2           DW          ØØØØ


                MOV         AL,LOC_1
                MOV         BX,LOC_2
                MOV         LOC_1,AH
                MOV         LOC_2,CX
```

As with the other addressing types, the values contained in the memory location or register to the right of the comma are copied into the memory location or register to the left of the comma.

Indirect Addressing

Indirect addressing is the most difficult addressing type to master but is also the most powerful. The three methods of indirect addressing are *register indirect*, *indexed* (or *based*), and *based and indexed with displacement*. We will not consider these methods individually, but will look at the general category of indirect addressing.

To illustrate the various indirect addressing methods, consider for a moment the following code fragments:

```
CMD_TABLE       EQU         THIS BYTE
                DW          OFFSET ACTION_CMD
                DW          OFFSET DOIT_CMD
                DW          OFFSET DRIVE_CMD
                DW          OFFSET PATH_CMD
                DW          OFFSET EXIT_CMD


ACTION_CMD      DB          'SELECT',Ø
DOIT_CMD        DB          'DELETE',Ø
DRIVE_CMD       DB          'DRIVE',Ø
PATH_CMD        DB          'PATH',Ø
EXIT_CMD        DB          'EXIT',Ø
CMD_NUM         DW          ØØØ3


                MOV         AX,CMD_NUM
                MOV         BX,OFFSET CMD_TABLE
                SHL         AX,1
                ADD         BX,AX
                MOV         SI,[BX]
```

Suppose that the variable CMD_NUM contains the value 3. The first instruction
in this fragment uses direct addressing to copy the contents of CMD_NUM (3)
into AX. Then immediate addressing is used to load BX with the offset address
of CMD_TABLE. Remember that when this code is assembled, the directive
OFFSET CMD_TABLE will be replaced with a literal number that represents the
desired offset. Then the contents of AX are multiplied by 2 (which *always*
happens when you shift the bits one position to the left), and this value is
added to what is already in BX. At this point, BX contains a value equal to 6
past the start of CMD_TABLE, which is the table entry for PATH_CMD.

The very next statement is a specific example of indirect addressing. This
statement results in SI being loaded with the contents of what is addressed by
BX, which is the address for the string PATH_CMD. This usage always assumes
that BX contains an address. *The brackets instruct the assembler to use the
value of the memory location pointed to by the register within the brackets.*
Only the registers BX, BP, SI, or DI may be used within brackets.

Clearly, this type of addressing is inherently powerful. As used in the routine
above, a different address can be loaded into SI simply by changing the number
in CMD_NUM. In this instance, BX is referred to as the *base register*.

Variations on this basic indirect-addressing method provide even greater
flexibility in addressing:

```
MOV      SI,[BX]
MOV      SI,[BP+2]
MOV      AX,[BX+SI+2]
```

The first instruction shows the indirect-addressing method already described.
The second and third examples, however, show some variations. The second
example uses the base register and a *displacement value* that is added to the
contents of the base register, producing a value that is assumed to be the
address of the source value to be copied to the destination.

The third example uses the base register, an *index register*, and a displacement
value that are all added together, resulting in a value that is again assumed to be
the address of the source value from which the destination is loaded.

In all of these indirect-addressing methods, the specifications of the source and
destination can be reversed, as with each of the other addressing schemes. Thus,

```
MOV      [BX],SI
MOV      [BP+2],SI
MOV      [BX+SI+2],AX
```

are all perfectly acceptable as destinations for data.

Segment Assumptions

When addressing data, the destination and source are always assumed to be in the data segment, or relative to the DS register. The exception to this assumption is when the base pointer, BP, is used as the base register in indirect addressing. In this instance the stack segment, SS, is used.

The default segment can be overridden by explicit use of the desired segment, as follows:

```
MOV        CS:LOC_2,5
MOV        AL,CS:LOC_1
MOV        CS:LOC_2,CX
MOV        SI,ES:[BX]
MOV        DS:[BP+2],SI
MOV        ES:[BX+SI+2],AX
```

Notice that in the fifth line of these examples, DS must be stated explicitly as an override segment because the BP register is being used as the base register. Normally, SS would be assumed, but in this case DS is used.

Subroutines and Procedures

Subroutines are essential to developing programs of any magnitude. They allow a programmer to break down a task into smaller tasks, and continue breaking it down as necessary for completion of the overall project. Using subroutines is much like outlining a book. You start with the main idea and break it down further and further until the entire topic is covered.

Depending on your programming background, a subroutine is basically the same as a procedure or function. Although some technical distinction may exist between subroutines, procedures, and functions, this book makes no such distinction and assumes that they are functionally the same. All of these terms are used to describe a portion of coding that is developed to perform a specialized task or set of tasks, and is called (either singularly or repetitively) from a higher-level controlling program.

In high-level languages you can easily define subroutines that other programs can call. BASIC uses the GOSUB command to invoke a subroutine, and the RETURN command to signal its end. Pascal and C allow you to call a procedure (or function) by using a user-defined name. In Pascal, control is subsequently returned to the calling program by use of the *end* marker; and in C, the closing brace (or optional *return* statement) marks the end of the function.

Because assembly language requires much more interaction on the programmer's part to accomplish a given task, and because the amount of source code written to accomplish the task can be prodigious, using procedures becomes even more important than with other languages. Two types of procedures (NEAR and FAR) are used in assembly language. They are procedurally the same, and differ only in how a CALL to and RETurn from each affects the stack and CS:IP registers.

NEAR procedures are those that are contained within the same code segment as that of the program invoking the procedure. The declaration of a NEAR procedure is accomplished by use of the PROC NEAR combination of directives. The following example shows a subroutine to load the AX register with the contents of the word that DS:SI points to, after which SI is incremented to point to the next word:

```
GET_WORD        PROC    NEAR
                MOV     AX,[SI]
                INC     SI
                INC     SI
                RET
GET_WORD        ENDP
```

This example is declared as a NEAR procedure because it will reside in the same code segment as the routine from which the procedure is being called. The only change necessary to this routine to make it a FAR procedure would be to change NEAR to FAR.

The following line will execute either a NEAR or FAR procedure:

```
CALL    GET_WORD
```

In the case of a NEAR procedure, this invocation results in the offset address of the instruction *following* the CALL being pushed on the stack, and the address of CS:GET_WORD being loaded into the IP (thus, execution begins at GET_WORD). When the subsequent RET is encountered, the value of the IP is retrieved from the stack, and execution continues from the point following the original CALL.

Because this is a NEAR routine, only offset addresses, one word long, are pushed on and subsequently popped from the stack.

A FAR procedure operates in exactly the same fashion, except that two address words (the value of the code segment and the offset address) are pushed on and later popped from the stack. Also, both the CS and IP registers are set to point to the beginning of the subroutine.

The vast majority of procedures you use will be of the NEAR persuasion. FAR procedures are generally used for controlling programs, for extremely large programs, and for interrupt handler routines.

The Assembly Language Subroutine Skeleton

By this point, programmers who have done most of their work with high-level languages are usually shaking their heads in amazement and starting to visualize assembly language programmers in padded cells with small, barred windows.

Don't despair! All this information about memory usage, program organization, data storage, and procedures is necessary so that you can start to see the structure and power of assembly language. The following statement may help to simplify everything discussed on the last several pages: Virtually all assembly language programs and subroutines can be written using a standard program skeleton. Through the use of a program skeleton, you can concentrate on task completion, rather than on administrative overhead.

A program skeleton is a template that gives a bare-bones (pardon the pun) outline of the program header, data declaration areas, and other "overhead" information. For example, most subroutines and .COM files have data and code in the same memory segment. Thus, the following program skeleton can be entered, saved as a file, and used as a starting point for future assembly language programs or subroutines:

```
    page 60,132
;   *****************************************************************
;   *                                                               *
;   * Author:   Allen L. Wyatt                                      *
;   * Date:     03/03/87                                            *
;   *                                                               *
;   * File:     [file name goes here]                              *
;   *                                                               *
;   * Descrpt:  [description of program or routine]                *
;   *                                                               *
;   * Format:   [syntax of calling statement]                      *
;   *                                                               *
;   *****************************************************************
```

```
; *** Public declaration of subroutines and data

          PUBLIC   XXXXXX

; *** External data needed by these subroutines

          EXTRN    [data and its type goes here]

; *** External subroutines called by these subroutines

          EXTRN    [routine and its type goes here]

          NAME     [routine name goes here]
CODE      SEGMENT BYTE PUBLIC 'CODE'
          ASSUME   CS:CODE

; *** Declaration of equates

PARMD     EQU      12            ;These are sample equates.
PARMC     EQU      1Ø            ;    The ones you use will
PARMB     EQU      Ø8            ;    vary as your program
PARMA     EQU      Ø6            ;    needs change.

; *** Declaration of data

DATA1     DW       ØØØØ          ;These are sample data
DATA2     DW       ØØØØ          ;    definitions. Yours
DATA3     DW       ØØØØ          ;    will vary.


; -------------------------------------------------------------
; START OF MAIN CODING
; -------------------------------------------------------------


XXXXXX         PROC    FAR

                             ;Your program statements are
                             ;    inserted at this point.


XXXXXX         ENDP
; -------------------------------------------------------------
CODE           ENDS
               END
```

Notice the liberal use of comments. Getting into the habit of documenting your programs will help make your job quite a bit easier. In assembly language, comments are denoted by a semicolon. When the program is assembled, everything following a semicolon is disregarded as a comment until the end of the current line is reached.

In this program skeleton, information within brackets is to be supplied when the skeleton is filled out into a real program. Also, the locations indicated by XXXXXX are to be replaced with the name of the routine or program. This is the name that will be used to call this routine from other programs, and that the Linker uses when the program modules are put together.

How you develop and use a program skeleton is up to you, as your own individual programming habits and needs will necessarily differ from those of others. If you do not have a skeleton developed already, develop one and store it in a computer file. Then you can recall the file and edit the skeleton to start new programs.

Summary

Assembly language is extremely quick, compact, and powerful. Because the "building blocks" that the language provides are so small, quite a few more blocks are needed to create a large structure. Resulting programs, however, can exhibit benefits—such as speed and compact code—that are not available with other languages. Other benefits are outlined in the introduction to this book.

This chapter has provided a quick overview of some features and basic tenets of the language. Detailed information on the usage of individual instructions can be gleaned from studying the examples through the rest of this book, or by referring to Part IV.

2

Interfacing Subroutines

When you interface assembly language subroutines with a high-level language, you must address

- How the subroutine is invoked
- How parameters are passed
- How values are returned

This chapter does not attempt to address the specifics of all these points. The nitty-gritty details of each of these considerations are covered in Chapters 3 through 5. The way you invoke an assembly language subroutine, for example, depends in large part on the high-level language from which that subroutine is called. The information in this chapter is more or less common to the process of interfacing assembly language subroutines, no matter which high-level language you may be using.

Let's look first at how parameters are passed to assembly language subroutines. Later in this chapter, you will see how values are returned to a high-level language.

Passing Parameters

Generally, you use the stack to pass parameters to subroutines. You learned from Chapter 1 that the stack is a general-purpose work area, and that using it correctly is critical to successful program execution.

Because each high-level language uses memory in different ways, a common area is needed for subroutine interfacing. The accepted standard for this area is the stack. If you push the parameters on the stack before you call a subroutine, the subroutine can access and modify the data. To prepare for the discussion of how parameters are accessed on the stack, let's look at how the data is placed on the stack and how parameters are formatted.

How Parameters Are Placed on the Stack

The specifics of how parameters are pushed on the stack depend on the type of data the parameter represents and on the high-level language you are using. However, individual parameters generally are passed either as data values or as pointers to the values.

Normally, if the parameter is a short numeric integer (16 bits or shorter), its data value is pushed on the stack. If the parameter is an alphanumeric string, a pointer to the string is passed. A parameter that is a large numeric integer or a floating-point number can be passed by either method.

Because parameter placement differs from language to language, later chapters cover the specifics for each language.

How Parameters Are Formatted

Individual parameter format may vary from language to language. For instance, if the data value of a floating-point number is being passed on the stack, the high-level language you are using determines the way in which the number is encoded.

Parameters must occupy at least one complete word (16 bits) on the stack (although, depending on the high-level language, additional words can be used). If that one word is a pointer to the variable (in the high-level language's data segment), the translation of the data at that memory location will differ from language to language. The number of bytes that each data element uses is particularly open to variation. Again, later chapters cover specifics for parameter format.

Accessing Parameters on the Stack

To access information passed through the stack, the routines in this book use the BP register (the Base Pointer, introduced in Chapter 1). This register is used as a secondary stack pointer, primarily for accessing data on the stack relative to a given location.

The specific way you use the BP register depends in large degree on the type of subroutine being called. Let's take a look at the contents of the stack when the assembly language subroutine is a NEAR procedure.

When the subroutine is invoked, the individual parameters are pushed on the stack, followed by the calling program's return address. In the case of a NEAR procedure, this return address is the segment offset—technically, the incremented contents of the IP (Instruction Pointer) register. Thus, at the start of the assembly language subroutine to which three 16-bit parameters are being passed, the stack would look like that shown in figure 2.1.

????
????
????
????
high byte of return address offset
low byte of return address offset

◀────stack pointer
(SP) is here

Fig. 2.1.
Stack at beginning of execution of a NEAR procedure.

If the routine being called were a FAR procedure, the stack contents would look like those in figure 2.2.

????
????
high byte of return address segment
low byte of return address segment
high byte of return address offset
low byte of return address offset

◀────stack pointer
(SP) is here

Fig. 2.2.
Stack at beginning of execution of a FAR procedure.

Notice that invoking a FAR procedure involves pushing one additional word of data. This word is the segment of the calling program, technically the contents of the CS (Code Segment) register.

Other than the number of bytes pushed for the return address, the information for both procedures is in the same format and in a predictable position on the stack. To access the information, you simply set the BP register and use offsets to retrieve values from the stack. The following code segment shows the proper way to do this in a NEAR procedure:

```
PARM_A          EQU     4
PARM_B          EQU     6
PARM_C          EQU     8

TEST            PROC    NEAR
                PUSH    BP
                MOV     BP,SP
```

```
            MOV     AX,[BP]+PARM_A
            MOV     BX,[BP]+PARM_B
            MOV     CX,[BP]+PARM_C

; REST OF PROGRAM GOES HERE

            POP     BP
            RET
TEST        ENDP
```

Notice that the three parameters are called PARM_A, PARM_B, and PARM_C in this subroutine. These symbols are equated with a specific offset value at the front of the program. When the subroutine executes, the first commands encountered set the base pointer so that it can be used with the offset values to access the parameters. Let's "walk through" what happens in this coding segment.

Remember that, on entry, the stack will look like the one shown in figure 2.1. At this point, the return address occupies the two bytes at stack offset 0, and the parameters begin with the byte at offset 2. To save the contents of the BP register, however, you must push the register on the stack. After you push BP on the stack, the value of BP occupies the two bytes at stack offset 0, followed by the two bytes of the return address and then by the parameters beginning at an offset of 4.

The next instruction sets BP equal to the current stack pointer (SP), which means that BP contains the stack offset address of the old BP value. Because you know that the parameters begin at offset 4, you can access them through indirect addressing, using BP and an offset.

At the end of the subroutine, it is imperative that you pop BP off the stack. Doing so leaves the stack clean and restores BP (in case it is used in the calling program).

Because a call to a FAR procedure results in an additional word on the stack, the only change necessary to the preceding coding segment is that of changing the equates (EQU) to

```
PARM_A        EQU     6
PARM_B        EQU     8
PARM_C        EQU     10
```

This change compensates for the additional word placed on the stack when the FAR procedure is called.

Most assembly language programmers use BP to access the contents of the stack—this method commonly is used to access parameters passed to assembly language subroutines.

Returning Values

Values generally are returned from an assembly language subroutine in one of the following ways:

- Through the stack
- Through a register
- Through memory

None of these methods is automatic; you must determine ahead of time how you will return values. The high-level language with which you are interfacing is the major determinant for selecting which method to use. Some languages require that you use a certain method. Others, such as C, allow some programming flexibility.

Let's take a look at each of these methods.

Returning Values through the Stack

The stack can be used not only for passing parameters but also for returning values. For example, assume that the calling program pushes four unsigned integer numbers on the stack before calling an assembly language subroutine. The subroutine can use (and even modify) these four words of data. On return to the controlling program, the four values remain on the stack. The controlling program can retrieve and use these values, which may have been altered by the subroutine. This is a common method for passing information both to and from a subroutine.

Returning Values through a Register

Some languages (such as C) let you provide a return value in a register. Because the expected register varies from language to language (and possibly from version to version), be sure to verify which registers to use for your particular language.

As an example of this method of returning values, assume that a calling program uses the following command line to invoke an assembly language subroutine:

```
x=whizbang();
```

Clearly, whatever the purpose of the whizbang subroutine, a return value is expected and will be assigned to the variable x. The value's expected format depends on the format of x. If we assume that x is a 16-bit integer, a value can be returned in a register, such as AX, and the high-level language then will assign the contents of AX to the variable x.

Returning Values through Memory

If your high-level language passes pointers to data instead of passing data values, you can modify high-level language variables directly.

When passing string variables to a subroutine, many high-level languages pass a pointer to the string's memory location. Because the length of the string may vary, passing the entire string on the stack is unrealistic. By using the pointer, you can access directly the contents of the string and even make changes directly to the string. Such changes are then available to the high-level language.

Although this method has powerful possibilities, it also has a drawback. For example, an assembly language subroutine cannot readily change the length of a string. Changing memory allocation is dangerous when that allocation is under the control of a high-level language. Many pointers and assumptions that affect the high-level language's use of the variable may be in play and, by changing the data length, you may overwrite other data or invalidate other pointers. Either of these possibilities is dangerous to successful program execution.

Other Stack Considerations

In addition to the previous observations about the stack and its proper usage, I want to point out several other considerations. Mainly, these are tips for you to recognize (and remember) in programming that will manipulate the stack.

As you've learned, additional data is pushed on the stack when a procedure is invoked. Common to all high-level languages, this additional data (which I call *overhead data*) is usually the return address for the calling program.

Inadvertently modifying this overhead data can have disastrous effects. For example, if the return address is modified, program execution will not resume at the proper point in the calling program—the entire system may "hang."

In another common error, information that should be removed is left pushed on the stack—leaving the stack "dirty." Figure 2.3 illustrates what may happen if you inadvertently leave an extra word of data on the stack.

????
????
????
????
12
6F
0C
A8
00
41

◄——actual return address

◄——stack pointer (SP) is here

Fig. 2.3.
Corrupted stack: too much data left at end of procedure.

When a RET (return) instruction is executed, execution will resume at 0CA8:0041 instead of resuming at 126F:0CA8 (the proper return address). The return address will vary, depending on what is left on the stack. And the results of this error will vary, depending on the memory contents beginning at the erroneous return address. This address may be in the program or, as in figure 2.3, it may be somewhere outside the program area. To solve the problem of program execution that does not continue as you want it to, make sure that everything pushed on the stack is subsequently popped off. Then execute the return.

A similar error occurs if you pop too much data from the stack—execution continues at an unintended memory address.

These two errors bring up an interesting (and potentially devastating) possibility. Many hard disk manufacturers include a set of low-level routines in ROM. These routines, which include low-level hard disk formatting and other preparation software, lie quietly in wait until you call them—either on purpose or inadvertently. It is possible (albeit unlikely) that an erroneous return address on the stack could cause program execution to resume at a memory address located at the start of the formatting (or other dangerous) code for the hard disk. The results could be devastating. To guard against such a possibility, back up your hard disk at regular intervals and make sure that your routines leave the proper return address undisturbed.

Tips for Data Manipulation

When working with data passed to assembly language subroutines, you should follow several safety guidelines:

1. Never manipulate data values unless you need to.

2. Use intermediate working variables or registers during execution of assembly language subroutines.

3. Always remember to leave the stack as it was when the routine was called. The stack should be free of extraneous data.

4. Make sure not to pop too much data from the stack.

5. Determine your subroutine procedure ahead of time, and make allowance for it. Is it NEAR or FAR? The type of subroutine affects how data is accessed.

6. Take care not to manipulate the calling program's return address.

Summary

Because different high-level languages use memory in different ways, a common method of passing information to assembly language subroutines is mandatory. The accepted method is to pass information on the stack, where that data can be accessed by the assembly language subroutines.

This chapter introduced and explained some general concepts, but did not cover language-specific information. In the following three chapters you will explore how to interface specific high-level languages with assembly language subroutines.

3

Interfacing with BASIC

BASIC (Beginner's All-purpose Symbolic Instruction Code) is perhaps the most popular of all computer languages. Its free-form structure, easy English-like vocabulary, and low cost make it the most widely distributed language in the world of microcomputers.

Although BASIC is popular, it has several shortcomings that have caused some people to disdain the language and others to adopt apparently unorthodox methods of circumventing the problem areas.

BASIC's slowness is its most serious and noticeable problem. By nature, BASIC is an interpretive language; every line of source code is parsed to its machine language equivalent when the code is executed, which ultimately slows down BASIC programs. The best way to get around this problem is to use a BASIC compiler, which translates the BASIC source code into machine language for subsequent execution. Although using a compiler greatly increases speed, it also increases development time and destroys the interactive nature of the language.

Some programmers have resorted to the technique of reducing time-consuming or slow procedures to their assembly language equivalent and then combining them with the interpretive BASIC program. This technique, which is certainly not without perils, is the type of assembly language interfacing covered in this chapter.

Those who turned to compiled BASIC seemed to solve the speed problem—for a while. IBM's BASIC compiler (introduced in the early 1980s and made to work with DOS versions prior to 2.0) did not support such features as hierarchical directories and path names, but programmers could use assembly language subroutines to sidestep these deficiencies. Many programmers converted other routines to assembly language; execution time for those routines was noticeably faster.

This chapter examines both interpretive and compiled BASIC. First, let's take a look at the process of interfacing with interpretive BASIC.

Interpretive BASIC

Shielded from the computer's day-to-day, machine-level intricacies, most interpretive BASIC programmers do not have to concern themselves with where code or data reside, or how peripherals are interfaced with the computer. The BASIC interpreter takes care of all these matters behind the scenes. However, a limited number of commands allow you to examine BASIC's internal workings more closely. These commands, which include VARPTR and DEF SEG, are not used frequently in the course of normal, BASIC-only programming.

You can use several methods to interface assembly language subroutines with BASIC. This chapter focuses on two methods: storing short routines in string variables, and storing long routines in a set position in memory. Each method is well suited for different types of subroutines, based on their length.

Interfacing Short Subroutines

You can enter short subroutines directly into memory by placing them in the variable space used by BASIC strings. These subroutines must (by definition) be short because, under interpretive BASIC, strings cannot be longer than 255 characters.

To place an assembly language subroutine into a string, follow these steps:

1. Determine the length (in bytes) of the machine language subroutine.

2. Set aside a string variable that is equal in length to the number of bytes determined in step 1.

3. Move the subroutine, byte by byte, into the memory space occupied by the string variable.

After completing these steps, you can call the subroutine at any time by simply calling the address associated with the string variable.

Now let's look at an example of this method of interfacing an assembly language subroutine. Let's assume that you want to call the following subroutine from BASIC:

```
      Page 60,132
;     ****************************************************************
;     *                                                              *
;     * Author:    Allen L. Wyatt                                    *
;     * Date:      7/28/87                                           *
;     *                                                              *
;     * File:      DELAY5.ASM                                        *
;     *                                                              *
;     * Descrpt:   Subroutine designed to delay 5 seconds, then      *
;     *            return to caller.  Designed to be called from     *
;     *            interpretive BASIC.                               *
;     *                                                              *
;     * Format:    CALL D5                                           *
;     *                D5:  Address of subroutine                    *
;     *                                                              *
;     ****************************************************************
;

                  PUBLIC  DELAY5

CODE              SEGMENT BYTE PUBLIC 'CODE'
                  ASSUME  CS:CODE


;     ----------------------------------------------------------------
DELAY5            PROC    FAR

                  MOV     CX,91           ;18.2 * 5 = 91 ticks

D1:               PUSH    CX

                  MOV     AH,0            ;Want to read time
                  INT     1Ah             ;Get initial ticks
D2:               PUSH    DX              ;Save tick count
                  MOV     AH,0            ;Want to read time again
                  INT     1Ah
                  POP     BX              ;Get back previous count
                  CMP     BX,DX           ;Are they the same?
                  JE      D2              ;Yes, so continue
```

```
                POP     CX
                LOOP    D1

                RET
DELAY5          ENDP

;   -------------------------------------------------------------
CODE            ENDS
                END     DELAY5
```

This simple little subroutine checks to make sure that an appropriate number of clock ticks has occurred, and then returns to the caller. The system clock ticks once every 0.0549 seconds, or 18.2065 times per second. This routine waits for 91 ticks (approximately five seconds) before returning.

Following the three steps outlined at the beginning of this section, you must first determine the number of bytes required by the preceding routine. Translated to assembly language, the routine consists of the following 22 bytes:

B9 5B 00 51 B4 00 CD 1A 52 B4 00 CD 1A 5B 3B DA 74 F6 59 E2 EE CB

Knowing this, you can create a string 22 bytes long for this routine. Of the many ways available for creating a string, one is as good as another—pick the method you find most comfortable. In the following sample BASIC program, I have used the SPACE instruction to create DELAY$ in line 130.

```
10 ' ********************************************************
15 ' *                                                      *
20 ' * Sample program to show poking an assembly language   *
25 ' * subroutine into BASIC's string variable space.       *
30 ' *                                                      *
35 ' * Assembly language routine pauses for 5 seconds, then *
40 ' * returns to BASIC.                                    *
45 ' *                                                      *
50 ' * Written by Allen L. Wyatt, 7/27/87                   *
55 ' *                                                      *
60 ' ********************************************************
```

```
100 DEF FN ADR(X$)=256*PEEK(VARPTR(X$)+2)+PEEK(VARPTR(X$)+1)
110 RESTORE 1000
120 READ NUMBYTES
130 DELAY$=SPACE$(NUMBYTES)
140 FOR J=1 TO NUMBYTES
150 READ VALUE$
160 MID$(DELAY$,J,1)=CHR$(VAL("&H"+VALUE$))
170 NEXT
180 PRINT "Starting pause at ";TIME$
190 D=FN ADR(DELAY$)
200 CALL D
210 PRINT "Finished at ";TIME$
220 END
1000 DATA 22
1010 DATA B9,5B,00,51,B4,00,CD,1A,52,B4
1020 DATA 00,CD,1A,5B,3B,DA,74,F6,59,E2
1030 DATA EE,CB
```

Notice that the byte values which make up the subroutine are contained in DATA statements at the end of the program. The first DATA statement (in line 1000) indicates the number of bytes in the subroutine.

Lines 120 through 170 read and act on the DATA statements. Line 160 stores the values into the variable space of DELAY$.

Lines 180 through 210 test the routine to show that it works. The TIME$ function is used to show that the assembly language subroutine pauses for five seconds.

Notice line 190, which is used to determine the physical address of DELAY$. Through the use of the function definition at line 100, the address is determined by using the string descriptor (maintained by BASIC) that specifies the length and location of variables. Look again at line 100:

```
100 DEF FN ADR(X$)=256*PEEK(VARPTR(X$)+2)+PEEK(VARPTR(X$)+1)
```

VARPTR returns the address of DELAY$. In this case, because we are working with a string, the address of the string descriptor is returned. This descriptor consists of three bytes that tell the string's length and address. Because the length is unimportant in this case, you need to use the first and second offset bytes at the descriptor address.

These offset bytes specify the address in memory of the first byte of DELAY$. The address is assigned (in line 190) to the numeric variable D. Because DELAY$ contains the machine language subroutine that should be called, line

200 passes control to that routine, starting at the first byte of DELAY$ (whose address is in D).

This subroutine has limited value because you cannot indicate how many seconds you want to pause. By slightly rewriting the routine, you can pass to assembly language a variable that specifies the number of seconds to pause (as in the following assembly language program):

```
     Page 60,132
;    *****************************************************************
;    *                                                               *
;    * Author:   Allen L. Wyatt                                      *
;    * Date:     7/28/87                                             *
;    *                                                               *
;    * File:     DELAYV.ASM                                          *
;    *                                                               *
;    * Descrpt:  Subroutine designed to delay a specified number     *
;    *           of seconds, then return to caller.  Designed to     *
;    *           be called from interpretive BASIC.                  *
;    *                                                               *
;    * Format:   CALL DE(S%)                                         *
;    *               DE:  Address of subroutine                      *
;    *               S%:  Number of seconds to delay                 *
;    *                                                               *
;    *****************************************************************

                 PUBLIC   DELAYV

CODE             SEGMENT BYTE PUBLIC 'CODE'
                 ASSUME   CS:CODE

;    ---------------------------------------------------------------
DELAYV           PROC     FAR
                 PUSH     BP
                 MOV      BP,SP              ;Get addressability

                 MOV      BX,[BP+6]          ;Get address of seconds
                 MOV      AX,[BX]            ;Move actual value to AX
```

```
              MOV     DX,Ø
              MOV     BX,182
              MUL     BX              ;Total ticks now in AX
              MOV     BX,1Ø           ;Divide by 1Ø
              DIV     BX
              MOV     CX,AX           ;And put it in CX
              CMP     DX,Ø            ;Was there any remainder?
              JE      D1              ;No
              INC     CX              ;Yes, so allow for fraction

D1:           PUSH    CX

              MOV     AH,Ø            ;Want to read time
              INT     1Ah             ;Get initial ticks
D2:           PUSH    DX              ;Save tick count
              MOV     AH,Ø            ;Want to read time again
              INT     1Ah
              POP     BX              ;Get back previous count
              CMP     BX,DX           ;Are they the same?
              JE      D2              ;Yes, so continue

              POP     CX
              LOOP    D1

              POP     BP
              RET     2               ;Return to BASIC
DELAYV        ENDP

; -------------------------------------------------------------------

CODE          ENDS
              END     DELAYV
```

The two versions of the assembly language routine are noticeably different. This rewritten version converts an input value (assumed to be in seconds) to clock ticks by multiplying the value by 182 and then dividing the result by 10. (In effect, this version multipies the original number by 18.2.)

Notice that the variable is passed through the stack. On entry to this routine through the CALL statement, BASIC pushes the variable's *pointer* on the stack. Thus, you can access the parameter value by retrieving the pointer from the stack and then loading AX with the parameter value itself.

Notice also that, in this version of the assembly language routine, you must use
RET (return from procedure) with a specification of the number of additional
bytes to pop from the stack. In this example, you use RET 2 because the
address BASIC pushed on the stack is two bytes long. If you don't use this
method of return when you pass parameters, the chances of getting back to
BASIC are slim.

You also need to change the BASIC program that uses this routine for passing a
value. The modified routine follows:

```
10  ' *********************************************************************
15  ' *                                                                   *
20  ' * Sample program to show poking an assembly language                *
25  ' * subroutine into BASIC's string variable space.                    *
30  ' *                                                                   *
35  ' * Assembly language routine pauses for a specified number           *
40  ' * of seconds, then returns to BASIC.                                *
45  ' *                                                                   *
50  ' * Written by Allen L. Wyatt, 7/27/87                                *
55  ' *                                                                   *
60  ' *********************************************************************
100 DEF FN ADR(X$)=256*PEEK(VARPTR(X$)+2)+PEEK(VARPTR(X$)+1)
110 RESTORE 1000
120 READ NUMBYTES
130 DELAY$=SPACE$(NUMBYTES)
140 FOR J=1 TO NUMBYTES
150 READ VALUE$
160 MID$(DELAY$,J,1)=CHR$(VAL("&H"+VALUE$))
170 NEXT
180 LINE INPUT "Pause value (in seconds): ";A$
190 SECS%=VAL(A$)
200 IF SECS%=0 THEN END
210 PRINT "Starting pause at ";TIME$
220 D=FN ADR(DELAY$)
230 CALL D(SECS%)
240 PRINT "Finished at ";TIME$
250 GOTO 180
1000 DATA 51
1010 DATA 55,8B,EC,8B,5E,06,8B,07,BA,00
```

```
1020 DATA 00,BB,B6,00,F7,E3,BB,0A,00,F7
1030 DATA F3,8B,C8,83,FA,00,74,01,41,51
1040 DATA B4,00,CD,1A,52,B4,00,CD,1A,5B
1050 DATA 3B,DA,74,F6,59,E2,EE,5D,CA,02
1060 DATA 00
```

Notice that the only modifications to the routine are in the invocation (line 230) and in the DATA statements that begin at line 1000 (after all, this assembly language routine is longer than the first).

Some new lines are added (lines 180 through 200) to allow user interaction in specifying how long to delay. If you input a delay of 0, the program will end. If you input a delay greater than 3,600 seconds, the execution of the program will not be as expected. 3,600 seconds converts to 65,520 clock ticks, which is just about the largest number that can be stored in a word register. Because the number of iterations is specified in CX (a word register), that number must be equal to or less than 65,535 clock ticks.

Notice in line 230 that the variable being passed to the routine (SECS%) is an integer variable. Integer variables are extremely easy to work with in assembly language. They require only two bytes in the BASIC variable area and can be accessed as word values in assembly language.

Interfacing Longer Subroutines

If the subroutine is more than 255 bytes long, or if you are not comfortable placing the subroutine into a string variable, you can place it directly into memory by following these steps:

1. Determine how much space to reserve for the assembly language subroutine.

2. Use the CLEAR command to set aside the necessary memory space.

3. Poke the subroutine into the reserved area of memory.

Even though this process is particularly well suited to subroutines longer than 255 bytes, I will use the following routine to illustrate the process:

```
    Page 60,132
;   *****************************************************************
;   *                                                               *
;   * Author:    Allen L. Wyatt                                     *
;   * Date:      7/28/87                                            *
;   *                                                               *
;   * File:      DELAYV.ASM                                         *
;   *                                                               *
;   * Descrpt:   Subroutine designed to delay a specified number    *
;   *            of seconds, then return to caller.  Designed to    *
;   *            be called from interpretive BASIC.                 *
;   *                                                               *
;   * Format:    CALL DE(S%)                                        *
;   *               DE:  Address of subroutine                      *
;   *               S%:  Number of seconds to delay                 *
;   *                                                               *
;   *****************************************************************

                    PUBLIC  DELAYV

CODE                SEGMENT BYTE PUBLIC 'CODE'
                    ASSUME  CS:CODE


;   ---------------------------------------------------------------------
DELAYV              PROC    FAR
                    PUSH    BP
                    MOV     BP,SP               ;Get addressability

                    MOV     BX,[BP+6]           ;Get address of seconds
                    MOV     AX,[BX]             ;Move actual value to AX

                    MOV     DX,0
                    MOV     BX,182
                    MUL     BX                  ;Total ticks now in AX
                    MOV     BX,10               ;Divide by 10
                    DIV     BX
                    MOV     CX,AX               ;And put it in CX
                    CMP     DX,0                ;Was there any remainder?
                    JE      D1                  ;No
                    INC     CX                  ;Yes, so allow for fraction
```

```
D1:             PUSH    CX

                MOV     AH,Ø            ;Want to read time
                INT     1Ah             ;Get initial ticks
D2:             PUSH    DX              ;Save tick count
                MOV     AH,Ø            ;Want to read time again
                INT     1Ah
                POP     BX              ;Get back previous count
                CMP     BX,DX           ;Are they the same?
                JE      D2              ;Yes, so continue

                POP     CX
                LOOP    D1

                POP     BP
                RET     2               ;Return to BASIC
DELAYV          ENDP

;       ------------------------------------------------------------
CODE            ENDS
                END     DELAYV
```

This routine, which has no coding that would render it static, is *relocatable* and will function properly, no matter where it is placed in memory. Interfacing is relatively easy. This type of routine gives programmers few headaches and little trouble.

To reserve memory for this routine, you use the CLEAR command with a designation which specifies the highest memory address that BASIC can access. BASIC ordinarily uses a full 64K segment. (To all intents and purposes, 64K is equivalent to FFFFh.) By subtracting (from this unlimited amount) the amount of space you want to reserve for your assembly language routines, you can determine a new ceiling limit to use in the CLEAR statement.

For example, the preceding subroutine occupies 51 bytes of memory. This subroutine and an additional 10 similar routines would need perhaps one full K of memory. Subtracting 400h (1K) from FFFFh results in FBFFh—the address (FBFFh, or 64511) to use with the CLEAR statement in the BASIC program. The process is shown in the following routine:

```
10  ' *******************************************************************
15  ' *                                                               *
20  ' * Sample program to show poking an assembly language            *
25  ' * subroutine into BASIC's high memory area.                     *
30  ' *                                                               *
35  ' * Assembly language routine pauses for a specified number       *
40  ' * of seconds, then returns to BASIC.                            *
45  ' *                                                               *
50  ' * Written by Allen L. Wyatt, 7/27/87                            *
55  ' *                                                               *
60  ' *******************************************************************
100 CLEAR ,64511
110 D=64512
120 RESTORE 1000
130 READ NUMBYTES
140 FOR J=1 TO NUMBYTES
150 READ VALUE$
160 POKE 64511+J,VAL("&H"+VALUE$)
170 NEXT
180 LINE INPUT "Pause value (in seconds): ";A$
190 SECS%=VAL(A$)
200 IF SECS%=0 THEN END
210 PRINT "Starting pause at ";TIME$
220 CALL D(SECS%)
230 PRINT "Finished at ";TIME$
240 GOTO 180
1000 DATA 51
1010 DATA 55,8B,EC,8B,5E,06,8B,07,BA,00
1020 DATA 00,BB,B6,00,F7,E3,BB,0A,00,F7
1030 DATA F3,8B,C8,83,FA,00,74,01,41,51
1040 DATA B4,00,CD,1A,52,B4,00,CD,1A,5B
1050 DATA 3B,DA,74,F6,59,E2,EE,5D,CA,02
1060 DATA 00
```

Notice the program coding at line 160. In this method of using an assembly language routine, the POKE statement is used to transfer the routine to the appropriate memory area.

This type of usage has clear advantages, the greatest of which is that BASIC can access long assembly language subroutines. The other advantage is that the subroutine resides at one static location. In this example, the assembly language subroutine will always reside at FC00h (64512). Clearly, this is preferable to having to calculate the beginning address whenever you want to invoke the routine.

Compiled BASIC

Although normal interpretive BASIC allows quick development time, compiled BASIC programs require that you run the source programs through the compiler and linker. Initially, you may have trouble getting used to these added steps— but the payoff is faster execution time for the final program.

Compiled and interpretive BASIC are different in several ways. The most noticeable differences are that strings may be up to 32,767 bytes long in compiled BASIC, and that assembly language subroutines do not have to be poked into memory. You can call subroutines by their names and then, using the LINK program, link them to the BASIC program.

Because longer strings are possible in compiled BASIC, the string descriptors that BASIC maintains must be of a different length than those in interpretive BASIC. Under compiled BASIC, string descriptors require not three bytes, but four: two for the length, followed by two for the starting address. During the CALL, the address of this descriptor is passed to the subroutine on the stack.

By taking into account this consideration for the string descriptors, you can handle assembly language subroutines as you would handle them under interpretive BASIC. They can be poked into high memory or stored in a string variable. However, a simpler, more straightforward method exists. This method involves using just the name of the assembly language subroutine that will be included during the LINK process.

As an example of how to interface assembly language subroutines with compiled BASIC programs, consider the following assembly language subroutine:

```
   Page 60,132
;  ****************************************************************
;  *                                                              *
;  * Author:   Allen L. Wyatt                                     *
;  * Date:     7/28/87                                            *
;  *                                                              *
;  * File:     ULCASE.ASM                                         *
;  *                                                              *
;  * Descrpt:  Subroutine designed to convert a string to upper  *
;  *           or lower case.  Designed to be called from         *
;  *           compiled BASIC.                                    *
;  *                                                              *
;  * Format:   CALL ULCASE(S$,X%)                                 *
;  *             S$:  Pointer to string to be converted           *
;  *             X%:  Controls conversion                         *
;  *                  0 = Convert to uppercase                    *
;  *                  ?   Any other signifies convert to lower-*
;  *                      case                                    *
;  *                                                              *
;  ****************************************************************

              PUBLIC    ULCASE

              NAME      ULCASE
CODE          SEGMENT   BYTE PUBLIC 'CODE'
              ASSUME    CS:CODE

PARMB         EQU       8
PARMA         EQU       6


;      ----------------------------------------------------------------
ULCASE        PROC      FAR
              PUSH      BP
              MOV       BP,SP

              MOV       BX,[BP]+PARMB         ;String descriptor address
              MOV       CX,[BX]               ;Get the string length
              JCXZ      EXIT                  ;Passed nul string, so exit
              MOV       DI,[BX+2]             ;Start of string to convert
```

```
          MOV     BX,[BP]+PARMA            ;Address of action variable
          MOV     AX,[BX]                  ;Get the actual number
          CMP     AX,Ø                     ;Converting to uppercase?
          JZ      UPPER                    ;Yes, so go handle

LOWER:    CMP     BYTE PTR [DI],'A'        ;Is it < A ?
          JB      L1                       ;Yes, so skip character
          CMP     BYTE PTR [DI],'Z'        ;Is it > Z ?
          JA      L1                       ;Yes, so skip character
          OR      BYTE PTR [DI],2Øh        ;Make lowercase (ØØ1ØØØØØb)
L1:       INC     DI                       ;Next character
          LOOP    LOWER                    ;Do it for all characters
          JMP     EXIT                     ;All done - exit

UPPER:    CMP     BYTE PTR [DI],'a'        ;Is it < a ?
          JB      U1                       ;Yes, so skip character
          CMP     BYTE PTR [DI],'z'        ;Is it > z ?
          JA      U1                       ;Yes, so skip character
          AND     BYTE PTR [DI],Ø5Fh       ;Make uppercase (Ø1Ø11111b)
U1:       INC     DI                       ;Next character
          LOOP    UPPER                    ;Do it for all characters

EXIT:     POP     BP
          RET     2*2
ULCASE    ENDP
;         ----------------------------------------------------------------
CODE      ENDS
          END     ULCASE
```

In this simple program, which converts a string to either all upper- or all lowercase, two parameters must be passed from BASIC: the string to be converted, and an integer number indicating whether the string is to be converted to upper- or lowercase.

Notice the calling syntax for the subroutine: ULCASE(S$,X%). When BASIC encounters the variables specified in the CALL statement, it places the variable addresses on the stack in the order encountered. Thus, the first address pushed is the descriptor for S$, and the second is the address for X%.

You'll notice that, in the body of the program, PARMA and PARMB specify the relative location on the stack of each parameter. PARMA represents the rightmost parameter in the calling list; PARMB, the second-to-rightmost parameter.

Here's the BASIC program that will use this subroutine:

```
10 ' *********************************************************
15 ' *                                                       *
20 ' * Sample program to show calling of assembly language   *
25 ' * subroutine from compiled BASIC.                       *
30 ' *                                                       *
35 ' * Assembly language routine converts string to upper- or *
40 ' * lowercase.                                            *
45 ' *                                                       *
50 ' * Written by Allen L. Wyatt, 7/28/87                    *
55 ' *                                                       *
60 ' *********************************************************
100 ZERO%=Ø:ONE%=1
110 LINE INPUT "String to convert: ";A$
120 IF A$="" THEN END
130 PRINT:PRINT "UPPERCASE:"
140 CALL ULCASE(A$,ZERO%)
150 PRINT A$
160 PRINT "lowercase:"
170 CALL ULCASE(A$,ONE%)
180 PRINT A$
190 GOTO 110
```

Notice that, because you don't need to worry about either poking or addresses, the procedure for calling assembly language subroutines in this program is a good deal simpler than the corresponding procedure for interpretive BASIC. Combining the assembly language subroutine with the BASIC program is accomplished through the LINK process (see Chapter 7).

Summary

Although BASIC is a readily available and extremely popular computer language, it has several shortcomings that make assembly language subroutines attractive and, in some instances, necessary to the viability of a program.

The process of interfacing assembly language subroutines depends, in large part, on whether the BASIC program is written in interpretive or compiled BASIC. Each type of BASIC has differences that affect how the language interacts with and passes variables to assembly language subroutines.

These subroutines are invoked through the versatile, easy-to-use CALL statement. But remember that, before calling an assembly language subroutine, BASIC does not remove the information it has pushed on the stack. You have to use the modified RET instruction to remove this information. BASIC is not very tidy in its handling of assembly language subroutines.

4

Interfacing with Pascal

Pascal, a relatively new programming language that first appeared in 1970, has a loyal following of users who enjoy the language's structured approach to programming. Pascal is readily available for most computer systems at a moderate cost, and several companies (such as Borland) supply a good, reasonably priced Pascal compiler. Such availability has added to the language's popularity.

Like any other computer language, Pascal "bogs down" in certain areas. I don't mean to imply that Pascal is unacceptable—it's just slower than assembly language in certain areas. As a result, many people have developed assembly language subroutines to interface with their Pascal programs.

General Interfacing Guidelines

The way assembly language subroutines are interfaced with Pascal programs depends (in large degree) on the Pascal compiler that you are using. For example, many Pascal compilers use a two-step approach to program development. After the source code is complete, it is *compiled* and then, in the second step, *linked*. If your Pascal uses this two-step approach, you can easily incorporate assembly language subroutines into your programs.

Other Pascal systems use a single-phase process that combines compiling and linking. The most notable of these systems is Borland's Turbo Pascal®. Although Turbo Pascal has many advantages over other types of Pascal compilers, it does not allow easy incorporation of external assembly language subroutines. Turbo Pascal has an *inline* assembly language generator (other Pascal compilers may not). Using assembly language in this manner is best left to a book dedicated to Turbo Pascal.

You can include external assembly language subroutines in Turbo Pascal programs if the subroutines are completely relocatable and self-contained. In other words, there can be no external references in the assembly language subroutine, and all branching must be short. Although this type of structure is possible in assembly language coding, it is severely limiting. To be truly useful, any notable assembly language subroutines require free access to memory and data areas. Such access is not available under Turbo Pascal.

If your Pascal compiler uses the two-phase development process of compiling and linking, there generally is only one stipulation for interfacing with assembly language subroutines: you must use the PROCEDURE statement to define the subroutine name and the variables to be passed. The format of this statement is

PROCEDURE function_name(arg1,arg2,arg3, . . . ,argn: dtype); EXTERNAL;

In this syntax, *function_name* is the publicly declared name of the assembly language subroutine. The *arguments* (*1* through *n*) are the names of the variables whose values are to be passed to the subroutine. For simplicity's sake, the parameters' data type (*dtype*) usually is INTEGER.

To indicate that pointers, rather than values, should be passed, the variable names can be modified with VAR or VARS prefixes. VAR indicates that only the offset address of the variable is to be passed; VARS indicates that both the segment and offset address are to be passed. Examples in this chapter show both types of data passing.

Interfacing Subroutines without Variable Passing

To help you better understand how an assembly language subroutine is interfaced with Pascal, let's look at a sample subroutine that does not require parameter passing. Consider the following assembly language program:

```
        Page 6Ø,132
;       ****************************************************************
;       *                                                              *
;       * Author:    Allen L. Wyatt                                    *
;       * Date:      7/28/87                                           *
;       *                                                              *
;       * File:      DELAY5P.ASM                                       *
;       *                                                              *
;       * Descrpt:   Subroutine designed to delay 5 seconds, then      *
;       *            return to caller.  Designed to be called from     *
;       *            Pascal.                                           *
;       *                                                              *
;       * Format:    DELAY5()                                          *
;       *                                                              *
;       ****************************************************************
;
```

```
                PUBLIC  DELAY5

CODE            SEGMENT BYTE PUBLIC 'CODE'
                ASSUME  CS:CODE

; -------------------------------------------------------------
DELAY5          PROC    FAR

                MOV     CX,91               ;18.2 * 5 = 91 ticks

D1:             PUSH    CX

                MOV     AH,Ø                ;Want to read time
                INT     1Ah                 ;Get initial ticks
D2:             PUSH    DX                  ;Save tick count
                MOV     AH,Ø                ;Want to read time again
                INT     1Ah
                POP     BX                  ;Get back previous count
                CMP     BX,DX               ;Are they the same?
                JE      D2                  ;Yes, so continue

                POP     CX
                LOOP    D1

                RET
DELAY5          ENDP

; -------------------------------------------------------------
CODE            ENDS
                END     DELAY5
```

This little subroutine simply checks to make sure that an appropriate number of clock ticks have occurred, and then returns to the caller. The system clock ticks once every 0.0549 seconds, or 18.2065 times per second. This routine waits for 91 clock ticks, or approximately 5 seconds, before returning.

The Pascal program written to test this routine is

```
{ Program to test the calling of DELAY5
  Written by Allen L. Wyatt
  Date: 7/28/87 }
```

```
PROGRAM DTESTP;
PROCEDURE DELAY5; EXTERNAL;
BEGIN
   WRITELN(' Starting delay... ');
   DELAY5;
   WRITE(' Finished');
END.
```

This simple, straightforward routine gives notice that the delay routine is going to be executed, invokes the delay routine, and then displays a finishing remark. Notice in this example that the routine is invoked as *DELAY5*. No parameters are included in the invocation because the routine doesn't require any.

Notice that there is nothing mystical or magical about the way this routine is called. The linker makes sure that the proper routines are linked to create the executable (.EXE) file. Invocation of the assembly language subroutine presupposes that this external procedure has been declared in the program header. Without such a PROCEDURE statement, an error would have been generated during the compilation process.

Interfacing Subroutines with Variable Passing

Pascal is one of the high-level languages (mentioned in Chapter 2) that use the stack for passing variables to assembly language. Values, short pointers, and long pointers can be passed, although you will find that long pointers are seldom necessary with most assembly language subroutines.

The value of the preceding subroutine (DELAY5) is limited because you cannot indicate how many seconds you want to pause. You can easily modify the routine so that it passes (to the assembly language subroutine) a variable specifying the number of seconds to pause. The following assembly language program includes this variable:

```
      Page 6Ø,132
;     ****************************************************************
;     *                                                              *
;     * Author:   Allen L. Wyatt                                     *
;     * Date:     7/28/87                                            *
;     *                                                              *
;     * File:     DELAYV1P.ASM                                       *
;     *                                                              *
;     * Descrpt:  Subroutine designed to wait a specified number    *
;     *           of seconds (value pushed on stack), then return   *
;     *           to caller.  Designed to be called from Pascal.    *
;     *                                                              *
;     * Format:   DELAY(VALUE)                                       *
;     *                                                              *
;     ****************************************************************

                  PUBLIC  DELAYV

                  NAME DELAYV
CODE              SEGMENT BYTE PUBLIC 'CODE'
                  ASSUME  CS:CODE


;     -------------------------------------------------------------------
DELAYV            PROC    FAR
                  PUSH    BP
                  MOV     BP,SP

                  MOV     AX,[BP+6]        ;Get number of seconds

                  MOV     DX,Ø
                  MOV     BX,182
                  MUL     BX               ;Get number of total ticks
                  MOV     BX,1Ø            ;Divide by 1Ø
                  DIV     BX
                  MOV     CX,AX            ;And put it in CX
                  CMP     DX,Ø             ;Was there any remainder?
                  JE      D1               ;No
                  INC     CX               ;Yes, allow fractional part
```

```
D1:             PUSH    CX

                MOV     AH,Ø            ;Want to read time
                INT     1Ah             ;Get initial ticks
D2:             PUSH    DX              ;Save tick count
                MOV     AH,Ø            ;Want to read time again
                INT     1Ah
                POP     BX              ;Get back previous count
                CMP     BX,DX           ;Are they the same?
                JE      D2              ;Yes, so continue

                POP     CX
                LOOP    D1

                POP     BP
                RET     2
DELAYV          ENDP

;    ---------------------------------------------------------------
CODE            ENDS
                END
```

This version of the assembly language routine is noticeably different from the preceding routine. This version converts an input value, assumed to be in seconds, to clock ticks by multiplying the input value by 182 and then dividing the result by 10 (in effect, multiplying the original number by 18.2).

Notice that the variable is passed through the stack, as described earlier and in Chapter 2. On entry to this routine, Pascal pushes the variable's *value* on the stack. Because the variable is an integer (it must be declared as such in the Pascal program), it can be accessed as a word on the stack.

Notice also that you must use RET (return from procedure) with a specification of the number of additional bytes to pop from the stack. RET 2 is used in this case because Pascal pushed an integer value (2 bytes long) on the stack. If you do not use this method of return when passing parameters, the chances of getting back to Pascal are slim.

You also must change the Pascal program that uses this routine to pass a value. The modified routine is

```
{ Program to test the calling of DELAYV()
  Written by Allen L. Wyatt
  Date: 7/28/87 }
```

```
PROGRAM DV1TESTP;
VAR SECS: INTEGER;
PROCEDURE DELAYV(SECS: INTEGER); EXTERNAL;
BEGIN
    SECS:=5;
    WHILE SECS>Ø DO BEGIN
        WRITE(' Delay value (seconds): '); READLN(SECS);
        IF SECS>Ø THEN BEGIN
            WRITELN(' Starting delay... ');
            DELAYV(SECS);
            WRITELN(' Finished');
        END;
    END;
END.
```

Notice that only a few modifications are made to the routine. The line that invokes the function uses a variable between the parentheses. Some new lines are added to allow user interaction in specifying the time to delay. If you input a delay of 0, the program will end; if you input a delay of more than 3600 seconds, the program will not execute as expected. 3,600 seconds converts to 65,520 clock ticks—just about the largest number that can be stored in a word register. Because the number of iterations is specified in CX (a word register), it must be equal to or less than 65,535 clock ticks.

Passing Variable Pointers

The preceding routine works well, provided that the variable being passed on the stack is a value. But a pointer to a variable would cause problems for the assembly language subroutine, which is not designed to handle a pointer. To allow passage of a pointer, you can modify the assembly language subroutine as follows:

```
        Page 6Ø,132
;       ***************************************************************
;       *                                                             *
;       * Author:    Allen L. Wyatt                                   *
;       * Date:      7/28/87                                          *
;       *                                                             *
;       * File:      DELAYV2P.ASM                                     *
;       *                                                             *
;       * Descrpt:   Subroutine designed to wait a specified number   *
;       *            of seconds (pointer pushed on stack), then       *
;       *            return to caller.  Designed to be called from    *
;       *            Pascal.                                          *
;       *                                                             *
;       * Format:    DELAYV(ADDRESS)                                  *
;       *                                                             *
;       ***************************************************************

                    PUBLIC   DELAYV

                    NAME DELAYV
CODE                SEGMENT BYTE PUBLIC 'CODE'
                    ASSUME   CS:CODE


;       ---------------------------------------------------------------------
DELAYV              PROC     FAR
                    PUSH     BP
                    MOV      BP,SP

                    MOV      BX,[BP+6]        ;Get address of seconds
                    MOV      AX,[BX]          ;Get actual seconds

                    MOV      DX,Ø
                    MOV      BX,182
                    MUL      BX               ;Get number of total ticks
                    MOV      BX,1Ø            ;Divide by 1Ø
                    DIV      BX
                    MOV      CX,AX            ;And put it in CX
                    CMP      DX,Ø             ;Was there any remainder?
                    JE       D1               ;No
                    INC      CX               ;Yes, allow fractional part
```

```
D1:             PUSH    CX

                MOV     AH,Ø            ;Want to read time
                INT     1Ah             ;Get initial ticks
D2:             PUSH    DX              ;Save tick count
                MOV     AH,Ø            ;Want to read time again
                INT     1Ah
                POP     BX              ;Get back previous count
                CMP     BX,DX           ;Are they the same?
                JE      D2              ;Yes, so continue

                POP     CX
                LOOP    D1

                POP     BP
                RET     2
DELAYV          ENDP

;       ----------------------------------------------------------------
CODE            ENDS
                END
```

In this routine, only the two lines that control retrieving the variable passed
from Pascal have been changed. Here, a *pointer* to the variable (rather than the
value) is assumed to be on the stack. Thus, you can access the parameter value
by first retrieving the pointer from the stack and then loading AX with the value
of the parameter.

Notice also that RET 2 is still used to return from this subroutine. Because the
address pushed on the stack is a simple offset address to the desired variable, it
occupies only two bytes. Again, including this type of return (with the proper
return value) is mandatory.

The Pascal program also must be changed (slightly) to indicate that an address
is to be passed to the subroutine. The following modifications reflect this
change:

```
{ Program to test the calling of DELAYV()
  Written by Allen L. Wyatt
  Date: 7/28/87 }
```

```
PROGRAM DV2TESTP;
VAR SECS: INTEGER;
PROCEDURE DELAYV(VAR SECS: INTEGER); EXTERNAL;
BEGIN
    SECS:=5;
    WHILE SECS>Ø DO BEGIN
        WRITE(' Delay value (seconds): '); READLN(SECS);
        IF SECS>Ø THEN BEGIN
            WRITELN(' Starting delay... ');
            DELAYV(SECS);
            WRITELN(' Finished');
        END;
    END;
END.
```

Notice that only the line declaring DELAYV( ) as an external procedure has been changed. This line indicates that DELAYV( ) expects a variable pointer rather than a value. The prefix VAR indicates to Pascal that the offset address for the variable is to be passed.

Why would passing a variable's address pointer be valuable, as opposed to passing only a value? Because, if you know the variable's location in memory, you can make direct changes to the variable's value in the assembly language subroutine. This capability can be invaluable if you are working with strings, as you can see from the following program:

```
        Page 6Ø,132
;       ***********************************************************
;       *                                                         *
;       * Author:    Allen L. Wyatt                               *
;       * Date:      7/28/87                                      *
;       *                                                         *
;       * File:      ULCASEP.ASM                                  *
;       *                                                         *
;       * Descrpt:   Subroutine designed to convert a string to upper-*
;       *            or lowercase.  Designed to be called from     *
;       *            Pascal.                                       *
;       *                                                         *
;       * Format:    ULCASE(S,X)                                   *
;       *                S:  Pointer to string to be converted     *
;       *                X:  Controls conversion                   *
;       *                    Ø = Convert to uppercase              *
;       *                    ?   Any other signifies convert to lower- *
;       *                    case                                  *
;       *                                                         *
;       ***********************************************************
;
```

```
          PUBLIC    ULCASE

          NAME      ULCASE
CODE      SEGMENT   BYTE PUBLIC 'CODE'
          ASSUME    CS:CODE

PARMA     EQU       8
PARMB     EQU       6


;     ------------------------------------------------------------
ULCASE    PROC      FAR
          PUSH      BP
          MOV       BP,SP
          PUSH      DI

          MOV       DI,[BP]+PARMA         ;Get string address
          INC       DI                    ;Point past length
          MOV       CX,[BP]+PARMA+2       ;Get length of string
          MOV       AX,[BP]+PARMB         ;Get action variable
          CMP       AX,Ø                  ;Converting to uppercase?
          JZ        UPPER                 ;Yes, so go handle

LOWER:    CMP       BYTE PTR [DI],Ø       ;Is this end of string?
          JE        EXIT                  ;Yes, so exit
          CMP       BYTE PTR [DI],'A'     ;Is it < A ?
          JB        L1                    ;Yes, so skip character
          CMP       BYTE PTR [DI],'Z'     ;Is it > Z ?
          JA        L1                    ;Yes, so skip character
          OR        BYTE PTR [DI],2Øh     ;Make lowercase (ØØ1ØØØØØb)
L1:       INC       DI                    ;Next character
          JMP       LOWER                 ;Do it again

UPPER:    CMP       BYTE PTR [DI],Ø       ;Is this end of string?
          JE        EXIT                  ;Yes, so exit
          CMP       BYTE PTR [DI],'a'     ;Is it < a ?
          JB        U1                    ;Yes, so skip character
          CMP       BYTE PTR [DI],'z'     ;Is it > z ?
          JA        U1                    ;Yes, so skip character
          AND       BYTE PTR [DI],Ø5Fh    ;Make uppercase (Ø1Ø11111b)
U1:       INC       DI                    ;Next character
          JMP       UPPER                 ;Do it again
```

```
EXIT:        POP     DI
             POP     BP
             RET     6                      ;Remove 6 bytes pushed
ULCASE       ENDP
;            ------------------------------------------------------------
CODE         ENDS
             END
```

This simple program, which converts a string to either all upper- or lowercase, expects two parameters to be passed from Pascal: a pointer to the string to be converted, and an integer value indicating whether the string is to be converted to upper- or lowercase.

You will notice that even though only two parameters are passed in this routine, six bytes are popped during the return sequence. This occurs because Pascal passes four bytes for an LSTRING variable—pushing first the two bytes representing the string length, and then pushing the offset address to the start of the string. Notice also that the conversion process begins at the string's second character, not its first, because the first position of an LSTRING variable always contains the number of characters in the string.

If you look at the calling syntax for the subroutine:

    ULCASE(S,X)

you will notice that Pascal places the function parameters on the stack in their order of occurrence, from left to right. Thus, the first value pushed is the offset address pointer for S, and the second is the value for X.

In the body of the program, PARMA and PARMB are used to specify the relative location of each parameter on the stack. PARMA represents the first (leftmost) parameter in the calling list; PARMB represents the second parameter.

The Pascal program that will use this subroutine follows:

```
{ Program to test the calling of ULCASE()
  Written by Allen L. Wyatt
  Date: 7/28/87
}
```

```
PROGRAM UTESTP;
VAR S:LSTRING(26);
PROCEDURE ULCASE(VAR S:LSTRING; X:INTEGER); EXTERNAL;
BEGIN
   S:='Original string value';
   WHILE S.LEN>Ø DO BEGIN
      WRITE('String to convert: '); READLN(S);
      IF S.LEN>Ø THEN BEGIN
         WRITELN('UPPERCASE: ');
         ULCASE(S,Ø);
         WRITELN(S);
         WRITELN('lowercase: ');
         ULCASE(S,1);
         WRITELN(S);
      END;
   END;
END.
```

Summary

Pascal is popular with a large section of the programming community. The ease with which you can combine assembly language subroutines with Pascal programs depends on the type of Pascal compiler used. If your compiler has a separate link phase, interfacing assembly language subroutines is relatively easy.

5

Interfacing with C

C is one of the fastest-growing high-level languages today. It has been said that nearly 75% of all commercial programs for personal computers are written in C—which is quite a plaudit for the popularity of the language.

Why is C so popular? Although the reasons vary from programmer to programmer, for most people, C seems to provide the right mix of ease of use, access to system-level functions, and transportability. These benefits make C an attractive development language.

Eventually, most serious C programmers must face the task of interfacing assembly language subroutines with the language. Because C is a compiled language, assembly language subroutines can be linked as the final step in program development. The trick is to make sure that the interface between C and assembly language is followed strictly, to allow proper passage of variables.

Most of the popular C compilers on the market today (including Microsoft® C, Lattice® C, Aztec C, and Turbo C) have similar functions and implementations of the language. Any notable differences between versions are mentioned as the examples in this chapter are developed.

General Interfacing Guidelines

To interface assembly language subroutines with C, you must follow a few general guidelines. First, you must give a specific segment name to the code segment of your assembly language subroutine. The name will vary, depending on which compiler you use. For example, Microsoft C requires either the segment name _TEXT (for small and compact memory model programs) or a segment name with the suffix _TEXT (for other memory models). Aztec C requires the segment name CODESEG.

Second, your C compiler may require specific names for data segments (if the data is being referenced outside the code segment). Microsoft C requires that the segment be named _DATA, whereas you must use the segment name

DATASEG with Aztec C. You must use these segment names, which are specific to C, to properly link and then execute the programs.

Third, you must realize how variables are passed to assembly language subroutines through the stack. In the function-calling syntax of

```
function_name(arg1,arg2,arg3,...,argn);
```

the value of argument n (*argn*) is pushed on the stack first, followed by the values of arguments 3 and 2 (*arg3* and *arg2*), with argument 1 (*arg1*) the last argument pushed. Either an actual value or a pointer can be passed to a variable on the stack. Although most values and pointers are passed as word-length stack elements, the longer data elements (such as long or unsigned long-type variables) require 32 bits (2 words) of stack space. If the memory model being used is compact, large, or huge, or if the data item has a segment override, data pointers also require 32 bits of stack space. Float-type variables use 64 bits (4 words) of stack space. Remember this distinction of stack usage by variable type—failure to do so can produce undesired results.

Fourth, in the assembly language source file, the assembly language routines to be called from C must begin (for Microsoft C) or end (for Aztec C) with an underline. However, the underline is not included when the routines are invoked in C. The examples in this chapter reflect this distinction.

Fifth, remember to save any special-purpose registers (such as CS, DS, SS, BP, SI, and DI) that your assembly language subroutine may disturb. Failure to save them may have undesired consequences when control is returned to the C program. You do not have to save the contents of AX, BX, CX, or DX because these registers are not considered nonchangeable by C.

The examples in this book are written specifically for Microsoft C. If you are using another C compiler, the only differences you will need to deal with should be in the required segment names for code and data, or in the naming of the subroutines. If you are not using Microsoft C, remember to make the appropriate changes if you enter the examples given here.

Interfacing Subroutines with No Variable Passing

To help you understand how an assembly language subroutine is interfaced with C, let's look at a sample subroutine that requires no parameter passing. Consider the following assembly language program:

```
      Page 60,132
;     ****************************************************************
;     *                                                              *
;     * Author:   Allen L. Wyatt                                     *
;     * Date:     7/28/87                                            *
;     *                                                              *
;     * File:     DELAY5C.ASM                                        *
;     *                                                              *
;     * Descrpt:  Subroutine designed to wait 5 seconds, then        *
;     *           return to caller.  Designed to be called from      *
;     *           Microsoft C.                                       *
;     *                                                              *
;     * Format:   delay()                                            *
;     *                                                              *
;     ****************************************************************

                  PUBLIC   _DELAY5

                  NAME DELAY5
_TEXT             SEGMENT BYTE PUBLIC 'CODE'
                  ASSUME  CS:_TEXT


;     ----------------------------------------------------------------
_DELAY5           PROC    NEAR
                  PUSH    BP
                  MOV     BP,SP

                  MOV     CX,91           ;18.2 * 5 = 91 ticks

D1:               PUSH    CX

                  MOV     AH,0            ;Want to read time
                  INT     1Ah             ;Get initial ticks
D2:               PUSH    DX              ;Save tick count
                  MOV     AH,0            ;Want to read time again
                  INT     1Ah
                  POP     BX              ;Get back previous count
                  CMP     BX,DX           ;Are they the same?
                  JE      D2              ;Yes, so continue
```

```
                    POP     CX
                    LOOP    D1

                    POP     BP
                    RET
_DELAY5             ENDP


;       ----------------------------------------------------------------
_TEXT               ENDS
                    END
```

This little subroutine simply checks to make sure that an appropriate number of clock ticks have occurred, and then returns to the caller. The system clock ticks once every 0.0549 seconds, or 18.2065 times per second. This routine waits for 91 clock ticks, or approximately 5 seconds, before returning.

Notice that the value of BP is saved on the stack (on entry to the subroutine) and restored (at the end of the program). Because the program does not modify the value of BP and has no variables to access, these steps are not necessary—but they are good programming practice.

The C program written to test this routine is

```
/* Program to test the calling of DELAY5()
   Written by Allen L. Wyatt
   Date: 7/28/87
*/

#include <stdio.h>
main()
{
printf("Starting delay...\n");
delay5();
printf("Finished\n");
}
```

This straightforward, simple routine displays a string, invokes the delay routine, and ends by printing another string. Notice that the routine invoked as delay5() in this example is called _DELAY5 in the assembly language source file. This difference is important for you to remember when you write programs and subroutines.

Interfacing Subroutines
with Variable Passing

As you probably remember from the discussions earlier in this chapter and in Chapter 2, variables are passed on the stack in C. This is C's normal method of variable passing.

You can easily modify the preceding subroutine so that it passes a variable to the assembly language subroutine. The value of this subroutine is limited because you cannot indicate how many seconds you want to pause. But with slight modification, the routine can accommodate passing a variable that specifies the number of seconds to pause. The following assembly language program includes this modification:

```
        Page 60,132
;       ************************************************************
;       *                                                          *
;       * Author:   Allen L. Wyatt                                 *
;       * Date:     7/28/87                                        *
;       *                                                          *
;       * File:     DELAYV1C.ASM                                   *
;       *                                                          *
;       * Descrpt:  Subroutine designed to wait a specified number *
;       *           of seconds (value pushed on stack), then return*
;       *           to caller.  Designed to be called from Microsoft*
;       *           C.                                             *
;       *                                                          *
;       * Format:   delay(value)                                   *
;       *                                                          *
;       ************************************************************

                PUBLIC  _DELAYV

                NAME DELAYV
_TEXT           SEGMENT BYTE PUBLIC 'CODE'
                ASSUME  CS:_TEXT
```

```
;       -------------------------------------------------------------------
_DELAYV         PROC    NEAR
                PUSH    BP
                MOV     BP,SP

                MOV     AX,[BP+4]               ;Get number of seconds

                MOV     DX,Ø
                MOV     BX,182
                MUL     BX                      ;Get number of total ticks
                MOV     BX,1Ø                   ;Divide by 1Ø
                DIV     BX
                MOV     CX,AX                   ;And put it in CX
                CMP     DX,Ø                    ;Was there any remainder?
                JE      D1                      ;No
                INC     CX                      ;Yes, allow fractional part

D1:             PUSH    CX

                MOV     AH,Ø                    ;Want to read time
                INT     1Ah                     ;Get initial ticks
D2:             PUSH    DX                      ;Save tick count
                MOV     AH,Ø                    ;Want to read time again
                INT     1Ah
                POP     BX                      ;Get back previous count
                CMP     BX,DX                   ;Are they the same?
                JE      D2                      ;Yes, so continue

                POP     CX
                LOOP    D1

                POP     BP
                RET
_DELAYV         ENDP

;       -------------------------------------------------------------------
_TEXT           ENDS
                END
```

This version of the assembly language routine is noticeably different from the first. This version converts an input value, assumed to be in seconds, to clock ticks by multiplying the value by 182 and then dividing the result by 10—or, in effect, by multiplying the original number by 18.2.

Notice that the variable is passed through the stack, as described earlier in this chapter and in Chapter 2. On entry to this routine, C pushes the variable's *value* on the stack. Because the variable is an integer (it must be declared as such in the C program), it can be accessed as a word on the stack.

The C program that uses this routine also was changed to pass a value. The modified routine appears as follows:

```
/* Program to test the calling of DELAYV()
   Written by Allen L. Wyatt
   Date: 7/28/87
*/

#include <stdio.h>
main()
{
unsigned short secs;
secs=5;
while (secs!=0)
    {
    printf("Delay value (seconds): ");
    scanf("%u",&secs);
    if (secs!=0)
        {
        printf("\nStarting delay...\n");
        delayv(secs);
        printf("Finished\n\n");
        }
    }
}
```

Notice that the invocation of the function now includes a variable between the parentheses, and that several lines have been added to allow user interaction in specifying how long to delay. If you input a delay of 0, the program will end. If you input a delay greater than 3,600 seconds, the program will not execute as expected because the number of iterations (which is specified in CX, a word register) must be less than or equal to 65,535 clock ticks. (3,600 seconds converts to 65,520 clock ticks, which is just about the largest number that can be stored in a word register.)

Passing Variable Pointers

The preceding routine works well, provided that the variable being passed on the stack is a value. But passing a pointer to a variable would cause problems for the assembly language subroutine, which is not designed for pointers. If you want to allow passing a pointer, you can modify the subroutine as follows:

```
      Page 60,132
;     *************************************************************
;     *                                                           *
;     * Author:   Allen L. Wyatt                                  *
;     * Date:     7/28/87                                         *
;     *                                                           *
;     * File:     DELAYV2C.ASM                                    *
;     *                                                           *
;     * Descrpt:  Subroutine designed to wait a specified number  *
;     *           of seconds (pointer pushed on stack), then      *
;     *           return to caller.  Designed to be called from   *
;     *           Microsoft C.                                    *
;     *                                                           *
;     * Format:   delay(address)                                  *
;     *                                                           *
;     *************************************************************

                PUBLIC  _DELAYV

                NAME DELAYV
_TEXT           SEGMENT BYTE PUBLIC 'CODE'
                ASSUME  CS:_TEXT

;     ---------------------------------------------------------------
_DELAYV         PROC    NEAR
                PUSH    BP
                MOV     BP,SP

                MOV     BX,[BP+4]          ;Get address of seconds
                MOV     AX,[BX]            ;Get actual seconds
```

```
                MOV     DX,Ø
                MOV     BX,182
                MUL     BX              ;Get number of total ticks
                MOV     BX,1Ø           ;Divide by 1Ø
                DIV     BX
                MOV     CX,AX           ;And put it in CX
                CMP     DX,Ø            ;Was there any remainder?
                JE      D1              ;No
                INC     CX              ;Yes, allow fractional part

D1:             PUSH    CX

                MOV     AH,Ø            ;Want to read time
                INT     1Ah             ;Get initial ticks
D2:             PUSH    DX              ;Save tick count
                MOV     AH,Ø            ;Want to read time again
                INT     1Ah
                POP     BX              ;Get back previous count
                CMP     BX,DX           ;Are they the same?
                JE      D2              ;Yes, so continue

                POP     CX
                LOOP    D1

                POP     BP
                RET
_DELAYV         ENDP


;       ----------------------------------------------------------------
_TEXT           ENDS
                END
```

In this routine, only the two lines that control retrieving the variable passed from C are changed. Here, not the value but rather a pointer to the actual variable is assumed to be on the stack. Thus, you can access the value of the parameter by first retrieving the pointer from the stack and then loading AX with the value pointed to by the parameter.

The C program also must be changed to indicate that an address is to be passed to the subroutine. The following program reflects this change:

```
/* Program to test the calling of DELAYV()
   Written by Allen L. Wyatt
   Date: 7/28/87
*/

#include <stdio.h>
main()
{
unsigned short secs;
secs=5;
while (secs!=0)
    {
    printf("Delay value (seconds): ");
    scanf("%u",&secs);
    if (secs!=0)
        {
        printf("\nStarting delay...\n");
        delayv(&secs);
        printf("Finished\n\n");
        }
    }
}
```

Notice that the only change is in the invocation of the subroutine. The ampersand before the variable name indicates to C that an address for the variable is to be passed.

Why would you want to pass a variable's address pointer instead of simply passing a value? Because if you know the variable's location in memory, you can make direct changes to the value of the variable in your assembly language subroutine. This capability can be invaluable if you are working with strings, as in the following example:

```
        Page 60,132
;       ****************************************************************
;       *                                                              *
;       * Author:   Allen L. Wyatt                                     *
;       * Date:     7/28/87                                            *
;       *                                                              *
;       * File:     ULCASEC.ASM                                        *
;       *                                                              *
;       * Descrpt:  Subroutine designed to convert a string to upper-*
;       *           or lowercase.  Designed to be called from          *
;       *           Microsoft C.                                       *
;       *                                                              *
;       * Format:   ulcase(s,x)                                        *
;       *               s:  Pointer to string to be converted         *
;       *               x:  Controls conversion                       *
;       *                   0 = Convert to uppercase                   *
;       *                   ?   Any other signifies convert to lower- *
;       *                       case                                   *
;       *                                                              *
;       ****************************************************************

                PUBLIC    _ULCASE

                NAME      ULCASE
_TEXT           SEGMENT   BYTE PUBLIC 'CODE'
                ASSUME    CS:_TEXT

PARMB           EQU       6
PARMA           EQU       4


;       ----------------------------------------------------------------
_ULCASE         PROC      NEAR
                PUSH      BP
                MOV       BP,SP
                PUSH      DI

                MOV       DI,[BP]+PARMA          ;Get string address
```

```
            MOV    AX,[BP]+PARMB        ;Get action variable
            CMP    AX,Ø                 ;Converting to uppercase?
            JZ     UPPER                ;Yes, so go handle

LOWER:      CMP    BYTE PTR [DI],Ø      ;Is this end of string?
            JE     EXIT                 ;Yes, so exit
            CMP    BYTE PTR [DI],'A'    ;Is it < A ?
            JB     L1                   ;Yes, so skip character
            CMP    BYTE PTR [DI],'Z'    ;Is it > Z ?
            JA     L1                   ;Yes, so skip character
            OR     BYTE PTR [DI],20h    ;Make lowercase (ØØ1ØØØØØb)
L1:         INC    DI                   ;Next character
            JMP    LOWER                ;Do it again

UPPER:      CMP    BYTE PTR [DI],Ø      ;Is this end of string?
            JE     EXIT                 ;Yes, so exit
            CMP    BYTE PTR [DI],'a'    ;Is it < a ?
            JB     U1                   ;Yes, so skip character
            CMP    BYTE PTR [DI],'z'    ;Is it > z ?
            JA     U1                   ;Yes, so skip character
            AND    BYTE PTR [DI],Ø5Fh   ;Make uppercase (Ø1Ø11111b)
U1:         INC    DI                   ;Next character
            JMP    UPPER                ;Do it again

EXIT:       POP    DI
            POP    BP
            RET
_ULCASE     ENDP
;           --------------------------------------------------------------
_TEXT       ENDS
            END
```

This simple program converts a string to either all upper- or lowercase. The program expects two parameters to be passed from C: a pointer to the string to be converted, and an integer value indicating whether the string is to be converted to upper- or lowercase.

Notice the calling syntax for the subroutine: ULCASE(S,X). Unlike some other languages, C places the function parameters onto the + stack in reverse order, from right to left. Thus, the first item pushed is the value for X, and the second item pushed is the pointer to S.

Notice that, in the body of the program, PARMA and PARMB are used to specify each parameter's relative location on the stack. PARMA represents the first (leftmost) parameter in the calling list and PARMB represents the second parameter.

The C program that uses this subroutine follows:

```
/* Program to test the calling of ULCASE()
   Written by Allen L. Wyatt
   Date: 7/28/87
*/

#include <stdio.h>
#include <string.h>
unsigned char s[]="This is the original string"
main()
{
while (strlen(s)!=Ø)
   {
   printf("String to convert: ");
   gets(s);
   if (strlen(s)!=Ø)
      {
      printf("\nUPPERCASE:\n");
      ulcase(s,Ø);
      printf("%s\nlowercase:\n",s);
      ulcase(s,1);
      printf("%s\n\n",s);
      }
   }
}
```

Summary

C is a popular language to which assembly language programs are easily interfaced. Although the specific interfacing syntax may vary from one compiler to another, the general guidelines are the same for all compilers. Code and data segments must conform to a specialized segment name, and public labels must adhere to a convention such as adding an underscore as a prefix or suffix.

Variables can be passed in C in many ways. You can pass variables on the stack as values or as pointers. Variables can be returned to C either by changing the variable value in the C data segment, or by returning a variable in the AX register. (This last method for returning a variable is not covered in this chapter but will be touched on in the developmental examples in Chapter 6 and particularly in Chapter 7.)

Part II

Assembly Language Tools

Includes

Using MASM
Using the Linker
Debugging Assembly Language Subroutines
Developing Libraries

6

Using MASM

Microsoft's *MASM* (for **M**acro **AS**se**M**bler) is one of the most popular assemblers for assembly language. Some other assemblers, such as the one with the IBM name on it, are actually the same MASM that Microsoft publishes. Still other assemblers are quite different from the Microsoft version.

To follow the instructions and examples in this chapter, you need either the Microsoft® Assembler (MASM.EXE) or the IBM Macro Assembler, both of which have virtually identical sets of commands.

Before getting into the specifics of how MASM operates, let's look at what an assembler does.

What an Assembler Does

As this book's Introduction points out, an *assembler* is a program that translates assembly language instructions into machine language. In concept, the assembler's job is simple. Its translation process simply converts assembly language mnemonics into a numeric equivalent that represents the proper machine language code—which sounds straightforward but frequently is not. Determining what the programmer wants can be tedious and tricky. This *parsing* process is what the assembler program spends the most time doing.

An assembler does not fully translate source code into machine language but creates instead an object code file which, by itself, is not executable. Although the assembler program parses and translates virtually every instruction, some instructions cannot be encoded at this point. Instead, a separate pass is required to translate the object file into an executable file. (This step, which is called *linking*, is covered in Chapter 7.)

MASM is a two-pass assembler that creates relocatable object code which subsequently can be linked and executed. A two-pass assembler must read the source code file twice to create the object code file. During the first pass, MASM

- parses the source code, calculating the offset for each line

- makes assumptions about undefined values

- does elementary error checking, displaying error messages if necessary

- generates a pass 1 listing file, if requested

During the second pass, MASM

- attempts to reconcile the value assumptions made during pass 1

- generates the assembly listing (LST) file, if specified

- generates the object code, storing it in the object (OBJ) file

- generates the cross-reference (CRF) file, if specified

- completes the error-checking process, displaying error messages if necessary

A Sample Program

To proceed through this chapter, we need a sample subroutine to assemble. This subroutine will be neither large nor complex, nor will it exemplify the best reasons for using assembly language. Although writing this routine in C would be easier than writing it in assembly language, we will use it to demonstrate how to assemble (and later link and debug) a subroutine.

Let's assume that you need to determine the total number of blocks in a pyramid in which each ascending row contains one less block than the row beneath it, with only one block in the top row (see fig. 6.1).

The bottom row contains 15 blocks, the next row, 14, and so on, with only 1 block in the top row. Your job is to calculate the total number of blocks needed, given only the number of blocks in the bottom row. You'll use the sample program to do the job.

The program (SUMS.ASM) is designed to be called from Microsoft C. The program, when passed a pointer to a 16-bit integer, calculates and returns the result in the same integer variable. The assembly language subroutine listing is as follows:

```
Page 60,132
; *********************************************************************
; *                                                                   *
; *   Program Name:    SUMS.ASM                                        *
; *   Written by:      Allen L. Wyatt    5/4/87                        *
; *                                                                    *
; *   Purpose:         Given an integer number X, find the sum of      *
; *                    X + (X-1) + (X-2) + (X-3) + (X-4) ... + 2 + 1    *
; *                    Designed to be called from Microsoft C.         *
; *                                                                    *
; *   Format:          SUMS(X)                                         *
; *                                                                    *
; *********************************************************************

                PUBLIC  _SUMS

                NAME    SUMS
_TEXT           SEGMENT BYTE PUBLIC 'CODE'
                ASSUME  CS:_TEXT

NUM_ADR         EQU     4

_SUMS           PROC    NEAR
                PUSH    BP
                MOV     BP,SP

                MOV     AX,0                ;INITIALIZE TO ZERO
                MOV     BX,[BP]+NUM_ADR     ;GET ADDRESS OF VALUE
                MOV     CX,[BX]             ;GET ACTUAL VALUE
                JCXZ    S3                  ;NUM=0, NO NEED TO DO
S1:             ADC     AX,CX               ;ADD ROW VALUE
                JC      S2                  ;QUIT IF AX OVERFLOWED
                LOOP    S1                  ;REPEAT PROCESS
                JMP     S3                  ;SUCCESSFUL COMPLETION
S2:             MOV     AX,0                ;FORCE A ZERO
S3:             MOV     [BX],AX             ;PLACE BACK IN VALUE

                POP     BP
                RET
_SUMS           ENDP

_TEXT           ENDS
                END
```

Fig. 6.1.
A sample pyramid.

If the number entered results in a sum that is greater than 65,535 (the largest unsigned integer number that can be held in 16 bits), the program sets the result to 0.

To prepare for the balance of this chapter (and for Chapters 7, 8, and 9), enter this subroutine as it is shown here. The controlling C program is listed in Chapter 7.

Using MASM Interactively

With your subroutine entered, you are ready to assemble the file. Make sure that SUMS.ASM (the subroutine file) and MASM.EXE are in your current disk directory. If MASM.EXE is not in your current directory, it should at least be available through your current search path.

At the DOS prompt, enter

MASM

to start the assembly process. You will see a notice and prompt similar to the following:

```
Microsoft (R) Macro Assembler  Version 4.00
Copyright (C) Microsoft Corp 1981, 1983, 1984, 1985.  All rights
reserved.

Source filename [.ASM]: _
```

The assembler is waiting for you to indicate which file you want to assemble. (The default answer, which is shown in brackets, is accepted if you simply press the Enter key.) Enter the root name of the file to assemble, *SUMS*. The extension .ASM is assumed. When you make this entry, the following should appear on the screen:

```
Source filename [.ASM]: SUMS
Object filename [SUMS.OBJ]: _
```

Notice that you are now prompted for the name of the .OBJ file to create. Because you want to use the default suggestion of SUMS.OBJ, simply press the Enter key. The following prompt is displayed:

```
Object filename [SUMS.OBJ]:
Source listing  [NUL.LST]: _
```

A *source listing* is an optional file that is created by the assembler as it assembles the .ASM file. (This file is explained later in the chapter.) Notice that the default is NUL.LST. If you press Enter, no file (NUL) will be created. But you need to create a file to use later. To create this file, called SUMS.LST, type *SUMS*. Then you will see the following prompt:

```
Source listing  [NUL.LST]: SUMS
Cross-reference [NUL.CRF]: _
```

This cross-reference file is another optional file that is explained later in the chapter. To indicate that you want to create the file SUMS.CRF, enter *SUMS* here.

Now that you have answered MASM's four questions, your disk drive will be active for a short time. Then you will see a message, similar to the following:

```
49922 Bytes symbol space free

   Ø Warning Errors
   Ø Severe  Errors
```

which indicates that the assembly process is complete. The important information here is that no errors occurred. Had there been errors, an error message indicating the type of error and the line number at which the error occurred would have appeared on the screen during assembly. The same errors also would be noted in the listing file (SUMS.LST). The number of total errors would be reflected in the final tally displayed on the screen.

If you receive any error messages, you must correct the errors before continuing. Check your source file (SUMS.ASM) against the listing file (SUMS.LST), correct any errors, and try the assembly process again. When you have corrected all the errors, you can proceed with this chapter.

Using the MASM Command Line

Instead of using MASM interactively, you can use MASM in another way. You can enter, directly from the MASM command line, any or all of the responses to individual prompts. For instance, entering (from DOS) either

    MASM SUMS, ,SUMS,SUMS;

or

    MASM SUMS, , , ;

will create the same files created by the interactive method described in the preceding section.

You'll remember that MASM asks four questions. In the preceding examples, the answers to those questions are parameters to the MASM command, with commas separating the parameters and a semicolon terminating the line.

Notice the two consecutive commas, which indicate blank parameters. In this case, MASM will use the first parameter (SUMS) as the implied parameter.

To enter parameters directly from the MASM command line, use the following syntax:

    MASM asm,obj,lst,crf

In this syntax, **MASM** is the command. *asm*, *obj*, *lst*, and *crf* are the file types that each parameter indicates. These file types, which were mentioned in the preceding section, are discussed in greater detail later in this chapter.

To indicate that you do not want a particular type of file, simply use NUL as the parameter for that file type. For instance, the following commands both instruct MASM to create an OBJ file, but no LST or CRF file.

    MASM SUMS, ,NUL,NUL;

    MASM SUMS, ;

Although the second command line is considerably shorter than the first, both have the same effect. The semicolon instructs MASM to begin processing without expecting additional parameters.

MASM Options

MASM accepts several parameters (referred to as *options* in the MASM documentation) that alter how MASM functions. You can enter these option directly from the command line or when you are running MASM interactively. The MASM options and their meanings are listed alphabetically in table 6.1.

Table 6.1
MASM Options

Option	Meaning
/A	Alphabetic segment order
/B*blocks*	Sets buffer size=number of *blocks*
/C	Cross-reference file
/D	Create a pass 1 listing
/D*x*	Define symbol=*x*
/E	Emulate floating-point instructions
/I*path*	Set include file path=*path*
/L	Listing file
/ML	Make case of names significant
/MU	Make all names uppercase
/MX	Make case of PUBLIC/EXTERNAL significant
/N	No tables included in listing file
/P	Check code purity
/R	Create code for 8087/80287
/S	Source-code segment order
/T	Suppress assembly completion messages
/V	Verbose—show extra assembly statistics
/X	Force inclusion of false conditionals
/Z	Display lines containing errors

You can include assembler options at any point in the MASM command or interactive format. Regardless of where you include them, the options affect all relevant files. The options usually are included at the end of the command line or at the end of your response to the last MASM prompt. You can enter the options as either upper- or lowercase.

You must include a delimiter before the option letter. This delimiter can be either a slash (/), as shown in table 6.1, or a hyphen (-). MASM does not differentiate between the two symbols.

Some of the assembler options (/S, /MU, /C, and /L) are superficial—they are included only for compatibility with earlier versions of MASM or with other operating systems, such as XENIX®. Other options control the way in which the OBJ file is generated. Still others control MASM's interaction with the programmer. Let's look at each of MASM's options.

Alphabetic Segment Order (/A)

This option controls the way MASM writes segments into the object (OBJ) file. MASM ordinarily writes segments in the order in which they occur in the source file. But some assemblers write segments in alphabetic order, regardless of how they occur in the source file. Because these files are in alphabetic order, they may not assemble and execute properly through MASM. To compensate, use the /A option to change the order in which MASM writes segments.

Set Buffer Size (/B*blocks*)

The size of the *buffer* (the work area MASM uses in memory) is normally 32K. Depending on the amount of free RAM available on your computer, you can set the buffer size to any amount between 1K and 63K.

blocks is the number of 1K blocks to set aside for the buffer area. Setting aside a buffer area larger than the source file accelerates the assembly process, because all operations can occur in memory.

Create Cross-Reference File (/C)

This option controls the creation of a cross-reference (CRF) file (described later in this chapter). When invoked, /C causes creation of a file with the same root name as the source file and an extension of .CRF. This option, which is included mainly for compatibility with XENIX, supersedes the answer you give to the cross-reference prompt or in the command line's CRF position.

Create Pass 1 Listing (/D)

This option instructs MASM to generate a pass 1 listing in the LST file. If you have not specified an LST file, this option simply lists pass 1 errors to the screen.

Because MASM, as a *two-pass assembler*, does two source code iterations to produce the finished object code, a pass 1 listing is beneficial if you need help locating phase errors. Phase errors are generated if MASM makes assumptions during the first pass that don't hold true in the second.

Define Symbol (/D*x*)

This option allows you to define an assembler symbol, where *x* is the symbol being defined. Because the symbol, which can be any valid assembly language symbol, is considered a null string, this option is similar to defining the symbol with an EQU directive in the source file.

Conditional assembly statements (IFDEF and IFNDEF) can use the symbol defined by this option to control how an assembly occurs. (Conditional assembly statements and procedures are discussed later in this chapter.)

Emulate Floating-Point Instructions (/E)

The /E option (which is the opposite of the /R option) directs MASM to emulate the floating-point capabilities of the 8087 or 80287 numeric coprocessors. MASM does not contain the actual emulation routines. Those routines are included when the object code is linked and a math-emulation library is used. Your high-level language (Microsoft C, for example) may include a library of this type because such libraries generally come from a third-party source.

When you use the /E option, the code that results can be executed on any compatible computer, regardless of whether you have an 8087 or 80287 coprocessor.

Include File Path (/I*path*)

This option lets you specify where MASM should look for files to be included in the source file. You can use the option to specify, one at a time, as many as 10 different paths.

If the INCLUDE directive in the source file contains a path specification, that explicit path overrides any paths set by the /I option. If the INCLUDE directive consists of only a file name, the /I option paths will be searched in the order they are invoked.

Create Listing File (/L)

This option controls creation of an assembly listing (LST) file. When invoked, the /L option creates a file with the same root name as the source file and a .LST extension. (The assembly listing file is described later in this chapter.)

This option, which is included primarily for compatibility with XENIX, supersedes the answer you give to the assembly listing prompt or place in the command line's LST position.

Make Case Significant (/ML)

Some programmers like to keep both upper- and lowercase in their code, and some high-level language compilers demand or expect this difference. Ordinarily, MASM converts to uppercase all symbol, variable, and label names. This option ensures that no such conversion occurs.

Make Uppercase (/MU)

The /MU option, which converts all symbol, variable, and label names to uppercase letters, is the default option. This option is included for compatibility with other assemblers and operating systems.

Make PUBLIC/EXTERNAL
Case Significant (/MX)

This option is similar to /ML, but affects only PUBLIC and EXTERNAL names. The /MX option ensures that, instead of being converted to uppercase, any symbol, variable, or label names defined as EXTERNAL or declared PUBLIC will remain in the case in which they were entered.

Exclude Tables from Listing File (/N)

Normally, MASM includes, at the end of an assembly listing (LST) file, several tables that recap the source file's structure. You can use /N to exclude those tables without changing the rest of the listing. Using /N causes MASM to function slightly faster.

Check Purity of Code (/P)

MASM creates protected mode coding for the Intel® 80286 microprocessor if the source file contains the .286p directive. The /P option specifies that MASM should check whether the source code is "pure" (that it contains no data moved in the code segment with a CS: override). If you use this option, an additional check is done and an additional error code may be generated.

Generate Numeric Coprocessor Code (/R)

Using this option causes MASM to generate coding that is compatible with either the 8087 or the 80287 numeric coprocessor. This generation of code affects only floating-point operations. Code created with the /R option can run only on computers that use one of these chips.

Occurrence Segment Ordering (/S)

This option, which is the opposite of /A, is the default option. /S specifies that segments be written in the order they occur in the source code. This option is included for compatibility with other assemblers and operating systems.

Suppress Assembly Messages (/T)

The /T (for *terse*) option suppresses all assembler messages if the assembly is successful. If at least one error occurs, the normal assembler copyright and version information will be displayed before the error is listed.

Include Extra Assembly Statistics (/V)

This option turns on MASM's verbose mode, which causes additional statistics to be generated when the file is assembled. For instance, using the /V option to assemble SUMS.ASM (refer to the "Using the MASM Command Line" section of this chapter) results in the following screen display:

```
MASM SUMS,,,/V;

Microsoft (R) Macro Assembler  Version 4.00
Copyright (C) Microsoft Corp 1981, 1983, 1984, 1985.  All
rights reserved.


    43 Source  Lines
    43 Total   Lines
    28 Symbols

 49926 Bytes symbol space free

     0 Warning Errors
     0 Severe  Errors
```

The additional information generated by the /V option includes the number of source lines, total lines, and symbols assembled.

List False Conditional Statements (/X)

If you request an LST file, and your source file includes conditional assembly directives, this option controls the listing of the code that would not normally be included in the LST file.

Normally, code that is not included in the OBJ file because the conditional assembly directives controlling its inclusion were FALSE is also not included in the assembly listing file. Using the /X option causes these source code lines to be included in the listing, even though no machine language code is generated.

Display Error Lines (/Z)

MASM ordinarily indicates compilation errors by displaying an error message and the line number at which the error(s) occurred. To display the source code line with the error, use the /Z option.

Files Created by MASM

I have referred throughout this chapter to the three file types that MASM creates: the *object*, *listing*, and *cross-reference* files.

The way you invoke MASM or answer MASM's prompts determines whether these files will be created. If you assembled SUMS.ASM and requested all files, you should see the following files displayed on your screen when you use DIR after assembly:

```
DIR SUMS.*

   Volume in drive C has no label
   Directory of  C:\ASSEMBLY

SUMS     ASM     178Ø     5-Ø4-87     7:58a
SUMS     LST     4652     5-Ø4-87    12:37p
SUMS     OBJ       91     5-Ø4-87    12:37p
SUMS     CRF      148     5-Ø4-87    12:37p
         4 File(s)   1514Ø864 bytes free
```

SUMS.ASM is the source code file. The other three files were created by MASM. Let's take a look at each of these files and what they represent.

The Object File (OBJ)

This file, which generally is the smallest and most important file created by MASM, is basically a machine language file. But because the linking pass must be performed to resolve external references, this file is not executable. Object files are discussed in greater detail in Chapter 7.

The List File (LST)

This file is the assembly language listing of the source file. It contains the source statements and the machine language instructions into which they translate. The SUMS.LST file follows:

```
Microsoft (R) Macro Assembler  Version 4.00      5/04/87 12:37:16


                                    Page    1-1


 1                           Page 60,132
 2                         ; ************************************************************
 3                         ; *                                                          *
 4                         ; *  Program Name:  SUMS.ASM                                 *
 5                         ; *  Written by:    Allen L. Wyatt   5/4/87                  *
 6                         ; *                                                          *
 7                         ; *  Purpose:       Given an integer number X, find the sum of *
 8                         ; *                 X + (X-1) + (X-2) + (X-3) + (X-4) ... + 2 + 1 *
 9                         ; *                 Designed to be called from Microsoft C.  *
10                         ; *                                                          *
11                         ; *  Format:        SUMS(X)                                  *
12                         ; *                                                          *
13                         ; ************************************************************
14
15                                   PUBLIC   _SUMS
16
17                                   NAME SUMS
18 0000         _TEXT      SEGMENT BYTE PUBLIC 'CODE'
19                                   ASSUME  CS:_TEXT
20
21 = 0004       NUM_ADR    EQU  4
22
23 0000         _SUMS      PROC NEAR
24 0000   55               PUSH BP
25 0001   8B EC            MOV  BP,SP
26
27 0003   B8 0000          MOV  AX,0            ;INITIALIZE TO ZERO
28 0006   8B 5E 04         MOV  BX,[BP]+NUM_ADR ;GET ADDRESS OF VALUE
29 0009   8B 0F            MOV  CX,[BX]         ;GET ACTUAL VALUE
```

```
30 000B  E3 0C                    S1:   JCXZ S3          ;NUM=0, NO NEED TO DO
31 000D  13 C1                          ADC  AX,CX       ;ADD ROW VALUE
32 000F  72 05                          JC   S2          ;QUIT IF AX OVERFLOWED
33 0011  E2 FA                          LOOP S1          ;REPEAT PROCESS
34 0013  EB 04 90                       JMP  S3          ;SUCCESSFUL COMPLETION
35 0016  B8 0000              S2:       MOV  AX,0        ;FORCE A ZERO
36 0019  89 07               S3:       MOV  [BX],AX     ;PLACE BACK IN VALUE
37
38 001B  5D                            POP  BP
39 001C  C3                            RET
40                           _SUMS     ENDP
41
42 001D                      _TEXT     ENDS
43                                     END
```

Microsoft (R) Macro Assembler   Version 4.00   5/04/87 12:37:16

Symbols-1

Segments and Groups:

N a m e	Size	Align	Combine	Class
_TEXT	001D	BYTE	PUBLIC	'CODE'

Symbols:

N a m e	Type	Value	Attr		
NUM_ADR	Number	0004			
S1	L NEAR	000D	_TEXT		
S2	L NEAR	0016	_TEXT		
S3	L NEAR	0019	_TEXT		
_SUMS	N PROC	0000	_TEXT	Global	Length 001D

```
    43 Source  Lines
    43 Total   Lines
    28 Symbols

 49926 Bytes symbol space free

     0 Warning Errors
     0 Severe  Errors
```

This file and listing are extremely helpful. You have the hard copy you need to debug a program effectively. And the listing is great for hard-copy archiving.

You already may know that not all printers print the same number of characters per line. This assembly listing file was formatted for 60-line pages, with 132 characters per line. The PAGE directive at the top of the file controls this format. If your printer handles only 80 characters per line, you easily can change the line to

```
PAGE 6Ø,8Ø
```

for a LST file formatted for 80 characters per line. How you change the line is up to you.

Notice also that the second page of this assembly listing lists information about the file just assembled. This status information includes a recap of the segments, groups, and symbols in the file. You can suppress the information (in this case, one page) by assembling the file with the /N option.

The Cross-Reference File (CRF)

The cross-reference file created by MASM (called SUMS.CRF in the example), contains information that Microsoft's cross-reference program (CREF.EXE) uses to create a cross-reference listing of symbols used in the source file.

By itself, SUMS.CRF is of little value. To create the actual cross-reference file, make sure that CREF.EXE is either in your current directory or accessible through the current search path.

CREF, like MASM, can be used interactively or on a single command line. Unlike MASM, which requires four responses, CREF requires only two: the name of the CRF file, and the name of the file that CREF is to create. Thus, the entire interactive dialog for CREF is

```
C>CREF

Microsoft (R) Cross-Reference Utility  Version 4.ØØ
Copyright (C) Microsoft Corp 1981, 1983, 1984, 1985.  All rights
reserved.

Cross [.CRF]: SUMS
Listing [sums.REF]:

7 Symbols
```

As with MASM, you can shorten this process. At the DOS prompt, simply enter

CREF SUMS,;

Either of these methods creates a file (called SUMS.REF) that contains a
formatted cross-reference of the symbols in SUMS.ASM. The contents of
SUMS.REF follow:

```
Microsoft Cross-Reference  Version 4.00              Mon May 11 13:05:02 1987


   Symbol Cross-Reference        (# is definition)                     Cref-1


   CODE . . . . . . . . . . . .  18

   NUM_ADR. . . . . . . . . . .  21      21#     28

   S1 . . . . . . . . . . . . .  31      31#     33
   S2 . . . . . . . . . . . . .  32      35      35#
   S3 . . . . . . . . . . . . .  30      34      36      36#

   _SUMS. . . . . . . . . . . .  15      23      23#
   _TEXT. . . . . . . . . . . .  18      18#     19      42


   7 Symbols
```

This listing shows that SUMS.ASM contains seven different symbols. SUMS.REF
lists each symbol with line numbers indicating where the symbol is referenced.
If a pound sign (#) is appended to the line number, the symbol is defined on
that line.

These line numbers refer to the line numbers generated in the assembly listing
(LST) file. If a LST file was not generated, all the line numbers will be
number 1.

One of the valuable ways that a cross-reference file can help you make your
assembly language coding more efficient is that you may be able to delete a
symbol that has only two references, one of which is the line where it is
defined.

Conditional Assembly

The capability of doing *conditional assemblies* is one of MASM's powerful features. Conditional assembly means that the assembler can decide, based on the values of certain symbols (or flags), whether to include specific blocks of code. This capability can greatly simplify the development process.

Table 6.2 lists the conditional assembly directives. These directives are not direct assembly language commands. Rather, they are commands to the assembler that control how the source code file is processed.

Table 6.2
Conditional Assembly Directives

Directive	Meaning
IF	Assemble if true
IFE	Assemble if false
IF1	Assemble if pass 1
IF2	Assemble if pass 2
IFDEF	Assemble if defined
IFNDEF	Assemble if not defined
IFB	Assemble if blank
IFNB	Assemble if not blank
IFIDN	Assemble if identical
IFDIF	Assemble if different
ELSE	Used with any of above
ENDIF	End of conditional block

Each of the conditional assembly directives listed in table 6.2 requires an expression or argument. MASM evaluates the expression or argument and, based on that evaluation, takes an appropriate action.

For instance, consider the following code segment:

```
ifdef debug
                INCLUDE DEBUG.ASM
endif
```

When this segment is coupled with the MASM command line invocation

```
MASM FILE,,,/DDEBUG;
```

the file DEBUG.ASM will be included in the object code. If you do not define debug, the code will not be included. This usage lets you include debugging code easily and flexibly to facilitate the development process. To create the proper object file after debugging, you simply omit the /D option from the MASM command line.

Conditional assembly statements can be used in numerous ways. Used wisely, they can make the development process faster and less painful. Just remember that they control only the assembler.

Using MASM through a Batch File

To make the assembly process easier, you can set up a batch file (as you can with many other development commands and programs). An example of such a file (ASM.BAT) follows:

```
ECHO OFF
CLS

:LOOP
REM - CHECK IF NO FILES AVAILABLE ON COMMAND LINE
IF %1/ == / GOTO DONE

REM - CHECK IF EXTENSION (.ASM) WAS ENTERED
IF NOT EXIST %1 GOTO CHKEXT
    ECHO Assembling ... %1
    MASM %1,; >NUL
    IF ERRORLEVEL 1 GOTO ERROR
    GOTO NEXT

:CHKEXT
REM - CHECK FOR ROOT PLUS ASSUMED EXTENSION
IF NOT EXIST %1.ASM GOTO NOT-FOUND
    ECHO Assembling ... %1.ASM
    MASM %1.ASM; >NUL
    IF ERRORLEVEL 1 GOTO ERROR
    GOTO NEXT

:NOT-FOUND
REM - FILE NOT LOCATED
ECHO File %1 Not Located or Found in Current Directory !
GOTO NEXT

:ERROR
ECHO Error detected while assembling %1
```

```
:NEXT
REM - CONTINUE WITH NEXT FILE - END OF LOOP
SHIFT
GOTO LOOP

:DONE
REM - FINAL MESSAGE AND ALL THROUGH
ECHO All Files have been Assembled !
```

This file assumes that you will enter the command line as

ASM file1 file2 file3 . . .

where *file1*, *file2*, *file3*, etc. are the names of the source code files to be assembled. You do not have to enter the .ASM extension, although this batch file checks to see whether an extension has been entered, and reacts accordingly. If none has been entered, the extension is assumed to be .ASM.

This batch file does not create an LST or CRF file, nor does it use any of the MASM options. If, because of your specific needs, you want to generate these files or use options, you will need to change only the two lines that invoke MASM.

When MASM terminates, an error level is returned to DOS. You can use this exit code to control how the batch file will function. This exit code is used simplistically (through the ERRORLEVEL batch command) in the sample batch file, which checks to see whether an exit code of at least 1 was returned and, if it was, displays a message indicating the status. But you can be quite elaborate in your implementation of an assembler batch file. Table 6.3 lists the possible exit codes for MASM version 4.0 and their meanings.

Provided that ASM.BAT can be located in your current search path, you can use it from any subdirectory. The source code file should be in the current directory, however, and the OBJ file will remain in the current directory.

Summary

This chapter covered the use of MASM, the Microsoft Macro Assembler. (The same principles apply to the IBM Macro Assembler, also created by Microsoft.) Using the assembler properly is essential to your success in using assembly language. MASM is not difficult to use, even though several options are available. You probably will use the options only in special situations.

In the next chapter, you will learn about the next step in developing assembly language routines, that of using the linker.

Table 6.3
MASM Exit Codes

Code	Meaning
0	No errors detected
1	Argument error
2	Can't open source file
3	Can't open LST file
4	Can't open OBJ file
5	Can't open CRF file
6	Can't open INCLUDE file
7	Assembly error
8	Memory allocation error
9	Unused
10	/D option error
11	Interrupted by user

7

Using the Linker

In Chapter 6, you learned how to use the Microsoft Macro Assembler (MASM). You learned also that an assembler (such as MASM) does not produce executable machine code. Instead, the OBJ file that MASM creates must be *linked* successfully in order to work properly.

This chapter covers using the LINK.EXE program. This program is available from a multitude of sources, most noticeably Microsoft and IBM. A copy of LINK.EXE usually is included with any MS-DOS or PC DOS computer system. You will need a copy of the program to complete this chapter.

Before we get started using LINK.EXE, let's take a look at what a linker does.

What a Linker Does

A *linker* is a program that translates relocatable object code (produced by an assembler or compiler) into executable machine code. The linker performs three main tasks:

- combines separate object modules into one executable file

- attempts to resolve references to external variables

- produces a listing (if you ask for one) showing how the object files were linked

Some people refer to these programs as linkers (as I have); others call them *linkage editors*. Whatever they are called, they do these three basic tasks. Many different linkers are available. The linker we use in this chapter (and throughout the rest of the book) is LINK.EXE, distributed by both Microsoft and IBM.

The Programs To Be Linked

To use LINK, you need at least one object code file. If you entered and assembled the SUMS.ASM program presented in Chapter 6, you already have access to SUMS.OBJ. The SUMS.OBJ file cannot be linked by itself, however, because it is designed to be called as a function from a Microsoft C program. To make a successful link, you must enter and compile the controlling C program.

Because we simply are doing some testing, the name of this program will be TEST.C. Enter the following program, and then compile it to produce an object code file called TEST.OBJ:

```
/* Program to test the calling of SUMS()
   Written by Allen L. Wyatt
   Date: 5/4/87
*/

#include <stdio.h>
main()
{
unsigned short j, x;
j=Ø;
while (j!=999)
    {
    printf("Initial Value: ");
    scanf("%u",&j);
    if (j!=999)
        {
        x=status(j);
        }
    }
for (j=1, x=1; x!=Ø; x=status(j++));
}

status(orig)
unsigned short orig;
{
unsigned short new;
new=orig;
sums(&new);
printf("%5u%1Øu\n",orig,new);
return (new);
}
```

This simple program performs two basic tasks. First, it allows you to enter a number that is used as a value for calling SUMS(). Both the original and derived number are displayed. Second, if you enter the number 999, the program exits the interactive portion and proceeds through a loop, starting at 1, that displays values and derived values until it reaches the limit of SUMS( ). You may remember from Chapter 6 that this limit is reached when the derived value is greater than 65,535. When this limit is exceeded, SUMS( ) returns a 0 and terminates execution of the controlling C program.

Although you can use LINK in several different ways, the principal ways are interactively or with just a command line. Let's look first at using LINK interactively.

Using LINK Interactively

Once you have the two object code files, TEST.OBJ and SUMS.OBJ, you are ready to link the files. Make sure that you have these files in your current directory. You should also have access to LINK.EXE, either in the current directory or in the search path. To start the linking process, enter the following at the DOS prompt:

LINK

When you press Enter, you'll see a notice and prompt similar to the following:

```
Microsoft (R) Overlay Linker   Version 3.51
Copyright (C) Microsoft Corp 1983, 1984, 1985, 1986.   All rights
reserved.

Object Modules [.OBJ]: _
```

The linker is waiting for you to specify the files to be linked. The default answer is shown in brackets; the linker accepts this answer if you simply press the Enter key. Enter the root names of the files to be linked, separated by either a space or a plus sign (+). Because the linker assumes an extension of .OBJ (unless you override it), you need to specify only the root names. When you make the proper entries, the following message should appear:

```
Object Modules [.OBJ]: TEST SUMS
Run File [TEST.EXE]: _
```

Notice that the linker now is prompting you for the name of the EXE file to create. (The EXE file is the executable run file that LINK.EXE creates.) The default answer is TEST.EXE, which is the name we will use. When you press the Enter key to signify that you accept the default, the linker asks the following:

```
Run File [TEST.EXE]:
List File [NUL.MAP]: _
```

A list file is optional, as the default of NUL.MAP indicates. List files for the linker have the extension of .MAP because they provide a "map" as to how the linker did its work. For later purposes, enter TEST to indicate that you want a list file named TEST.MAP. When you do, you will see the following prompt:

```
List File [NUL.MAP]: TEST
Libraries [.LIB]: _
```

LINK needs some direction about which library files to use for external references that it cannot resolve from within the object code files. (Libraries are covered in Chapter 9, and there are no consequential external references in this example. LINK will search automatically and use some C libraries, but again, those are covered in Chapter 9.) Simply press the Enter key to indicate that no explicit libraries are to be used.

LINK has now asked its four questions, and you have responded. Notice that your disk drive is active for a short time; then the DOS prompt returns. The return of the DOS prompt indicates that the linking process is complete, and no errors occurred. If an error had occurred, an error message would have appeared during linking, indicating the type of error and the source file for the error.

If you receive any error messages, you must correct the errors before continuing. Check your files against the listings in Chapter 6 and in the previous section; then try to assemble, compile, and link again. When you have corrected the errors, you can proceed with this chapter.

Using the LINK Command Line

As mentioned earlier, you also can use LINK from the DOS command line. You can enter any or all of the responses to individual prompts directly after the LINK command. For instance, entering either of the following produces the same results as those achieved in the last section:

```
LINK TEST SUMS, ,TEST;
LINK TEST+SUMS, , ;
```

Remember that LINK asks four questions during an interactive session. The parameters in either of these command lines provide answers to the questions. The parameters are separated by commas, and the line ends with a semicolon.

Notice that some parameters are left blank, as the two consecutive commas indicate. In this case, LINK uses the first parameter (TEST) as the implied parameter.

The following syntax is used to enter parameters directly from the MASM command line:

LINK *obj,exe,map,lib*

Here, *obj, exe, map*, and *lib* indicate the file type that each parameter designates. These file types were touched on in the last section and are discussed in more detail later in this chapter.

How do you indicate that you do not want a particular type of file? Simply by using NUL as the parameter for that file type. For instance, both of the following commands instruct MASM to create an EXE file but no MAP file:

LINK TEST SUMS, ,NUL;
LINK TEST+SUMS, ;

Notice that the second command line, although shorter than the first, is effectively the same. The semicolon instructs LINK to begin processing without expecting any more parameters.

The LINK Response File

You can respond to the four LINK questions within a file, logically called a *response file*. This method of using LINK is beneficial when you know that you will be linking the same program over and over again during development; repeatedly typing answers to each question can be tiresome.

To use this method of providing input to LINK, create a normal ASCII text file, with any name you want, that has the answers to each question. Each question's answer should be on a separate line. For instance, using our sample programs, the response file would have only four lines:

```
TEST SUMS

TEST
;
```

LINK uses this response file to link TEST.OBJ and SUMS.OBJ, producing the default output file TEST.EXE. Also, the list file TEST.MAP is created and no libraries are specified.

To use a response file with LINK, simply invoke LINK using the following command syntax:

LINK @*filename.ext*

filename.ext is the name of the response file LINK is to use. Notice the @ symbol directly before the file name. This symbol is the signal that LINK needs to differentiate between a response file and a source file.

If our sample response file is named TEST.LNK, then the following command will run LINK and provide input to LINK from our response file:

    LINK @TEST.LNK

The more you use LINK, the more you will understand the value of using response files.

Using LINK Options

LINK has several parameters that alter how LINK functions. The Microsoft documentation refers to these parameters as *options*. You can enter them either directly from the command line or when you are running LINK interactively. Table 7.1 lists alphabetically the different LINK options and their meaning.

Table 7.1
LINK Options

Option	*Meaning*
/CO	Create CodeView compatible file
/CP:para	Set maximum allocation space
/DO	Use MS-DOS segment ordering
/DS	Place DGROUP data at high end of group
/E	Pack the .EXE file created by LINK
/HE	List LINK options
/HI	Load program in high memory
/I	Island
/L	Include line numbers in list file
/M	Include global symbol table in list file
/NOD	Do not use default libraries
/NOG	Do not associate groups
/NOI	Do not ignore case differences
/O:int	Set overlay loader interrupt number
/P	Pause for disk change
/SE:seg	Specify maximum segments
/ST:size	Override stack size

Some of these options may not be available in your version of LINK.EXE. Microsoft, IBM, and others have distributed many different versions of LINK, each with different parameters. This group of parameters comes with version 3.51 of LINK as distributed with Microsoft C, version 4.0. This set is used here because it seems to be a complete set of the available options. Your version of LINK probably has many of these options.

You can include linker options at any point in the LINK command or during the interactive format. Regardless of the inclusion point, options affect all the relevant files. Usually, you include the options at the end of the command line or at the end of your response to the last LINK prompt. You can enter the options in either upper- or lowercase.

You must include a delimiter before the actual option letter. Table 7.1 shows this delimiter as a slash, but you can also use a hyphen (-); to LINK, they are equivalent.

Let's look at each of LINK's options.

Create CodeView Compatible File (/CO)

This special option instructs LINK to create an EXE file that is compatible with Microsoft's CodeView™ debugger. (CodeView is distributed with version 4.0 of the Microsoft C Compiler.) For more information on using CodeView, refer to the *Microsoft CodeView and C Language Reference Manual*.

Set Allocation Space (/CP:para)

This option allows you to specify the amount of memory (in paragraphs) the program is to use. MS-DOS requires that programs request a block of memory for program use so that there are no memory conflicts. Usually, LINK requests all memory, or 65,535 paragraphs. Because this much memory is never available, MS-DOS returns the largest contiguous block of memory for program use.

Using this option lets you state explicitly how much memory should be requested. *para* is the number of paragraphs (16-byte memory blocks) that your program's code and data need. Because the amount of memory you designate probably will be an amount smaller than LINK normally allocates, memory will be freed for other purposes.

If *para* is smaller than the amount of memory the program actually needs, LINK ignores the *para* parameter and requests the maximum memory area.

Use MS-DOS Segment Ordering (/DO)

The /DO option instructs LINK to process files using the MS-DOS segment ordering rules. These rules are as follows:

1. Segments with a class name of CODE are placed at the start of the linked file.

2. Segments with a class name of DGROUP are placed at the end of the linked file.

3. All other segments are placed after the CODE class segments, but before the DGROUP class.

Normally, LINK copies segments to the file in the order that they occur in the object files.

Place DGROUP at High End (/DS)

LINK normally assigns data in DGROUP (a program's data group) to a low address, starting at an offset of 0. This option causes LINK to start data assignments so that the last byte in DGROUP is at an offset of FFFFh, or the top of memory. Usually, this option is used in conjunction with the /HI option.

Pack EXE File (/E)

The /E option causes LINK to create an EXE file that is optimized for size. Using this option may result in a more compact EXE file. How much, if any, space this option will save through packing the executable file depends on the number of repeated bytes used in the file. If your program requires a considerable amount of relocation upon loading, this option causes the relocation table to be optimized for size. If the resulting EXE file is smaller, it logically will load more quickly than a file linked without this option.

If you plan to convert your EXE file to a COM file, do not use this option. If you pack your EXE file, you cannot convert it to a COM file.

List LINK Options (/HE)

The /HE option is LINK's help function. If you enter

    LINK /HE

LINK responds with a listing of the available options. The screen appears similar to the following:

```
Microsoft (R) Overlay Linker   Version 3.51
Copyright (C) Microsoft Corp 1983, 1984, 1985, 1986.  All rights
reserved.

Valid switches are:
  CODEVIEW
  CPARMAXALLOC
  DOSSEG
  DSALLOCATE
  EXEPACK
  HELP
  HIGH
  ISLAND
  LINENUMBERS
  MAP
  NODEFAULTLIBRARYSEARCH
  NOGROUPASSOCIATION
  NOIGNORECASE
  OVERLAYINTERRUPT
  PAUSE
  SEGMENTS
  STACK
```

Notice that the verbose option names are listed. When you enter the options,
only enough characters are required so that the desired option is not confused
with another.

Load Program in High Memory (/HI)

Normally, LINK assumes that a program is to be loaded at the lowest free
memory address. The /HI option instructs LINK to load the linked program as
high in memory as possible. This option typically is used in conjunction with
the /DS option.

Island (/I)

The /I option seems to be available only in version 3.51 of the Microsoft
Overlay Linker. There is no documentation or information available explaining
what the option does or represents. When I asked the technicians at Microsoft
about this option, they indicated that it was left over from a development
version of the linker and "slipped into" the release of LINK, version 3.51. It had
to do with linking files for use with CodeView, and was subsequently replaced
with the /CO option.

Include Line Numbers in List File (/L)

If you specified a listing file when responding to the LINK prompts, you can use the /L option to include a list of all source code line memory addresses in the list file. Including such a list is helpful when you are debugging.

This option is useful only if the OBJ file includes a line number, which depends on how the OBJ file was created. MASM does not include line numbers in the OBJ file, but many high-level languages do. If the OBJ file does not include line number information, no extra information is generated in the MAP file.

Include Global Symbol Table in List File (/M)

When you include the /M option, LINK creates a public symbol listing. Using this option is similar to responding to LINK's *listing file* question, except that you have no opportunity to override the default file name. Instead, the listing file will have the name of the first OBJ file and the extension .MAP.

Do Not Use Default Libraries (/NOD)

Some high-level languages include in the OBJ file the name(s) of default libraries for LINK to search when linking the file. This option overrides those specifications, so that LINK ignores any libraries that the language specified in the OBJ files.

Do Not Associate Groups (/NOG)

The /NOG option instructs LINK to ignore GROUP associations when it assigns memory addresses for data and program code. The option is intended specifically for use with object code generated by old versions of the Microsoft FORTRAN and Pascal compilers.

Do Not Ignore Case Differences (/NOI)

The /NOI option causes LINK to differentiate between upper- and lowercase letters.

Set Overlay Loader Interrupt Number (/O:int)

The /O: option allows you to specify the interrupt number used by an overlay loader. Use this option with object code generated by compilers that support overlays, such as Microsoft C (but not MASM). *int* is the number (between 0 and 255) of the MS-DOS interrupt to use for the overlay loader.

Pause for Disk Change (/P)

Using this option causes LINK to display a message and wait for you to switch disks before it writes the EXE file. This option is particularly useful if you have a limited number of disk drives or disk space. When LINK has completely written the EXE file, LINK prompts you to return the original disk.

Specify Maximum Segments (/SE:seg)

This option directs LINK to process no more than a specific number of segments. Typically, this option is used if the program being linked has a large number of segments; LINK, by default, handles up to 128 segments only. *seg* can be a number between 1 and 1024, inclusive.

Stack Size Override (/ST:size)

Normally, LINK determines the stack size in the finished, linked program based on any stack declarations in the OBJ file. The /ST:size option overrides this value. To use this option you must substitute a number for *size* between 1 and 65,535, representing the desired stack size.

Files Created by LINK

Throughout this chapter we have referred to the different file types that LINK creates: the *executable* and *listing* files.

Whether these files are actually created depends on how you invoke MASM or answer MASM's prompts. Assuming that you assembled SUMS.ASM and requested all files, you should notice the following three files when you use DIR after assembly:

```
C>DIR

Volume in drive C has no label
Directory of  C:\ASSEMBLY
```

```
  .              <DIR>      5-Ø1-87    3:Ø5p
  . .            <DIR>      5-Ø1-87    3:Ø5p
SUMS    ASM      1932       5-Ø4-87    7:58a
SUMS    LST      48Ø4       5-Ø4-87   12:37p
SUMS    OBJ        91       5-Ø4-87   12:37p
SUMS    CRF       148       5-Ø4-87   12:37p
SUMS    REF       574       5-Ø4-87    1:Ø5p
TEST    C         464       5-Ø4-87    1:53p
TEST    OBJ       525       5-Ø4-87    1:55p
TEST    MAP      14Ø3       5-Ø4-87    1:56p
TEST    EXE      9356       5-Ø4-87    1:56p
    11 File(s)   14232832 bytes free
```

You may remember, from Chapter 6, that SUMS.ASM is the assembly language source code file. SUMS.LST, SUMS.OBJ, and SUMS.CRF were created by MASM. SUMS.REF was created by CREF.EXE. TEST.C is the C source code, and TEST.OBJ is the object code file generated by the Microsoft C compiler. The remaining files, TEST.MAP and TEST.EXE, were created by LINK. Sometimes LINK also creates a temporary file, VM.TMP. Let's take a look at each of the three types of files created by LINK.

The Executable File (EXE)

The EXE file is usually the end result of the development process that you seek: an executable file. If the source files' logic and construction were correct, and no debugging or further development is needed, the EXE file is the finished program that you can invoke from DOS.

The List File (MAP)

The MAP file is the listing that the linker produced as it processed each object code file. The MAP file contains the beginning and ending addresses of the segments that LINK processed to create TEST.EXE. The file TEST.MAP is as follows:

```
Start   Stop    Length  Name            Class
ØØØØØH  Ø1E1EH  Ø1E1FH  _TEXT           CODE
Ø1E1FH  Ø1E1FH  ØØØØØH  C_ETEXT         ENDCODE
Ø1E2ØH  Ø1E55H  ØØØ36H  NULL            BEGDATA
Ø1E56H  Ø2173H  ØØ31EH  _DATA           DATA
Ø2174H  Ø2181H  ØØØØEH  CDATA           DATA
Ø2182H  Ø2182H  ØØØØØH  XIB             DATA
Ø2182H  Ø2182H  ØØØØØH  XI              DATA
Ø2182H  Ø2182H  ØØØØØH  XIE             DATA
```

```
Ø2182H  Ø2182H  ØØØØØH  XPB              DATA
Ø2182H  Ø2183H  ØØØØ2H  XP               DATA
Ø2184H  Ø2184H  ØØØØØH  XPE              DATA
Ø2184H  Ø2184H  ØØØØØH  XCB              DATA
Ø2184H  Ø2184H  ØØØØØH  XC               DATA
Ø2184H  Ø2184H  ØØØØØH  XCE              DATA
Ø2184H  Ø2184H  ØØØØØH  CONST            CONST
Ø2184H  Ø218BH  ØØØØ8H  HDR              MSG
Ø218CH  Ø2288H  ØØØFDH  MSG              MSG
Ø2289H  Ø228AH  ØØØØ2H  PAD              MSG
Ø228BH  Ø228BH  ØØØØ1H  EPAD             MSG
Ø228CH  Ø22D1H  ØØØ46H  _BSS             BSS
Ø22D2H  Ø22D2H  ØØØØØH  XOB              BSS
Ø22D2H  Ø22D2H  ØØØØØH  XO               BSS
Ø22D2H  Ø22D2H  ØØØØØH  XOE              BSS
Ø22EØH  Ø26DFH  ØØ4ØØH  c_common         BSS
Ø26EØH  Ø2EDFH  ØØ8ØØH  STACK            STACK


Origin    Group
Ø1E2:Ø    DGROUP


Program entry point at ØØØØ:ØØD4
```

Notice that C automatically included a number of segments. As your programs grow larger, you may find this listing file to be of increasingly greater value in your debugging efforts.

The Temporary File (VM.TMP)

Notice that nothing in your disk directory looks like a temporary (TMP) file. LINK creates this type of file, specifically named VM.TMP, only if necessary.

LINK normally attempts to perform all operations in memory. If this is not possible, because of the large size of the program or the large amount of data being processed, LINK creates a temporary file on the DOS default drive. LINK uses this intermediate work file to store the linked portions of the final program.

If LINK needs to create VM.TMP, a message similar to the following is displayed, where drive B is the default drive:

```
VM.TMP has been created
Do not change diskette in drive B:
```

If you are using floppy disks or working in a networked environment, deleting or moving the VM.TMP file while LINK is working can have unpredictable results.

When LINK is finished, it automatically deletes VM.TMP.

For most practical development purposes, you will never see LINK create this temporary file; most operations can be done in memory. I have used LINK routinely with object files of 54K and libraries of 30K to create a 41K EXE file, and all operations were still performed in memory.

The Finished TEST.EXE

Now that LINK has created TEST.EXE, we can try our program to see if it works. Enter the following at the DOS prompt to start execution of the program:

TEST

The result should be a prompt asking you for an initial value. Enter an integer number, such as 7. You have just asked TEST to calculate the number of blocks in a seven-level pyramid, as shown in figure 7.1.

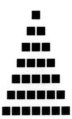

Fig. 7.1.
A seven-level pyramid.

The program dialog and results should appear as follows:

```
C>TEST
Initial Value: 7
    7         28
Initial Value: _
```

Of course, this program is designed for utility, not attractiveness. The returned values indicate the original value entered (7) and the total number of blocks in the pyramid (28).

This program is designed to continue asking for values and returning results until you enter a value of 999. Then the program will generate a list showing the initial values and resulting values for pyramids between one row high and the maximum number of rows the program can handle. A partial program dialog follows:

```
C>TEST
Initial Value: 7
    7          28
Initial Value: 5
    5          15
Initial Value: 22
   22         253
Initial Value: 103
  1Ø3         5356
Initial Value: 999
    1           1
    2           3
    3           6
    4          1Ø
    5          15
    6          21
    7          28
    8          36
    9          45
   1Ø          55
```

(intermediate values deleted to conserve space)

```
  353       62481
  354       62835
  355       6319Ø
  356       63546
  357       639Ø3
  358       64261
  359       6462Ø
  36Ø       6498Ø
  361       65341
  362           Ø
```

```
C>_
```

Notice that the upper limit the routine can handle represents a 361-row pyramid. A 362-row pyramid contains 65,703 blocks, a number too large to be stored in the unsigned integer that is used to return values from the assembly language subroutine.

Summary

The linking step is vital to completion of any program. Using LINK is easy because during ordinary use you don't need to worry about using options or other complicating factors.

The only use of LINK not covered in this chapter is using LINK with libraries. That topic is discussed in Chapter 9. The next chapter deals with debugging programs.

8

Debugging Assembly Language Subroutines

We all know what *bugs* are. The bane of programmers everywhere, bugs seem to crop up at the most inopportune times (such as when the program you are working on is supposed to be shipped out the door) and have been known to keep frustrated programmers from sleeping at night.

If you have been programming for any length of time, you are already familiar with debugging tools for high-level languages. Anyone who has stared at program listings for hours on end knows that debugging software can make the job of debugging much faster and easier. Assembly language is no different from other high-level languages in this respect. The type and amount of programming you do are important factors in determining the type (and price) of the debugging tool you need. Hundreds of debugging tools, which run the gamut of features and prices, are available.

Software and hardware *debuggers* are development tools that simplify the task of tracking and exterminating software bugs. Software debuggers (such as DEBUG) are memory resident and work from within memory. Hardware debuggers generally combine a hardware computer card with software to provide external debugging capabilities.

Which group of debuggers is "better" depends on the nature of the problem. If you are an applications programmer, software debuggers generally fill the bill. But for system-level programmers, as well as for applications programmers who develop software that's designed to operate in real-time, using interrupts, hardware debuggers can make life easier. The types of problems and glitches that crop up in such programs can easily lock up a computer, rendering software debuggers useless.

You should already have access to one or two software debuggers: DEBUG (or DEBUG.COM) is available with both PC DOS and MS-DOS; SYMDEB.EXE (SYMDEB stands for **SYM**bolic **DEB**ugger) is available with the Microsoft Assembler. But because some readers may not be using the Microsoft Assembler package, this book does not cover SYMDEB (which does everything that DEBUG does, and then some). If you are familiar with DEBUG, you can easily learn how to use SYMDEB. Most DEBUG commands work also with SYMDEB.

This chapter describes DEBUG, a rudimentary software debugger, and walks you through a sample debugging session. The chapter concludes with a brief overview of the differences between software and hardware debuggers, and lists possible sources for both types of development aids.

Let's look at the DEBUG program and its use.

Starting and Quitting DEBUG

You can begin a DEBUG session with or without a file. The simplest way to start is without a file. At the DOS prompt, enter:

DEBUG

After you enter this command, a dash will appear on the screen at the left edge of the next line. This dash, which is DEBUG's prompt character, lets you know that DEBUG is functioning and awaiting your command. If you see any other message, chances are that you have misspelled DEBUG or that DEBUG.COM is not available on the current disk drive.

At the DEBUG prompt, type the letter *R* (in either upper- or lowercase) and press Enter. The display on your screen should be similar to the following:

```
C>debug
-r
AX=0000  BX=0000  CX=0000  DX=0000  SP=FFEE  BP=0000  SI=0000  DI=0000
DS=1206  ES=1206  SS=1206  CS=1206  IP=0100   NV UP EI PL NZ NA  PO NC
1206:0100 FB            STI
-
```

This entire display is the basic DEBUG "status line." (On your screen, the numbers and letters on the line that starts with DS= may be different from those shown here.) The *R* that you entered is DEBUG's Register command, which causes DEBUG to display the contents of the CPU registers.

As you learned in Chapter 1, AX, BX, CX, and DX are general-purpose registers. Ordinarily, they are the ones used for direct data manipulation. The other registers (SP, BP, SI, DI, DS, ES, SS, CS, and IP) are specialized registers. When you start DEBUG, the registers AX, BX, CX, DX, BP, SI, and DI are all set to zero.

The characters NV, UP, EI, PL, NZ, NA, PO, and NC are the settings of each of the status register's status flags. Table 8.1 shows the possible display values for each flag, depending on the flag setting. Note that in the Condition column, set denotes a value of 1 in the corresponding register bit, and clear denotes a value of 0.

Table 8.1
Status Flag Display Characteristics for DEBUG

Status Flag	Condition	Meaning	Display
Overflow	set	yes	OV
	clear	no	NV
Direction	set	decrement	DN
	clear	increment	UP
Interrupt	set	enabled	EI
	clear	disabled	DI
Sign	set	negative	NG
	clear	positive	PL
Zero	set	yes	ZR
	clear	no	NZ
Auxiliary Carry	set	yes	AC
	clear	no	NA
Parity	set	even	PE
	clear	odd	PO
Carry	set	yes	CY
	clear	no	NC

The current disassembled values of the code segment and the offset are displayed in the bottom line. 1206, the value of the code segment (CS) register, is used as the segment; 0100, the value of the instruction pointer (IP) register is used as the offset.

When you enter DEBUG without a file, the value shown for disassembly could be almost anything because you have not instructed DEBUG to initialize the memory area. In this instance, the byte at 1206:0100 contains the value *FBh*, which is the numeric value for the mnemonic instruction *STI*.

To end the DEBUG session and return to DOS, type the letter *Q* (for Quit) and press Enter.

Now let's look at the other way to start DEBUG.

Starting DEBUG with a File

The other way to begin a DEBUG session is to specify the file that you want to debug. Suppose, for example, that you want to debug a file called TEST.COM. To load DEBUG and then TEST.COM, enter the following line at the DOS prompt:

DEBUG TEST.COM

If DEBUG cannot find the specified file, you will see an error message. DEBUG will continue as though you had not entered a file name. Should this happen, you must do one of two things: either use the Q command to exit DEBUG and then, using the proper file specification, start over (I prefer this option); or use the L command to load the correct file. (The L command is described in the following section.)

If the program you are debugging requires command line parameters in order to function, simply add the parameters to the line invoking DEBUG. For instance, if TEST.COM needed a drive specification as a parameter, you would enter:

DEBUG TEST.COM B:

After DEBUG has loaded TEST.COM, you will see the dash prompt—DEBUG is ready and waiting for a command. If you enter the Register command, the status display will be similar to the one shown in the preceding section. But this time the BX:CX register pair will be equal to the number of bytes loaded from the file TEST.COM. All other registers and flags should be equivalent to the default settings that DEBUG uses when no file has been loaded.

The DEBUG Command Set

To perform necessary debugging functions, you can use DEBUG's set of 18 commands (see table 8.2).

To invoke any of these commands, enter the command character (in either upper- or lowercase) and then enter any parameters that the command may require. In this chapter's examples of DEBUG commands, the command and any required parameters are shown in **boldface**, with optional parameters in *italics*.

DEBUG does not require any delimiters between commands and parameters, except when two hexadecimal numbers are entered as separate parameters. In all other instances, delimiters are optional, although you may find that using them makes the commands you enter more readable. A delimiter can be either a space or comma; use a colon as the delimiter between the segment and offset of a hexadecimal address.

Table 8.2
The DEBUG Command Set

Command	Meaning
A	Assemble
C	Compare
D	Dump
E	Enter
F	Fill
G	Go
H	Hexadecimal Arithmetic
I	Input
L	Load
M	Move
N	Name
O	Output
Q	Quit
R	Register
S	Search
T	Trace
U	Unassemble
W	Write

Commands are executed when you press Enter, not as you type them. You can change a line by pressing the backspace key to delete what you have typed and then typing the correct characters. When the command line is as you want it, press Enter to execute the entire line.

DEBUG does not detect errors until you have pressed Enter. If you make a syntax error in an entry, the command line is redisplayed with the word *error* added at the point at which the error was detected. If a command line contains more than one error, only the first error will be detected and indicated, and execution will cease at that point.

Let's examine each of the DEBUG commands.

Assemble (A)

The Assemble command is used for entering assembly language mnemonics and for having them translated directly into machine language instructions in memory. This capability is extremely helpful for making on-the-fly changes to a program and for entering short test programs. The syntax for this command is

A *address*

address is an optional beginning address (hexadecimal) at which the assembled machine language instructions will be placed. If you do not specify an address, DEBUG will start placing the instructions either at CS:0100 or after the last machine language instruction entered through Assemble.

Virtually every assembly language mnemonic, including segment override specifiers (CS:, DS:, ES:, SS:), is supported. There are one or two differences, however, between the standard mnemonics and DEBUG's implementation of them. First, because DEBUG cannot differentiate between NEAR and FAR returns, RET is assumed to be a near return, and RETF to be a far return.

Also, when a command line you enter refers to memory locations, DEBUG cannot always determine whether you want to act on a byte or on a word at that location. In the following example:

    DEC [42B]

it is not clear whether a byte or a word should be decremented at that location. To overcome this ambiguity, you must indicate explicitly which you intend. To do so, use *BYTE PTR* or *WORD PTR*, as in the following amended example:

    DEC BYTE PTR [42B]

Clearly, such explicitness is not always necessary, as in this example:

    MOV AL,[42B]

Because only a byte can be moved into AL, using BYTE PTR here would be redundant.

The Assemble command lets you use DB and DW (in addition to the regular 8088 and 8087 assembly language mnemonics) to define data areas.

Each line is assembled after you press Enter. If DEBUG cannot determine what you want when you enter a certain mnemonic, it flags the error and does not assemble that line.

When you have finished using the Assemble command, press Enter to return to the DEBUG dash prompt.

Compare (C)

The Compare command compares and reports on any differences between the contents of two memory blocks. The syntax for this command is

    C block1 address

block1 is either both the beginning and ending addresses or, if preceded by an **l**, the beginning address and length of the first memory block. **address** is the start of the second memory block. The length of the second block is assumed to be equal to the length of the first. The memory blocks can overlap, and the second block can lie physically before the first.

The command compares the two blocks, byte-by-byte, and reports any differences in the following format:

> address1   value1   value2   address2

Dump (D)

The Dump command displays the contents of a series of memory locations. The syntax for the command is

> **D** *address1 address2*

You must specify *address1*, an optional starting address for the display, before you can specify *address2*, an optional ending address.

If no addresses are specified, DEBUG will start displaying memory locations either with DS:0100 or (if Dump has already been used) with the byte following the last byte displayed by the most recent Dump command.

Dump always displays 16 bytes per line, beginning with the nearest paragraph (16-byte) boundary. This display rule may differ with the first and last lines displayed, because you may have asked DEBUG to start the dump with a memory location that was not on a paragraph boundary.

If you do not specify an ending address, DEBUG always displays 128 bytes of memory. Each byte is shown in both hexadecimal and ASCII representation, as in the following example:

```
-D 2C5
126F:02C0              0F 00 03-D1 52 57 36 FF 2E AC 04      ....RW6....
126F:02D0  58 5F 07 8B DE BE 00 05-8B 0E 40 05 3D 53 59 74  X_........@.=SYt
126F:02E0  4F 3D 48 50 74 4A 3D 49-4E 74 45 BE 54 04 8B 0E  O=HPtJ=INtE.T...
126F:02F0  51 04 3D 42 4F 74 39 26-80 3D 00 74 16 26 80 7D  Q.=BOt9&.=.t.&.}
126F:0300  01 3A 75 0F 26 8A 15 80-CA 20 80 EA 60 8A C2 FE  .:u.&.... ..'...
126F:0310  C8 EB 06 B4 19 CD 21 32-D2 04 41 AA B8 3A 5C AB  ......!2..A..:\.
126F:0320  8C C0 8E D8 87 FE B4 47-CD 21 87 FE 73 12 EB 0D  .......G.!..s...
126F:0330  83 F9 03 74 01 49 D1 E9-73 01 A4 F3 A5 32 C0 AA  ...t.I..s....2..
126F:0340  8B F3 36 FF 2E                                    ..6..
```

Reading from left to right, notice that each line shows the address of the first byte, followed by eight bytes, a hyphen, and the remaining eight bytes of the paragraph. The rightmost characters on each line are the ASCII representation of the hexadecimal values in the paragraph. Note also that if a specific hexadecimal value has no corresponding ASCII character, a period is used as a placeholder.

Enter (E)

The Enter command allows you to change the contents of specific memory locations. The syntax for this command is

E address *changes*

address is the beginning address for entering changes, and *changes* is an optional list of the changes to be made.

You can specify *changes* on the command line in any combination of hexadecimal numbers or ASCII characters. (ASCII characters must be enclosed in quotation marks.)

If you do not specify changes on the command line, DEBUG enters a special entry mode in which the values of memory locations, beginning at **address**, are displayed. You can change these values, one byte at a time. (Be sure to enter the changes as hexadecimal numbers.) After each entry, press the space bar to effect the change. The next byte will then be displayed so that you can make any necessary changes. To exit entry mode and return to DEBUG command mode, press Enter.

If you enter a minus sign or hyphen as part of a change to a byte, DEBUG will go back one byte to the preceding memory location. You can then make additional changes to that byte.

If you have not made any changes to a byte, press the space bar to proceed to the next byte. The unchanged byte retains its original value.

Fill (F)

Use this command to fill a block of memory with a specific value or series of values. The syntax for this command is

F block fillvalue

block is either both the beginning and ending addresses or, if preceded by an **l**, the beginning address and length of the memory block. **fillvalue** is the byte value(s) that should be used to fill the memory block. If **fillvalue** represents fewer bytes than are needed to fill the **block**, the series is repeated until the **block** is completed.

fillvalue may be any combination of hexadecimal numbers or ASCII characters. (Any ASCII characters must be enclosed in quotation marks.)

As an example, either of the following command lines will fill (with a nul value) the memory block DS:0000 through DS:00FF:

    F DS:0000 DS:00FF 0
    F DS:0000 LFF 0

To fill the same area with the hexadecimal equivalents of the ASCII characters "ALW", followed by a carriage return and a line feed, you would use either of the following command lines:

    F DS:0000 DS:00FF "ALW" D A
    F DS:0000 LFF "ALW" D A

Remember that the five values (41, 4C, 57, 0D, and 0A) will be repeated again and again until all 256 bytes have been filled.

Go (G)

The Go command, which causes machine language statements to be executed, is one of the most frequently used DEBUG commands. If you are debugging a program, this command executes the program you have loaded. It also lets you specify optional *breakpoints*, which are addresses at which program execution will stop. The syntax for the Go command is

    G =start break1 break2 . . . break10

=*start* is an optional starting address, and *break1* through *break10* are optional breakpoint addresses. If the starting address is not specified, Go will begin program execution with the current address contained in CS:IP.

If the breakpoints are not reached, execution continues until the program ends. If you specify only an offset for a breakpoint address, CS is assumed to be the segment.

To facilitate a breakpoint, DEBUG replaces the code at the breakpoint address with the hexadecimal value CC, which is the code for an interrupt. If DEBUG reaches the interrupt (the breakpoint), all breakpoints are returned to their original values, the registers are displayed (as though by the R command) and program execution stops. If DEBUG never reaches the breakpoint, the values at the breakpoints remain in their changed state.

Hexadecimal Arithmetic (H)

This convenience command does simple hexadecimal addition and subtraction. If you are using a hexadecimal calculator, you may never need to issue this command. The syntax for this command is

H value1 value2

value1 and **value2** are hexadecimal numbers. This command returns a result line, which shows two values: the sum of **value1** and **value2**, and the difference between **value1** and **value2**. This command does not alter any registers or flags.

The following examples show how the **H** command is used. In the first example:

```
-H AE BF
016D   FFEF
```

AHh and BFh are added (which results in 016Dh) and then subtracted (resulting in FFEFh). The second example:

```
-H 96 C2
0158   FFD4
```

performs the same operations with 96h and C2h.

Input (I)

The Input command (the opposite of the Output command) fetches a byte from a port. The syntax is

I port

port is the address of the specified port to read. The Input command fetches a byte from the desired port and then displays it as a hexadecimal value. This command does not change any registers or flags.

Load (L)

The Load command (the opposite of the Write command) is used to load a file or disk sectors into memory. The syntax is

L *buffer drivenum startsector numsector*

buffer is the destination memory address for the information to be loaded. *drivenum* is an optional numeric disk-drive designator. *startsector* is the absolute disk sector (a hexadecimal number) with which to begin reading, and *numsector* is the total number of disk sectors (a hexadecimal number) to read.

In *drivenum*, the drive specification, 0=A, 1=B, 2=C, etc. In *numsector*, no more than 128 (80h) sectors can be loaded.

If you do not provide the *drivenum startsector numsector* combination, DEBUG assumes that you want to load a file, in which case the *buffer* address is optional. If you do not specify an address, DEBUG loads the file at CS:0100. Use the Name command (described shortly) to specify the name of the file.

After a file has been loaded, BX:CX contains the number of bytes successfully read, provided that the file does not have an EXE extension. If the file has an EXE extension, BX:CX is set to the size of the program.

Move (M)

The Move command moves a block of memory from one location to another. The syntax is

M block1 address

block1 is either both the beginning and ending addresses or, if preceded by an **l**, the beginning address and length of the first memory block. **address** is the destination address for the move. The destination address and the source block can overlap. The bytes from the source block are moved, one at a time, to the destination address.

Name (N)

The Name command is used to specify a filename that will be used either by the Load and Write commands or by the program you are debugging. The syntax of this command is

N filename1 *filename2*

filename1 is the complete file specification that will be parsed and placed in a file control block at CS:005C. *filename2* is the complete file specification that will be parsed and placed in a file control block at CS:006C.

In addition to parsing the file specifications, DEBUG places them (as entered) at CS:0081, preceded by a byte indicating the number of bytes entered. DEBUG then sets AX to indicate the parsing status (validity) of the file specifications, with AL corresponding to the first file and AH to the second. If either file name is invalid, its corresponding byte is set to 1; otherwise, it is set to 0.

Output (O)

The Output command (the opposite of the Input command) outputs a byte to a specified port. The syntax is

O port value

port is the address of the specified port, and **value** is the hexadecimal byte to write. This command does not change any registers or flags.

Quit (Q)

The Quit command is used to quit DEBUG and return control of your computer to DOS. You simply press *Q*. There are no parameters for this command, which does not save the programs on which you were working.

Register (R)

The Register command displays the microprocessor's register and flag values, and allows you to change individual register values. The command's syntax is

R *register*

register, the optional name of the register to modify, may be any of the following: AX, BX, CX, DX, SP, BP, SI, DI, DS, ES, SS, CS, IP, PC, or F. IP and PC are synonymous; both refer to the instruction pointer register. F refers to the flags register.

If you enter the Register command with no parameters, DEBUG responds by displaying a register summary similar to the following:

```
-r
AX=ØØØØ  BX=ØØØØ  CX=ØØØØ  DX=ØØØØ  SP=FFEE  BP=ØØØØ  SI=ØØØØ  DI=ØØØØ
DS=12Ø6  ES=12Ø6  SS=12Ø6  CS=12Ø6  IP=Ø1ØØ     NV UP EI PL NZ NA PO NC
12Ø6:Ø1ØØ FB          STI
-
```

If you enter a register name as a parameter, DEBUG displays the current register value and waits for you to enter a new value. If you enter a value, it is assumed to be in hexadecimal. If you do not enter a value, no change is made to the register value.

(For more information on the Register command, refer to this chapter's "Starting and Quitting DEBUG" section.)

Search (S)

The Search command allows you to search a block of memory for a specific sequence of values. The syntax is

S block searchvalue

block is either both the beginning and ending addresses or, if preceded by an **l**, the beginning address and length of the first memory block. **searchvalue** is the byte value(s) that you want to search for in the memory block.

The values that DEBUG searches for can be any combination of hexadecimal numbers and ASCII characters. (ASCII characters must be enclosed in quotation marks.)

If DEBUG locates any exact matches, it displays the address of the beginning of the match. If no matches are found, no message is displayed.

Trace (T)

The Trace command allows the single-step execution of machine language instructions, after which the register status is displayed (as with the Register command). The syntax of the Trace command is

T =*start count*

Both of these parameters are optional; =*start* is a starting address, and *count* is a hexadecimal number that signifies how many individual instructions must be traced through. If =*start* is not specified, execution will begin with the current address contained in CS:IP. If *count* is excluded, only one machine language instruction will be executed.

Unassemble (U)

The Unassemble command decodes the values of a group of memory locations into 8088 mnemonics. One of the most frequently used DEBUG commands, Unassemble allows you to view the instructions that will be executed during the DEBUG operation. The syntax is as follows:

U *range*

range, which is optional, is either both the beginning and ending addresses or, if preceded by an *l*, the beginning address and length of the area to be unassembled.

If you do not specify an address or range, unassembly begins with the memory location indicated by CS:IP or (if Unassemble has already been used) with the byte following the last byte displayed by the most recent Unassemble command. The unassembly proceeds for 16 bytes. The number of instruction lines this process represents depends on the number of bytes used in each instruction line. If you specify an address range, all bytes within that block are unassembled.

(The Unassemble command is used extensively in this chapter's "Debugging TEST.EXE" section.)

Write (W)

The Write command (the opposite of the Load command) is used to write a file or individual disk sectors to a disk. The syntax is

> **W** *buffer drivenum startsector numsector*

buffer is the memory address of the information to be written; *drivenum* is an optional numeric disk-drive designator; *startsector* is the absolute disk sector (a hexadecimal number) at which writing is to begin; and *numsector* is the total number of disk sectors (a hexadecimal number) to be written.

The drive specification, *drivenum*, is such that 0=A, 1=B, 2=C, etc. In *numsector*, the number of sectors loaded cannot exceed 128, or 80h.

If you do not provide the *drivenum startsector numsector* combination, DEBUG assumes that you want to write a file; the buffer address is then optional. If you do not specify an address, DEBUG assumes the start-of-file to be CS:0100. (Use the Name command to specify the name of the file.)

Before a file is written, BX:CX must be set to the number of bytes to be written. DEBUG cannot write to files with an EXE or HEX extension.

Debugging TEST.EXE

Now that you are familiar with starting and quitting DEBUG and with the DEBUG commands, it's time to see how DEBUG functions in a real-life debugging session. Using DEBUG, we will step through the TEST.EXE program (developed in Chapters 6 and 7). But before we do, we need to put a "bug" in the assembly language subroutine so that there's a reason for our search.

To do so, modify SUMS.ASM (refer to Chapter 6) by changing the line labeled S1. The modified listing follows:

Page 6Ø,132
```
;  *********************************************************************
;  *                                                                  *
;  *  Program Name:  SUMS.ASM                                         *
;  *  Written by:    Allen L. Wyatt   5/4/87                          *
;  *                                                                  *
;  *  Purpose:       Given an integer number X, find the sum of       *
;  *                 X + (X-1) + (X-2) + (X-3) + (X-4) ... + 2 + 1     *
;  *                 Designed to be called from Microsoft C.          *
;  *                                                                  *
;  *  Format:        SUMS(X)                                          *
;  *                                                                  *
;  *********************************************************************

                PUBLIC  _SUMS

                NAME    SUMS
_TEXT           SEGMENT BYTE PUBLIC 'CODE'
                ASSUME  CS:_TEXT

NUM_ADR         EQU     4

_SUMS           PROC    NEAR
                PUSH    BP
                MOV     BP,SP

                MOV     AX,Ø             ;Initialize to zero
                MOV     BX,[BP]+NUM_ADR  ;Get address of value
                MOV     CX,[BX]          ;Get actual value
                JCXZ    S3               ;Number is zero, so exit
S1:             ADC     CX,AX            ;Add row value
                JC      S2               ;Quit if AX overflowed
                LOOP    S1               ;Repeat process
                JMP     S3               ;Successful completion
S2:             MOV     AX,Ø             ;Force a zero
S3:             MOV     [BX],AX          ;Place back in value

                POP     BP
                RET
_SUMS           ENDP

_TEXT           ENDS
                END
```

The change you've made will cause the routine to always return an answer of 0. From this point on, pretend that you do not know what is causing this error. Put yourself in the place of a programmer who has discovered an honest-to-goodness bug in a program.

Assemble the modified routine and then link it to TEST.OBJ to form a new TEST.EXE. Next, test this version of TEST.EXE to see what happens. If you use the inputs shown in Chapter 7, the following results occur:

```
TEST
Initial Value: 7
    7           Ø
Initial Value: 5
    5           Ø
Initial Value: 22
   22           Ø
Initial Value: 1Ø3
  1Ø3           Ø
Initial Value: 999
    1           Ø


c>_
```

This is not the intent of the program! Clearly, a problem exists. But where in the program or routine is it occurring? We need to start looking. Deductively, we can determine that the SUMS routine (where the returned value always appears to be 0) is a good place to begin the search.

To begin using DEBUG with TEST.EXE, enter

    DEBUG TEST.EXE

DEBUG should respond with the dash prompt, signaling that it is ready and awaiting a command. To get an idea of where you are in the program, enter the Register command (press *R*).

```
DEBUG TEST.EXE
-R
AX=ØØØØ  BX=ØØØØ  CX=228C  DX=ØØØØ  SP=Ø8ØØ  BP=ØØØØ  SI=ØØØØ  DI=ØØØØ
DS=128C  ES=128C  SS=15ØA  CS=129C  IP=ØØD4   NV UP EI PL NZ NA PO NC
129C:ØØD4 B43Ø          MOV   AH,3Ø
-
```

This display tells you that TEST.EXE has been loaded, the segment registers have been set properly, and the IP register is loaded correctly with the address of the first program instruction to be executed. Notice that the offset entry address is 00D4h, which is the entry address noted in the MAP file produced by LINK.EXE (refer to Chapter 7). Notice also the values of the segment registers, particularly CS and DS. (The values in your segment registers may be different from those shown here, depending on where in your computer's memory DEBUG has loaded the program.)

Next, use the Unassemble command so that you can look at the first portions of program code:

```
-U
129C:00D4 B430          MOV   AH,30
129C:00D6 CD21          INT   21
129C:00D8 3C02          CMP   AL,02
129C:00DA 730E          JNB   00EA
129C:00DC B80400        MOV   AX,0004
129C:00DF 50            PUSH  AX
129C:00E0 E8110B        CALL  0BF4
129C:00E3 92            XCHG  DX,AX
129C:00E4 B409          MOV   AH,09
129C:00E6 CD21          INT   21
129C:00E8 CD20          INT   20
129C:00EA BF7E14        MOV   DI,147E
129C:00ED 8B360200      MOV   SI,[0002]
129C:00F1 2BF7          SUB   SI,DI
129C:00F3 81FE0010      CMP   SI,1000
-U
129C:00F7 7203          JB    00FC
129C:00F9 BE0010        MOV   SI,1000
129C:00FC FA            CLI
129C:00FD 8ED7          MOV   SS,DI
129C:00FF 81C4BE08      ADD   SP,08BE
129C:0103 FB            STI
129C:0104 730B          JNB   0111
129C:0106 33C0          XOR   AX,AX
129C:0108 50            PUSH  AX
129C:0109 E8180B        CALL  0C24
129C:010C B8FF4C        MOV   AX,4CFF
129C:010F CD21          INT   21
129C:0111 81E4FEFF      AND   SP,FFFE
129C:0115 36            SS:
129C:0116 89265800      MOV   [0058],SP
-
```

This code is the assembly language translation of the machine language to which the C program (TEST.C) was converted. However, you have deduced that the bug probably is not in the C program—it is in the assembly language subroutine. How do you find it?

The quickest way to find the right subroutine is to use the Search command. But first you must determine what to search for. To do so, you need to look at the contents of the file TEST.LST (shown in Chapter 6) to see what the first several bytes of machine language *should* be. The appropriate code follows:

```
15                              PUBLIC  _SUMS
16
17                              NAME    SUMS
18 0000              _TEXT      SEGMENT BYTE PUBLIC 'CODE'
19                              ASSUME  CS:_TEXT
20
21 = 0004            NUM_ADR    EQU     4
22
23 0000              _SUMS      PROC    NEAR
24 0000    55                   PUSH    BP
25 0001    8B EC                MOV     BP,SP
26
27 0003    B8 0000              MOV     AX,0        ;Initialize to zero
28 0006    8B 5E 04             MOV     BX,[BP]+NUM_ADR  ;Get address of value
```

Notice that, beginning in line 24, the first machine code bytes generated by the assembler were 55, 8B, EC, B8, 00, 00, 8B, 5E, and 04. You will search for these nine bytes—a combination unique enough to pinpoint the start of the SUMS subroutine.

Using the Search command, search for these bytes from the beginning of the code segment. Be sure to search an area that is at least equal to the length of the file.

When you enter:

   –S CS:00 L248C 55 8B EC B8 00 00 8B 5E 04

the computer responds

   129C:00A1

   –

Sure enough, this series of bytes occurs at only one point in memory—at offset 00A1h, the entry point for the SUMS subroutine. To view the code, use the Unassemble command. When you press *U A1*, the following code will be displayed:

```
-U A1
129C:00A1 55            PUSH   BP
129C:00A2 8BEC          MOV    BP,SP
129C:00A4 B80000        MOV    AX,0000
129C:00A7 8B5E04        MOV    BX,[BP+04]
129C:00AA 8B0F          MOV    CX,[BX]
129C:00AC E30C          JCXZ   00BA
129C:00AE 13C8          ADC    CX,AX
129C:00B0 7205          JB     00B7
129C:00B2 E2FA          LOOP   00AE
129C:00B4 EB04          JMP    00BA
129C:00B6 90            NOP
129C:00B7 B80000        MOV    AX,0000
129C:00BA 8907          MOV    [BX],AX
129C:00BC 5D            POP    BP
129C:00BD C3            RET
129C:00BE 59            POP    CX
129C:00BF 8BDC          MOV    BX,SP
-
```

This code is the unassembled SUMS routine, beginning at offset 00A1h and continuing through offset 00BDh. Following this routine, a different one begins at offset 00BEh.

Now, because you want to see what happens in this routine, simply use the Go command to execute the program through the beginning of SUMS. Because the program will run normally until it reaches the breakpoint, you must answer the question asked by TEST.EXE—for test purposes, enter a 5 at the prompt for an initial value.

```
-G A1
Initial Value: 5

AX=1098  BX=1098  CX=007A  DX=0000  SP=1094  BP=109A  SI=00A3  DI=116D
DS=147E  ES=147E  SS=147E  CS=129C  IP=00A1   NV UP EI PL NZ NA PE NC
129C:00A1 55            PUSH   BP
-
```

When DEBUG reaches the specified breakpoint of CS:00A1 (the CS is assumed), program execution stops and the register values are displayed. Now, using the Trace command to step through the routine, you can examine what is happening to the number being passed from C.

```
-T

AX=1098  BX=1098  CX=007A  DX=0000  SP=1092  BP=109A  SI=00A3  DI=116D
DS=147E  ES=147E  SS=147E  CS=129C  IP=00A2   NV UP EI PL NZ NA PE NC
129C:00A2 8BEC          MOV    BP,SP
-
```

After each Trace command is entered, DEBUG executes the previously displayed instruction (which is shown on the unassembled status line) and displays the registers again, as in the following code:

```
-T

AX=1098  BX=1098  CX=007A  DX=0000  SP=1092  BP=1092  SI=00A3  DI=116D
DS=147E  ES=147E  SS=147E  CS=129C  IP=00A4   NV UP EI PL NZ NA PE NC
129C:00A4 B80000          MOV    AX,0000
-
```

In this display, you can see that the base pointer has been set so that the passed parameters can be accessed. The next Trace instruction will result in execution of the MOV AX,0000 instruction, which simply clears the AX register. Soon, AX will be used to accumulate the count of pyramid blocks. Go ahead and Trace through the next step:

```
-T

AX=0000  BX=1098  CX=007A  DX=0000  SP=1092  BP=1092  SI=00A3  DI=116D
DS=147E  ES=147E  SS=147E  CS=129C  IP=00A7   NV UP EI PL NZ NA PE NC
129C:00A7 8B5E04          MOV    BX,[BP+04]    SS:1096=1098
-
```

Notice that AX has been cleared, and that you now are ready to pull the parameter (an integer pointer) from the stack. As you can see, DEBUG displays the value at SS:[BP+04]. (Remember that DEBUG assumes the SS unless your coding explicitly overrides it.) Two additional traces result in the following:

```
-T

AX=0000  BX=1098  CX=007A  DX=0000  SP=1092  BP=1092  SI=00A3  DI=116D
DS=147E  ES=147E  SS=147E  CS=129C  IP=00AA   NV UP EI PL NZ NA PE NC
129C:00AA 8B0F            MOV    CX,[BX]    DS:1098=0005
-T
```

```
AX=ØØØØ  BX=1Ø98  CX=ØØØ5  DX=ØØØØ  SP=1Ø92  BP=1Ø92  SI=ØØA3  DI=116D
DS=147E  ES=147E  SS=147E  CS=129C  IP=ØØAC    NV UP EI PL NZ NA PE NC
129C:ØØAC E3ØC          JCXZ   ØØBA
-
```

Executing the two instructions (MOV BX,[BP+04] and MOV CX,[BX]) placed the correct value of the parameter (5) in CX. So far, the routine is functioning properly, with no problems. The next instruction (JCXZ 00BA) checks whether the parameter passed was a 0. If it was, DEBUG performs no calculations.

```
-T

AX=ØØØØ  BX=1Ø98  CX=ØØØ5  DX=ØØØØ  SP=1Ø92  BP=1Ø92  SI=ØØA3  DI=116D
DS=147E  ES=147E  SS=147E  CS=129C  IP=ØØAE    NV UP EI PL NZ NA PE NC
129C:ØØAE 13C8          ADC    CX,AX
-
```

The instruction to be executed next (ADC CX,AX) is supposed to add the row value (5, which also represents the number of blocks on the row) to the value in AX.

But as you can see from the following display:

```
-T

AX=ØØØØ  BX=1Ø98  CX=ØØØ5  DX=ØØØØ  SP=1Ø92  BP=1Ø92  SI=ØØA3  DI=116D
DS=147E  ES=147E  SS=147E  CS=129C  IP=ØØBØ    NV UP EI PL NZ NA PE NC
129C:ØØBØ 72Ø5          JB     ØØB7
-
```

the value in AX did not change. The problem must be occurring here—the value is not being added to AX. As written, the program results in the sum of AX and CX being deposited in the wrong register—CX.

To test this hypothesis, change the coding here by using the Assemble command and entering the following code:

```
-A AE
129C:ØØAE ADC AX,CX
129C:ØØBØ
-
```

Now the corrected coding is in place, but the instruction pointer register still points to the wrong location. You need to have the computer execute this

newly entered instruction. The following dialog shows how to use the Register
command to change the IP register, and then use the command again to view
the register contents.

```
-RIP
IP ØØBØ
:AE
-R
AX=ØØØØ  BX=1Ø98  CX=ØØØ5  DX=ØØØØ  SP=1Ø92  BP=1Ø92  SI=ØØA3  DI=116D
DS=147E  ES=147E  SS=147E  CS=129C  IP=ØØAE   NV UP EI PL NZ NA PE NC
129C:ØØAE 11C8         ADC    AX,CX
-
```

RIP allowed the IP register to be changed to AE, the memory offset of the
instructions just entered. Finally, the Register command causes DEBUG to
display the registers so that you can verify that the computer is indeed ready to
execute the proper instruction. Now you will trace through this step (ADC
AX,CX) to verify its effect on the AX register.

As you can see from the following display:

```
-T

AX=ØØØ5  BX=1Ø98  CX=ØØØ5  DX=ØØØØ  SP=1Ø92  BP=1Ø92  SI=ØØA3  DI=116D
DS=147E  ES=147E  SS=147E  CS=129C  IP=ØØBØ   NV UP EI PL NZ NA PE NC
129C:ØØBØ 72Ø5          JB     ØØB7
-
```

the AX register has been updated to the correct value. Now, so that you can
quit DEBUG, execute the rest of the program by using the Go command:

```
-G
     5           15
Initial Value: 3
     3            6
Initial Value: 7
     7           28
Initial Value: 999
     1            1
     2            3
     3            6
     4           1Ø
     5           15
```

```
*** Portion of output deleted for space ***

    358      64261
    359      64620
    360      64980
    361      65341
    362          0

Program terminated normally

-Q

c>_
```

Well, you've done it! You have just used DEBUG to track down a bug in a program. This example may be simple, but the precepts don't change. Whatever the task, you must step through the coding to make sure that all is going as expected.

By the way, DEBUG did not change the source or executable files. Now that you have discovered what the problem was, you will have to change SUMS.ASM, reassemble, and then link, to produce a corrected version of TEST.EXE.

Now that you have learned about DEBUG, the rudimentary software debugger accessible to virtually every PC DOS or MS-DOS user, let's take a look at other debuggers, both software and hardware.

Software Debuggers

Other software debuggers expand on DEBUG's capabilities to provide more powerful development environments. Table 8.3 lists a few of these software debuggers and the companies that publish them.

Some software debuggers are packaged with language development systems: SYMDEB comes with the Microsoft Macro Assembler, for example, and Codeview is packaged with the Microsoft C Compiler.

Software debuggers range in price from free (DEBUG) to more than $500. Generally, higher-priced debuggers offer advanced features that may make the investment worthwhile. For example, if your programming time is worth $40 an hour, just a few hours lost to manual debugging (using a free debugger) would justify the cost of a higher-priced commercial system. Many programmers have found that the time saved locating a single bug more than offsets the cost of the debugger.

Table 8.3
Software Debuggers

Product	Source
Advanced Trace86	Morgan Computing Co., Inc. P.O. Box 112730 Carrollton, TX 75011 (214) 416-6101
CodeSmith-86	Visual Age 642 N. Larchmont Blvd. Los Angeles, CA 90004 (800) 732-2345
CodeView SYMDEB	Microsoft Corp. 16011 NE 36th Way Redmond, WA 98073 (206) 882-8080
DEBUG	PC DOS or MS-DOS suppliers
Periscope II-X	The Periscope Co., Inc. 14 Bonnie Lane Atlanta, GA 30328 (404) 256-3860
Pfix86+	Phoenix Technologies Ltd. 320 Norwood Park South Norwood, MA 02062 (617) 769-7020
RBUG86	Answer Software Corp. 20045 Stevens Creek Blvd. Cupertino, CA 95014 (408) 253-7515
Software Source Probe	Atron Corp. 20665 Fourth St. Saratoga, CA 95070 (408) 741-5900
Soft-Scope	Concurrent Sciences, Inc. P.O. Box 9666 Moscow, ID 83843 (208) 882-0445

Generally, software debuggers are written to monitor (in a controlled fashion) the operation of the target program. These debuggers load themselves in RAM and then load the program to be debugged into a work area from which the debugger can control execution of the program.

Benign observers, software debuggers ignorantly follow instructions. If you instruct the debugger to execute a section of code, it will attempt to do so, sometimes destroying itself in the process. For example, if an errant program causes a sector to be loaded from disk into RAM at the place where the debugging software resides, the debugging session will come to a screeching halt, and the debugger will do nothing to stop the error. Totally isolating a software-only debugger is impossible.

Hardware Debuggers

Hardware debuggers come in a variety of shapes, sizes, and capabilities. Generally, they consist of both hardware and software components. Usually, the hardware component is either a card that fits in an expansion slot of the computer, or a device that is placed between the microprocessor and the system board. The software component may be similar to the previously described software debuggers, or it may reside in ROM on the hardware board. Table 8.4 lists a few hardware debuggers and where you can get them.

Hardware debuggers, which are much more expensive than software debuggers, can range in price from close to $1,000 to almost $8,000. The prices vary according to the type of hardware debugger, any additional options, and the type of computer you will use.

The more expensive systems generally require the use of a second computer to monitor the functioning of the first. These systems (called *in-circuit emulators* or *in-circuit devices*), which are virtually isolated from the target program, include the Microcosm™ In-Circuit Emulator, I²ICE™, and the ICD-286™.

As with software debuggers, the time saved in the development process may justify the cost of a hardware debugger. Hardware debuggers are best suited for systems-level or interrupt-driven software programs, which are prone to bugs that are virtually impossible to ferret out with software debuggers only.

And hardware debuggers offer greater control over the program environment than do their software-only counterparts. Through the use of the *non-maskable interrupt* (NMI) line of the processor, hardware debuggers usually provide a way for you to recover system control at virtually any time, even if the computer has "hung." There are very few occasions when such a brute-force method of seizing control of the computer will not work.

Table 8.4
Hardware Debuggers

Product	Source
I²ICE PSCOPE-86	Intel Corp. 3065 Bowers Ave. Santa Clara, CA 95051 (800) 548-4725
In-Circuit Emulator	Microcosm Inc. 15275 Southwest Koll Parkway, Suite E Beaverton, OR 97006 (503) 626-6100
PC Probe AT Probe Mini Probe I, II, III	Atron Corp. 20665 Fourth St. Saratoga, CA 95070 (408) 741-5900
PDTPC PDTAT ICD286	Answer Software Corp. 20045 Stevens Creek Blvd. Cupertino, CA 95014 (408) 253-7515
Periscope I Periscope II Periscope III	The Periscope Co., Inc. 14 Bonnie Lane Atlanta, GA 30328 (404) 256-3860

Summary

In this chapter, you first learned how to use DEBUG. You learned what the DEBUG commands are and how to use them to help uncover errors in your subroutines. As you work with DEBUG, try to become familiar with all of the available commands so that you can make your debugging sessions as efficient and productive as possible.

Although DEBUG is helpful, it is not the answer to every debugging need. You may discover errors that completely lock up your computer, so that the only way to regain control is to turn off the computer. In these instances, software debuggers such as DEBUG are virtually useless because they assume that you will always have some control, such as being able to enter keyboard commands.

Professional debuggers that combine hardware and software also are available. These debuggers provide a virtually independent way to monitor and debug programs. Professional debuggers may be expensive, but in many development environments they are the only viable option for effective debugging.

The ideal debugging system, regardless of type, will perform as a benign observer until you instruct it to perform a task. A debugger that interferes with the operation of the program is of little use because examining how the program operates without the debugger is impossible.

9

Developing Libraries

When it's time to link your assembly language subroutines, the process of specifying each file name can be unwieldy if you use an increasingly large number of routines. Consider, for example, the following external declaration section from one (and *only* one) subroutine:

```
;  ****   OUTSIDE SUBROUTINES CALLED   ****
            EXTRN       SET_DI:NEAR
            EXTRN       CURSOR_ON:NEAR
            EXTRN       CURSOR_OFF:NEAR
            EXTRN       HORIZ_LINE:NEAR
            EXTRN       PRINT_CHAR:NEAR
            EXTRN       PRINT_STRING:NEAR
            EXTRN       ERASE_LINE:NEAR
            EXTRN       BOOP:NEAR
            EXTRN       CALC_LEN:NEAR
```

keeping in mind that these external subroutines call other subroutines, which may call still other subroutines. As you can imagine, the list of possible subroutines can become extensive.

To solve this problem, you can place your assembly language OBJ files into a *library*, a special file that is searched at linkage time.

When the LINK command finds an external declaration, it looks for the external reference in the explicit OBJ file names you entered. If the external reference is not contained in one of those files, LINK searches the library for the reference. If the reference is located, LINK extracts the OBJ module and combines it into the executable file being created.

This library concept relieves the programmer of several potential headaches (and errors) in the program development process. If you change a source file, you can simply update the library and recompile (or reassemble) all files that use that routine—quick, simple, and effective.

Creating a Library

You create a library by using library-management software. Because of the wide diversity of available library-management software, this book focuses on a single system: a program called LIB.EXE, which is distributed with the Microsoft and IBM assembler packages. Other library-management software packages, most with commands similar to those offered in the Microsoft and IBM systems, are available from various vendors.

Let's look at how you use the software from Microsoft and IBM to create and modify libraries.

If you have done the examples in this book, you have created several assembly language subroutines that can be joined together into a library (see table 9.1). Be sure that these routines are available, because you will use them in this session.

Table 9.1
Available Files To Be Placed in a Library File

File Name	Chapter
ULCASEC . ASM	5
DELAYV1C . ASM	5
DELAY5C . ASM	5
SUMS . ASM	7

Make sure that you have the LIB.EXE program on a floppy disk, in the current directory, or accessible through a search path. Then, at the DOS prompt, enter the following command:

    LIB

to execute the LIB.EXE program. If you are using the Microsoft version of LIB.EXE, you will see on your screen a notice and prompt similar to the following:

```
C>LIB

Microsoft (R) Library Manager  Version 3.02
Copyright (C) Microsoft Corp 1983, 1984, 1985. All rights reserved.

Library name: _
```

If you are using the IBM version of LIB.EXE, your screen will look a little different. However, because the prompts are similar, you should be able to follow this session.

Now, enter *TEST*, the name of the library file that you want to create. (Because the standard library extension (.LIB) is appended automatically unless another extension is entered, the full name of this library will be TEST.LIB.) When you press Enter, the following prompt is displayed:

```
Library name: TEST
Library does not exist. Create? _
```

This prompt is just a precaution, in case you misspelled the name of the library. Because you are creating a new library, press *Y*. Your screen will look like this:

```
Library does not exist. Create? Y
Operations: _
```

LIB is requesting information about the operations you want to perform with TEST.LIB. There are three basic operations: adding, deleting, and copying. By combining these basic commands, you can perform two additional operations. For instance, you can replace a library entry by deleting and then adding it; or you can move the entry by deleting and then copying it. Table 9.2 lists the available LIB operations.

Table 9.2
LIB Operations

Operation	Function
+	Add an OBJ file as a library entry
-	Delete a library entry
*	Copy a library entry
-+	Replace a library entry
-*	Move a library entry

Because you are creating a new library, you don't need to delete, copy, replace, or move an entry. You want to add OBJ files to the new library. To do so, enter the following at the Operations: prompt:

+SUMS +DELAY5C +DELAYV1C +ULCASEC

This entry instructs LIB to add to the library the object code files you created in Chapters 5 and 7: SUMS.OBJ, DELAY5C.OBJ, DELAYV1C.OBJ, and ULCASEC.OBJ (.OBJ is the default file extension).

If you used the BASIC examples in Chapter 3 to create your files, you should substitute the names of those files in the preceding response line. Include only those files that were developed for use with compiled BASIC, because interpretive BASIC files are not suited for use with a library. Interpretive BASIC does not go through a linkage phase in development.

In Chapter 3, only one file (ULCASE.ASM) was developed for use with compiled BASIC. The chapter's other routines (those for interpretive BASIC) can be modified so that they work with compiled BASIC, and are thus suited for inclusion in a library. Whether to modify them is up to you.

If you used the Pascal examples in Chapter 4 to create your files, you should substitute the names of those files in the LIB response line. The appropriate file names are detailed in table 9.3.

Table 9.3
Available Files To Be Placed in a Library (For Use with Pascal)

File Name	Chapter
DELAY5P.ASM	4
DELAYV1P.ASM	4
DELAYV2P.ASM	4
ULCASEP.ASM	4

Notice that each file requires an individual command—a plus sign. Notice also that each command is separated from the others by a space. Although you can use commas as command delimiters, I prefer spaces.

Alternatively, you can enter the commands on individual lines in the following manner:

```
Operations: +SUMS +DELAY5C &
Operations: +DELAYV1C +ULCASEC
```

The ampersand (&) at the end of the first line signifies that more follows. Use it if you cannot fit all the desired operations onto one command line.

Finally, the following prompt will appear on your screen:

```
Operations: +SUMS +DELAY5C +DELAYV1C +ULCASEC
List file: _
```

A *list file*, which is optional, contains reference information that you may find interesting and helpful. If you do not want one, simply press Enter. But here, for the sake of illustration, enter *TEST.LST* as a file name. Be sure to specify the *.LST* file extension, because LIB does not provide a default extension for list files.

After a few moments, the DOS prompt returns to the screen, signifying that LIB has created the library TEST.LIB. If any errors occur during the process of creating a library, an error message is displayed. (In some instances, notification of the action taken by LIB is displayed also.)

To get an idea of what happened during the process of creating the library, look at the list file that was created. If you type *TEST.LST*, you should see the following display:

```
C>TYPE TEST.LST


_DELAY5..........DELAY5C          _DELAYV..........DELAYV1C
_SUMS...........SUMS              _ULCASE..........ULCASEC



SUMS              Offset: 00000010H  Code and data size: 1dH
  _SUMS


DELAY5C           Offset: 00000070H  Code and data size: 1aH
  _DELAY5


DELAYV1C          Offset: 000000d0H  Code and data size: 2fH
  _DELAYV


ULCASEC           Offset: 00000150H  Code and data size: 3cH
  _ULCASE


C>_
```

The list file (in this case, TEST.LST) contains information about the newly created library: the names of the modules in the library, as well as information about where each module begins and the length of each module. From this TEST.LST file, you can see that the file SUMS (the .OBJ extension is assumed) contains the public label _SUMS, that the module begins at a file offset of 10h, and that its length is 1Dh.

Linking with a Library

As you may recall from Chapter 7, one of the LINK prompts asked which libraries to use in the linking process. Because libraries had not yet been discussed, the discussion of linking libraries was deferred to this chapter.

Now that you have created a library (TEST.LIB), you can perform the linking process again to see how TEST.LIB affects the process.

When you enter the LINK command at the DOS prompt, your screen should look like this:

```
C>LINK
Microsoft (R) Overlay Linker  Version 3.51
Copyright (C) Microsoft Corp 1983, 1984, 1985, 1986. All rights
reserved.

Object Modules [.OBJ]: _
```

Enter *TEST.ASM* (the name of the object file used in Chapter 7). Then, to signify that the run file will be the default file, press Enter. Your screen should look like this:

```
Object Modules [.OBJ]: TEST
Run File [TEST.EXE]:
List File [NUL.MAP]: _
```

Because you do not need a list file for this example, simply press Enter.

Now comes the important question:

```
List File [NUL.MAP]:
Libraries [.LIB]: _
```

In response to this prompt, enter the name of the library (or libraries) that you want to use to link this file. If you enter several library names, use spaces to separate them. You don't have to include a file extension (.LIB is assumed).

To continue with the sample library (TEST.LIB), simply type *TEST* and press Enter.

LINK asks no further questions, but goes to work on the tasks you specified. First, all of the specified object files are linked together (in this case, there is only one: TEST.OBJ). Then, if any unresolved external references remain, the library files are searched to see whether the references are included as public label declarations. Thus, when _SUMS cannot be located in TEST.OBJ, TEST.LIB is examined to ascertain whether it contains the label. If (as in this case) the library file contains the label, the module containing the label is extracted from TEST.LIB and linked to TEST.OBJ.

If any secondary unresolved external references remain (in other words, if the _SUMS routine contains any references that cannot be satisfied internally to _SUMS or in the TEST.OBJ file), the library is searched again. This search-and-include cycle continues until all possible references have been resolved. If some references cannot be resolved, LINK generates an error message, and the linkage process stops.

If an error message such as the following occurs:

```
C>LINK
Microsoft (R) Overlay Linker  Version 3.51
Copyright (C) Microsoft Corp 1983, 1984, 1985, 1986. All rights
reserved.

Object Modules [.OBJ]: TEST
Run File [TEST.EXE]:
List File [NUL.MAP]:
Libraries [.LIB]: TEST

Unresolved externals:


_sums in file(s):
TEST.OBJ(test.C)

There was 1 error detected

C>_
```

you know that LINK could not find the subroutine in the object file (TEST.OBJ) or in the library (TEST.LIB). Usually, this means that you have forgotten to include all necessary files in the library. Check your work again and try the linking procedure one more time.

Making Changes to a Library

Changing a library file is as easy as creating one. By using the commands to delete, add, copy, replace, or move, you can update an existing library to reflect current needs. For example, suppose that you need to update the file SUMS in TEST.LIB. To do so, you would carry on the following dialog:

```
C>LIB

Microsoft (R) Library Manager  Version 3.02
Copyright (C) Microsoft Corp 1983, 1984, 1985. All rights
reserved.

Library name: TEST
Operations: -+SUMS
List file:

C>_
```

This process updates TEST.LIB with the new version of SUMS.OBJ. But what if the new version of the file is in another directory or on another disk? You simply provide the necessary information at the Operations: prompt, as in the following dialog:

C>*LIB*

```
Microsoft (R) Library Manager  Version 3.02
Copyright (C) Microsoft Corp 1983, 1984, 1985. All rights
reserved.

Library name: TEST
Operations: -SUMS +B:\OBJ\SUMS
List file:
```

C>_

Notice that you indicate the deletion and addition as two separate steps. The result, however, is the same as in the previous example.

To modify the library in other ways, simply specify the operation you want performed (refer to table 9.2) and the name of the file module you want to modify.

Creating and Using Library Response Files

With LIB, as with LINK, you can provide a file (cleverly called a *response file*) of responses to questions. Because repeatedly typing answers to each question is tiresome, this method of using LIB is beneficial when you know that you will be adjusting a library time and again during development.

To use this method of providing input to LIB, create an ASCII text file that contains the answers to each question. You can give this file whatever name you want. Just be sure to place the answer to each question on a separate line. For instance, I regularly create a new library of all my assembly language subroutines by using the following LIB response file:

```
\assemble\huge.lib
Y
+ \assemble\obj\asciibin &
+ \assemble\obj\box &
+ \assemble\obj\boxita &
+ \assemble\obj\calclen &
```

```
+  \assemble\obj\cdir &
+  \assemble\obj\clrwndow &
+  \assemble\obj\cls &
+  \assemble\obj\conascii &
+  \assemble\obj\conhex &
+  \assemble\obj\concase &
+  \assemble\obj\crc &
+  \assemble\obj\cursoff &
+  \assemble\obj\curson &
+  \assemble\obj\dait &
+  \assemble\obj\dayt &
+  \assemble\obj\direct &
+  \assemble\obj\eraselne &
+  \assemble\obj\findcard &
+  \assemble\obj\fmenu &
+  \assemble\obj\fsize &
+  \assemble\obj\getkey &
+  \assemble\obj\getline &
+  \assemble\obj\getlinea &
+  \assemble\obj\getyn &
+  \assemble\obj\horiz &
+  \assemble\obj\invert &
+  \assemble\obj\mbindiv &
+  \assemble\obj\mencom &
+  \assemble\obj\menuar &
+  \assemble\obj\menubox &
+  \assemble\obj\message &
+  \assemble\obj\motr &
+  \assemble\obj\pauztick &
+  \assemble\obj\pauztime &
+  \assemble\obj\pchar &
+  \assemble\obj\pmsg &
+  \assemble\obj\pnum &
+  \assemble\obj\pstrng &
+  \assemble\obj\pstrng2 &
+  \assemble\obj\qscreen &
+  \assemble\obj\sbox &
+  \assemble\obj\scrn &
+  \assemble\obj\scrnbas &
+  \assemble\obj\seekey &
+  \assemble\obj\setcolor &
+  \assemble\obj\setdi &
+  \assemble\obj\soundasm &
```

```
+ \assemble\obj\soundbas &
+ \assemble\obj\tbox &
+ \assemble\obj\timer &
+ \assemble\obj\vidbas &
+ \assemble\obj\viddata
\assemble\huge.lst
;
```

Notice the response on the second line of this file, the letter *Y*, which is there to answer the following question:

```
Library does not exist. Create? _
```

LIB asks this question if it cannot find HUGE.LIB. The construction of this response file presupposes that the original library (if any) has been deleted. The *Y* response causes LIB to combine into HUGE.LIB the 52 specified object code files. The ampersand (&) at the end of each line (except the final file specification line) tells LIB that additional commands follow. Finally, LIB is directed to create a list file called HUGE.LST.

To use a response file with LIB, simply invoke LIB with the following command syntax:

    LIB @filename.ext

filename.ext is the name of the response file to be used. Notice the @ symbol directly before the file name. LIB needs this key symbol to differentiate between a response file and a library name.

If the sample response file were called HUGE.LRF, you could use it by issuing the following command:

    LIB @HUGE.LRF

As you use LIB repeatedly, you will appreciate being able to use response files.

Managing a Library

As you add files to your library, you can follow either of two avenues usually taken by programmers: you can create one large library containing (in one convenient location) all of your subroutines, or you can create several smaller libraries, each representing a specialized category of subroutine.

Let's assume that you want to manage only one large library and that, from time to time, you would like to be able to update one of the subroutines in the library. Updating the library is simple if you combine the procedures that you have learned in this chapter with the capabilities of DOS batch files. You can apply the same techniques to smaller libraries, as well.

The usual process for updating a library is

1. Assemble the source file.

2. Delete the original OBJ file from the library.

3. Add the new OBJ file to the library.

Let's assume that your library is called HUGE.LIB and that, to make matters more complicated, you need to update several files. You can update your library by using the following batch file (UPDATE.BAT) to perform the three steps:

```
echo off
 cls
 del *.obj >nul
 del \assemble\hugelib.txt
 :loop
      if %1\ == \ goto exit
          echo Working on %1.asm
          masm %1,; >nul
          lib \assemble\huge -+%1; >\assemble\hugelib.txt
          shift
          goto loop
 :exit
 del *.obj >nul
```

This batch file assumes that MASM and LIB are in either your current directory or the search path; that the source file (.ASM) is in the current directory; and that you want HUGE.LIB to be in the subdirectory ASSEMBLE.

The proper syntax for this batch file is

UPDATE file1 file2 file3 file4 . . .

file1 is the root file name of the ASM file to be updated in the library. *file2, file3, file4,* etc. are the optional names of other source files that you want updated to the library.

After this batch file has completed its job, the dialog normally presented by LIB.EXE will be saved (in the ASSEMBLE subdirectory) in a file called HUGELIB.TXT. Any errors will be noted in this file.

Summary

This chapter has shown you how to create, change, and manage libraries, and how libraries fit into the linking process.

Libraries, which are intended to make the programmer's life easier, can be a headache if they are not managed properly or logically. Take time to think through your library needs. Consider how to fit library use into your normal methods for program development. Then develop some batch files (such as the one described in this chapter) that will help you make the most of libraries.

As you become adept at using libraries, you will find that they can make your tasks much easier.

Part III

Advanced Assembly Language Topics

Includes

Video Memory
Accessing Hardware Ports
Accessing BIOS Services
Accessing DOS Services

10

Video Memory

Writing information to a video display monitor is, perhaps, the biggest bottleneck in most high-level languages. The sad thing is, most programmers do not even realize that it is a bottleneck.

The video display is simply a representation of what is contained in a specific area of memory. This type of display is referred to as a *memory-mapped* display; the display memory area is called a *video buffer* because it holds what will be displayed on the monitor. Changes occur constantly in the video buffer, and affect what is seen on the video display. The buffer's location in memory depends on the type of display adapter that is being used. A discussion of the buffer's location is included in this chapter in the discussion of each type of display adapter.

Each text screen's video buffer occupies 4,000 bytes (0FA0h) of data—a number derived from an 80-column, 25-line screen. Each character position on the screen uses two bytes of memory—one for the character and one for the character's attribute. The *attribute byte* controls how the character will be displayed (in color, with underlining, blinking, etc.). Thus, one text screen requires 4,000 bytes (80 times 25 times 2) of memory.

Certain BIOS and DOS interrupts allow you to display either individual characters or strings, but tend to be rather slow. You can use BIOS and DOS functions to gain some (but not much) speed advantage over high-level language display techniques. You do not gain much of an advantage because, to guarantee portability and compatibility, most high-level languages ordinarily use the BIOS and DOS interrupts in their display library routines.

Because of the way the BIOS, and subsequently the DOS, routines were written, they repeat several tasks during a display operation. Although this repetition may have been necessary to maintain the general-purpose design of the routines, it has the undesirable effect of slowing down display operations so much that they almost become unacceptable. For example, an examination of the BIOS video routines shows that, in more than one instance, the individual routines which make up INT 10h call themselves to determine necessary information for the completion of the current task. This results in much more pushing, popping, and overhead than if the video routines had been written with a specific purpose in mind.

Because a video display is simply a representation of a special memory area, you can alter the display by altering that memory area directly. As you know, you can transfer large blocks of memory quickly from one location to another. By using the string-manipulation mnemonics, you can use the following subroutine to transfer an entire video screen in approximately 80,100 clock cycles:

```
MOVE_BLOCK      PROC    NEAR
                PUSH    CX                      ;Save all used registers
                PUSH    SI
                PUSH    DI
                PUSH    ES

                MOV     SI,OFFSET SOURCE_DAT    ;Image data to be moved
                MOV     ES,VIDEO_BUFFER         ;Segment of video buffer
                MOV     DI,Ø                    ;Start at beginning
                                                ;  of video buffer
                MOV     CX,ØFAØh                ;Size of video screen
                REP     MOVSB                   ;Move it

                POP     ES                      ;Restore all used registers
                POP     DI
                POP     SI
                POP     CX
                RET
MOVE_BLOCK      ENDP
```

Stated in clock cycles, this may sound like a long time for transferring data. However, you must remember that on a standard IBM PC, running at 4.772727 MHz, one clock cycle is only 0.0000002095238 seconds long; therefore, the entire process takes approximately 0.01678307 seconds. The speed increases significantly on an AT- or 80386-based machine.

No matter which machine you use, displaying an entire screen in less than 1/50 of a second causes the screen to display instantaneously. Compare that to a high-level language and the way you have to clear the screen and then move data elements individually to the screen!

For those of us who use high-level languages, the capability of displaying things quickly on the screen is one of the attractions of using assembly language.

Because the physical location of the video memory depends on which display adapter is used, let's take just a moment to examine the display adapters commonly used on IBM microcomputers.

Differences between Display Adapters

The IBM family of personal computers (and major clones) use a variety of display devices. Several have been around for years, and new ones crop up periodically. In this section, I discuss the methods and conventions used to display information on the four most popular display devices:

- the IBM Monochrome Display Adapter (MDA)
- the Hercules Graphics Adapter (HGA), which allows monochrome graphics
- the IBM Color Graphics Adapter (CGA)
- the IBM Enhanced Graphics Adapter (EGA)

The way you program your application depends, in large part, on which of these display devices you use. You should do some advance research to ensure that you know which device(s) you will use. If several different display types are likely to be used, you can program your software to make intelligent choices about which type of display is currently in use. You will learn about one such method later in this chapter.

All of these display adapters (except the MDA) can display true graphics data. As I stated in the "Introduction," I will not delve into specific graphics routines. Rather, I will discuss the way in which each type of display adapter stores and displays textual data.

The Monochrome Display Adapter (MDA)

The IBM Monochrome Display Adapter made its debut when the IBM Personal Computer was introduced in 1981. As the name implies, the MDA displays information in monochrome (one color). Which color depends on the type of monitor you have; most monochrome monitors display data in either green or amber, although other colors can be displayed.

The MDA offers a resolution of 720 by 350 pixels—a total of 252,000 picture elements. This total is segmented into 2,000 character cells (each with a resolution of 9 by 14 pixels) arranged in 25 rows of 80 cells each.

The contents of each character cell are stored in memory as a single byte of information. Each character cell has a corresponding attribute byte that controls the way in which the character is displayed. The composition and use of the attribute byte is discussed later in this chapter.

The video buffer used by the MDA holds a single text screen and consists of 4K of RAM, beginning at B0000h (segment address B000:0000). The characters and their attribute bytes are interlaced so that the video memory is mapped beginning at the upper left corner of the screen and proceeding across and down the display (see table 10.1).

Table 10.1
Memory Locations for MDA Display Data

Segment Address	Character/Attribute
B000:0000	Character for row 1, column 1
B000:0001	Attribute for row 1, column 1
B000:0002	Character for row 1, column 2
B000:0003	Attribute for row 1, column 2
B000:0004	Character for row 1, column 3
B000:0005	Attribute for row 1, column 3
B000:009C	Character for row 1, column 79
B000:009D	Attribute for row 1, column 79
B000:009E	Character for row 1, column 80
B000:009F	Attribute for row 1, column 80
B000:00A0	Character for row 2, column 1
B000:00A1	Attribute for row 2, column 1
B000:00A2	Character for row 2, column 2
B000:00A3	Attribute for row 2, column 2
B000:0EFC	Character for row 24, column 79
B000:0EFD	Attribute for row 24, column 79
B000:0EFE	Character for row 24, column 80
B000:0EFF	Attribute for row 24, column 80
B000:0F00	Character for row 25, column 1
B000:0F01	Attribute for row 25, column 1
B000:0F02	Character for row 25, column 2
B000:0F03	Attribute for row 25, column 2
B000:0F9C	Character for row 25, column 79
B000:0F9D	Attribute for row 25, column 79
B000:0F9E	Character for row 25, column 80
B000:0F9F	qAttribute for row 25, column 80

Each character-display position can contain a value of 1 through 256, with each value equivalent to a specific character code. The character code used by the MDA is a superset of ASCII (see fig. 10.1).

0=	32=	64=@	96=`	128=Ç	160=á	192=L	224=α
1=☺	33=!	65=A	97=a	129=ü	161=í	193=⊥	225=β
2=☻	34="	66=B	98=b	130=é	162=ó	194=┬	226=Γ
3=♥	35=#	67=C	99=c	131=â	163=ú	195=├	227=π
4=♦	36=$	68=D	100=d	132=ä	164=ñ	196=─	228=Σ
5=♣	37=%	69=E	101=e	133=à	165=Ñ	197=┼	229=σ
6=♠	38=&	70=F	102=f	134=å	166=ª	198=╞	230=μ
7=•	39='	71=G	103=g	135=ç	167=º	199=╟	231=τ
8=◘	40=(	72=H	104=h	136=ê	168=¿	200=╚	232=Φ
9=○	41=)	73=I	105=i	137=ë	169=⌐	201=╔	233=Θ
10=◙	42=*	74=J	106=j	138=è	170=¬	202=╩	234=Ω
11=♂	43=+	75=K	107=k	139=ï	171=½	203=╦	235=δ
12=♀	44=,	76=L	108=l	140=î	172=¼	204=╠	236=∞
13=♪	45=-	77=M	109=m	141=ì	173=¡	205=═	237=φ
14=♫	46=.	78=N	110=n	142=Ä	174=«	206=╬	238=ε
15=☼	47=/	79=O	111=o	143=Å	175=»	207=╧	239=∩
16=►	48=0	80=P	112=p	144=É	176=░	208=╨	240=≡
17=◄	49=1	81=Q	113=q	145=æ	177=▒	209=╤	241=±
18=↕	50=2	82=R	114=r	146=Æ	178=▓	210=╥	242=≥
19=‼	51=3	83=S	115=s	147=ô	179=│	211=╙	243=≤
20=¶	52=4	84=T	116=t	148=ö	180=┤	212=╘	244=⌠
21=§	53=5	85=U	117=u	149=ò	181=╡	213=╒	245=⌡
22=▬	54=6	86=V	118=v	150=û	182=╢	214=╓	246=÷
23=↨	55=7	87=W	119=w	151=ù	183=╖	215=╫	247=≈
24=↑	56=8	88=X	120=x	152=ÿ	184=╕	216=╪	248=°
25=↓	57=9	89=Y	121=y	153=Ö	185=╣	217=┘	249=∙
26=→	58=:	90=Z	122=z	154=Ü	186=║	218=┌	250=·
27=←	59=;	91=[	123={	155=¢	187=╗	219=█	251=√
28=∟	60=<	92=\	124=|	156=£	188=╝	220=▄	252=ⁿ
29=↔	61==	93=]	125=}	157=¥	189=╜	221=▌	253=²
30=▲	62=>	94=^	126=~	158=₧	190=╛	222=▐	254=■
31=▼	63=?	95=_	127=⌂	159=ƒ	191=┐	223=▀	255=

Fig. 10.1.
ASCII character code for MDA.

The character codes shown in figure 10.1 are created by an 8K character generator on the MDA interface board. To generate a character, simply place the character in the proper memory location in the MDA buffer. The internal hardware of the MDA takes care of the rest.

The Hercules Graphics Adapter (HGA)

The Hercules Graphics Adapter, which is similar to the MDA, comes from a company called Hercules Computer Technology. This device is supported by a great deal of software and is the standard for monochrome graphics.

Ordinarily, the HGA behaves exactly like the MDA, except that the HGA includes a monochrome graphics capability. In bit-mapped graphics mode, the HGA provides a resolution of 720 by 348 pixels—the highest resolution of any adapter discussed in this book. In text mode, the HGA operates exactly like the MDA. (For additional information, refer to the section on the MDA.)

The Color Graphics Adapter (CGA)

IBM's first offering for color graphics capability on the IBM family of microcomputers, the Color Graphics Adapter, can operate in text mode (like the MDA) or in a bit-mapped graphics mode. I will focus on the display of textual data because, as I stated in the Introduction, the bit-mapped graphics mode is beyond the scope of this book.

The high resolution offered by the CGA is 640 by 200 pixels, a total of 128,000 picture elements. As with the MDA, this total can be segmented into 2,000 character cells, which are arranged in 25 rows of either 40 or 80 cells each. But the resolution of each cell is significantly less with the CGA—only 8 by 8 pixels, which renders characters that are not as readable or crisp as those on the MDA.

In text mode, the CGA functions much like the MDA. This is understandable— the CGA and MDA both use the Motorola® 6845 CRT Controller chip. With the CGA as with the MDA, the contents of each character cell are stored in memory as a single byte of information. Each character cell has a corresponding attribute byte that controls how the character is displayed. The composition and use of the attribute byte is different in the CGA and the MDA, as you will learn later in this chapter.

The video buffer used by the CGA consists of 16K of RAM, beginning at B8000h (segment address B800:0000). Because a 40 by 25 text screen requires only 2K of memory, the video buffer can hold as many as eight text screens, or pages. With an 80 by 25 text screen, which requires 4K of memory, as many as four video pages can be contained in the video buffer.

The currently displayed video page can be changed easily; to do so, you modify the buffer start address used by the 6845 CRTC. Normally, this address is set to point to the memory block starting at B8000h. The current video page is changed through the use of BIOS function calls (see Chapter 12).

As with the MDA, the characters and their attribute bytes are interlaced, beginning at the upper left corner of the screen and proceeding across and down the display. Table 10.2 shows how the video memory for the first page of an 80 by 25 screen is mapped.

Table 10.2
Memory Locations for First Page of an 80 by 25 CGA

Segment Address	Character/Attribute
B800:0000	Character for row 1, column 1
B800:0001	Attribute for row 1, column 1
B800:0002	Character for row 1, column 2
B800:0003	Attribute for row 1, column 2
B800:0004	Character for row 1, column 3
B800:0005	Attribute for row 1, column 3
B800:009C	Character for row 1, column 79
B800:009D	Attribute for row 1, column 79
B800:009E	Character for row 1, column 80
B800:009F	Attribute for row 1, column 80
B800:00A0	Character for row 2, column 1
B800:00A1	Attribute for row 2, column 1
B800:00A2	Character for row 2, column 2
B800:00A3	Attribute for row 2, column 2
B800:0EFC	Character for row 24, column 79
B800:0EFD	Attribute for row 24, column 79
B800:0EFE	Character for row 24, column 80
B800:0EFF	Attribute for row 24, column 80
B800:0F00	Character for row 25, column 1
B800:0F01	Attribute for row 25, column 1
B800:0F02	Character for row 25, column 2
B800:0F03	Attribute for row 25, column 2
B800:0F9C	Character for row 25, column 79
B800:0F9D	Attribute for row 25, column 79
B800:0F9E	Character for row 25, column 80
B800:0F9F	Attribute for row 25, column 80

Each character-display position can contain a value of 1 through 256, with each value equivalent to a specific character code. The character codes used by the CGA are the same as those used by the MDA, and are a superset of ASCII. The CGA also uses a ROM character generator.

The Enhanced Graphics Adapter (EGA)

IBM introduced the Enhanced Graphics Adapter in late 1984. To date, not much software is available that takes advantage of the full capabilities of the EGA. Most software treats the EGA as though it were a Color Graphics Adapter—which is not unlike using a sledgehammer to drive picture hooks into the wall—it works, but why the overkill?

The real power of the EGA card is evident when you work with its enhanced graphics capabilities. But, even in text mode, there are several noticeable differences between the EGA and the Color Graphics Adapter. With an EGA card:

- More colors can be displayed

- Text information, displayed in color, can blink

- Resolution is improved

- More display modes are available

- User-defined character sets are available

Before proceeding, let's examine this last point. As you can see from table 10.3, the EGA offers 12 display modes.

Table 10.3
EGA Display Modes

Mode Number	Mode Type	Display Type	Pixel Resolution	Characters	Box Size	Colors
0	Text	Color	320 × 200	40 × 25	8 × 8	16
		Enhanced	320 × 350	40 × 25	8 × 14	16/64
1	---------- Same as mode 0 ----------					
2	Text	Color	640 × 200	80 × 25	8 × 8	16
		Enhanced	640 × 350	80 × 25	8 × 14	16/64
3	---------- Same as mode 2 ----------					
4	Graph	Clr/Enh	320 × 200	40 × 25	8 × 8	4
5	---------- Same as mode 4 ----------					
6	Graph	Clr/Enh	640 × 200	80 × 25	8 × 14	2

Table 10.3—cont.

Mode Number	Mode Type	Display Type	Pixel Resolution	Characters	Box Size	Colors
7	Text	Mono	720 × 350	80 × 25	9 × 14	4
13	Graph	Clr/Enh	320 × 200	40 × 25	8 × 8	16
14	Graph	Clr/Enh	640 × 200	80 × 25	8 × 8	16
15	Graph	Mono	640 × 350	80 × 25	8 × 14	4
16	Graph	Enhanced	640 × 350	80 × 25	8 × 14	varies

Notice that the resolution offered by the EGA is not quite as good as that offered by the MDA and HGA boards. EGA resolution is 640 by 350 pixels—a total of 224,000 picture elements.

The possibilities of using this resolution in a color graphics mode are quite impressive, but these capabilities are beyond the scope of this book. Because the effective use of the EGA would fill an entire book, I will focus only on using the EGA in text mode.

Like the other video adapters, the EGA segments the text screen into 2,000 character cells, each with a resolution of 8 by 14 pixels. These character cells are arranged in 25 rows of 80 cells each. The contents of each character cell are stored in memory as a single byte of information. Each character cell has a corresponding attribute byte that controls how the character is displayed. (The composition and use of the attribute byte are discussed later in this chapter.)

Which video buffer is used by the EGA depends on the amount of memory available on the card. Most of the higher memory capabilities are used only in multipage graphics software or in animation. In text mode, however, the EGA is capable of emulating either the MDA or CGA in memory usage. If connected to a monochrome monitor, the video buffer begins at absolute address B0000h (segment address B000:0000), as does the MDA. If connected to a color monitor, the video buffer begins at absolute address B8000h (segment address B800:0000), as does the CGA.

As with other text screens, the characters and their attribute bytes are interlaced so that, beginning at the upper left corner of the screen and proceeding across and down the display, the video memory is mapped as shown in table 10.4. The question mark is replaced by 0 if the EGA is connected to a monochrome monitor; by 8 if connected to a color monitor.

Table 10.4
Memory Locations for EGA Display Data

Segment Address	Character/Attribute
B?00:0000	Character for row 1, column 1
B?00:0001	Attribute for row 1, column 1
B?00:0002	Character for row 1, column 2
B?00:0003	Attribute for row 1, column 2
B?00:0004	Character for row 1, column 3
B?00:0005	Attribute for row 1, column 3
B?00:009C	Character for row 1, column 79
B?00:009D	Attribute for row 1, column 79
B?00:009E	Character for row 1, column 80
B?00:009F	Attribute for row 1, column 80
B?00:00A0	Character for row 2, column 1
B?00:00A1	Attribute for row 2, column 1
B?00:00A2	Character for row 2, column 2
B?00:00A3	Attribute for row 2, column 2
B?00:0EFC	Character for row 24, column 79
B?00:0EFD	Attribute for row 24, column 79
B?00:0EFE	Character for row 24, column 80
B?00:0EFF	Attribute for row 24, column 80
B?00:0F00	Character for row 25, column 1
B?00:0F01	Attribute for row 25, column 1
B?00:0F02	Character for row 25, column 2
B?00:0F03	Attribute for row 25, column 2
B?00:0F9C	Character for row 25, column 79
B?00:0F9D	Attribute for row 25, column 79
B?00:0F9E	Character for row 25, column 80
B?00:0F9F	Attribute for row 25, column 80

The EGA can display the same character set that each of the other display
adapters can display. There is a difference in how the characters are displayed,
however. The EGA uses a RAM character generator, not one that is ROM based.
This means that users can design and download custom fonts based on their
own needs. As many as four fonts of 256 characters each can be developed and
subsequently used by the EGA, but only two of the fonts can be used at any
given time. Detailed information on the development and use of alternate fonts
is beyond the scope of this book.

Determining the Type of Display Installed

Because the way in which text is displayed depends on the type of display adapter installed, your first task is to determine which type of adapter is installed in the computer.

To communicate with the peripherals that are attached to it, the computer must know what those peripherals are—this includes display adapters.

BIOS cannot display information unless it knows what type of display adapter is currently being used. BIOS keeps a list of video-related information beginning at memory locations 0449h through 0489h (see table 10.5).

Table 10.5
BIOS Video Data Area

Memory Location	Length	Purpose
0410h	byte	POST equipment list 1
0411h	byte	POST equipment list 2
0449h	byte	BIOS video mode
044Ah	word	Columns
044Ch	word	Page length
044Eh	word	Page beginning
0460h	word	Cursor start/end
0462h	byte	Page number
0463h	word	Current adapter base port
0465h	byte	Mode selection
0466h	byte	Palette

Currently, two of the memory locations shown in table 10.5 are of interest. The byte at 0410h tells what the system board switch settings were when the POST (Power-On Self Test) was performed at booting. Each bit of the word denotes a different setting. Table 10.6 shows the bit meanings of the value at 0410h.

Table 10.6
Meaning of Bits at Memory Location 0410h

Bits 76543210	Meaning of Bits
00	1 disk drive installed, if bit 0=1
01	2 disk drives installed, if bit 0=1
10	3 disk drives installed, if bit 0=1
11	4 disk drives installed, if bit 0=1
01	Initial video mode is color, 40 by 25
10	Initial video mode is color, 80 by 25
11	Initial video mode is monochrome, 80 by 25
00	64K system board RAM installed
01	128K system board RAM installed
10	192K system board RAM installed
11	256K system board RAM installed
x	Position not used
0	No disk drives installed
1	Disk drives installed, see bits 7–6

The value of bits 5-4 tells you what type of card (color or monochrome) is installed, according to the system board dip switch settings. But you can't tell whether the monochrome board is an MDA or HGA, or whether the color board is a CGA or EGA. (The distinction is not germane to this discussion, however, because we are dealing only with textual display of data.) A monochrome adapter, such as the MDA, the HGA, or the EGA in monochrome mode, uses a video buffer starting at B0000h, whereas a color adapter, such as the CGA or EGA in a text color mode, uses a video buffer starting at B8000h.

The other memory location that is of interest is the one at 0463h, which provides the information needed to determine where in memory textual data should be stored. The different base port adapter values are shown in table 10.7.

Table 10.7
Adapter Base Port Values Stored at 0463h

Adapter	Base port
MDA	03B4h
CGA	03D4h
HGA	03B4h
EGA	03D4h

Notice that the same values are stored at 0463h for the MDA/HGA and the CGA/EGA. This information tells you which class of adapter is being used. Color-capable adapters have a base port address of 03D4h, whereas monochrome adapters have a base port address of 03B4h. Coupled with the data obtained from memory location 0410h (whether the computer is in monochrome or color mode), you easily and safely can assume which type of monitor the computer is using.

Now let's use this information in a subroutine to determine the segment address that should be used for display of textual information. This routine is a "building block" that will be called by other (still to be developed) assembly language subroutines; as such, the following routine is written as a NEAR procedure:

```
;   ********************************************************************
;   *                                                                  *
;   *  Author:   Allen L. Wyatt                                        *
;   *  Date:     3/11/87                                               *
;   *                                                                  *
;   *  Program:  FIND CARD.ASM                                         *
;   *                                                                  *
;   *  Purpose:  Determine type of video card and save info.          *
;   *            To be called from other assembly language routines.  *
;   *                                                                  *
;   ********************************************************************

; NEAR PUBLIC ROUTINES
              PUBLIC    FIND_CARD

; PUBLIC DATA
              PUBLIC    MONITOR_ADDR
              PUBLIC    STATUS_PORT
```

```
                    NAME     FIND_CARD
        CODE        SEGMENT  BYTE PUBLIC 'CODE'
                    ASSUME   CS:CODE


; EQUATES

        MONO        EQU      ØBØØØh              ;Mono video buffer start
        COLOR       EQU      ØB8ØØh              ;Color video buffer start

; DATA

MONITOR_ADDR        DW       ØØØØ                ;Offset of video buffer
STATUS_PORT         DW       ØØØØ                ;Address of card status port
; -----------------------------------------------------------------
FIND_CARD           PROC     NEAR
                    PUSH     BX                  ;Store all the registers
                    PUSH     DX                  ;     used in this
                    PUSH     ES                  ;     routine

                    MOV      BX,ØØ4Øh            ;Look at base port value
                    MOV      ES,BX               ;     Ø3B4h = monochrome
                    MOV      DX,ES:63h           ;     Ø3D4h = color
                    ADD      DX,6                ;Point to card's status port
                    MOV      STATUS_PORT,DX      ;Save the status port

                    MOV      MONITOR_ADDR,COLOR  ;Default to color card
                    MOV      BX,ES:1Øh           ;Get equipment list
                    AND      BX,3Øh              ;Only want bits 5-4
                    CMP      BX,3Øh              ;Is it monochrome (bits=11)?
                    JNE      FC1                 ;No, so keep as color
                    MOV      MONITOR_ADDR,MONO   ;Yes, set for monochrome

FC1:                POP      ES                  ;Restore the registers
                    POP      DX
                    POP      BX
                    RET                          ;Return to caller
FIND_CARD           ENDP


; -----------------------------------------------------------------
        CODE        ENDS
                    END
```

At the conclusion of this routine, the address of the display adapter's status port is saved in STATUS_PORT, and the segment offset for the video buffer is stored in MONITOR_ADDR. These variables are declared PUBLIC so that they can be used by the routine that actually moves a character of data to the video buffer. (You soon will find out why determination of the adapter's status port location is important.)

Displaying a Character in Video Memory

The next task is to develop a routine to move a character directly into video memory. You may remember that the IBM family of computers uses a memory-mapped video display. Consequently, changing the video memory results in a display change.

You can move data moved directly into the video buffer area, but doing so may result in an undesirable side effect of "snow," or glitches, on the display screen. This effect, which is particularly noticeable on a CGA in text color mode, is caused by accessing the video controller in a way that conflicts with other demands placed on the controller.

All of the IBM display adapters are based on the Motorola 6845 CRT Controller chip. The chip used in the EGA is different, but is based on the 6845. This chip controls the video buffer area. The chip fetches characters from the video buffer, translates them, and subsequently displays them. If you are depositing a character into a memory location at the same time that the 6845 is trying to read it for display, the interference causes the snow.

To compensate for this potential conflict, a routine must verify that a character is deposited only when the 6845 is not reading video memory. This "safe" time occurs during what is referred to as a *horizontal retrace condition* (HRC). While this condition is in effect, depositing a character in a video memory location will not result in interference.

The adapter card's status port contains information about the current state of the 6845. One of the items that can be determined by reading this port is whether the adapter is currently in a horizontal retrace condition. If bit 0 is set to 0, the 6845 has video enabled and is accessing memory. If bit 0 is set to 1, a horizontal retrace condition exists and video memory is not being accessed.

To display a single character in a non-conflict manner, you must write a low-level routine such as PCHAR. Remember that the following is a low-level routine, designed to be called from other assembly language routines:

```
;    ******************************************************************
;    *                                                                *
;    *  Author:      Allen L. Wyatt                                   *
;    *  Date:        3/11/87                                          *
;    *                                                                *
;    *  Program:     PCHAR.ASM                                        *
;    *                                                                *
;    *  Purpose:     To print a character on the video screen.       *
;    *                                                                *
;    *  Enter with: AL = ASCII value of character to print           *
;    *              DI = video buffer offset at which to place AL     *
;    *                                                                *
;    ******************************************************************
;

;    NEAR PUBLIC ROUTINES
             PUBLIC  PCHAR

;    EXTERNAL DATA:
             EXTRN   MONITOR_ADDR:WORD
             EXTRN   STATUS_PORT:WORD

             NAME    PCHAR
CODE         SEGMENT BYTE PUBLIC 'CODE'
             ASSUME  CS:CODE


;    ------------------------------------------------------------------
PCHAR        PROC    NEAR
             PUSH    DX
             PUSH    ES

             MOV     ES,CS:MONITOR_ADDR
             MOV     DX,CS:STATUS_PORT

             CLI                         ;Don't allow interrupts
             PUSH    AX                  ;Store the character
RETRACE:     IN      AL,DX               ;Get card status
             TEST    AL,1                ;Are we in a retrace state?
             JNZ     RETRACE             ;Yes, so check again
                                         ;On fall-through, just
                                         ;   exited retrace state
```

```
NO_RETRACE:     IN      AL,DX              ;Get card status
                TEST    AL,1               ;Are we in a retrace state?
                JZ      NO_RETRACE         ;No, so check again
                                           ;On fall-through, just
                                           ;   entered retrace state
                POP     AX                 ;Yes, get character back
                MOV     ES:[DI],AL         ;OK to write it now
                STI                        ;OK to have interrupts now

                INC     DI                 ;Point to attribute
                INC     DI                 ;Next screen location

                POP     ES
                POP     DX
                RET
PCHAR           ENDP

; ----------------------------------------------------------------
CODE            ENDS
                END
```

Notice that the 6845 status port is read in two separate loops. The first,
RETRACE, tests bit 0 to determine whether an HRC currently exists. If bit 0 is
equal to 1, the zero flag will be clear, and the JNZ is executed to check again
for an HRC. The loop is exited only when the HRC does not exist. This may
sound backwards, because I pointed out earlier that accessing video memory
during the retrace is safe. It *is* safe, but the instructions to pop the character
from the stack and deposit it in video memory take time—the HRC could be
over by the time the character is deposited.

When this routine is entered, you have no idea how long the HRC has been in
effect or when it will end. Thus, the first loop waits until any existing HRC is
completed. The second loop waits for an HRC and then accesses the memory at
the start of the HRC. The result is the least possible snow.

After verifying that an HRC has begun, PCHAR places a character at the video
buffer offset position determined by DI. The following section shows how to
determine the value of DI from simple X-Y coordinates.

PCHAR returns with all registers (except DI) intact. DI is incremented to point
at the next character position in the video buffer. After completion of this
routine, you can develop a routine (callable from a high-level language) to
display a string of ASCII characters quickly and at any position on the display
screen.

Displaying an ASCII String

You now know what type of display adapter is installed, you have saved the segment address of the video buffer, and you know how to display a single character. All that remains is to determine the correct offset address so that you know where to begin displaying information.

From the details presented earlier in this chapter, you can easily derive a formula for determining the offset for displaying a character at any given location on the screen. This formula can be expressed as

[(ROW-1) * 80 + (COLUMN-1)] * 2

In this equation, ROW is assumed to be in the range of 1 through 25, and COLUMN is assumed to be in the range of 1 through 80. The offset for the attribute for any given character can be located by the formula

[(ROW-1) * 80 + (COLUMN-1)] * 2 + 1

Notice that the character addresses are always even, whereas the attribute addresses are always odd.

Basically, all you need to calculate the memory offset are the X (COLUMN) and Y (ROW) coordinates. Based on this equation and the routines developed in the two preceding sections, you can write a routine that displays a string at any given position on the text screen. The following routine, which is called from compiled BASIC, will perform this task:

```
;       **********************************************************************
;       *                                                                    *
;       *  Author:     Allen L. Wyatt                                         *
;       *  Date:       3/11/87                                                *
;       *                                                                    *
;       *  Program:    PSTRNG.ASM                                             *
;       *                                                                    *
;       *  Purpose:    To display a string directly to video memory from     *
;       *              compiled BASIC.                                        *
;       *                                                                    *
;       *  Formats:    CALL PSTRNG(A$,X%,Y%)                                  *
;       *                                                                    *
;       *  Variables: A$:  The BASIC string to be displayed.                 *
;       *             X%:  The integer column value.                         *
;       *             Y%:  The integer row value.                            *
;       *                                                                    *
;       **********************************************************************
```

```
; FAR PUBLIC ROUTINES
                PUBLIC   PSTRNG


; EXTERNAL ROUTINES
                EXTRN    FIND_CARD:NEAR
                EXTRN    PCHAR:NEAR

                NAME     PSTRNG
CODE            SEGMENT  BYTE PUBLIC 'CODE'
                ASSUME   CS:CODE


; EQUATES

PARMC           EQU      1Ø
PARMB           EQU      Ø8
PARMA           EQU      Ø6


; DATA

STORE_DS        DW       ØØØØ                 ;Storage for BASIC's DS
STORE_BP        DW       ØØØØ                 ;Storage for BASIC's BP


; -------------------------------------------------------------------
PSTRNG          PROC     FAR                  ;Always FAR PROC from BASIC
                PUSH     BP
                MOV      BP,SP                ;Point to stack
                PUSH     ES
                MOV      CS:STORE_DS,DS       ;Store BASIC data segment
                MOV      CS:STORE_BP,BP       ;Store stack pointer
                MOV      AX,CS                ;Make sure data segment
                MOV      DS,AX                ;     is properly set

                CALL     FIND_CARD            ;Locate the video buffer
                MOV      BP,STORE_BP          ;Get back stack pointer
                MOV      DS,STORE_DS          ;Point to BASIC data area
                MOV      BX,[BP+PARMC]        ;Get BASIC's string pointer
                MOV      CX,[BX]              ;Get the string's length
                JCXZ     EXIT                 ;No length, so don't print
                MOV      SI,[BX+2]            ;SI points to string

                MOV      BX,[BP+PARMB]        ;Get address for row
                MOV      AX,[BX]              ;Get row value
                DEC      AX                   ;Put as a zero offset
```

```
            MOV      BX,[BP+PARMA]         ;Get address for column
            MOV      DI,[BX]               ;Get column value
            DEC      DI                    ;Put as zero offset
            MOV      BX,8Ø                  ;8Ø characters/row
            MUL      BX                    ;Now have rows in AX
            ADD      DI,AX                 ;Add to column number
            SHL      DI,1                  ;Multiply by 2, DI=offset

PSLOOP:     MOV      AL,[SI]               ;Get the string character
            INC      SI                    ;Point to the next character
            CALL     PCHAR                 ;No, so print the character
            LOOP     PSLOOP                ;Redo for length of string

EXIT:       MOV      DS,CS:STORE_DS        ;Restore data segment
            MOV      BP,CS:STORE_BP        ;Restore base pointer
            POP      ES
            POP      BP
            RET      3*2                   ;Return to BASIC
PSTRNG      ENDP

; -------------------------------------------------------------------
CODE        ENDS
            END
```

When you pass parameters from compiled BASIC to this routine, it is important to remember that the X-Y coordinates must be integer values. Unpredictable results may occur if integers are not used.

Using the Attribute Byte

You may recall that each displayed character in the video buffer requires two bytes of information—the ASCII value of the character and the character's display attribute.

This attribute byte controls how the character is displayed. Each bit of the attribute byte has a different function and, regardless of the type of display adapter you are using, the purpose of each bit is the same. However, the *effect* produced by different settings varies according to the type of adapter.

Generally, bits 0–3 and 7 control the foreground, whereas bits 4–6 control the background. The foreground is the character itself. The background is the area of the character cell surrounding the character. Although the use of these bits is the same on both color and monochrome adapters, their effect is different. Table 10.8 shows the meanings and possible settings of the bits in each character's attribute byte on a monochrome monitor. Table 10.9 shows the same information for attribute bytes on a color monitor.

Table 10.8
Meaning of the Bits in a Monochrome Attribute Byte

Bits 76543210	Meaning of Bit Setting
0	Character does not blink
1	Character blinks
000	Black background (normal)
111	White foreground (inversed)
0	Normal intensity
1	High intensity
001	Underlined white foreground
111	White foreground (normal)
000	Black foregound (inverse)

Table 10.9
Meaning of the Bits in a Color Attribute Byte

Bits 76543210	Meaning of Bit Setting
0	Normal foreground
1	Blinking foreground
bbb	Background (see table 10.10)
ffff	Foreground (see table 10.10)

You can see from table 10.10 that, with the color attribute, only the first eight colors (0–7) can be used for background values, whereas all 16 colors can be used for foreground. When you use both the monochrome and color attributes, certain combinations of foreground and background will result in characters that are invisible. (Invisible characters, although useless to humans, are valid to the computer.) You can test for different color combinations that you may find pleasing for different applications.

Table 10.10
Background and Foreground Colors for Color Attribute Byte

Bit Setting	Decimal Value	Color
0000	0	Black
0001	1	Blue
0010	2	Green
0011	3	Cyan
0100	4	Red
0101	5	Magenta
0110	6	Brown
0111	7	White
1000	8	Gray
1001	9	Light blue
1010	10	Light green
1011	11	Light cyan
1100	12	Light red
1101	13	Light magenta
1110	14	Yellow
1111	15	White (high intensity)

How can you apply this to enhance the routines developed in this chapter? You do not need to change the FIND_CARD routine, which simply locates the type of card and sets two variables for use in the other routines. But PCHAR and PSTRNG can be changed so that they use a specified attribute value.

PCHAR is written to display a character on either a monochrome or color monitor. It would be nice to be able to use the original routine, but allow the routine to make an intelligent decision about converting attribute values. If the routine were modified in this way, the high-level program could be written to take advantage of a color monitor, but PCHAR would translate the character attribute to a display format appropriate for a monochrome display. This new implementation of PCHAR is as follows:

```
;   ****************************************************************
;   *                                                              *
;   *   Author:      Allen L. Wyatt                                *
;   *   Date:        3/11/87                                       *
;   *                                                              *
;   *   Program:     PCHAR.ASM                                     *
;   *                                                              *
;   *   Purpose:     To print a character on the video screen.     *
;   *                                                              *
;   *   Enter with:  AL = ASCII value of character to print        *
;   *                DI = video buffer offset at which to place AL *
;   *                ATTRIBUTE is initialized by calling program   *
;   *                                                              *
;   *                Sets the video attribute according to the color *
;   *                table values if using a monochrome display.   *
;   *                                                              *
;   ****************************************************************
;

;   NEAR PUBLIC ROUTINES
                PUBLIC  PCHAR

;   PUBLIC DATA
                PUBLIC ATTRIBUTE

;   EXTERNAL DATA
                EXTRN    MONITOR_ADDR:WORD
                EXTRN    STATUS_PORT:WORD

                NAME    PCHAR
CODE            SEGMENT BYTE PUBLIC 'CODE'
                ASSUME  CS:CODE

; EQUATES

MONO            EQU      ØBØØØh                 ;Mono video buffer start
COLOR           EQU      ØB8ØØh                 ;Color video buffer start

; DATA

ATTRIBUTE       DB       ØØ
ATTR_TEST       DB       ØØ
```

```
COLOR_TABLE     EQU     THIS BYTE
BWT_BLK         DB      ØFh,ØFh                 ;Black background
BLU_BLK         DB      Ø1h,Ø1h
YEL_BLU         DB      1Eh,7Øh
BLU_WHT         DB      71h,7Øh
GRN_WHT         DB      72h,7Øh
CYN_WHT         DB      73h,7Øh
RED_WHT         DB      74h,7Øh
MAG_WHT         DB      75h,7Øh
BRN_WHT         DB      76h,7Øh
GRY_WHT         DB      78h,7Øh
LBL_WHT         DB      79h,7Øh
LGR_WHT         DB      7Ah,7Øh
LCY_WHT         DB      7Bh,7Øh
LRD_WHT         DB      7Ch,7Øh
LMG_WHT         DB      7Dh,7Øh
YEL_WHT         DB      7Eh,7Øh
BWT_WHT         DB      7Fh,7Øh
TABLE_END       DB      ØØh,Ø7h                 ;End of table


; -------------------------------------------------------------------
PCHAR           PROC    NEAR
                PUSH    BX
                PUSH    DX
                PUSH    SI
                PUSH    ES

                MOV     ES,MONITOR_ADDR
                MOV     DX,STATUS_PORT

; HANDLE TRANSLATION FOR MONOCHROME MONITORS

                MOV     AH,ATTRIBUTE            ;Get video attribute
                CMP     MONITOR_ADDR,COLOR     ;Is it a color monitor?
                JE      POK                     ;Yes, assume correct
                CMP     AH,ATTR_TEST           ;Is it the same as before?
                JE      POK                     ;Yes, so keep going
                MOV     SI,OFFSET COLOR_TABLE
COLOR_LOOP:     MOV     BH,[SI]                 ;Get the first color
                INC     SI                      ;Point to mono equivalent
                CMP     BH,Ø                    ;End of table?
                JE      SET_COLOR               ;Yes, so use default
```

```
                CMP     AH,BH                   ;Should we translate?
                JE      SET_COLOR               ;Yes, so set new color
                INC     SI                      ;Skip the mono equivalent
                JMP     SHORT COLOR_LOOP
SET_COLOR:      MOV     AH,[SI]                 ;Get mono equivalent
                MOV     ATTR_TEST,AH            ;Reset the test byte

POK:            CLI                             ;Don't allow interrupts
                PUSH    AX                      ;Store the character
RETRACE:        IN      AL,DX                   ;Get card status
                TEST    AL,1                    ;Are we in a retrace state?
                JNZ     RETRACE                 ;Yes, so check again
                                                ;On fall-through, just
                                                ;   exited retrace state
NO_RETRACE:     IN      AL,DX                   ;Get card status
                TEST    AL,1                    ;Are we in a retrace state?
                JZ      NO_RETRACE              ;No, so check again
                                                ;On fall-through, just
                                                ;   entered retrace state
                POP     AX                      ;Yes, get character back
                MOV     ES:[DI],AX              ;OK to write it now
                STI                             ;OK to have interrupts now

                INC     DI                      ;Point to attribute
                INC     DI                      ;Next screen location

                POP     ES
                POP     SI
                POP     DX
                POP     BX
                RET
PCHAR           ENDP

; -----------------------------------------------------------------
CODE            ENDS
                END
```

This new version of the routine is only slightly different from the earlier
PCHAR. The modified routine has the additional data areas needed for the
attribute and the attribute translation.

The translation table begins at the label COLOR_TABLE. Each color attribute to be translated is listed, followed by the monochrome equivalent of the attribute. For instance, the color attribute for a yellow foreground on a blue background (YEL_BLU) translates to an inverse (black on white) attribute in monochrome.

A 0 in the color attribute position signifies the end of the table. Any translation that has not been caught specifically in the table is translated to normal monochrome white on black.

This translation process is handled in PCHAR by the coding beginning at the line

```
; HANDLE TRANSLATION FOR MONOCHROME MONITORS
```

First, PCHAR checks to see whether a monochrome monitor is in use. If not, no translation is needed, and processing continues. If a monochrome monitor is in use, the old attribute (ATTR_TEST) is checked against the new one. If the two attributes are the same, no translation is needed, and processing continues.

If a translation is indicated, PCHAR loads the offset of COLOR_TABLE into SI. Next, the attribute byte at that location (SI) is loaded and SI is incremented to point at the monochrome equivalent of the color attribute. Then PCHAR checks for the end-of-table flag. If the end has been reached, the routine is exited, the default attribute (white on black) is loaded, and the character is displayed. If a valid translation is needed, the new attribute is loaded from the table, and the character is displayed.

Notice that in this version of PCHAR, an entire word (both the ASCII value and its attribute) is moved into the video buffer; in the earlier version of the routine, only the ASCII character was moved to memory.

The overhead associated with the changes to this routine is a small price to pay for the added value received. Now you can control not only *which* character is displayed but also *how* a character is displayed.

Notice that ATTRIBUTE is assumed to have been set before entry into PCHAR. ATTRIBUTE is a video attribute that can be set in PSTRNG with a value passed from a high-level language. The new version of PSTRNG, which is written for compiled BASIC and allows for setting ATTRIBUTE, follows:

```
;   ****************************************************************
;   *                                                              *
;   *   Author:     Allen L. Wyatt                                 *
;   *   Date:       3/11/87                                        *
;   *                                                              *
;   *   Program:    PSTRNG.ASM                                     *
;   *                                                              *
;   *   Purpose:    To display a string directly to video memory from *
;   *               compiled BASIC.                                *
;   *                                                              *
;   *   Formats:    CALL PSTRNG(A$,X%,Y%,Z%)                       *
;   *                                                              *
;   *   Variables: A$:  The BASIC string to be displayed.          *
;   *               X%:  The integer column value.                 *
;   *               Y%:  The integer row value.                    *
;   *               Z%:  The integer video attribute.              *
;   *                                                              *
;   ****************************************************************

; FAR PUBLIC ROUTINES
                PUBLIC  PSTRNG

; EXTERNAL ROUTINES
                EXTRN   FIND_CARD:NEAR
                EXTRN   PCHAR:NEAR

; EXTERNAL DATA
                EXTRN   ATTRIBUTE:BYTE

                NAME    PSTRNG
CODE            SEGMENT BYTE PUBLIC 'CODE'
                ASSUME  CS:CODE

; EQUATES

PARMD           EQU     12
PARMC           EQU     1Ø
PARMB           EQU     Ø8
PARMA           EQU     Ø6

; DATA
```

```
STORE_DS        DW      ØØØØ                    ;Storage for BASIC's DS
STORE_BP        DW      ØØØØ                    ;Storage for BASIC's BP


; ------------------------------------------------------------------
PSTRNG          PROC    FAR                     ;Always FAR PROC from BASIC
                PUSH    BP
                MOV     BP,SP                   ;Point to stack
                PUSH    ES
                MOV     CS:STORE_DS,DS          ;Store BASIC data segment
                MOV     CS:STORE_BP,BP          ;Store stack pointer
                MOV     AX,CS                   ;Make sure data segment
                MOV     DS,AX                   ;    is properly set

                CALL    FIND_CARD               ;Locate the video buffer
                MOV     BP,STORE_BP             ;Get back stack pointer
                MOV     DS,STORE_DS             ;Point to BASIC data area
                MOV     BX,[BP+PARMA]           ;Address of attribute value
                MOV     AX,[BX]                 ;Get attribute value
                MOV     ATTRIBUTE,AL            ;Only working with a byte

                MOV     BX,[BP+PARMD]           ;Get BASIC's string pointer
                MOV     CX,[BX]                 ;Get the string's length
                JCXZ    EXIT                    ;No length, so don't print
                MOV     SI,[BX+2]               ;SI points to string

                MOV     BX,[BP+PARMC]           ;Get address for row
                MOV     AX,[BX]                 ;Get row value
                DEC     AX                      ;Put as a zero offset
                MOV     BX,[BP+PARMB]           ;Get address for column
                MOV     DI,[BX]                 ;Get column value
                DEC     DI                      ;Put AS zero offset
                MOV     BX,8Ø                   ;8Ø characters/row
                MUL     BX                      ;Now have rows in AX
                ADD     DI,AX                   ;Add to column number
                SHL     DI,1                    ;Multiply by 2, DI=offset

PSLOOP:         MOV     AL,[SI]                 ;Get the string character
                INC     SI                      ;Point to the next character
                CALL    PCHAR                   ;Print the character
                LOOP    PSLOOP                  ;Redo for length of string
```

```
EXIT:           MOV     DS,CS:STORE_DS      ;Restore data segment
                MOV     BP,CS:STORE_BP      ;Restore base pointer
                POP     ES
                POP     BP
                RET     4*2                 ;Return to BASIC
PSTRNG          ENDP

; ---------------------------------------------------------------
CODE            ENDS
                END
```

There is only one difference between this and the earlier version of PSTRNG. This version allows an additional variable to be passed by BASIC to specify the attribute of the string being printed. This attribute is placed in the variable ATTRIBUTE for subsequent use by PCHAR.

Notice that even though a word (16-bit integer) is passed from BASIC, only the lower byte of the word is used for the attribute. As you will recall from the memory-mapped display of the IBM computer family, only one byte is used to specify a character's attribute.

Text-Based Graphics Routines

Now that you know how information is stored on the screen, and how the appearance of the information is controlled, you can use these building blocks to create routines for handling text-based graphics. Such routines are helpful when you create attractive menus or data-input screens. Using assembly language to paint appealing screens that enhance the image of your program allows you to display them quickly. An added bonus is that the screens and menus are created with one call from your high-level language.

In the ASCII character set of the IBM family of microcomputers, several characters are well-suited for ASCII graphics. These characters were designed for the very task I am talking about—creating screen forms and display outlines. Figure 10.2 shows the different groups of ASCII graphics characters.

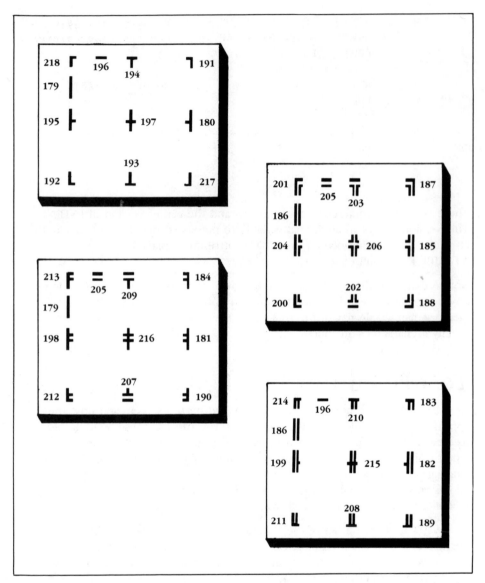

Fig. 10.2.
ASCII graphics characters.

Let's create a routine that uses some of these ASCII graphics characters to display a double-lined box anywhere on the screen. All you have to do is pass the coordinates for the upper left and lower right corners of the box, along with the display attribute to use when creating the box. This routine (named BOX) is coded as follows when called from compiled BASIC:

```
;     ****************************************************************
;     *                                                              *
;     *  Author:    Allen L. Wyatt                                   *
;     *  Date:      3/11/87                                          *
;     *                                                              *
;     *  Program:   BOX.ASM                                          *
;     *                                                              *
;     *  Purpose:   To display a string directly to video memory from *
;     *             compiled BASIC.                                  *
;     *                                                              *
;     *  Formats:   CALL BOX(TLC%,BRC%,Z%)                           *
;     *                                                              *
;     *  Variables: TLC%:  The top left screen coordinate.           *
;     *             BRC%:  The bottom right screen coordinate.       *
;     *             Z%:    The integer video attribute.              *
;     *                                                              *
;     ****************************************************************
;

; FAR PUBLIC ROUTINES
                PUBLIC   BOX

; EXTERNAL ROUTINES
                EXTRN    FIND_CARD:NEAR
                EXTRN    SET_DI:NEAR
                EXTRN    PCHAR:NEAR

; EXTERNAL DATA
                EXTRN    ATTRIBUTE:BYTE

                NAME     BOX
CODE            SEGMENT BYTE PUBLIC 'CODE'
                ASSUME   CS:CODE

; EQUATES

PARMC           EQU      1Ø
PARMB           EQU      Ø8
PARMA           EQU      Ø6

; DATA
```

```
BOX_CHAR        DB      ′£àè¥¤ë′
BOX_ULC         EQU     THIS WORD
UL_COL          DB      ØØ
UL_ROW          DB      ØØ
BOX_LRC         EQU     THIS WORD
LR_COL          DB      ØØ
LR_ROW          DB      ØØ


; --------------------------------------------------------------------
BOX             PROC    FAR
                PUSH    BP
                MOV     BP,SP                   ;Get addressability
                PUSH    DS
                PUSH    ES

                MOV     BX,[BP+PARMA]           ;Get address of attribute
                MOV     AX,[BX]                 ;Get value of attribute
                MOV     CS:ATTRIBUTE,AL         ;Store the attribute
                MOV     BX,[BP+PARMB]           ;Get address of BRC
                MOV     AX,[BX]                 ;Get value of BRC
                MOV     CS:BOX_LRC,AX           ;Store the value
                MOV     BX,[BP+PARMC]           ;Get address of TLC
                MOV     AX,[BX]                 ;Get value of TLC
                MOV     CS:BOX_ULC,AX           ;Store the value

                MOV     AX,CS                   ;Set proper data segment
                MOV     DS,AX

                CALL    FIND_CARD               ;Locate the monitor info

; PRINT SIDES OF BOX, TOP TO BOTTOM

                MOV     BH,UL_ROW               ;Get upper left (row only)
                INC     BH                      ;Start next row down
                MOV     AL,BOX_CHAR+4           ;Character for side of box
                MOV     CH,UL_ROW               ;Top row
                MOV     CL,LR_ROW               ;Bottom row
                SUB     CL,CH                   ;Height is left in CL
                SUB     CH,CH                   ;Zero out CH
                DEC     CX                      ;Adjust for actual height
V1:             MOV     BL,UL_COL               ;Set left column
                CALL    SET_DI                  ;Position offset
```

```
                CALL    PCHAR
                MOV     BL,LR_COL           ;Set right column
                CALL    SET_DI              ;Position offset
                CALL    PCHAR
                INC     BH                  ;Next row
                LOOP    V1
```

; PRINT TOP OF BOX

```
                MOV     BX,BOX_ULC          ;Get upper left column
                INC     BX                  ;Next space right
                CALL    SET_DI              ;Position offset
                MOV     AL,BOX_CHAR+5       ;Top/bottom character
                MOV     CL,LR_COL           ;Left column
                MOV     CH,UL_COL           ;Right column
                SUB     CL,CH
                SUB     CH,CH               ;Zero out
                DEC     CX                  ;Width of box is in CX
                PUSH    CX                  ;Store width for later
TB1:            CALL    PCHAR
                LOOP    TB1                 ;Do it again
```

; PRINT BOTTOM OF BOX

```
                MOV     BH,LR_ROW
                MOV     BL,UL_COL           ;Now have bottom left corner
                INC     BX                  ;Next space right
                CALL    SET_DI              ;Position offset
                POP     CX                  ;Get width back
                MOV     AL,BOX_CHAR+5       ;Top/bottom character
TB2:            CALL    PCHAR
                LOOP    TB2                 ;Do it again
```

; PRINT CORNERS

```
                MOV     BX,BOX_ULC          ;Upper left
                CALL    SET_DI              ;Position offset
                MOV     AL,BOX_CHAR+2       ;Upper left character
                CALL    PCHAR

                MOV     BX,BOX_LRC          ;Upper right
                CALL    SET_DI              ;Position offset
                MOV     AL,BOX_CHAR+3       ;Lower right character
                CALL    PCHAR
```

```
           MOV      BH,UL_ROW
           MOV      BL,LR_COL                 ;Upper right
           CALL     SET_DI                    ;Position offset
           MOV      AL,BOX_CHAR               ;Upper right character
           CALL     PCHAR

           MOV      BH,LR_ROW
           MOV      BL,UL_COL                 ;Lower left
           CALL     SET_DI                    ;Position offset
           MOV      AL,BOX_CHAR+1             ;Lower left character
           CALL     PCHAR

           POP      ES
           POP      DS
           POP      BP
           RET      2*5                       ;Return to BASIC
BOX        ENDP

; -------------------------------------------------------------------

CODE       ENDS
           END
```

This routine displays a double-lined box at the specified location on the video screen (without erasing the area within the box). Using the following equation, the controlling program (in compiled BASIC) passes the coordinates through an integer variable that contains the row/column coordinates:

$$COORD\% = ROW * 256 + COLUMN$$

The controlling program's use of this equation results in less need for number manipulation during the execution of this routine. Using this equation, the coordinates are passed in a format that places the row in the upper byte of the integer parameter, and the column in the lower byte.

This routine is designed so that you easily can change the type of border used for the box. To draw a different type of box, you simply change the contents of BOX_CHAR to the six appropriate drawing bytes.

The FIND_CARD and PCHAR subroutines are both used in this routine, as well as another subroutine, SET_DI. The SET_DI subroutine converts a row/column coordinate, which is held in BX, into an offset into the video buffer. The coding for SET_DI follows:

```
;    ******************************************************************
;    *                                                                *
;    *  Author:    Allen L. Wyatt                                     *
;    *  Date:      3/14/87                                            *
;    *                                                                *
;    *  Program:   SETDI.ASM                                          *
;    *                                                                *
;    *  Purpose:   To set DI from BX. On entry, BX contains the       *
;    *             desired screen row/column. On exit, DI contains    *
;    *             the screen memory offset. All other registers      *
;    *             are unchanged.                                     *
;    *                                                                *
;    ******************************************************************

; NEAR PUBLIC ROUTINES:
                PUBLIC  SET_DI

                NAME    SET_DI
CODE            SEGMENT BYTE PUBLIC 'CODE'
                ASSUME  CS:CODE


; ----------------------------------------------------------------------
SET_DI          PROC    NEAR

                PUSH    DX
                PUSH    BX              ;Save row/column
                PUSH    AX

                MOV     AH,Ø            ;Don't need AH now
                MOV     AL,BH           ;Move the row
                MOV     BH,Ø            ;And zero it out
                MOV     DI,BX           ;Move the column
                MOV     BX,8Ø           ;columns per row
                MUL     BX              ;AX = row * 8Ø
                ADD     DI,AX           ;Add to column
                SHL     DI,1            ;Multiply by 2

                POP     AX              ;Restore all registers
                POP     BX
                POP     DX
```

```
                    RET
SET_DI          ENDP

; --------------------------------------------------------------------

CODE            ENDS
                END
```

By studying BOX, you can see how easily you can place graphics on the video screen. Using ASCII characters, you can change the routine to create any type of screen graphics you want. The speed with which assembly language paints entire screens may surprise you.

Window Techniques: Saving and Restoring Windows

Now that you know how to create boxes, you can take the next logical step—that of creating routines to allow pop-up windows from compiled BASIC.

To create pop-up windows, you need to follow these steps:

- Determine the rectangular coordinates of the area to contain the window.

- Save the current screen contents within that area.

- Clear the defined area.

- Draw a box around the area.

Perhaps the most important step is that of saving the video information under the pop-up window. A complete routine must not only save this information but also be able to restore previous video information. Re-creating the entire screen after the user is finished with the window is unacceptable—and, in many cases, impossible.

The routines described in this section will perform all of these tasks. These routines allow you to use a "window stack" to save and create multiple windows. This stack concept allows the windows to be removed from the screen in reverse order.

The following listing includes two callable routines: SAVSCRN, which is similar to the process used in BOX, requires the passing of the upper left corner and lower right corner of the window area; GETSCRN removes the previously created window. The listing is as follows:

```
        page        60,132
;       ****************************************************************
;       *                                                              *
;       *  Author:    Allen Wyatt                                      *
;       *  Date:      10/16/86                                         *
;       *                                                              *
;       *  Program:   SCRN.ASM                                         *
;       *                                                              *
;       *  Purpose:   To save and restore a portion of the screen to a *
;       *             buffer from BASIC.                               *
;       *                                                              *
;       *  Format:    CALL SAVSCRN(TLC%,BRC%)                          *
;       *             CALL GETSCRN                                     *
;       *                                                              *
;       ****************************************************************

; FAR PUBLIC ROUTINES
                PUBLIC  SAVSCRN
                PUBLIC  GETSCRN


; EXTERNAL ROUTINES
                EXTRN   SET_DI:NEAR
                EXTRN   PCHAR:NEAR


; EXTERNAL DATA
                EXTRN   MONITOR_ADDR:WORD
                EXTRN   STATUS_PORT:WORD


                NAME    SCRN
CODE            SEGMENT PARA PUBLIC 'CODE'
                ASSUME  CS:CODE


; EQUATES

PARMB           EQU     08
PARMA           EQU     06


; DATA

TEMP            DW      0000
WND_WIDTH       DW      0000
```

```
BOX_CHAR        DB      'fàè¥¤ë'
BOX_ULC         EQU     THIS WORD
UL_COL          DB      ØØ
UL_ROW          DB      ØØ
BOX_LRC         EQU     THIS WORD
LR_COL          DB      ØØ
LR_ROW          DB      ØØ


SCREENS         DB      4 DUP(1Ø24 DUP(Ø))  ;Screen stack space
END_SCREENS     DB      ØØ                  ;End of screen stack space


; ----------------------------------------------------------------------
SAVSCRN         PROC    FAR
                PUSH    BP
                MOV     BP,SP                 ;Get addressability
                PUSH    DS
                PUSH    ES

                MOV     BX,[BP+PARMA]         ;Get pointer to BRC
                MOV     AX,[BX]               ;Get BRC value
                MOV     CS:BOX_LRC,AX         ;Save it
                MOV     BX,[BP+PARMB]         ;Get pointer to TLC
                MOV     AX,[BX]               ;Get TLC value
                MOV     CS:BOX_ULC,AX         ;Save it

                MOV     AX,CS
                MOV     DS,AX

                CALL    CALCSIZE              ;Calculate space for save
                CALL    FINDFREE              ;Find free space in screen
                                              ;   stack area
                JNC     SS_CONT               ;Continue
                JMP     SS_EXIT               ;Sorry, no space left

SS_CONT:        PUSH    SI                    ;Save area
                ADD     SI,6                  ;Set past pointer area
                MOV     AX,BOX_ULC            ;Move upper left corner
                MOV     TEMP,AX               ;   into work area

SS_LOOP:        MOV     BX,TEMP
                CALL    SET_DI                ;Set offset
                MOV     ES,CS:MONITOR_ADDR
                MOV     CX,WND_WIDTH
```

```
SS_L2:          MOV     AX,ES:[DI]          ;Get character/attribute
                MOV     [SI],AX             ;Place into screen stack
                INC     DI                  ;Point to next display set
                INC     DI
                INC     SI                  ;Increment stack pointer
                INC     SI
                LOOP    SS_L2               ;Do for entire line
                ADD     TEMP,Ø1ØØh          ;Proceed to next line
                MOV     AX,TEMP
                MOV     BX,BOX_LRC
                CMP     AH,BH               ;Are we too far down?
                JLE     SS_LOOP             ;No, so continue

                MOV     BX,SI               ;Get end of screen in stack
                POP     SI                  ;Get start of area
                MOV     AX,BOX_ULC          ;Store upper left corner
                MOV     [SI],AX             ;   coordinates
                INC     SI                  ;Point to next coordinate
                INC     SI                  ;   location
                MOV     AX,BOX_LRC          ;Store lower right corner
                MOV     [SI],AX             ;   coordinates
                INC     SI                  ;Point to next coordinate
                INC     SI                  ;   location
                MOV     [SI],BX             ;Store pointer to start of
                                            ;   stack free space

; PRINT SIDES OF BOX, TOP TO BOTTOM

                MOV     BH,UL_ROW           ;Get upper left (row only)
                INC     BH                  ;Start next row down
                MOV     AL,BOX_CHAR+4       ;Character for side of box
                MOV     CH,UL_ROW           ;Top row
                MOV     CL,LR_ROW           ;Bottom row
                SUB     CL,CH               ;Height is left in CL
                SUB     CH,CH               ;Zero out CH
                DEC     CX                  ;Adjust for actual height
V1:             MOV     BL,UL_COL           ;Set left column
                CALL    SET_DI              ;Position offset
                CALL    PCHAR
                MOV     BL,LR_COL           ;Set right column
                CALL    SET_DI              ;Position offset
                CALL    PCHAR
                INC     BH                  ;Next row
                LOOP    V1
```

```
; PRINT TOP OF BOX

                MOV     BX,BOX_ULC          ;Get upper left column
                INC     BX                  ;Next space right
                CALL    SET_DI              ;Position offset
                MOV     AL,BOX_CHAR+5       ;Top/bottom character
                MOV     CL,LR_COL           ;Left column
                MOV     CH,UL_COL           ;Right column
                SUB     CL,CH
                SUB     CH,CH               ;Zero out
                DEC     CX                  ;Width of box is in CX
                PUSH    CX                  ;Store width for later
TB1:            CALL    PCHAR
                LOOP    TB1                 ;Do it again

; PRINT BOTTOM OF BOX

                MOV     BH,LR_ROW
                MOV     BL,UL_COL           ;Now have bottom left corner
                INC     BX                  ;Next space right
                CALL    SET_DI              ;Position offset
                POP     CX                  ;Get width back
                MOV     AL,BOX_CHAR+5       ;Top/bottom character
TB2:            CALL    PCHAR
                LOOP    TB2                 ;Do it again

; PRINT CORNERS

                MOV     BX,BOX_ULC          ;Upper left
                CALL    SET_DI              ;Position offset
                MOV     AL,BOX_CHAR+2       ;Upper left character
                CALL    PCHAR

                MOV     BX,BOX_LRC          ;Upper right
                CALL    SET_DI              ;Position offset
                MOV     AL,BOX_CHAR+3       ;Lower right character
                CALL    PCHAR

                MOV     BH,UL_ROW
                MOV     BL,LR_COL           ;Upper right
                CALL    SET_DI              ;Position offset
                MOV     AL,BOX_CHAR         ;Upper right character
                CALL    PCHAR
```

```
                MOV     BH,LR_ROW
                MOV     BL,UL_COL               ;Lower left
                CALL    SET_DI                  ;Position offset
                MOV     AL,BOX_CHAR+1           ;Lower left character
                CALL    PCHAR

                MOV     CX,BOX_ULC              ;Upper left corner
                ADD     CX,0101h                ;Don't erase box
                MOV     DX,BOX_LRC              ;Bottom right corner
                SUB     DX,0101h                ;Don't erase box

                MOV     BH,07h                  ;Normal white/black
                MOV     AH,6                    ;Clear upwards
                MOV     AL,0                    ;Clear the window
                INT     10h                     ;Call BIOS interrupt

                CLC                             ;No errors

SS_EXIT:        POP     ES
                POP     DS
                POP     BP
                RET     2*2                     ;Return to BASIC
SAVSCRN         ENDP
; --------------------------------------------------------------------
GETSCRN         PROC    FAR
                PUSH    BP
                MOV     BP,SP                   ;Get addressability
                PUSH    DS
                PUSH    ES

                MOV     AX,CS                   ;Reset data area
                MOV     DS,AX

                CALL    FINDLAST                ;Find last saved screen
                JC      GS_EXIT                 ;Sorry, none there

                PUSH    SI
                MOV     AX,[SI]                 ;Get upper left corner
                MOV     BOX_ULC,AX              ;Store in this area
                MOV     TEMP,AX                 ;Store in work area
                INC     SI                      ;Point to next coordinate
                INC     SI                      ;  location
```

```
            MOV     AX,[SI]             ;Get lower right corner
            MOV     BOX_LRC,AX          ;  and store it
            INC     SI                  ;Point to next coordinate
            INC     SI                  ;  location

            MOV     AX,[SI]             ;Get pointer to next area
            PUSH    AX                  ;Save temporarily
            INC     SI                  ;Point to next coordinate
            INC     SI                  ;  location

            CALL    CALCSIZE            ;This will set the width
GS_LOOP:    MOV     BX,TEMP
            CALL    SET_DI              ;Position cursor there
            MOV     CX,WND_WIDTH
GS_L2:      MOV     AX,[SI]             ;Get from stack area
            CALL    MCHAR               ;Move the character
            INC     SI                  ;Point to next character
            INC     SI                  ;  group
            LOOP    GS_L2               ;Repeat for entire line
            ADD     TEMP,0100h          ;Point to next line
            MOV     AX,TEMP
            MOV     BX,BOX_LRC
            CMP     AH,BH               ;Are we too far down?
            JLE     GS_LOOP             ;No, so continue

            POP     BX                  ;Get back next area pointer
            POP     SI                  ;Get back start
            SUB     BX,SI               ;Size of area
            INC     BX
            MOV     AX,0                ;Zero out entire area
            MOV     CX,BX
FL:         MOV     [SI],AL
            INC     SI
            LOOP    FL
            CLC                         ;Set for no errors

GS_EXIT:    POP     ES
            POP     DS
            POP     BP
            RET                         ;Return to BASIC
GETSCRN     ENDP
```

```
; -------------------------------------------------------------------
; SUBROUTINES FOR SAVSCRN AND GETSCRN
; -------------------------------------------------------------------


; -------------------------------------------------------------------
; FINDFREE - FIND A BLOCK ON SCREEN STACK LARGE ENOUGH TO HOLD WINDOW
;            ENTER WITH CX SET TO SIZE NEEDED, IN BYTES
; -------------------------------------------------------------------

FINDFREE        PROC    NEAR
                MOV     SI,OFFSET SCREENS       ;Start of screen stack
FF_LOOP:        MOV     BX,[SI+4]               ;Get pointer to next area
                CMP     BX,Ø                    ;Is there anything here?
                                                ;  BX equal to 1 past end
                                                ;  of saved screen if so
                JE      FOUND_FREE              ;Nothing here
                MOV     SI,BX                   ;Point to next screen set
                JMP     FF_LOOP                 ;Keep looking

FOUND_FREE:     MOV     AX,SI                   ;Set to beginning of entry
                ADD     AX,12                   ;Add enough for two sets of
                                                ;  pointers
                ADD     AX,CX                   ;Add length of save
                MOV     DX,OFFSET END_SCREENS   ;End of screen stack
                CMP     AX,DX                   ;Are we past end of stack?
                JGE     FF_NOPE                 ;Yes, too big (can't save)
                CLC                             ;Return without error
                JNC     FF_EXIT
FF_NOPE:        STC
FF_EXIT:        RET                             ;Return to caller
FINDFREE        ENDP


; -------------------------------------------------------------------
; CALCSIZE - CALCULATE THE SPACE NEEDED FOR THE WINDOW AREA
;            RETURNS WITH CX SET TO NUMBER OF BYTES
; -------------------------------------------------------------------
CALCSIZE        PROC    NEAR
                MOV     AX,BOX_ULC              ;Get upper left corner
                MOV     BX,BOX_LRC              ;Lower right corner
                SUB     BX,AX                   ;Absolute rows/columns
```

```
                ADD     BX,0101h            ;Set to actual numbers
                MOV     AX,0
                MOV     AL,BH               ;Number of rows in AX
                MOV     BH,0                ;Number of columns in BX
                MOV     WND_WIDTH,BX        ;Save width for later use
                MUL     BX                  ;Character positions in AX
                SHL     AX,1                ;Number of bytes in block
                MOV     CX,AX               ;Put in proper register
                RET                         ;Return to caller
CALCSIZE        ENDP


; --------------------------------------------------------------
; FINDLAST - LOCATES THE LAST SAVED SCREEN ON THE SCREEN STACK
; --------------------------------------------------------------
FINDLAST        PROC    NEAR
                MOV     SI,OFFSET SCREENS
                MOV     AX,0
                PUSH    AX                  ;Save original pointer
FL_LOOP:        MOV     BX,[SI+4]           ;Get pointer to next area
                CMP     BX,0                ;Is there anything here?
                                           ;   BX equal to 1 past end
                                           ;   of saved screen if so
                JE      FOUND_LAST          ;Nothing here, at end
                POP     AX                  ;Get back old pointer
                PUSH    SI                  ;Save where we are now
                MOV     SI,BX               ;Point to next screen set
                JMP     FL_LOOP             ;Keep looking

FOUND_LAST:     POP     SI                  ;Get back the good pointer
                CMP     SI,0                ;Was it zero (nothing to
                                           ;   restore)?
                JE      FL_NOPE             ;Yes, so error
                CLC                         ;Return without error
                JNC     FL_EXIT
FL_NOPE:        STC
FL_EXIT:        RET
FINDLAST        ENDP
```

```
; ------------------------------------------------------------------
; MCHAR - MOVE A CHARACTER INTO THE VIDEO BUFFER (SIMILAR TO PCHAR)
; ------------------------------------------------------------------
MCHAR           PROC    NEAR
                PUSH    ES
                PUSH    DX

                MOV     ES,CS:MONITOR_ADDR
                MOV     DX,CS:STATUS_PORT

                CLI                     ;Don't allow interrupts
                PUSH    AX              ;Store the character
RETRACE:        IN      AL,DX           ;Get card status
                TEST    AL,1            ;Are we in a retrace state?
                JNZ     RETRACE         ;Yes, so check again
                                        ;On fall-through, just
                                        ;   exited retrace state
NO_RETRACE:     IN      AL,DX           ;Get card status
                TEST    AL,1            ;Are we in a retrace state?
                JZ      NO_RETRACE      ;No, so check again
                                        ;On fall-through, just
                                        ;   entered retrace state
                POP     AX              ;Yes, get character back
                MOV     ES:[DI],AX      ;OK to write it now
                STI                     ;OK to have interrupts now

                INC     DI              ;Point to attribute
                INC     DI              ;Next screen location

                POP     DX
                POP     ES
                RET
MCHAR           ENDP
; ------------------------------------------------------------------

CODE            ENDS
                END
```

This set of routines is an example of the point made at the beginning of this book—that source code for assembly language routines takes a great deal of space. When assembled, however, the resulting object code is significantly smaller than a similar routine written entirely in BASIC.

Notice that these routines, particularly SAVSCRN, do not use the SI and DI registers in the usual manner: in these routines, DI points to the source, whereas SI points to the destination. I did this so that maximum use could be made of existing routines, such as SET_DI. I hope that the purists among you will not become incensed.

SAVSCRN allows for as much as 4K of screen data (the size of the entire screen) to be saved. Because most pop-up windows do not use the whole screen, you can save several windows. If you find that you need a larger screen stack area, you can increase the area by changing the number of bytes defined by SCREENS.

Notice that GETSCRN uses a subroutine called MCHAR. You will find, on examination, that MCHAR seems similar to PCHAR, the routine developed earlier in this chapter. Right you are! The routines are similar because they do almost the same thing—they store information into the video buffer. A new routine was warranted because, instead of using the default ATTRIBUTE (as PCHAR does), you are retrieving data one word at a time.

Summary

The wide range of display adapters and monitors available for the IBM family of microcomputers can all be classified in one of two categories—monochrome or color. Because the classification of display devices can be determined by software, you can write routines that quickly display video data on either category of display adapter.

Video display routines written in assembly language execute faster and take less object code space than those written in high-level languages. Adding assembly language display subroutines to a high-level language program increases the overall speed of the program, especially one that is heavily screen-dependent.

The routines in this chapter have all been written for compiled BASIC. These routines could have been written just as easily for any other high-level language. If you change the parameter passing coding, the routines should work with C and Pascal as well as with compiled BASIC.

11

Accessing Hardware Ports

To communicate with peripheral devices, the 8086/8088 uses *hardware ports*. These ports are memory areas that the 8086/8088 accesses by using special assembly language instructions. This chapter discusses specific hardware ports and the assembly language instructions that apply to them. In addition, the chapter covers several significant hardware port addresses, addresses that are important because they are used for direct control of such computer devices as the keyboard, the video monitor, and the speaker.

The 8086/8088 has the capability of addressing as many as 65,536 hardware ports. However, because of way the 8086/8088 is implemented in the IBM PC family of microcomputers, the microprocessor uses only the first 1K of I/O addresses (hardware I/O port addresses 0 through 3FFh). These addresses (memory locations) are accessible to both the microprocessor and the I/O device. Before we see how the I/O ports are used, let's look at the specific manner in which the ports are accessed.

The IN and OUT Assembly Language Instructions

The IN and OUT assembly language instructions handle the transfer of data to and from hardware ports. These mnemonics allow the transfer of a single byte of information to or from a port address.

Because the I/O ports are simply specialized memory locations, you may wonder why you cannot use the MOV instruction to transfer the appropriate information. There is no good reason, except that the architecture of the IBM PC does not mix these two kinds of memory areas—RAM and I/O port memory are kept separate. The IN and OUT instructions cause different pins of the microprocessor to be activated for the data transfer. Therefore, when the 8086/8088 microprocessor executes the instructions, it "knows" to access the specialized I/O memory. If the peripheral device were designed to interface through main RAM, the IN/OUT instructions would not be needed.

How, then, do you access these individual I/O ports? If the address of the port you are accessing is less than 256, you can code the address explicitly into the instruction, as in the following example:

```
IN      AL,50           ;Get a byte from the port
```

Notice that the byte is read from the port address specified by the source operand (50), and placed in the destination operand, or AL register. All IN/OUT instructions assume that the data transfer will be between the port address and the AL register. Attempting to transfer data to a different register results in an error during the assembly process.

Because the IBM can access directly more than 256 I/O addresses, there must be a way to access these other ports. That method is to use the DX register to specify the port address. For example, the following coding facilitates writing a byte to a port with a higher address:

```
         MOV      DX,CS:STATUS_PORT

         CLI                       ;Don't allow interrupts
         PUSH     AX               ;Store the character
RETRACE: IN       AL,DX            ;Get card status
```

You may recognize this coding as a section from the listings in Chapter 10. The I/O port address, which is assumed to be larger than 255, is loaded into DX and then used (in the RETRACE line) to fetch a byte from that port and place it into the AL register.

OUT works in the same fashion as IN, except that the data flows in the other direction—data is transferred from the source operand (AL) to the destination operand (the I/O port address). As you can see from the following examples, port addresses that are lower than 256 can be coded explicitly; those that are higher than 255 must be specified in the DX register:

```
OUT      50,AL
OUT      DX,AL
```

The IN and OUT statements are analogous with the MOV statement—they all transfer information. The main difference is that the MOV statement works on RAM memory, whereas the IN and OUT statements work with I/O address memory.

IN and OUT attempt to transfer information, regardless of the meaning of the port address supplied. Even if no device is using the port address, IN places a byte of information in AL, and OUT writes a byte of information from AL. The statements do not check to see whether a device is at the port address, or whether the specified information was written successfully to a device. Because a peripheral device ordinarily uses more than one port address (perhaps one for input, one for output, and one for status), you can check different ports to verify the success of any interfacing.

There is no standard among devices to stipulate how the interfacing will occur. For instance, the procedure for communicating with the monochrome display adapter is different from that for communicating with the asynchronous communications adapter. Each adapter or device uses different combinations of ports and addresses for different purposes.

The I/O Port Map

IBM has defined some of the I/O port addresses for specific I/O purposes. The first 256 I/O ports (0-FFh) are reserved for use by the system board. Peripheral devices that control such areas as memory refresh, timers, interrupt controllers, and coprocessor utilization are linked to the main system at these ports.

The remaining I/O ports (100h-3FFh) are used for other general-purpose I/O, with some areas set aside for specialized usage. Table 11.1 details the currently defined hardware I/O addresses.

Table 11.1
Hardware I/O Port Addresses and Their Usage

I/O Port Range	Use/purpose
0 – 0Fh	8237-A Direct Memory Access (DMA) controller
10h	Manufacturing test point
20h – 23h	8259 Interrupt controller
40h – 43h	8253 timer
60h – 64h	8255 programmable peripheral interface
80h – 83h	DMA page registers
A0h – AFh	Nonmaskable interrupt registers
E0h – FFh	Numeric coprocessor usage
1F0h – 1F8h	AT fixed disk interface
200h – 20Fh	Game controller
210h – 217h	Expansion unit

Table 11.1—cont.

I/O Port Range	Use/purpose
220h – 24Fh	Reserved
278h – 27Fh	LPT3:
2E8h – 2EFh	COM4:
2F0h – 2F7h	Reserved
2F8h – 2FFh	COM2:
300h – 31Fh	Prototype cards
320h – 32Fh	XT fixed disk interface
378h – 37Fh	LPT2:
380h – 38Ch	SDLC/secondary bi-sync interface
3A0h – 3A9h	Primary bi-sync interface
3B0h – 3BBh	Monochrome display
3BCh – 3BFh	LPT1:
3C0h – 3CFh	EGA display control
3D0h – 3DFh	Color/graphics display
3E0h – 3E7h	Reserved
3E8h – 3EFh	COM3:
3F0h – 3F7h	Floppy disk controller
3F8h – 3FFh	COM1:

Areas that are not shown as defined or in use in table 11.1 are available for other I/O devices. Some third-party interface devices may use other I/O addresses that are not shown. However, port addresses below 256 (FFh) are reserved for exclusive use by the system board.

Because there is no real standard for communicating with external devices, and because such interfacing varies according to the type of device, the use of most I/O ports is not well documented in the IBM literature. In some cases, specialized books or manuals from either Intel or the specific peripheral manufacturer may contain relevant information. In the next few sections, we will take a brief look at some of the specific ports.

Some Significant Hardware Ports

Several hardware port addresses are significant to assembly language programmers—those for the ports most often accessed through assembly language programs.

Some hardware ports are used predominantly by the internal workings of BIOS and DOS routines (see Chapters 12 and 13). Other ports are available for different interface devices. Although the exact way in which all of these ports may interact with your program is beyond the scope of this book, a quick look at some of the hardware port addresses may be helpful.

The 8259 Interrupt Controller

The computer uses the 8259 Programmable Interrupt Controller to control interrupts. The Interrupt Controller handles as many as eight interrupts, according to their priority sequence, presenting them to the microprocessor in prioritized order.

As you can see from table 11.1, the 8259 Interrupt Controller uses four port addresses (20h through 23h). Although IBM documentation indicates that these four port addresses are reserved for the 8259, only the two lower ports (20h and 21h) are documented as usable by programmers. The use of the other two ports (22h and 23h) remains something of a mystery.

I/O address 20h is referred to as the 8259 command port because it is used to send commands to the 8259. Programmers most commonly use this port in conjunction with *interrupt handlers*—assembly language routines that control how the computer will react when presented with a system interrupt. Before issuing an IRET, the programmer is responsible for informing the system that it can process other interrupts. To do so, a 20h is sent to I/O address 20h in the following manner:

```
MOV     AL,20h          ;Signal other interrupts OK
OUT     20h,AL
```

Port 21h is the interrupt mask register for the 8259. Specific interrupts can be either enabled or disabled, depending on the settings of the bits in this register. Table 11.2 lists the meaning of the bits at the port.

Table 11.2
Meaning of 8259 Interrupt Mask Register Bits for I/O Port 21h

Bits 76543210	Meaning
0	IRQ 7 (parallel printer) interrupt enabled
1	IRQ 7 (parallel printer) interrupt disabled
0	IRQ 6 (floppy disk controller) interrupt enabled
1	IRQ 6 (floppy disk controller) interrupt disabled
0	IRQ 5 (XT fixed disk controller) interrupt enabled
1	IRQ 5 (XT fixed disk controller) interrupt disabled
0	IRQ 4 (COM1:) interrupt enabled
1	IRQ 4 (COM1:) interrupt disabled
0	IRQ 3 (COM2:) interrupt enabled
1	IRQ 3 (COM2:) interrupt disabled
0	IRQ 2 Reserved
1	IRQ 2 Reserved
0	IRQ 1 (keyboard) interrupt enabled
1	IRQ 1 (keyboard) interrupt disabled
0	IRQ 0 (system timer) interrupt enabled
1	IRQ 0 (system timer) interrupt disabled

The 8253 Timer

The IBM PC family of microcomputers uses an 8253 timer chip to control certain system functions. This chip, which operates at a frequency of 1.19318 MHz, provides for three independent timer channels and six separate operation modes.

The 8253 is interfaced through I/O port addresses 40h through 43h. Port 40h is used for timer channel 0 I/O, port 41h for timer channel 1 I/O, and port 42h for timer channel 2 I/O. Port 43h is used for mode control (see table 11.3).

The 8253's three timer channels are used for different purposes within the computer. Each channel has an associated divisor (one word long) that indicates how often the channel generates an interrupt. This divisor may range from 1 to 65,536. A divisor of 0 is equivalent to 65,536. To derive the channel interrupt frequency, you divide 1,193,180 (the chip operating frequency) by the divisor.

Channel 0, which is used for the system timer, uses a divisor of 0. The resulting interrupt (INT 8, IRQ0) frequency of 1,193,180/65,536 is approximately 18.2065 times per second, or once every 54.9 milliseconds. This channel is used to update the BIOS clock counter and the controls that turn off the floppy disk drive motor. This channel operates in mode 3, which signifies that the timer generates a square wave.

Table 11.3
Meaning of 8253 Mode Control Bits for I/O Port 43h

Bits 76543210	Meaning
00	Channel 0
01	Channel 1
10	Channel 2
00	Latch present counter value
01	Read/write only MSB
10	Read/write only LSB
11	Read/write LSB followed by MSB
000	Operation mode 0
001	Operation mode 1
010	Operation mode 2
011	Operation mode 3
100	Operation mode 4
101	Operation mode 5
0	Binary counter operation
1	BCD counter operation

Channel 1 is used for DMA memory-refresh operations. It uses a divisor of 18, resulting in a frequency of 1,193,180/18, or approximately 66,287.7778 times per second. This is equivalent to a DMA interrupt being generated approximately once every 15.086 microseconds. Operation of this channel is in mode 2, which signifies that a pulse is generated once every period.

Channel 2, which is available for general use, is used most often in conjunction with the speaker port. A specific example of this type of use is covered in the following section.

The 8255 Programmable Peripheral Interface (PPI)

The 8255A Programmable Peripheral Interface (PPI) is used to control the keyboard, the speaker, and the configuration switches. Four port addresses, 60h through 63h, (or more, depending on the computer) are associated with this device.

Because the use of each of these port addresses varies by computer, be sure to check your computer's technical documentation if you plan to program the addresses directly. This section provides some general information and direction, but should not be accepted as "the gospel truth."

I/O port 60h is used for keyboard input and (on some versions of the IBM) for reading the configuration switches from the system board. If port 60h is used for reading the configuration switches, bit 7 of I/O port 61h should be set. If this bit is cleared, port 60h is used strictly for keyboard input. This port and port 61h are used in the examples shown later in this section.

I/O port 61h is used for configuration information for various devices, most notably the keyboard. Table 11.4 lists the meaning of the bit settings for this port.

Table 11.4
Meaning of I/O Port 61h Bit Settings

Bits 76543210	Meaning
0	Keyboard enabled
1	PC – Read configuration switches
1	XT – Keyboard acknowledge
0	Keyboard click off
1	Keyboard click on
0	Parity errors from expansion ports enabled
1	Parity errors from expansion ports disabled

Table 11.4—cont.

Bits 76543210	Meaning
0	RAM parity errors enabled
1	RAM parity errors disabled
0	PC – Cassette motor on
1	PC – Cassette motor off
0	XT – Read high nibble, configuration switches, port 62h
1	XT – Read low nibble, configuration switches, port 62h
0	PC – Read spare switches, port 62h
1	PC – Read RAM size switches, port 62h
x	XT – Unused
0	Speaker off
1	Speaker on
0	Direct speaker control through bit 1
1	Speaker control through 8253 timer (channel 2)

You use I/O port 62h to input a variety of system information (see table 11.5).

Table 11.5
Meaning of I/O Port 62h Bit Settings

Bits 76543210	Meaning
1	RAM parity error
1	Expansion slot error
?	8253 timer channel 2 output
?	PC – Cassette data input
x	XT – Unused
????	PC – Input according to bit 2, port 61h
????	XT – Input according to bit 3, port 61h

I/O port 63h is used as a mode-control register to control the other three I/O ports for this device. Table 11.6 details the individual bit settings and their meaning.

Table 11.6
Meaning of I/O Port 63h Bit Settings

Bits 76543210	Meaning
0	Port active
1	Port inactive
00	Port 60h mode 0
01	Port 60h mode 1
10	Port 60h mode 2
0	Port 60h used for output
1	Port 60h used for input
0	Port 62h, bits 7–4 used for output
1	Port 62h, bits 7–4 used for input
0	Port 61h mode 0
1	Port 61h mode 1
0	Port 61h used for output
1	Port 61h used for input
0	Port 62h, bits 3–0 used for output
1	Port 62h, bits 3–0 used for input

I/O port 64h is used as a status port for the keyboard on the IBM Personal Computer AT, as you will learn in the following section.

Controlling the Keyboard

Controlling hardware devices directly (through I/O ports) is possible. Because the process generally entails more work than most programmers choose to tackle, programmers usually elect to use either BIOS or DOS functions to control standard devices (see Chapters 12 and 13). Nevertheless, you should be aware that direct control of hardware devices is possible. Some programmers may even need to use direct control programming for specific applications.

This section includes an example of such programming—a program that directly controls the keyboard. I chose this particular device because not every reader may have a speaker or a video monitor, but you're sure to be able to get your hands on a keyboard.

The following sample program reads the information presented by the keyboard and then outputs the information as a decimal scan code (originally contained in the AL register).

Although this particular example is written as a stand-alone assembly language program, you can convert and modify it easily if you want to run it as a subroutine of a high-level language.

```
        page 60,132
;       ****************************************************************
;       *   Author:   Allen L. Wyatt                                  *
;       *     Date:   06/29/87                                        *
;       *                                                             *
;       *     File:   KEYHARD.ASM                                     *
;       *                                                             *
;       *  Program:   KEYHARD.COM                                     *
;       *                                                             *
;       *  Purpose:   This intercepts and prints the value returned by the  *
;       *             keyboard each time a key is pressed.  Once installed,  *
;       *             the only way out of this program is to turn off  *
;       *             the computer.                                   *
;       *                                                             *
;       ****************************************************************

CODE            SEGMENT BYTE PUBLIC 'CODE'
                ORG     100H
; ---------------------------------------------------------------------
KEYHARD         PROC    FAR

                ASSUME  CS:CODE,DS:CODE
                JMP     KEY_BEGIN               ;Starts the program

KB_DATA         EQU     60h
STATUS_PORT     EQU     64h
INPT_BUF_FULL   EQU     02h
DIS_KBD         EQU     0ADh
ENA_KBD         EQU     0AEh

KEY_NORMAL      DD      0                       ;Holds the normal keyboard
                                                ;  interrupt vector address
OK_MSG          DB      'Program is installed$'
```

```
; ------------------------------------------------------------------------
PNUM            PROC    NEAR
                PUSH    AX
                PUSH    BX
                PUSH    CX
                PUSH    DX

                MOV     CX,0FFFFh               ;Push our ending flag
                PUSH    CX
                MOV     CX,10                   ;Always dividing by 10
DIVLP:          MOV     DX,0
                DIV     CX
                ADD     DX,30h                  ;Change to ASCII character
                PUSH    DX                      ;Save remainder
                CMP     AX,0
                JA      DIVLP

NPLOOP:         POP     AX                      ;Get number back
                CMP     AX,0FFFFh               ;Is it our ending flag?
                JE      PNUM_EXIT               ;Yes, so go on our way
                CALL    PCHAR                   ;Go print the character
                JMP     NPLOOP                  ;Do next one

PNUM_EXIT:      POP     DX
                POP     CX
                POP     BX
                POP     AX
                RET
PNUM            ENDP


; ------------------------------------------------------------------------
PCHAR           PROC    NEAR
                PUSH    AX
                PUSH    BX

                MOV     BH,0
                MOV     AH,0Eh                  ;Display character
                INT     10h                     ;BIOS interrupt

                POP     BX
                POP     AX
                RET
PCHAR           ENDP
```

```
; -------------------------------------------------------------------
SEND_IT         PROC    NEAR
                PUSH    AX                      ;Save byte to send
                CLI                             ;Disable interrupts
SIO:            IN      AL,STATUS_PORT          ;Get keyboard status
                TEST    AL,INPT_BUF_FULL        ;Is the coding complete?
                LOOPNZ  SIO                     ;No, so continue waiting
                POP     AX                      ;Retrieve byte to send
                OUT     STATUS_PORT,AL          ;Send the byte
                STI                             ;Enable interrupts
                RET
SEND_IT         ENDP


; -------------------------------------------------------------------
NEW_KBD_INT:    PUSHF                           ;Save the flags
                PUSH    AX                      ;Only messing with AX

                MOV     AL,DIS_KBD
                CALL    SEND_IT                 ;Go disable keyboard

                CLI                             ;Disable interrupts
GET_KB_STAT:    IN      AL,STATUS_PORT          ;Get keyboard status
                TEST    AL,INPT_BUF_FULL        ;Is the coding complete?
                LOOPNZ  GET_KB_STAT             ;No, so continue waiting
                IN      AL,KB_DATA              ;Yes, so get code
                STI                             ;Enable interrupts

                TEST    AL,80h                  ;Is it an acknowledgment?
                JNZ     END_IT                  ;Yes, so ignore it

                PUSH    AX                      ;Save code
                MOV     AL,'A'                  ;Print 'AL='
                CALL    PCHAR
                MOV     AL,'L'
                CALL    PCHAR
                MOV     AL,'='
                CALL    PCHAR
                POP     AX                      ;Retrieve code
```

```
                MOV     AH,Ø                ;Only want AL
                CALL    PNUM                ;Print decimal value
                MOV     AL,13               ;Print carriage return
                CALL    PCHAR
                MOV     AL,1Ø               ;Print line feed
                CALL    PCHAR

END_IT:         MOV     AL,2Øh              ;Signify end of interrupt
                OUT     2Øh,AL

                MOV     AL,ENA_KBD
                CALL    SEND_IT             ;Go enable keyboard again

                POP     AX                  ;Restore AX register
                POPF                        ;  and the flags
                IRET

; --------------------------------------------------------------------
KEY_BEGIN:      MOV     AL,9h               ;Get keyboard interrupt
                MOV     AH,35h
                INT     21h
                MOV     SI,OFFSET KEY_NORMAL  ;Store it here
                MOV     [SI],BX             ;Offset address
                MOV     [SI+2],ES           ;Segment address
                MOV     AX,CS               ;New segment address
                MOV     DS,AX
                MOV     DX,OFFSET NEW_KBD_INT  ;New offset address
                MOV     AL,9h               ;Change keyboard vector
                MOV     AH,25h              ;  to point to NEW_KBD_INT
                INT     21h

                MOV     DX,OFFSET OK_MSG    ;Installation complete
                MOV     AH,9                ;Print message at DS:DX
                INT     21h
                MOV     DX,OFFSET KEY_BEGIN ;End of resident portion
                INT     27h                 ;Terminate but stay resident

KEYHARD         ENDP
; --------------------------------------------------------------------
CODE            ENDS
                END     KEYHARD
```

After it has been entered, assembled, and executed, this program takes control of the keyboard by redirecting the keyboard interrupt vector to the new interrupt handler, NEW_KBD_INT. This handler intercepts and prints the decimal value of every keystroke; thus, every key on the keyboard returns a code, with no intervening translation by BIOS.

Because this routine prints the keyboard scan code for *every* key (without exception), the only way to disable the program is to turn off the computer. This routine, although of limited value and usefulness, does give you a rudimentary way to control the keyboard.

Notice that this program directly reads and interprets signals from I/O ports 60h and 64h. Because the program was designed to work on an IBM Personal Computer AT or COMPAQ 386, the address values may be different if you are using a different type of computer.

Controlling the Speaker

This example, which shows how you can control the speaker directly, uses both the 8253 timer and the 8255 PPI. The WARBLE subroutine provides a good sound for error routines; BOOP provides a gentle sound when the wrong key is pressed.

You can call these routines directly from C. To modify them so that they work with compiled BASIC, simply remove the underscores that precede the labels, and change WARBLE and BOOP from NEAR to FAR routines.

```
        page 60,132
;       ****************************************************************
;       *    Author:   Allen L. Wyatt                                  *
;       *      Date:   7/21/87                                         *
;       *                                                              *
;       *    File Name:   SOUND.ASM                                    *
;       *                                                              *
;       *      Purpose:   Provide common error sounds from C.          *
;       *                                                              *
;       * Subroutines:                                                 *
;       *    WARBLE - Sound used in error routines                     *
;       *    BOOP - Sound used when wrong key pressed                  *
;       *                                                              *
;       ****************************************************************
```

```
                PUBLIC  _WARBLE
                PUBLIC  _BOOP

                NAME    SOUND
_TEXT           SEGMENT BYTE PUBLIC 'CODE'
                ASSUME  CS:_TEXT


; -----------------------------------------------------------------
_WARBLE         PROC    NEAR
                PUSH    BP
                MOV     BP,SP

                IN      AL,61h          ;Save speaker port contents
                PUSH    AX

                MOV     DX,0Bh
MAIN:           MOV     BX,477          ;1,193,180 / 2500
                CALL    WARBCOM
                MOV     CX,2600h
DELAY1:
                LOOP    DELAY1
                MOV     BX,36           ;1,193,180 / 32767
                CALL    WARBCOM
                MOV     CX,1300h
DELAY2:
                LOOP    DELAY2
                DEC     DX
                JNZ     MAIN

                POP     AX              ;Restore speaker port
                OUT     61h,AL          ;   contents (turn it off)

                POP     BP
                RET
_WARBLE         ENDP
; -----------------------------------------------------------------
_BOOP           PROC    NEAR
                PUSH    BP
                MOV     BP,SP
                PUSH    AX
                PUSH    BX
                PUSH    CX
```

```
                IN      AL,61h              ;Save speaker port contents
                PUSH    AX

                MOV     BX,6818             ;1,193,180 / 175
                CALL    WARBCOM
                MOV     CX,4B4Bh
DELAY3:
                LOOP    DELAY3

                POP     AX                  ;Restore speaker port
                OUT     61h,AL              ;  contents (turn it off)

                POP     CX
                POP     BX
                POP     AX
                POP     BP
                RET
_BOOP           ENDP
; ------------------------------------------------------------------
WARBCOM         PROC    NEAR
                MOV     AL,10110110b        ;Channel 2, write LSB/MSB,
                OUT     43h,AL              ;  operation mode 3, binary
                MOV     AX,BX               ;Send counter LSB
                OUT     42h,AL
                MOV     AL,AH               ;Send counter MSB
                OUT     42h,AL
                IN      AL,61h              ;Get 8255 port contents
                OR      AL,00000011b        ;Enable speaker and use
                OUT     61h,AL              ;  clock channel 2 for input
                RET
WARBCOM         ENDP
; ------------------------------------------------------------------

_TEXT           ENDS
                END
```

The root of these subroutines is the procedure WARBCOM, which turns on the
speaker at a specific frequency, specified in BX. The procedure sets channel 2
of the 8253 timer chip (ports 42h and 43h) and then ties timer output to
speaker input through the 8255 PPI (port 61h).

Unlike many other port addresses (which may change with succeeding
generations of computers), IBM has seen fit to leave unchanged the port

addresses used in SOUND.ASM. Because of this, the routines should work on any IBM or true compatible.

Video Controller Ports

The addresses of the video controller ports vary, depending on whether you are using a monochrome or color adapter card. If you are using a monochrome adapter card, the port addresses range from 3B0h to 3BBh; with the color adapter card, the ports range from 3D0h to 3DCh. Your programs can determine which card is in use, and modify their behavior accordingly. This section simply outlines the specific port uses (monochrome and color). (For an in-depth discussion of this process, refer to Chapter 10.)

The Monochrome Adapter

Although IBM lists the port addresses from 3B0h to 3BBh as being reserved for the monochrome adapter, the only ports used to control the monochrome display adapter are 3B4h, 3B5h, 3B8h, and 3BAh. The adapter does not use 3B0h through 3B3h, 3B6h, and 3B7h, and ports 3B9h and 3BBh are reserved.

Port 3B4h, the index register, is used to specify the register to be accessed through port 3B5h. You use the OUT instruction to output the desired register (0 through 17) to this port.

Port 3B5h, the data register, is used for communication with the adapter's internal registers. The desired register is specified through port 3B4h. Table 11.7 details the individual adapter registers.

Table 11.7
The Internal Monochrome Display Adapter Registers

Register	Use/Meaning
0	Total horizontal characters
1	Total displayed horizontal characters
2	Horizontal sync position
3	Horizontal sync width
4	Total vertical rows
5	Vertical scan line adjust value
6	Total displayed vertical rows
7	Vertical sync position
8	Interlace mode
9	Maximum scan line address
10	Scan line at which cursor starts

Table 11.7—cont.

Register	Use/Meaning
11	Scan line at which cursor ends
12	High-byte start address
13	Low-byte start address
14	High-byte cursor address
15	Low-byte cursor address
16	Light pen (high byte)
17	Light pen (low byte)

Port 3B8h, the CRT control port, is set during power-up and should never be changed. Only three bits in the byte are significant (see table 11.8).

Table 11.8
Bit Meanings in Monochrome Adapter Mode-Control Register, Port 3B8h

Bits 76543210	Meaning
xx	Not used
0	Disable blink
1	Enable blink
x	Not used
0	Video disable
1	Video enable
xx	Not used
1	80 × 25 display mode

Port 3BAh, the CRT status port, is a read-only address. This byte has only two significant bits, with bit 0 (when clear) indicating that video is enabled. Bit 3 is set when a vertical retrace condition exists.

The Color/Graphics Adapter

IBM lists the port addresses from 3D0h to 3DFh as being reserved for the color/graphics adapter. But, as with the monochrome adapter, the color/graphics adapter uses only some of these ports; 3D4h, 3D5h, and 3D8h through 3DCh are the only ports used to control the color/graphics adapter.

Port 3D4h, the index register, is used to specify the register to be accessed through port 3D5h. The desired register (0 through 17) is output to this port.

Port 3D5h, the data register, is used for communication with the adapter's internal registers. The desired register is specified through port 3D4h.

Because both adapters use the same chip for display control, the register meanings for the color/graphics adapter are identical to those for the monochrome display adapter (refer to table 11.7).

Port 3D8h is the mode-control register. Only six bits in the byte are significant (see table 11.9).

Table 11.9
Bit Meanings in Color/Graphics Adapter
Mode-Control Register, Port 3D8h

Bits 76543210	*Meaning*
xx	Not used
0	Disable blink
1	Enable blink
0	Normal resolution
1	High resolution (640 × 200)
0	Video disabled
1	Video enabled
0	Color mode
1	Black-and-white mode
0	Alphanumeric mode
1	320 × 200 graphics mode
0	40 × 25 alphanumeric display mode
1	80 × 25 alphanumeric display mode

Port 3D9h, the color-select register, is used to specify the colors used in various display modes. Only the lower six bits are significant (see table 11.10).

Table 11.10
Bit Meanings in Color/Graphics Adapter Color-Select Register, Port 3D9h

Bits 76543210	*Meaning*
xx	Not used
1	Selects cyan/magenta/white color set
0	Selects green/red/brown color set
1	Selects intensified color set in graphics modes, or background colors in alphanumeric display mode
1	Selects intensified border color in 40 × 25 alphanumeric display mode, intensified background color in 320 × 200 graphics mode, or red foreground color in 640 × 200 graphics mode
1	Selects red border color in 40 × 25 alphanumeric display mode, red background color in 320 × 200 graphics mode, or red foreground color in 640 × 200 graphics mode
1	Selects green border color in 40 × 25 alphanumeric display mode, green background color in 320 × 200 graphics mode, or green foreground color in 640 × 200 graphics mode
1	Selects blue border color in 40 × 25 alphanumeric display mode, blue background color in 320 × 200 graphics mode, or blue foreground color in 640 × 200 graphics mode

Port 3DAh, a read-only address, is the CRT status port. This byte has only four significant bits, which are shown in table 11.11.

Table 11.11
Bit Meanings in Color/Graphics Adapter Status Register, Port 3DAh

Bits 76543210	Meaning
xxxx	Not used
1	Vertical retrace condition
0	Light pen triggered
1	Light pen not triggered
1	Light pen trigger set
0	Video disabled
1	Video enabled

Port 3DBh, a strobe, is used to clear the light pen latch; any writing to this port clears bit 1 at port 3DAh. Port 3DCh is a strobe used to preset the light pen latch.

Printer Ports

The line-printer interface ports vary according to the number of printer interface cards installed in the system. Normally, the three printer ports are addressed as indicated in table 11.12.

Table 11.12
Normal Printer-Port Addressing

Designation	Port address range
LPT1:	3BCh - 3BFh
LPT2:	378h - 37Fh
LPT3:	278h - 27Fh

The addresses shown in table 11.12 are general guidelines, and will vary from installation to installation. If instead of installing a printer interface that uses the addresses normally assigned to LPT1:, for example, you install an interface card that uses one of the other port ranges, that card becomes known to the system as LPT1:.

The first port in each address range (3BCh, 378h, or 278h) is used to output information to the printer. The bits of information are output directly on the parallel port. Bit 0 corresponds to pin 2, bit 1 to pin 3, and so on through bit 7, which corresponds to pin 9 of the parallel connector.

Port 3BDh (or 379h, or 279h) is the printer-status register. The bits at this port indicate the status of various line signals for the parallel connector. The meaning of each bit is indicated in table 11.13.

Table 11.13
Bit Meanings for Parallel Printer Adapter Status Register,
Port 3BDh/379h/279h

Bits 76543210	Meaning
0	Printer busy
0	Acknowledged
1	Out of paper
1	On-line (printer selected)
1	Printer error
xx	Not used
1	Time out

Port 3BEh (or 37Ah, or 27Ah) is the printer-control register. The bits at this port are used to control the printer, as indicated in table 11.14.

Table 11.14
Bit Meanings for Parallel Printer Adapter Control Register,
Port 3BEh/37Ah/27Ah

Bits 76543210	Meaning
xxx	Not used
1	Enable IRQ7 interrupt for printer acknowledge
1	Printer reads output
1	Initialize printer
1	Enable auto-linefeed
1	Output data to printer (strobe)

The remaining ports (3BFh, 37Bh through 37Fh, and 27Bh through 27Fh) are not used by the parallel interface.

Asynchronous Communications Ports

The serial communications interface ports vary according to the number of asynchronous interface cards installed in the system. Ordinarily, BIOS and DOS allow no more than two communications ports to be used (see table 11.15).

Table 11.15
Normal Printer-Port Addressing

Designation	Port address range
COM1:	3F8h - 3FFh
COM2:	2F8h - 2FFh
COM3:	3E8h - 3EFh
COM4:	2E8h - 2EFh

Notice that table 11.15 lists the addresses for four communications ports. Although neither BIOS nor DOS supports the addresses for COM3: and COM4:, many communications devices do support four communications ports; software can be written to enable use of the two additional ports.

Because the intricacies and complexities of programming for asynchronous communications are astounding, a detailed explanation of the communications ports, their use, programming, and functions is best left for another book. The balance of this section simply details the meanings of the ports used by asynchronous communications devices.

Port 3F8h, which ordinarily is used to transmit and receive data, can be used also (if bit 7 of port 3FBh is set) to specify the low-order byte of the baud-rate divisor.

The baud-rate divisor is used to specify the baud rate of the communications device; the divisor is a number that, divided into the clock speed of a specific device, results in the proper number of bits-per-second for the baud rate of that device.

Port 3F9h also is used for different purposes. If bit 7 of port 3FBh is set, this port is used to specify the high-order byte of the baud-rate divisor.

Table 11.16 details several popular baud rates and their proper baud-rate divisor settings. The port addresses shown are for COM1:. Other communications ports should use the corresponding port addresses of 2F9h/2F8h, 3E9h/3E8h, or 2E9h/2E8h.

Table 11.16
Baud-Rate Divisor Settings for Standard 1.8432 MHz Clock Speed

| *Baud-Rate Divisors* | | |
| *MSB* | *LSB* | *Resulting* |
3F9h	*3F8h*	*Baud Rate*
4	17h	110 bps
1	80h	300 bps
0	60h	1,200 bps
0	30h	2,400 bps
0	18h	4,800 bps
0	0Ch	9,600 bps
0	07h	19,200 bps

The proper procedure for setting the baud rate is to set bit 7 of port 3FBh, output the proper divisors to the appropriate ports, and then clear bit 7 of port 3FBh.

If bit 7 of port 3FBh is clear, port 3F9h serves as the interrupt-enable register. The interrupt-enable register lets you specify which communications events will generate interrupts to the microprocessor. The bit meanings for this register are indicated in table 11.17.

Table 11.17
Bit Meanings for the Interrupt-Enable Register,
Port 3F9h (or 2F9h, 3E9h, or 2E9h)

Bits 76543210	*Meaning*
0000	Not used, set to 0
1	Enable interrupt on modem status change
1	Enable interrupt on receive line status change
1	Enable interrupt on transmit holding register empty
1	Enable interrupt on data available

Port 3FAh is the interrupt identification register. When the microprocessor receives an interrupt generated by the communications device, the program reads this register to determine exactly what caused the interrupt. Only the three least significant bits are meaningful (see table 11.18).

**Table 11.18
Bit Meanings for the Interrupt-Identification Register,
Port 3FAh (or 2FAh, 3EAh, or 2EAh)**

Bits 76543210	Meaning
00000	Not used, set to 0
11	Receiver line status interrupt
10	Received data available
01	Transmitter holding register empty
00	Modem status change
1	Interrupt not pending
0	Interrupt pending

Port 3FBh, the line-control register, is used to specify the format of the data that is transmitted and received through the communications port. Table 11.19 lists the meanings of the bit settings for this register.

Port 3FCh, the modem-control register, is used for controlling the modem interface. The bit meanings for this register are detailed in table 11.20.

Port 3FDh, the line-status register, is used to indicate the condition of data transfer. The meanings of the bits in this register are detailed in table 11.21.

Port 3FEh, the modem-status register, is used to reflect the state of the modem-control lines. Table 11.22 shows its bit meanings.

Ordinarily, the communications device uses port 3FFh internally as a "scratch pad."

Summary

The organization and use of hardware ports were discussed in this chapter. Hardware ports are necessary for computers to be able to communicate with outside devices such as video monitors, keyboards, printers, mice, etc. By writing software, you can access these hardware devices directly (through the IN and OUT mnemonic instructions).

To use hardware ports properly, you must know which ports are used by the device you want to control. Certain devices (such as the keyboard, speaker, and video monitors) use standardized hardware port addresses that can be readily accessed and programmed through assembly language.

Such intimate control of the individual device has drawbacks, however. Future releases of DOS or future generations of computers may abandon the currently accepted standard I/O addresses in favor of a different standard. In that event, software that directly controls devices through I/O ports would have to be changed. The BIOS and DOS services in Chapters 12 and 13 insulate programmers from such vagaries of change.

Table 11.19
Bit Meanings for the Line-Control Register,
Port 3FBh (or 2FBh, 3EBh, or 2EBh)

Bits 76543210	Meaning
0	Normal access to ports 3F8h/3F9h
1	Use ports 3F8h/3F9h to specify baud-rate divisor
1	Transmit break condition
0	Parity held at value in bit 4
1	Parity operates normally
0	Odd parity
1	Even parity
0	Parity disabled
1	Parity enabled
0	1 stop bit
1	2 stop bits (1.5 if bits 0-1 are clear)
00	5-bit data length
01	6-bit data length
10	7-bit data length
11	8-bit data length

Table 11.20
Bit Meanings for the Modem-Control Register,
Port 3FCh (or 2FCh, 3ECh, or 2ECh)

Bits 76543210	Meaning
000	Not used, set to 0
0	Normal modem functioning
1	Operate in loop-back test mode
?	Control for auxiliary output 2
?	Control for auxiliary output 1
0	RTS clear
1	RTS set
0	DTR clear
1	DTR set

Table 11.21
Bit Meanings for the Line-Status Register,
Port 3FDh (or 2FDh, 3EDh, or 2DCh)

Bits 76543210	Meaning
0	Not used, set to 0
0	Transmitter shift register full
1	Transmitter shift register empty
0	Transmitter holding register full
1	Transmitter holding register empty
1	Break condition detected
1	Framing error detected
1	Parity error detected
1	Overrun error detected
0	No character ready
1	Received character ready

Table 11.22
Bit Meanings for the Modem-Status Register,
Port 3FEh (or 2FEh, 3EEh, or 2DEh)

Bits 76543210	Meaning
1	Receive line signal detected
1	Ring detected
1	DSR set
1	CTS set
1	Change in receive line signal detect state
1	Change in ring indicator state
1	Change in DSR state
1	Change in CTS state

12

Accessing BIOS Services

BIOS (Basic Input/Output System) is the lowest software level for communicating with hardware. Because the BIOS software usually is contained in the computer's read-only memory (ROM), BIOS is often referred to as ROM-BIOS.

The BIOS contains a series of functions that are easily accessible to an outside program—such as one you may develop. These functions, which are nothing more than callable subroutines, are invoked through software interrupts. Interrupts are generated by the assembly language instruction INT, which causes the microprocessor to use an address fetched from an interrupt table in low memory as the address for this special type of subroutine.

Specifically, INT pushes the flag(s) register on the stack and then resets the interrupt and trap flags. The full return address (CS:IP) is placed on the stack and then the desired interrupt vector (address) is retrieved from the interrupt table and placed in CS:IP. Execution of the interrupt then continues until an IRET instruction is encountered, at which point the return address is popped from the stack and placed in CS:IP. The flags register is then restored from the stack, and program execution continues from the point at which the interrupt was invoked.

Notice that the number of the interrupt being invoked determines which interrupt address is fetched from the interrupt table. Thus, the full syntax for calling an interrupt is

    INT XX

(The XX represents the number of the appropriate interrupt.)

This chapter covers the BIOS interrupt services, listing in detail the different BIOS interrupt numbers and the tasks they perform. (Chapter 13 covers the DOS interrupt services.)

As you will recall, Chapter 11 describes how to access the computer's hardware ports directly. Ordinarily, BIOS does most of this direct accessing. The concept of allowing BIOS to perform hardware interfacing, instead of performing the interfacing in your software, is readily justifiable. Although the chips that make up the computer hardware (or their related port address) may change or vary from one computer to another, the BIOS interfaces should not change. Any given BIOS function should produce identical results, regardless of which computer you're using. The way BIOS performs a task will differ, depending on the hardware. But because of the insulation provided by BIOS, this difference does not affect you (the programmer).

The universality of the BIOS applies only to the world of IBM microcomputers or close clones. Some computers that are purported to be IBM compatible are not. And there are different levels of compatibility—some computers are hardware compatible, some are DOS compatible, and others are BIOS compatible. The BIOS services listed in this chapter should work on any machine that is BIOS-compatible with the IBM.

The interface layer that BIOS introduces between the hardware and software levels has definite benefits. The primary benefit should be immediately apparent—software development time is greatly enhanced. (Programmers can spend less time developing software.) Because of the BIOS, you don't have to develop a different interface for every possible hardware combination. Other benefits include the security of knowing that your software will work on a variety of hardware configurations.

The BIOS Service Categories

The services offered by BIOS can be divided into several broad categories. Generally, these categories are determined by the I/O devices supported by the BIOS functions. Some categories, however, contain BIOS functions that deal with the internal workings of the computer rather than an external peripheral. (As used in this chapter, the interrupt itself is a function; a subfunction, or subinterrupt—such as AH= ?—is a service.)

The BIOS function categories include

- Video services
- Disk services
- Communications services
- Cassette tape services
- Keyboard services
- Printer services
- Date/Time services
- System services

The BIOS Services

The rest of this chapter is designed as a convenient reference. Each BIOS function call is described in detail, with the following information listed:

- *Function name.* A name based on the BIOS function names selected and listed by IBM in various technical documentation. Where appropriate, names have been modified or expanded to more accurately reflect the true purpose of the service.

- *Category.* The general classification of the function

- *Registers on entry.* BIOS function parameters generally are passed through registers. The expected register settings are detailed here.

- *Registers on return.* Knowing how registers are affected by interrupts is important for proper operation of software. Because BIOS functions frequently return values through registers, such information is detailed here. For most BIOS operations, all registers (except the AX and flags registers) remain intact.

- *Memory areas affected.* Some BIOS functions modify memory. Any affected memory is detailed here.

- *Syntax for calling.* A coding section that shows the proper method for calling the interrupt

- *Description.* Details of the purpose, benefits, and special considerations of the function

The functions are arranged in ascending numerical order. Each function can be identified by the primary interrupt number and a service number. (Each service number is specified by the contents of the AH register.) In this notation scheme, any BIOS service can be denoted by a hexadecimal number pair, *II/SS*, in which *II* is the interrupt number and *SS* is the service number. For example, the service used to set video mode, service 10/0, has an interrupt number of 10h, and a service number (specified through AH) of 0.

Print Screen (Interrupt 5)

Category: Printer services

Registers on Entry: Not significant

Registers on Return: Unchanged

Memory Affected: None

Syntax:

```
INT     5h            ;BIOS print screen interrupt
```

Description: To invoke this BIOS interrupt, press the PrtSc key. The interrupt causes the ASCII contents of the video screen to be sent to the printer.

Because most programs do not need a verbatim copy of the screen being sent to the printer, this interrupt normally is not called by a user program. However, the interrupt is designed for this type of use, and there is no problem in calling it from software control. The effect is the same as if the user had pressed the PrtSc key.

By changing the vector for this interrupt, you can create a custom version of the print screen service or disable it completely. For information on changing an interrupt vector, see DOS service 21/25 (Chapter 13).

When you call this interrupt, the contents of the registers are not significant; they remain unchanged on return. This routine does not change the position of the video cursor.

The status of this operation is contained in the single byte at memory address 50:0, which is 1 while printing is in progress. It is 0 if the print operation was successful, and OFFH if an error occured during the last print screen operation.

Set Video Mode (Interrupt 10h, service 0)

Category: Video services

Registers on Entry:

AH: 0
AL: Desired video mode

Registers on Return: Unchanged

Memory Affected: Ordinarily, the video memory area for the desired mode is cleared, unless the high-order bit of AL is set and an Enhanced Graphics Adapter card is in use.

Syntax:

```
MOV     AH,Ø          ;Specify service Ø
MOV     AL,3          ;8Øx25 color, TEXT (CGA display adapter)
INT     1Øh           ;BIOS video interrupt
```

Description: This service is used to set a specific video mode. The acceptable modes will vary, depending on the type of display adapter installed in the computer. Table 12.1 shows the possible settings for video modes.

Table 12.1
Video Mode Settings for BIOS Service 10/0

Mode Number	Mode Type	Display Adapter	Pixel Resolution	Characters	Colors
0	Text	CGA	320 × 200	40 × 25	16(gray)
1	Text	CGA	320 × 200	40 × 25	16
		EGA	320 × 350	40 × 25	16/64
2	Text	CGA	640 × 200	80 × 25	16(gray)
3	Text	CGA	640 × 200	80 × 25	16
		EGA	640 × 350	80 × 25	16/64
4	Graph	CGA/EGA	320 × 200		4
5	Graph	CGA/EGA	320 × 200		4(gray)
6	Graph	CGA/EGA	640 × 200		2
7	Text	MDA	720 × 350	80 × 25	
		EGA(mono)	720 × 350	80 × 25	4
8	Graph	PCjr	160 × 200		16
9	Graph	PCjr	320 × 200		16
10	Graph	PCjr	640 × 200		4
13	Graph	CGA/EGA	320 × 200		16
14	Graph	CGA/EGA	640 × 200		16
15	Graph	EGA(mono)	640 × 350		
16	Graph	EGA	640 × 350		4/16

Normally, setting the video mode causes the video buffer to be cleared. If you are using an EGA card, however, you can add the value 128 to any video mode value to indicate that the video display memory should not be cleared. Adding 128 is equivalent to setting the high-order bit of AL.

As new types of display adapters become available, the list of video modes listed in table 12.1 will probably change or grow. Depending on the amount of RAM available to the display adapter, the colors available with the EGA card in the various video modes will vary.

The results of using a mode which is not supported by the display adapter that you are using can be unpredictable. Ordinarily, the result is that no characters are displayed.

Set Cursor Size (Interrupt 10h, service 1)

Category: Video services

Registers on Entry:

> AH: 1
> CH: Beginning scan line of cursor
> CL: Ending scan line of cursor

Registers on Return: Unchanged

Memory Affected: None

Syntax:

```
MOV    AH,1        ;Specify service 1
MOV    CH,Ø        ;Start on scan line Ø
MOV    CL,7        ;End on scan line 7
INT    1Øh         ;BIOS video interrupt
```

Description: Depending on the type of display adapter used, the number of scan lines used by a text character can vary. The MDA and EGA adapters use characters that are 14 pixels high. The CGA uses a character box that is 8 pixels high. Each of these pixels corresponds to a *scan line* (the horizontal path traced by the electron beam that paints a character on the video monitor).

This service allows you to specify where in the character box the cursor should start and end. These positions, which are the beginning and ending scan lines, can vary from 0 to 7 lines (for the CGA) or from 0 to 13 lines (for the MDA and EGA). Within the valid numeric range, you can specify any combination of beginning and ending scan lines. If the beginning scan line is greater than the ending scan line, the cursor will wrap around the bottom of the character box, resulting in an apparent two-part cursor. A normal cursor occupies only the bottom one or two scan lines in the character box.

Set Cursor Position (Interrupt 10h, service 2)

Category: Video services

Registers on Entry:

> AH: 2
> BH: Video page number
> DH: Cursor row
> DL: Cursor column

Registers on Return: Unchanged

Memory Affected: None

Syntax:

```
MOV    AH,2         ;Specify service 2
MOV    DH,Ø         ;Place cursor at top left
MOV    DL,Ø         ;  corner of screen (Ø,Ø)
MOV    BH,Ø         ;Primary text page
INT    1Øh          ;BIOS video interrupt
```

Description: This service, which sets the position of the video cursor, is based on a screen-coordinate system. The cursor row, stored in DH, can vary from 0 to 24 for normal 25-line monitors. The cursor column, stored in DL, can vary from 0 to 39 or from 0 to 79, depending on the type of display adapter used and on the currently set video mode.

If you are using graphics mode, the video page number stored in BH should be set for 0. In text modes, which can accommodate more than one video page, the number usually varies from 0 to 3. If you are operating in 40-column mode, the video page number can vary from 0 to 7. The cursor position for each video page is independent of the other pages.

Read Cursor Position and Size (Interrupt 10h, service 3)

Category: Video services

Registers on Entry:

AH: 3
BH: Video page number

Registers on Return:

BH: Video page number
CH: Beginning scan line of cursor
CL: Ending scan line of cursor
DH: Cursor row
DL: Cursor column

Memory Affected: None

Syntax:

```
MOV    AH,3                    ;Specify service 3
MOV    BH,Ø                    ;Primary text page
INT    1Øh                     ;BIOS video interrupt
MOV    CUR_SIZE,CX             ;Save current cursor size
MOV    CUR_POSITION,DX         ;Save current position
```

Description: Use this service to determine the cursor's current status. Be sure to save the values so that, after manipulation, the program can restore the cursor condition.

If you are using graphics mode, the video page number stored in BH should be set for 0. In text modes, which can accommodate more than one video page, the video page number usually varies from 0 to 3. If you are operating in 40-column mode, the video page can vary from 0 to 7. The cursor position for each video page is independent of the other pages.

In this service (which is the opposite of services 10/1 and 10/2) the cursor size and position for a desired video page number are returned in CX and DX.

Ordinarily, the scan lines returned in CH and CL will vary from 0 to 7 (for the CGA adapter) or from 0 to 13 (for the MDA and EGA adapters). For additional information on scan line designations, refer to service 10/1.

The cursor row returned in DH normally varies from 0 to 24, and the cursor column returned in DL varies either from 0 to 39 or from 0 to 79, depending on which video mode currently is set.

Read Light Pen Position
(Interrupt 10h, service 4)

Category: Video services

Registers on Entry:

AH: 4

Registers on Return:

AH: Light pen trigger status
BX: Pixel column
CX: Raster line (pixel row)
DH: Light pen row
DL: Light pen column

Memory Affected: None

Syntax:

```
MOV     AH,4          ;Specify service 4
INT     1Øh           ;BIOS video interrupt
```

Description: If you have a light pen attached to your computer, this service allows you to determine the status of the light pen. Even though the hardware for using a light pen exists on the MDA, its use effectively is defeated by the long retention time of the phosphor used in monochrome monitors.

On return from this interrupt, you should check the value in AH. If the value is 0, the light pen has not been triggered. Because the other values will be meaningless, do not attempt further analysis and action based on the light pen's status.

If the value in AH is 1, the light pen has been triggered and two sets of coordinates (pixel and text) are returned. The video mode you are using determines which set of coordinates you should use: the pixel coordinates are appropriate for graphics screens; the text coordinates, for text screens.

The register pair CX:BX contains the set of pixel coordinates. CX is the *raster line*, or vertical pixel position, which varies from 0 to 199 or, for some EGA modes, from 0 to 349. BX (the horizontal pixel position) can vary from 0 to 319 or from 0 to 639, depending on the resolution of the video adapter used in the computer.

The accuracy of the pixel coordinates returned by this BIOS service varies. Because the vertical (raster line) coordinate is always a multiple of 2, only even lines are returned, even if an odd number line triggered the pen. Similarly, if the video mode currently allows for a horizontal resolution of 320 pixels, the horizontal coordinate returned is a multiple of 2. If the horizontal resolution is 640 pixels, the horizontal coordinate is a multiple of 4. Thus, this BIOS function precludes use of a light pen for precise graphics work.

If you are working in text mode, you will want to use the other set of light pen coordinates: the row (DH) and column (DL) coordinates. The row coordinate normally varies from 0 to 24; the column coordinate varies either from 0 to 39, or from 0 to 80, depending on the video adapter. 0,0 is the coordinate for the upper left corner of the display area.

Select Active Display Page (Interrupt 10h, service 5)

Category: Video services

Registers on Entry:

AH: 5
AL: Desired display page

Registers on Return: Unchanged

Memory Affected: This service determines which area of video memory is displayed.

Syntax:

```
MOV    AH,5        ;Specify service 5
MOV    AL,1        ;Want page 1 video
INT    1Øh         ;BIOS video interrupt
```

Description: Depending on the current display mode and the video adapter you are using, you can use multiple, independent display pages. This BIOS service allows you to specify which video page is to be active, or displayed.

The desired display page is specified in AL. This value will vary within a range determined by the current display mode and the type of adapter you are using (see table 12.2). The video mode numbers indicated in table 12.2 correlate directly to those shown in table 12.1.

Table 12.2
Video Display Pages for Various Display Modes and Video Adapters

Mode Number	Display Adapter	Page Range
0	CGA	0 – 7
1	CGA	0 – 7
	EGA	0 – 7
2	CGA	0 – 3
3	CGA	0 – 3
	EGA	0 – 7
13	EGA	0 – 7
14	EGA	0 – 3
15	EGA	0 – 1
16	EGA	0 – 1

Notice that you can set the active display page only if you are operating in text mode. The contents of the different display pages are not modified if you switch between pages.

Scroll Window Up (Interrupt 10h, service 6)

Category: Video services

Registers on Entry:

AH: 6
AL: Number of lines to scroll
BH: Display attribute for blank lines
CH: Row for upper left corner of window
CL: Column for upper left corner of window
DH: Row for lower right corner of window
DL: Column for lower right corner of window

Registers on Return: Unchanged

Memory Affected: This service modifies the desired video buffer area of the active display page.

Syntax:

```
MOV    AH,6              ;Specify service 6
MOV    AL,3              ;Want to scroll 3 lines
MOV    BH,7              ;Normal white-on-black
MOV    CH,5              ;Upper left = 5,5
MOV    CL,5
MOV    DH,15             ;Lower right - 15,74
MOV    DL,74
INT    10h               ;BIOS video interrupt
```

Description: Use this service (which is the opposite of service 10/7) to selectively scroll up portions of the text screen. Only the currently active text display page is affected. The number of lines to scroll, contained in AL, is set for the desired value. If this value is set to 0, or to a value greater than the height of the specified window, the entire window area is cleared.

CX and DX should contain the upper left and lower right coordinates for the window, respectively. The high byte of each register is the row, normally in the range of 0 to 24. The low byte is the column, normally either 0 to 39 or 0 to 79, depending on the current display mode. If the rectangle specified is inverted so that the value in CX is greater than the value in DX, the results will be unpredictable.

The information scrolled off the top of the window is lost. The blank lines scrolled on the bottom of the window consist of spaces with the character attribute specified by the byte value in BH. Table 12.3 lists the character attributes available for a CGA or EGA video adapter; other values may be available, depending on which video adapter card you use.

Table 12.3
Character Attribute Byte Values

Foreground	Background	Hex Value	Decimal Value
Blue	Black	01h	1
Green	Black	02h	2
Cyan	Black	03h	3
Red	Black	04h	4
Magenta	Black	05h	5
Brown	Black	06h	6
White	Black	07h	7
Gray	Black	08h	8
Light Blue	Black	09h	9
Light Green	Black	0Ah	10
Light Cyan	Black	0Bh	11
Light Red	Black	0Ch	12
Light Magenta	Black	0Dh	13
Yellow	Black	0Eh	14
Bright White	Black	0Fh	15
Black	Blue	10h	16
Green	Blue	12h	18
Cyan	Blue	13h	19
Red	Blue	14h	20
Magenta	Blue	15h	21
Brown	Blue	16h	22
White	Blue	17h	23
Gray	Blue	18h	24
Light Blue	Blue	19h	25
Light Green	Blue	1Ah	26
Light Cyan	Blue	1Bh	27
Light Red	Blue	1Ch	28
Light Magenta	Blue	1Dh	29
Yellow	Blue	1Eh	30
Bright White	Blue	1Fh	31

Table 12.3—cont.

Foreground	Background	Hex Value	Decimal Value
Black	Green	20h	32
Blue	Green	21h	33
Cyan	Green	23h	25
Red	Green	24h	26
Magenta	Green	25h	27
Brown	Green	26h	28
White	Green	27h	29
Gray	Green	28h	40
Light Blue	Green	29h	41
Light Green	Green	2Ah	42
Light Cyan	Green	2Bh	43
Light Red	Green	2Ch	44
Light Magenta	Green	2Dh	45
Yellow	Green	2Eh	46
Bright White	Green	2Fh	47
Black	Cyan	30h	48
Blue	Cyan	31h	49
Green	Cyan	32h	50
Red	Cyan	34h	52
Magenta	Cyan	35h	53
Brown	Cyan	36h	54
White	Cyan	37h	55
Gray	Cyan	38h	56
Light Blue	Cyan	39h	57
Light Green	Cyan	3Ah	58
Light Cyan	Cyan	3Bh	59
Light Red	Cyan	3Ch	60
Light Magenta	Cyan	3Dh	61
Yellow	Cyan	3Eh	62
Bright White	Cyan	3Fh	63
Black	Red	40h	64
Blue	Red	41h	65
Green	Red	42h	66
Cyan	Red	43h	67
Magenta	Red	45h	69
Brown	Red	46h	70
White	Red	47h	71
Gray	Red	48h	72

Table 12.3—cont.

Foreground	Background	Hex Value	Decimal Value
Light Blue	Red	49h	73
Light Green	Red	4Ah	74
Light Cyan	Red	4Bh	75
Light Red	Red	4Ch	76
Light Magenta	Red	4Dh	77
Yellow	Red	4Eh	78
Bright White	Red	4Fh	79
Black	Magenta	50h	80
Blue	Magenta	51h	81
Green	Magenta	52h	82
Cyan	Magenta	53h	83
Red	Magenta	54h	84
Brown	Magenta	56h	86
White	Magenta	57h	87
Gray	Magenta	58h	88
Light Blue	Magenta	59h	89
Light Green	Magenta	5Ah	90
Light Cyan	Magenta	5Bh	91
Light Red	Magenta	5Ch	92
Light Magenta	Magenta	5Dh	93
Yellow	Magenta	5Eh	94
Bright White	Magenta	5Fh	95
Black	Brown	60h	96
Blue	Brown	61h	97
Green	Brown	62h	98
Cyan	Brown	63h	99
Red	Brown	64h	100
Magenta	Brown	65h	101
White	Brown	67h	103
Gray	Brown	68h	104
Light Blue	Brown	69h	105
Light Green	Brown	6Ah	106
Light Cyan	Brown	6Bh	107
Light Red	Brown	6Ch	108
Light Magenta	Brown	6Dh	109
Yellow	Brown	6Eh	110
Bright White	Brown	6Fh	111

Table 12.3—cont.

Foreground	Background	Hex Value	Decimal Value
Black	White	70h	112
Blue	White	71h	113
Green	White	72h	114
Cyan	White	73h	115
Red	White	74h	116
Magenta	White	75h	117
Brown	White	76h	118
Gray	White	78h	120
Light Blue	White	79h	121
Light Green	White	7Ah	122
Light Cyan	White	7Bh	123
Light Red	White	7Ch	124
Light Magenta	White	7Dh	125
Yellow	White	7Eh	126
Bright White	White	7Fh	127

Scroll Window Down (Interrupt 10h, service 7)

Category: Video services

Registers on Entry:

AH: 7
AL: Number of lines to scroll
BH: Display attribute for blank lines
CH: Row for upper left corner of window
CL: Column for upper left corner of window
DH: Row for lower right corner of window
DL: Column for lower right corner of window

Registers on Return: Unchanged

Memory Affected: This service modifies the desired video buffer area of the active display page.

Syntax:

```
MOV     AH,7        ;Specify service 7
MOV     AL,5        ;Want to scroll 5 lines
MOV     BH,7        ;Normal white-on-black
MOV     CH,1Ø       ;Upper left = 1Ø,5
MOV     CL,5
MOV     DH,2Ø       ;Lower right - 2Ø,74
MOV     DL,74
INT     1Øh         ;BIOS video interrupt
```

Description: Use this service (which is the opposite of service 10/6) to selectively scroll down portions of the text screen. Only the currently active text display page is affected. The number of lines to scroll, contained in AL, is set for the desired value. If this value is set to 0, or to a value greater than the height of the specified window, the entire window area is cleared.

CX and DX should contain the upper left and lower right coordinates for the window, respectively. The high byte of each register is the row, normally in the range of 0 to 24. The low byte is the column, normally either 0 to 39 or 0 to 79, depending on the current display mode. If the rectangle specified is inverted so that the value in CX is greater than that in DX, the results will be unpredictable.

The information scrolled off the bottom of the window is lost, and the blank lines scrolled on the top of the window consist of spaces with the character attribute specified by the value in BH. (Some of the possible video attributes are listed in table 12.3.)

Read Character and Attribute (Interrupt 10h, service 8)

Category: Video services

Registers on Entry:

AH: 8
BH: Video page number

Registers on Return:

AH: Attribute byte
AL: ASCII character code

Memory Affected: None

Syntax:

```
; POSITION CURSOR AT DESIRED LOCATION PRIOR TO USING THIS SERVICE
; (SEE SERVICE 10/2)
    MOV     AH,2            ;Specify service 2
    MOV     DH,0            ;Place cursor at top left
    MOV     DL,0            ;  corner of screen (0,0)
    MOV     BH,0            ;Primary text page
    INT     10h             ;BIOS video interrupt

; NOW USE SERVICE 10/8 TO READ THE CHARACTER/ATTRIBUTE WORD

    MOV     AH,8            ;Specify service 8
    MOV     BH,0            ;Primary text page
    INT     10h             ;BIOS video interrupt
```

Description: Because this service reads (from *any* display page) the character and attribute at the cursor's current position, you are not limited to the currently visible display page.

This service works in both text and graphics modes, although the character attribute has significance only in text mode. In text mode, the value returned in AH represents the character's video attribute (refer to table 12.3). In graphics mode, the color of the character is returned in AH. NULL (ASCII 0) is returned in AL if the character at the cursor's current position (in graphics mode) does not match any valid ASCII character.

Write Character and Attribute (Interrupt 10h, service 9)

Category: Video services

Registers on Entry:

AH: 9
AL: ASCII character code
BH: Video page number
BL: Video attribute of character in AL
CX: Number of character/attribute words to display

Registers on Return: Unchanged

Memory Affected: This service modifies the desired area of the active display page's video buffer.

Syntax:

```
MOV   AH,9            ;Specify service 9
MOV   AL,'-'          ;Want to display a dash
MOV   BH,Ø            ;Primary text page
MOV   BL,ØEh          ;Yellow on black attribute
MOV   CX,5Øh          ;Print 8Ø characters
INT   1Øh             ;BIOS video interrupt
```

Description: This service displays a specific number of characters at the cursor's current position on any valid video page.

The character in AL is displayed with the video attribute specified in BL (which is valid only for text modes). (For a list of possible video attributes, refer to table 12.3.) In graphics modes, the color of the character (foreground) should be specified in BL. If bit 7 of BL is set to 1, then the color in BL is XORed with the background color where the character is to be displayed. If the same character (AL) is displayed at the same position with the same color (BL) and bit 7 of BL set, the character will be erased and the background will remain undisturbed.

The character displayed by this service can be displayed on any valid video page (not just on the currently visible one). By using this service and service 10/0Ah, you can create a page of text on a background (not displayed) page, and then display the entire page at once through service 10/5.

This service can be used to display any number of characters from 1 through 65,536. Setting the value in CX to 0 signifies 65,536 characters, the ultimate number of character repetitions. In text mode, if the number being displayed extends beyond the right margin, the characters progress from line to line. In graphics mode, however, no line-wrap occurs—only those characters on the current line are displayed.

Even though this service displays a specified number of characters at the current cursor position, the cursor position does not advance. To subsequently change the cursor position, use service 10/2.

Write Character (Interrupt 10h, service 0Ah)

Category: Video services

Registers on Entry:

AH: 0Ah
AL: ASCII character code
BH: Video page number
BL: Graphic color of character in AL (only in graphic modes)
CX: Number of character/attribute words to display

Registers on Return: Unchanged

Memory Affected: This service modifies the desired area of the active display page's video buffer.

Syntax:

```
MOV    AH,ØAh         ;Specify service ØAh
MOV    AL,'*'         ;Want to display an asterisk
MOV    BH,Ø           ;Primary text page
MOV    CX,1           ;Print only 1 character
INT    1Øh            ;BIOS video interrupt
```

Description: This service is effectively the same as service 10/9, but uses the existing video attribute values. In graphics modes, the color of the character (foreground) should be specified in BL. If bit 7 of BL is set to 1, the color in BL is XORed with the background color where the character will be displayed. If the same character (AL) is displayed at the same position with the same color (BL) and bit 7 of BL set, the character will be erased and the background will remain undisturbed.

The character can be displayed on any valid video page (not just on the currently visible video page). Using this service and service 10/9, you can create a page of text on a background (not displayed) page, and then display then entire page at once through service 10/5.

This service can be used to display any number of characters from 1 through 65,536. Setting the value in CX to 0 signifies 65,536 characters, the ultimate number of character repetitions. In text mode, if the number being displayed extends beyond the right margin, the characters progress from line to line. In graphics mode, however, no line wrap occurs—only those characters on the current line are displayed.

Even though this service displays a specified number of characters at the current cursor position, the cursor position does not advance. To subsequently change the cursor position, use service 10/2.

Set Color Palette (Interrupt 10h, service 0Bh)

Category: Video services

Registers on Entry:

AH: 0Bh
BH: Palette ID
BL: Palette ID color value

Registers on Return: Unchanged

Memory Affected: None

Syntax:

```
MOV    AH,ØBh         ;Specify service ØBh
MOV    BH,1           ;Setting palette
MOV    BL,Ø           ;Green/red/brown palette
INT    1Øh            ;BIOS video interrupt
```

Description: This service, which is used primarily to set the color palette used by medium-resolution graphics services, has significance only in a few video modes, most notably mode 4. (For more information on video modes, see the service 10/0 description.)

This service does not affect the video memory. It only changes the way that the 6845 CRT Controller chip on the CGA board interprets and displays pixel values already in video memory.

If BH contains 0, the value of BL is used as both the background and border colors. If BH contains a 1, the value in BL specifies which color palette to use; BL can be set to any value, but only the contents of the low bit are significant. This bit value determines one or the other of the following palettes:

Value	Palette
0	Green, red, and brown
1	Cyan, magenta, and white

Notice the colors for palette 0. The technical specifications for the CGA card and the 6845 CRT Controller show that these are the proper colors (although the system BIOS reference in the *IBM Technical Reference* manual states that the colors for this palette are green, red, and yellow).

A palette specifies the display colors to be used for various bit combinations. Changing the palette changes the screen display immediately. Rapidly using this service and alternately changing the palette can result in a flashing screen. The pixel bit determination is as follows:

Pixel Value	Palette 0 Color	Palette 1 Color
00	Background	Background
01	Green	Cyan
10	Red	Magenta
11	Brown	White

You can use this service also to set the border color in text mode. In text mode, if BH is 0, the value in BL is used as the border color.

Write Pixel Dot (Interrupt 10h, service 0Ch)

Category: Video services

Registers on Entry:

AH: 0Ch
AL: Pixel value
CX: Pixel column
DX: Raster line (pixel row)

Registers on Return: Unchanged

Memory Affected: This service modifies the desired area of the active display page's video buffer.

Syntax:

```
MOV    AH,ØCh        ;Specify service ØCh
MOV    AL,11b        ;Pixel value to use
MOV    CX,AØh        ;Position at 1ØØ,16Ø
MOV    DX,64h        ;
INT    1Øh           ;BIOS video interrupt
```

Description: This general-purpose graphics plotting service (the opposite of service 10/0Dh) works in either medium- or high-resolution graphics modes, although the effects in each are different.

In medium-resolution graphics modes on the CGA, the contents of AL can vary from 0 to 3. The display effect of these pixel values depends on the color palette in use (see service 10/0Bh). The results of the various setting of AL are

Pixel Value	Palette 0 Color	Palette 1 Color
00	Background	Background
01	Green	Cyan
10	Red	Magenta
11	Brown	White

In high-resolution graphics modes on the CGA, the value of AL can vary between 0 and 1. These values correspond to whether the pixel is off (black) or on (white).

If the high-order bit of AL is set (1), the pixel color is XORed with the pixel's current contents. Because of the behavior of XORing values, this capability provides a quick way to display a pixel and then to erase it (by again writing the same pixel value to the location). If the high-order bit of AL is set (0), the pixel value is written to the pixel location.

The register pair DX:CX contains the pixel's plotting coordinates. DX is the *raster line*, or vertical pixel position; its value can range from 0 to 199, or from 0 to 349 for some EGA video modes. The value of CX (the horizontal pixel position) can range either from 0 to 319 (medium-resolution) or from 0 to 639 (high-resolution). Coordinates are numbered from top to bottom and from left to right; 0,0 is the top left screen corner and either 199,319 or 199,639 is the bottom right corner, depending on the resolution of the video mode. If you specify coordinates outside the legal range for the current graphics mode, the results can be unpredictable.

Read Pixel Dot (Interrupt 10h, service 0Dh)

Category: Video services

Registers on Entry:

AH: 0Dh
CX: Pixel column
DX: Raster line (pixel row)

Registers on Return:

AL: Pixel value
CX: Pixel column
DX: Raster line (pixel row)

Memory Affected: None

Syntax:

```
MOV     AH,ØDh          ;Specify service ØDh
MOV     CX,AØh          ;Want pixel value at
MOV     DX,64h          ;  coordinate 1ØØ,16Ø
INT     1Øh             ;BIOS video interrupt
```

Description: This service (the opposite of 10/0Ch) is used in either medium- or high-resolution graphics modes to determine the pixel value of the pixel at any given screen location.

The desired pixel coordinates are specified in the register pair DX:CX. DX is the *raster line*, or vertical pixel position; its value can range from 0 to 199, or from 0 to 349 for some EGA video modes. The value of CX (the horizontal pixel position) can range either from 0 to 319 (medium-resolution) or from 0 to 639 (high-resolution). Notice that this horizontal resolution is in a 16-bit register but that the other coordinate is in an 8-bit register. Coordinates are numbered from top to bottom and from left to right; 0,0 is the top left screen corner and either 199,319, 199,639, or 349,639 is the bottom right corner, depending on the resolution of the video mode. If you specify coordinates outside the legal range for the current graphics mode, the results can be unpredictable.

The pixel value returned in AL depends on the current video mode. In medium-resolution graphics modes on the CGA, the value of AL can vary from 0 to 3. In high-resolution graphics modes on the CGA, the value of AL can vary between 0 and 1. (For more information about pixel values, see the description for service 10/0Ch.)

TTY Character Output (Interrupt 10h, service 0Eh)

Category: Video services

Registers on Entry:

AH: 0Eh
AL: ASCII character code
BH: Video page number
BL: Character color (graphics foreground)

Registers on Return: Unchanged

Memory Affected: This service modifies the desired area of the active display page's video buffer.

Syntax:

```
MOV    AH,ØEh         ;Specify service ØEh
MOV    AL,'.'         ;Output a period
MOV    BH,Ø           ;Primary video page
INT    1Øh            ;BIOS video interrupt
```

Description: This service is similar to service 10/9, except that the output is in *teletype* mode (a limited amount of character processing is performed on the output). The ASCII codes for bell (07), backspace (08), linefeed (10), and carriage return (13) are all intercepted and translated to the appropriate actions. Line wrap and scrolling are performed if the printed characters exceed the right display margin or the bottom display line.

Because the ASCII value of the character to be output is loaded in AL, and the video page number loaded in BH, this output service can be used for display pages other than the current one. By using this service and service 10/0Ah, you can create a page of text on a background (not displayed) page, and then display the entire page at once through service 10/5. If output is to a background page, the processing of the bell character (ASCII 07) will still result in the familiar "beep."

The foreground color, which is specified in BL, has significance only in graphics modes. Notice that the syntax example for this service does not specify BL. In text mode, the current video attributes for the screen location are used. With this service, you cannot specify a video attribute other than the current one.

You can use this service, which advances the cursor position, to display multiple characters in series. With this service, you do not have to set the cursor position before displaying each character.

Get Current Video State
(Interrupt 10h, service 0Fh)

Category: Video services

Registers on Entry:

AH: 0Fh

Registers on Return:

AH: Screen width
AL: Display mode
BH: Active display page

Memory Affected: None

Syntax:

```
MOV     AH,ØFh              ;Specify service ØFh
INT     1Øh                 ;BIOS video interrupt
MOV     COLUMNS,AH          ;Save number of columns
MOV     MODE,AL             ;Save display mode
MOV     PAGE,BH             ;Save display page
```

Description: This service, which is used to determine the current video state of the computer, returns three pieces of information: the width in columns of the display screen (AH), the current video display mode (AL), and the current video display page (BH). Table 12.4 lists possible video-mode settings.

Table 12.4
Possible Video Mode Settings Returned by BIOS Service 10/0F

Mode Number	Mode Type	Display Adapter	Pixel Resolution	Characters	Colors
0	Text	CGA	320 × 200	40 × 25	16(gray)
1	Text	CGA	320 × 200	40 × 25	16
		EGA	320 × 350	40 × 25	16/64
2	Text	CGA	640 × 200	80 × 25	16(gray)
3	Text	CGA	640 × 200	80 × 25	16
		EGA	640 × 350	80 × 25	16/64
4	Graph	CGA/EGA	320 × 200		4
5	Graph	CGA/EGA	320 × 200		4(gray)
6	Graph	CGA/EGA	640 × 200		2
7	Text	MDA	720 × 350	80 × 25	
		EGA(mono)	720 × 350	80 × 25	4
8	Graph	PCjr	160 × 200		16
9	Graph	PCjr	320 × 200		16
10	Graph	PCjr	640 × 200		4
13	Graph	CGA/EGA	320 × 200		16
14	Graph	CGA/EGA	640 × 200		16
15	Graph	EGA(mono)	640 × 350		
16	Graph	EGA	640 × 350		4/16

Reserved (Interrupt 10H, services 10h, 11h, 12h)

These services are listed as reserved in the IBM Personal Computer AT BIOS. The assigned code returns directly to the caller and no intervening functions are performed. Clearly, this condition will not always hold true. As peripherals and capabilities are added, these services will more than likely be used.

Write String (Interrupt 10h, service 13h)

Category: Video services

Registers on Entry:

AH: 13h
AL: Mode
BH: Video page number

BL: Character attribute (depending on AL)
CX: Length of string
DH: Cursor row where string is to be displayed
DL: Cursor column where string is to be displayed
BP: Offset address of string
ES: Segment address of string

Registers on Return: Unchanged

Memory Affected: This service modifies the desired area of the active display page's video buffer.

Syntax:

```
MOV     BH,Ø                    ;Primary video page
MOV     BL,Ø7h                  ;Normal attributes
MOV     DH,5                    ;Display string at
MOV     DL,5                    ;   coordinates 5,5
PUSH    DS                      ;Make ES same as DS
POP     ES
MOV     BP,OFFSET ES:MSG_1      ;Point to message offset
MOV     CX,1Øh                  ;Standard string length
MOV     AH,13h                  ;Specify service 13h
INT     1Øh                     ;BIOS video interrupt
```

Description: *This service is available only on the Personal Computer AT.* Use this service, which is a logical extension of the BIOS character display functions, to display an entire string on any video page.

The mode specified in AL determines how BIOS will treat the string that is to be displayed. Table 12.5 lists this service's four modes.

Table 12.5
Modes for Service 10/13

Mode	Cursor	Attribute	*String Composition* (C=Character, A=Attribute)
0	Not moved	in BL	CCCCCCCC...CC
1	Moved	in BL	CCCCCCCC...CC
2	Not moved	in string	CACACACA...CA
3	Moved	in string	CACACACA...CA

Notice that the display attributes can be specified either in BL or in the string, depending on the contents of AL. If you are using mode 2 or 3, the contents of BL are not significant. The mode determines also whether the cursor is moved when the string is displayed.

The string's address is specified in ES:BP. CX contains the length of the string. The service displays the string until CX reaches 0. Do not use a length of 0. If you do, 65,536 characters will be displayed, and the effects of displaying this number of characters probably will be undesirable.

Because this service makes limited use of BIOS service 10/0E, some character processing is performed on the individual string characters. The ASCII codes for bell (07), backspace (08), linefeed (10), and carriage return (13) are all intercepted and directed to service 10/0E, where they are translated to the appropriate actions. Line wrap and scrolling are performed if the printed characters exceed the right display margin or the bottom display line. If the string character is not a bell, backspace, linefeed, or carriage return, it is displayed by service 10/9.

Although this service is neither particularly fast nor efficient, it is convenient. The routines in Chapter 10 result in faster displays but entail more work for the programmer. Only you can decide which to use.

Get Equipment Status (Interrupt 11h)

Category: System services

Registers on Entry: Not significant

Registers on Return:

  AX: Equipment status

Memory Affected: None

Syntax:

```
INT    11h            ;Invoke BIOS interrupt
```

Description: Use this rudimentary service, which returns a minimal amount of information, to determine what equipment is attached to the computer. The equipment status word is set up during the booting process and does not change. The meaning of each bit in the returned word is shown in table 12.6.

Table 12.6
Bit Meanings for Equipment Status Word Returned by Interrupt 11

Bits		Meaning of Bits
FEDCBA98	76543210	*Meaning of Bits*
xx		Number of printers attached
x		Not used
0		Game adapter not installed
1		Game adapter installed
xxx		Number of serial cards attached
x		Not used
	00	1 disk drive attached (if bit 0=1)
	01	2 disk drives attached (if bit 0=1)
	10	3 disk drives attached (if bit 0=1)
	11	4 disk drives attached (if bit 0=1)
	01	Initial video mode – 40 × 25 BW/color card
	10	Initial video mode – 80 × 25 BW/color card
	11	Initial video mode – 80 × 25 BW/mono card
	00	16K system board RAM
	01	32K system board RAM
	10	48K system board RAM
	11	64K system board RAM
	1	Math coprocessor installed
	0	No disk drives installed (bits 6–7 insignificant)
	1	Disk drives installed (bits 6–7 significant)

Depending on the computer you are using, certain portions of this equipment status word may not be significant. If you are using an IBM Personal Computer AT, for example, the value of bits 2 and 3 have no meaning. These bits are relics of the days when 64K of RAM was considered as much as anyone could possibly want in a microcomputer.

You can see that the register contents on entry are not significant, and that AX is the only register changed on return.

Get Memory Size (Interrupt 12h)

Category: System services

Registers on Entry: Not significant

Registers on Return:

   AX: Memory blocks

Memory Affected: None

Syntax:

```
INT     12h             ;Invoke BIOS interrupt
```

Description: Use this service to return the number of contiguous 1K blocks of memory installed in the computer. The memory size, which is determined when you power-up the computer, is returned in AX.

Notice that the number of contiguous memory blocks is returned. If the power-on self test (POST) determines that defective RAM chips are installed in the computer, the value returned by this interrupt will be equal to the number of 1K blocks counted before the defective memory area was encountered.

The register contents on entry of this interrupt are not significant. AX is the only register changed on return.

Reset Disk Drives (Interrupt 13h, service 0)

Category: Disk services

Registers on Entry:

   AH: 0

Registers on Return: Unchanged

Memory Affected: None

Syntax:

```
MOV     AH,Ø            ;Specify service Ø
INT     13h             ;BIOS disk interrupt
```

Description: Use this service to reset the floppy disk drive controller. (The service works on the NEC series of floppy disk drive controllers specified as standard equipment by IBM.)

Calling this service has no apparent effect on the disk drives. The recalibrate command is sent directly to the floppy drive controller in use, and a reset flag is set to recalibrate all the drives the next time they are used. This recalibration retracts the read/write head to track 0, causing the familiar "grinding" sound often heard after a disk error. The read/write head is forced to track 0 and then must seek out the desired track.

Used primarily in routines that handle critical errors on disks, this service forces the controller to recalibrate itself on the subsequent operation. If a critical error occurs, the service is necessary for reliable disk operation; it forces the disk controller to make no assumptions about its position or condition—assumptions that may be wrong because of the critical error condition.

Get Floppy Disk Status
(Interrupt 13h, service 1)

Category: Disk services

Registers on Entry:

AH: 1

Registers on Return:

AL: Status byte

Memory Affected: None

Syntax:

```
MOV     AH,1            ;Specify service 1
INT     13h             ;BIOS disk interrupt
```

Description: This service returns the status of the floppy disk drive controller. The status, which is set after each disk operation (such as reading, writing, or formatting), is returned in AL. The meaning of each bit in the returned status byte is shown in table 12.7.

Read Disk Sectors (Interrupt 13h, service 2)

Category: Disk services

Registers on Entry:

AH: 2
AL: Number of sectors
BX: Offset address of data buffer
CH: Track
CL: Sector
DH: Head (side) number
DL: Drive number
ES: Segment address of data buffer

Table 12.7
Meaning of the Status Byte Returned by Service 13/1

Bits 76543210	Hex	Decimal	Meaning of Bits
1	80	128	Time out—drive did not respond
1	40	64	Seek failure—couldn't move to requested track
1	20	32	Controller malfunction
1	10	16	Bad CRC detected on disk read
1 1	9	9	DMA error—64K boundary crossed
1	8	8	DMA overrun
1	4	4	Bad sector/sector not found
11	3	3	Write protect error
1	2	2	Bad sector ID (address) mark
1	1	1	Bad command

Registers on Return:

AH: Return code

Memory Affected: RAM buffer area specified by address starting at ES:BX is overwritten by sectors requested from disk.

Syntax:

```
MOV    AL,1                     ;Reading 1 sector
MOV    CH,TRACK                 ;Specify track
MOV    CL,SECTOR                ;  and sector
MOV    DH,SIDE                  ;Specify side
MOV    DL,DRIVE                 ;Specify drive
PUSH   DS                       ;Point ES to proper
POP    ES                       ;  segment address
MOV    BX,OFFSET ES:BUFFER      ;Offset of buffer area
MOV    AH,2                     ;Specify service 2
INT    13h                      ;BIOS disk interrupt
```

Description: Use this service to control reading from the disk. (This service is the opposite of service 13/3, which controls writing to the disk.)

To use this service, you must specify the precise physical location on the disk at which you want to begin reading. The drive is specified in DL (A=0, B=1, C=2, etc.). The side, or head, is specified in DH and can be 0 or 1. CH and CL contain the track and sector, respectively. These values will vary depending on the type of disk drive in use. The number of sectors to be read is specified in AL.

The final registers to be set up specify which RAM area will be used as a buffer for the sectors that are read. This address is specified in ES:BX. You need to know the size of each disk sector ahead of time, because this information determines how large the RAM buffer should be. For instance, if each disk sector contains 512 bytes, and you are going to read 4 sectors, the length of your buffer should be 2K, or 2048 bytes.

This service checks parameters only on the requested drive number (DL); all other passed parameters are not checked for validity. If you pass invalid parameters, the results are unpredictable. Table 12.8 shows some typical parameter ranges for this service.

Table 12.8
Parameter Ranges for Service 13/2 Using a 360K Disk

Parameter	Register	Valid Range
# of sectors	AL	1 through 9
Track	CH	0 through 39
Sector	CL	1 through 9
Head (side)	DH	0 or 1
Drive	DL	0=A, 1=B, 2=C, etc.

On return from this service, the carry flag signifies whether an error occurred. If the carry flag is not set, AH will contain a zero (0). If the carry flag is set, AH will contain the disk status byte described under service 13/1 (refer to table 12.7). If an error occurs during reading, use service 13/0 to reset the disk system before you attempt another read.

Note: In this service and service 13/3, a particularly confusing error may occur. DMA boundary error (AH=9) means that an illegal boundary was crossed when the information was placed into RAM. DMA (Direct Memory Access) is used by the disk service routines to place information into RAM. If a memory offset address ending in 3 zeros (ES:1000, ES:2000, ES:3000, etc.) falls in the middle of the area being overlaid by a sector, this error will occur. You must calculate and read a much smaller chunk so that this type of memory boundary corresponds with a sector boundary. I don't know why this happens—it is simply frustrating as heck to a programmer.

Write Disk Sectors (Interrupt 13h, service 3)

Category: Disk services

Registers on Entry:

AH: 3
AL: Number of sectors
BX: Offset address of data buffer
CH: Track
CL: Sector
DH: Head (side) number
DL: Drive number
ES: Segment address of data buffer

Registers on Return:

AH: Return code

Memory Affected: None

Syntax:

```
MOV     AL,9                    ;Write entire track
MOV     CH,TRACK                ;Specify track
MOV     CL,SECTOR               ;  and sector
MOV     DH,SIDE                 ;Specify side
MOV     DL,DRIVE                ;Specify drive
PUSH    DS                      ;Point ES to proper
POP     ES                      ;  segment address
MOV     BX,OFFSET ES:BUFFER     ;Offset of buffer area
MOV     AH,3                    ;Specify service 3
INT     13h                     ;BIOS disk interrupt
```

Description: This service, which controls writing to the disk, is the opposite of service 13/2, which controls reading from the disk.

To use this service, you must specify (in ES:BX) which RAM area will be used as the buffer for the sectors that are written. This buffer area must contain all of the information that you want written to the disk. You must know the size of the sectors being written on the disk because this service calculates, based on the sector size and the number of sectors to write (AH), the amount of RAM to read and subsequently write. The preceding example requires a buffer of 4068 bytes (4.5K), assuming that each sector requires 512 bytes.

By setting up the other registers, you determine the precise physical location on the disk at which you wish to begin writing. The drive is specified in DL (A=0,

B=1, C=2, etc.). The side, or head, is specified in DH, which can be 0 or 1. CH and CL contain the track and sector, respectively. (These values will vary, depending on the type of disk drive in use.) In AL, specify the number of sectors to be written.

This service checks parameters only on the requested drive number (DL); all other passed parameters are not checked for validity. If you pass invalid parameters, the results are unpredictable and may result in errors or damaged disks. (For some typical parameter ranges for this service, refer to table 12.8.)

On return from this service, the carry flag signifies whether an error occurred. If the carry flag is not set, AH contains a zero (0). If the carry flag is set, AH contains the disk status byte as detailed in service 13/1 (refer to table 12.7). If an error occurs during the writing operation, use service 13/0 to reset the disk system before you attempt another write operation.

Note: In this service and service 13/2, a particularly confusing error may occur. DMA boundary error (AH=9) means that an illegal boundary was crossed when the information was placed into RAM. DMA (Direct Memory Access) is used by the disk service routines to place information into RAM. This error will occur if a memory offset address ending in 3 zeros (ES:1000, ES:2000, ES:3000, etc.) is crossed before this service completes reading an entire sector of information. You must calculate and reread so that this type of memory boundary corresponds with a sector boundary.

Verify Disk Sectors (Interrupt 13h, service 4)

Category: Disk services

Registers on Entry:

AH: 4
AL: Number of sectors
CH: Track
CL: Sector
DH: Head (side) number
DL: Drive number

Registers on Return:

AH: Return code

Memory Affected: None

Syntax:

```
MOV     AL,9            ;Verify entire track
MOV     CH,TRACK        ;Specify track
MOV     CL,SECTOR       ;  and sector
MOV     DH,SIDE         ;Specify side
MOV     DL,DRIVE        ;Specify drive
MOV     AH,4            ;Specify service 4
INT     13h             ;BIOS disk interrupt
```

Description: Use this service to verify the contents of sectors on the disk. Notice that this function has no buffer specification. Unlike services 13/2 and 13/3, this service does not compare the sectors with memory; it simply verifies that the sectors can be read and that the CRC checksum for each sector agrees with the data.

The CRC, or Cyclic Redundancy Check, is a sophisticated checksum that detects a high percentage of any errors that may occur. When a sector is written to disk, an original CRC is calculated and written along with the sector data. The verification service reads the sector, recalculates the CRC, and compares the recalculated CRC with the original CRC. If they agree, there is a high probability that the data is correct; if they disagree, an error condition is generated.

You set up the registers to determine the precise physical location on the disk at which you wish to begin verification. The drive is specified in DL (A=0, B=1, C=2, etc.). The side, or head, is specified in DH and can be 0 or 1. CH and CL contain the track and sector, respectively. These values will vary, depending on the type of disk drive in use. Specify in AL the number of sectors to be verified.

This service checks parameters only on the requested drive number (DL); all other passed parameters are not checked for validity. If you pass invalid parameters, the results are unpredictable and may result in errors or damaged disks. (For some typical parameter ranges for this service, refer to table 12.8.)

On return from this service, the carry flag signifies whether an error occurred. If the carry flag is not set, AH contains a zero (0). If the carry flag is set, AH contains the disk status bits as detailed in service 13/1 (refer to table 12.7). If an error occurs during the writing operation, use service 13/0 to reset the disk system before attempting another read, write, or verify operation.

Format Disk Track (Interrupt 13h, service 5)

Category: Disk services

Registers on Entry:

AH: 5
BX: Offset address of track address fields
CH: Track
DH: Head (side) number
DL: Drive number
ES: Segment address of track address fields

Registers on Return:

AH: Return code

Memory Affected: None

Syntax:

```
MOV    CH,TRACK                   ;Specify track
MOV    DH,SIDE                    ;Specify side
MOV    DL,DRIVE                   ;Specify drive
PUSH   DS                         ;Point ES to proper
POP    ES                         ;  segment address
MOV    BX,OFFSET ES:ADR_FIELD     ;Offset of address fields
MOV    AH,5                       ;Specify service 5
INT    13h                        ;BIOS disk interrupt
```

Description: Use this service to format a specific track on a disk. To format an entire disk, you must "step through" each track, invoking this service for each track.

The registers to be set up specify the disk track to be formatted (CH) and the side, or head. Specify the side (which can be 0 or 1) in DH. Specify the drive in DL (A=0, B=1, C=2, etc.). Because an entire track is formatted at one time, this service does not require a specification for the starting sector or the number of sectors.

Notice that ES:BX contains the address of an area referred to as the *track address fields*, a collection of fields that indicate specific information about each sector on the track. Some of this information is written to the sector header so that the sector being formatted can subsequently be located with read, write, or verify operations.

The track address fields consist of four bytes for each sector on the track. These four bytes detail the following information in the following order:

Cylinder (track)
Head (side)
Record (sector number)
Size code

In common computerese, the *cylinder*, *head*, and *record* information are the track, side, and sector numbers, respectively. Clearly, the sector number will vary. But the track and side numbers are the same for all of the track address fields. These numbers do not have to be in sequential order; they can be interleaved to enhance disk performance or for some other special purpose. Regardless of the order denoted by this entry (the record field) into the track address fields, the sectors are placed physically on the disk in the order indicated by the position of the address field. Although this description may sound confusing, it corresponds to physical and logical placement of sectors on the disk.

Physically, the sectors are always arranged in sequential order (for example, from 1 through 9 for a 360K DS/DD disk). Logically, however, physical sector 1 may have a sector address mark that is not 1. The following example shows two typical interleave schemes in which consecutive logical sectors are placed physically either two or five sectors apart. The logical numbers are those entered in the address fields.

Physical order	1	2	3	4	5	6	7	8	9
Logical order	1	6	2	7	3	8	4	9	5
Logical order	1	3	5	7	9	2	4	6	8

IBM microcomputers read sectors from the disk logically, by their sector address, not physically, by their placement on the disk.

The *size code* is nothing more than an indicator of the number of bytes the sector will contain. The size code may vary from 0 to 3 (see table 12.9).

Table 12.9
Valid Size Codes for Use in Service 13/5 Track Address Fields

Size Code	Bytes per Sector
0	128
1	256
2	512
3	1024

If you understand the make-up of the track address fields, you easily can compose the 36 bytes necessary for formatting a 360K DS/DD disk. If you were writing the sectors in sequential order on side 0 of track 5, the bytes would appear as follows (for clarity, an extra space has been inserted between every four bytes):

    5012 5022 5032 5042 5052 5062 5072 5082 5092

If you were constructing the same track address fields for an interleaved track with an interleave factor of 5, the bytes would appear as follows:

    5012 5032 5052 5072 5092 5022 5042 5062 5082

On return from this service, the carry flag signifies whether an error occurred. If the carry flag is not set, AH contains a zero (0). If the carry flag is set, AH contains the disk status bits as detailed in service 13/1 (refer to table 12.7). If an error occurs during the formatting operation, use service 13/0 to reset the disk system before you attempt to reformat the track.

The following stripped-down, bare-bones routine to format any given track of a disk was written to format a DS/DD 360K disk on an IBM PC, PC XT, or compatible computer. To format different types of disks, you would have to change the data beginning at ADR_FIELD, as well as the logic that changes this area and controls the formatting of both sides of the disk.

To format a DS/DD 360K disk on an IBM Personal Computer AT or compatible, you must use additional BIOS services to ensure that the parameters are set properly for the formatting operation. To do this setup work and to perform the formatting properly, you would call the subroutine FMT_AT_TRK.

Note: The following routine is a subroutine only; you must incorporate it into another program.

```
TRUE            EQU     -1
FALSE           EQU      Ø

FMT_TYPE        DB       Ø1              ;1=36ØK in 36ØK drive
                                        ;2=36ØK in 1.2M drive

CUR_DISK        DB       ØØ
CUR_TRACK       DB       ØØ
RETRY_CNT       DB       ØØ

RECOVERABLE     DB       ØØ              ;Flag: TRUE=recoverable
                                        ;      FALSE=not recoverable
```

```
BAD_SPOT_FLAG    DB      ØØ              ;FLAG: TRUE=bad spots
                                         ;      FALSE=none bad

ADR_FIELD        DW      ØØØØ            ;Track/side
                 DB      Ø1              ;Sector number
                 DB      Ø2              ;Size code=512 bytes/sector

                 DW      ØØØØ            ;Track/side
                 DB      Ø2              ;Sector number
                 DB      Ø2              ;Size code=512 bytes/sector

                 DW      ØØØØ            ;Track/side
                 DB      Ø3              ;Sector number
                 DB      Ø2              ;Size code=512 bytes/sector

                 DW      ØØØØ            ;Track/side
                 DB      Ø4              ;Sector number
                 DB      Ø2              ;Size code=512 bytes/sector

                 DW      ØØØØ            ;Track/side
                 DB      Ø5              ;Sector number
                 DB      Ø2              ;Size code=512 bytes/sector

                 DW      ØØØØ            ;Track/side
                 DB      Ø6              ;Sector number
                 DB      Ø2              ;Size code=512 bytes/sector

                 DW      ØØØØ            ;Track/side
                 DB      Ø7              ;Sector number
                 DB      Ø2              ;Size code=512 bytes/sector

                 DW      ØØØØ            ;Track/side
                 DB      Ø8              ;Sector number
                 DB      Ø2              ;Size code=512 bytes/sector

                 DW      ØØØØ            ;Track/side
                 DB      Ø9              ;Sector number
                 DB      Ø2              ;Size code=512 bytes/sector
```

```
; ----------------------------------------------------------------
; HANDLE FORMATTING A SINGLE TRACK ON AN AT - 360K DS/DD
;       BEFORE CALLING, MAKE SURE FMT_TYPE IS SET TO THE PROPER
;       VALUE BASED ON THE TYPE OF DRIVE BEING USED TO FORMAT
;       THE 360K DISK
; ----------------------------------------------------------------


FMT_AT_TRK      PROC    NEAR
                PUSH    AX
                PUSH    BX
                PUSH    DX
                PUSH    ES

                MOV     AL,FMT_TYPE         ;Set DASD for drive
                MOV     DL,CUR_DISK         ;Set for drive
                MOV     AH,11h              ;Set for function 11h
                INT     13h                 ;Call BIOS disk service

                MOV     AH,35h              ;Get interrupt vector
                MOV     AL,1Eh              ;Disk base table vector
                INT     21h                 ;DOS service to get vector
                ADD     BX,7                ;Offset to format gap length
                MOV     AL,ES:[BX]          ;Get current gap length
                PUSH    AX                  ;Store original value
                MOV     ES:[BX],50h         ;Set TO appropriate gap
                DEC     BX                  ;Point to proper field:
                DEC     BX                  ;  last sector (sectors
                DEC     BX                  ;  per track
                MOV     AL,ES:[BX]          ;Get current last sector
                PUSH    AX                  ;Store original value
                MOV     ES:[BX],9           ;Set for 9 sectors/track
                PUSH    BX                  ;Save offset address
                PUSH    ES                  ;Save segment address

                CALL    FMT_TRACK           ;Go format the track

                POP     ES                  ;Get segment back
                POP     BX                  ;Get offset back
                POP     AX                  ;Get original value back
                MOV     ES:[BX],AL          ;Restore last sector value
                INC     BX                  ;Point to proper field:
                INC     BX                  ;  format gap length
                INC     BX                  ;
```

```
                POP     AX                      ;Get original value back
                MOV     ES:[BX],AL              ;Restore last sector value

                POP     ES
                POP     DX
                POP     BX
                POP     AX
                RET

FMT_AT_TRK      ENDP


; ------------------------------------------------------------------
; HANDLE FORMATTING A SINGLE TRACK - 360K DS/DD
; ------------------------------------------------------------------

FMT_TRACK       PROC    NEAR
                PUSH    AX
                PUSH    BX
                PUSH    CX
                PUSH    DX
                PUSH    ES

                PUSH    CS                      ;Data and code segments
                POP     ES                      ;  are the same

                MOV     AL,CUR_TRACK            ;Move track number
                MOV     AH,1                    ;Counter for heads done

FD_A:           MOV     DH,AH                   ;Formatting two sides
                MOV     RETRY_CNT,3             ;Allow 3 retries/track

                MOV     CX,9                    ;Want to do 9 fields
                MOV     BX,OFFSET ADR_FIELD     ;Starting here
FD_B:           MOV     [BX],AX
                ADD     BX,4                    ;Point at next field
                LOOP    FD_B

FD_C:           MOV     BX,OFFSET ADR_FIELD     ;Data area for formatting
                MOV     DL,CUR_DISK             ;Set for drive
                MOV     CH,CUR_TRACK            ;Move track number
                MOV     CL,1ep
```

```
                MOV     AH,5                    ;Want to format a track
                INT     13h                     ;ROM BIOS diskette services
                JC      FMT_ERROR               ;If error, go handle

                MOV     AX,ADR_FIELD            ;Get current track/head
                DEC     AH                      ;Decrement head
                JZ      FD_A                    ;If zero, loop

FD_EXIT:        POP     ES
                POP     DX
                POP     CX
                POP     BX
                POP     AX
                RET

FMT_ERROR:      CALL    DO_ERROR
                CMP     RECOVERABLE,TRUE        ;Was the error recoverable?
                JE      FD_C                    ;Yes, do it again
                DEC     RETRY_CNT_FMT
                JNZ     FD_C
                MOV     BAD_SPOT_FLAG,TRUE      ;Set flag for bad spots
                JMP     FD_EXIT

FMT_TRACK       ENDP

; ------------------------------------------------------------
; HANDLE ERRORS THAT OCCUR DURING FORMATTING A TRACK
; ------------------------------------------------------------

DO_ERROR        PROC    NEAR
                MOV     RECOVERABLE,FALSE       ;Assume non-recoverable
                PUSH    AX                      ;Save current status byte
                XOR     AX,AX                   ;Zero out, reset disk system
                INT     13h                     ;ROM BIOS diskette services
                POP     AX                      ;Get status byte back
                CMP     AH,Ø3h                  ;Was it a write protect?
                JE      DE_C                    ;Yes, go handle
                CMP     AH,8Øh                  ;Was it time out?
                JNE     DE_EXIT                 ;No, so exit
DE_C:           MOV     RECOVERABLE,TRUE        ;Recoverable error

DE_EXIT:        RET
DO_ERROR        ENDP
```

If an error is detected during formatting, the routine DO_ERROR is called. This routine can be improved. For example, although DO_ERROR considers write-protect and timeout errors as recoverable, no allowance is made for the program to pause while the operator corrects the source of the errors. You can easily add a pause in your programs.

(For additional information about the disk base table, see Appendix B.)

Unused (Interrupt 13H, services 6, 7)

Although these services are listed as unused in the Personal Computer AT BIOS, they will more than likely be used as peripherals and capabilities are added.

Return Drive Parameters (Interrupt 13h, service 8)

Category: Disk services

Registers on Entry:

AH: 8
DL: Fixed disk drive number

Registers on Return:

CH: Number of tracks/side
CL: Number of sectors/track
DH: Number of sides
DL: Number of consecutive drives attached

Memory Affected: None

Syntax:

```
MOV    DL,80h        ;Use first disk drive
MOV    AH,8          ;Specify service 8
INT    13h           ;BIOS disk interrupt
```

Description: Use this service to retrieve disk parameters for a fixed disk drive. (*This service is available only on the Personal Computer AT and works only with fixed disks.*)

Notice that when you call this service, you will specify the fixed disk drive number in DL (80h for the first fixed disk, 81h for the second, etc.) These numbers do not correspond to the standard BIOS disk-number scheme. If you attempt the service with any out-of-range fixed disk drive numbers (those below 80h), an error will be returned.

On return from this service, the carry flag signifies whether an error occurred. If the carry flag is not set, AH contains a zero (0). If the carry flag is set, AH contains the disk status bits as detailed in service 13/1 (refer to table 12.7).

Initialize Fixed Disk Table (Interrupt 13h, service 9)

Category: Disk services

Registers on Entry:

AH: 9
DL: Fixed disk drive number

Registers on Return: Unchanged

Memory Affected: None

Syntax:

```
MOV    DL,8Øh        ;Use first disk drive
MOV    AH,9          ;Specify service 9
INT    13h           ;BIOS disk interrupt
```

Description: Use this service to initialize the fixed disk parameter tables for a specific drive. (*This service is available only on the Personal Computer AT and works only with fixed disks.*)

Notice that when you call this service, you will specify the fixed disk drive number in DL (80h for the first fixed disk, 81h for the second, etc.) These numbers do not correspond to the standard BIOS disk numbering scheme. If you attempt the service with any out-of-range fixed disk drive numbers (those below 80h), an error will be returned.

On return from this service, the carry flag signifies whether an error occurred. If the carry flag is not set, AH contains a zero (0). If the carry flag is set, AH contains the disk status byte as detailed in service 13/1 (refer to table 12.7).

The fixed disk parameter tables for as many as two fixed disks are contained in RAM at the memory addresses pointed to by interrupt vectors 41h and 46h.

Read Long Sectors
(Interrupt 13h, service 0Ah)

Category: Disk services

Registers on Entry:

AH: 0Ah
AL: Number of sectors
BX: Offset address of data buffer
CH: Track
CL: Sector
DH: Head (side) number
DL: Fixed disk drive number
ES: Segment address of data buffer

Registers on Return:

AH: Return code

Memory Affected: RAM data buffer starting at memory address ES:BX is overwritten by sectors requested from the fixed disk.

Syntax:

```
MOV     AL,1                    ;Reading 1 sector
MOV     CH,LOW_TRACK            ;Specify low-order track
MOV     CL,HIGH_TRACK           ;Specify high-order track
MOV     BL,6                    ;Want to shift 6 bits
SHL     CL,BL                   ;  left, place in bits 6/7
OR      CL,SECTOR               ;Place sector in bits 0-5
MOV     DH,SIDE                 ;Specify side
MOV     DL,80h                  ;Use first disk drive
PUSH    DS                      ;Point ES to proper
POP     ES                      ;  segment address
MOV     BX,OFFSET ES:BUFFER     ;Offset of buffer area
MOV     AH,0Ah                  ;Specify service 0Ah
INT     13h                     ;BIOS disk interrupt
```

Description: Use this service to control reading long sectors from the IBM Personal Computer AT's 20M fixed disk drive. (This service, *which is available only on the Personal Computer AT and works only with fixed disks*, is the opposite of service 13/0B, which controls writing long sectors to the fixed disk.) A long sector consists of a regular sector of data and four bytes of error-correction information (used to verify the information that is read from the fixed disk).

To use this service, you must specify the precise physical location on the fixed disk at which you want to begin reading. In DL, specify the fixed disk drive number (80h for the first fixed disk, 81h for the second, etc.). These numbers do not correspond to the standard BIOS disk numbering scheme. If you attempt the service with any out-of-range fixed disk drive numbers (those below 80h), an error will be returned.

In DH, specify the side, or head, which may vary from 0 to 15. CH and CL contain the track and sector, respectively. These values, which will vary depending on the size of fixed disk used, are normally in the range specified in table 12.10. Track (CH) and sector (CL) information in the table are encoded according to the description for this service.

Table 12.10
Parameter Ranges for Service 13/A on an IBM Personal Computer AT

Parameter	Register	Valid Range
# of sectors	AL	1 through 121
Track	CH/CL	0 through 1023
Sector	CL	1 through 17
Head (side)	DH	0 through 15
Drive	DL	80=first, 81=second, etc.

As you can see, the track range (CH) can be greater than 255, the largest number that can be contained in a single byte. Actually, the track is specified as a 10-bit number, with the two high-order bits stored in bits 7 and 6 of CL. The sector specification is stored in bits 0 through 5 of CL.

The final registers to be set up specify which RAM area will be used as a buffer for the sectors that are read. This address is specified in ES:BX. To determine the size of the RAM buffer, you must know ahead of time how large each disk sector is. For instance, if each disk sector contains 512 bytes, and you are going to read four sectors, your buffer should be 2048 bytes (2K) long.

This service checks parameters on the requested drive number (DL) only; all other passed parameters are not checked for validity. If you pass invalid parameters, the results are unpredictable.

On return from this service, the carry flag signifies whether an error occurred. If the carry flag is not set, AH will contain a zero (0). If the carry flag is set, AH will contain the disk status bits as detailed in service 13/1 (refer to table 12.7). If an error occurs during the reading operation, use service 13/0 (with the fixed disk drive number in DL) to reset the fixed disk system before you attempt another read operation.

Note: In this service, a particularly confusing error may occur. DMA boundary error (AH=9) means that an illegal boundary was crossed when the information was placed into RAM. DMA (Direct Memory Access) is used by the disk service routines to place information into RAM. This error will occur if a memory offset address ending in three zeros (ES:1000, ES:2000, ES:3000, etc.) falls in the middle of the area being overlaid by a sector. You must calculate and reread so that this type of memory boundary corresponds with a sector boundary. I don't know why this happens, but it is frustrating as all get out to a programmer. (This error code consideration applies also to services 13/2, 13/3, and 13/0Bh.)

Write Long Sectors
(Interrupt 13h, service 0Bh)

Category: Disk services

Registers on Entry:

AH: 0Bh
AL: Number of sectors
BX: Offset address of data buffer
CH: Track
CL: Sector
DH: Head (side) number
DL: Fixed disk drive number
ES: Segment address of data buffer

Registers on Return:

AH: Return code

Memory Affected: None

Syntax:

```
MOV    AL,17              ;Writing entire track
MOV    CH,LOW_TRACK       ;Specify low-order track
MOV    CL,HIGH_TRACK      ;Specify high-order track
MOV    BL,6               ;Want to shift 6 bits
SHL    CL,BL              ;  left, place in bits 6/7
OR     CL,SECTOR          ;Place sector in bits 0-5
MOV    DH,SIDE            ;Specify side
```

```
MOV     DL,80h                  ;Use first disk drive
PUSH    DS                      ;Point ES to proper
POP     ES                      ;  segment address
MOV     BX,OFFSET ES:BUFFER     ;Offset of buffer area
MOV     AH,0Bh                  ;Specify service 0Bh
INT     13h                     ;BIOS disk interrupt
```

Description: This service, which controls writing long sectors to the IBM Personal Computer AT 20M fixed disk drive, *is available only on the Personal Computer AT and works only with fixed disks.* (It is the opposite of service 13/0Ah, which controls reading long sectors from the fixed disk.) A long sector consists of a regular sector of data and four bytes of error-correction information, which is used to verify the information that is read from the fixed disk.

To use this service, you must specify (in ES:BX) which RAM area is used as the buffer for the sectors written. The area should be initialized with the desired data, in the right amount. Because this service calculates the amount of RAM to read and subsequently write, based on the number of sectors to write (AH) and the sector size, you must know the size of the sectors being written on the disk. Assuming that each sector requires 512 bytes, the example shown in the syntax section requires a buffer of 8,704 bytes (8.5K).

You set up other registers to determine the precise physical location on the fixed disk at which you wish to begin writing. Specify the fixed disk drive number in DL (80h for the first fixed disk, 81h for the second, etc.). These numbers do not correspond to the standard BIOS disk numbering scheme. If you attempt the service with any out-of-range fixed disk drive numbers (those below 80h), an error will be returned.

The side, or head, is specified in DH and may vary from 0 to 15. CH and CL contain the track and sector, respectively. These values, which will vary depending on the size of fixed disk used, are normally in the range specified in table 12.10 (refer to service 13/0Ah).

The track range (CH) can be greater than 255, the largest number that can be contained in a single byte. Actually, the track is specified as a 10-bit number, with the two high-order bits stored in bits 7 and 6 of CL. The sector specification is stored in bits 0 through 5 of CL.

This service checks parameters on the requested drive number (DL) only; all other passed parameters are not checked for validity. If you pass invalid parameters, the results are unpredictable.

On return from this service, the carry flag signifies whether an error occurred. If the carry flag is not set, AH contains a zero (0). If the carry flag is set, AH contains the disk status bits as detailed in service 13/1 (refer to table 12.7). If an error occurs during the reading operation, use service 13/0 (with the fixed disk drive number in DL) to reset the fixed disk system before you attempt another write operation.

Note: In this service (and services 13/2, 13/3, and 13/0Ah) a particularly confusing error may occur. DMA boundary error (AH=9) means that an illegal boundary was crossed as the information was read from the RAM buffer. DMA (Direct Memory Access) is used by the disk service routines to place information into RAM. This error will occur if a memory offset address ending in three zeros (ES:1000, ES:2000, ES:3000, etc.) is crossed before this service completes reading an entire sector of information. You must calculate and reread so that this type of memory boundary corresponds with a sector boundary.

Seek Cylinder (Interrupt 13h, service 0Ch)

Category: Disk services

Registers on Entry:

AH: 0Ch
CH: Low-order track
CL: High-order track
DH: Head (side) number
DL: Fixed disk drive number

Registers on Return:

AH: Return code

Memory Affected: None

Syntax:

```
MOV     CH,LOW_TRACK            ;Specify low-order track
MOV     CL,HIGH_TRACK           ;Specify high-order track
MOV     BL,6                    ;Want to shift 6 bits
SHL     CL,BL                   ;  left, place in bits 6/7
MOV     DH,SIDE                 ;Specify side
MOV     DL,80h                  ;Use first disk drive
MOV     AH,0Ch                  ;Specify service 0Ch
INT     13h                     ;BIOS disk interrupt
```

Description: Use this service to move the read/write heads of the fixed disk drive to a specific track (cylinder). *This service is available only on the Personal Computer AT and works only with fixed disks.*

To use this service, you must specify the fixed disk drive number (80h for the first fixed disk, 81h for the second, etc.) in DL. These numbers do not correspond to the standard BIOS disk numbering scheme. If you attempt the service with any out-of-range fixed disk drive numbers (those below 80h), an error will be returned.

The side, or head, is specified in DH and may vary from 0 to 15. CH and CL contain the track and sector, respectively. These values, which will vary depending on the size of fixed disk used, are normally in the range specified in table 12.10 (refer to service 13/0Ah).

The track range (CH) can be greater than 255, the largest number that can be contained in a single byte. Actually, the track is specified as a 10-bit number, with the two high-order bits stored in bits 7 and 6 of CL.

This service checks parameters on the requested drive number only (DL); all other passed parameters are not checked for validity. If you pass invalid parameters, the results are unpredictable.

On return from this service, the carry flag signifies whether an error occurred. If the carry flag is not set, AH contains a zero (0). If the carry flag is set, AH contains the disk status byte as detailed in service 13/1 (refer to table 12.7).

Alternate Reset (Interrupt 13h, service 0Dh)

Category: Disk services

Registers on Entry:

AH: 0Dh
DL: Fixed disk drive number

Registers on Return:

AH: Return code

Memory Affected: None

Syntax:

```
MOV    DL,8Øh        ;Use first disk drive
MOV    AH,ØDh        ;Specify service Dh
INT    13h           ;BIOS disk interrupt
```

Description: This service (*which is available only on the Personal Computer AT*) resets the fixed disk drive.

The IBM Personal Computer AT BIOS shows that, after compensating for the fixed disk drive specification, this service is hard-coded to the same routine address as service 13/0; there is absolutely no difference between the two services. (This service apparently was included for future expansion—for the day when identical reset routines could not be used for both fixed and floppy disks.)

To use this service, you must specify the fixed disk drive number (80h for the first fixed disk, 81h for the second, etc.) in DL. These numbers do not correspond to the standard BIOS disk numbering scheme. If you attempt the service with any out-of-range fixed disk drive numbers (those below 80h), an error will be returned.

When this service is called, its effect on the fixed disk drive is not apparent. The recalibrate command is sent directly to the fixed disk controller, and a reset flag is set to recalibrate the drive the next time it is used. (This recalibration consists primarily of retracting the read/write head to track 0.)

Used primarily in routines that handle critical errors, this service forces the controller to recalibrate itself on the subsequent operation. If a critical error occurs, this service is necessary for reliable operation of the fixed disk. The service forces the controller to make no assumptions about its position or condition—assumptions that may be wrong because of the previously experienced critical-error condition.

On return from this service, the carry flag signifies whether an error occurred. If the carry flag is not set, AH will contain a zero (0). If the carry flag is set, AH contains the disk status byte as detailed in service 13/1 (refer to table 12.7).

Unused (Interrupt 13H, services Eh, Fh)

These services, which are listed as unused in the Personal Computer AT BIOS, will more than likely be used as peripherals and capabilities are added.

Read DASD Type (Interrupt 13h, service 15h)

Category: Disk services

Registers on Entry:

AH: 15h
DL: Drive number

Registers on Return:

AH: Return code
CX: High byte—number of fixed disk sectors
DX: Low byte—number of fixed disk sectors

Memory Affected: None

Syntax:

```
MOV     DL,Ø            ;Use drive A:
MOV     AH,15h          ;Specify service 15h
INT     13h             ;BIOS disk interrupt
```

Description: This service (*available only on the Personal Computer AT*) is used to determine the DASD type of a given disk drive. DASD represents the type of disk drive indicated by the return value in AH.

DL can contain either a normal BIOS disk drive number (0=A, 1=B, 2=C, etc.) or a fixed disk drive number (80h for the first fixed disk, 81h for the second, etc.).

On return from this service, the carry flag signifies whether an error occurred. If the carry flag is set, AH contains the disk status byte as detailed in service 13/ 1 (refer to table 12.7). If an error occurs, use service 13/0 to reset the disk system before you attempt to use this service again.

If the carry flag is clear, the return code in AH indicates the DASD type of the drive. Table 12.11 lists the possible return codes and their meanings.

Table 12.11
DASD Types for Service 13/15

Code	Meaning
0	The drive requested (DL) is not present
1	Drive present, cannot detect disk change
2	Drive present, can detect disk change
3	Fixed disk

If the return code indicates a DASD type of 3 (fixed disk), the register pair CX:DX will indicate the number of sectors on the fixed disk.

Read Disk Change Line Status (Interrupt 13h, service 16h)

Category: Disk services

Registers on Entry:

AH: 16h
DL: Drive number

Registers on Return:

AH: Return code

Memory Affected: None

Syntax:

```
MOV    DL,Ø          ;Use drive A:
MOV    AH,16h        ;Specify service 16h
INT    13h           ;BIOS disk interrupt
```

Description: Use this service (*which is available only on the Personal Computer AT*) to determine whether the disk in a drive has been changed.

The result code in AH will be either a zero (0) or a 6; a 0 means that the disk has not been changed, a 6 means that it has. If the disk has not been changed, the carry flag will be clear; if the disk has been changed, the carry flag will be set.

The use of the carry flag can have strange consequences in this service: the carry flag is set not only if an error has occurred but also if the disk has been changed. Because having two uses for the carry flag can be confusing, be sure to check the contents of AH for the true result code. If AH is 0, and the carry flag is set, you know that an error has occurred. AH can then be assumed to contain the disk status byte as detailed in service 13/1 (refer to table 12.7).

Even if there is no disk in the drive, this service works and does not generate an error. The drive is activated and checked and, if no disk is present, a result of 6 is returned. If this service is called several times with no intervening disk access, the same result code is returned repetitively. For instance, if you request a disk's directory and then invoke this service, a result code of 0 will be returned. If you then change the disk, a result code of 6 is generated. If you leave the same disk in the drive and again call this service, a result code of 6 will again be returned. A result code of 0, indicating that there has been no change, will be returned only after the disk has been read.

Set DASD Type for Format
(Interrupt 13h, service 17h)

Category: Disk services

Registers on Entry:

AH: 17h
AL: DASD format type
DL: Drive number

Registers on Return: Unchanged

Memory Affected: None

Syntax:

```
MOV    AL,3          ;Set DASD for 1.2M
MOV    DL,Ø          ;Set drive A:
MOV    AH,17h        ;Specify service 17h
INT    13h           ;BIOS disk interrupt
```

Description: Use this service in conjunction with service 13/5 to format a disk. You must use this service, *which is available only on the Personal Computer AT,* to specify not only the type of disk to format but also the type of drive in which that disk will be formatted.

The DASD format type specified in AL can be a number from 1 to 3 (see table 12.12).

Table 12.12
DASD Format Types for Service 13/17

Type	Meaning
1	Formatting a 320/360K disk in a 320/360K drive
2	Formatting a 320/360K disk in a 1.2M drive
3	Formatting a 1.2M disk in a 1.2M drive

For more information on the proper use of this service, see the discussion and sample routines for service 13/5.

Initialize Communications Port (Interrupt 14h, service 0)

Category: Communications services

Registers on Entry:

AH: 0
AL: Initialization parameter
DX: Communications port

Registers on Return:

AH: Line status
AL: Modem status

Memory Affected: None

Syntax:

```
MOV     AL,10000011b            ;Set for 1200/N/8/1
MOV     DX,0                    ;Set COM1:
MOV     AH,0                    ;Specify service 0
INT     14h                     ;BIOS comm. interrupt
```

Description: This service is used to initialize the communications (RS-232) port specified in DX. The contents of DX can vary from 0 to 3 (corresponding to COM1:, COM2:, COM3:, and COM4:).

In AL, you specify how the communications port should be initialized. This service allows you to set the baud rate, parity, data length, and stop bits. Specify these settings through the bits of register AL, according to the coding scheme shown in table 12.13.

Table 12.13
Meaning of AL Bits for Service 14/0

Bits 76543210	Meaning
000	110 baud
001	150 baud
010	300 baud
011	600 baud
100	1200 baud
101	2400 baud
110	4800 baud
111	9600 baud
00	No parity
01	Odd parity
10	No parity
11	Even parity
0	1 stopbit
1	2 stopbits
10	7-bit data length
11	8-bit data length

This service returns two values, which correspond to the asynchronous chip's line status (AH) and modem status (AL) registers. These return values, which indicate the status and condition of the asynchronous communications adapter, are the same as those returned in service 14/3. The meaning of each bit of the line status register is shown in table 12.14; table 12.15 lists the meaning of the modem status register.

Table 12.14
The Line Status Register Bit Meanings

Bits 76543210	Meaning
1	Time-out error
1	Transfer shift register (TSR) empty
1	Transfer holding register (THR) empty
1	Break interrupt detected
1	Framing error
1	Parity error
1	Overrun error
1	Data ready

Table 12.15
The Modem Status Register Bit Meanings

Bits 76543210	Meaning
1	Receive line signal detect
1	Ring indicator
1	Data set ready (DSR)
1	Clear to send (CTS)
1	Delta receive line signal detect
1	Trailing edge ring detector
1	Delta data set ready (DDSR)
1	Delta clear to send (DCTS)

Note that the value in AH, which corresponds to the line status register, has an added bit. Although the meaning of bit 7 in the line status register ordinarily is undefined, BIOS uses this bit to signal that an excessive amount of time has passed since a character has been received.

Although this book does not attempt to explain the purpose, use, and interpretation of each bit in these registers, many books on asynchronous communications are available on the market.

Transmit Character (Interrupt 14h, service 1)

Category: Communications services

Registers on Entry:

AH: 1
AL: ASCII character
DX: Communications port

Registers on Return:

AH: Return code

Memory Affected: None

Syntax:

```
MOV     AL,'T'          ;Send the letter 'T'
MOV     DX,Ø            ;Set COM1:
MOV     AH,1            ;Specify service 1
INT     14h             ;BIOS comm. interrupt
```

Description: This service sends a character to the communications (RS-232) port specified in DX. The contents of DX can vary from 0 to 3 (corresponding to COM1:, COM2:, COM3:, and COM4:). Before calling this service for the first time, make sure that service 14/0 has been used to initialize the communications port.

The character to be sent should be loaded in AL. The transmission was successful if the high-order bit of AH is clear (AH < 80h) on return. Table 12.16 shows the balance of the bits in AH after a successful transmission.

If the transmission was unsuccessful, the high-order bit will be set (AH > 7Fh) and the balance of AH will appear as in table 12.16.

Receive Character (Interrupt 14h, service 2)

Category: Communications services

Registers on Entry:

AH: 2
DX: Communications port

Registers on Return:

AH: Return code

Table 12.16
The Return Code Values for Service 14/1

Bits 76543210	Meaning
X	Error indicator
1	Transfer shift register (TSR) empty
1	Transfer holding register (THR) empty
1	Break interrupt detected
1	Framing error
1	Parity error
1	Overrun error
1	Data ready

Memory Affected: None

Syntax:

```
MOV     DX,Ø         ;Set COM1:
MOV     AH,2         ;Specify service 2
INT     14h          ;BIOS comm. interrupt
```

Description: This service is used to receive a character from the communications (RS-232) port specified in DX. The contents of DX can vary from 0 to 3 (corresponding to COM1:, COM2:, COM3:, and COM4:). Before calling this service for the first time, make sure that you have used service 14/0 to initialize the communications port.

Because this service waits for a character, other computer processing is suspended until the character is received or until the communications port returns an error.

On return, AH contains a return code. In this return code, which is analogous to the line control register return values of service 14/3, only the error bits are used (see table 12.17).

If you set AL to 0 before calling this service, you can quickly test to see whether a character was received. Because most receiving software discards NULL characters (ASCII value of 0), no action need be taken (even if a null character is received)—your routine can continue to await an incoming character.

Table 12.17
The Return Code Values for Service 14/2

Bits 76543210	Meaning
1	Time-out error
?	Unused
?	Unused
1	Break interrupt detected
1	Framing error
1	Parity error
1	Overrun error
?	Unused

Get Communications Port Status (Interrupt 14h, service 3)

Category: Communications services

Registers on Entry:

AH: 3
DX: Communications port

Registers on Return:

AH: Line status
AL: Modem status

Memory Affected: None

Syntax:

```
MOV    DX,Ø        ;Set COM1:
MOV    AH,3        ;Specify service 3
INT    14h         ;BIOS comm. interrupt
```

Description: Use this service to check the status of the communications line and the modem. The communications (RS-232) port is specified in DX. The contents of DX can vary from 0 to 3 (corresponding to COM1:, COM2:, COM3:, and COM4:).

This service returns two values, which correspond to the asynchronous chip's line status (AH) and modem status (AL) registers. The meaning of each line status register bit is shown in table 12.18; that of each modem status register bit, in table 12.19.

Table 12.18
Meanings of Line Status Register Bits

Bits 76543210	Meaning
1	Time-out error
1	Transfer shift register (TSR) empty
1	Transfer holding register (THR) empty
1	Break interrupt detected
1	Framing error
1	Parity error
1	Overrun error
1	Data ready

Table 12.19
Meanings of Modem Status Register Bits

Bits 76543210	Meaning
1	Receive line signal detect
1	Ring indicator
1	Data set ready (DSR)
1	Clear to send (CTS)
1	Delta receive line signal detect
1	Trailing edge ring detector
1	Delta data set ready (DDSR)
1	Delta clear to send (DCTS)

Notice that the value in AH, which corresponds to the line status register, has an added bit. Although the meaning of bit 7 in the line status register is undefined, BIOS uses this bit to signal that an excessive amount of time has passed since a character has been received.

Although this book does not attempt to explain the purpose, use, and interpretation of each bit in these registers, many books on asynchronous communications are available on the market.

Turn On Cassette Motor
(Interrupt 15h, service 0)

Category: Cassette services

Registers on Entry:

AH: 0

Registers on Return:

AH: Return code

Memory Affected: None

Syntax:

```
MOV    AH,Ø        ;Specify service Ø
INT    15h         ;BIOS cassette interrupt
```

Description: This service (the opposite of service 15/1) turns on the cassette motor. Because this service works only on older models of the PC, using it on the IBM PC XT or Personal Computer AT causes the return of an 86h in AH and sets the carry flag.

Turn Off Cassette Motor
(Interrupt 15h, service 1)

Category: Cassette services

Registers on Entry:

AH: 1

Registers on Return:

AH: Return code

Memory Affected: None

Syntax:

```
MOV    AH,1        ;Specify service 1
INT    15h         ;BIOS cassette interrupt
```

Description: This service (the opposite of service 15/0) turns off the cassette motor. Because this service works only on older models of the PC, using it on the IBM PC XT or Personal Computer AT causes the return of an 86h in AH and sets the carry flag.

Read Data Blocks from Cassette (Interrupt 15h, service 2)

Category: Cassette services

Registers on Entry:

AH: 2
BX: Offset address of data buffer
CX: Number of bytes to read
ES: Segment address of data buffer

Registers on Return:

AH: Return code
DX: Number of bytes read

Memory Affected: RAM buffer area specified by address starting at ES:BX is overwritten with bytes requested from cassette.

Syntax:

```
MOV     CX,NUM_BYTES              ;Read this many bytes
PUSH    DS                       ;Point ES to proper
POP     ES                       ;  segment address
MOV     BX,OFFSET ES:BUFFER      ;Offset of buffer area
MOV     AH,2                     ;Specify service 2
INT     15h                      ;BIOS cassette interrupt
```

Description: This service reads data from the cassette tape port. Because this service works only on older models of the PC, using it on the IBM PC XT or Personal Computer AT causes the return of an 86h in AH and sets the carry flag.

Information is read from the cassette in 256-byte blocks, but only the number of bytes requested in CX are transferred to the memory address pointed to by ES:BX.

On completion, DX is set to the number of bytes actually read. If no error occurred, the carry flag is clear; if an error occurred, the carry flag is set and AH will contain an error code. The error codes shown in table 12.20 are valid only if the carry flag is set.

Table 12.20
Error Codes Returned in AH for Service 15/2

AH	Meaning
0h	Invalid command
1h	CRC error
2h	Data transitions lost
3h	No data located on tape
86h	No cassette port available

Write Data Blocks to Cassette (Interrupt 15h, service 3)

Category: Cassette services

Registers on Entry:

AH: 3
BX: Offset address of data buffer
CX: Number of bytes to write
ES: Segment address of data buffer

Registers on Return:

AH: Return code

Memory Affected: None

Syntax:

```
MOV    CX,NUM_BYTES              ;Write this many bytes
PUSH   DS                       ;Point ES to proper
POP    ES                       ;  segment address
MOV    BX,OFFSET ES:BUFFER      ;Offset of buffer area
MOV    AH,3                     ;Specify service 3
INT    15h                      ;BIOS cassette interrupt
```

Description: This service writes data to the cassette tape port. Because this service works only on older models of the PC, using it on the IBM PC XT or Personal Computer AT causes the return of an 86h in AH and sets the carry flag.

Information is written to the cassette in 256-byte blocks, but only the number of bytes indicated in CX are transferred from the memory address pointed to by ES:BX.

If an error is detected when this service is invoked, the carry flag is set and AH will contain an error code (see table 12.21). These error codes, which are valid only if the carry flag is set, indicate only syntactical errors. Neither of the errors returned indicates that information was written improperly to the cassette.

Table 12.21
Error Codes Returned in AH for Service 15/3

AH	Meaning
0h	Invalid command
86h	No cassette port available

Read Keyboard Character
(Interrupt 16h, service 0)

Category: Keyboard services

Registers on Entry:

AH: 0

Registers on Return:

AH: Keyboard scan code
AL: ASCII value of keystroke

Memory Affected: None

Syntax:

```
MOV     AH,Ø             ;Specify service Ø
INT     16h              ;BIOS keyboard interrupt
MOV     SCAN_CODE,AH     ;Store scan code
MOV     ASCII_KEY,AL     ;Store ASCII value
```

Description: This service, which is similar to service 16/1, examines the keyboard buffer to determine whether a keystroke is available. If no keystoke is available, the service waits until a key is pressed; otherwise the service returns the ASCII value of the keystroke in AL and the scan code value in AH.

Several keys or key combinations on a standard IBM PC keyboard do not have a corresponding ASCII value. If these keys are pressed, this service returns a 0 (zero) in AL; the value in AH still represents the appropriate scan code value. (For a list of keyboard scan codes and ASCII values, see Appendix C.)

You cannot use this service to return a scan code for every possible keystroke on the keyboard. It does not return scan codes for some keys (such as the Shift, Ctrl, and Alt keys) that cause modification to the key(s) which follow. When these keys alone are pressed, no scan code is returned. However, key combinations such as Alt-T or Ctrl-A cause scan code/ASCII combinations to be returned.

Some keys (such as system request, PrtSc, and Ctrl-Alt-Del) also cause an interrupt to occur. This service does not trap and return these keys.

Through this service, any ASCII value from 0 to 255 can be derived by combining the Alt key with the numeric keypad. For example, holding the Alt key while pressing 153 on the keypad, and then releasing the Alt key, causes 0 to be returned in AH (scan code) and 153 to be returned in AL (ASCII value). Pressing, in this fashion, a keypad number larger than 255 causes the value returned in AL to be the modulo of that number divided by 256. For example, if you use the preceding Alt-key procedure but press 8529 on the keypad, a value of 81 (the modulo of 8529 divided by 256) will be returned in AL.

Read Keyboard Status
(Interrupt 16h, service 1)

Category: Keyboard services

Registers on Entry:

AH: 1

Registers on Return:

AH: Keyboard scan code
AL: ASCII value of keypress

Memory Affected: None

Syntax:

```
          MOV    AH,1              ;Specify service 1
          INT    16h               ;BIOS keyboard interrupt
          JZ     NO_KEY            ;No key available
          MOV    SCAN_CODE,AH      ;Store scan code
          MOV    ASCII_KEY,AL      ;Store ASCII value
NO_KEY:
```

Description: This service, which is similar to service 16/0, examines the keyboard buffer to determine whether a keystroke is available. If a key is available, the zero flag is cleared, the ASCII value of the keystroke is returned in AL, and the scan code value is returned in AH. If no keystroke is waiting, the zero flag is set on return; the contents of AH and AL are not significant.

Several keys or key combinations on a standard IBM PC keyboard do not have a corresponding ASCII value. If these keys are pressed, this service returns a 0 (zero) in AL; the value in AH still represents the appropriate scan code value. (For a list of keyboard scan codes and ASCII values, see Appendix C.)

You cannot use this service to return a scan code for every possible keystroke on the keyboard. It does not return scan codes for some keys (such as the Shift, Ctrl, and Alt keys) that cause modification to the key(s) which follow. When these keys alone are pressed, no scan code is returned. However, key combinations such as Alt-T or Ctrl-A cause scan code/ASCII combinations to be returned.

Some keys (such as system request, PrtSc, and Ctrl-Alt-Del) also cause an interrupt to occur. This service does not trap and return these keys.

Through this service, any ASCII value from 0 to 255 can be derived by combining the Alt key with the numeric keypad. For example, holding the Alt key while pressing 153 on the keypad, and then releasing the Alt key, causes 0 to be returned in AH (scan code) and 153 to be returned in AL (ASCII value). Pressing, in this fashion, a keypad number larger than 255 causes the value returned in AL to be the modulo of that number divided by 256. For example, if you use the preceding Alt-key procedure but press 8529 on the keypad, a value of 81 (the modulo of 8529 divided by 256) will be returned in AL. The value is not placed into the keyboard buffer until you release the Alt key.

Read Keyboard Shift Status (Interrupt 16h, service 2)

Category: Keyboard services

Registers on Entry:

   AH: 2

Registers on Return:

   AL: Shift status

Memory Affected: None

Syntax:

```
MOV   AH,2        ;Specify service 2
INT   16h         ;BIOS keyboard interrupt
```

Description: This service returns (in AL) the keyboard's current shift status. Each bit of the returned value represents the state of a specific keyboard shift key (see table 12.22).

Table 12.22
Keyboard Shift Status Values Returned by Service 16/2

Bits 76543210	Hex	Decimal	Meaning of Bits
1	80	128	Insert on
1	40	64	Caps Lock on
1	20	32	Num Lock on
1	10	16	Scroll Lock on
1	8	8	Alt key down
1	4	4	Ctrl key down
1	2	2	Left Shift key down
1	1	1	Right Shift key down

Your programs can use this function to check for exotic key combinations that serve as a signal to perform a certain task. For instance, you may want to minimize the possibility of accidentally exiting your program. Instead of using the Esc key (which is easy to press accidentally) to exit the program, you can set up your program so that the user can exit only by pressing the Ctrl-Alt-Left Shift key combination. It is unlikely that this combination will be entered by accident.

The BIOS controls the setting of this status byte through the keyboard interrupt. Whenever someone presses the Ins, Shift, Ctrl, Alt, Num Lock, or Scroll Lock key, BIOS changes the appropriate bits in the keyboard status byte and resumes waiting for another key to be pressed.

Print Character (Interrupt 17h, service 0)

Category: Printer services

Registers on Entry:

AH: 0
AL: Character to print
DX: Printer to be used

Registers on Return:

AH: Printer status

Memory Affected: None

Syntax:

```
MOV    AL,'*'         ;Print an asterisk
MOV    DX,Ø           ;Use first printer
MOV    AH,Ø           ;Specify service Ø
INT    17h            ;BIOS printer interrupt
```

Description: This service outputs a character to a printer port. The character to be printed is loaded in AL; the printer to use is designated in DX. A printer designation of 0 to 2 is valid (0 corresponds to LPT1:, 1 to LPT2:, and 2 to LPT3:).

The value that this service returns in AH is the printer status byte. (Services 17/1 and 17/2 also return the printer status byte in AH.) Table 12.23 lists the meaning of the bits in this returned byte.

Table 12.23
Meaning of Bits Returned in AH for Services 17/0, 17/1, and 17/2

Bits 76543210	Meaning of Bits
1	Printer not busy
0	Printer busy
1	Printer acknowledgment
1	Out of paper
1	Printer selected
1	I/O error
??	Unused
1	Time-out

Initialize Printer (Interrupt 17h, service 1)

Category: Printer services

Registers on Entry:

AH: 1
DX: Printer to be used

Registers on Return:

AH: Printer status

Memory Affected: None

Syntax:

```
MOV    DX,∅        ;Use first printer
MOV    AH,1        ;Specify service 1
INT    17h         ;BIOS printer interrupt
```

Description: The outputs from this service initialize the IBM- or EPSON®-compatible printer connected to the port specified in DX. A printer designation of 0 to 2 is valid (0 corresponds to LPT1:, 1 to LPT2:, and 2 to LPT3:).

Two values (08h and 0Ch) are output to initialize the printer. The printer interprets these values as a command to perform a reset. Note that this series works only on IBM- and EPSON-compatible printers. Other printers may not understand this series and may produce unwanted results.

The value that this service returns in AH is the printer status byte. (Refer to table 12.23 for the meaning of the bits in this returned byte.)

Get Printer Status (Interrupt 17h, service 2)

Category: Printer services

Registers on Entry:

AH: 2
DX: Printer to be used

Registers on Return:

AH: Printer status

Memory Affected: None

Syntax:

```
MOV    DX,∅        ;Use first printer
MOV    AH,2        ;Specify service 2
INT    17h         ;BIOS printer interrupt
```

Description: This service retrieves the status of the printer specified in DX. A printer designation of 0 to 2 is valid (0 corresponds to LPT1:, 1 to LPT2:, and 2 to LPT3:).

The value that this service returns in AH is the printer status byte. (Refer to table 12.23 for the meaning of the bits in this returned byte.)

Warm Boot (Interrupt 19h)

Category: System services

Registers on Entry: Not significant

Registers on Return: Not applicable (no return)

Memory Affected: Contents of memory after invocation will reflect normal memory conditions after a warm-booting procedure. The contents of any given free memory area are unpredictable.

Syntax:

```
INT     19h             ;BIOS warm boot
```

Description: This interrupt, which performs a warm reboot of the computer system, is functionally the same as pressing Ctrl-Alt-Del or turning off the computer and then turning it back on.

There are differences between this method and the other methods of starting the computer system, however. This interrupt does not go through the power-on self test (POST) procedures, nor does it reset the equipment status word in memory (refer to Interrupt 11h).

Get Clock Counter (Interrupt 1Ah, service 0)

Category: Date/time services

Registers on Entry:

AH: 0

Registers on Return:

AL: Midnight flag
CX: Clock count high-order word
DX: Clock count low-order word

Memory Affected: None

Syntax:

```
MOV     AH,Ø            ;Specify service Ø
INT     1Ah             ;BIOS date/time interrupt
```

Description: This service retrieves the current value of the system software clock counter. This value is a double word register that is incremented approximately 18.2065 times per second, starting from 0 (midnight). Midnight is assumed when the value of the counter reaches 1800B0h or when the counter has been incremented 1,573,040 times. Dividing this counter value by 18.2065 indicates that this clock count represents 86,399.9121 seconds (a fairly accurate representation of a full day, because there are 86,400 seconds in a 24-hour period).

AL is set to 1 if midnight has been passed since the last read of the clock. If midnight has not been passed, AL is set to 0 (zero). Invoking this service always causes the midnight flag to be reset to 0.

Set Clock Counter (Interrupt 1Ah, service 1)

Category: Date/time services

Registers on Entry:

AH: 1
CX: Clock count high-order word
DX: Clock count low-order word

Registers on Return: Unchanged

Memory Affected: None

Syntax:

```
MOV     CX,HIGH_COUNT               ;Clock high-order word
MOV     DX,LOW_COUNT                ;Clock low-order word
MOV     AH,1                        ;Specify service 1
INT     1Ah                         ;BIOS date/time interrupt
```

Description: This service sets the current value of the system software clock counter. This value is a double word register that is incremented approximately .2065 times per second, starting from 0 (midnight).

To determine the proper settings for any given time of the day, simply determine the number of seconds since midnight and then multiply this number by 18.2065. For instance, the clock value for 14:22:17.39 (military time) would be determined as follows:

14 hours =	14 * 60 * 60	= 50400	seconds
22 minutes =	22 * 60	= 1320	seconds
17.39 seconds =	17.39	= 17.39	seconds
Total:		51737.39	seconds
Clock ticks per second =		18.2065	ticks
Ticks represented:		941956.7910	ticks

Because fractional ticks cannot be represented, the number of ticks is rounded to 941,957 (0E5F85h). CX is loaded with 0Eh; DX, with 5F85h.

Be careful. Because this service performs no range checks on the values you specify in CX and DX, you can inadvertently specify an invalid time without any indication from BIOS that you have done so. (An invalid time is any value greater than 1800B0h, the number of ticks in a full 24-hour period.)

Read Real-Time Clock
(Interrupt 1Ah, service 2)

Category: Date/time services

Registers on Entry:

AH: 2

Registers on Return:

CH: Hours (BCD)
CL: Minutes (BCD)
DH: Seconds (BCD)

Memory Affected: None

Syntax:

```
MOV     AH,2            ;Specify service 2
INT     1Ah             ;BIOS date/time interrupt
MOV     HOUR,CH         ;Save current hour
MOV     MINUTE,CL       ;Save current minute
MOV     SECOND,DH       ;Save current second
```

Description: This service, *which is available only on the Personal Computer AT*, retrieves the value of the real-time clock. Remember that the values returned in CH, CL, and DH are in *binary coded decimal* (BCD) and that you must make allowances for subsequent calculations that use these return values.

If the clock is not functioning, the carry flag is set on return; otherwise, the carry flag is clear.

Set Real-Time Clock
(Interrupt 1Ah, service 3)

Category: Date/time services

Registers on Entry:

AH: 3
CH: Hours (BCD)
CL: Minutes (BCD)
DH: Seconds (BCD)
DL: Daylight saving time

Registers on Return: Unchanged

Memory Affected: None

Syntax:

```
MOV     CH,HOUR              ;Get current hour
MOV     CL,MINUTE            ;Get current minute
MOV     DH,SECOND            ;Get current second
MOV     DL,Ø                 ;Normal time
MOV     AH,3                 ;Specify service 3
INT     1Ah                  ;BIOS date/time interrupt
```

Description: This service, *which is available only on the Personal Computer AT*, sets the real-time clock. Remember that the values specified in CH, CL, and DH should be in *binary coded decimal* (BCD).

DL should be set to indicate whether the time being set is daylight saving time. If DL is 0 (zero), standard time is indicated; if DL is 1, daylight saving time is indicated.

Read Date from Real-Time Clock
(Interrupt 1Ah, service 4)

Category: Date/time services

Registers on Entry:

AH: 4

Registers on Return:

CH: Century (BCD)
CL: Year (BCD)
DH: Month (BCD)
DL: Day (BCD)

Memory Affected: None

Syntax:

```
MOV     AH,4        ;Specify service 4
INT     1Ah         ;BIOS date/time interrupt
```

Description: This service, *which is available only on the Personal Computer AT*, retrieves the date from the real-time clock. Remember that all values returned are in *binary coded decimal* (BCD) and that you must make allowances for subsequent calculations which use these return values.

For instance, if the date is July 1, 1987, the value returned in CH is 19h, the value in CL is 87h, the value in DH is 07h, and the value in DL is 01h.

If the clock is not functioning, the carry flag is set on return; otherwise, the carry flag is clear.

Set Date of Real-Time Clock (Interrupt 1Ah, service 5)

Category: Date/time services

Registers on Entry:

AH: 5
CH: Century (BCD, 19 or 20)
CL: Year (BCD)
DH: Month (BCD)
DL: Day (BCD)

Registers on Return: Unchanged

Memory Affected: None

Syntax:

```
MOV     CX,1986h    ;Year in BCD
MOV     DH,12h      ;December (BCD)
MOV     DL,25h      ;Day in BCD
MOV     AH,5        ;Specify service 5
INT     1Ah         ;BIOS date/time interrupt
```

Description: This service, *which is available only on the Personal Computer AT*, sets the date of the real-time clock. Remember that all values used by this service should be in *binary coded decimal* (BCD).

Because no range checking is performed on the registers for this service, all range checking should be performed by the user program.

Set Alarm (Interrupt 1Ah, service 6)

Category: Date/time services

Registers on Entry:

AH: 6
CH: Hours (BCD)
CL: Minutes (BCD)
DH: Seconds (BCD)

Registers on Return: Unchanged

Memory Affected: None

Syntax:

```
MOV     CH,Ø1h          ;1 hour
MOV     CL,3Øh          ;3Ø minutes (BCD)
MOV     DH,Ø            ;Ø seconds
MOV     AH,6            ;Specify service 6
INT     1Ah             ;BIOS date/time interrupt
```

Description: This service, *which is available only on the Personal Computer AT*, sets the BIOS alarm function. Remember that all values used by this service are expected to be in *binary coded decimal* (BCD). The time specified in the registers (CH, CL, DH) is the elapsed time before the alarm will occur. In the preceding syntax example, the alarm will occur 1 hour, 30 minutes, 0 seconds from the time the service is invoked.

The BIOS alarm function simply generates an interrupt signal after the appropriate period of time has elapsed. The address of the routine that you want to perform should be vectored to interrupt 4Ah.

Because no range checking is performed on the registers for this service, all range checking should be performed by the user program.

If the clock is not functioning or if the alarm is already enabled, the carry flag is set on return; otherwise, the carry flag is clear. To reset the alarm to another time, you must first disable the alarm by invoking service 1A/7; then reset the alarm.

Disable Alarm (Interrupt 1Ah, service 7)

Category: Date/time services

Registers on Entry:

AH: 7

Registers on Return: Unchanged

Memory Affected: None

Syntax:

```
MOV     AH,7            ;Specify service 7
INT     1Ah             ;BIOS date/time interrupt
```

Description: This service, *which is available only on the Personal Computer AT*, disables an alarm interrupt enabled through service 1A/6. This service must be called before the alarm can be reset.

13

Accessing DOS Services

DOS is an acronym for Disk Operating System. In this book, DOS is also short for MS-DOS (distributed by Microsoft) or PC DOS (distributed by IBM). Because both operating systems are effectively the same, with the same assembly language function calls available through both, this book refers to either dialect as DOS.

DOS, like BIOS, contains a series of functions that are accessible to outside programs. You invoke these functions (callable subroutines) through the use of software *interrupts*, which are generated through the INT assembly language instruction. INT causes the microprocessor to use an address from an interrupt table in low memory as the address for this special type of subroutine.

Specifically, INT pushes the flags register on the stack and then resets the interrupt and trap flags. The full return address (CS:IP) is placed on the stack, at which point the desired interrupt vector (address) is retrieved from the interrupt table and placed in CS:IP. Execution of the interrupt then continues until an IRET instruction is encountered. At this point, the return address is popped from the stack and placed in CS:IP. The flags register is then restored from the stack, and program execution continues from the point at which the interrupt was invoked.

Notice that the interrupt address is fetched from the interrupt table based on the number of the interrupt being invoked. The full syntax for calling an interrupt is

    INT XX

where XX is replaced by the number of the appropriate interrupt.

The preceding chapter detailed many BIOS functions that are callable through various interrupts. This chapter provides the same kind of information for DOS services.

The DOS Service Categories

The interrupts and services offered by DOS can be divided into several broad categories, which generally are specified by the task classification of the function. The DOS function categories include

- I/O services

- Printer services

- Disk services

- System services

- Network services

- Date/time services

Some of these categories may look familiar to readers who have referred to Chapter 12. Although the categories are similar to the BIOS services, their operations may vary considerably. The largest single category of DOS services is, understandably, the disk services; after all, these services are Disk Operating System services.

The number of DOS services available depends necessarily on the version of DOS you are using. The services explained in this chapter work with DOS Version 3.3. Earlier versions of DOS may not include all the functions detailed. If you have questions, consult your DOS technical manual.

The DOS Services

The rest of this chapter forms a convenient reference section. Each DOS service is described in detail in an organized manner. The following information is provided for each service:

- *Service name.* This name is based on the DOS function names selected by IBM or Microsoft and listed in various technical documentation. Where appropriate, the name has been modified or expanded to reflect more accurately the purpose of the service.

- *Service category.* The general classification of the service, as previously listed

- *Registers on entry.* DOS service parameters generally are passed through registers. The expected register settings are given here.

- *Registers on return.* For proper operation of software, you must know how registers are affected by interrupts. Frequently, DOS functions return values through registers. Such information is detailed here.

- *Memory areas affected.* Some DOS functions modify memory based on the desired service. Any affected memory is given.

- *Syntax for calling.* A coding section showing the proper method for calling the interrupt is shown.

- *Description.* The purpose, benefits, and special considerations of the service are given in this section.

The services are arranged in ascending numerical order. Each service can be identified by the primary interrupt number and an individual service number. The service number is specified by the contents of the AH register. In this notation scheme, any DOS service can be denoted by a hexadecimal number pair, *II/SS*, where *II* is the interrupt number and *SS* is the service number. For instance, the service used to remove a subdirectory, service 21/3A, has an interrupt number of 21h, and a service number (specified through register AH) of 3Ah.

Other services may be specified as *II/SS/FF*, where the appended *FF* indicates the function number. For instance, the service used to read from a block device, service 21/44/4, has an interrupt number of 21h, a service number (specified through register AH) of 44h, and a function number (specified through register AL) of 4.

Terminate Program (Interrupt 20h)

Category: System services

Registers on Entry: Not significant

Registers on Return: Unspecified (does not return)

Memory Affected: None

Syntax:

```
INT     2Øh     ;Terminate program
```

Description: You can use this interrupt to terminate a program and return control to DOS. Internally, DOS restores several critical vector addresses (Ctrl-C and critical error handlers), flushes the file buffers, and transfers control to the termination handler address. This interrupt is equivalent to service 21/0.

This service does not allow you to pass a return code to DOS or to a parent program. For that capability, see services 21/31 and 21/4C.

Terminate Program (Interrupt 21h, service 0)

Category: System services

Registers on Entry:

AH: 0
CS: Segment address of program's PSP

Registers on Return: Unspecified (does not return)

Memory Affected: None

Syntax:

```
MOV     AH,Ø        ;Want service Ø
INT     21h         ;DOS services interrupt
```

Description: You can use this service to terminate a program and return control to DOS. Internally, DOS restores several critical vector addresses (Ctrl-C and critical error handlers), flushes the file buffers, and transfers control to the termination handler address. This service is equivalent to issuing an INT 20h.

AH is the only functional register that you need to load before calling this service. Because CS, in all likelihood, will not have changed since the program began, CS should already be set to the proper value.

This service does not allow you to pass a return code to DOS or to a parent program. For that capability, see services 21/31 and 21/4C.

Character Input with Echo (Interrupt 21h, service 1)

Category: I/O services

Registers on Entry:

AH: 1

Registers on Return:

AL: Character

Memory Affected: The appropriate areas of video memory are altered to reflect the displayed (echoed) character.

Syntax:

```
MOV     AH,1        ;Want service 1
INT     21h         ;DOS services interrupt
```

Description: Originally, this service was designed to fetch a character from the keyboard and display that character on the video monitor. Intermediate versions of DOS, however, have modified this service so that I/O redirection is possible. If the standard input device or console has been redirected, this service fetches a character from the specified device. Regardless of the device, the character is echoed to the video monitor.

Even though this service waits for a character to be returned by the keyboard (or redirected I/O device), the service differs significantly from the BIOS keyboard routines in that only one character code is returned in AL. If an extended ASCII code is generated by the keyboard (such as codes generated by the function keys or cursor-control keys), interrupt 21h, service 1 returns a zero in AL. If you invoke the service again, it returns the scan code in AL.

Output Character (Interrupt 21h, service 2)

Category: I/O services

Registers on Entry:

AH: 2
DL: Character (ASCII value)

Registers on Return: Unchanged

Memory Affected: If I/O has not been redirected, the appropriate areas of video memory are altered to reflect the displayed character.

Syntax:

```
MOV    DL,'*'      ;Output an asterisk
MOV    AH,2        ;Want service 2
INT    21h         ;DOS services interrupt
```

Description: Originally, this service was designed to output a character to the video monitor. Intermediate versions of DOS, however, have modified this service so that I/O redirection is possible. If the standard output device has been redirected, this service sends a character to the specified device.

Auxiliary Input (Interrupt 21h, service 3)

Category: I/O services

Registers on Entry:

AH: 3

Registers on Return:

   AL: Character

Memory Affected: None

Syntax:

```
MOV    AH,3          ;Want service 3
INT    21h           ;DOS services interrupt
```

Description: This service returns a character from the standard auxiliary device, which, if not redirected, is set to be COM1:.

This service is a poor way to read the communications port. More precise and error-free communication is possible through the BIOS communications functions (services 14/0—14/2) or, better yet, through a custom interrupt-driven communications interface. This interface, however, is beyond the scope of this book.

Auxiliary Output (Interrupt 21h, service 4)

Category: I/O services

Registers on Entry:

   AH: 4
   DL: Character (ASCII value)

Registers on Return: Unchanged

Memory Affected: None

Syntax:

```
MOV    DL,'_'        ;Output an underscore
MOV    AH,4          ;Want service 4
INT    21h           ;DOS services interrupt
```

Description: This service sends a character to the standard auxiliary device, which, if not redirected, is set to COM1:.

This service is a poor way to control the communications port. More precise and error-free communication is possible through the BIOS communications functions (services 14/0—14/2), or better yet through a custom interrupt-driven communications interface. This interface, however, is beyond the scope of this book.

Printer Output (Interrupt 21h, service 5)

Category: Printer services

Registers on Entry:

AH: 5
DL: Character (ASCII value)

Registers on Return: Unchanged

Memory Affected: None

Syntax:

```
MOV    DL,'_'              ;Print an underscore
MOV    AH,5                ;Want service 5
INT    21h                 ;DOS services interrupt
```

Description: This service sends a character to the standard list device. Unless redirected, this device is LPT1:.

Direct Console I/O (Interrupt 21h, service 6)

Category: I/O services

Registers on Entry:

AH: 6
DL: Character (ASCII value) or input flag

Registers on Return:

AL: Input character

Memory Affected: If the service is outputting a character to the video monitor, the appropriate video memory areas are changed to reflect the character being displayed.

Syntax:

```
INP_LOOP:      MOV    DL,ØFFh              ;Want to input
               MOV    AH,6                 ;Want service 6
               INT    21h                  ;DOS services interrupt
               JZ     NO_CHAR              ;No character ready
               CMP    AL,Ø                 ;Was it extended ASCII?
               JNE    GOT_CHAR             ;No, treat as character
               MOV    EXTEND_FLAG,1        ;Yes, so set appropriately
               JMP    INP_LOOP             ;Get scan code
GOT_CHAR:      MOV    CHAR,AL              ;Store character
```

Description: You can use this service for character input or output, depending on the contents of DL. If DL is a value between 0 and 254 (0FEh), the contents of DL are sent to the console (unless redirected, the video screen). If DL contains 255 (0FFh), input is fetched from the console (unless redirected, the keyboard).

When you request input through this service, the zero flag is set on return to indicate the presence of a character. Zero in AL means that a key generating an extended ASCII code has been pressed and this service should be invoked again to retrieve the scan code.

Direct Character Input without Echo (Interrupt 21h, service 7)

Category: I/O services

Registers on Entry:

AH: 7

Registers on Return:

AL: Character

Memory Affected: None

Syntax:

```
MOV    AH,7          ;Want service 7
INT    21h           ;DOS services interrupt
```

Description: Originally, this service was designed simply to fetch a character from the keyboard. Intermediate versions of DOS, however, have modified this service so that I/O redirection is possible. If the standard input device or console has been redirected, this service fetches a character from the specified device.

Even though this service waits for a character to be returned by the keyboard (or redirected I/O device), the service differs significantly from the BIOS keyboard routines in that only one character code is returned in AL. If the keyboard generates an extended ASCII code (such as codes generated by the function keys or cursor-control keys), this service returns a 0 in AL. A second invocation returns the scan code in AL.

Character Input without Echo
(Interrupt 21h, service 8)

Category: I/O services

Registers on Entry:

AH: 8

Registers on Return:

AL: Character

Memory Affected: None

Syntax:

```
MOV    AH,8         ;Want service 8
INT    21h          ;DOS services interrupt
```

Description: Originally, this service was designed simply to fetch a character from the keyboard. Intermediate versions of DOS, however, have modified this service so that I/O redirection is possible. If the standard input device or console has been redirected, this service fetches a character from the specified device.

Even though this service waits for a character to be returned by the keyboard (or redirected I/O device), the service differs significantly from the BIOS keyboard routines in that only one character code is returned in AL. If the keyboard generates an extended ASCII code (such as codes generated by the function keys or cursor-control keys), this service returns a 0 in AL. A second invocation returns the scan code in AL.

This service differs from 21/7 in that it performs some interpretation on the characters received. For instance, if Ctrl-C and Ctrl-Break are received, they are translated and acted on by this service.

Output Character String
(Interrupt 21h, service 9)

Category: I/O services

Registers on Entry:

AH: 9
DX: Offset address of string
DS: Segment address of string

Registers on Return: Unchanged

Memory Affected: If output is directed to the video display, the contents of the video memory buffers are changed appropriately to reflect the characters displayed.

Syntax:

```
PUSH    CS                          ;Code segment and
POP     DS                          ;   data segment are same
MOV     DX,OFFSET MSG_1             ;Offset address of string
MOV     AH,9                        ;Want service 9
INT     21h                         ;DOS services interrupt
```

Description: This service displays (or outputs) a string on the standard output device. If I/O has been redirected, the string is sent to the specified device.

Each character of the string at DS:DX—up to (but not including) the first occurrence of a dollar sign (ASCII 36)—is displayed by this service. Because of this strange convention (a carryover from CP/M), you cannot display the dollar sign when you are using this service.

Buffered Input (Interrupt 21h, service 0Ah)

Category: I/O services

Registers on Entry:

AH: 0Ah
DX: Offset address of buffer
DS: Segment address of buffer

Registers on Return: Unchanged

Memory Affected: The memory area beginning at DS:DX is overlaid with characters input from the standard input device.

Syntax:

```
PUSH    CS                          ;Code segment and
POP     DS                          ;   data segment are same
MOV     DX,OFFSET BUFFER            ;Offset address of buffer
MOV     AH,ØAh                      ;Want service ØAh
INT     21h                         ;DOS services interrupt
```

Description: This service allows the input of a specified number of characters from the standard input device. You can change the device (which, originally, is the keyboard) through I/O redirection.

The input characters are stored at the buffer specified by DS:DX. The value of the first byte of this buffer must indicate the maximum number of characters the buffer can contain. DOS sets the value of the second byte to indicate the number of characters this service returns. Therefore, if your maximum input length is 80 characters, you should set aside 82 bytes for the buffer.

This service does not return until you press the Enter key. If the buffer is filled before the service detects the carriage return, the extra characters are ignored and the bell sounds with each extra keypress. Remember that each extended ASCII character (function keys, etc.) occupies two bytes in the buffer area.

Check for Character Waiting (Interrupt 21h, service 0Bh)

Category: I/O services

Registers on Entry:

AH: 0Bh

Registers on Return:

AL: Waiting flag

Memory Affected: None

Syntax:

```
KEY_LOOP:       MOV     AH,ØBh          ;Want service ØBh
                INT     21h             ;DOS services interrupt
                CMP     AL,Ø            ;Was there a keypress?
                JE      KEY_LOOP        ;No, continue to wait
```

Description: This service simply checks the status of the standard input device (usually the keyboard) to determine whether a character is available for input. If a character is available, AL equals FFh. If no character is available, AL equals 0.

Clear Buffer and Get Input
(Interrupt 21h, service 0Ch)

Category: I/O services

Registers on Entry:

AH: 0Ch
AL: Desired input service
DX: Offset address of buffer
DS: Segment address of buffer

Registers on Return:

AL: Character (ASCII value)

Memory Affected: If AL is loaded with 0Ah, the memory area beginning at DS:DX is overlaid with characters input from the standard input device. Otherwise, memory is not affected.

Syntax:

```
PUSH    CS                      ;Code segment and
POP     DS                      ;   data segment are same
MOV     DX,OFFSET BUFFER        ;Offset address of buffer
MOV     AL,ØAh                  ;Want input service ØAh
MOV     AH,ØCh                  ;Want service ØCh
INT     21h                     ;DOS services interrupt
```

Description: This compound service forms a gateway to input services 21/1, 21/6, 21/7, 21/8, and 21/A. You invoke any of these input services by loading the desired service number (1, 6, 7, 8, Ah) into AL. After the type-ahead buffer is cleared, the specified service is invoked.

If AL is set to 0Ah, DS:DX must point to a buffer that is constructed in the fashion described under service 21/A. If AL is set to one of the other services, the contents of DS:DX are not significant.

If AL is set to 1, 6, 7, or 8, on return AL contains the ASCII value of the character fetched. The other characteristics of these DOS services are maintained. Please refer to the appropriate service descriptions for further information.

Reset Disk (Interrupt 21h, service 0Dh)

Category: Disk services

Registers on Entry:

   AH: 0Dh

Registers on Return: Unchanged

Memory Affected: None

Syntax:

```
MOV    AH,ØDh          ;Want service ØDh
INT    21h             ;DOS services interrupt
```

Description: This service flushes the DOS disk buffers. If a DOS file buffer contains information to be written to a disk file, that information is written to disk. The service does not close the files.

This service does not change the default drive and has no physical effect on the disk drives or their controllers.

Set Default Drive (Interrupt 21h, service 0Eh)

Category: Disk services

Registers on Entry:

   AH: 0Eh
   DL: Drive wanted

Registers on Return:

   AL: Logical drives

Memory Affected: None

Syntax:

```
MOV    DL,2            ;Set for drive C:
MOV    AH,ØEh          ;Want service ØEh
INT    21h             ;DOS services interrupt
```

Description: This service has two purposes: (1) to set the default drive designation by specifying the desired drive in DL, where 0=A, 1=B, 2=C, etc.; and (2) to find out how many logical disk drives are connected to the computer.

Logical disk drives include RAM disks, disk emulators, and multisegmented hard disk drives. For instance, if you have two floppy drives (A: and B:), a 40M hard disk that is partitioned to two disks (C: and D:), and a RAM disk (E:), this service returns a value of 5 in AL even though only three physical drives are connected to the computer.

Clearly, knowing how many logical drives are connected to a computer without actually changing the default disk drive may be beneficial. You can get this information by determining the current default drive (through service 21/19) and then using that information to call this service. The following code segment performs this task:

```
MOV     AH,19h                  ;Want service 19h
INT     21h                     ;DOS services interrupt
MOV     CUR_DRIVE,AL            ;Store current drive (Ø-?)
MOV     DL,AL                   ;Set for default drive
MOV     AH,ØEh                  ;Want service ØEh
INT     21h                     ;DOS services interrupt
MOV     NUM_DRIVES,AL          ;Store number of drives
```

For more information about service 21/19, refer to the description for that service.

Open File, Using FCB
(Interrupt 21h, service 0Fh)

Category: Disk services

Registers on Entry:

AH: 0Fh
DX: Offset address of FCB
DS: Segment address of FCB

Registers on Return:

AL: Status byte

Memory Affected: If the service opens the file successfully, DOS fills in the FCB area specified by DS:DX to reflect the status of the file opened.

Syntax:

```
PUSH   CS                      ;Code segment and
POP    DS                      ;  data segment are same
MOV    DX,OFFSET FCB_1         ;Offset address of FCB
MOV    AH,ØFh                  ;Want service ØFh
INT    21h                     ;DOS services interrupt
```

Description: This service opens a disk file, based on a *file control block*, or FCB. The FCB is a block of information that is set initially by the programmer and then completed by DOS. The FCB consists of 44 bytes constructed in the following manner:

```
FCB_PRE        DB     ØFFh                   ;Extension flag
               DB     5 DUP(Ø)               ;Unused
               DB     ØØ                     ;File attribute
FCB_1          DB     ØØ                     ;Set for default drive
FILE_ROOT      DB     'FILENAME'             ;File name root
FILE_EXT       DB     'EXT'                  ;File name extension
BLOCK_NUM      DW     ØØØØ                   ;Current block number
REC_SIZE       DW     ØØØØ                   ;Record size
FILE_SIZE      DD     ØØØØØØØØ               ;File size
FILE_DATE      DW     ØØØØ                   ;File date
FILE_TIME      DW     ØØØØ                   ;File time
               DB     8 DUP(Ø)               ;DOS work area
REC_NUM        DB     ØØ                     ;Current record number
RANDOM_REC     DD     ØØØØØØØØ               ;Random record number
```

The offset address of FCB_1 is the address you specify in DS:DX when you invoke this service. If you are using an extended FCB, use the offset address of FCB_PRE. To call this service, the values for FCB_1 (the drive designator), FILE_ROOT, and FILE_EXT must be specified. Notice that the drive designator is different from the normal method for DOS and BIOS drive designation: 0 equals the default drive, and 1=A, 2=B, 3=C, etc.

If the open operation is successful, DOS returns a 0 in AL and sets FCB_1 to reflect the drive number (1=A, 2=B, 3=C, etc.). DOS also sets BLOCK_NUM to 0; REC_SIZE to 80h; and FILE_SIZE, FILE_DATE, and FILE_TIME to the equivalent of the directory entry for the file. If the open operation is unsuccessful, DOS returns FFh in AL, and the FCB is not filled in.

Notice that this service allows you to use only FCBs. Because FCB file encoding does not allow for path names, any file operations must be performed in the current disk subdirectory. With floppy disks, this limitation may not be a problem. With fixed disks, however, the limitation can be serious. Refer to service 21/3D for a file-opening method that does not have this limitation.

Close File, Using FCB
(Interrupt 21h, service 10h)

Category: Disk services

Registers on Entry:

AH: 10h
DX: Offset address of FCB
DS: Segment address of FCB

Registers on Return:

AL: Status byte

Memory Affected: None

Syntax:

```
PUSH    CS                      ;Code segment and
POP     DS                      ;  data segment are same
MOV     DX,OFFSET FCB_1         ;Offset address of FCB
MOV     AH,10h                  ;Want service 10h
INT     21h                     ;DOS services interrupt
```

Description: This service closes a disk file, based on a file control block, or
FCB. The FCB consists of 44 bytes constructed in the following manner:

```
FCB_PRE         DB      0FFh                ;Extension flag
                DB      5 DUP(0)            ;Unused
                DB      00                  ;File attribute
FCB_1           DB      00                  ;Set for default drive
FILE_ROOT       DB      'FILENAME'          ;File name root
FILE_EXT        DB      'EXT'               ;File name extension
BLOCK_NUM       DW      0000                ;Current block number
REC_SIZE        DW      0000                ;Record size
FILE_SIZE       DD      00000000            ;File size
FILE_DATE       DW      0000                ;File date
FILE_TIME       DW      0000                ;File time
                DB      8 DUP(0)            ;DOS work area
REC_NUM         DB      00                  ;Current record number
RANDOM_REC      DD      00000000            ;Random record number
```

The offset address of FCB_1 is the address you specify in DS:DX when you
invoke this service. If you are using an extended FCB, use the offset address of
FCB_PRE. To call this service, you must specify the values for FCB_1 (the drive

designator), FILE_ROOT, and FILE_EXT. Notice that the drive designator is different from the normal method for DOS and BIOS drive designation. In this instance, 0 equals the default drive, and 1=A, 2=B, 3=C, etc.

If the close operation is successful, DOS returns a 0 in AL; if the operation is unsuccessful, AL contains FFh.

Notice that this service allows you to use only FCBs. Because FCB file encoding does not allow for path names, any file operations must be performed in the current disk subdirectory. With floppy disks, this limitation may not be a problem. With fixed disks, however, the limitation can be serious. (Service 21/ 3E, another method of closing files, does not have this limitation.)

Search for First File Name Match, Using FCB (Interrupt 21h, service 11h)

Category: Disk services

Registers on Entry:

AH: 11h
DX: Offset address of FCB
DS: Segment address of FCB

Registers on Return:

AL: Status byte

Memory Affected: If a file name match is located, DOS fills in the memory area specified as the disk transfer area (DTA) so that it reflects a completed FCB for the file. DOS alters the original FCB area to allow subsequent searching with service 21/12.

Syntax:

```
PUSH   CS                    ;Code segment and
POP    DS                    ;   data segment are same
MOV    DX,OFFSET FCB_1       ;Offset address of FCB
MOV    AH,11h                ;Want service 11h
INT    21h                   ;DOS services interrupt
```

Description: This service locates a file with a specified name in the current directory of a disk drive, based on a file control block, or FCB. The FCB consists of 44 bytes constructed in the following manner:

```
FCB_PRE        DB      ØFFh                    ;Extension flag
               DB      5 DUP(Ø)                ;Unused
FILE_ATTR      DB      ØØ                      ;File attribute
FCB_1          DB      ØØ                      ;Set for default drive
FILE_ROOT      DB      'FILENAME'              ;File name root
FILE_EXT       DB      '???'                   ;File name extension
BLOCK_NUM      DW      ØØØØ                    ;Current block number
REC_SIZE       DW      ØØØØ                    ;Record size
FILE_SIZE      DD      ØØØØØØØØ                ;File size
FILE_DATE      DW      ØØØØ                    ;File date
FILE_TIME      DW      ØØØØ                    ;File time
               DB      8 DUP(Ø)                ;DOS work area
REC_NUM        DB      ØØ                      ;Current record number
RANDOM_REC     DD      ØØØØØØØØ                ;Random record number
```

The offset address of FCB_1 is the address you specify in DS:DX when you invoke this service. If you are using an extended FCB, you should use the offset address of FCB_PRE. To call the service, you must specify the values for FCB_1 (the drive designator), FILE_ROOT, and FILE_EXT. Notice that the drive designator is different from the normal method for DOS and BIOS drive designation. In this instance, 0 equals the default drive, and 1=A, 2=B, 3=C, etc.

One useful feature of this service is that you can use the question mark (?) as a wildcard in the file name specification of the FCB. In the sample FCB, any file with the name FILENAME and any extension constitutes a match.

If you are searching for non-normal files (that is, hidden, system, etc.), you must use an extended FCB, which is the sample portion beginning with FCB_PRE. FCB_PRE is set to FFh, signaling that the FCB extension is active. You set the FILE_ATTR file attribute to specify the combination of file attributes you want to search for. Table 13.1 shows possible settings of this byte.

Table 13.1
Extended FCB Attribute Byte Settings for Service 21/11

Value	Types of Files Searched
0	Normal files
2	Normal and hidden files
4	Normal and system files
6	Normal, system, and hidden files
8	Volume labels only
16	Directory files

If the search is successful, DOS returns a 0 in AL and constructs a full FCB (either normal or extended) at the DTA location specified through service 21/1A. If the search is unsuccessful, AL contains FFh and the DTA remains undisturbed.

Notice that this service allows you to use only FCBs. Because FCB file encoding does not allow for path names, any file operations must be performed in the current disk subdirectory. With floppy disks, this limitation may not be a problem. With fixed disks, however, the limitation can be serious. Refer to service 21/4E, another method of searching for files, which does not have this limitation.

Search for Next File Name Match, Using FCB (Interrupt 21h, service 12h)

Category: Disk services

Registers on Entry:

AH: 12h
DX: Offset address of FCB
DS: Segment address of FCB

Registers on Return:

AL: Status byte

Memory Affected: If a file name match is located, DOS fills in the memory area specified as the DTA so that it reflects a completed FCB for the file. DOS alters the original FCB area to allow subsequent searching with service 21/12.

Syntax:

```
PUSH    CS                      ;Code segment and
POP     DS                      ;   data segment are same
MOV     DX,OFFSET FCB_1         ;Offset address of FCB
MOV     AH,12h                  ;Want service 12h
INT     21h                     ;DOS services interrupt
```

Description: Use this service to locate (in the current directory of a disk drive) a file with a specified name, based on a file control block, or FCB. Before you invoke this service, you must set the FCB by a call to service 21/11. If the FCB is not set, the results can be unpredictable. For more information, see the description for service 21/11.

Because any given directory must contain unique file names, this service is useless if the file specification for which you are searching does not contain the question-mark wildcard (?).

Delete File Using FCB
(Interrupt 21h, service 13h)

Category: Disk services

Registers on Entry:

AH: 13h
DX: Offset address of FCB
DS: Segment address of FCB

Registers on Return:

AL: Status byte

Memory Affected: None

Syntax:

```
PUSH    CS                      ;Code segment and
POP     DS                      ;   data segment are same
MOV     DX,OFFSET FCB_1         ;Offset address of FCB
MOV     AH,13h                  ;Want service 13h
INT     21h                     ;DOS services interrupt
```

Description: Use this service to delete files by means of a file control block, or FCB. The FCB consists of 44 bytes constructed in the following manner:

```
FCB_PRE       DB     ØFFh            ;Extension flag
              DB     5 DUP(Ø)        ;Unused
FILE_ATTR     DB     ØØ              ;File attribute
FCB_1         DB     ØØ              ;Set for default drive
FILE_ROOT     DB     'FILENAME'      ;File name root
FILE_EXT      DB     '???'           ;File name extension
BLOCK_NUM     DW     ØØØØ            ;Current block number
REC_SIZE      DW     ØØØØ            ;Record size
FILE_SIZE     DD     ØØØØØØØØ        ;File size
FILE_DATE     DW     ØØØØ            ;File date
FILE_TIME     DW     ØØØØ            ;File time
              DB     8 DUP(Ø)        ;DOS work area
REC_NUM       DB     ØØ              ;Current record number
RANDOM_REC    DD     ØØØØØØØØ        ;Random record number
```

When you invoke this service, specify the offset address of FCB_1 in DS:DX. If you are using an extended FCB, use the offset address of FCB_PRE. To call this service, you must specify the values for FCB_1 (the drive designator), FILE_ROOT, and FILE_EXT. Notice that the drive designator is different from the normal method for DOS and BIOS drive designation. In this instance, 0 equals the default drive, and 1=A, 2=B, 3=C, etc.

A useful feature of this service is that you can use the question mark (?) as a wildcard in the file name specification of the FCB. In the sample FCB, any file with the name FILENAME and any extension is deleted.

Notice that this service allows you to use only FCBs. Because FCB file encoding does not allow for path names, any files deleted must reside in the current disk subdirectory. With floppy disks, this limitation may not be a problem, but with fixed disks, the limitation can be serious. Refer to service 21/41, a method of deleting files that does not have this limitation.

Sequential Read Using FCB (Interrupt 21h, service 14h)

Category: Disk services

Registers on Entry:

AH: 14h
DX: Offset address of FCB
DS: Segment address of FCB

Registers on Return:

AL: Status byte

Memory Affected: The memory area designated as DTA is overwritten with information read from the disk.

Syntax:

```
PUSH    CS                      ;Code segment and
POP     DS                      ;  data segment are same
MOV     DX,OFFSET FCB_1         ;Offset address of FCB
MOV     AH,14h                  ;Want service 14h
INT     21h                     ;DOS services interrupt
```

Description: This service is used to read a block of information from a file that has been opened to the DTA. You designate the block size through the file control block, or FCB. The FCB consists of 44 bytes constructed in the following manner:

```
        FCB_PRE         DB      ØFFh                    ;Extension flag
                        DB      5 DUP(Ø)                ;Unused
        FILE_ATTR       DB      ØØ                      ;File attribute
        FCB_1           DB      ØØ                      ;Set for default drive
        FILE_ROOT       DB      'FILENAME'              ;File name root
        FILE_EXT        DB      'DAT'                   ;File name extension
        BLOCK_NUM       DW      ØØØØ                    ;Current block number
        REC_SIZE        DW      ØØØØ                    ;Record size
        FILE_SIZE       DD      ØØØØØØØØ                ;File size
        FILE_DATE       DW      ØØØØ                    ;File date
        FILE_TIME       DW      ØØØØ                    ;File time
                        DB      8 DUP(Ø)                ;DOS work area
        REC_NUM         DB      ØØ                      ;Current record number
        RANDOM_REC      DD      ØØØØØØØØ                ;Random record number
```

When you invoke this service, specify the offset address of FCB_1 in DS:DX. If you are using an extended FCB, use the offset address of FCB_PRE. Before you open the file, set the values for FCB_1 (the drive designator), FILE_ROOT, and FILE_EXT. Specify the size of the block to be read in the REC_SIZE field. The values in BLOCK_NUM and REC_NUM designate where in the file the read is to begin; these fields are incremented automatically after a successful read.

When the service is completed, the value of AL indicates the status of the operation. If AL is 0, the read was successful. If AL is 1, no data was read because the end of file was already reached. If AL is 2, the DTA crossed a *segment boundary* (a memory address ending in 000), which resulted in an error condition. If AL is 3, the end of file had already been reached when the read began and the service could not read the entire block (the partial block was read and placed in the DTA area).

Sequential Write Using FCB (Interrupt 21h, service 15h)

Category: Disk services

Registers on Entry:

AH: 15h
DX: Offset address of FCB
DS: Segment address of FCB

Registers on Return:

AL: Status byte

Memory Affected: None

Syntax:

```
PUSH    CS                          ;Code segment and
POP     DS                          ;  data segment are same
MOV     DX,OFFSET FCB_1             ;Offset address of FCB
MOV     AH,15h                      ;Want service 15h
INT     21h                         ;DOS services interrupt
```

Description: This service is used to write a block of information from the DTA to an open file. You designate the block size through the file control block, or FCB. The FCB consists of 44 bytes constructed in the following manner:

```
FCB_PRE       DB      ØFFh          ;Extension flag
              DB      5 DUP(Ø)      ;Unused
FILE_ATTR     DB      ØØ            ;File attribute
FCB_1         DB      ØØ            ;Set for default drive
FILE_ROOT     DB      'FILENAME'    ;File name root
FILE_EXT      DB      'DAT'         ;File name extension
BLOCK_NUM     DW      ØØØØ          ;Current block number
REC_SIZE      DW      ØØØØ          ;Record size
FILE_SIZE     DD      ØØØØØØØØ      ;File size
FILE_DATE     DW      ØØØØ          ;File date
FILE_TIME     DW      ØØØØ          ;File time
              DB      8 DUP(Ø)      ;DOS work area
REC_NUM       DB      ØØ            ;Current record number
RANDOM_REC    DD      ØØØØØØØØ      ;Random record number
```

You specify the offset address of FCB_1 in DS:DX when you invoke this service. If you are using an extended FCB, you should use the offset address of FCB_PRE. You should set the values for FCB_1 (the drive designator), FILE_ROOT, and FILE_EXT before you open the file. You specify the size of the block to be written in the REC_SIZE field. The values in BLOCK_NUM and REC_NUM designate where in the file the writing is to begin. After a successful write, these fields are incremented automatically.

When the service is completed, the value of AL indicates the status of the operation. If AL is 0, the write was successful. If AL is 1, a disk-full error was detected during the write. If AL is 2, the DTA crossed a segment boundary, a memory address ending in 000, and an error was generated.

Create File Using FCB
(Interrupt 21h, service 16h)

Category: Disk services

Registers on Entry:

AH: 16h
DX: Offset address of FCB
DS: Segment address of FCB

Registers on Return:

AL: Status byte

Memory Affected: If the file is created successfully, DOS fills in the FCB area
(specified by DS:DX) to reflect the status of the file.

Syntax:

```
PUSH    CS                      ;Code segment and
POP     DS                      ;   data segment are same
MOV     DX,OFFSET FCB_1         ;Offset address of FCB
MOV     AH,16h                  ;Want service 16h
INT     21h                     ;DOS services interrupt
```

Description: This service uses the information in the file control block, or FCB,
to create or truncate a disk file. This FCB is a block of information that the
programmer initially sets and DOS subsequently completes. The FCB consists of
44 bytes constructed in the following manner:

```
FCB_PRE         DB      ØFFh            ;Extension flag
                DB      5 DUP(Ø)        ;Unused
                DB      ØØ              ;File attribute
FCB_1           DB      ØØ              ;Set for default drive
FILE_ROOT       DB      'FILENAME'      ;File name root
FILE_EXT        DB      'EXT'           ;File name extension
BLOCK_NUM       DW      ØØØØ            ;Current block number
REC_SIZE        DW      ØØØØ            ;Record size
FILE_SIZE       DD      ØØØØØØØØ        ;File size
FILE_DATE       DW      ØØØØ            ;File date
FILE_TIME       DW      ØØØØ            ;File time
                DB      8 DUP(Ø)        ;DOS work area
REC_NUM         DB      ØØ              ;Current record number
RANDOM_REC      DD      ØØØØØØØØ        ;Random record number
```

You specify the offset address of FCB_1 in DS:DX when you invoke this service. If you are using an extended FCB, you should use the offset address of FCB_PRE. To call this service, you must specify the values for FCB_1 (the drive designator), FILE_ROOT, and FILE_EXT. Notice that the drive designator is different from the normal method for DOS and BIOS drive designation. In this instance, 0 equals the default drive, and 1=A, 2=B, 3=C, etc.

If you use the FCB extension area, you can specify the attribute of the file being created. In the example, the extended FCB begins with the area shown as FCB_PRE. FCB_PRE is set to FFh, signaling that the FCB extension is active. The FILE_ATTR file attribute is set to specify the file attribute for the new file.

If the file name specified in the FCB already exists in the current directory, the file is opened and its length is truncated to 0.

If the file is created successfully, DOS returns a 0 in AL. In addition, the service sets FCB_1 to reflect the drive number (1=A, 2=B, 3=C, etc.), and sets BLOCK_NUM to 0, REC_SIZE to 80h, and FILE_SIZE, FILE_DATE, and FILE_TIME to their appropriate values for the new file. If the open operation is unsuccessful, DOS returns FFh in AL and does not fill in the FCB.

When this service is completed, the specified file is left open. You do not need to open the file, but you must remember to close it.

Notice that this service allows you to use only FCBs. Because FCB file encoding does not allow for path names, any file operations must be performed in the current disk subdirectory. With floppy disks, this limitation may not be a problem. With fixed disks, however, the limitation can be serious. Refer to service 21/3C; this method of creating files does not have this limitation.

Rename File Using FCB (Interrupt 21h, service 17h)

Category: Disk services

Registers on Entry:

   AH: 17h
   DX: Offset address of modified FCB
   DS: Segment address of modified FCB

Registers on Return:

   AL: Status byte

Memory Affected: None

Syntax:

```
PUSH    CS                          ;Code segment and
POP     DS                          ;   data segment are same
MOV     DX,OFFSET FCB_1             ;Offset address of FCB
MOV     AH,17h                      ;Want service 17h
INT     21h                         ;DOS services interrupt
```

Description: This service uses information contained in a modified file control block, or FCB, to rename a file in the current directory. This modified FCB consists of 44 bytes constructed in the following manner:

```
MOD_FCB     DB      ØØ              ;Set for default drive
OLD_ROOT    DB      'OLD_FILE'      ;Original file root
OLD_EXT     DB      'EXT'           ;Original file extension
            DB      5 DUP(Ø)        ;DOS work area
NEW_ROOT    DB      'NEW_FILE'      ;New file root
NEW_EXT     DB      'EXT'           ;New file extension
            DB      16 DUP(Ø)       ;DOS work area
```

You specify the offset address of MOD_FCB in DS:DX when you invoke this service. To call this service, you must specify the values for MOD_FCB (the drive designator), OLD_ROOT, and OLD_EXT. Notice that the drive designator is different from the normal method for DOS and BIOS drive designation. In this instance, 0 equals the default drive, and 1=A, 2=B, 3=C, etc.

If the renaming operation is successful, DOS returns a 0 in AL. If the operation is unsuccessful, DOS returns FFh in AL.

This service does not allow you to rename files outside of the current directory. With floppy disks, this limitation may not be a problem. With fixed disks, however, the limitation can be serious. Refer to service 21/56; this method of creating files does not have this limitation.

Reserved (Interrupt 21h, service 18h)

Description: This service is listed by IBM and Microsoft as reserved for the internal use of DOS. The service, which is not publicized or documented, is subject to modification in future versions of DOS.

Get Current Drive (Interrupt 21h, service 19h)

Category: Disk services

Registers on Entry:

AH: 19h

Registers on Return:

AL: Drive code

Memory Affected: None

Syntax:

```
MOV     AH,19h           ;Want service 19h
INT     21h              ;DOS services interrupt
MOV     CUR_DRIVE,AL     ;Store drive designator
```

Description: This service is used to determine the current default disk drive. The service has no calling parameters, and the returned value in AL is a drive code in which 0=A, 1=B, 2=C, etc.

Generally, the default disk drive is the drive from which the computer was booted, or the drive last set with service 21/0E.

Set Disk Transfer Area (DTA) (Interrupt 21h, service 1Ah)

Category: Disk services

Registers on Entry:

AH: 1Ah
DX: Offset address of DTA
DS: Segment address of DTA

Registers on Return: Unchanged

Memory Affected: None

Syntax:

```
PUSH    CS               ;Code segment and
POP     DS               ;   data segment are same
MOV     DX,OFFSET FCB_1  ;Offset address of FCB
MOV     AH,1Ah           ;Want service 1Ah
INT     21h              ;DOS services interrupt
```

Description: When DOS works with file control blocks (FCBs), DOS transfers information to and from the disk through a block of memory called the DTA.

Normally, this DTA is set as a 128-byte memory area at offset 80h in the program segment prefix (PSP). You can, however, set aside for the DTA an area of memory within your program. If the size of the blocks you will be reading and writing is larger than 128 bytes, you need to specify your own DTA through this service.

Get FAT (File Allocation Table) Information for Default Drive (Interrupt 21h, service 1Bh)

Category: Disk services

Registers on Entry:

AH: 1Bh

Registers on Return:

AL: Sectors per cluster
BX: Offset address of FAT ID byte
CX: Bytes per sector
DX: Clusters per disk
DS: Segment address of FAT ID byte

Memory Affected: None

Syntax:

```
MOV     AH,1Bh          ;Want service 1Bh
INT     21h             ;DOS services interrupt
```

Description: This service returns basic information about the disk in the default drive. The information includes the number of bytes per sector (CX), the number of sectors per cluster (AL), the number of clusters per disk (DX), and the address of the file allocation table identification (ID) byte (DS:BX).

Once you know this information, deriving other valuable information is easy. For instance, to determine the byte capacity of the disk, you simply multiply CX by AL by DX.

The File Allocation Table (FAT) identification byte to which DS:BX points indicates the type of disk in use. Actually, this byte indicates only how the disk was formatted. Table 13.2 shows some possible values for the FAT ID byte.

Table 13.2
Some Possible FAT ID Byte Values

Value	Disk characteristics
F0	Not identifiable
F8	Fixed disk
F9	Double sided, 15 sectors/track
F9	Double sided, 9 sectors/track (720K)
FC	Single sided, 9 sectors/track
FD	Double sided, 9 sectors/track (360K)
FE	Single sided, 8 sectors/track
FF	Double sided, 8 sectors/track

Get FAT Information for Drive (Interrupt 21h, service 1Ch)

Category: Disk services

Registers on Entry:

AH: 1Ch
DL: Drive code

Registers on Return:

AL: Sectors per cluster
BX: Offset address of FAT ID byte
CX: Bytes per sector
DX: Clusters per disk
DS: Segment address of FAT ID byte

Memory Affected: None

Syntax:

```
MOV    DL,Ø         ;Drive A:
MOV    AH,1Ch       ;Want service 1Ch
INT    21h          ;DOS services interrupt
```

Description: This service returns basic information about the disk in the drive specified by DL. The drive number is specified as A=0, B=1, C=2, etc.

The information returned by this service is identical to that for service 21/1B. The information includes the number of bytes per sector (CX), the number of sectors per cluster (AL), the number of clusters per disk (DX), and the address of the file allocation table ID byte (DS:BX).

Once you know this information, deriving other valuable information is easy. For instance, to determine the byte capacity of the disk, you simply multiply CX by AL by DX.

The FAT ID byte to which DS:BX points indicates the type of disk in use. Actually, this byte indicates only how the disk was formatted. (Refer to table 13.2 for some possible values for the FAT ID byte.)

Reserved (Interrupt 21h, services 1Dh, 1Eh, 1Fh, 20h)

Description: These services are listed by IBM and Microsoft as reserved for the internal use of DOS. Because their purpose and use are not publicized or documented, these services are subject to modification in future versions of DOS.

Random Read, Using FCB (Interrupt 21h, service 21h)

Category: Disk services

Registers on Entry:

AH: 21h
DX: Offset address of FCB
DS: Segment address of FCB

Registers on Return:

AL: Status byte

Memory Affected: The memory area designated as DTA is overwritten with information read from the disk.

Syntax:

```
PUSH    CS                      ;Code segment and
POP     DS                      ;  data segment are same
MOV     DX,OFFSET FCB_1         ;Offset address of FCB
MOV     AH,21h                  ;Want service 21h
INT     21h                     ;DOS services interrupt
```

Description: This service is used to read a data record from an open file and place the information in the DTA. You designate the record size through the file control block, or FCB. The FCB consists of 44 bytes constructed in the following manner:

```
FCB_PRE       DB    ØFFh          ;Extension flag
              DB    5 DUP(Ø)      ;Unused
FILE_ATTR     DB    ØØ            ;File attribute
FCB_1         DB    ØØ            ;Set for default drive
FILE_ROOT     DB    'FILENAME'    ;File name root
FILE_EXT      DB    'DAT'         ;File name extension
BLOCK_NUM     DW    ØØØØ          ;Current block number
REC_SIZE      DW    ØØØØ          ;Record size
FILE_SIZE     DD    ØØØØØØØØ      ;File size
FILE_DATE     DW    ØØØØ          ;File date
FILE_TIME     DW    ØØØØ          ;File time
              DB    8 DUP(Ø)      ;DOS work area
REC_NUM       DB    ØØ            ;Current record number
RANDOM_REC    DD    ØØØØØØØØ      ;Random record number
```

You specify the offset address of FCB_1 in DS:DX when you invoke this service. If you are using an extended FCB, you should use the offset address of FCB_PRE. You should set the values for FCB_1 (the drive designator), FILE_ROOT, and FILE_EXT before the file is opened. You specify the file's record size in the REC_SIZE field. The area set aside as the DTA should be as large as a record. The values in REC_SIZE and RANDOM_REC specify where the file read is to begin. After a successful read, the values in BLOCK_NUM and REC_NUM are updated to the proper values. RANDOM_REC, which is not incremented by this service, remains the same as before the invocation.

When this service is completed, the value of AL indicates the status of the operation. If AL is 0, the read was successful. If AL is 1, no data was read because the end of file was already reached. If AL is 2, the DTA crossed a segment boundary, a memory address ending in 000, which resulted in an error condition. If AL is 3, the system reached the end of file during the read and could not read an entire block (the partial block was read and placed in the DTA area).

Random Write Using FCB
(Interrupt 21h, service 22h)

Category: Disk services

Registers on Entry:

AH: 22h
DX: Offset address of FCB
DS: Segment address of FCB

Registers on Return:

AL: Status byte

Memory Affected: Certain FCB values are modified.

Syntax:

```
PUSH    CS                      ;Code segment and
POP     DS                      ;  data segment are same
MOV     DX,OFFSET FCB_1         ;Offset address of FCB
MOV     AH,22h                  ;Want service 22h
INT     21h                     ;DOS services interrupt
```

Description: This service is used to write a data record to a previously opened
file. The information to be written is contained in the DTA. The record size is
designated through the file control block, or FCB. The FCB consists of 44 bytes
constructed in the following manner:

```
FCB_PRE         DB      ØFFh            ;Extension flag
                DB      5 DUP(Ø)        ;Unused
FILE_ATTR       DB      ØØ              ;File attribute
FCB_1           DB      ØØ              ;Set for default drive
FILE_ROOT       DB      'FILENAME'      ;File name root
FILE_EXT        DB      'DAT'           ;File name extension
BLOCK_NUM       DW      ØØØØ            ;Current block number
REC_SIZE        DW      ØØØØ            ;Record size
FILE_SIZE       DD      ØØØØØØØØ        ;File size
FILE_DATE       DW      ØØØØ            ;File date
FILE_TIME       DW      ØØØØ            ;File time
                DB      8 DUP(Ø)        ;DOS work area
REC_NUM         DB      ØØ              ;Current record number
RANDOM_REC      DD      ØØØØØØØØ        ;Random record number
```

You specify the offset address of FCB_1 in DS:DX when you invoke this service.
If you are using an extended FCB, you should use the offset address of

FCB_PRE. You should set the values for FCB_1 (the drive designator), FILE_ROOT, and FILE_EXT before the file is opened. You specify the file's record size in the REC_SIZE field. This size is the number of bytes that will be written by this service. The values in REC_SIZE and RANDOM_REC specify the location in the file at which writing is to begin. After a successful write, the values in BLOCK_NUM and REC_NUM are updated to the proper values. RANDOM_REC, which is not incremented by this service, remains the same as before the invocation.

When this service is completed, the value of AL indicates the status of the operation. If AL is 0, the write was successful. If AL is 1, a disk-full error was detected during the write. If AL is 2, the DTA crossed a segment boundary, a memory address ending in 000, and an error was generated.

Get File Size Using FCB (Interrupt 21h, service 23h)

Category: Disk services

Registers on Entry:

AH: 23h
DX: Offset address of FCB
DS: Segment address of FCB

Registers on Return:

AL: Status byte

Memory Affected: Certain FCB values are modified.

Syntax:

```
PUSH    CS                      ;Code segment and
POP     DS                      ;   data segment are same
MOV     DX,OFFSET FCB_1         ;Offset address of FCB
MOV     AH,23h                  ;Want service 23h
INT     21h                     ;DOS services interrupt
CMP     AL,ØFFh                 ;Was the file found?
JE      FILE_ERR                ;No, so handle error
```

Description: This service searches for a specific file name in the current directory and returns the number of records in that file. You specify the file name to be used in the file control block, or FCB. The FCB consists of 44 bytes constructed in the following manner:

```
FCB_PRE         DB      ØFFh            ;Extension flag
                DB      5 DUP(Ø)        ;Unused
FILE_ATTR       DB      ØØ              ;File attribute
FCB_1           DB      ØØ              ;Set for default drive
FILE_ROOT       DB      'FILENAME'      ;File name root
FILE_EXT        DB      'DAT'           ;File name extension
BLOCK_NUM       DW      ØØØØ            ;Current block number
REC_SIZE        DW      ØØØØ            ;Record size
FILE_SIZE       DD      ØØØØØØØØ        ;File size
FILE_DATE       DW      ØØØØ            ;File date
FILE_TIME       DW      ØØØØ            ;File time
                DB      8 DUP(Ø)        ;DOS work area
REC_NUM         DB      ØØ              ;Current record number
RANDOM_REC      DD      ØØØØØØØØ        ;Random record number
```

You specify the offset address of FCB_1 in DS:DX when you invoke this service. If you are using an extended FCB, you should use the offset address of FCB_PRE. To use this service, you should set the values for FCB_1 (the drive designator), FILE_ROOT, and FILE_EXT. The value in REC_SIZE indicates the record size in the file and has a direct bearing on the returned value. If this field is set to 1, the value returned by this service is equal to the number of bytes in the file.

On return, the value of AL indicates the status of the operation. If AL is 0, the file was located, and the value in RANDOM_REC indicates the number of records (of size REC_SIZE) in the file. If AL is FFh, the requested file could not be located, and the FCB values are not significant.

Set Random Record Field in FCB (Interrupt 21h, service 24h)

Category: Disk services

Registers on Entry:

    AH: 24h
    DX: Offset address of FCB
    DS: Segment address of FCB

Registers on Return: Unchanged

Memory Affected: Certain FCB values are modified.

Syntax:

```
PUSH    CS                      ;Code segment and
POP     DS                      ;   data segment are same
MOV     DX,OFFSET FCB_1         ;Offset address of FCB
MOV     AH,24h                  ;Want service 24h
INT     21h                     ;DOS services interrupt
```

Description: This service modifies the contents of the random record field in the file control block (FCB) of an open file. The FCB is a 44-byte area constructed as follows:

```
FCB_PRE       DB    ØFFh            ;Extension flag
              DB    5 DUP(Ø)        ;Unused
FILE_ATTR     DB    ØØ              ;File attribute
FCB_1         DB    ØØ              ;Set for default drive
FILE_ROOT     DB    'FILENAME'      ;File name root
FILE_EXT      DB    'DAT'           ;File name extension
BLOCK_NUM     DW    ØØØØ            ;Current block number
REC_SIZE      DW    ØØØØ            ;Record size
FILE_SIZE     DD    ØØØØØØØØ        ;File size
FILE_DATE     DW    ØØØØ            ;File date
FILE_TIME     DW    ØØØØ            ;File time
              DB    8 DUP(Ø)        ;DOS work area
REC_NUM       DB    ØØ              ;Current record number
RANDOM_REC    DD    ØØØØØØØØ        ;Random record number
```

You specify the offset address of FCB_1 in DS:DX when you invoke this service. If you are using an extended FCB, you should use the offset address of FCB_PRE. Before you call the service, set the values for FCB_1 (the drive designator), FILE_ROOT, and FILE_EXT for the open file. Also set the values in REC_SIZE, REC_NUM, and BLOCK_NUM before calling this service. These values are used to compute the value in RANDOM_REC.

Set Interrupt Vector
(Interrupt 21h, service 25h)

Category: System services

Registers on Entry:

AH: 25h
AL: Interrupt number
DX: Offset address of new interrupt handler
DS: Segment address of new interrupt handler

Registers on Return: Unchanged

Memory Affected: The values in the interrupt vector table in low memory are altered.

Syntax:

```
PUSH    DS                      ;Save current data segment
MOV     AL,5                    ;Print-screen interrupt
PUSH    CS                      ;Code segment and
POP     DS                      ;  data segment are same
MOV     DX,OFFSET PS_HANDLER    ;Offset address of handler
MOV     AH,25h                  ;Want service 25h
INT     21h                     ;DOS services interrupt
POP     DS                      ;Restore data segment
```

Description: This service provides a uniform method for altering the interrupt vector table in low memory. Such a method is useful if you want to alter or replace the way the system currently handles interrupts.

An important consideration is that, once changed, the old interrupt vector is lost. You can use service 21/35 to determine the current vector so that you can save the vector before changing it. Then, on program completion, you can reset the vector to the original value.

Create Program Segment Prefix (PSP) (Interrupt 21h, service 26h)

Category: System services

Registers on Entry:

AH: 26h
DX: Segment address of new PSP

Registers on Return: Unchanged

Memory Affected: The 256 bytes of memory at the desired segment address are altered.

Syntax:

```
MOV     DX,OFFSET CS:PROG_END   ;Point to end of program
MOV     AH,26h                  ;Want service 26h
INT     21h                     ;DOS services interrupt
```

Description: This service, which is used to facilitate overlays and subprograms to the current program, copies the current PSP contents to the desired paragraph and then sets the PSP vector contents to match the contents of the interrupt vector table.

The new DOS technical reference manuals (DOS 3.3) recommend that this service not be used; they recommend using service 21/4B.

Read Random Record(s) Using FCB (Interrupt 21h, service 27h)

Category: Disk services

Registers on Entry:

AH: 27h
CX: Number of records to read
DX: Offset address of FCB
DS: Segment address of FCB

Registers on Return:

AL: Status byte
CX: Number of records read

Memory Affected: The memory designated by DTA is overlaid with information read from the disk.

Syntax:

```
PUSH    CS                      ;Code segment and
POP     DS                      ;  data segment are same
MOV     DX,OFFSET FCB_1         ;Offset address of FCB
MOV     CX,8                    ;Read 8 records
MOV     AH,27h                  ;Want service 27h
INT     21h                     ;DOS services interrupt
```

Description: This service is used to read a specified number of data records from a previously opened file and to place the information in the DTA. You specify the number of records to read in CX. Designate the record size through the file control block, or FCB. The FCB consists of 44 bytes constructed in the following manner:

```
FCB_PRE     DB      ØFFh            ;Extension flag
            DB      5 DUP(Ø)        ;Unused
FILE_ATTR   DB      ØØ              ;File attribute
FCB_1       DB      ØØ              ;Set for default drive
FILE_ROOT   DB      'FILENAME'      ;File name root
FILE_EXT    DB      'DAT'           ;File name extension
```

```
        BLOCK_NUM       DW      ØØØØ              ;Current block number
        REC_SIZE        DW      ØØØØ              ;Record size
        FILE_SIZE       DD      ØØØØØØØØ          ;File size
        FILE_DATE       DW      ØØØØ              ;File date
        FILE_TIME       DW      ØØØØ              ;File time
                        DB      8 DUP(Ø)          ;DOS work area
        REC_NUM         DB      ØØ                ;Current record number
        RANDOM_REC      DD      ØØØØØØØØ          ;Random record number
```

You specify the offset address of FCB_1 in DS:DX when you invoke this service. If you are using an extended FCB, you should use the offset address of FCB_PRE. You set the values for FCB_1 (the drive designator), FILE_ROOT, and FILE_EXT before the file is opened. You specify the file's record size in the REC_SIZE field. The area set aside as the DTA should be large enough to contain the number of records being requested. The values in REC_SIZE and RANDOM_REC specify the location in the file at which the read is to begin. After a successful read, the service updates the values in BLOCK_NUM, REC_NUM, and RANDOM_REC.

When this service is completed, the value of AL indicates the status of the operation. If AL is 0, the read was successful. If AL is 1, no data was read because the end of file was already reached. If AL is 2, the DTA crossed a segment boundary, a memory address ending in 000, which resulted in an error condition. If AL is 3, the end of file was reached during the read; the service could not read an entire block (the partial block is still read and placed in the DTA area). CX contains the number of records read.

Write Random Record(s) Using FCB (Interrupt 21h, service 28h)

Category: Disk services

Registers on Entry:

  AH: 28h
  CX: Number of records to write
  DX: Offset address of FCB
  DS: Segment address of FCB

Registers on Return:

  AL: Status byte
  CX: Number of records written

Memory Affected: Certain FCB values are modified.

Syntax:

```
PUSH    CS                      ;Code segment and
POP     DS                      ;  data segment are same
MOV     DX,OFFSET FCB_1         ;Offset address of FCB
MOV     CX,8                    ;Write 8 records
MOV     AH,28h                  ;Want service 28h
INT     21h                     ;DOS services interrupt
```

Description: This service is used to write a specific number of data records to a previously opened file. The information to be written is contained in the DTA. You specify the number of records to be written in CX. You designate the record size through the file control block, or FCB. The FCB consists of 44 bytes constructed in the following manner:

```
FCB_PRE         DB      ØFFh            ;Extension flag
                DB      5 DUP(Ø)        ;Unused
FILE_ATTR       DB      ØØ              ;File attribute
FCB_1           DB      ØØ              ;Set for default drive
FILE_ROOT       DB      'FILENAME'      ;File name root
FILE_EXT        DB      'DAT'           ;File name extension
BLOCK_NUM       DW      ØØØØ            ;Current block number
REC_SIZE        DW      ØØØØ            ;Record size
FILE_SIZE       DD      ØØØØØØØØ        ;File size
FILE_DATE       DW      ØØØØ            ;File date
FILE_TIME       DW      ØØØØ            ;File time
                DB      8 DUP(Ø)        ;DOS work area
REC_NUM         DB      ØØ              ;Current record number
RANDOM_REC      DD      ØØØØØØØØ        ;Random record number
```

You specify the offset address of FCB_1 DS:DX when you invoke this service. If you are using an extended FCB, you should use the offset address of FCB_PRE. You set the values for FCB_1 (the drive designator), FILE_ROOT, and FILE_EXT before the file is opened. Specify the file's record size in the REC_SIZE field. The values in REC_SIZE and RANDOM_REC specify the location in the file at which the writing is to begin. After a successful write, the service updates the values in BLOCK_NUM, REC_NUM, and RANDOM_REC.

When this service is completed, the value of AL indicates the status of the operation. If AL is 0, the write was successful. If AL is 1, a disk-full error was detected during the write. If AL is 2, the DTA crossed a segment boundary, a memory address ending in 000, and an error was generated. CX contains the number of records written.

Parse File Name Using FCB
(Interrupt 21h, service 29h)

Category: Disk services

Registers on Entry:

AH: 29h
AL: Parsing control byte
SI: Offset address of string to be parsed
DI: Offset address of FCB
DS: Segment address of string to be parsed
ES: Segment address of FCB

Registers on Return:

AL: Status byte
SI: Offset address of first character following parsed string
DI: Offset address of FCB
DS: Segment address of first character following parsed string
ES: Segment address of FCB

Memory Affected: Certain values in the FCB are altered.

Syntax:

```
PUSH    DS                      ;Save data segment
PUSH    ES                      ;Save extra segment
MOV     AX,CS                   ;Code, data, and extra
MOV     DS,AX                   ;  segments are all
MOV     ES,AX                   ;  the same
MOV     SI,OFFSET INPUT         ;Offset address of string
MOV     DI,OFFSET FCB_1         ;Offset address of FCB
MOV     AL,00001111b            ;Set proper parse control
MOV     AH,29h                  ;Want service 29h
INT     21h                     ;DOS services interrupt
POP     ES                      ;Restore extra segment
POP     DS                      ;Restore data segment
```

Description: This service is used to parse (translate) a text string in order to pick out a valid drive designator, file name, and file extension. The service parses for simple drive/file name designations only, not for path names.

DS:SI points to the text string to be parsed, and ES:DI points to the memory area that will hold the constructed FCB. This area should be at least 44 bytes in length.

The four low-order bits of AL control how the text string is parsed. Table 13.3 details the meanings of the bit settings.

Table 13.3
Bit Settings for AL Register, Service 21/29

Bits 76543210	*Meaning*
0000	Reserved—must be set to 0
0	File extension in FCB is set either to parsed value or blanks.
1	File extension in FCB is set only if 1 is detected in the text string and the parsed file name is valid.
0	File name in FCB is set either to parsed value or blanks.
1	File name in FCB is set only if a valid file name exists in the text string.
0	Drive ID byte is set either to parsed value or 0.
1	Drive ID byte is set only if a valid drive designator is parsed in the text string.
0	Leading separators are not ignored.
1	Leading separators are ignored.

This service correctly translates wildcard characters (* and ?) to the appropriate FCB values.

On return, AL indicates the parsing status. If AL=0, no wildcard characters were located in the text string. If AL=1, the text string contained wildcard characters. If AL=FFh, the drive specifier was invalid. In all instances, ES:DI points to the first byte of the new FCB.

Get System Date (Interrupt 21h, service 2Ah)

Category: Date/time services

Registers on Entry:

AH: 2Ah

Registers on Return:

AL: Day of week
CX: Year
DH: Month
DL: Day

Memory Affected: None

Syntax:

```
MOV     AH,2Ah                  ;Want service 2Ah
INT     21h                     ;DOS services interrupt
```

Description: This service, which returns the system date, returns the month (DH), day (DL), and year (CX), along with the day of the week for this date. The day of the week is returned in AL as 0=Sunday, 1=Monday, 2=Tuesday, etc.

Set System Date (Interrupt 21h, service 2Bh)

Category: Date/time services

Registers on Entry:

AH: 2Bh
CX: Year (1980–2099)
DH: Month (1–12)
DL: Day (1–31)

Registers on Return:

AL: Status byte

Memory Affected: None

Syntax:

```
            MOV     DH,MONTH        ;Get current month
            MOV     DL,DAY          ;Get current day
            MOV     CX,YEAR         ;Get current year
            CMP     CX,100          ;Does CX include century?
            JA      OK_GO           ;Yes, so continue
            ADD     CX,1900         ;No, so adjust
OK_GO:      MOV     AH,2Bh          ;Want service 2Bh
            INT     21h             ;DOS services interrupt
            CMP     AL,0            ;Was there an error?
            JNE     DATE_ERROR      ;Yes, go handle
```

Description: This service allows the DOS date (system software clock) to be set but does not set the real-time hardware clock on the IBM Personal Computer AT or compatibles.

To use this service, you must load a valid month, day, and year into DH, DL, and CX, respectively. On return, AL contains either a 0 (indicating that the date was valid and has been set) or FFh (indicating that the specified date is invalid).

Get System Time (Interrupt 21h, service 2Ch)

Category: Date/time services

Registers on Entry:

AH: 2Ch

Registers on Return:

CH: Hour
CL: Minute
DH: Second
DL: Hundredths of a second

Memory Affected: None

Syntax:

```
MOV     AH,2Ch          ;Want service 2Ch
INT     21h             ;DOS services interrupt
```

Description: This service converts the value of the computer's system-software clock counter to values that humans readily understand: hours (CH), minutes (CL), seconds (DH), and hundredths of seconds (DL). The hours (CH), which are returned in military time, range from 0 to 23.

Set Time (Interrupt 21h, service 2Dh)

Category: Date/time services

Registers on Entry:

AH: 2Dh
CH: Hour (0–23)
CL: Minute (0–59)
DH: Second (0–59)
DL: Hundredths of a second (0–99)

Registers on Return:

AL: Status byte

Memory Affected: None

Syntax:

```
MOV    CH,HOUR        ;Get current hour
MOV    CL,MINUTE      ;Get current minute
MOV    DH,SECOND      ;Get current second
MOV    DL,Ø           ;Hundredths doesn't matter
MOV    AH,2Dh         ;Want service 2Dh
INT    21h            ;DOS services interrupt
CMP    AL,Ø           ;Was there an error?
JNE    TIME_ERROR     ;Yes, go handle
```

Description: This service converts a specified time to the corresponding number of clock ticks, and stores the resulting value in the computer's software clock counter. This service does not reset the real-time clock on the IBM Personal Computer AT or compatibles.

This service determines, through a series of multiplications, the number of clock ticks represented by the specified time. The entered values are converted to a total number of seconds, which then is multiplied by 18.2065 (the approximate number of clock ticks per second). For example, if you are setting the time to 14:22:17.39 (military time), the computer goes through conversions similar to the following:

14 hours =	14 * 60 * 60	= 50400	seconds
22 minutes =	22 * 60	= 1320	seconds
17.39 seconds =	17.39	= 17.39	seconds
Total:		51737.39	seconds
Clock ticks per second =		18.2065	ticks
Ticks represented:		941956.7910	ticks

Because fractional ticks cannot be represented, the total number is rounded to 941,957 ticks. The system software clock is then set to this value. This is the same type of process that sets the system clock with the BIOS date/time services (refer to Chapter 12, service 1A/4). As a programmer, you can easily see the added value of some of these DOS services.

On return, AL contains either a 0 (indicating that the time was valid and has been set) or FFh (indicating that the specified time is invalid).

Set Verify Flag (Interrupt 21h, service 2Eh)

Category: Disk services

Registers on Entry:

AH: 2Eh
AL: Verify setting
DL: 0

Registers on Return: Unchanged

Memory Affected: None

Syntax:

```
MOV     AL,1            ;Set verify on
MOV     DL,Ø
MOV     AH,2Eh          ;Want service 2Eh
INT     21h             ;DOS services interrupt
```

Description: This service sets the system flag that determines whether DOS performs a verify operation after each disk write to ensure that the information has been recorded accurately. In most applications, the reliability of DOS operations is such that you safely can leave the verify flag set to off (the default setting).

The setting of DL is not important if you are working with DOS 3.0 or later versions but, for earlier versions, DL must be set to 0. This is an undocumented necessity; no reason is given for this setting.

If you are working with a network system, verification is not supported—the setting has no meaning.

Get Disk Transfer Area
(Interrupt 21h, service 2Fh)

Category: Disk services

Registers on Entry:

AH: 2Fh

Registers on Return:

BX: Offset address of DTA
ES: Segment address of DTA

Memory Affected: None

Syntax:

```
MOV    AH,2Fh           ;Want service 2Fh
INT    21h              ;DOS services interrupt
```

Description: This service returns the address of the current DOS disk transfer area (DTA). DOS uses this area to transfer information between the computer and the disk. The address is returned in ES:BX.

Get DOS Version Number
(Interrupt 21h, service 30h)

Category: System services

Registers on Entry:

AH: 30h

Registers on Return:

AL: Major version number
AH: Minor version number
BX: 0
CX: 0

Memory Affected: None

Syntax:

```
MOV    AH,30h           ;Want service 30h
INT    21h              ;DOS services interrupt
CMP    AL,2             ;At least version 2.0?
JB     DOS_BAD          ;No, so exit early
```

Description: This service determines the version number of the DOS that is operating within the computer (the DOS used during booting).

The major purpose of this service is to allow programs to determine whether the proper version of DOS is in use for certain functions and services. AL contains the major version number (2 or 3). If AL contains 0, the DOS version is earlier than 2.0. The minor version number returned in AH is the number to the right of the decimal point (to two decimal places). BX and CX are also set to 0, suggesting that future versions of DOS may use this service to return expanded or additional information.

Terminate and Stay Resident (Interrupt 21h, service 31h)

Category: System services

Registers on Entry:

AH: 31h
AL: Return code
DX: Memory paragraphs to reserve

Registers on Return: Indeterminable (does not return)

Memory Affected: The available free memory is decreased by the number of paragraphs specified in DX.

Syntax:

```
MOV    AL,Ø          ;Return code of Ø
MOV    DX,1ØØh        ;Reserve 4K of info
MOV    AH,31h         ;Want service 31h
INT    21h            ;DOS services interrupt
```

Description: This service is used to exit a program, leaving all or part of the program's memory intact. The service is used by a wide variety of TSR (terminate and stay resident) programs such as SideKick, ProKey, etc.

The return code you specify in AL when you invoke this service is passed to the parent program or to DOS. From DOS command level, the return code is available through the ERRORLEVEL batch command; from programs, the return code can be determined through service 21/4D.

The number of paragraphs requested in DX are reserved by DOS and unavailable to other programs.

Reserved (Interrupt 21h, service 32h)

Description: This service is listed by IBM and Microsoft as reserved for the internal use of DOS. The service, which is not publicized or documented, is subject to modification in future versions of DOS.

Ctrl-Break Flag Control (Interrupt 21h, service 33h)

Category: System services

Registers on Entry:

AH: 33h
AL: Get/set flag
DL: Ctrl-Break flag setting

Registers on Return:

DL: Ctrl-Break flag setting

Memory Affected: None

Syntax:

```
MOV     AL,1                ;Setting flag
MOV     DL,Ø                ;Turn off Ctrl-Break check
MOV     AH,33h              ;Want service 33h
INT     21h                 ;DOS services interrupt
```

Description: This service gets or sets the flag that controls how often DOS checks whether the Ctrl-Break key combination has been pressed. Other documentation for this service implies that this flag turns Ctrl-Break checking on or off completely—not true: this flag controls only the frequency of checking. Even with this flag set to off, checking is performed during certain DOS operations, such as performing video output.

To set the Ctrl-Break flag, load AL with 1 and DL with the desired state of the flag. If DL is 0, Ctrl-Break checking is at the minimum. If DL is 1, checking is more frequent during virtually every DOS operation.

To get the current state of the flag, load AL with 0. On return, DL contains 0 or 1, depending on whether the flag is off or on.

Reserved (Interrupt 21h, service 34h)

Description: This service is listed by IBM and Microsoft as reserved for the internal use of DOS. The service, which is not publicized or documented, is subject to modification in future versions of DOS.

Get Interrupt Vector (Interrupt 21h, service 35h)

Category: System services

Registers on Entry:

AH: 35h
AL: Interrupt number

Registers on Return:

BX: Offset address of interrupt handler
ES: Segment address of interrupt handler

Memory Affected: None

Syntax:

```
PUSH    ES                      ;Save registers
PUSH    BX
MOV     AL,5                    ;Print-screen interrupt
MOV     AH,35h                  ;Want service 35h
INT     21h                     ;DOS services interrupt
MOV     I5_SEG_OLD,ES           ;Store old segment
MOV     I5_OFF_OLD,BX           ;Store old offset
POP     BX                      ;Restore registers
POP     ES
```

Description: This service allows a uniform method for retrieving the address of an interrupt handler from the interrupt vector table in low memory. This service is used to determine current values so that they can be saved before changing; then service 21/25 can be used to alter the vector.

Get Disk Free Space
(Interrupt 21h, service 36h)

Category: Disk services

Registers on Entry:

AH: 36h
DL: Drive code

Registers on Return:

AX: Sectors per cluster
BX: Available clusters
CX: Bytes per sector
DX: Clusters per drive

Memory Affected: None

Syntax:

```
MOV     AH,36h          ;Want service 36h
INT     21h             ;DOS services interrupt
CMP     AX,ØFFFFh       ;Was there an error?
JE      ERROR           ;Yes, so go handle
PUSH    AX              ;Save sectors/cluster
MUL     DX              ;AX=sectors/drive
MUL     CX              ;DX:AX=bytes/drive
MOV     BPD_HI,DX       ;Save high word
MOV     BPD_LO,AX       ;Save low word
POP     AX              ;Get back sectors/cluster
MUL     BX              ;AX=free sectors/drive
MUL     CX              ;DX:AX=free bytes/drive
MOV     FBPD_HI,DX      ;Save high word
MOV     FBPD_LO,AX      ;Save low word
```

Description: This service returns basic information about space on the disk in the drive specified by DL. Notice that the drive code is different from the normal method for DOS and BIOS drive designation. In this instance, 0 equals the default drive, and 1=A, 2=B, 3=C, etc.

On return from this service, the calling program checks AX to determine whether an error has occurred. If AX contains FFFFh, the drive code is invalid, and the balance of the registers are undefined.

If AX does not indicate an error, the information this service returns is similar to that provided by services 21/1B and 21/1C. This information includes the number of bytes per sector (CX), the number of sectors per cluster (AX), the number of clusters per disk (DX), and the number of free clusters on the disk (BX).

Once you know this information, deriving other valuable information is easy. For instance, to determine the byte capacity of the disk, you simply multiply CX by AX by DX.

Reserved (Interrupt 21h, service 37h)

Description: This service is listed by IBM and Microsoft as reserved for the internal use of DOS. The service, which is not publicized or documented, is subject to modification in future versions of DOS.

Get/Set Country-Dependent Information (Interrupt 21h, service 38h)

Category: System services

Registers on Entry:

AH: 38h
AL: Country specifier
BX: Country specifier
DS: Segment address of information block
DX: Offset address of information block

Registers on Return: Unchanged

AX: Error code
BX: Country specifier
DS: Segment address of information block
DX: Offset address of information block

Memory Affected: If country information is retrieved, the memory block to which DS:DX points is overwritten with the country-dependent information.

Syntax:

```
MOV   AL,Ø                    ;Info for current country
PUSH  CS                      ;Code segment and
POP   DS                      ;  data segment are same
MOV   DX,OFFSET INFO_BLOCK    ;Offset address of block
MOV   AH,38h                  ;Want service 38h
INT   21h                     ;DOS services interrupt
```

Description: This powerful service allows you to retrieve or set a great deal of system information. The purposes and function of this service have changed over the course of several different versions of DOS. The description here conforms with the function of the service according to DOS 3.00.

DOS uses the country information governed by this service to control elements such as the display of dates and numbers. This service allows a program great flexibility in handling display formats, flexibility that is particularly useful if the software is being used for a market other than the United States. However, because most computers sold in the United States come configured for this country, this service may have little value for programmers whose sole market is the United States.

To get country-dependent information, simply load DS:DX with the segment:offset address of the 34-byte memory block that will be used to store the retrieved information. Load AL with the country code to be retrieved, as indicated in table 13.4.

Table 13.4
Country Codes

Country	Code
Currently installed	0
United States	1
Netherlands	31
Belgium	32
France	33
Spain	34
Italy	39
Switzerland	41
United Kingdom	44
Denmark	45
Sweden	46
Norway	47
Germany	49
Australia	61
Finland	358
Israel	972

If the country code is greater than 255 (as it is for Finland and Israel), you enter FFh in AL and set BX to the country code value. If AL is less than FFh, the contents of BX are not significant. Notice that if AL is 0, the country information table reflects the current country's information. If a different country is selected, that country's information is returned with no effect on the currently configured country.

On return, the carry flag indicates whether an error has occurred. If the carry flag is set, AX contains the error code, which can be handled through service 21/59. If the carry is clear, DS:DX points to the information table.

The following code segment illustrates a typical pattern for setting up the information table area. The code segment details the fields of the returned information:

```
COUNTRY_TABLE   EQU     THIS BYTE
DATE_FORMAT     DW      ØØØØ            ;Numeric code
CURRENCY_SYM    DB      5 DUP(Ø)        ;ASCIIZ--zero terminated
THOUSANDS_SEP   DB      ØØ              ;ASCIIZ--zero terminated
                DB      ØØ              ;  this byte will be nul
DECIMAL_SEP     DB      ØØ              ;ASCIIZ--zero terminated
                DB      ØØ              ;  this byte will be nul
DATE_SEP        DB      ØØ              ;ASCIIZ--zero terminated
                DB      ØØ              ;  this byte will be nul
TIME_SEP        DB      ØØ              ;ASCIIZ--zero terminated
                DB      ØØ              ;  this byte will be nul
CURRENCY_FMT    DB      ØØ              ;Numeric code
CURRENCY_SD     DB      ØØ              ;Sig. decimals in currency
TIME_FMT        DB      ØØ              ;Ø=normal, 1=military
MAP_CALL        DD      ØØØØØØØØ        ;Map call address
DATALIST_SEP    DB      ØØ              ;ASCIIZ--zero terminated
                DB      ØØ              ;  this byte will be nul
                DB      5 DUP(Ø)        ;Reserved area
```

To use this code segment, load DS:DX with the segment:offset of COUNTRY_TABLE before calling this service. On return, the information table is filled in, and individual fields can be addressed by field name.

DATE_FMT is a numeric code indicating the format to be used to display the date. Table 13.5 gives the possible values for this field. Notice also that this field is one word long, which may indicate significant expansion in future versions of DOS.

Table 13.5
Date Format Codes and Their Meanings

Code	Date Format	Country Affiliation
0	mm dd yy	United States
1	dd mm yy	Europe
2	yy mm dd	Japan and the Far East

Now, refer again to the code segment. CURRENCY_SYM is a nul-terminated string that indicates the currency symbol for the country. This symbol can be no more than four characters long because the last character has a value of 0 (thus the designation *nul-terminated*, or *ASCIIZ* string).

THOUSANDS_SEP, DECIMAL_SEP, DATE_SEP, TIME_SEP, and DATALIST_SEP also are ASCIIZ strings. They indicate, respectively, the characters to be used to separate thousands in number displays, to indicate the decimal point, to separate date components, to separate time components, and to separate items in a data list. Each field is two bytes long, with the second byte set to nul. Why the writers of DOS felt that a single-byte string needed to be set up as an ASCIIZ string is a mystery.

CURRENCY_FMT is a numeric code indicating the format to be used to display the currency. Table 13.6 gives the possible values for this field.

Table 13.6
Currency Format Codes and Their Meanings

Code	Meaning
0	Currency symbol immediately precedes currency value
1	Currency symbol immediately follows currency value
2	Currency symbol and space immediately precede currency value
3	Currency symbol and space immediately follow currency value
4	Currency symbol replaces decimal separator

CURRENCY_SD indicates the number of significant decimal places in the country's currency displays.

Bit 0 of TIME_FMT indicates how the hours of a time display are handled. If bit 0 is 0, a 12-hour clock is used. If bit 0 is 1, a military (or 24-hour) clock is used.

MAP_CALL is the full segment:offset address of a DOS subroutine that converts foreign ASCII lowercase characters to their uppercase equivalents. This routine is intended for ASCII codes with values greater than 7Fh. The original ASCII code is specified in AL; then this routine is called, and the converted ASCII code is returned in AL.

This service returns the country code in BX as well as the information in the country table. This code is meaningful only if you invoked the service with AL set to 0. In this manner you can determine the country for which the computer is configured.

To set country-dependent information, simply load DX with FFFFh, the signal that informs DOS that the country-dependent information is being set. You load AL with the country code (refer to table 13.4) to be retrieved. If the country code is greater than 255 (as for Finland and Israel), you enter FFh in AL and set BX to the country code value. If AL is less than FFh, the contents of BX are not significant.

On return, the carry flag indicates whether an error has occurred. If the carry flag is set, AX contains the error code, which can be handled through service 21/59. If the carry is clear, no error has occurred, and the contents of AX are not significant.

Create Subdirectory (Interrupt 21h, service 39h)

Category: Disk services

Registers on Entry:

AH: 39h
DX: Offset address of path name
DS: Segment address of path name

Registers on Return:

AX: Error code

Memory Affected: None

Syntax:

```
PUSH    CS                      ;Code segment and
POP     DS                      ;  data segment are same
MOV     DX,OFFSET PATH_NAME     ;Offset address of path
MOV     AH,39h                  ;Want service 39h
INT     21h                     ;DOS services interrupt
JC      ERROR                   ;Carry set, handle error
```

Description: This service (the opposite of service 21/3A) allows the creation of a subdirectory. The result is the same as the result of using the DOS command MKDIR or MD. On entry, DS:DX points to an ASCIIZ (nul-terminated ASCII) string that contains the name of the directory.

On return, if the carry flag is set, an error has occurred, and the error code is in AX. Service 21/59 can be used to get detailed error information. If the carry flag is not set, the operation was successful, and AX is undefined.

Remove Subdirectory (Interrupt 21h, service 3Ah)

Category: Disk services

Registers on Entry:

AH: 3Ah
DX: Offset address of path name
DS: Segment address of path name

Registers on Return:

AX: Error code

Memory Affected: None

Syntax:

```
PUSH   CS                      ;Code segment and
POP    DS                      ;  data segment are same
MOV    DX,OFFSET PATH_NAME     ;Offset address of path
MOV    AH,3Ah                  ;Want service 3Ah
INT    21h                     ;DOS services interrupt
JC     ERROR                   ;Carry set, handle error
```

Description: This service (the opposite of service 21/39) is used to remove existing subdirectories. The result is the same as the result of using the DOS command RMDIR or RD. On entry, DS:DX points to an ASCIIZ (nul-terminated ASCII) string that contains the name of the directory.

On return, if the carry flag is set, an error has occurred, and the error code is in AX. Service 21/59 can be used to get detailed error information. If the carry flag is not set, the operation was successful, and AX is undefined.

Set Directory (Interrupt 21h, service 3Bh)

Category: Disk services

Registers on Entry:

AH: 3Bh
DX: Offset address of path name
DS: Segment address of path name

Registers on Return:

AX: Error code

Memory Affected: None

Syntax:

```
PUSH    CS                      ;Code segment and
POP     DS                      ;  data segment are same
MOV     DX,OFFSET PATH_NAME     ;Offset address of path
MOV     AH,3Bh                  ;Want service 3Bh
INT     21h                     ;DOS services interrupt
JC      ERROR                   ;Carry set, handle error
```

Description: This service is used to change the default directory setting. The result is the same as that of using the DOS command CHDIR or CD. On entry, DS:DX points to an ASCIIZ (nul-terminated ASCII) string that contains the name of the directory.

On return, if the carry flag is set, an error has occurred, and the error code is in AX. Service 21/59 can be used to get detailed error information. If the carry flag is not set, the operation was successful, and AX is undefined.

Create File (Interrupt 21h, service 3Ch)

Category: Disk services

Registers on Entry:

AH: 3Ch
CX: File attribute
DX: Offset address of path name
DS: Segment address of path name

Registers on Return:

AX: Return code

Memory Affected: None

Syntax:

```
PUSH    CS                      ;Code segment and
POP     DS                      ;  data segment are same
MOV     DX,OFFSET PATH_NAME     ;Offset address of path
MOV     CX,Ø                    ;File attribute is normal
MOV     AH,3Ch                  ;Want service 3Ch
INT     21h                     ;DOS services interrupt
JC      ERROR                   ;Carry set, handle error
MOV     FILE_HANDLE,AX          ;Store returned handle
```

Description: This service is used to create or truncate a disk file. On entry, DS:DX points to an ASCIIZ (nul-terminated ASCII) string that contains the full name of the file, including any applicable path name. CX is set equal to the desired attribute for the file.

This service is identical to service 21/5B, except that if the file name specified in the ASCIIZ string already exists, the file is opened and its length is truncated to 0.

On return, if the carry flag is set, an error has occurred, and the error code is in AX. Service 21/59 can be used to get detailed error information. If the carry flag is not set, the operation was successful, and AX contains the file handle for the newly opened file. This number (file handle) can be used in many other DOS file operations.

When this service is completed, the specified file is left open. You do not need to open the file, but you must remember to close it.

Open File (Interrupt 21h, service 3Dh)

Category: Disk services

Registers on Entry:

AH: 3Dh
AL: Open code
DX: Offset address of path name
DS: Segment address of path name

Registers on Return:

AX: File handle or error code

Memory Affected: None

Syntax:

```
PUSH    CS                      ;Code segment and
POP     DS                      ;  data segment are same
MOV     DX,OFFSET PATH_NAME     ;Offset address of path
MOV     AL,11000010b            ;Set proper open mode
MOV     AH,3Dh                  ;Want service 3Dh
INT     21h                     ;DOS services interrupt
JC      ERROR                   ;Carry set, handle error
MOV     FILE_HANDLE,AX          ;Save file handle
```

Description: This service opens a disk file. On entry, DS:DX points to an ASCIIZ (nul-terminated ASCII) string that contains the full name of the file, including any applicable path name. AL is set to equal the mode to be used for the open file. Each bit in AL has significance. Table 13.7 gives detailed information.

Table 13.7
Open Mode Bit Settings for Service 21/3D

Bits 76543210	Meaning
0	File is inherited by a child process
1	File is not inherited by a child process
000	Sharing mode—allow compatible access
001	Sharing mode—exclusive access
010	Sharing mode—deny others write access
011	Sharing mode—deny others read access
100	Sharing mode—allow others full access
0	Reserved—set to 0
000	Open for read access
001	Open for write access
010	Open for read/write access

On return, if the carry flag is set, an error has occurred, and the error code is in AX. Service 21/59 can be used to get detailed error information. If the carry flag is not set, the operation was successful, and AX contains the file handle for the newly opened file. This number (file handle) can be used in many other DOS file operations.

Close File (Interrupt 21h, service 3Eh)

Category: Disk services

Registers on Entry:

AH: 3Eh
BX: File handle

Registers on Return:

AX: Error code

Memory Affected: None

Syntax:

```
MOV     BX,FILE_HANDLE          ;Get file handle
MOV     AH,3Eh                  ;Want service 3Eh
INT     21h                     ;DOS services interrupt
JC      ERROR                   ;Carry set, handle error
```

Description: This service closes a previously opened file. The file handle must be loaded in BX.

On return, if the carry flag is set, an error has occurred, and the error code is in AX. Service 21/59 can be used to get detailed error information. If the carry flag is not set, the operation was successful.

Read File (Interrupt 21h, service 3Fh)

Category: Disk services

Registers on Entry:

AH: 3Fh
BX: File handle
CX: Bytes to read
DX: Offset address for buffer
DS: Segment address for buffer

Registers on Return:

AX: Return code

Memory Affected: The memory area specified by DS:DX is overlaid with information read from the disk.

Syntax:

```
MOV     BX,FILE_HANDLE          ;Get file handle
PUSH    CS                      ;Code segment and
POP     DS                      ;   data segment are same
MOV     DX,OFFSET BUFFER        ;Offset address of buffer
MOV     CX,1000h                ;Read 4K of info
MOV     AH,3Fh                  ;Want service 3Fh
INT     21h                     ;DOS services interrupt
JC      ERROR                   ;Carry set, handle error
```

Description: This service reads information from a disk file. The file handle is specified in BX, with DS:DX pointing to the input buffer. CX is set to the number of bytes to be read.

Reading from the file is done based on the value of the file pointer. If the file has just been opened, reading begins from the beginning of the file. Subsequent reads begin at the point where the last read finished.

On return, if the carry flag is set, an error has occurred, and the error code is in AX. Service 21/59 can be used to get detailed error information. If the carry flag is not set, the operation was successful, and AX contains the number of bytes actually read.

Write File (Interrupt 21h, service 40h)

Category: Disk services

Registers on Entry:

AH: 40h
BX: File handle
CX: Bytes to write
DX: Offset address for buffer
DS: Segment address for buffer

Registers on Return:

AX: Return code

Memory Affected: None

Syntax:

```
MOV     BX,FILE_HANDLE          ;Get file handle
PUSH    CS                      ;Code segment and
POP     DS                      ;  data segment are same
MOV     DX,OFFSET BUFFER        ;Offset address of buffer
MOV     CX,1000h                ;Write 4K of info
PUSH    CX                      ;Save for later reference
MOV     AH,40h                  ;Want service 40h
INT     21h                     ;DOS services interrupt
JC      ERROR                   ;Carry set, handle error
POP     CX                      ;Get original bytes back
CMP     AX,CX                   ;Are they the same?
JNE     ERROR                   ;No, go handle
```

Description: This service writes information to a disk file. The file handle is specified in BX, with DS:DX pointing to the buffer area. CX is set to the number of bytes to be copied from the buffer to the disk.

Writing is done based on the value of the file pointer. If the file has just been opened, writing begins at the front of the file. Subsequent writes begin at the point where the last write finished.

On return, if the carry flag is set, an error has occurred, and the error code is in AX. Service 21/59 can be used to get detailed error information. If the carry flag is not set, the operation was successful, and AX contains the number of bytes actually written. If AX does not equal the number of bytes that should have been written, an error (such as the disk being full) has occurred, even though the carry flag is not set.

Delete File (Interrupt 21h, service 41h)

Category: Disk services

Registers on Entry:

AH: 41h
DX: Offset address of path name
DS: Segment address of path name

Registers on Return:

AX: Error code

Memory Affected: None

Syntax:

```
PUSH    CS                      ;Code segment and
POP     DS                      ;  data segment are same
MOV     DX,OFFSET PATH_NAME     ;Offset address of path
MOV     AH,41h                  ;Want service 41h
INT     21h                     ;DOS services interrupt
JC      ERROR                   ;Carry set, handle error
```

Description: This service deletes a disk file. On entry, DS:DX points to an ASCIIZ (nul-terminated ASCII) string that contains the full name of the file, including any applicable path name. Wildcards cannot be used in the file designation. If the file being deleted has a read-only attribute, this service returns an error.

On return, if the carry flag is set, an error has occurred, and the error code is in AX. Service 21/59 can be used to get detailed error information. If the carry flag is not set, the operation was successful.

Move File Pointer (Interrupt 21h, service 42h)

Category: Disk services

Registers on Entry:

AH: 42h
AL: Movement code
BX: File handle
CX: High-order word of distance to move
DX: Low-order word of distance to move

Registers on Return:

AX: Low-order word of new pointer location or error code
DX: High-order word of new pointer location

Memory Affected: None

Syntax:

```
MOV     BX,FILE_HANDLE          ;Get file handle
MOV     AL,Ø                    ;Relative to start of file
MOV     CX,DIST_HIGH            ;Distance to move
MOV     DX,DIST_LOW             ;
MOV     AH,42h                  ;Want service 42h
INT     21h                     ;DOS services interrupt
JC      ERROR                   ;Carry set, handle error
```

Description: This service causes the file pointer to move to a new location. The file handle is specified in BX, and the distance to move (in bytes) is specified in CX:DX. A movement code is specified in AL (see table 13.8).

Table 13.8
Movement Code for Service 21/42

Value	Meaning
0	Move relative to beginning of file
1	Move relative to current pointer location
2	Move relative to end of file

If the offset specified in CX:DX is too large, you can move the file pointer past the beginning or the end of the file. Doing so does not generate an immediate error but does cause an error when reading or writing is attempted later.

On return, if the carry flag is set, an error has occurred, and the error code is in AX. Service 21/59 can be used to get detailed error information. If the carry flag is not set, the operation was successful, and DX:AX contains the new file pointer value.

Get/Set File Attributes
(Interrupt 21h, service 43h)

Category: Disk services

Registers on Entry:

> AH: 43h
> AL: Function code
> CX: Desired attribute
> DX: Offset address of path name
> DS: Segment address of path name

Registers on Return:

> AX: Error code
> CX: Current attribute

Memory Affected: None

Syntax:

```
MOV    AL,Ø                  ;Get current attribute
PUSH   CS                    ;Code segment and
POP    DS                    ;  data segment are same
MOV    DX,OFFSET PATH_NAME   ;Offset address of PATH
MOV    AH,43h                ;Want service 43h
INT    21h                   ;DOS services interrupt
JC     ERROR                 ;Go handle error
```

Description: This service allows you to determine or set a file's attribute. The desired function is specified in AL. If AL=0, the file attribute is retrieved; if AL=1, the file attribute is set.

DS:DX should point to an ASCIIZ (nul-terminated ASCII) string that contains the full name of the file, including any applicable path name. Wildcards cannot be used in the file designation. If you are setting the file attribute (AL=1), place the desired value in CX. Actually, because the file attribute is only a byte in length, the new setting is placed in CL, and CH is set to 0. Table 13.9 shows the possible file attribute settings. In this table, a 1 in a bit position indicated by an *x* means that the attribute is selected; a 0 means that the attribute is not selected.

You cannot change the volume label or subdirectory bits of the file attribute. If you attempt to do so or if these bits are not set to 0, an error is generated. If you are retrieving the file attribute (AL=0), the contents of CX are not significant.

Table 13.9
Bit Settings for File Attribute, Service 21/43

Bits 76543210	Meaning
00	Reserved—set to 0
x	Archive
0	Subdirectory—set to 0 for this service
0	Volume label—set to 0 for this service
x	System
x	Hidden
x	Read-only

On return, if the carry flag is set, an error has occurred, and the error code is in AX. Service 21/59 can be used to get detailed error information. If the carry flag is not set, the operation was successful. If you were retrieving the file attribute, CX contains the requested information.

Device I/O Control
(Interrupt 21h, service 44h)

Description: This service controls I/O with DOS device drivers. This service has 12 individual functions, which are selected by the value in AL. The following several service/function sections describe the functions for this service.

Get Device Information
(Interrupt 21h, service 44h, function 0)

Category: System services

Registers on Entry:

AH: 44h
AL: 0
BX: Device handle

Registers on Return:

DX: Device information

Memory Affected: None

Syntax:

```
MOV    AL,Ø                    ;Want function Ø
MOV    BX,DEVICE_HANDLE        ;Use this handle
MOV    AH,44h                  ;Want service 44h
INT    21h                     ;DOS services interrupt
```

Description: This function retrieves information about the device. On calling, AL should contain 0 and BX should contain the device handle. On return, DX contains the requested information, as given in table 13.10.

Table 13.10
Device Information Returned by Function 21/44/0

Bits FEDCBA98 76543210	*Meaning*
?	Reserved
0	Control strings not allowed for services 21/44/2, 21/44/3, 21/44/4, and 21/44/5. This bit is significant only if bit 7 is 1.
1	Control strings acceptable for services 21/44/2, 21/44/3, 21/44/4, and 21/44/5. This bit is significant only if bit 7 is 1.
??????	Reserved
0	This channel is a disk file.
1	This channel is a device.
0	End of file
1	Not end of file
0	Using ASCII mode
1	Using binary mode
?	Reserved
0	Not a clock device
1	Clock device
0	Normal device
1	Null device
0	Not console output device
1	Console output device
0	Not console input device
1	Console input device

This function is not supported on network devices.

Set Device Information
(Interrupt 21h, service 44h, function 1)

Category: System services

Registers on Entry:

AH: 44h
AL: 1
BX: Device handle
DH: 0
DL: Device information

Registers on Return: Unchanged

Memory Affected: None

Syntax:

```
MOV    AL,1                    ;Want function 1
MOV    DH,Ø                    ;Must be set to Ø
MOV    DL,DEVICE_INFO          ;Desired configuration
MOV    BX,DEVICE_HANDLE        ;For this device
MOV    AH,44h                  ;Want service 44h
INT    21h                     ;DOS services interrupt
```

Description: This function is used to set information about the device. On calling, AL should contain 1, BX should contain the device handle, and DL should contain the device information, as given in table 13.11. DH must be set to 0.

This function is not supported on network devices.

Character Device Read
(Interrupt 21h, service 44h, function 2)

Category: System services

Registers on Entry:

AH: 44h
AL: 2
BX: Device handle
CX: Bytes to read
DX: Offset address of buffer
DS: Segment address of buffer

Table 13.11
Device Information for Function 21/44/1

Bits 76543210	Meaning
0	This channel is a disk file.
1	This channel is a device.
0	End of file
1	Not end of file
0	Using binary mode
1	Using ASCII mode
0	Not a clock device
1	Clock device
0	Normal device
1	Null device
0	Not console output device
1	Console output device
0	Not console input device
1	Console input device

Registers on Return:

AX: Bytes read

Memory Affected: The buffer area at DS:DX is overwritten with information read from the device driver.

Syntax:

```
PUSH    CS                      ;Code segment and
POP     DS                      ;   data segment are same
MOV     DX,OFFSET BUFFER        ;Address of input buffer
MOV     AL,2                    ;Want function 2
MOV     BX,DEVICE_HANDLE        ;Want this device
MOV     CX,NUM_BYTES            ;Read this many bytes
MOV     AH,44h                  ;Want service 44h
INT     21h                     ;DOS services interrupt
```

Description: This function reads a control string from the device. The buffer specified by DS:DX stores the information from device BX. Only CX bytes are read from the device.

For this function to be usable, bit 14 of the device information word (as returned in the DX register through service 21/44/0) must be 1. (Refer to table 13.10 for the makeup of the device information word.) This service is not supported on network devices.

Character Device Write
(Interrupt 21h, service 44h, function 3)

Category: System services

Registers on Entry:

AH: 44h
AL: 3
BX: Device handle
CX: Bytes to write
DX: Offset address of buffer
DS: Segment address of buffer

Registers on Return:

AX: Bytes written

Memory Affected: None

Syntax:

```
PUSH    CS                  ;Code segment and
POP     DS                  ;   data segment are same
MOV     DX,OFFSET BUFFER    ;Address of input buffer
MOV     BX,DEVICE_HANDLE    ;Want this device
MOV     CX,NUM_BYTES        ;Write this many bytes
PUSH    CX                  ;Store for later check
MOV     AL,3                ;Want function 3
MOV     AH,44h              ;Want service 44h
INT     21h                 ;DOS services interrupt
POP     CX                  ;Get back original number
CMP     AX,CX               ;Was everything written?
JE      ERROR               ;No, go handle
```

Description: This function writes a control string to a device. CX bytes of information stored at the buffer address specified by DS:DX are written to device BX.

For this function to be usable, bit 14 of the device information word (as returned in the DX register through service 21/44/0) must be 1. (Refer to table 13.10 for the makeup of the device information word.) This service is not supported on network devices.

Block Device Read (Interrupt 21h, service 44h, function 4)

Category: System services

Registers on Entry:

AH: 44h
AL: 4
BL: Drive number
CX: Bytes to read
DX: Offset address of buffer
DS: Segment address of buffer

Registers on Return:

AX: Bytes read

Memory Affected: The buffer area at DS:DX is overwritten with information read from the drive.

Syntax:

```
PUSH   CS                       ;Code segment and
POP    DS                       ;   data segment are same
MOV    DX,OFFSET BUFFER         ;Address of input buffer
MOV    AL,4                     ;Want function 4
MOV    BL,DRIVE                 ;Want this drive
MOV    CX,NUM_BYTES             ;Read this many bytes
MOV    AH,44h                   ;Want service 44h
INT    21h                      ;DOS services interrupt
```

Description: This function reads a control string from a block device, typically a disk drive. BL is used to specify which drive to use, where 0=default, 1=A, 2=B, 3=C, etc. The information is stored at the buffer specified by DS:DX. Only CX bytes are read.

For this function to be usable, bit 14 of the device information word (as returned in the DX register through service 21/44/0) must be 1. (Refer to table 13.10 for the makeup of the device information word.) This service is not supported on network devices.

Block Device Write (Interrupt 21h, service 44h, function 5)

Category: System services

Registers on Entry:

AH: 44h
AL: 5
BL: Drive number
CX: Bytes to write
DX: Offset address of buffer
DS: Segment address of buffer

Registers on Return:

AX: Bytes written

Memory Affected: None

Syntax:

```
PUSH   CS                    ;Code segment and
POP    DS                    ;  data segment are same
MOV    DX,OFFSET BUFFER      ;Address of input buffer
MOV    BL,DRIVE              ;Want this drive
MOV    CX,NUM_BYTES          ;Write this many bytes
PUSH   CX                    ;Store for later check
MOV    AL,5                  ;Want function 5
MOV    AH,44h                ;Want service 44h
INT    21h                   ;DOS services interrupt
POP    CX                    ;Get back original number
CMP    AX,CX                 ;Was everything written?
JE     ERROR                 ;No, go handle
```

Description: This function writes a control string to a block device, typically a disk drive. BL is used to specify which drive to use, where 0=default, 1=A, 2=B, 3=C, etc. CX bytes of information stored at the buffer address specified by DS:DX are written.

For this function to be usable, bit 14 of the device information word (as returned in the DX register through service 21/44/0) must be 1. (Refer to table 13.10 for the makeup of the device information word.) This service is not supported on network devices.

Get Input Status (Interrupt 21h, service 44h, function 6)

Category: System services

Registers on Entry:

AH: 44h
AL: 6
BX: Device handle

Registers on Return:

AL: Status

Memory Affected: None

Syntax:

```
MOV     BX,DEVICE_HANDLE        ;Use this device
MOV     AL,6                    ;Want function 6
MOV     AH,44h                  ;Want service 44h
INT     21h                     ;DOS services interrupt
```

Description: This service determines whether the device is ready for input. If the device is ready, AL returns 0Fh. If the device is not ready, AL returns 0.

If the device specified in BX is a file, AL always returns FFh until the end of file is reached, at which point AL is equal to 0.

This function is not supported on network devices.

Get Output Status (Interrupt 21h, service 44h, function 7)

Category: System services

Registers on Entry:

AH: 44h
AL: 7
BX: Device handle

Registers on Return:

AL: Status

Memory Affected: None

Syntax:

```
MOV     BX,DEVICE_HANDLE        ;Use this device
MOV     AL,7                    ;Want function 7
MOV     AH,44h                  ;Want service 44h
INT     21h                     ;DOS services interrupt
```

Description: This service determines whether the device is ready for output. If the device is ready, AL returns 0Fh. If the device is not ready, AL returns 0.

If the device specified in BX is a file, AL always returns FFh until the end of file is reached, at which point AL is equal to 0.

This function is not supported on network devices.

Block Device Changeable? (Interrupt 21h, service 44h, function 8)

Category: System services

Registers on Entry:

AH: 44h
AL: 8
BL: Drive number

Registers on Return:

AX: Status

Memory Affected: None

Syntax:

```
MOV     BL,Ø            ;Check on default drive
MOV     AL,8            ;Want function 8
MOV     AH,44h          ;Want service 44h
INT     21h             ;DOS services interrupt
CMP     AX,1            ;Is it fixed?
JE      FIXED           ;Yes, so treat accordingly
```

Description: This function allows your program to determine whether the block device (typically a disk drive) supports removable media. BL is used to specify which drive to check, where 0=default, 1=A, 2=B, 3=C, etc.

On return, AX is equal to 0 if removable media is supported, and equal to 1 if the media is not removable (fixed disk). If AX is equal to 0Fh, the value specified in BL is an invalid drive.

This function is not supported on network devices.

Logical Device Local/Remote Determination (Interrupt 21h, service 44h, function 9)

Category: System services

Registers on Entry:

AH: 44h
AL: 9
BL: Drive number

Registers on Return:

DX: Status

Memory Affected: None

Syntax:

```
MOV    BL,Ø         ;Check on default drive
MOV    AL,9         ;Want function 9
MOV    AH,44h       ;Want service 44h
INT    21h          ;DOS services interrupt
```

Description: This function is used in a networking environment to determine whether the block device (usually a disk drive) specified in BL is local or remote. BL is used to specify which drive to check, where 0=default, 1=A, 2=B, 3=C, etc.

On return, bit 12 of DX is set if the device is remote. If the device is local or if redirection is paused, bit 12 is clear.

Handle Local/Remote Determination (Interrupt 21h, service 44h, function 0Ah)

Category: System services

Registers on Entry:

AH: 44h
AL: 0Ah
BX: File handle

Registers on Return:

DX: Status

Memory Affected: None

Syntax:

```
MOV    BX,FILE_HANDLE          ;Checking this file
MOV    AL,ØAh                  ;Want function ØAh
MOV    AH,44h                  ;Want service 44h
INT    21h                     ;DOS services interrupt
```

Description: This function is used in a networking environment to determine whether a given file handle (specified in BX) represents a local or a remote file.

On return, bit 15 of DX is set if the device is remote. If the device is local, bit 15 is clear.

Set Sharing Retry Count (Interrupt 21h, service 44h, function 0Bh)

Category: System services

Registers on Entry:

AH: 44h
AL: 0Bh
CX: Delay loop counter
DX: Retries

Registers on Return:

AX: Error code

Memory Affected: None

Syntax:

```
MOV    CX,3                    ;3 delay loops
MOV    DX,8                    ;8 retries
MOV    AL,ØBh                  ;Want function ØBh
MOV    AH,44h                  ;Want service 44h
INT    21h                     ;DOS services interrupt
JC     ERROR                   ;Error, go handle
```

Description: This function is used in a networking environment to specify the number of attempts at file access and the delay between retries. If a file is locked or if a sharing conflict exists, DOS attempts to access the file three times with one delay loop between attempts before returning an error.

On return, the carry flag indicates an error if one has occurred. If the carry flag is set, AX contains the error code, which can be handled through service 21/59.

Handle Generic Code Page Switching
(Interrupt 21h, service 44h, function 0Ch)

Category: System services

Registers on Entry:

AH: 44h
AL: 0Ch
BX: Device handle
CH: Major subfunction code
CL: Minor subfunction code
DX: Offset address of parameter block
DS: Segment address of parameter block

Registers on Return:

AX: Error code

Memory Affected: This function can have various effects on memory, depending on the major and minor subfunctions requested.

Syntax:

```
PUSH    CS                      ;Code segment and
POP     DS                      ;  data segment are same
MOV     DX,OFFSET PARM_BLOCK    ;Address of parameter block
MOV     BX,DEVICE_HANDLE        ;Device handle in use
MOV     CH,MAJOR                ;Major subfunction desired
MOV     CL,MINOR                ;Minor subfunction desired
MOV     AL,0Ch                  ;Want function Ch
MOV     AH,44h                  ;Want service 44h
INT     21h                     ;DOS services interrupt
```

Description: This service allows device driver support for subfunctions that enable code page switching. You specify the device handle in BX, a major subfunction code in CH, and a minor code in CL. Currently, the service has four major codes and five minor codes, for a total of 20 possible combinations of major/minor codes. Each minor code requires a different set of parameters, which are passed through a parameter block. DS:DX points to this parameter block.

On return, the carry flag indicates an error if one has occurred. If the carry flag is set, AX contains the error code, which can be handled through service 21/59.

Because of the detail and complexity involved with this function, its discussion is best left to another publication. Detailed information about this function is available in the DOS 3.3 *Technical Reference Manual*.

Generic IOCTL Block Device Request
(Interrupt 21h, service 44h, function 0Dh)

Category: System services

Registers on Entry:

AH: 44h
AL: 0Dh
BL: Drive number
CH: Major subfunction code
CL: Minor subfunction code
DX: Offset address of parameter block
DS: Segment address of parameter block

Registers on Return:

AX: Error code

Memory Affected: This function can have various effects on memory, depending on the major and minor subfunctions requested.

Syntax:

```
PUSH    CS                      ;Code segment and
POP     DS                      ;   data segment are same
MOV     DX,OFFSET PARM_BLOCK    ;Address of parameter block
MOV     BL,Ø                    ;Check on default drive
MOV     CH,8                    ;Always 8
MOV     CL,MINOR                ;Minor subfunction desired
MOV     AL,ØDh                  ;Want function Dh
MOV     AH,44h                  ;Want service 44h
INT     21h                     ;DOS services interrupt
```

Description: This service allows uniform device support for a number of block device functions—typically, disk drive functions. The drive number is specified in BL. BL is used to specify the drive, where 0=default, 1=A, 2=B, 3=C, etc.

A major subfunction code is specified in CH, which is always 8 (as of DOS 3.3). A minor subfunction code is specified in CL. The possible minor codes are detailed in table 13.12.

Each minor code requires a different set of parameters, which are passed through a parameter block. DS:DX points to this parameter block.

On return, the carry flag indicates whether an error has occurred. If the carry flag is set, AX contains the error code, which can be handled through service 21/59.

Table 13.12
Minor Subfunction Codes (CL) for Service 21/44/D

Value	Meaning
40h	Set device parameters
41h	Write logical device track
42h	Format and verify logical device track
60h	Get device parameters
61h	Read logical device track
62h	Verify logical device track

Because of the detail and complexity involved with this function, its discussion is best left to another publication. Detailed information about this function, its subfunctions, and the parameter setup is available in the DOS 3.3 *Technical Reference Manual*.

Get Logical Device (Interrupt 21h, service 44h, function 0Eh)

Category: System services

Registers on Entry:

AH: 44h
AL: 0Eh
BL: Drive number

Registers on Return:

AX: Return code

Memory Affected: None

Syntax:

```
MOV   BL,0         ;Use default drive
MOV   AL,0Eh       ;Want function 0Eh
MOV   AH,44h       ;Want service 44h
INT   21h          ;DOS services interrupt
```

Description: This function determines whether a block device (typically, a disk drive) has more than one logical drive assigned to it. Use BL to specify which drive to check, where 0=default, 1=A, 2=B, 3=C, etc.

On return, the carry flag indicates whether an error has occurred. If the carry flag is set, AX contains the error code, which can be handled through service 21/59. If the carry flag is not set, AL contains the result code. If AL is 0, the block device has only one logical drive assigned. If AL contains another number, that number represents the drive letter last used to reference the device. In this case, 1=A, 2=B, 3=C, etc.

Set Logical Device (Interrupt 21h, service 44h, function 0Fh)

Category: System services

Registers on Entry:

> AH: 44h
> AL: 0Fh
> BL: Drive number

Registers on Return:

> AX: Return code

Memory Affected: None

Syntax:

```
MOV    BL,Ø            ;Use default drive
MOV    AL,ØFh          ;Want function ØFh
MOV    AH,44h          ;Want service 44h
INT    21h             ;DOS services interrupt
```

Description: This function assigns a logical drive letter to a block device (typically a disk drive). Use BL to specify the drive letter, where 1=A, 2=B, 3=C, etc. You use this function where more than one logical drive letter can be assigned to a single physical block device. An example is a system with a single floppy drive. Even though the system has only one block device (the floppy drive), that device can be addressed logically as two devices (drives A: and B:). This function causes DOS to view the system as either A: or B: in subsequent I/O functions.

On return, the carry flag indicates whether an error has occurred. If the carry flag is set, AX contains the error code, which can be handled through service 21/59.

Duplicate File Handle
(Interrupt 21h, service 45h)

Category: Disk services

Registers on Entry:

AH: 45h
BX: File handle

Registers on Return:

AX: Return code

Memory Affected: None

Syntax:

```
MOV    BX,FILE_HANDLE_1        ;Use current file handle
MOV    AH,45h                  ;Want service 45h
INT    21h                     ;DOS services interrupt
JC     ERROR                   ;Go handle error
MOV    FILE_HANDLE_2,AX        ;Save new handle
```

Description: This service, which duplicates a file handle, results in two handles that point to the same file at the same file position.

There is no clear need or use for this function—you simply can use two different handles to refer to one file. These handles operate in tandem, not independently, because any change that you make to the file pointer by using one of the handles is reflected in the other handle. The most common use for this function is in connection with service 21/46, where you duplicate a handle before reassigning it. This use allows redirection at a later time.

On return, the carry flag indicates whether an error has occurred. If the carry flag is set, AX contains the error code, which can be handled through service 21/59.

Force Handle Duplication
(Interrupt 21h, service 46h)

Category: Disk services

Registers on Entry:

AH: 46h
BX: File handle
CX: File handle to be forced

Registers on Return:

AX: Error code

Memory Affected: None

Syntax:

```
MOV    BX,FILE_HANDLE          ;Original handle
MOV    CX,4                    ;Standard printer handle
MOV    AH,46h                  ;Want service 46h
INT    21h                     ;DOS services interrupt
JC     ERROR                   ;Branch if error
```

Description: This service forces one file handle to point to the same device (file, etc.) another handle points to. In the syntax example, BX represents an open file. CX is loaded with the standard printer handle, and through this service handle 4 is made to point to the open file. Anything sent to handle 4 (normally sent to the printer) is sent to the open file.

On return, the carry flag indicates whether an error has occurred. If the carry flag is set, AX contains the error code, which can be handled through service 21/59.

Get Directory Path
(Interrupt 21h, service 47h)

Category: Disk services

Registers on Entry:

AH: 47h
DL: Drive number
SI: Offset address of buffer area
DS: Segment address of buffer area

Registers on Return: Unchanged

AX: Error code
SI: Offset address of buffer area
DS: Segment address of buffer area

Memory Affected: The memory area pointed to by DS:SI is overwritten with the requested directory information.

Syntax:

```
PUSH   CS                   ;Code segment and
POP    DS                   ;  data segment are same
MOV    SI,OFFSET DIR_BUFFER ;Address of 64-byte buffer
MOV    DL,Ø                 ;Use default drive
MOV    AH,47h               ;Want service 47h
INT    21h                  ;DOS services interrupt
```

Description: This service determines the ASCIIZ string path for the current directory of the drive specified in DL, where 0=default, 1=A, 2=B, 3=C, etc.

The returned string is not the complete path name because the drive designator and root directory backslash are not returned. These characters, however, can be added to the beginning of the string to create a complete path for the directory. Because an ASCIIZ string is returned, it ends with an ASCII 0 (nul).

Because path names can be as many as 64 bytes long, a good practice is to make sure that the buffer area to which DS:SI points is 64 bytes long.

On return, the carry flag indicates whether an error has occurred. If the carry flag is set, AX contains the error code, which can be handled through service 21/59. If the carry flag is not set, the address to which DS:SI points is the start of the returned ASCIIZ string.

Allocate Memory (Interrupt 21h, service 48h)

Category: System services

Registers on Entry:

AH: 48h
BX: Paragraphs to allocate

Registers on Return:

AX: Return code
BX: Maximum paragraphs available

Memory Affected: Although the contents of the requested memory are not changed, the amount of free memory is reduced by the requested number of paragraphs.

Syntax:

```
MOV    BX,1ØØh          ;Request 4K block of memory
MOV    AH,48h           ;Want service 48h
INT    21h              ;DOS services interrupt
JC     ERROR            ;Branch if error
MOV    BLOCK_SEG,AX     ;Save segment address
```

Description: This service is used to set aside blocks of memory for program use. You specify the number of contiguous paragraphs required in BX.

On return, the carry flag indicates whether an error has occurred. If the carry flag is set, AX contains the error code, which can be handled through service 21/59. If an error has occurred, BX contains the maximum number of contiguous paragraphs available.

If the carry flag is not set, AX points to the paragraph or segment address where the memory block begins. This memory block must later be freed (before program completion) through service 21/49.

Free Allocated Memory (Interrupt 21h, service 49h)

Category: System services

Registers on Entry:

AH: 49h
ES: Segment address of memory block

Registers on Return:

AX: Error code

Memory Affected: Although the contents of the requested memory are not changed, the amount of free memory is increased by the size of the block being relinquished.

Syntax:

```
PUSH    ES                      ;Save current segment
MOV     ES,BLOCK_SEG            ;Set to segment to free
MOV     AH,49h                 ;Want service 49h
INT     21h                    ;DOS services interrupt
POP     ES                      ;Get register back
JC      ERROR                   ;Branch if error
MOV     BLOCK_SEG,Ø            ;Zero out variable
```

Description: This service frees memory blocks allocated through service 21/48. You specify the segment address of the block in ES.

On return, the carry flag indicates whether an error has occurred. If the carry flag is set, AX contains the error code, which can be handled through service 21/59.

Change Memory Block Allocation (Interrupt 21h, service 4Ah)

Category: System services

Registers on Entry:

AH: 4Ah
BX: Total paragraphs to allocate
ES: Segment address of memory block

Registers on Return:

AX: Error code
BX: Maximum paragraphs available

Memory Affected: Although the contents of the requested memory are not changed, the amount of free memory is reduced by the difference between the number of paragraphs already allocated to the block and the requested number of paragraphs.

Syntax:

```
MOV    BX,200h              ;Change to 8K block
MOV    AH,4Ah               ;Want service 4Ah
INT    21h                  ;DOS services interrupt
JC     ERROR                ;Branch if error
MOV    BLOCK_SEG,AX         ;Save segment address
```

Description: This service changes the size of a previously allocated memory block (through service 21/48). You specify the segment address of the existing block in ES.

On return, the carry flag indicates whether an error has occurred. If the carry flag is set, AX contains the error code, which can be handled through service 21/59. If an error has occurred and an increase in block size was requested, BX contains the maximum number of contiguous paragraphs available; however, the original block allocation is not changed.

Load or Execute Program (Interrupt 21h, service 4Bh)

Category: System services

Registers on Entry:

AH: 4Bh
AL: Function code
BX: Offset address of parameter block
DX: Offset address of path name
DS: Segment address of path name
ES: Segment address of parameter block

Registers on Return:

AX: Error code

Memory Affected: The desired file, if located, is loaded into memory, overwriting previous memory contents.

Syntax:

```
MOV     AX,CS               ;Code segment is same as
MOV     DS,AX               ;  data segment and
MOV     ES,AX               ;  extra segment
MOV     DX,OFFSET FILE_PATH ;Offset address of path
MOV     BX,OFFSET LOAD_EXECUTE ;Offset address of parameters
MOV     AL,Ø                ;Load and execute
MOV     AH,4Bh              ;Want service 4Bh
INT     21h                 ;DOS services interrupt
```

Description: This service allows a disk file to be loaded, or loaded and executed. You specify the desired function in AL; the only valid functions are indicated by a 0 or a 3. If AL=0, the file is loaded and executed; if AL=3, the file is only loaded. This last function is valuable when you use program overlays.

DS:DX should point to an ASCIIZ (nul-terminated ASCII) string that contains the full name of the file, including any applicable path name. Wildcards cannot be used in the file designation.

ES:BX should point to a parameter block that provides necessary information for loading the file. The two possible parameter blocks are organized as follows:

```
LOAD_EXECUTE    DW      SEG ENV_STRING      ;Environment string segment
                DW      OFFSET CMD_LINE     ;Offset of default command
                DW      SEG CMD_LINE        ;Segment of default command
                DW      OFFSET FCB_1        ;Offset of default FCB 1
                DW      SEG FCB_1           ;Segment of default FCB 1
                DW      OFFSET FCB_2         ;Offset of default FCB 2
                DW      SEG FCB_2           ;Segment of default FCB 2

LOAD_ONLY       DW      SEG LOAD_POINT      ;Segment of loading point
                DW      0000                ;Relocation factor for file
```

Notice that the parameter table for the load-and-execute function (AL=0) is significantly larger than that for the load-only function (AL=3).

The loaded file or program is called a *child* of the original program, which is referred to as the *parent*. All open files (except files with their inheritance bit set) are available for the child program. Because this service destroys all registers, remember to save all registers before using this service and restore them after returning.

On return, the carry flag indicates whether an error has occurred. If the carry flag is set, AX contains the error code, which can be handled through service 21/59.

Process Terminate (Interrupt 21h, service 4Ch)

Category: System services

Registers on Entry:

AH: 4Ch
AL: Return code

Registers on Return: Undefined (does not return)

Memory Affected: Although not altered, the memory area used by the program is made available to future programs.

Syntax:

```
MOV     AL,RETURN_CODE          ;Return code to pass
MOV     AH,4Ch                  ;Want service 4Ch
INT     21h                     ;DOS services interrupt
```

Description: This service terminates a program and returns control to either a parent program or DOS. This service allows passing a return code to the parent or to DOS. If the program invoking this service is a child program, the return code is retrievable (by the parent program) through service 21/4D. If control is returned to DOS, the return code is available through the ERRORLEVEL batch-file command.

Get Return Code of a Subprocess (Interrupt 21h, service 4Dh)

Category: System services

Registers on Entry:

AH: 4Dh

Registers on Return:

AX: Return code

Memory Affected: None

Syntax:

```
MOV     AH,4Dh              ;Want service 4Dh
INT     21h                 ;DOS services interrupt
```

Description: This service retrieves the return code that a child program passes through service 21/4C. A reliable return code can be retrieved only once.

The returned value, in AX, is divided into two parts. AL contains the value passed by the child program, and AH contains one of the values shown in table 13.13.

Table 13.13
AH Return Codes for Service 21/4D

Value	Termination Meaning
0	Normal
1	Ctrl-Break
2	Critical error
3	Terminate and stay resident (TSR)

Search for First File Name Match (Interrupt 21h, service 4Eh)

Category: Disk services

Registers on Entry:

AH: 4Eh
CX: File attribute
DX: Offset address of file name
DS: Segment address of file name

Registers on Return:

AX: Error code

Memory Affected: If the service locates a file name match, DOS fills the memory area specified as the DTA with 43 bytes of file information.

Syntax:

```
PUSH    CS                          ;Code segment and
POP     DS                          ;  data segment are same
MOV     DX,OFFSET PATH_NAME         ;Offset address of path
MOV     AH,4Eh                      ;Want service 4Eh
INT     21h                         ;DOS services interrupt
JC      ERROR                       ;Branch if error
```

Description: This service locates a file with a specified file name. DS:DX should point to an ASCIIZ (nul-terminated ASCII) string that contains the full name of the file, including any applicable path name. Wildcards can be used in the file designation.

You place the desired file attribute value in CX. Actually, because the file attribute is only one byte long, you should place the new setting in CL, and set CH to 0. Table 13.14 shows bit meanings of the file attribute byte. In this table, a 1 in a bit position indicated by an x means that the attribute is selected; a 0 means that the attribute is not selected.

DOS follows a peculiar logic when searching for files with matching attributes. If CX is set to 0, DOS locates normal files (files with no special attributes). Selecting an attribute byte with any combination of subdirectory, system, or hidden bits set results in those files and normal files being selected. If the volume label bit is set, only files with a volume label attribute match.

On return, the carry flag indicates whether an error has occurred. If the carry flag is set, AX contains the error code, which can be handled through service

Table 13.14
Bit Settings for File Attribute, Service 21/43

Bits 76543210	Meaning
00	Reserved—set to 0
0	Archive—does not apply to this service
x	Subdirectory
x	Volume label
x	System
x	Hidden
0	Read-only—does not apply to this service

21/59. If the carry flag is not set, the service fills in the DTA with 43 bytes of information about the located file. This information is detailed as follows:

```
           DB     21 DUP(Ø)          ;Reserved—used by DOS
FILE_ATTR  DB     ØØ                 ;File attribute
FILE_TIME  DW     ØØØØ               ;File time
FILE_DATE  DW     ØØØØ               ;File date
FILE_SIZE  DD     ØØØØØØØØ           ;File size
FILE_NAME  DB     13 DUP(Ø)          ;ASCIIZ of file name
```

The file name returned in FILE_NAME is left-justified, with a period between the root and extension.

Search for Next File Name Match
(Interrupt 21h, service 4Fh)

Category: Disk services

Registers on Entry:

AH: 4Fh

Registers on Return:

AX: Error code

Memory Affected: If the service locates a file name match, DOS fills in the memory area specified as the DTA with 43 bytes of file information.

Syntax:

```
MOV    AH,4Fh             ;Want service 4Fh
INT    21h                ;DOS services interrupt
JC     ERROR              ;Branch if error
```

Description: This service locates the next file with a specified file name. Before you invoke this service, the DTA must be set by a call to service 21/4E. Otherwise, the results can be unpredictable. For more information, see the description for service 21/4E.

Because any given directory must contain unique file names, this service is useless if the file specification for which you are searching does not contain the question-mark wildcard (?).

Reserved (Interrupt 21h, services 50h, 51h, 52h, 53h)

Description: These services are listed by IBM and Microsoft as reserved for the internal use of DOS. Because their purpose and use are not publicized or documented, they are subject to modification in future versions of DOS.

Get Verify Setting (Interrupt 21h, service 54h)

Category: System services

Registers on Entry:

AH: 54h

Registers on Return:

AL: Verify flag

Memory Affected: None

Syntax:

```
MOV     AH,54h                  ;Want service 54h
INT     21h                     ;DOS services interrupt
```

Description: This service returns the system flag that specifies whether DOS verifies after each disk write to ensure that the information has been recorded accurately. The return value, in AL, signifies the state of the verify flag. If AL=0, the verify flag is off. If AL=1, the verify flag is on.

If you are working with a network system, verification is not supported; therefore, the return value has no meaning.

Reserved (Interrupt 21h, service 55h)

Description: This service is listed by IBM and Microsoft as reserved for the internal use of DOS. The service, which is not publicized or documented, is subject to modification in future versions of DOS.

Rename File (Interrupt 21h, service 56h)

Category: Disk services

Registers on Entry:

AH: 56h
DX: Offset address of old file name
DI: Offset address of new file name
DS: Segment address of old file name
ES: Segment address of new file name

Registers on Return:

AX: Error code

Memory Affected: None

Syntax:

```
MOV     AX,CS                   ;Code segment is same as
MOV     DS,AX                   ;   data segment and
MOV     ES,AX                   ;   extra segment
MOV     DX,OFFSET OLD_FILE      ;Offset address of old file
MOV     DI,OFFSET NEW_FILE      ;Offset address of new file
MOV     AH,56h                  ;Want service 56h
INT     21h                     ;DOS services interrupt
```

Description: This service allows you to rename files, using ASCIIZ strings. DS:DX should point to an ASCIIZ (nul-terminated ASCII) string that contains the full name of the old file, including any applicable path name. ES:DI should point to a similar string for the new file.

Because the directory paths for the files may differ, you can rename files across directories. The only restriction is that both files must reside on the same drive.

On return, the carry flag indicates whether an error has occurred. If the carry flag is set, AX contains the error code, which can be handled through service 21/59.

Get/Set File Date and Time (Interrupt 21h, service 57h)

Category: Disk services

Registers on Entry:

AH: 57h
AL: Function code
BX: File handle
CX: New file time
DX: New file date

Registers on Return:

AX: Error code
CX: File time
DX: File date

Memory Affected: None

Syntax:

```
MOV    AL,Ø                 ;Get file date and time
MOV    BX,FILE_HANDLE       ;Use this handle
MOV    AH,57h               ;Want service 57h
INT    21h                  ;DOS services interrupt
```

Description: This service allows you to retrieve or set the date and time for an open file, based on the function code in AL. If AL=0, the service retrieves the file date and time; if AL=1, the service sets the file date and time.

If you are setting the file date and time, specify the time in CX and the date in DX.

On return, the carry flag indicates whether an error has occurred. If the carry flag is set, AX contains the error code, which can be handled through service 21/59. If the carry flag is clear and AL=0, CX and DX reflect, on return, the file time and date, respectively.

Reserved (Interrupt 21h, service 58h)

Description: This service is listed by IBM and Microsoft as reserved for the internal use of DOS. The service, which is not publicized or documented, is subject to modification in future versions of DOS.

Get Extended Error Information
(Interrupt 21h, service 59h)

Category: System services

Registers on Entry:

  AH: 59h
  BX: 0

Registers on Return:

  AX: Extended error code
  BH: Error class
  BL: Suggested remedy
  CH: Locus

Memory Affected: None

Syntax:

```
ERROR:     PUSH    AX                  ;Store all registers
           PUSH    BX
           PUSH    CX
           PUSH    DX
           PUSH    DI
           PUSH    SI
           PUSH    ES
           PUSH    DS
           MOV     BX,Ø
           MOV     AH,59h              ;Want service 59h
           INT     21h                 ;DOS services interrupt
           MOV     ERROR_CODE,AX       ;Store returned values
           MOV     ERROR_CLASS,BH
           MOV     ACTION,BL
           MOV     LOCUS,CH
           POP     DS                  ;Restore all registers
           POP     ES
           POP     SI
           POP     DI
           POP     DX
           POP     CX
           POP     BX
           POP     AX
```

Description: This service returns detailed information on system errors that have occurred. The service is used for DOS service calls that return errors through use of the carry flag.

The *error code* is the general system error code. The *classes* provide further information about the error classification. The suggested *actions* provide remedies that DOS "thinks" are appropriate for the type of error and the circumstances of its occurrence. The *locus* is the general hardware area where the error occurred.

Because this service destroys virtually all registers, you should save all the registers if you need their contents.

The error code returned in AX is one of the values shown in table 13.15. The possible error classes returned in BH are shown in table 13.16; possible suggested actions returned in BL are shown in table 13.17; and table 13.18 details the locus returned in CH.

Table 13.15
Possible Extended Error Codes Returned in AX for Service 21/59

Value	Meaning
1	Invalid function
2	File not found
3	Path not found
4	Too many file handles open
5	Access denied
6	Invalid handle
7	Memory control blocks destroyed
8	Insufficient memory
9	Invalid memory block address
10	Invalid environment
11	Invalid format
12	Invalid access code
13	Invalid data
14	Reserved
15	Invalid drive
16	Attempt to remove current directory
17	Not same device
18	No more files
19	Disk write-protected
20	Unknown unit
21	Drive not ready
22	Unknown command

Table 13.15—cont.

Value	Meaning
23	CRC error
24	Bad request structure length
25	Seek error
26	Unknown media type
27	Sector not found
28	Out of paper
29	Write fault
30	Read fault
31	General failure
32	Sharing violation
33	Lock violation
34	Invalid disk change
35	FCB unavailable
36	Sharing buffer overflow
37	Reserved
38	Reserved
39	Reserved
40	Reserved
41	Reserved
42	Reserved
43	Reserved
44	Reserved
45	Reserved
46	Reserved
47	Reserved
48	Reserved
49	Reserved
50	Network request not supported
51	Remote computer not listening
52	Duplicate name on network
53	Network name not found
54	Network busy
55	Network device no longer exists
56	Net BIOS command limit exceeded
57	Network adapter error
58	Incorrect network response
59	Unexpected network error
60	Incompatible remote adapter
61	Print queue full
62	Not enough space for print file

Table 13.15—cont.

Value	Meaning
63	Print file deleted
64	Network name deleted
65	Access denied
66	Network device type incorrect
67	Network name not found
68	Network name limit exceeded
69	Net BIOS session limit exceeded
70	Temporarily paused
71	Network request not accepted
72	Print or disk redirection is paused
73	Reserved
74	Reserved
75	Reserved
76	Reserved
77	Reserved
78	Reserved
79	Reserved
80	File exists
81	Reserved
82	Cannot make directory entry
83	Fail on INT 24
84	Too many redirections
85	Duplicate redirection
86	Invalid password
87	Invalid parameter
88	Network data fault

Table 13.16
Possible Error Classes Returned in BH for Service 21/59

Value	Meaning
1	Out of resource
2	Temporary situation
3	Authorization
4	Internal
5	Hardware failure
6	System failure
7	Application program error
8	Not found
9	Bad format
10	Locked
11	Media
12	Already exists
13	Unknown

Table 13.17
Possible Suggested Actions Returned in BL for Service 21/59

Value	Meaning
1	Retry
2	Delay then retry
3	Reconsider user input
4	Abort with cleanup
5	Immediate exit without cleanup
6	Ignore
7	Retry after action taken

Table 13.18
Possible Locus Values Returned in CH for Service 21/59

Value	Meaning
1	Unknown
2	Block device
3	Network
4	Serial device
5	Memory

Create Temporary File
(Interrupt 21h, service 5Ah)

Category: Disk services

Registers on Entry:

AH: 5Ah
CX: File attribute
DX: Offset address of path name
DS: Segment address of path name

Registers on Return:

AX: Return code
DX: Offset address of completed path name
DS: Segment address of completed path name

Memory Affected: The ASCIIZ string specified by DS:DX is appended with the file name of the unique file created.

Syntax:

```
PUSH    CS                      ;Code segment and
POP     DS                      ;   data segment are same
MOV     DX,OFFSET PATH_NAME     ;Offset address of path
MOV     CX,Ø                    ;Normal file
MOV     AH,5Ah                  ;Want service 5Ah
INT     21h                     ;DOS services interrupt
JC      ERROR                   ;Branch if error
MOV     FILE_HANDLE,AX          ;Store returned handle
```

Description: This service causes a file with a unique file name to be created in the specified directory. DS:DX should point to an ASCIIZ (nul-terminated ASCII) string that contains the path name of the directory which will contain the file. This path name should end with a backslash.

You should place the file attribute in CX. Actually, because the file attribute is only one byte long, place the new setting in CL, and set CH to 0. Table 13.19 shows the possible file attribute settings. In this table, a 1 in a bit position indicated by an x means that the attribute is selected; a 0 means that the attribute is not selected.

This service is helpful for programs that need temporary files for program purposes. It generates a unique file name and opens the file for read/write operations. The file stays open until you close it, and is not deleted unless you delete it.

Table 13.19
Bit Settings for File Attribute, Service 21/43

Bits 76543210	Meaning
00	Reserved—set to 0
x	Archive
0	Subdirectory—set to 0 for this service
0	Volume label—set to 0 for this service
x	System
x	Hidden
x	Read-only

On return, the carry flag indicates whether an error has occurred. If the carry flag is set, AX contains the error code, which can be handled through service 21/59. If the carry flag is clear, AX contains the file handle for the newly created file, and DS:DX points to an ASCIIZ string that represents the full path name of the created file.

Create File (Interrupt 21h, service 5Bh)

Category: Disk services

Registers on Entry:

AH: 5Bh
CX: File attribute
DX: Offset address of path name
DS: Segment address of path name

Registers on Return:

AX: Return code

Memory Affected: None

Syntax:

```
PUSH    CS                      ;Code segment and
POP     DS                      ;  data segment are same
MOV     DX,OFFSET PATH_NAME     ;Offset address of path
MOV     CX,Ø                    ;File attribute is normal
MOV     AH,5Bh                  ;Want service 5Bh
INT     21h                     ;DOS services interrupt
JC      ERROR                   ;Carry set, handle error
MOV     FILE_HANDLE,AX          ;Store returned handle
```

Description: This service creates a disk file. On entry, DS:DX points to an ASCIIZ (nul-terminated ASCII) string that contains the full name of the file, including any applicable path name. You set CX to equal the desired attribute for the file.

This service is identical to service 21/3C except that if the file name specified in the ASCIIZ string already exists, an error code is returned.

On return, if the carry flag is set, an error has occurred, and the error code is in AX. Service 21/59 can be used to get detailed error information. If the carry flag is not set, the operation was successful, and AX contains the file handle for the newly opened file. This number (file handle) can be used in many other DOS file operations.

When this service is completed, the specified file is left open. You do not need to open the file, but you must remember to close it.

File Access Control
(Interrupt 21h, service 5Ch)

Category: Disk services

Registers on Entry:

AH: 5Ch
AL: Function code
BX: File handle
CX: Region offset high
DX: Region offset low
DI: Region length low
SI: Region length high

Registers on Return:

AX: Error code

Memory Affected: None

Syntax:

```
MOV     AL,Ø                    ;Lock region
MOV     BX,FILE_HANDLE          ;Use this file
MOV     CX,PTR_HIGH             ;Offset into file
MOV     DX,PTR_LOW
MOV     SI,Ø                    ;Only lock 1 record
MOV     DI,REC_LEN
MOV     AH,5Ch                  ;Want service 5Ch
INT     21h                     ;DOS services interrupt
JC      ERROR                   ;Branch if error
```

Description: This service provides a simple access-limitation convention for files. The user can lock or unlock regions of a file, thereby limiting or expanding access to the file contents. This service is most useful in networked or multitasking environments.

AL should contain either a 0 or a 1. AL=0 means to lock the file specified in BX; AL=1 means to unlock the file. CX:DX contains a byte offset into the file that specifies the start of the region to be locked. SI:DI contains the length of the region to be locked.

On return, if the carry flag is set, an error has occurred, and the error code is in AX. Service 21/59 can be used to get detailed error information.

Before exiting a program, be sure to remember to unlock any regions that have been locked. Failure to do so can have unpredictable results.

Reserved (Interrupt 21h, service 5Dh)

Description: This service is listed by IBM and Microsoft as reserved for the internal use of DOS. The service, which is not publicized or documented, is subject to modification in future versions of DOS.

Get Machine Name
(Interrupt 21h, service 5Eh, function 0)

Category: Network services

Registers on Entry:

> AH: 5Eh
> AL: 0
> DX: Offset address of buffer
> DS: Segment address of buffer

Registers on Return:

> AX: Error code
> CH: Indicator flag
> CL: NETBIOS number
> DX: Offset address of buffer
> DS: Segment address of buffer

Memory Affected: The memory area specified by DS:DX is overwritten with the returned string.

Syntax:

```
MOV     AL,Ø                  ;Get machine name
PUSH    CS                    ;Code segment and
POP     DS                    ;  data segment are same
MOV     DX,OFFSET BUFFER      ;Offset address of buffer
MOV     AH,5Eh                ;Want service 5Eh
INT     21h                   ;DOS services interrupt
JC      ERROR                 ;Branch if error
```

Description: You use this function when you are working under local area network (LAN) software. This function returns a 15-byte string indicating the name of the computer on which the software is operating. The string is padded with spaces and is nul-terminated, rendering 16 bytes in total.

On return, if the carry flag is set, an error has occurred, and the error code is in AX. Service 21/59 can be used to get detailed error information.

If the carry is clear, CH contains a flag to indicate whether the name is actually returned. If CH is 0, no name has been defined for this computer. If CH<>0, DS:DX defines and points to the name. CL then contains a number that represents the NETBIOS number for the name at DS:DX.

Set Printer Setup (Interrupt 21h, service 5Eh, function 2)

Category: Network services

Registers on Entry:

AH: 5Eh
AL: 2
BX: Redirection list index
CX: Setup string length
SI: Offset address of buffer
DS: Segment address of buffer

Registers on Return:

AX: Error code

Memory Affected: None

Syntax:

```
MOV    AL,2                  ;Set printer setup
PUSH   CS                    ;Code segment and
POP    DS                    ;  data segment are same
MOV    SI,OFFSET SETUP_STR   ;Offset of setup string
MOV    CX,SETUP_LENGTH       ;Length of setup string
MOV    BX,INDEX              ;Redirection list
MOV    AH,5Eh                ;Want service 5Eh
INT    21h                   ;DOS services interrupt
JC     ERROR                 ;Branch if error
```

Description: You use this service when you are operating under local area network (LAN) software. This service allows you to specify a string to precede all files sent from the local node to a network printer. The designed purpose of the string is to allow the printer to be set up according to individual node requirements. DS:SI points to the string, which can be up to 64 bytes in length (length specified in CX). BX contains the redirection list index pointer, which is determined through service 21/5F/2.

On return, if the carry flag is set, an error has occurred, and the error code is in AX. Service 21/59 can be used to get detailed error information.

Get Printer Setup (Interrupt 21h, service 5Eh, function 3)

Category: Network services

Registers on Entry:

AH: 5Eh
AL: 3
BX: Redirection list index
DI: Offset address of buffer
ES: Segment address of buffer

Registers on Return:

AX: Error code
CX: Setup string length
DI: Offset address of buffer
ES: Segment address of buffer

Memory Affected: The memory area specified by ES:DI is overwritten with the requested network information.

Syntax:

```
MOV     AL,3                   ;Get printer setup
PUSH    CS                     ;Code segment and
POP     ES                     ;  extra segment are same
MOV     DI,OFFSET SETUP_STR    ;Offset of setup string
MOV     BX,INDEX               ;Redirection list
MOV     AH,5Eh                 ;Want service 5Eh
INT     21h                    ;DOS services interrupt
JC      ERROR                  ;Branch if error
```

Description: You use this service when you are operating under local area network (LAN) software. This service returns the printer setup string specified with service 21/5E/2. The returned value, which is stored at the buffer specified by ES:DI, may be up to 64 bytes in length. Be sure that you set aside a large enough buffer area. BX contains the redirection list index pointer, which is determined through service 21/5F/2.

On return, if the carry flag is set, an error has occurred, and the error code is in AX. Service 21/59 can be used to get detailed error information. If the carry flag is not set, the buffer area to which ES:DI points contains the printer setup string, with CX set to the string length.

Get Redirection List Entry (Interrupt 21h, service 5Fh, function 2)

Category: Network services

Registers on Entry:

AH: 5Fh
AL: 2
BX: Redirection list index
DI: Offset address of network name buffer
SI: Offset address of local name buffer
DS: Segment address of local name buffer
ES: Segment address of network name buffer

Registers on Return:

AX: Error code
BH: Device status
BL: Device type
CX: Parameter value
DI: Offset address of network name buffer

SI: Offset address of local name buffer
DS: Segment address of local name buffer
ES: Segment address of network name buffer

Memory Affected: The buffers to which DS:SI and ES:DI point are overwritten with the requested network information.

Syntax:

```
MOV    AX,CS                    ;Code segment is same as
MOV    DS,AX                    ;   data segment and
MOV    ES,AX                    ;   extra segment
MOV    SI,OFFSET LOCAL_BUF      ;Offset address of buffer
MOV    DI,OFFSET NET_BUF        ;Offset address of buffer
MOV    BX,1                     ;Start with this entry
MOV    AL,2                     ;Get list entry
MOV    AH,5Fh                   ;Want service 5Fh
INT    21h                      ;DOS services interrupt
JC     ERROR                    ;Branch if error
```

Description: You use this service when you are operating under local area network (LAN) software. This service returns an entry from the redirection list, which is set up by service 21/5F/3. The buffers to which DS:SI and ES:DI point should each be 128 bytes in length.

On return, if the carry flag is set, an error has occurred, and the error code is in AX. Service 21/59 can be used to get detailed error information. If the carry flag is not set, DS:SI and ES:DI point to ASCIIZ strings of the requested information; and BH, BL, and CX all contain additional device information. This function destroys DX and BP.

Redirect Device (Interrupt 21h, service 5Fh, function 3)

Category: Network services

Registers on Entry:

AH: 5Fh
AL: 3
BL: Device type
CX: Caller value
DI: Offset address of network path
SI: Offset address of device name
DS: Segment address of device name
ES: Segment address of network path

Registers on Return:

AX: Error code

Memory Affected: None

Syntax:

```
MOV     AX,CS                   ;Code segment is same as
MOV     DS,AX                   ;  data segment and
MOV     ES,AX                   ;  extra segment
MOV     SI,OFFSET DEVICE        ;Offset of device name
MOV     DI,OFFSET NET_PATH      ;Offset of network path
MOV     AL,3                    ;Redirect
MOV     AH,5Fh                  ;Want service 5Fh
INT     21h                     ;DOS services interrupt
JC      ERROR                   ;Branch if error
```

Description: You use this service when you are operating under local area network (LAN) software. The service allows you to add devices to the network redirection list. DS:SI and ES:DI both specify ASCIIZ strings.

On return, if the carry flag is set, an error has occurred, and the error code is in AX. Service 21/59 can be used to get detailed error information.

Cancel Redirection (Interrupt 21h, service 5Fh, function 4)

Category: Network services

Registers on Entry:

AH: 5Fh
AL: 4
SI: Offset address of device name/path
DS: Segment address of device name/path

Registers on Return:

AX: Error code

Memory Affected: None

Syntax:

```
PUSH    CS                      ;Code segment and
POP     DS                      ;  data segment are same
MOV     SI,OFFSET DEVICE        ;Offset of device name
MOV     AL,4                    ;Get list entry
```

```
MOV     AH,5Fh              ;Want service 5Fh
INT     21h                 ;DOS services interrupt
JC      ERROR               ;Branch if error
```

Description: You use this service when you are operating under local area network (LAN) software. The service allows for deleting devices from the network redirection list. DS:SI specifies an ASCIIZ string.

On return, if the carry flag is set, an error has occurred, and the error code is in AX. Service 21/59 can be used to get detailed error information.

Reserved (Interrupt 21h, service 60h, 61h)

Description: These services are listed by IBM and Microsoft as reserved for the internal use of DOS. Their purpose and use, which are not publicized or documented, are subject to modification in future versions of DOS.

Get Program Segment Prefix (PSP) Address (Interrupt 21h, service 62h)

Category: System services

Registers on Entry:

AH: 62h

Registers on Return:

BX: PSP segment address

Memory Affected: None

Syntax:

```
MOV     AH,62h              ;Want service 62h
INT     21h                 ;DOS services interrupt
```

Description: This service returns the program segment prefix (PSP) address for the current program. The PSP segment address is returned in BX.

Reserved (Interrupt 21h, service 63h, 64h)

Description: These services are listed by IBM and Microsoft as reserved for the internal use of DOS. Their purpose and use, which are not publicized or documented, are subject to modification in future versions of DOS.

Get Extended Country Information (Interrupt 21h, service 65h)

Category: System services

Registers on Entry:

AH: 65h
AL: Information code
BX: Code page
CX: Length of information to return
DX: Country ID
DI: Offset address of buffer
ES: Segment address of buffer

Registers on Return:

AX: Error code
DI: Offset address of buffer
ES: Segment address of buffer

Memory Affected: The buffer area to which ES:DI points is overlaid with the requested country information.

Syntax:

```
MOV     AL,1                    ;Want country info
MOV     BX,-1                   ;Use current console device
MOV     DX,-1                   ;Use current country
MOV     CX,41                   ;Want all the information
PUSH    CS                      ;Code segment and
POP     ES                      ;  Extra segment are same
MOV     DI,OFFSET BUFFER        ;Offset address of buffer
MOV     AH,63h                  ;Want service 63h
INT     21h                     ;DOS services interrupt
```

Description: This service returns information similar to that provided by service 21/38. With service 63/64, you specify the information to be returned in AL and the destination in ES:DI. Because the amount of information is specified in CX, only partial information retrieval is possible.

The country code is specified in DX, as shown in table 13.20.

If the country code (DX) does not match the code page (BX) or if either is invalid, an error is generated and returned in AX.

You request the desired information in AL. This information code can be 1, 2, 4, or 6. The possible amount of information returned by each information type

Table 13.20
Country Codes

Country	Code
Currently installed	−1
United States	1
Netherlands	31
Belgium	32
France	33
Spain	34
Italy	39
Switzerland	41
United Kingdom	44
Denmark	45
Sweden	46
Norway	47
Germany	49
Australia	61
Finland	358
Israel	972

specifier varies, but you can limit the information (to no less than 5 bytes) by the value placed in CX. Tables 13.21 through 13.24 detail the information returned at ES:DI by each possible value for AL. Notice, in table 13.21, the similarities to information returned by service 21/38.

Table 13.21
Information Returned for Service 21/65 if AL=1

Bytes	Purpose
1	Information specifier (1)
2	Size
2	Country ID
2	Code page
2	Date format
5	Currency symbol
2	Thousands separator
2	Decimal separator
2	Date separator
2	Time separator

Table 13.21—cont.

Bytes	Purpose
1	Currency format
1	Currency decimal digits
1	Time format
4	Map call address
2	Data list separator
10	Nul bytes

Table 13.22
Information Returned for Service 21/65 if AL=2

Bytes	Purpose
1	Information specifier (2)
4	Uppercase table address

Table 13.23
Information Returned for Service 21/65 if AL=4

Bytes	Purpose
1	Information specifier (4)
4	File name uppercase table address

Table 13.24
Information Returned for Service 21/65 if AL=6

Bytes	Purpose
1	Information specifier (6)
4	Collate table address

Get/Set Global Code Page
(Interrupt 21h, service 66h)

Category: System services

Registers on Entry:

AH: 66h
AL: Function code
BX: Code page

Registers on Return:

AX: Error code
BX: Code page
DX: Boot code page

Memory Affected: None

Syntax:

```
MOV    AL,1         ;Get global code page
MOV    AH,66h       ;Want service 66h
INT    21h          ;DOS services interrupt
JC     ERROR        ;Branch if error
```

Description: This service retrieves or changes the code page for the currently selected country information. If AL=1, the code page is retrieved. If AL=2, the code page is set.

If you are retrieving the code page (AL=1), the contents of BX are not significant on service entry. BX and DX return the requested information.

If you are setting the code page (AL=2), you specify the desired code page in BX. The only return value when setting the code page is the error code in AX (if the carry flag is set).

On return, if the carry flag is set, an error has occurred, and the error code is in AX. Service 21/59 can be used to get detailed error information.

Change Handle Count
(Interrupt 21h, service 67h)

Category: System services

Registers on Entry:

AH: 67h
BX: Number of handles

Registers on Return:

AX: Error code

Memory Affected: None

Syntax:

```
MOV     BX,5Ø               ;Want 5Ø handles
MOV     AH,67h              ;Want service 67h
INT     21h                 ;DOS services interrupt
```

Description: This service allows you to specify the number of file handles available to DOS. You specify this number, which must be between 20 and 65,535, in BX. The number can be larger than 255, which is the maximum definable in the CONFIG.SYS file.

On return, if the carry flag is set, an error has occurred, and the error code is in AX. Service 21/59 can be used to get detailed error information.

Flush Buffer (Interrupt 21h, service 68h)

Category: Disk services

Registers on Entry:

AH: 68h
BX: File handle

Registers on Return:

AX: Error code

Memory Affected: None

Syntax:

```
MOV     BX,FILE_HANDLE      ;Use this file
MOV     AH,68h              ;Want service 68h
INT     21h                 ;DOS services interrupt
JC      ERROR               ;Branch if error
```

Description: With this service, the file buffer of the specified file (BX) is written to disk.

On return, if the carry flag is set, an error has occurred, and the error code is in AX. Service 21/59 can be used to get detailed error information.

Terminate Address (Interrupt 22h)

Description: This interrupt is not a serviceable interrupt. Rather, it is a vector to the termination handler for DOS. It is the address to which control passes when a program ends.

Ctrl-Break Handler Address (Interrupt 23h)

Description: This interrupt is not a serviceable interrupt. Rather, it is a vector to the address of the routine that receives control from DOS when a Ctrl-Break key combination is detected.

Critical Error Handler Address (Interrupt 24h)

Description: This interrupt is not a serviceable interrupt. Rather, it is a vector to the address of the routine that receives control from DOS when a critical error is detected.

Absolute Disk Read (Interrupt 25h)

Category: Disk services

Registers on Entry:

> AL: Drive number
> BX: Offset address of buffer
> CX: Sectors to read
> DX: Logical starting sector
> DS: Segment address of buffer

Registers on Return:

> AX: Error code

Memory Affected: The buffer area specified by DS:BX is overlaid with information read from the disk.

Syntax:

```
MOV    AL,2                    ;Drive C:
MOV    DX,Ø                    ;Starting with sector Ø
MOV    CX,3                    ;Read 3 sectors
MOV    BX,OFFSET DS:BUFFER     ;Offset of buffer area
INT    25h                     ;Read sectors
POP    DX                      ;Clean up stack
JC     ERROR                   ;Branch if error
```

Description: This interrupt, which allows DOS to read any sector from the disk, is the opposite of interrupt 26h (and similar to BIOS service 13/2).

To use this service, you must specify the precise physical location on the disk at which you want to begin reading. Specify the drive in AL, where A=0, B=1, C=2, etc. DX is the logical starting sector. (All sectors on the disk are numbered logically in sequential order, starting with 0.) CX is the number of sectors to read. The final registers to be set up specify which RAM area will be used as a buffer for the sectors that are read. This address is specified in DS:BX.

On return, if the carry flag is set, an error has occurred, and the error code is in AX. You must realize that, on return from this interrupt, the flags are still on the stack. They must be removed from the stack before the program continues.

Absolute Disk Write (Interrupt 26h)

Category: Disk services

Registers on Entry:

AL: Drive number
BX: Offset address of buffer
CX: Sectors to write
DX: Logical starting sector
DS: Segment address of buffer

Registers on Return:

AX: Error code

Memory Affected: None

Syntax:

```
MOV    AL,2                ;Drive C:
MOV    DX,Ø                ;Starting with sector Ø
MOV    CX,3                ;Write 3 sectors
MOV    BX,OFFSET DS:BUFFER ;Offset of buffer area
INT    26h                 ;Write sectors
POP    DX                  ;Clean up stack
JC     ERROR               ;Branch if error
```

Description: This interrupt, which is the opposite of interrupt 25h (and similar to BIOS service 13/3), allows DOS to write any sector to the disk.

To use this service, you must specify the precise physical location on the disk at which you want to begin writing. You specify the drive in AL, where A=0, B=1, C=2, etc. DX is the logical starting sector. (All sectors on the disk are logically numbered in sequential order starting with 0.) CX is the number of sectors to write. The final registers to be set up specify the RAM area from which to take the information to be written. This address is specified in DS:BX.

On return, if the carry flag is set, an error has occurred, and the error code is in AX. You must realize that, on return from this interrupt, the flags are still on the stack. They must be removed from the stack before the program continues.

Terminate and Stay Resident (Interrupt 27h)

Category: System services

Registers on Entry:

  DX: Pointer to last byte of program

Registers on Return: Unknown (does not return)

Memory Affected: None

Syntax:

```
MOV    DX,OFFSET CS:END_BYTE  ;Point to end of program
INT    27h                    ;TSR
```

Description: This interrupt, which is similar to the preferred TSR service of 21/31, allows the program to exit to DOS without freeing the program memory space.

Because only one register is used to point to the program endpoint, the maximum usable program size for this interrupt is obviously 64K. Any files created or opened by the program remain open after this interrupt is invoked.

Reserved (Interrupts 28h, 29h, 2Ah, 2Bh, 2Ch, 2Dh, 2Eh)

Description: These interrupts are listed by IBM and Microsoft as reserved for the internal use of DOS. Their purpose and use, which are not publicized or documented, are subject to modification in future versions of DOS.

Multiplex Interrupt (Interrupt 2Fh)

Category: System services

Registers on Entry: Varies

Registers on Return: Varies

Memory Affected: Varies

Description: This interrupt allows user-defined routines to share the space set aside for special DOS programs such as PRINT, ASSIGN, and SHARE.

The use and function of this interrupt are beyond the scope of this book. For more information, please refer to the DOS 3.3 *Technical Reference Manual*.

Reserved (Interrupts 30h through 3Fh)

Description: These interrupts are listed by IBM and Microsoft as reserved for the internal use of DOS. Their purpose and use, which are not publicized or documented, are subject to modification in future versions of DOS.

Part IV

Intel Processor Instruction Sets

Includes

Instruction Set for the Intel 8088
Instruction Set for the Intel 80286
Instruction Set for the Intel 80386
Instruction Set for the Intel 8087
Instruction Set for the Intel 80287

Instruction Set for the Intel 8088

The Intel 8088 Instruction Set is explained in detail in this section. The instruction set for the Intel 8088 is the same as the instruction set for the Intel 8086.

Instruction Set Groupings

The 8086/8088 instructions can be grouped according to the purpose of the instruction. The six general classifications of instructions are

Data transfer
Arithmetic
Bit manipulation
String manipulation
Control transfer
Flag and processor control

Table 8088.1 shows how the individual instructions within these categories are grouped.

Table 8088.1
Instruction Set Groupings

Instruction	Meaning
Data Transfer	
IN	Input from port
LAHF	Load AH register with flags
LDS	Load DS register
LEA	Load effective address
LES	Load ES register
MOV	Move
OUT	Output to port
POP	Remove data from stack
POPF	Remove flags from stack
PUSH	Place data on stack
PUSHF	Place flags on stack
SAHF	Store AH into flag register
XCHG	Exchange
XLAT	Translate

Table 8088.1—cont.

Instruction	Meaning

Arithmetic

AAA	ASCII adjust for addition
AAD	ASCII adjust for division
AAM	ASCII adjust for multiplication
AAS	ASCII adjust for subtraction
ADC	Add with carry
ADD	Add
CBW	Convert byte to word
CMP	Compare
CWD	Convert word to doubleword
DAA	Decimal adjust for addition
DAS	Decimal adjust for subtraction
DEC	Decrement
DIV	Divide
IDIV	Integer divide
IMUL	Integer multiply
INC	Increment
MUL	Multiply
NEG	Negate
SBB	Subtract with carry
SUB	Subtract

Bit Manipulation

AND	Logical AND on bits
NOT	Logical NOT on bits
OR	Logical OR on bits
RCL	Rotate left through carry
RCR	Rotate right through carry
ROL	Rotate left
ROR	Rotate right
SAL	Arithmetic shift left
SAR	Arithmetic shift right
SHL	Shift left
SHR	Shift right
TEST	Test bits
XOR	Logical exclusive-or on bits

Table 8088.1—cont.

Instruction	Meaning

String Manipulation

CMPSB	Compare strings byte for byte
CMPSW	Compare strings word for word
LODSB	Load a byte from string into AL
LODSW	Load a word from string into AX
MOVSB	Move string byte-by-byte
MOVSW	Move string word-by-word
REP	Repeat
REPE	Repeat if equal
REPNE	Repeat if not equal
REPNZ	Repeat if not zero
REPZ	Repeat if zero
SCASB	Scan string for byte
SCASW	Scan string for word
STOSB	Store byte in AL at string
STOSW	Store word in AX at string

Control Transfer

CALL	Perform subroutine
INT	Software interrupt
INTO	Interrupt on overflow
IRET	Return from interrupt
JA	Jump if above
JAE	Jump if above or equal
JB	Jump if below
JBE	Jump if below or equal
JC	Jump on carry
JCXZ	Jump if CX=0
JE	Jump if equal
JG	Jump if greater
JGE	Jump if greater or equal
JL	Jump if less than
JLE	Jump if less than or equal
JMP	Jump
JNA	Jump if not above
JNAE	Jump if not above or equal
JNB	Jump if not below
JNBE	Jump if not below or equal
JNC	Jump on no carry

Table 8088.1—cont.

Instruction	Meaning
JNE	Jump if not equal
JNG	Jump if not greater than
JNGE	Jump if not greater than or equal
JNL	Jump if not less than
JNLE	Jump if not less than or equal
JNO	Jump on no overflow
JNP	Jump on no parity
JNS	Jump on not sign
JNZ	Jump on not zero
JO	Jump on overflow
JP	Jump on parity
JPE	Jump on parity even
JPO	Jump on parity odd
JS	Jump on sign
JZ	Jump on zero
LOOP	Loop
LOOPE	Loop while equal
LOOPNE	Loop while not equal
LOOPNZ	Loop while not zero
LOOPZ	Loop while zero
RET	Return from subroutine

Flag and Processor Control

CLC	Clear carry flag
CLD	Clear direction flag
CLI	Clear interrupt flag
CMC	Complement carry flag
ESC	Escape
HLT	Halt
LOCK	Lock bus
NOP	No operation
STC	Set carry flag
STD	Set direction flag
STI	Set interrupt flag
WAIT	Wait

Detailed Instruction Information

In the balance of this reference section for the 8086/8088 instruction set, each instruction is described in detail. The following information is given for each instruction:

- *Instruction name.* This name is based on the standard mnemonic code designed by Intel.

- *Instruction category.* The general classification for the instruction is provided.

- *Flags affected.* The majority of the instructions change the status of the bits in the flags register. The individual flags affected are listed in the following format:

F	E	D	C	B	A	9	8	7	6	5	4	3	2	1	Ø
				OF	DF	IF	TF	SF	ZF		AF		PF		CF
				?				?	?		X		?		X

In this format, an X indicates that the flag is changed, and a question mark (?) indicates that the flag is undefined after the instruction is issued. The flags are as follows:

Abbreviation	Flag	Location
OF	Overflow	Bit Bh
DF	Direction	Bit Ah
IF	Interrupt	Bit 9
TF	Trap	Bit 8
SF	Sign	Bit 7
ZF	Zero	Bit 6
AF	Auxiliary Carry	Bit 4
PF	Parity	Bit 2
CF	Carry	Bit 0

- *Coding examples.* Brief examples of the use of the instruction are given.

- *Description.* A narrative description of each instruction is provided.

The instructions are arranged in ascending alphabetical order.

AAA: ASCII Adjust for Addition

Category: Arithmetic instructions

Flags affected:

F	E	D	C	B	A	9	8	7	6	5	4	3	2	1	Ø
				OF	DF	IF	TF	SF	ZF		AF		PF		CF
				?				?	?		X		?		X

Coding example:

    AAA

Description: AAA changes the contents of AL to a valid unpacked decimal number with the high-order nibble zeroed.

AAD: ASCII Adjust for Division

Category: Arithmetic instructions

Flags affected:

F	E	D	C	B	A	9	8	7	6	5	4	3	2	1	Ø
				OF	DF	IF	TF	SF	ZF		AF		PF		CF
				?				X	X		?		X		?

Coding example:

    AAD

Description: AAD multiplies the contents of AH by 10, adds the result to the contents of AL, and places the result in AL. The instruction then sets AH to 0. You use this instruction before you divide unpacked decimal numbers.

AAM: ASCII Adjust for Multiplication

Category: Arithmetic instructions

Flags affected:

F	E	D	C	B	A	9	8	7	6	5	4	3	2	1	Ø
				OF	DF	IF	TF	SF	ZF		AF		PF		CF
				?				X	X		?		X		?

Coding example:

```
AAM
```

Description: After multiplying two unpacked decimal numbers, you use AAM to correct the result to an unpacked decimal number. For the instruction to work properly, each number multiplied must have had its high-order nibbles set to 0.

AAS: ASCII Adjust for Subtraction

Category: Arithmetic instructions

Flags affected:

F	E	D	C	B	A	9	8	7	6	5	4	3	2	1	Ø
				OF	DF	IF	TF	SF	ZF		AF		PF		CF
				?				?	?		X		?		X

Coding example:

```
AAS
```

Description: AAS corrects the result of a previous unpacked decimal subtraction so that the value in AL is a true unpacked decimal number.

ADC: Add with Carry

Category: Arithmetic instructions

Flags affected:

F	E	D	C	B	A	9	8	7	6	5	4	3	2	1	Ø
				OF	DF	IF	TF	SF	ZF		AF		PF		CF
				X				X	X		X		X		X

Coding examples:

```
ADC        AX,BX            ;AX=AX+BX+CF
ADC        AX,TEMP          ;AX=AX+TEMP+CF
ADC        SUM,BX           ;SUM=SUM+BX+CF
ADC        CL,1Ø            ;CL=CL+1Ø+CF
ADC        AX,TEMP[BX]      ;Indirect address example
```

Description: ADC adds the contents of the source operand to (and stores the result in) the destination operand. If the carry flag is set, the result changes in increments of 1. In this routine, the values being added are assumed to be binary.

ADD: Add

Category: Arithmetic instructions

Flags affected:

F	E	D	C	B	A	9	8	7	6	5	4	3	2	1	Ø
				OF	DF	IF	TF	SF	ZF		AF		PF		CF
				X				X	X		X		X		X

Coding examples:

```
ADD        AX,BX            ;AX=AX+BX
ADD        AX,TEMP          ;AX=AX+TEMP
ADD        SUM,BX           ;SUM=SUM+BX
ADD        CL,1Ø            ;CL=CL+1Ø
ADD        AX,TEMP[BX]      ;Indirect address example
```

Description: ADD adds the contents of the source operand to (and stores the result in) the destination operand. In this routine the values being added are assumed to be binary.

AND: Logical AND on Bits

Category: Bit-manipulation instructions

Flags affected:

F	E	D	C	B	A	9	8	7	6	5	4	3	2	1	Ø
				OF	DF	IF	TF	SF	ZF		AF		PF		CF
				X				X	X		?		X		X

Coding examples:

```
AND      AX,BX           ;
AND      AX,TEMP         ;TEMP must be a word
AND      SUM,BX          ;SUM must be a word
AND      CL,ØØØØ1111b     ;Zero high nibble
AND      AX,TEMP[BX]     ;Indirect address example
```

Description: This instruction performs a logical AND of the operands and stores the result in the destination operand. Each bit of the resultant byte or word is set to 1 only if the corresponding bit of each operand is set to 1.

CALL: Perform Subroutine

Category: Control-transfer instructions

Flags affected: None

Coding examples:

```
CALL    WHIZ_BANG       ;WHIZ_BANG is a subroutine
CALL    [BX]            ;Perform subroutine with
                        ;   address at [BX]
CALL    AX              ;Subroutine address in AX
```

Description: CALL does the following:

• Pushes offset address of following instruction on the stack

- If procedure being called is declared as FAR, pushes segment address of following instruction on the stack

- Loads IP with the offset address of the procedure being called

- If procedure being called is declared as FAR, loads CS with the segment address of the procedure being called

Execution then continues at the newly loaded CS:IP address until a RET instruction is encountered.

CBW: Convert Byte to Word

Category: Arithmetic instructions

Flags affected: None

Coding example:

```
CBW
```

Description: CBW converts the byte value in AL to a word value in AX by extending the high-order bit value of AL through all bits of AH.

CLC: Clear Carry Flag

Category: Flag- and processor-control instructions

Flags affected:

F	E	D	C	B	A	9	8	7	6	5	4	3	2	1	Ø
				OF	DF	IF	TF	SF	ZF		AF		PF		CF
															X

Coding example:

```
CLC
```

Description: CLC clears the flags register's carry flag by setting it to 0.

CLD: Clear Direction Flag

Category: Flag- and processor-control instructions

Flags affected:

F	E	D	C	B	A	9	8	7	6	5	4	3	2	1	Ø
					OF	DF	IF	TF	SF	ZF		AF		PF		CF
					X										

Coding example:

```
CLD
```

Description: CLD clears the direction flag of the flags register by setting the flag to 0.

CLI: Clear Interrupt Flag

Category: Flag- and processor-control instructions

Flags affected:

F	E	D	C	B	A	9	8	7	6	5	4	3	2	1	Ø
					OF	DF	IF	TF	SF	ZF		AF		PF		CF
					X										

Coding example:

```
CLI
```

Description: CLI clears the interrupt flag of the flags register by setting the flag to 0. While the interrupt flag is cleared, the CPU recognizes no maskable interrupts.

CMC: Complement Carry Flag

Category: Flag- and processor-control instructions

Flags affected:

F	E	D	C	B	A	9	8	7	6	5	4	3	2	1	Ø
				OF	DF	IF	TF	SF	ZF		AF		PF		CF
															X

Coding example:

```
CMC
```

Description: CMC switches the carry flag of the flags register to the opposite of the flag's current setting.

CMP: Compare

Category: Arithmetic instructions

Flags affected:

F	E	D	C	B	A	9	8	7	6	5	4	3	2	1	Ø
				OF	DF	IF	TF	SF	ZF		AF		PF		CF
				X				X	X		X		X		X

Coding examples:

```
CMP   AX,BX           ;
CMP   AX,TEMP         ;TEMP must be a word
CMP   SUM,BX          ;SUM must be a word
CMP   CL,3            ;Compare to constant
CMP   AX,TEMP[BX]     ;Indirect address example
```

Description: CMP is considered an arithmetic instruction because the source operand is subtracted from the destination operand. The result, however, is used for setting the flags—it is not stored anywhere. You can use subsequent testing of the flags for program control.

CMPSB: Compare Strings, Byte-for-Byte

Category: String-manipulation instructions

Flags affected:

F	E	D	C	B	A	9	8	7	6	5	4	3	2	1	Ø
				OF	DF	IF	TF	SF	ZF		AF		PF		CF
				X				X	X		X		X		X

Coding examples:

```
CMPSB              ;Compare strings
REPE CMPSB         ;Repeat a comparison loop
```

Description: This instruction compares strings, byte-by-byte. DI and SI change in increments or decrements of 1, depending on the setting of the direction flag. Ordinarily, this instruction is used with the REPE, REPNE, REPNZ, or REPZ instructions to repeat the comparison for a maximum of CX number of bytes. Intel lists this command as CMPS, but the Microsoft Macro Assembler makes the byte (CMPSB) and word (CMPSW) distinctions. This instruction affects only the flags; no changes are made to the operands.

CMPSW: Compare Strings, Word-for-Word

Category: String-manipulation instructions

Flags affected:

F	E	D	C	B	A	9	8	7	6	5	4	3	2	1	Ø
				OF	DF	IF	TF	SF	ZF		AF		PF		CF
				X				X	X		X		X		X

Coding examples:

```
CMPSW              ;Compare strings
REPe CMPSW         ;Repeat a comparison loop
```

Description: This instruction compares strings, word-for-word. DI and SI change in increments or decrements of 2, depending on the setting of the direction flag. Ordinarily, this instruction is used along with REPE, REPNE,

REPNZ, or REPZ instructions to repeat the comparison for a maximum of CX number of words. Intel lists this command as CMPS, but the Microsoft Macro Assembler makes the byte (CMPSB) and word (CMPSW) distinctions. This instruction affects only the flags; no changes are made to the operands.

CWD: Convert Word to Doubleword

Category: Arithmetic instructions

Flags affected: None

Coding example:

```
CWD
```

Description: CWD converts the word value in AX to a double word value in DX:AX by extending the high-order bit value of AX through all bits of DX.

DAA: Decimal Adjust for Addition

Category: Arithmetic instructions

Flags affected:

F	E	D	C	B	A	9	8	7	6	5	4	3	2	1	0
				OF	DF	IF	TF	SF	ZF		AF		PF		CF
				?				X	X		X		X		X

Coding example:

```
DAA
```

Description: DAA corrects the result (AL) of a previous binary-coded decimal (BCD) addition operation.

DAS: Decimal Adjust for Subtraction

Category: Arithmetic instructions

Flags affected:

F	E	D	C	B	A	9	8	7	6	5	4	3	2	1	Ø
				OF	DF	IF	TF	SF	ZF		AF		PF		CF
				?				X	X		X		X		X

Coding example:

```
DAS
```

Description: DAS corrects the result (AL) of a previous binary-coded decimal (BCD) subtraction operation.

DEC: Decrement

Category: Arithmetic instructions

Flags affected:

F	E	D	C	B	A	9	8	7	6	5	4	3	2	1	Ø
				OF	DF	IF	TF	SF	ZF		AF		PF		CF
				X				X	X		X		X		

Coding examples:

```
DEC     AX
DEC     SUM
DEC     CL
DEC     TEMP[SI]
```

Description: DEC changes, in decrements of 1, the contents of the operand. The operand is assumed to be an unsigned binary value.

DIV: Divide

Category: Arithmetic instructions

Flags affected:

F	E	D	C	B	A	9	8	7	6	5	4	3	2	1	Ø
				OF	DF	IF	TF	SF	ZF		AF		PF		CF
				?				?	?		?		?		?

Coding examples:

```
DIV        BX              ;AX=DX:AX/BX
DIV        WORD_TEMP       ;AX=DX:AX/WORD_TEMP
DIV        BYTE_SUM        ;AL=AX/BYTE_SUM
DIV        WORD_TBL[BX]    ;Indirect address example
```

Description: If the operand is a byte value, DIV divides the contents of AX by the contents of the operand, stores the result in AL, and the remainder in AH. If the operand is a word value, DIV divides the contents of DX:AX by the contents of the operand, stores the result in AX, and the remainder in DX. This instruction treats numbers as unsigned binary values.

ESC: Escape

Category: Flag- and processor-control instructions

Flags affected: None

Coding examples:

```
ESC        6,TEMP
ESC        15,CL
```

Description: This instruction provides a means for coprocessors (such as the 8087) to access data in the 8086/8088 data stream. When this instruction is encountered, it causes the 8086/8088 to place the operand on the data bus and perform an NOP internally.

HLT: Halt

Category: Flag- and processor-control instructions

Flags affected: None

Coding example:

```
HLT
```

Description: HLT causes the 8086/8088 to stop execution, and leaves the CS:IP registers pointing to the instruction following the HLT. This halt condition is terminated only after the system receives an interrupt or the RESET line is activated.

IDIV: Integer Divide

Category: Arithmetic instructions

Flags affected:

F	E	D	C	B	A	9	8	7	6	5	4	3	2	1	Ø
				OF	DF	IF	TF	SF	ZF		AF		PF		CF
				?				?	?		?		?		?

Coding examples:

```
IDIV      BX              ;AX=DX:AX/BX
IDIV      WORD_TEMP       ;AX=DX:AX/WORD_TEMP
IDIV      BYTE_SUM        ;AL=AX/BYTE_SUM
IDIV      WORD_TBL[BX]    ;Indirect address example
```

Description: If the operand is a byte value, IDIV divides the contents of AX by the contents of the operand, stores the result in AL, and the remainder in AH. If the operand is a word value, IDIV divides the contents of DX:AX by the contents of the operand, stores the result in AX, and the remainder in DX. This instruction treats numbers as signed binary values.

IMUL: Integer Multiply

Category: Arithmetic instructions

Flags affected:

F	E	D	C	B	A	9	8	7	6	5	4	3	2	1	Ø
				OF	DF	IF	TF	SF	ZF		AF		PF		CF
				X				?	?		?		?		X

Coding examples:

```
IMUL      BX              ;DX:AX=AX*BX
IMUL      WORD_TEMP       ;DX:AX=AX*WORD_TEMP
IMUL      BYTE_SUM        ;AX=AL*BYTE_SUM
IMUL      WORD_TBL[BX]    ;Indirect address example
```

Description: If the operand is a byte value, IMUL multiplies the contents of AL by the contents of the operand, and stores the result in AX. If the operand is a word value, IMUL multiplies the contents of AX by the contents of the operand, and stores the result in DX:AX. This instruction treats numbers as signed binary values.

IN: Input from Port

Category: Data-transfer instructions

Flags affected: None

Coding examples:

```
IN    AL,64h
IN    AX,DX
```

Description: IN loads a byte or a word from the specified hardware I/O port address to AL or AX, respectively. A port number smaller than 256 may be specified either as a constant or as a variable in the DX register, but a port number greater than 255 *must* be specified in the DX register.

INC: Increment

Category: Arithmetic instructions

Flags affected:

F	E	D	C	B	A	9	8	7	6	5	4	3	2	1	Ø
				OF	DF	IF	TF	SF	ZF		AF		PF		CF
				X				X	X		X		X		

Coding examples:

```
INC      AX
INC      SUM
INC      CL
INC      TEMP[SI]
```

Description: INC changes, by increments of 1, the contents of the operand. The operand is assumed to be an unsigned binary value.

INT: Software Interrupt

Category: Control-transfer instructions

Flags affected:

F	E	D	C	B	A	9	8	7	6	5	4	3	2	1	Ø
						OF	DF	IF	TF	SF	ZF		AF		PF		CF
						X	X									

Coding examples:

```
INT        1Øh
INT        13h
```

Description: INT initiates a software interrupt of the 8086/8088 CPU. INT initiates the following functions:

- Pushing the flags on the stack

- Clearing the TF and IF flags

- Pushing the value of CS on the stack

- Loading CS with the segment address of the interrupt being invoked. This segment address is found at the calculated address in the interrupt vector table.

- Pushing the value of IP on the stack

- Loading IP with the offset address of the interrupt being invoked. This offset address is found at the calculated address in the interrupt vector table.

Execution then continues at the newly loaded CS:IP address until an IRET instruction is encountered.

INTO: Interrupt on Overflow

Category: Control-transfer instructions

Flags affected: None

Coding example:

```
INTO
```

Description: If the overflow flag (OF) is set, INTO executes an interrupt 4 and control proceeds as though an INT 4 had been issued. Be aware that, in this case, the flags register is affected as described for the INT instruction.

IRET: Return from Interrupt

Category: Control-transfer instructions

Flags affected:

F	E	D	C	B	A	9	8	7	6	5	4	3	2	1	Ø
				OF	DF	IF	TF	SF	ZF		AF		PF		CF
X	X	X	X	X	X	X	X	X	X	X	X	X	X	X	X

Coding example:

```
IRET
```

Description: IRET causes termination of an interrupt procedure and, by popping the values of IP, CS, and the flags register from the stack, returns control to the point at which the interrupt occurred.

JA: Jump if Above

Category: Control-transfer instructions

Flags affected: None

Coding example:

```
JA    NEXT_STEP
```

Description: JA causes program execution to branch to the operand address if the carry and zero flags are both clear. This instruction is functionally the same as JNBE.

JAE: Jump if Above or Equal

Category: Control-transfer instructions

Flags affected: None

Coding example:

```
JAE   NEXT_STEP
```

Description: JAE causes program execution to branch to the operand address if the carry flag is clear. This instruction is functionally the same as JNB or JNC.

JB: Jump if Below

Category: Control-transfer instructions

Flags affected: None

Coding example:

```
JB    NEXT_STEP
```

Description: JB causes program execution to branch to the operand address if the carry flag is set. This instruction is functionally the same as JC or JNAE.

JBE: Jump if Below or Equal

Category: Control-transfer instructions

Flags affected: None

Coding example:

```
JBE   NEXT_STEP
```

Description: JBE causes program execution to branch to the operand address if either the carry or zero flag is set. This instruction is functionally the same as JNA.

JC: Jump on Carry

Category: Control-transfer instructions

Flags affected: None

Coding example:

```
JC    NEXT_STEP
```

Description: JC causes program execution to branch to the operand address if the carry flag is set. This instruction is functionally the same as JB or JNAE.

JCXZ: Jump if CX=0

Category: Control-transfer instructions

Flags affected: None

Coding example:

```
JCXZ        SKIP_LOOP
```

Description: JCXZ causes program execution to branch to the operand address if the value of CX is 0.

JE: Jump if Equal

Category: Control-transfer instructions

Flags affected: None

Coding example:

```
JE   NEXT_STEP
```

Description: JE causes program execution to branch to the operand address if the zero flag is set. This instruction is functionally the same as JZ.

JG: Jump if Greater

Category: Control-transfer instructions

Flags affected: None

Coding example:

```
JG   NEXT_STEP
```

Description: JG causes program execution to branch to the operand address if the sign flag equals the overflow flag or if the zero flag is clear. This instruction is functionally the same as JNLE.

JGE: Jump if Greater or Equal

Category: Control-transfer instructions

Flags affected: None

Coding example:

```
JGE         NEXT_STEP
```

Description: JGE causes program execution to branch to the operand address if the sign flag equals the overflow flag. This instruction is functionally the same as JNL.

JL: Jump if Less Than

Category: Control-transfer instructions

Flags affected: None

Coding example:

```
JL    NEXT_STEP
```

Description: JL causes program execution to branch to the operand address if the sign flag does not equal the overflow flag. This instruction is functionally the same as JNGE.

JLE: Jump if Less Than or Equal

Category: Control-transfer instructions

Flags affected: None

Coding example:

```
JLE        NEXT_STEP
```

Description: JLE causes program execution to branch to the operand address if the sign flag does not equal the overflow flag or if the zero flag is set. This instruction is functionally the same as JNG.

JMP: Jump

Category: Control-transfer instructions

Flags affected: None

Coding examples:

```
JMP        EXIT_CODE
JMP        [BX]            ;Jump to address at [BX]
JMP        AX              ;Jump to address in AX
```

Description: JMP causes program execution to begin execution at the designated operand address. JMP affects the CS and IP registers as necessary in order to cause this unconditional branch.

JNA: Jump if Not Above

Category: Control-transfer instructions

Flags affected: None

Coding example:

```
JNA          NEXT_STEP
```

Description: JNA causes program execution to branch to the operand address if either the carry or zero flag is set. This instruction is functionally the same as JBE.

JNAE: Jump if Not Above or Equal

Category: Control-transfer instructions

Flags affected: None

Coding example:

```
JNAE         NEXT_STEP
```

Description: JNAE causes program execution to branch to the operand address if the carry flag is set. This instruction is functionally the same as JB or JC.

JNB: Jump if Not Below

Category: Control-transfer instructions

Flags affected: None

Coding example:

```
JNB          NEXT_STEP
```

Description: JNB causes program execution to branch to the operand address if the carry flag is clear. This instruction is functionally the same as JAE or JNC.

JNBE: Jump if Not Below or Equal

Category: Control-transfer instructions

Flags affected: None

Coding example:

```
JNBE         NEXT_STEP
```

Description: JNBE causes program execution to branch to the operand address if both the carry and zero flags are clear. This instruction is functionally the same as JA.

JNC: Jump on No Carry

Category: Control-transfer instructions

Flags affected: None

Coding example:

```
JNC        NEXT_STEP
```

Description: JNC causes program execution to branch to the operand address if the carry flag is clear. This instruction is functionally the same as JAE or JNB.

JNE: Jump if Not Equal

Category: Control-transfer instructions

Flags affected: None

Coding example:

```
JNE        NEXT_STEP
```

Description: JNE causes program execution to branch to the operand address if the zero flag is clear. This instruction is functionally the same as JNZ.

JNG: Jump if Not Greater Than

Category: Control-transfer instructions

Flags affected: None

Coding example:

```
JNG        NEXT_STEP
```

Description: JNG causes program execution to branch to the operand address if the sign flag does not equal the overflow flag or if the zero flag is set. This instruction is functionally the same as JLE.

JNGE: Jump if Not Greater Than or Equal

Category: Control-transfer instructions

Flags affected: None

Coding example:

```
JNGE        NEXT_STEP
```

Description: JNGE causes program execution to branch to the operand address if the sign flag does not equal the overflow flag. This instruction is functionally the same as JL.

JNL: Jump if Not Less Than

Category: Control-transfer instructions

Flags affected: None

Coding example:

```
JNL         NEXT_STEP
```

Description: JNL causes program execution to branch to the operand address if the sign flag equals the overflow flag. This instruction is functionally the same as JGE.

JNLE: Jump if Not Less Than or Equal

Category: Control-transfer instructions

Flags affected: None

Coding example:

```
JNLE        NEXT_STEP
```

Description: JNLE causes program execution to branch to the operand address if the sign flag equals the overflow flag or the zero flag is clear. This instruction is functionally the same as JG.

JNO: Jump on No Overflow

Category: Control-transfer instructions

Flags affected: None

Coding example:

```
JNO        NEXT_STEP
```

Description: JNO causes program execution to branch to the operand address if the overflow flag is clear.

JNP: Jump on No Parity

Category: Control-transfer instructions

Flags affected: None

Coding example:

```
JNP        NEXT_STEP
```

Description: JNP causes program execution to branch to the operand address if the parity flag is clear. This instruction is functionally the same as JPO.

JNS: Jump on Not Sign

Category: Control-transfer instructions

Flags affected: None

Coding example:

```
JNS        NEXT_STEP
```

Description: JNS causes program execution to branch to the operand address if the sign flag is clear.

JNZ: Jump on Not Zero

Category: Control-transfer instructions

Flags affected: None

Coding example:

```
JNZ        NEXT_STEP
```

Description: JNZ causes program execution to branch to the operand address if the zero flag is clear. This instruction is functionally the same as JNE.

JO: Jump on Overflow

Category: Control-transfer instructions

Flags affected: None

Coding example:

```
JO    NEXT_STEP
```

Description: JO causes program execution to branch to the operand address if the overflow flag is set.

JP: Jump on Parity

Category: Control-transfer instructions

Flags affected: None

Coding example:

```
JP    NEXT_STEP
```

Description: JP causes program execution to branch to the operand address if the parity flag is set. This instruction is functionally the same as JPE.

JPE: Jump on Parity Even

Category: Control-transfer instructions

Flags affected: None

Coding example:

```
JPE        NEXT_STEP
```

Description: JPE causes program execution to branch to the operand address if the parity flag is set. This instruction is functionally the same as JP.

JPO: Jump on Parity Odd

Category: Control-transfer instructions

Flags affected: None

Coding example:

```
JPO        NEXT_STEP
```

Description: JPO causes program execution to branch to the operand address if the parity flag is clear. This instruction is functionally the same as JNP.

JS: Jump on Sign

Category: Control-transfer instructions

Flags affected: None

Coding example:

```
JS    NEXT_STEP
```

Description: JS causes program execution to branch to the operand address if the sign flag is set.

JZ: Jump on Zero

Category: Control-transfer instructions

Flags affected: None

Coding example:

```
JZ    NEXT_STEP
```

Description: JZ causes program execution to branch to the operand address if the zero flag is set. This instruction is functionally the same as JE.

LAHF: Load AH Register with Flags

Category: Data-transfer instructions

Flags affected: None

Coding example:

```
LAHF
```

Description: LAHF copies the low-order byte of the flags register to AH. After execution of this instruction, bits 7, 6, 4, 2, and 1 of AH are equal to SF, ZF, AF, PF, and CF, respectively.

LDS: Load DS Register

Category: Data-transfer instructions

Flags affected: None

Coding example:

```
LDS       SI,SOURCE_BUFFER
```

Description: LDS performs two distinct operations: it loads DS with the segment address of the source operand, and loads the destination operand with the offset address of the source operand.

LEA: Load Effective Address

Category: Data-transfer instructions

Flags affected: None

Coding example:

```
LEA        AX,MESSAGE_1
```

Description: LEA transfers the offset address of the source operand to the destination operand. The destination operand must be a general word register.

LES: Load ES Register

Category: Data-transfer instructions

Flags affected: None

Coding example:

```
LES        DI,DEST_BUFFER
```

Description: LES performs two distinct operations: it loads ES with the segment address of the source operand, and loads the destination operand with the offset address of the source operand.

LOCK: Lock Bus

Category: Flag- and processor-control instructions

Flags affected: None

Coding example:

```
LOCK XLAT
```

Description: LOCK prohibits interference from any other coprocessors during the execution of the next instruction issued. LOCK is a prefix to be used with other operations.

LODSB: Load a Byte from String into AL

Category: String-manipulation instructions

Flags affected: None

Coding example:

```
LODSB
```

Description: This instruction loads AL with the contents of the address pointed to by SI. SI then changes in increments or decrements of 1, depending on the setting of the direction flag. Intel lists this command as LODS; however, the Microsoft Macro Assembler distinguishes between byte (LODSB) and word (LODSW).

LODSW: Load a Word from String into AX

Category: String-manipulation instructions

Flags affected: None

Coding example:

```
LODSW
```

Description: This instruction loads AX with the contents of the address pointed to by SI. SI then changes in increments or decrements of 2, depending on the setting of the direction flag. Intel lists this command as LODS; however, the Microsoft Macro Assembler distinguishes between byte (LODSB) and word (LODSW).

LOOP: Loop

Category: Control-transfer instructions

Flags affected: None

Coding example:

```
LOOP      PRINT_LOOP
```

Description: Based on the contents of CX, program execution branches to the address of the destination operand. If CX does not equal 0, CX changes in decrements of 1, and the branch occurs. If CX is 0, no decrements or branching occur, and execution proceeds to the next instruction.

LOOPE: Loop While Equal

Category: Control-transfer instructions

Flags affected: None

Coding example:

```
LOOPE    TEST_LOOP
```

Description: Based on the contents of CX and the zero flag, program execution branches to the address of the destination operand. If CX does not equal 0 and the zero flag is set, CX changes in decrements of 1, and the branch occurs. If CX is 0 or the zero flag is clear, no decrements or branching occur, and execution proceeds to the next instruction. This instruction is functionally equivalent to LOOPZ.

LOOPNE: Loop While Not Equal

Category: Control-transfer instructions

Flags affected: None

Coding example:

```
LOOPNE   TEST_LOOP
```

Description: Based on the contents of CX and the zero flag, program execution branches to the address of the destination operand. If CX does not equal 0 and the zero flag is clear, CX changes in decrements of 1, and the branch occurs. If CX is 0 or the zero flag is set, no decrements or branching occur, and execution proceeds to the next instruction. This instruction is functionally equivalent to LOOPNZ.

LOOPNZ: Loop While Not Zero

Category: Control-transfer instructions

Flags affected: None

Coding example:

```
LOOPNZ   TEST_LOOP
```

Description: Based on the contents of CX and the zero flag, program execution branches to the address of the destination operand. If CX does not equal 0 and the zero flag is clear, CX changes in decrements of 1, and the branch occurs. If

CX is 0 or the zero flag is set, no decrements or branching occur, and execution proceeds to the next instruction. This instruction is functionally equivalent to LOOPNE.

LOOPZ: Loop While Zero

Category: Control-transfer instructions

Flags affected: None

Coding example:

```
LOOPZ   TEST_LOOP
```

Description: Based on the contents of CX and the zero flag, program execution branches to the address of the destination operand. If CX does not equal 0 and the zero flag is set, CX changes in decrements of 1, and the branch occurs. If CX is 0 or the zero flag is clear, no decrements or branching occur, and execution proceeds to the next instruction. This instruction is functionally equivalent to LOOPE.

MOV: Move

Category: Data-transfer instructions

Flags affected: None

Coding examples:

```
MOV       AX,BX          ;AX=BX
MOV       AX,TEMP        ;AX=TEMP (TEMP is a word)
MOV       SUM,BX         ;SUM=BX (SUM is a word)
MOV       CL,57          ;CL=57
MOV       DEC,1Ø         ;DEC=1Ø
MOV       AX,TEMP[BX]    ;Indirect address example
```

Description: MOV copies the contents of the source operand to the destination operand. Both operands must be the same length.

MOVSB: Move String, Byte-by-Byte

Category: String-manipulation instructions

Flags affected: None

Coding examples:

```
MOVSB
REP MOVSB        ;Repeat a move loop
```

Description: This instruction moves strings, byte-by-byte. The values of SI and DI change in increments or decrements of 1, depending on the setting of the direction flag. Usually, this instruction is used with the REP instruction to repeat the move for a maximum of CX bytes. Intel lists this command as MOVS; however, the Microsoft Macro Assembler makes the byte/word distinctions.

MOVSW: Move String, Word-by-Word

Category: String-manipulation instructions

Flags affected: None

Coding examples:

```
MOVSW
REP MOVSW        ;Repeat a move loop
```

Description: This instruction moves strings, word-by-word. The values of SI and DI change in increments or decrements of 2, depending on the setting of the direction flag. Usually, this instruction is used with the REP instruction to repeat the move for a maximum of CX words. Intel lists this command as MOVS; however, the Microsoft Macro Assembler makes the byte/word distinctions.

MUL: Multiply

Category: Arithmetic instructions

Flags affected:

F	E	D	C	B	A	9	8	7	6	5	4	3	2	1	Ø
				OF	DF	IF	TF	SF	ZF		AF		PF		CF
				X				?	?		?		?		X

Coding examples:

```
MUL    BX              ;DX:AX=AX*BX
MUL    WORD_TEMP       ;DX:AX=AX*WORD_TEMP
MUL    BYTE_SUM        ;AX=AL*BYTE_SUM
MUL    WORD_TBL[BX]    ;Indirect address example
```

Description: If the operand is a byte value, MUL multiplies the contents of AL by the contents of the operand and stores the result in AX. If the operand is a word value, MUL multiplies the contents of AX by the contents of the operand and stores the result in DX:AX. This instruction treats numbers as unsigned binary values.

NEG: Negate

Category: Arithmetic instructions

Flags affected:

F	E	D	C	B	A	9	8	7	6	5	4	3	2	1	Ø
				OF	DF	IF	TF	SF	ZF		AF		PF		CF
				X				X	X		X		X		X

Coding examples:

```
NEG     TEMP
NEG     CL
```

Description: NEG calculates the two's complement of the destination operand and stores the result in the destination operand. This calculation is effectively the same as subtracting the destination operand from 0.

NOP: No Operation

Category: Flag- and processor-control instructions

Flags affected: None

Coding example:

```
NOP
```

Description: NOP simply takes space and time. It causes the CPU to do nothing.

NOT: Logical NOT on Bits

Category: Bit-manipulation instructions

Flags affected: None

Coding examples:

```
NOT     CL
NOT     TEMP
NOT     AX
```

Description: NOT inverts the bits in the destination operand (0 becomes 1, and 1 becomes 0) and stores the inverted bits in the destination operand.

OR: Logical OR on Bits

Category: Bit-manipulation instructions

Flags affected:

F	E	D	C	B	A	9	8	7	6	5	4	3	2	1	Ø
				OF	DF	IF	TF	SF	ZF		AF		PF		CF
				X				X	X		?		X		X

Coding examples:

```
OR      AL,BL
OR      AL,10000000b
OR      DX,TEMP
OR      AX,CX
```

Description: This instruction performs a logical OR of the operands and stores the result in the destination operand. Each bit of the resultant byte or word is set to 1 if either or both of the corresponding bits of each operand are set to 1.

OUT: Output to Port

Category: Data-transfer instructions

Flags affected: None

Coding examples:

```
OUT     AL,64h
OUT     AX,DX
```

Description: OUT sends a byte (AL) or word (AX) to the specified hardware I/O port address. A port number below 256 may be specified either as a constant or as a variable in the DX register. A port number above 255, however, *must* be specified in the DX register.

POP: Remove Data from Stack

Category: Data-transfer instructions

Flags affected: None

Coding examples:

```
POP        AX
POP        DS
POP        HOLD_REG
```

Description: POP removes a word from the stack and places that word in the desired destination operand.

POPF: Remove Flags from Stack

Category: Data-transfer instructions

Flags affected:

F	E	D	C	B	A	9	8	7	6	5	4	3	2	1	Ø
				OF	DF	IF	TF	SF	ZF		AF		PF		CF
X	X	X	X	X	X	X	X	X	X	X	X	X	X	X	X

Coding example:

```
POPF
```

Description: POPF removes a word from the stack and places the word in the flags register.

PUSH: Place Data on Stack

Category: Data-transfer instructions

Flags affected: None

Coding examples:

```
PUSH       AX
PUSH       DS
PUSH       HOLD_REG
```

Description: PUSH places a copy of the value of the operand on the stack.

PUSHF: Place Flags on Stack

Category: Data-transfer instructions

Flags affected: None

Coding example:

```
PUSHF
```

Description: PUSHF places a copy of the flags register on the stack.

RCL: Rotate Left through Carry

Category: Bit-manipulation instructions

Flags affected:

F	E	D	C	B	A	9	8	7	6	5	4	3	2	1	Ø
				OF	DF	IF	TF	SF	ZF		AF		PF		CF
				X											X

Coding examples:

```
RCL        AX,1
RCL        BL,3
RCL        TEMP,CL
```

Description: RCL rotates all bits in the destination operand to the left by the number of places specified in the source operand. The rotation is performed through the carry flag in an order that rotates the most significant bit of the destination operand to the carry flag and rotates the carry flag to the least significant bit of the destination operand.

RCR: Rotate Right through Carry

Category: Bit-manipulation instructions

Flags affected:

F	E	D	C	B	A	9	8	7	6	5	4	3	2	1	Ø
				OF	DF	IF	TF	SF	ZF		AF		PF		CF
				X											X

Coding examples:

```
RCR     AX,1
RCR     BL,3
RCR     TEMP,CL
```

Description: RCR rotates all bits in the destination operand to the right by the number of places specified in the source operand. The rotation is performed through the carry flag in an order that rotates the least significant bit of the destination operand to the carry flag and rotates the carry flag to the most significant bit of the destination operand.

REP: Repeat

Category: String-manipulation instructions

Flags affected: None

Coding example:

```
REP MOVSB
```

Description: REP causes string-manipulation instructions to be repeated the number of iterations specified in CX.

REPE: Repeat if Equal

Category: String-manipulation instructions

Flags affected: None

Coding example:

```
REPE CMPSW
```

Description: REPE causes string-manipulation instructions to be repeated the number of iterations specified in CX. When used with CMPSB, CMPSW, SCASB, or SCASW, this instruction repeats only while the zero flag is set. This instruction is functionally equivalent to REPZ.

REPNE: Repeat if Not Equal

Category: String-manipulation instructions

Flags affected: None

Coding example:

```
REPNE CMPSW
```

Description: REPNE causes string-manipulation instructions to be repeated the number of iterations specified in CX. When used with CMPSB, CMPSW, SCASB, or SCASW, this instruction repeats only while the zero flag is clear. This instruction is functionally equivalent to REPNZ.

REPNZ: Repeat if Not Zero

Category: String-manipulation instructions

Flags affected: None

Coding example:

```
REPNZ CMPSW
```

Description: REPNZ causes string-manipulation instructions to be repeated the number of iterations specified in CX. When used with CMPSB, CMPSW, SCASB, or SCASW, this instruction repeats only while the zero flag is clear. This instruction is functionally equivalent to REPNE.

REPZ: Repeat if Zero

Category: String-manipulation instructions

Flags affected: None

Coding example:

```
REPZ CMPSW
```

Description: REPZ causes string-manipulation instructions to be repeated the number of iterations specified in CX. When used with CMPSB, CMPSW, SCASB, or SCASW, this instruction repeats only while the zero flag is set. This instruction is functionally equivalent to REPE.

RET: Return from Subroutine

Category: Control-transfer instructions

Flags affected: None

Coding examples:

```
RET
RET        2
```

Description: By popping IP from the stack, RET transfers program control back to the point where a CALL was issued. If the CALL was to a FAR procedure, both CS:IP are popped from the stack.

If the RET has a specified return value (2, in the coding example), the stack is adjusted by that number of bytes. The coding example shows that a word is discarded from the stack after either IP or CS:IP is popped.

ROL: Rotate Left

Category: Bit-manipulation instructions

Flags affected:

F	E	D	C	B	A	9	8	7	6	5	4	3	2	1	Ø
				OF	DF	IF	TF	SF	ZF		AF		PF		CF
				X											X

Coding examples:

```
ROL        AX,1
ROL        BL,3
ROL        TEMP,CL
```

Description: ROL rotates all bits in the destination operand to the left by the number of places specified in the source operand.

ROR: Rotate Right

Category: Bit-manipulation instructions

Flags affected:

F	E	D	C	B	A	9	8	7	6	5	4	3	2	1	Ø
				OF	DF	IF	TF	SF	ZF		AF		PF		CF
				X											X

Coding examples:

```
ROR        AX,1
ROR        BL,3
ROR        TEMP,CL
```

Description: ROR rotates all bits in the destination operand to the right by the number of places specified in the source operand.

SAHF: Store AH into Flag Register

Category: Data-transfer instructions

Flags affected:

F	E	D	C	B	A	9	8	7	6	5	4	3	2	1	Ø
				OF	DF	IF	TF	SF	ZF		AF		PF		CF
								X	X	X	X	X	X	X	X

Coding example:

```
SAHF
```

Description: SAHF copies the the contents of AH to the low-order byte of the flags register. After execution of this instruction, SF, ZF, AF, PF, and CF are equal to bits 7, 6, 4, 2, and 1 of AH, respectively.

SAL: Arithmetic Shift Left

Category: Bit-manipulation instructions

Flags affected:

F	E	D	C	B	A	9	8	7	6	5	4	3	2	1	Ø
				OF	DF	IF	TF	SF	ZF		AF		PF		CF
				X				X	X		?		X		X

Coding examples:

```
SAL        AX,1
SAL        BL,3
SAL        TEMP,CL
```

Description: SAL shifts all bits in the destination operand to the left by the number of places specified in the source operand. High-order bits are lost, and low-order bits are cleared.

SAR: Arithmetic Shift Right

Category: Bit-manipulation instructions

Flags affected:

F	E	D	C	B	A	9	8	7	6	5	4	3	2	1	Ø
				OF	DF	IF	TF	SF	ZF		AF		PF		CF
				X				X	X		?		X		X

Coding examples:

```
SAR      AX,1
SAR      BL,3
SAR      TEMP,CL
```

Description: SAR shifts all bits in the destination operand to the right by the number of places specified in the source operand. Low-order bits are lost, and high-order bits are set equal to the existing high-order bit.

SBB: Subtract with Carry

Category: Arithmetic instructions

Flags affected:

F	E	D	C	B	A	9	8	7	6	5	4	3	2	1	Ø
				OF	DF	IF	TF	SF	ZF		AF		PF		CF
				X				X	X		X		X		X

Coding examples:

```
SBB      AX,BX          ;AX=AX-AX-CF
SBB      AX,TEMP        ;AX=AX-TEMP-CF
SBB      SUM,BX         ;SUM=SUM-BX-CF
SBB      CL,1Ø          ;CL=CL-1Ø-CF
SBB      AX,TEMP[BX]    ;Indirect address example
```

Description: SBB subtracts the contents of the source operand from (and stores the result in) the destination operand. If the carry flag is set, the result changes in decrements of 1. In this instruction, the values being added are assumed to be binary.

SCASB: Scan String for Byte

Category: String-manipulation instructions

Flags affected:

F	E	D	C	B	A	9	8	7	6	5	4	3	2	1	Ø
				OF	DF	IF	TF	SF	ZF		AF		PF		CF
				X				X	X		X		X		X

Coding examples:

```
SCASB
REPNZ SCASB      ;Repeat a scan loop
```

Description: This instruction subtracts the destination operand string byte (pointed to by DI) from the value of AL. The result is not stored, but the flags are updated. Then, the value of DI changes in increments or decrements of 1, depending on the setting of the direction flag. Usually, this instruction is used with the REPE, REPNE, REPNZ, or REPZ instructions to repeat the scan for a maximum of CX bytes, or until SCASB finds a match or difference. Intel lists this command as SCAS; however, the Microsoft Macro Assembler makes the byte/word distinctions.

SCASW: Scan String for Word

Category: String-manipulation instructions

Flags affected:

F	E	D	C	B	A	9	8	7	6	5	4	3	2	1	Ø
				OF	DF	IF	TF	SF	ZF		AF		PF		CF
				X				X	X		X		X		X

Coding examples:

```
SCASW
REPNZ SCASW    ;Repeat a scan loop
```

Description: This instruction subtracts the destination operand string word (pointed to by DI) from the value of AX. The result is not stored, but the flags are updated. Then, the value of DI changes in increments or decrements of 2, depending on the setting of the direction flag. Usually, this instruction is used with the REPE, REPNE, REPNZ, or REPZ instructions to repeat the scan for a maximum of CX bytes, or until SCASW finds a match or difference. Intel lists this command as SCAS; however, the Microsoft Macro Assembler makes the byte/word distinctions.

SHL: Shift Left

Category: Bit-manipulation instructions

Flags affected:

F	E	D	C	B	A	9	8	7	6	5	4	3	2	1	Ø
				OF	DF	IF	TF	SF	ZF		AF		PF		CF
				X				X	X		?		X		X

Coding examples:

```
SHL    AX,1
SHL    BL,3
SHL    TEMP,CL
```

Description: SHL shifts all bits in the destination operand to the left by the number of places specified in the source operand. High-order bits are lost, and low-order bits are cleared.

SHR: Shift Right

Category: Bit-manipulation instructions

Flags affected:

F	E	D	C	B	A	9	8	7	6	5	4	3	2	1	Ø
				OF	DF	IF	TF	SF	ZF		AF		PF		CF
				X				X	X		?		X		X

Coding examples:

```
SHR        AX,1
SHR        BL,3
SHR        TEMP,CL
```

Description: SHR shifts all bits in the destination operand to the right by the number of places specified in the source operand. Low-order bits are lost, and high-order bits are cleared.

STC: Set Carry Flag

Category: Flag- and processor-control instructions

Flags affected:

F	E	D	C	B	A	9	8	7	6	5	4	3	2	1	Ø
				OF	DF	IF	TF	SF	ZF		AF		PF		CF
															X

Coding example:

```
STC
```

Description: STC sets the carry flag, regardless of the flag's present condition.

STD: Set Direction Flag

Category: Flag- and processor-control instructions

Flags affected:

F	E	D	C	B	A	9	8	7	6	5	4	3	2	1	Ø
				OF	DF	IF	TF	SF	ZF		AF		PF		CF
				X											

Coding example:

```
STD
```

Description: STD sets the direction flag, regardless of the flag's present condition. This setting has effect on the string instructions.

STI: Set Interrupt Flag

Category: Flag- and processor-control instructions

Flags affected:

F	E	D	C	B	A	9	8	7	6	5	4	3	2	1	Ø
					OF	DF	IF	TF	SF	ZF		AF		PF		CF
						X									

Coding example:

```
STI
```

Description: STI sets the interrupt flag, regardless of the flag's present condition. While this flag is set, the 8086/8088 CPU responds to maskable interrupts.

STOSB: Store Byte in AL at String

Category: String-manipulation instructions

Flags affected: None

Coding example:

```
STOSB
```

Description: This instruction copies the contents of AL to the byte address pointed to by DI. DI then changes in increments or decrements of 1, depending on the setting of the direction flag. Intel lists this command as STOS; however, the Microsoft Macro Assembler makes the byte/word distinctions.

STOSW: Store Word in AX at String

Category: String-manipulation instructions

Flags affected: None

Coding example:

```
STOSW
```

Description: This instruction copies the contents of AX to the word address pointed to by DI. DI then changes in increments or decrements of 2, depending on the setting of the direction flag. Intel lists this command as STOS; however, the Microsoft Macro Assembler makes the byte/word distinctions.

SUB: Subtract

Category: Arithmetic instructions

Flags affected:

F	E	D	C	B	A	9	8	7	6	5	4	3	2	1	Ø
				OF	DF	IF	TF	SF	ZF		AF		PF		CF
				X				X	X		X		X		X

Coding examples:

```
SUB        AX,BX           ;AX=AX-AX
SUB        AX,TEMP         ;AX=AX-TEMP
SUB        SUM,BX          ;SUM=SUM-BX
SUB        CL,1Ø           ;CL=CL-1Ø
SUB        AX,TEMP[BX]     ;Indirect address example
```

Description: SUB subtracts the contents of the source operand from (and stores the result in) the destination operand. In this instruction, the values being added are assumed to be binary.

TEST: Test Bits

Category: Bit-manipulation instructions

Flags affected:

F	E	D	C	B	A	9	8	7	6	5	4	3	2	1	Ø
				OF	DF	IF	TF	SF	ZF		AF		PF		CF
				X				X	X		?		X		X

Coding examples:

```
TEST    AX,BX         ;
TEST    AX,TEMP       ;TEMP must be a word
TEST    SUM,BX        ;SUM must be a word
TEST    CL,00001111b  ;
TEST    AX,TEMP[BX]   ;Indirect address example
```

Description: TEST performs a logical AND of the operands, but the result is not stored. Only the flags are affected. Each bit of the resultant byte or word is set to 1 only if the corresponding bit of each operand is set to 1.

WAIT: Wait

Category: Flag- and processor-control instructions

Flags affected: None

Coding example:

```
WAIT
```

Description: WAIT causes the 8086/8088 CPU to wait for an external interrupt on the TEST line before continuing.

XCHG: Exchange

Category: Data-transfer instructions

Flags affected: None

Coding examples:

```
XCHG    AX,BX    ;Swap AX with BX
XCHG    CL,CH    ;Swap CL with CH
XCHG    AX,TEMP  ;Swap AX with TEMP (word)
```

Description: XCHG swaps the contents of the source and destination operands.

XLAT: Translate

Category: Data-transfer instructions

Flags affected: None

Coding example:

```
XLAT
```

Description: Assuming that the offset address of a 256-byte translation table is contained in BX, this instruction uses the value in AL as a zero-based offset into the table, and subsequently loads AL with the byte value at that calculated offset. This instruction is helpful for translation tables.

XOR: Logical Exclusive-Or on Bits

Category: Bit-manipulation instructions

Flags affected:

F	E	D	C	B	A	9	8	7	6	5	4	3	2	1	Ø
				OF	DF	IF	TF	SF	ZF		AF		PF		CF
				X				X	X		?		X		X

Coding examples:

```
XOR     AX,BX           ;
XOR     AX,TEMP         ;TEMP must be a word
XOR     SUM,BX          ;SUM must be a word
XOR     CL,ØØØØ1111b     ;
XOR     AX,TEMP[BX]     ;Indirect address example
```

Description: This instruction performs a logical XOR of the operands and stores the result in the destination operand. Each bit of the resultant byte or word is set to 1 only if the corresponding bit of each operand contains opposite values.

Instruction Set for the Intel 80286

The Intel 80286 Instruction Set is an extension of the instruction set for the Intel 8086/8088. Some of the approximately 27 additional instructions included here are not designed for use in applications software; rather, they are used for developing operating systems software.

Instruction Set Groupings

The 80286 instructions may be grouped according to the purpose of the instruction. The six general classifications of instructions are

Data transfer
Arithmetic
Bit manipulation
String manipulation
Control transfer
Flag and processor control

The individual instructions within these categories are listed in table 80286.1.

Table 80286.1
80286 Instruction Set Groupings

Instruction	Meaning
Data Transfer	
IN	Input from port
INS	Input string from port
INSB	Input string byte from port
INSW	Input string word from port
LAHF	Load AH register with flags
LAR	Load access-rights byte
LDS	Load DS register
LEA	Load effective address
LES	Load ES register
LGDT	Load global descriptor table register
LIDT	Load interrupt descriptor table register
LLDT	Load local descriptor table register
LMSW	Load machine status word

Table 80286.1—cont.

Instruction	Meaning
LSL	Load segment limit
LTR	Load task register
MOV	Move
OUT	Output to port
OUTS	Output string to port
OUTSB	Output string byte to port
OUTSW	Output string word to port
POP	Remove data from stack
POPA	Pop all general registers
POPF	Remove flags from stack
PUSH	Place data on stack
PUSHA	Push all general registers
PUSHF	Place flags on stack
SAHF	Store AH into flag register
SGDT	Store global descriptor table register
SIDT	Store interrupt descriptor table register
SLDT	Store local descriptor table register
SMSW	Store machine status word
STR	Store task register
XCHG	Exchange
XLAT	Translate

Arithmetic

AAA	ASCII adjust for addition
AAD	ASCII adjust for division
AAM	ASCII adjust for multiplication
AAS	ASCII adjust for subtraction
ADC	Add with carry
ADD	Add
CBW	Convert byte to word
CMP	Compare
CWD	Convert word to doubleword
DAA	Decimal adjust for addition
DAS	Decimal adjust for subtraction
DEC	Decrement
DIV	Divide
IDIV	Integer divide
IMUL	Integer multiply
INC	Increment

Table 80286.1—cont.

Instruction	Meaning
MUL	Multiply
NEG	Negate
SBB	Subtract with carry
SUB	Subtract

Bit Manipulation

AND	Logical AND on bits
ARPL	Adjust RPL field of selector
NOT	Logical NOT on bits
OR	Logical OR on bits
RCL	Rotate left through carry
RCR	Rotate right through carry
ROL	Rotate left
ROR	Rotate right
SAL	Arithmetic shift left
SAR	Arithmetic shift right
SHL	Shift left
SHR	Shift right
TEST	Test bits
XOR	Logical exclusive-or on bits

String Manipulation

CMPSB	Compare strings, byte for byte
CMPSW	Compare strings, word for word
LODSB	Load a byte from string into AL
LODSW	Load a word from string into AX
MOVSB	Move string, byte-by-byte
MOVSW	Move string, word-by-word
REP	Repeat
REPE	Repeat if equal
REPNE	Repeat if not equal
REPNZ	Repeat if not zero
REPZ	Repeat if zero
SCASB	Scan string for byte
SCASW	Scan string for word
STOSB	Store byte in AL at string
STOSW	Store word in AX at string

Table 80286.1—cont.

Instruction	Meaning

Control Transfer

CALL	Perform subroutine
INT	Software interrupt
INTO	Interrupt on overflow
IRET	Return from interrupt
JA	Jump if above
JAE	Jump if above or equal
JB	Jump if below
JBE	Jump if below or equal
JC	Jump on carry
JCXZ	Jump if CX=0
JE	Jump if equal
JG	Jump if greater
JGE	Jump if greater or equal
JL	Jump if less than
JLE	Jump if less than or equal
JMP	Jump
JNA	Jump if not above
JNAE	Jump if not above or equal
JNB	Jump if not below
JNBE	Jump if not below or equal
JNC	Jump on no carry
JNE	Jump if not equal
JNG	Jump if not greater than
JNGE	Jump if not greater than or equal
JNL	Jump if not less than
JNLE	Jump if not less than or equal
JNO	Jump on no overflow
JNP	Jump on no parity
JNS	Jump on not sign
JNZ	Jump on not zero
JO	Jump on overflow
JP	Jump on parity
JPE	Jump on parity even
JPO	Jump on parity odd
JS	Jump on sign
JZ	Jump on zero

Table 80286.1—cont.

Instruction	Meaning
LOOP	Loop
LOOPE	Loop while equal
LOOPNE	Loop while not equal
LOOPNZ	Loop while not zero
LOOPZ	Loop while zero
RET	Return from subroutine

Flag and Processor Control

BOUND	Check array index against bounds
CLC	Clear carry flag
CLD	Clear direction flag
CLI	Clear interrupt flag
CLTS	Clear task switched flag
CMC	Complement carry flag
ENTER	Make stack frame for procedure parameters
ESC	Escape
HLT	Halt
LEAVE	High-level procedure exit
LOCK	Lock bus
NOP	No operation
STC	Set carry flag
STD	Set direction flag
STI	Set interrupt flag
VERR	Verify a segment for reading
VERW	Verify a segment for writing
WAIT	Wait

Detailed Instruction Information

The balance of this section is designed as a reference for the 80286 instruction set. Each instruction is described in detail. The following information is listed for each instruction:

- *Instruction name*. This name is based on the standard mnemonic code designed by Intel.

- *Instruction category*. The general classification for the instruction is given.

- *Flags affected.* The majority of the instructions change the status of the bits in the flags register. The individual flags affected are listed in the following format:

F	E	D	C	B	A	9	8	7	6	5	4	3	2	1	Ø
	NT	IOPL		OF	DF	IF	TF	SF	ZF		AF		PF		CF
				?				?	?		X		?		X

In this format, an X indicates that the flag is changed, and a question mark (?) indicates that the flag is undefined after the instruction is issued. The flags are as follows:

Abbreviation	Flag	Location
NT	Nested task	Bit Eh
IOPL	I/O privilege level	Bits Ch/Dh
OF	Overflow	Bit Bh
DF	Direction	Bit Ah
IF	Interrupt	Bit 9
TF	Trap	Bit 8
SF	Sign	Bit 7
ZF	Zero	Bit 6
AF	Auxiliary carry	Bit 4
PF	Parity	Bit 2
CF	Carry	Bit 0

- *Coding examples.* One or two lines of code show how the instruction is used.

- *Description.* A narrative description of the instruction completes the detail.

The instructions are arranged in ascending alphabetical order.

AAA: ASCII Adjust for Addition

Category: Arithmetic instructions

Flags affected:

F	E	D	C	B	A	9	8	7	6	5	4	3	2	1	Ø
	NT	IOPL		OF	DF	IF	TF	SF	ZF		AF		PF		CF
				?				?	?		X		?		X

Coding example:

    AAA

Description: AAA changes the contents of AL to a valid unpacked decimal number with the high-order nibble zeroed.

AAD: ASCII Adjust for Division

Category: Arithmetic instructions

Flags affected:

F	E	D	C	B	A	9	8	7	6	5	4	3	2	1	Ø
	NT	IOPL		OF	DF	IF	TF	SF	ZF		AF		PF		CF
				?				X	X		?		X		?

Coding example:

    AAD

Description: AAD multiplies the contents of AH by 10, adds the result to the contents of AL, and places the final result in AL. The instruction then sets AH to 0. Use this instruction before dividing unpacked decimal numbers.

AAM: ASCII Adjust for Multiplication

Category: Arithmetic instructions

Flags affected:

F	E	D	C	B	A	9	8	7	6	5	4	3	2	1	Ø
	NT	IOPL		OF	DF	IF	TF	SF	ZF		AF		PF		CF
				?				X	X		?		X		?

Coding example:

    AAM

Description: After multiplying two unpacked decimal numbers, use this instruction to correct the result to an unpacked decimal number. For AAM to work properly, each number multiplied must have had its high-order nibbles set to 0.

AAS: ASCII Adjust for Subtraction

Category: Arithmetic instructions

Flags affected:

F	E	D	C	B	A	9	8	7	6	5	4	3	2	1	Ø
	NT	IOPL		OF	DF	IF	TF	SF	ZF		AF		PF		CF
				?				?	?		X		?		X

Coding example:

```
AAS
```

Description: AAS corrects the result of a previous unpacked decimal subtraction so that the value in AL is a true unpacked decimal number.

ADC: Add with Carry

Category: Arithmetic instructions

Flags affected:

F	E	D	C	B	A	9	8	7	6	5	4	3	2	1	Ø
	NT	IOPL		OF	DF	IF	TF	SF	ZF		AF		PF		CF
				X				X	X		X		X		X

Coding examples:

```
ADC        AX,BX            ;AX=AX+BX+CF
ADC        AX,TEMP          ;AX=AX+TEMP+CF
ADC        SUM,BX           ;SUM=SUM+BX+CF
ADC        CL,1Ø            ;CL=CL+1Ø+CF
ADC        AX,TEMP[BX]      ;Indirect address example
```

Description: ADC adds the contents of the source operand to (and stores the result in) the destination operand. If the carry flag is set, the result is changed in an increment of 1. In this routine, the values being added are assumed to be binary.

ADD: Add

Category: Arithmetic instructions

Flags affected:

F	E	D	C	B	A	9	8	7	6	5	4	3	2	1	Ø
	NT	IOPL		OF	DF	IF	TF	SF	ZF		AF		PF		CF
				X				X	X		X		X		X

Coding examples:

```
ADD     AX,BX           ;AX=AX+BX
ADD     AX,TEMP         ;AX=AX+TEMP
ADD     SUM,BX          ;SUM=SUM+BX
ADD     CL,1Ø           ;CL=CL+1Ø
ADD     AX,TEMP[BX]     ;Indirect address example
```

Description: ADD adds the contents of the source operand to (and stores the result in) the destination operand. In this routine, the values being added are assumed to be binary.

AND: Logical AND on Bits

Category: Bit-manipulation instructions

F	E	D	C	B	A	9	8	7	6	5	4	3	2	1	Ø
	NT	IOPL		OF	DF	IF	TF	SF	ZF		AF		PF		CF
				X				X	X		?		X		X

Coding examples:

```
AND     AX,BX           ;
AND     AX,TEMP         ;TEMP must be a word
AND     SUM,BX          ;SUM must be a word
AND     CL,ØØØØ1111b     ;Zero high nibble
AND     AX,TEMP[BX]     ;Indirect address example
```

Description: AND performs a logical AND of the operands and stores the result in the destination operand. Each bit of the resultant byte or word is set to 1, only if the corresponding bit of each operand is set to 1.

ARPL: Adjust RPL Field of Selector

Category: Bit-manipulation instructions

Flags affected:

F	E	D	C	B	A	9	8	7	6	5	4	3	2	1	Ø
	NT	IOPL		OF	DF	IF	TF	SF	ZF		AF		PF		CF
									X						

Coding examples:

```
ARPL        SELECTOR,AX
ARPL        AX,CX
```

Description: ARPL compares the RPL bits (bits 0 and 1) of the first operand with those of the second. If the RPL bits of the first operand are less than those of the second, the two bits of the first operand are set equal to the two bits of the second, and the zero flag is set. Otherwise, the zero flag is cleared. This instruction is used only in operating system software (not used in applications software).

BOUND: Check Array Index against Bounds

Category: Flag- and processor-control instructions

Flags affected: None

Coding example:

```
BOUND       BX,LIMITS
```

Description: BOUND determines whether the signed value in the first operand falls between the two boundaries specified by the second operand. The word at the second operand is assumed to be the lower boundary, and the following word is assumed to be the upper boundary. An interrupt 5 occurs if the value in the first operand is less than the lower limit or greater than the upper limit.

CALL: Perform Subroutine

Category: Control-transfer instructions

Flags affected: None

Coding examples:

```
CALL       WHIZ_BANG      ;WHIZ_BANG is a subroutine
CALL       [BX]           ;Perform subroutine with
                          ;  address at [BX]
CALL       AX             ;Subroutine address in AX
```

Description: CALL causes the following to happen:

- Pushes offset address of following instruction on the stack

- If procedure being called is declared as FAR, pushes segment address of following instruction on the stack

- Loads IP with the offset address of the procedure being called

- If procedure being called is declared as FAR, loads CS with the segment address of the procedure being called

Execution then continues at the newly loaded CS:IP address until a RET instruction is encountered.

CBW: Convert Byte to Word

Category: Arithmetic instructions

Flags affected: None

Coding example:

```
CBW
```

Description: CBW converts the byte value in AL to a word value in AX by extending the high-order bit value of AL through all bits of AH.

CLC: Clear Carry Flag

Category: Flag- and processor-control instructions

Flags affected:

F	E	D	C	B	A	9	8	7	6	5	4	3	2	1	Ø
	NT	IOPL		OF	DF	IF	TF	SF	ZF		AF		PF		CF
															X

Coding example:

```
CLC
```

Description: CLC clears the carry flag of the flags register by setting the flag to 0.

CLD: Clear Direction Flag

Category: Flag- and processor-control instructions

Flags affected:

F	E	D	C	B	A	9	8	7	6	5	4	3	2	1	Ø
	NT	IOPL		OF	DF	IF	TF	SF	ZF		AF		PF		CF
					X										

Coding example:

```
CLD
```

Description: CLD clears the direction flag of the flags register by setting the flag to 0.

CLI: Clear Interrupt Flag

Category: Flag- and processor-control instructions

Flags affected:

F	E	D	C	B	A	9	8	7	6	5	4	3	2	1	Ø
	NT	IOPL		OF	DF	IF	TF	SF	ZF		AF		PF		CF
					X										

Coding example:

```
CLI
```

Description: CLI clears the interrupt flag of the flags register by setting the flag to 0. While the flag is cleared, no maskable interrupts are recognized by the CPU.

CLTS: Clear Task Switched Flag

Category: Flag- and processor-control instructions

Flags affected: None in flags register—affects machine status word

Coding example:

```
CLTS
```

Description: CLTS clears the task switched flag of the machine status register. This instruction is used only in operating system software (not in applications software).

CMC: Complement Carry Flag

Category: Flag- and processor-control instructions

Flags affected:

F	E	D	C	B	A	9	8	7	6	5	4	3	2	1	Ø
	NT	IOPL		OF	DF	IF	TF	SF	ZF		AF		PF		CF
															X

Coding example:

```
CMC
```

Description: CMC switches the carry flag of the flags register to the opposite of the flag's current setting.

CMP: Compare

Category: Arithmetic instructions

Flags affected:

F	E	D	C	B	A	9	8	7	6	5	4	3	2	1	Ø
	NT	IOPL		OF	DF	IF	TF	SF	ZF		AF		PF		CF
				X				X	X		X		X		X

Coding examples:

```
CMP   AX,BX         ;
CMP   AX,TEMP       ;TEMP must be a word
CMP   SUM,BX        ;SUM must be a word
CMP   CL,3          ;Compare to constant
CMP   AX,TEMP[BX]   ;Indirect address example
```

Description: CMP is considered an arithmetic instruction because the source operand is subtracted from the destination operand. The result is not stored anywhere, however; it is used for setting the flags. Subsequent testing of the flags can be used for program control.

CMPSB: Compare Strings, Byte-for-Byte

Category: String-manipulation instructions

Flags affected:

F	E	D	C	B	A	9	8	7	6	5	4	3	2	1	Ø
	NT	IOPL		OF	DF	IF	TF	SF	ZF		AF		PF		CF
				X				X	X		X		X		X

Coding examples:

```
CMPSB            ;Compare strings
REPE CMPSB       ;Repeat a comparison loop
```

Description: CMPSB compares strings byte-for-byte. DI and SI change in an increment or decrement of 1, depending on the setting of the direction flag. Usually, this instruction is used with the REPE, REPNE, REPNZ, or REPZ instructions to repeat the comparison for a maximum of CX number of bytes. Intel lists this command as CMPS; however, the Microsoft Macro Assembler makes the byte/word distinctions. This instruction affects only the flags; no changes are made to the operands.

CMPSW: Compare Strings, Word-for-Word

Category: String-manipulation instructions

Flags affected:

F	E	D	C	B	A	9	8	7	6	5	4	3	2	1	Ø
	NT	IOPL		OF	DF	IF	TF	SF	ZF		AF		PF		CF
				X				X	X		X		X		X

Coding examples:

```
CMPSW              ;Compare strings
REPE CMPSW         ;Repeat a comparison loop
```

Description: CMPSW compares strings word-for-word. DI and SI change in increments or decrements of 2, depending on the setting of the direction flag. Usually, this instruction is used with REPE, REPNE, REPNZ, or REPZ instructions to repeat the comparison for a maximum of CX number of words. Intel lists this command as CMPS; however, the Microsoft Macro Assembler makes the byte/word distinctions. This instruction affects only the flags; no changes are made to the operands.

CWD: Convert Word to Doubleword

Category: Arithmetic instructions

Flags affected: None

Coding example:

```
CWD
```

Description: CWD converts the word value in AX to a double word value in DX:AX by extending the high-order bit value of AX through all bits of DX.

DAA: Decimal Adjust for Addition

Category: Arithmetic instructions

Flags affected:

F	E	D	C	B	A	9	8	7	6	5	4	3	2	1	Ø
	NT	IOPL		OF	DF	IF	TF	SF	ZF		AF		PF		CF
				?				X	X		X		X		X

Coding example:

```
DAA
```

Description: DAA corrects the result (AL) of a previous binary-coded decimal (BCD) addition operation.

DAS: Decimal Adjust for Subtraction

Category: Arithmetic instructions

Flags affected:

F	E	D	C	B	A	9	8	7	6	5	4	3	2	1	Ø
	NT	IOPL		OF	DF	IF	TF	SF	ZF		AF		PF		CF
				?				X	X		X		X		X

Coding example:

```
DAS
```

Description: DAS corrects the result (AL) of a previous binary-coded decimal (BCD) subtraction operation.

DEC: Decrement

Category: Arithmetic instructions

Flags affected:

F	E	D	C	B	A	9	8	7	6	5	4	3	2	1	Ø
	NT	IOPL		OF	DF	IF	TF	SF	ZF		AF		PF		CF
				X				X	X		X		X		

Coding examples:

```
DEC     AX
DEC     SUM
DEC     CL
DEC     TEMP[SI]
```

Description: DEC changes the contents of the operand in a decrement of 1. The operand is assumed to be an unsigned binary value.

DIV: Divide

Category: Arithmetic instructions

Flags affected:

F	E	D	C	B	A	9	8	7	6	5	4	3	2	1	Ø
	NT	IOPL		OF	DF	IF	TF	SF	ZF		AF		PF		CF
				?				?	?		?		?		?

Coding examples:

```
DIV     BX              ;AX=DX:AX/BX
DIV     WORD_TEMP       ;AX=DX:AX/WORD_TEMP
DIV     BYTE_SUM        ;AL=AX/BYTE_SUM
DIV     WORD_TBL[BX]    ;Indirect address example
```

Description: If the operand is a byte value, DIV divides the contents of AX by the contents of the operand, then stores the result in AL and the remainder in AH. If the operand is a word value, DIV divides the contents of DX:AX by the contents of the operand, then stores the result in AX and the remainder in DX. This instruction treats numbers as unsigned binary values.

ENTER: Make Stack Frame for Procedure Parameters

Category: Flag- and processor-control instructions

Flags affected: None

Coding examples:

```
ENTER   PPTR,3
ENTER   DS:BX,Ø
```

Description: ENTER modifies the stack appropriately for entry to a high-level language procedure. The first operand specifies the number of bytes of storage to be allocated on the stack; the second operand specifies the nesting level of the routine. The effects of this instruction are undone by the LEAVE instruction.

ESC: Escape

Category: Flag- and processor-control instructions

Flags affected: None

Coding examples:

```
ESC   6,TEMP
ESC   15,CL
```

Description: This instruction is a means for coprocessors (such as the 80287) to access data in the 80286 data stream. When this instruction is encountered, it causes the 80286 to place the operand on the data bus and perform an NOP internally.

HLT: Halt

Category: Flag- and processor-control instructions

Flags affected: None

Coding example:

```
HLT
```

Description: HLT causes the 80286 to stop execution and leaves the CS:IP registers pointing to the instruction following the HLT. This halt condition is terminated only after receipt of an interrupt or activation of the RESET line.

IDIV: Integer Divide

Category: Arithmetic instructions

Flags affected:

F	E	D	C	B	A	9	8	7	6	5	4	3	2	1	Ø
	NT	IOPL		OF	DF	IF	TF	SF	ZF		AF		PF		CF
			?					?	?		?		?		?

Coding examples:

```
IDIV       BX              ;AX=DX:AX/BX
IDIV       WORD_TEMP       ;AX=DX:AX/WORD_TEMP
IDIV       BYTE_SUM        ;AL=AX/BYTE_SUM
IDIV       WORD_TBL[BX]    ;Indirect address example
```

Description: If the operand is a byte value, IDIV divides the contents of AX by the contents of the operand, then stores the result in AL and the remainder in AH. If the operand is a word value, IDIV divides the contents of DX:AX by the contents of the operand, then stores the result in AX and the remainder in DX. This instruction treats numbers as signed binary values.

IMUL: Integer Multiply

Category: Arithmetic instructions

Flags affected:

F	E	D	C	B	A	9	8	7	6	5	4	3	2	1	Ø
	NT	IOPL		OF	DF	IF	TF	SF	ZF		AF		PF		CF
				X				?	?		?		?		X

Coding examples:

```
IMUL    BX              ;DX:AX=AX*BX
IMUL    WORD_TEMP       ;DX:AX=AX*WORD_TEMP
IMUL    BYTE_SUM        ;AX=AL*BYTE_SUM
IMUL    WORD_TBL[BX]    ;Indirect address example
```

Description: If the operand is a byte value, IMUL multiplies the contents of AL by the contents of the operand and stores the result in AX. If the operand is a word value, IMUL multiplies the contents of AX by the contents of the operand and stores the result in DX:AX. This instruction treats numbers as signed binary values.

IN: Input from Port

Category: Data-transfer instructions

Flags affected: None

Coding examples:

```
IN   AL,64h
IN   AX,DX
```

Description: IN loads a byte or a word from the specified hardware I/O port address to AL or AX, respectively. A port number below 256 may be specified as a constant or as a variable in the DX register. A port number above 255, however, *must* be specified in the DX register.

INC: Increment

Category: Arithmetic instructions

Flags affected:

F	E	D	C	B	A	9	8	7	6	5	4	3	2	1	Ø
	NT	IOPL		OF	DF	IF	TF	SF	ZF		AF		PF		CF
				X				X	X		X		X		

Coding examples:

```
INC        AX
INC        SUM
INC        CL
INC        TEMP[SI]
```

Description: INC changes the contents of the operand in an increment of 1. The operand is assumed to be an unsigned binary value.

INS: Input String from Port

Category: Data-transfer instructions

Flags affected: None

Coding examples:

```
INS        CX,DX        ;Load word
INS        BL,DX        ;Load byte
```

Description: INS loads a byte or a word from the specified hardware I/O port address to the destination operand. The size of the destination operand determines whether a byte or a word is transferred. The port number may range from 0 to 65,535.

INSB: Input String Byte from Port

Category: Data-transfer instructions

Flags affected: None

Coding example:

```
INSB
```

Description: INSB loads a byte from the hardware I/O port address specified in DX to the address specified by ES:[DI]. The port number may range from 0 to 65,535. After the transfer, DI changes in an increment or decrement of 1, depending on the setting of the direction flag.

INSW: Input String Word from Port

Category: Data-transfer instructions

Flags affected: None

Coding example:

```
INSW
```

Description: INSW loads a word from the hardware I/O port address specified in DX to the address specified by ES:[DI]. The port number may range from 0 to 65,535. After the transfer, DI changes in increments or decrements of 2, depending on the setting of the direction flag.

INT: Software Interrupt

Category: Control-transfer instructions

Flags affected:

F	E	D	C	B	A	9	8	7	6	5	4	3	2	1	Ø
	NT	IOPL		OF	DF	IF	TF	SF	ZF		AF		PF		CF
						X	X								

Coding examples:

```
INT     1Øh
INT     13h
```

Description: INT initiates a software interrupt of the 80286 CPU. The instruction initiates the following:

- Pushes the flags on the stack

- Clears the TF and IF flags

- Pushes the value of CS on the stack

- Loads CS with the segment address of the interrupt being invoked. This segment address is found at the calculated address in the interrupt vector table.

- Pushes the value of IP on the stack

- Loads IP with the offset address of the interrupt being invoked. This offset address is found at the calculated address in the interrupt vector table.

Execution then continues at the newly loaded CS:IP address until an IRET instruction is encountered.

INTO: Interrupt on Overflow

Category: Control-transfer instructions

Flags affected: None

Coding example:

```
INTO
```

Description: If the overflow flag (OF) is set, an interrupt 4 is executed and control proceeds as though an INT 4 had been issued. Be aware that, in this case, the flags register is affected as described for the INT instruction.

IRET: Return from Interrupt

Category: Control-transfer instructions

Flags affected:

F	E	D	C	B	A	9	8	7	6	5	4	3	2	1	Ø
	NT	IOPL		OF	DF	IF	TF	SF	ZF		AF		PF		CF
X	X	X	X	X	X	X	X	X	X	X	X	X	X	X	X

Coding example:

```
IRET
```

Description: By popping the values of IP, CS, and the flags register from the stack, IRET causes termination of an interrupt procedure and returns control to the point at which the interrupt occurred.

JA: Jump if Above

Category: Control-transfer instructions

Flags affected: None

Coding example:

```
JA    NEXT_STEP
```

Description: JA causes program execution to branch to the operand address if both the carry and zero flags are clear. This instruction is functionally the same as JNBE.

JAE: Jump if Above or Equal

Category: Control-transfer instructions

Flags affected: None

Coding example:

```
JAE        NEXT_STEP
```

Description: JAE causes program execution to branch to the operand address if the carry flag is clear. This instruction is functionally the same as JNB or JNC.

JB: Jump if Below

Category: Control-transfer instructions

Flags affected: None

Coding example:

```
JB    NEXT_STEP
```

Description: JB causes program execution to branch to the operand address if the carry flag is set. This instruction is functionally the same as JC or JNAE.

JBE: Jump if Below or Equal

Category: Control-transfer instructions

Flags affected: None

Coding example:

```
JBE    NEXT_STEP
```

Description: JBE causes program execution to branch to the operand address if either the carry or zero flag is set. This instruction is functionally the same as JNA.

JC: Jump on Carry

Category: Control-transfer instructions

Flags affected: None

Coding example:

```
JC    NEXT_STEP
```

Description: JC causes program execution to branch to the operand address if the carry flag is set. This instruction is functionally the same as JB or JNAE.

JCXZ: Jump if CX=0

Category: Control-transfer instructions

Flags affected: None

Coding example:

```
JCXZ     SKIP_LOOP
```

Description: JCXZ causes program execution to branch to the operand address if the value of CX is 0.

JE: Jump if Equal

Category: Control-transfer instructions

Flags affected: None

Coding example:

```
JE       NEXT_STEP
```

Description: JE causes program execution to branch to the operand address if the zero flag is set. This instruction is functionally the same as JZ.

JG: Jump if Greater

Category: Control-transfer instructions

Flags affected: None

Coding example:

```
JG          NEXT_STEP
```

Description: JG causes program execution to branch to the operand address if either the sign flag equals the overflow flag or the zero flag is clear. This instruction is functionally the same as JNLE.

JGE: Jump if Greater or Equal

Category: Control-transfer instructions

Flags affected: None

Coding example:

```
JGE         NEXT_STEP
```

Description: JGE causes program execution to branch to the operand address if the sign flag equals the overflow flag. This instruction is functionally the same as JNL.

JL: Jump if Less Than

Category: Control-transfer instructions

Flags affected: None

Coding example:

```
JL    NEXT_STEP
```

Description: JL causes program execution to branch to the operand address if the sign flag does not equal the overflow flag. This instruction is functionally the same as JNGE.

JLE: Jump if Less Than or Equal

Category: Control-transfer instructions

Flags affected: None

Coding example:

```
JLE        NEXT_STEP
```

Description: JLE causes program execution to branch to the operand address if the sign flag does not equal the overflow flag or the zero flag is set. This instruction is functionally the same as JNG.

JMP: Jump

Category: Control-transfer instructions

Flags affected: None

Coding examples:

```
JMP        EXIT_CODE
JMP        [BX]              ;Jump to address at [BX]
JMP        AX               ;Jump to address in AX
```

Description: JMP causes program execution to begin at the designated operand address. JMP affects the CS and IP registers as necessary to cause this unconditional branch.

JNA: Jump if Not Above

Category: Control-transfer instructions

Flags affected: None

Coding example:

```
JNA     NEXT_STEP
```

Description: JNA causes program execution to branch to the operand address if either the carry or zero flag is set. This instruction is functionally the same as JBE.

JNAE: Jump if Not Above or Equal

Category: Control-transfer instructions

Flags affected: None

Coding example:

```
JNAE       NEXT_STEP
```

Description: JNAE causes program execution to branch to the operand address if the carry flag is set. This instruction is functionally the same as JB or JC.

JNB: Jump if Not Below

Category: Control-transfer instructions

Flags affected: None

Coding example:

```
JNB        NEXT_STEP
```

Description: JNB causes program execution to branch to the operand address if the carry flag is clear. This instruction is functionally the same as JAE or JNC.

JNBE: Jump if Not Below or Equal

Category: Control-transfer instructions

Flags affected: None

Coding example:

```
JNBE       NEXT_STEP
```

Description: JNBE causes program execution to branch to the operand address if both the carry and zero flags are clear. This instruction is functionally the same as JA.

JNC: Jump on No Carry

Category: Control-transfer instructions

Flags affected: None

Coding example:

```
JNC        NEXT_STEP
```

Description: JNC causes program execution to branch to the operand address if the carry flag is clear. This instruction is functionally the same as JAE or JNB.

JNE: Jump if Not Equal

Category: Control-transfer instructions

Flags affected: None

Coding example:

```
JNE        NEXT_STEP
```

Description: JNE causes program execution to branch to the operand address if the zero flag is clear. This instruction is functionally the same as JNZ.

JNG: Jump if Not Greater Than

Category: Control-transfer instructions

Flags affected: None

Coding example:

```
JNG        NEXT_STEP
```

Description: JNG causes program execution to branch to the operand address if the sign flag does not equal the overflow flag or the zero flag is set. This instruction is functionally the same as JLE.

JNGE: Jump if Not Greater Than or Equal

Category: Control-transfer instructions

Flags affected: None

Coding example:

```
JNGE       NEXT_STEP
```

Description: JNGE causes program execution to branch to the operand address if the sign flag does not equal the overflow flag. This instruction is functionally the same as JL.

JNL: Jump if Not Less Than

Category: Control-transfer instructions

Flags affected: None

Coding example:

```
JNL        NEXT_STEP
```

Description: JNL causes program execution to branch to the operand address if the sign flag equals the overflow flag. This instruction is functionally the same as JGE.

JNLE: Jump if Not Less Than or Equal

Category: Control-transfer instructions

Flags affected: None

Coding example:

```
JNLE       NEXT_STEP
```

Description: JNLE causes program execution to branch to the operand address if the sign flag equals the overflow flag or the zero flag is clear. This instruction is functionally the same as JG.

JNO: Jump on No Overflow

Category: Control-transfer instructions

Flags affected: None

Coding example:

```
JNO        NEXT_STEP
```

Description: JNO causes program execution to branch to the operand address if the overflow flag is clear.

JNP: Jump on No Parity

Category: Control-transfer instructions

Flags affected: None

Coding example:

```
JNP        NEXT_STEP
```

Description: JNP causes program execution to branch to the operand address if the parity flag is clear. This instruction is functionally the same as JPO.

JNS: Jump on Not Sign

Category: Control-transfer instructions

Flags affected: None

Coding example:

```
JNS        NEXT_STEP
```

Description: JNS causes program execution to branch to the operand address if the sign flag is clear.

JNZ: Jump on Not Zero

Category: Control-transfer instructions

Flags affected: None

Coding example:

```
JNZ        NEXT_STEP
```

Description: JNZ causes program execution to branch to the operand address if the zero flag is clear. This instruction is functionally the same as JNE.

JO: Jump on Overflow

Category: Control-transfer instructions

Flags affected: None

Coding example:

```
JO         NEXT_STEP
```

Description: JO causes program execution to branch to the operand address if the overflow flag is set.

JP: Jump on Parity

Category: Control-transfer instructions

Flags affected: None

Coding example:

```
JP       NEXT_STEP
```

Description: JP causes program execution to branch to the operand address if the parity flag is set. This instruction is functionally the same as JPE.

JPE: Jump on Parity Even

Category: Control-transfer instructions

Flags affected: None

Coding example:

```
JPE      NEXT_STEP
```

Description: JPE causes program execution to branch to the operand address if the parity flag is set. This instruction is functionally the same as JP.

JPO: Jump on Parity Odd

Category: Control-transfer instructions

Flags affected: None

Coding example:

```
JPO      NEXT_STEP
```

Description: JPO causes program execution to branch to the operand address if the parity flag is clear. This instruction is functionally the same as JNP.

JS: Jump on Sign

Category: Control-transfer instructions

Flags affected: None

Coding example:

```
JS       NEXT_STEP
```

Description: JS causes program execution to branch to the operand address if the sign flag is set.

JZ: Jump on Zero

Category: Control-transfer instructions

Flags affected: None

Coding example:

```
JZ          NEXT_STEP
```

Description: JZ causes program execution to branch to the operand address if the zero flag is set. This instruction is functionally the same as JE.

LAHF: Load AH Register with Flags

Category: Data-transfer instructions

Flags affected: None

Coding example:

```
LAHF
```

Description: LAHF copies the low-order byte of the flags register to AH. After execution of this instruction, bits 7, 6, 4, 2, and 1 of AH are equal to SF, ZF, AF, PF, and CF, respectively.

LAR: Load Access-Rights Byte

Category: Data-transfer instructions

Flags affected:

F	E	D	C	B	A	9	8	7	6	5	4	3	2	1	Ø
	NT	IOPL		OF	DF	IF	TF	SF	ZF		AF		PF		CF
									X						

Coding example:

```
LAR         AX,SELECT
```

Description: Based on the selection in the second operand, the high byte of the destination register is overwritten by the value of the access-rights byte, and the low byte is zeroed. The loading is done only if the descriptor is visible at the current privilege level and at the selector RPL. The zero flag is set if the loading operation is successful.

LDS: Load DS Register

Category: Data-transfer instructions

Flags affected: None

Coding example:

```
LDS      SI,SOURCE_BUFFER
```

Description: LDS performs two distinct operations: it loads DS with the segment address of the source operand and loads the destination operand with the offset address of the source operand.

LEA: Load Effective Address

Category: Data-transfer instructions

Flags affected: None

Coding example:

```
LEA      AX,MESSAGE_1
```

Description: LEA transfers the offset address of the source operand to the destination operand. The destination operand must be a general word register.

LEAVE: High-Level Procedure Exit

Category: Flag- and processor-control instructions

Flags affected: None

Coding example:

```
LEAVE
```

Description: LEAVE undoes the changes performed by the ENTER instruction. This instruction is used for exiting high-level language subroutines.

LES: Load ES Register

Category: Data-transfer instructions

Flags affected: None

Coding example:

```
LES      DI,DEST_BUFFER
```

Description: LES performs two distinct operations: it loads ES with the segment address of the source operand and then loads the destination operand with the offset address of the source operand.

LGDT: Load Global Descriptor Table Register

Category: Data-transfer instructions

Flags affected: None

Coding example:

```
LGDT        TEMP[BX]
```

Description: LGDT loads the six bytes associated with the global descriptor table from the memory address specified in the operand. This instruction is for use in protected-mode operating system software; it is not used in applications software.

LIDT: Load Interrupt Descriptor Table Register

Category: Data-transfer instructions

Flags affected: None

Coding example:

```
LIDT        TEMP[BX]
```

Description: LIDT loads the six bytes associated with the interrupt descriptor table from the memory address specified in the operand. This instruction is for use in protected-mode operating system software; it is not used in applications software.

LLDT: Load Local Descriptor Table Register

Category: Data-transfer instructions

Flags affected: None

Coding example:

```
LLDT        AX
```

Description: Based on the selector specified in the operand, LLDT transfers the valid global descriptor table entry to the local descriptor table. This instruction is for use in protected-mode operating system software and is not used in applications software.

LMSW: Load Machine Status Word

Category: Data-transfer instructions

Flags affected: None

Coding example:

```
LMSW        AX
```

Description: LMSW copies the value of the operand to the machine status word. This instruction is for use only in operating system software (not in applications software).

LOCK: Lock Bus

Category: Flag- and processor-control instructions

Flags affected: None

Coding example:

```
LOCK        XLAT
```

Description: LOCK prohibits interference from any other coprocessors during the execution of the next instruction. This instruction is a prefix to be used with other operations.

LODSB: Load a Byte from String into AL

Category: String-manipulation instructions

Flags affected: None

Coding example:

```
LODSB
```

Description: This instruction loads AL with the contents of the address pointed to by SI. SI then changes in an increment or decrement of 1, depending on the setting of the direction flag. Intel lists this command as LODS; however, the Microsoft Macro Assembler makes the byte/word distinctions.

LODSW: Load a Word from String into AX

Category: String-manipulation instructions

Flags affected: None

Coding example:

```
LODSW
```

Description: This instruction loads AX with the contents of the address pointed to by SI. SI then changes in increments or decrements of 2, depending on the setting of the direction flag. Intel lists this command as LODS; however, the Microsoft Macro Assembler makes the byte/word distinctions.

LOOP: Loop

Category: Control-transfer instructions

Flags affected: None

Coding example:

```
LOOP        PRINT_LOOP
```

Description: Based on the contents of CX, program execution branches to the address of the destination operand. If CX does not equal 0, CX changes in a decrement of 1, and the branch occurs. If CX is 0, no decrement or branching occurs, and execution proceeds to the next instruction.

LOOPE: Loop While Equal

Category: Control-transfer instructions

Flags affected: None

Coding example:

```
LOOPE TEST_LOOP
```

Description: Based on the contents of CX and the zero flag, program execution branches to the address of the destination operand. If CX does equal 0 and the zero flag is set, CX changes in a decrement of 1, and the branch occurs. If CX is 0 or the zero flag is clear, no decrement or branching occurs, and execution proceeds to the next instruction. This instruction is functionally equivalent to LOOPZ.

LOOPNE: Loop While Not Equal

Category: Control-transfer instructions

Flags affected: None

Coding example:

```
LOOPNE TEST_LOOP
```

Description: Based on the contents of CX and the zero flag, program execution branches to the address of the destination operand. If CX does not equal 0 and the zero flag is clear, CX changes in a decrement of 1, and the branch occurs. If CX is 0 or the zero flag is set, no decrement or branching occurs, and execution proceeds to the next instruction. This instruction is functionally equivalent to LOOPNZ.

LOOPNZ: Loop While Not Zero

Category: Control-transfer instructions

Flags affected: None

Coding example:

```
LOOPNZ TEST_LOOP
```

Description: Based on the contents of CX and the zero flag, program execution branches to the address of the destination operand. If CX does not equal 0 and the zero flag is clear, CX changes in a decrement of 1, and the branch occurs. If CX is 0 or the zero flag is set, no decrement or branching occurs, and execution proceeds to the next instruction. This instruction is functionally equivalent to LOOPNE.

LOOPZ: Loop While Zero

Category: Control-transfer instructions

Flags affected: None

Coding example:

```
LOOPZ  TEST_LOOP
```

Description: Based on the contents of CX and the zero flag, program execution branches to the address of the destination operand. If CX does not equal 0 and the zero flag is set, CX changes in a decrement of 1, and the branch occurs. If CX is 0 or the zero flag is clear, no decrement or branching occurs, and execution proceeds to the next instruction. This instruction is functionally equivalent to LOOPE.

LSL: Load Segment Limit

Category: Data-transfer instructions

Flags affected:

F	E	D	C	B	A	9	8	7	6	5	4	3	2	1	Ø
	NT	IOPL		OF	DF	IF	TF	SF	ZF		AF		PF		CF
									X						

Coding example:

```
LSL        AX,SELECTOR
```

Description: Based on the selector specified in the source operand, LSL loads the descriptor's limit field into the target operand (register). The descriptor denoted by the selector must be visible. If the loading is successful, the zero flag is set; otherwise, it is cleared.

LTR: Load Task Register

Category: Data-transfer instructions

Flags affected: None

Coding examples:

```
LTR        DX
LTR        TEMP[BX]
```

Description: LTR loads the task register from the value of the source operand. This instruction is for use in operating system software only and is not used in applications software.

MOV: Move

Category: Data-transfer instructions

Flags affected: None

Coding examples:

```
MOV        AX,BX           ;AX=BX
MOV        AX,TEMP         ;AX=TEMP (TEMP is a word)
MOV        SUM,BX          ;SUM=BX (SUM is a word)
MOV        CL,57           ;CL=57
MOV        DEC,1Ø          ;DEC=1Ø
MOV        AX,TEMP[BX]     ;Indirect address example
```

Description: MOV copies the contents of the source operand to the destination operand. Both operands must be the same length.

MOVSB: Move String, Byte-by-Byte

Category: String-manipulation instructions

Flags affected: None

Coding examples:

```
MOVSB
REP MOVSB          ;Repeat a move loop
```

Description: This instruction moves strings, byte-by-byte. The values of SI and DI change in an increment or decrement of 1, depending on the setting of the direction flag. Usually, this instruction is used with the REP instruction to repeat the move for a maximum of CX bytes. Intel lists this command as MOVS; however, the Microsoft Macro Assembler makes the byte/word distinctions.

MOVSW: Move String, Word-by-Word

Category: String-manipulation instructions

Flags affected: None

Coding examples:

```
MOVSW
REP MOVSW          ;Repeat a move loop
```

Description: This instruction moves strings, word-by-word. The values of SI and DI change in increments or decrements of 2, depending on the setting of the direction flag. Usually, this instruction is used with the REP instruction to repeat the move for a maximum of CX words. Intel lists this command as MOVS; however, the Microsoft Macro Assembler makes the byte/word distinctions.

MUL: Multiply

Category: Arithmetic instructions

Flags affected:

F	E	D	C	B	A	9	8	7	6	5	4	3	2	1	Ø
	NT	IOPL		OF	DF	IF	TF	SF	ZF		AF		PF		CF
				X				?	?		?		?		X

Coding examples:

```
MUL       BX              ;DX:AX=AX*BX
MUL       WORD_TEMP       ;DX:AX=AX*WORD_TEMP
MUL       BYTE_SUM        ;AX=AL*BYTE_SUM
MUL       WORD_TBL[BX]    ;Indirect address example
```

Description: If the operand is a byte value, MUL multiplies the contents of AL by the contents of the operand and stores the result in AX. If the operand is a word value, MUL multiplies the contents of AX by the contents of the operand and stores the result in DX:AX. This instruction treats numbers as unsigned binary values.

NEG: Negate

Category: Arithmetic instructions

Flags affected:

F	E	D	C	B	A	9	8	7	6	5	4	3	2	1	Ø
	NT	IOPL		OF	DF	IF	TF	SF	ZF		AF		PF		CF
				X				X	X		X		X		X

Coding examples:

```
NEG       TEMP
NEG       CL
```

Description: NEG calculates the two's complement of the destination operand and stores the result in the destination operand. This calculation is effectively the same as subtracting the destination operand from 0.

NOP: No Operation

Category: Flag- and processor-control instructions

Flags affected: None

Coding example:

```
NOP
```

Description: NOP does nothing but take space and time. It causes the CPU to do nothing.

NOT: Logical NOT on Bits

Category: Bit-manipulation instructions

Flags affected: None

Coding examples:

```
NOT        CL
NOT        TEMP
NOT        AX
```

Description: NOT inverts the bits in the destination operand (0 becomes 1, and 1 becomes 0) and stores them in the destination operand.

OR: Logical OR on Bits

Category: Bit-manipulation instructions

Flags affected:

F	E	D	C	B	A	9	8	7	6	5	4	3	2	1	Ø
	NT	IOPL		OF	DF	IF	TF	SF	ZF		AF		PF		CF
				X				X	X		?		X		X

Coding examples:

```
OR     AL,BL
OR     AL,10000000b
OR     DX,TEMP
OR     AX,CX
```

Description: OR performs a logical OR of the operands and stores the result in the destination operand. Each bit of the resultant byte or word is set to 1 if either or both of the corresponding bits of each operand are set to 1.

OUT: Output to Port

Category: Data-transfer instructions

Flags affected: None

Coding examples:

```
OUT        AL,64h
OUT        AX,DX
```

Description: OUT sends a byte (AL) or a word (AX) to the specified hardware I/O port address. A port number below 256 may be specified as a constant or as a variable in the DX register. A port number above 255, however, *must* be specified in the DX register.

OUTS: Output String to Port

Category: Data-transfer instructions

Flags affected: None

Coding examples:

```
OUTS       DX,CX        ;Output word
OUTS       DX,BL        ;Output byte
```

Description: OUTS sends a byte or a word (length is specified by the size of the source operand) to the hardware I/O port address specified in DX. The port number may range from 0 to 65,535.

OUTSB: Output String Byte to Port

Category: Data-transfer instructions

Flags affected: None

Coding example:

```
OUTSB
```

Description: OUTSB sends a byte from the address specified by DS:[SI] to the hardware I/O port address specified in DX. The port number may range from 0 to 65,535. After the transfer, DI changes in an increment or decrement of 1, depending on the setting of the direction flag.

OUTSW: Output String Word to Port

Category: Data-transfer instructions

Flags affected: None

Coding example:

```
OUTSW
```

Description: OUTSW sends a word from the address specified by DS:[SI] to the hardware I/O port address specified in DX. The port number may range from 0 to 65,535. After the transfer, DI changes in increments or decrements of 2, depending on the setting of the direction flag.

POP: Remove Data from Stack

Category: Data-transfer instructions

Flags affected: None

Coding examples:

```
POP       AX
POP       DS
POP       HOLD_REG
```

Description: POP removes a word from the stack and places the word in the desired destination operand.

POPA: Pop All General Registers

Category: Data-transfer instructions

Flags affected: None

Coding example:

```
POPA
```

Description: POPA removes the general-purpose registers and loads them from the stack in this order: DI, SI, BP, SP, BX, DX, CX, AX. The SP register is discarded when it is popped.

POPF: Remove Flags from Stack

Category: Data-transfer instructions

Flags affected:

F	E	D	C	B	A	9	8	7	6	5	4	3	2	1	Ø
	NT	IOPL		OF	DF	IF	TF	SF	ZF		AF		PF		CF
X	X	X	X	X	X	X	X	X	X	X	X	X	X	X	X

Coding example:

```
POPF
```

Description: POPF removes a word from the stack and places the word in the flags register.

PUSH: Place Data on Stack

Category: Data-transfer instructions

Flags affected: None

Coding examples:

```
PUSH      AX
PUSH      DS
PUSH      HOLD_REG
```

Description: PUSH places a copy of the value of the operand on the stack.

PUSHA: Push All General Registers

Category: Data-transfer instructions

Flags affected: None

Coding example:

```
PUSHA
```

Description: The general-purpose registers are pushed on the stack in this order: AX, CX, DX, BX, SP, BP, SI, DI. The SP value that is pushed is the value existing before this instruction is executed.

PUSHF: Place Flags on Stack

Category: Data-transfer instructions

Flags affected: None

Coding example:

```
PUSHF
```

Description: PUSHF places a copy of the flags register on the stack.

RCL: Rotate Left through Carry

Category: Bit-manipulation instructions

Flags affected:

F	E	D	C	B	A	9	8	7	6	5	4	3	2	1	Ø
	NT	IOPL		OF	DF	IF	TF	SF	ZF		AF		PF		CF
				X											X

Coding examples:

```
RCL      AX,1
RCL      BL,3
RCL      TEMP,CL
```

Description: RCL rotates all bits in the destination operand to the left by the number of places specified in the source operand. The rotation is performed through the carry flag in an order that rotates the most significant bit of the destination operand to the carry flag and the carry flag to the least significant bit of the destination operand.

RCR: Rotate Right through Carry

Category: Bit-manipulation instructions

Flags affected:

F	E	D	C	B	A	9	8	7	6	5	4	3	2	1	Ø
	NT	IOPL		OF	DF	IF	TF	SF	ZF		AF		PF		CF
				X											X

Coding examples:

```
RCR        AX,1
RCR        BL,3
RCR        TEMP,CL
```

Description: RCR rotates all bits in the destination operand to the right by the number of places specified in the source operand. The rotation is performed through the carry flag in an order that rotates the least significant bit of the destination operand to the carry flag and the carry flag to the most significant bit of the destination operand.

REP: Repeat

Category: String-manipulation instructions

Flags affected: None

Coding example:

```
REP MOVSB
```

Description: REP causes string-manipulation instructions to be repeated the number of iterations specified in CX.

REPE: Repeat if Equal

Category: String-manipulation instructions

Flags affected: None

Coding example:

```
REPE CMPSW
```

Description: REPE causes string-manipulation instructions to be repeated the number of iterations specified in CX. When used with CMPSB, CMPSW, SCASB, or SCASW, this instruction repeats only while the zero flag is set. This instruction is functionally equivalent to REPZ.

REPNE: Repeat if Not Equal

Category: String-manipulation instructions

Flags affected: None

Coding example:

```
REPNE CMPSW
```

Description: REPNE causes string-manipulation instructions to be repeated the number of iterations specified in CX. When used with CMPSB, CMPSW, SCASB, or SCASW, this instruction repeats only while the zero flag is clear. This instruction is functionally equivalent to REPNZ.

REPNZ: Repeat if Not Zero

Category: String-manipulation instructions

Flags affected: None

Coding example:

```
REPNZ CMPSW
```

Description: REPNZ causes string-manipulation instructions to be repeated the number of iterations specified in CX. When used with CMPSB, CMPSW, SCASB, or SCASW, this instruction repeats only while the zero flag is clear. This instruction is functionally equivalent to REPNE.

REPZ: Repeat if Zero

Category: String-manipulation instructions

Flags affected: None

Coding example:

```
REPZ CMPSW
```

Description: REPZ causes string-manipulation instructions to be repeated the number of iterations specified in CX. When used with CMPSB, CMPSW, SCASB, or SCASW, this instruction repeats only while the zero flag is set. This instruction is functionally equivalent to REPE.

RET: Return from Subroutine

Category: Control-transfer instructions

Flags affected: None

Coding examples:

```
RET
RET      2
```

Description: By popping IP from the stack, RET transfers program control back to the point at which a CALL was issued. If the CALL was to a FAR procedure, both CS:IP are popped from the stack.

If the RET has a specified return value (2, in the coding example), the stack is adjusted by that number of bytes. The example shows a word discarded from the stack after either IP or CS:IP has been popped.

ROL: Rotate Left

Category: Bit-manipulation instructions

Flags affected:

F	E	D	C	B	A	9	8	7	6	5	4	3	2	1	Ø
	NT	IOPL		OF	DF	IF	TF	SF	ZF		AF		PF		CF
				X											X

Coding examples:

```
ROL        AX,1
ROL        BL,3
ROL        TEMP,CL
```

Description: ROL rotates all bits in the destination operand to the left by the number of places specified in the source operand.

ROR: Rotate Right

Category: Bit-manipulation instructions

Flags affected:

F	E	D	C	B	A	9	8	7	6	5	4	3	2	1	Ø
	NT	IOPL		OF	DF	IF	TF	SF	ZF		AF		PF		CF
				X											X

Coding examples:

```
ROR        AX,1
ROR        BL,3
ROR        TEMP,CL
```

Description: ROR rotates all bits in the destination operand to the right by the number of places specified in the source operand.

SAHF: Store AH into Flag Register

Category: Data-transfer instructions

Flags affected:

F	E	D	C	B	A	9	8	7	6	5	4	3	2	1	Ø
	NT	IOPL		OF	DF	IF	TF	SF	ZF		AF		PF		CF
								X	X	X	X	X	X	X	X

Coding example:

```
SAHF
```

Description: SAHF copies the contents of AH into the low-order byte of the flags register. After execution of this instruction, SF, ZF, AF, PF, and CF are equal to bits 7, 6, 4, 2, and 1 of AH, respectively.

SAL: Arithmetic Shift Left

Category: Bit-manipulation instructions

Flags affected:

F	E	D	C	B	A	9	8	7	6	5	4	3	2	1	Ø
	NT	IOPL		OF	DF	IF	TF	SF	ZF		AF		PF		CF
				X				X	X		?		X		X

Coding examples:

```
SAL     AX,1
SAL     BL,3
SAL     TEMP,CL
```

Description: SAL shifts all bits in the destination operand to the left by the number of places specified in the source operand. High-order bits are lost, and low-order bits are cleared.

SAR: Arithmetic Shift Right

Category: Bit-manipulation instructions

Flags affected:

F	E	D	C	B	A	9	8	7	6	5	4	3	2	1	Ø
	NT	IOPL		OF	DF	IF	TF	SF	ZF		AF		PF		CF
				X				X	X		?		X		X

Coding examples:

```
SAR        AX,1
SAR        BL,3
SAR        TEMP,CL
```

Description: SAR shifts all bits in the destination operand to the right by the number of places specified in the source operand. Low-order bits are lost, and high-order bits are set equal to the existing high-order bit.

SBB: Subtract with Carry

Category: Arithmetic instructions

Flags affected:

F	E	D	C	B	A	9	8	7	6	5	4	3	2	1	Ø
	NT	IOPL		OF	DF	IF	TF	SF	ZF		AF		PF		CF
				X				X	X		X		X		X

Coding examples:

```
SBB        AX,BX          ;AX=AX-AX-CF
SBB        AX,TEMP        ;AX=AX-TEMP-CF
SBB        SUM,BX         ;SUM=SUM-BX-CF
SBB        CL,1Ø          ;CL=CL-1Ø-CF
SBB        AX,TEMP[BX]    ;Indirect address example
```

Description: SBB subtracts the contents of the source operand from (and stores the result in) the destination operand. If the carry flag is set, the result changes in a decrement of 1. In this instruction, the values being added are assumed to be binary.

SCASB: Scan String for Byte

Category: String-manipulation instructions

Flags affected:

F	E	D	C	B	A	9	8	7	6	5	4	3	2	1	Ø
	NT	IOPL		OF	DF	IF	TF	SF	ZF		AF		PF		CF
				X				X	X		X		X		X

Coding examples:

```
SCASB
REPNZ SCASB      ;Repeat a scan loop
```

Description: This instruction subtracts the destination operand string byte (pointed to by DI) from the value of AL. The result is not stored, but the flags are updated. Then the value of DI changes in an increment or decrement of 1, depending on the setting of the direction flag. Usually, this instruction is used with the REPE, REPNE, REPNZ, or REPZ instructions to repeat the scan for a maximum of CX bytes, or until a match or difference is found. Intel lists this command as SCAS; however, the Microsoft Macro Assembler makes the byte/word distinctions.

SCASW: Scan String for Word

Category: String-manipulation instructions

Flags affected:

F	E	D	C	B	A	9	8	7	6	5	4	3	2	1	Ø
	NT	IOPL		OF	DF	IF	TF	SF	ZF		AF		PF		CF
				X				X	X		X		X		X

Coding examples:

```
SCASW
REPNZ SCASW      ;Repeat a scan loop
```

Description: This instruction subtracts the destination operand string word (pointed to by DI) from the value of AX. The result is not stored, but the flags are updated. Then the value of DI changes in increments or decrements of 2, depending on the setting of the direction flag. Usually, this instruction is used with the REPE, REPNE, REPNZ, or REPZ instructions to repeat the scan for a maximum of CX bytes, or until a match or difference is found. Intel lists this command as SCAS; however, the Microsoft Macro Assembler makes the byte/word distinctions.

SGDT: Store Global Descriptor Table Register

Category: Data-transfer instructions

Flags affected: None

Coding example:

```
SGDT    TEMP[BX]
```

Description: SGDT transfers the six bytes of the global descriptor table to the memory address specified in the operand. This instruction is for use in protected-mode operating system software and is not used in applications software.

SHL: Shift Left

Category: Bit-manipulation instructions

Flags affected:

F	E	D	C	B	A	9	8	7	6	5	4	3	2	1	Ø
	NT	IOPL		OF	DF	IF	TF	SF	ZF		AF		PF		CF
				X				X	X		?		X		X

Coding examples:

```
SHL     AX,1
SHL     BL,3
SHL     TEMP,CL
```

Description: SHL shifts all bits in the destination operand to the left by the number of places specified in the source operand. High-order bits are lost, and low-order bits are cleared.

SHR: Shift Right

Category: Bit-manipulation instructions

Flags affected:

F	E	D	C	B	A	9	8	7	6	5	4	3	2	1	Ø
	NT	IOPL		OF	DF	IF	TF	SF	ZF		AF		PF		CF
				X				X	X		?		X		X

Coding examples:

```
SHR        AX,1
SHR        BL,3
SHR        TEMP,CL
```

Description: SHR shifts all bits in the destination operand to the right by the number of places specified in the source operand. Low-order bits are lost, and high-order bits are cleared.

SIDT: Store Interrupt Descriptor Table Register

Category: Data-transfer instructions

Flags affected: None

Coding example:

```
SIDT       TEMP[BX]
```

Description: SIDT transfers the six bytes of the interrupt descriptor table to the memory address specified in the operand. This instruction is for use in protected-mode operating system software and is not used in applications software.

SLDT: Store Local Descriptor Table Register

Category: Data-transfer instructions

Flags affected: None

Coding examples:

```
SLDT       AX
SLDT       LDT_TEMP
```

Description: SLDT copies the contents of the local descriptor table to the two bytes of the operand. This instruction is for use in protected-mode operating system software and is not used in applications software.

SMSW: Store Machine Status Word

Category: Data-transfer instructions

Flags affected: None

Coding examples:

```
SMSW      AX
SMSW      MSW_TEMP
```

Description: SMSW copies the value of machine status word to the operand. This instruction is for use in operating system software only and is not used in applications software.

STC: Set Carry Flag

Category: Flag- and processor-control instructions

Flags affected:

F	E	D	C	B	A	9	8	7	6	5	4	3	2	1	Ø
	NT	IOPL		OF	DF	IF	TF	SF	ZF		AF		PF		CF
															X

Coding example:

```
STC
```

Description: STC sets the carry flag, regardless of its present condition.

STD: Set Direction Flag

Category: Flag- and processor-control instructions

Flags affected:

F	E	D	C	B	A	9	8	7	6	5	4	3	2	1	Ø
	NT	IOPL		OF	DF	IF	TF	SF	ZF		AF		PF		CF
					X										

Coding example:

```
STD
```

Description: STD sets the direction flag, regardless of the flag's present condition. The setting of this flag has an effect on the string instructions.

STI: Set Interrupt Flag

Category: Flag- and processor-control instructions

Flags affected:

F	E	D	C	B	A	9	8	7	6	5	4	3	2	1	Ø
	NT	IOPL		OF	DF	IF	TF	SF	ZF		AF		PF		CF
						X									

Coding example:

```
STI
```

Description: STI sets the interrupt flag, regardless of its present condition. While this flag is set, the 80286 CPU responds to maskable interrupts.

STOSB: Store Byte in AL at String

Category: String-manipulation instructions

Flags affected: None

Coding example:

```
STOSB
```

Description: STOSB copies the contents of AL to the byte address pointed to by DI. DI then changes in an increment or decrement of 1, depending on the setting of the direction flag. Intel lists this command as STOS; however, the Microsoft Macro Assembler makes the byte/word distinctions.

STOSW: Store Word in AX at String

Category: String-manipulation instructions

Flags affected: None

Coding example:

```
STOSW
```

Description: STOSW copies the contents of AX to the word address pointed to by DI. DI then changes in increments or decrements of 2, depending on the setting of the direction flag. Intel lists this command as STOS; however, the Microsoft Macro Assembler makes the byte/word distinctions.

STR: Store Task Register

Category: Data-transfer instructions

Flags affected: None

Coding examples:

```
STR        AX
STR        MSW_TEMP
```

Description: STR copies the value of the task register to the operand. This instruction is for use in operating system software only and is not used in applications software.

SUB: Subtract

Category: Arithmetic instructions

Flags affected:

F	E	D	C	B	A	9	8	7	6	5	4	3	2	1	Ø
	NT	IOPL		OF	DF	IF	TF	SF	ZF		AF		PF		CF
				X				X	X		X		X		X

Coding examples:

```
SUB      AX,BX          ;AX=AX-AX
SUB      AX,TEMP        ;AX=AX-TEMP
SUB      SUM,BX         ;SUM=SUM-BX
SUB      CL,10          ;CL=CL-10
SUB      AX,TEMP[BX]    ;Indirect address example
```

Description: SUB subtracts the contents of the source operand from (and stores the result in) the destination operand. In this instruction, the values being added are assumed to be binary.

TEST: Test Bits

Category: Bit-manipulation instructions

Flags affected:

F	E	D	C	B	A	9	8	7	6	5	4	3	2	1	0
	NT	IOPL		OF	DF	IF	TF	SF	ZF		AF		PF		CF
				X				X	X		?		X		X

Coding examples:

```
TEST     AX,BX          ;
TEST     AX,TEMP        ;TEMP must be a word
TEST     SUM,BX         ;SUM must be a word
TEST     CL,00001111b   ;
TEST     AX,TEMP[BX]    ;Indirect address example
```

Description: TEST performs a logical AND of the operands, but the result is not stored. Only the flags are affected. Each bit of the resultant byte or word is set to 1 only if the corresponding bit of each of the operands is set to 1.

VERR: Verify a Segment for Reading

Category: Flag- and processor-control instructions

Flags affected:

F	E	D	C	B	A	9	8	7	6	5	4	3	2	1	Ø
	NT	IOPL		OF	DF	IF	TF	SF	ZF		AF		PF		CF
									X						

Coding examples:

```
VERR       TEMP
VERR       AX
```

Description: VERR determines whether the selector specified in the operand is visible at the current privilege level and is readable. The zero flag is set if the selector is accessible.

VERW: Verify a Segment for Writing

Category: Flag- and processor-control instructions

Flags affected:

F	E	D	C	B	A	9	8	7	6	5	4	3	2	1	Ø
	NT	IOPL		OF	DF	IF	TF	SF	ZF		AF		PF		CF
									X						

Coding examples:

```
VERW       TEMP
VERW       AX
```

Description: VERW determines whether the selector specified in the operand is visible at the current privilege level and can be written. The zero flag is set if the selector is accessible.

WAIT: Wait

Category: Flag- and processor-control instructions

Flags affected: None

Coding example:

```
WAIT
```

Description: WAIT causes the 80286 CPU to wait for an external interrupt on the TEST line before continuing.

XCHG: Exchange

Category: Data-transfer instructions

Flags affected: None

Coding examples:

```
XCHG        AX,BX       ;Swap AX with BX
XCHG        CL,CH       ;Swap CL with CH
XCHG        AX,TEMP     ;Swap AX with TEMP (word)
```

Description: XCHG swaps the contents of the source and destination operands.

XLAT: Translate

Category: Data-transfer instructions

Flags affected: None

Coding example:

```
XLAT
```

Description: Assuming that the offset address of a 256-byte translation table is contained in BX, this instruction uses the value in AL as a zero-based offset into the table. XLAT subsequently loads AL with the byte value at that calculated offset. This instruction is helpful for translation tables.

XOR: Logical Exclusive-Or on Bits

Category: Bit-manipulation instructions

Flags affected:

F	E	D	C	B	A	9	8	7	6	5	4	3	2	1	Ø
	NT	IOPL		OF	DF	IF	TF	SF	ZF		AF		PF		CF
				X				X	X		?		X		X

Coding examples:

```
XOR        AX,BX           ;
XOR        AX,TEMP         ;TEMP must be a word
XOR        SUM,BX          ;SUM must be a word
XOR        CL,00001111b    ;
XOR        AX,TEMP[BX]     ;Indirect address example
```

Description: XOR performs a logical XOR of the operands and stores the result in the destination operand. Each bit of the resultant byte or word is set to 1 only if the corresponding bits of each operand contain opposite values.

Instruction Set
for the Intel 80386

The Intel 80386 Instruction Set, detailed in this section, is an extension of the instruction set for the Intel 80286 and, subsequently, for the Intel 8086/8088. The 80386 instruction set has approximately 57 more instructions than are available for the 80286. Some of these new instructions are used for developing operating systems software; none is designed for use in applications software.

Registers

Unlike its 8-bit and 16-bit predecessors, the 80386 is a 32-bit microprocessor. The registers in the 80386 reflect this enlarged structure. The 80386 still uses the same general-purpose registers as the 8086/8088 and the 80286 (AX, BX, CX, and DX), but the registers' full 32-bit counterparts are addressed by use of the E (extended) prefix. EAX, EBX, ECX, and EDX are 32-bit general-purpose registers. Without the E, only the lower 16 bits of each register are accessed. Using the traditional AL, AH, BL, BH, CL, CH, DL, or DH allows access to 8-bit chunks of the lower 16 bits of the registers.

This use of the E prefix to denote 32-bit register size also applies to other microprocessor registers, such as BP, SI, DI, and SP, which become EBP, ESI, EDI, and ESP, respectively.

The other segment registers—CS, DS, SS, and ES—are intact as implemented in earlier Intel microprocessors. These registers still are 16 bits in width. They are joined, however, by two new segment registers (also 16 bits in width): the FS and GS registers, which operate the same as the ES register.

As in earlier microprocessors, the 80386 uses a flags register, but it is 32 bits wide. The upper 14 bits of this register are reserved, however, and are not available to programmers. The remaining 18 bits are the ones about which programmers must be concerned. The detailed description of each instruction indicates how these 18 flag bits are affected by execution of the instruction.

Instruction Set Groupings

The 80386 instructions can be grouped according to the purpose of the instruction. The six general classifications of instructions are

Data transfer
Arithmetic
Bit manipulation
String manipulation
Control transfer
Flag and processor control

The individual instructions that comprise these categories are given in table 80386.1.

Table 80386.1
Instruction Set Groupings for the 80386

Instruction	Meaning
Data Transfer	
IN	Input from port
INS	Input string from port
INSB	Input string byte from port
INSD	Input string doubleword from port
INSW	Input string word from port
LAHF	Load AH register with flags
LAR	Load access-rights byte
LDS	Load DS register
LEA	Load effective address
LES	Load ES register
LFS	Load FS register
LGDT	Load global descriptor table register
LGS	Load GS register
LIDT	Load interrupt descriptor table register
LLDT	Load local descriptor table register
LMSW	Load machine status word
LSL	Load segment limit
LSS	Load SS register
LTR	Load task register
MOV	Move
MOVSX	Move with sign extended
MOVZX	Move with zero extended
OUT	Output to port

Table 80386.1—cont.

Instruction	Meaning
OUTS	Output string to port
OUTSB	Output string byte to port
OUTSD	Output string doubleword to port
OUTSW	Output string word to port
POP	Remove data from stack
POPA	Pop all general registers
POPAD	Pop all general doubleword registers
POPF	Remove flags from stack
POPFD	Remove extended flags from stack
PUSH	Place data on stack
PUSHA	Push all general registers
PUSHAD	Push all general doubleword registers
PUSHF	Place flags on stack
PUSHFD	Place extended flags on stack
SAHF	Store AH into flag register
SETA	Set byte if above
SETAE	Set byte if above or equal
SETB	Set byte if below
SETBE	Set byte if below or equal
SETC	Set byte on carry
SETE	Set byte if equal
SETG	Set byte if greater
SETGE	Set byte if greater or equal
SETL	Set byte if less than
SETLE	Set byte if less than or equal
SETNA	Set byte if not above
SETNAE	Set byte if not above or equal
SETNB	Set byte if not below
SETNBE	Set byte if not below or equal
SETNC	Set byte on no carry
SETNE	Set byte if not equal
SETNG	Set byte if not greater than
SETNGE	Set byte if not greater than or equal
SETNL	Set byte if not less than
SETNLE	Set byte if not less than or equal
SETNO	Set byte on no overflow
SETNP	Set byte on no parity
SETNS	Set byte on not sign
SETNZ	Set byte if not zero

Table 80386.1—cont.

Instruction	Meaning
SETO	Set byte on overflow
SETP	Set byte on parity
SETPE	Set byte on parity even
SETPO	Set byte on parity odd
SETS	Set byte on sign
SETZ	Set byte if zero
SGDT	Store global descriptor table register
SIDT	Store interrupt descriptor table register
SLDT	Store local descriptor table register
SMSW	Store machine status word
STR	Store task register
XCHG	Exchange
XLAT	Translate

Arithmetic

AAA	ASCII adjust for addition
AAD	ASCII adjust for division
AAM	ASCII adjust for multiplication
AAS	ASCII adjust for subtraction
ADC	Add with carry
ADD	Add
CBW	Convert byte to word
CDQ	Convert doubleword to quadword
CMP	Compare
CWD	Convert word to doubleword
CWDE	Convert word to doubleword
DAA	Decimal adjust for addition
DAS	Decimal adjust for subtraction
DEC	Decrement
DIV	Divide
IDIV	Integer divide
IMUL	Integer multiply
INC	Increment
MUL	Multiply
NEG	Negate
SBB	Subtract with carry
SUB	Subtract

Table 80386.1—cont.

Instruction	Meaning

Bit Manipulation

AND	Logical AND on bits
ARPL	Adjust RPL field of selector
BSF	Bit scan forward
BSR	Bit scan reverse
BT	Bit test
BTC	Bit test and complement
BTR	Bit test and reset
BTS	Bit test and set
NOT	Logical NOT on bits
OR	Logical OR on bits
RCL	Rotate left through carry
RCR	Rotate right through carry
ROL	Rotate left
ROR	Rotate right
SAL	Arithmetic shift left
SAR	Arithmetic shift right
SHL	Shift left
SHLD	Shift left, double precision
SHR	Shift right
SHRD	Shift right, double precision
TEST	Test bits
XOR	Logical exclusive-OR on bits

String Manipulation

CMPSB	Compare strings, byte-for-byte
CMPSW	Compare strings, word-for-word
CMPSD	Compare strings, doubleword-for-doubleword
LODSB	Load a byte from string into AL
LODSD	Load a doubleword from string into EAX
LODSW	Load a word from string into AX
MOVSB	Move string, byte-by-byte
MOVSD	Move string, doubleword-by-doubleword
MOVSW	Move string, word-by-word
REP	Repeat
REPE	Repeat if equal
REPNE	Repeat if not equal
REPNZ	Repeat if not zero
REPZ	Repeat if zero

Table 80386.1—cont.

Instruction	Meaning
SCASB	Scan string for byte
SCASD	Scan string for doubleword
SCASW	Scan string for word
STOSB	Store byte in AL at string
STOSD	Store doubleword in EAX at string
STOSW	Store word in AX at string

Control Transfer

Instruction	Meaning
CALL	Perform subroutine
INT	Software interrupt
INTO	Interrupt on overflow
IRET	Return from interrupt
JA	Jump if above
JAE	Jump if above or equal
JB	Jump if below
JBE	Jump if below or equal
JC	Jump on carry
JCXZ	Jump if CX=0
JE	Jump if equal
JECXZ	Jump if ECX=0
JG	Jump if greater
JGE	Jump if greater or equal
JL	Jump if less than
JLE	Jump if less than or equal
JMP	Jump
JNA	Jump if not above
JNAE	Jump if not above or equal
JNB	Jump if not below
JNBE	Jump if not below or equal
JNC	Jump on no carry
JNE	Jump if not equal
JNG	Jump if not greater than
JNGE	Jump if not greater than or equal
JNL	Jump if not less than
JNLE	Jump if not less than or equal
JNO	Jump on no overflow
JNP	Jump on no parity
JNS	Jump on not sign
JNZ	Jump on not zero

Table 80386.1—cont.

Instruction	Meaning
JO	Jump on overflow
JP	Jump on parity
JPE	Jump on parity even
JPO	Jump on parity odd
JS	Jump on sign
JZ	Jump on zero
LOOP	Loop
LOOPE	Loop while equal
LOOPNE	Loop while not equal
LOOPNZ	Loop while not zero
LOOPZ	Loop while zero
RET	Return from subroutine

Flag and Processor Control

Instruction	Meaning
BOUND	Check array index against bounds
CLC	Clear carry flag
CLD	Clear direction flag
CLI	Clear interrupt flag
CLTS	Clear task switched flag
CMC	Complement carry flag
ENTER	Make stack frame for procedure parameters
ESC	Escape
HLT	Halt
LEAVE	High-level procedure exit
LOCK	Lock bus
NOP	No operation
STC	Set carry flag
STD	Set direction flag
STI	Set interrupt flag
VERR	Verify a segment for reading
VERW	Verify a segment for writing
WAIT	Wait

Detailed Instruction Information

The balance of this section is designed as a reference to the 80386 instruction set. Each instruction is described in detail. The following information is listed for each instruction:

- *Instruction name*. This name is based on the standard mnemonic code designed by Intel.

- *Instruction category*. The general classification for the instruction is given.

- *Flags affected*. The majority of the instructions change the status of the bits in the flags register. The individual flags affected are listed here in the following format:

11	10	F	E	D	C	B	A	9	8	7	6	5	4	3	2	1	0
VM	R		NT	IOPL		OF	DF	IF	TF	SF	ZF		AF		PF		CF
						?				?	?		X		?		X

In this format, an X indicates that the flag is changed, and a question mark (?) indicates that the flag is undefined after the instruction is executed. The flags are as follows:

Abbreviation	Flag	Location
VM	Virtual mode	Bit 11h
R	Resume	Bit 10h
NT	Nested task	Bit Eh
IOPL	I/O privilege level	Bits Ch/Dh
OF	Overflow	Bit Bh
DF	Direction	Bit Ah
IF	Interrupt	Bit 9
TF	Trap	Bit 8
SF	Sign	Bit 7
ZF	Zero	Bit 6
AF	Auxiliary carry	Bit 4
PF	Parity	Bit 2
CF	Carry	Bit 0

- *Coding examples*. An example shows how the instruction is used.

- *Description*. A narrative description of the instruction is included.

The instructions are arranged in ascending alphabetical order.

AAA: ASCII Adjust for Addition

Category: Arithmetic instructions

Flags affected:

11	1Ø	F	E	D	C	B	A	9	8	7	6	5	4	3	2	1	Ø
VM	R		NT	IOPL		OF	DF	IF	TF	SF	ZF		AF		PF		CF
						?				?	?		X		?		X

Coding example:

AAA

Description: AAA changes the contents of AL to a valid unpacked decimal number with the high-order nibble zeroed.

AAD: ASCII Adjust for Division

Category: Arithmetic instructions

Flags affected:

11	1Ø	F	E	D	C	B	A	9	8	7	6	5	4	3	2	1	Ø
VM	R		NT	IOPL		OF	DF	IF	TF	SF	ZF		AF		PF		CF
						?				X	X		?		X		?

Coding example:

AAD

Description: AAD multiplies the contents of AH by 10, adds the result to the contents of AL, and places the final result in AL. AH then is set to 0. Use this instruction before dividing unpacked decimal numbers.

AAM: ASCII Adjust for Multiplication

Category: Arithmetic instructions

Flags affected:

11	1Ø	F	E	D	C	B	A	9	8	7	6	5	4	3	2	1	Ø
VM	R		NT	IOPL		OF	DF	IF	TF	SF	ZF		AF		PF		CF
						?				X	X		?		X		?

Coding example:

```
AAM
```

Description: After multiplying two unpacked decimal numbers, use this instruction to correct the result to an unpacked decimal number. For AAM to work properly, each number multiplied must have had its high-order nibbles set to 0.

AAS: ASCII Adjust for Subtraction

Category: Arithmetic instructions

Flags affected:

11	1Ø	F	E	D	C	B	A	9	8	7	6	5	4	3	2	1	Ø
VM	R		NT	IOPL		OF	DF	IF	TF	SF	ZF		AF		PF		CF
						?				?	?		X		?		X

Coding example:

```
AAS
```

Description: AAS corrects the result of a previous unpacked decimal subtraction so that the value in AL is a true unpacked decimal number.

ADC: Add with Carry

Category: Arithmetic instructions

Flags affected:

11	1Ø	F	E	D	C	B	A	9	8	7	6	5	4	3	2	1	Ø
VM	R		NT	IOPL		OF	DF	IF	TF	SF	ZF		AF		PF		CF
						X				X	X		X		X		X

Coding Examples

```
ADC     AX,BX          ;AX=AX+BX+CF
ADC     EAX,TEMP       ;EAX=EAX+TEMP+CF
ADC     SUM,EBX        ;SUM=SUM+EBX+CF
ADC     CL,1Ø          ;CL=CL+1Ø+CF
ADC     AX,TEMP[BX]    ;Indirect address example
```

Description: ADC adds the contents of the source operand to (and stores the result in) the destination operand. If the carry flag is set, the result changes in an increment of 1. In this routine, the values being added are assumed to be binary.

ADD: Add

Category: Arithmetic instructions

Flags affected:

11	1Ø	F	E	D	C	B	A	9	8	7	6	5	4	3	2	1	Ø
VM	R			NT	IOPL	OF	DF	IF	TF	SF	ZF		AF		PF		CF
						X				X	X		X		X		X

Coding examples:

```
ADD     AX,BX          ;AX=AX+BX
ADD     EAX,TEMP       ;EAX=EAX+TEMP
ADD     SUM,EBX        ;SUM=SUM+EBX
ADD     CL,1Ø          ;CL=CL+1Ø
ADD     AX,TEMP[BX]    ;Indirect address example
```

Description: ADD adds the contents of the source operand to (and stores the result in) the destination operand. In this routine, the values being added are assumed to be binary.

AND: Logical AND on Bits

Category: Bit-manipulation instructions

Flags affected:

11	1Ø	F	E	D	C	B	A	9	8	7	6	5	4	3	2	1	Ø
VM	R			NT	IOPL	OF	DF	IF	TF	SF	ZF		AF		PF		CF
						X				X	X		?		X		X

Coding examples:

```
AND        AX,BX              ;
AND        EAX,TEMP           ;TEMP must be a doubleword
AND        SUM,EBX            ;SUM must be a doubleword
AND        CL,00001111b       ;Zero high nibble
AND        AX,TEMP[BX]        ;Indirect address example
```

Description: This instruction performs a logical AND of the operands and stores the result in the destination operand. Each bit of the resultant byte or word is set to 1, only if the corresponding bit of each operand is set to 1. The carry and overflow flags are cleared by this operation.

ARPL: Adjust RPL Field of Selector

Category: Bit-manipulation instructions

Flags affected:

11	10	F	E	D	C	B	A	9	8	7	6	5	4	3	2	1	0
VM	R		NT	IOPL		OF	DF	IF	TF	SF	ZF		AF		PF		CF
											X						

Coding examples:

```
ARPL       SELECTOR,AX
ARPL       AX,CX
```

Description: ARPL compares the RPL bits (bits 0 and 1) of the first operand against those of the second. If the RPL bits of the first operand are less than those of the second, the two bits of the first operand are set equal to those of the second, and the zero flag is set; otherwise, the zero flag is cleared. This instruction is used in operating system software but not in applications software.

BOUND: Check Array Index against Bounds

Category: Flag- and processor-control instructions

Flags affected: None

Coding example:

```
BOUND      BX,LIMITS
```

Description: BOUND determines whether the signed value in the first operand falls between the two boundaries specified by the second operand. The word at the second operand is assumed to be the lower boundary, and the following word is assumed to be the upper boundary. An interrupt 5 occurs if the value in the first operand is less than the lower limit or greater than the upper limit.

BSF: Bit Scan Forward

Category: Bit-manipulation instructions

Flags affected:

11	1Ø	F	E	D	C	B	A	9	8	7	6	5	4	3	2	1	Ø
VM	R		NT	IOPL		OF	DF	IF	TF	SF	ZF		AF		PF		CF
											X						

Coding examples:

```
BSF        EAX,TEMP
BSF        CX,BX
```

Description: BSF scans the bits of the second operand (starting with bit 0) to see whether any are set. If all bits are clear (second operand is 0), the first operand is not changed, and the zero flag is set. If any bit is set, the zero flag is cleared, and the first operand is set equal to the bit number of the bit that is set.

BSR: Bit Scan Reverse

Category: Bit-manipulation instructions

Flags affected:

11	1Ø	F	E	D	C	B	A	9	8	7	6	5	4	3	2	1	Ø
VM	R		NT	IOPL		OF	DF	IF	TF	SF	ZF		AF		PF		CF
											X						

Coding examples:

```
BSR      EAX,TEMP
BSR      CX,BX
```

Description: BSR scans the bits of the second operand (starting with the high-order bit) to see whether any are set. If all bits are clear (second operand is 0), the first operand is not changed, and the zero flag is set. If any bit is set, the zero flag is cleared, and the first operand is set equal to the bit number of the bit that is set.

BT: Bit Test

Category: Bit-manipulation instructions

Flags affected:

11	1Ø	F	E	D	C	B	A	9	8	7	6	5	4	3	2	1	Ø
VM	R		NT	IOPL		OF	DF	IF	TF	SF	ZF		AF		PF		CF
																	X

Coding examples:

```
BT     TEMP,EAX
BT     BX,CX
BT     TEMP,3            ;Test 3rd bit
```

Description: BT uses the value of the second operand as a bit index into the value of the first operand. The bit at the indexed position of the first operand is copied into the carry flag.

BTC: Bit Test and Complement

Category: Bit-manipulation instructions

Flags affected:

11	1Ø	F	E	D	C	B	A	9	8	7	6	5	4	3	2	1	Ø
VM	R		NT	IOPL		OF	DF	IF	TF	SF	ZF		AF		PF		CF
																	X

Coding examples:

```
BTC        TEMP,EAX
BTC        BX,CX
BTC        TEMP,3          ;Opposite of 3rd bit
```

Description: BTC uses the value of the second operand as a bit index into the value of the first operand. The opposite value of the bit at the indexed position of the first operand is copied into the carry flag.

BTR: Bit Test and Reset

Category: Bit-manipulation instructions

Flags affected:

11	1Ø	F	E	D	C	B	A	9	8	7	6	5	4	3	2	1	Ø
VM	R		NT	IOPL		OF	DF	IF	TF	SF	ZF		AF		PF		CF
																	X

Coding examples:

```
BTR        TEMP,EAX
BTR        BX,CX
BTR        TEMP,3          ;Value of 3rd bit
```

Description: BTR uses the value of the second operand as a bit index into the value of the first operand. The bit at the indexed position of the first operand is copied into the carry flag, and then the original bit value is cleared.

BTS: Bit Test and Set

Category: Bit-manipulation instructions

Flags affected:

11	1Ø	F	E	D	C	B	A	9	8	7	6	5	4	3	2	1	Ø
VM	R		NT	IOPL		OF	DF	IF	TF	SF	ZF		AF		PF		CF
																	X

Coding examples:

```
BTS        TEMP,EAX
BTS        BX,CX
BTS        TEMP,3              ;Value of 3rd bit
```

Description: BTS uses the value of the second operand as a bit index into the value of the first operand. The bit at the indexed position of the first operand is copied into the carry flag, and then the original bit value is set.

CALL: Perform Subroutine

Category: Control-transfer instructions

Flags affected: None

Coding examples:

```
CALL       WHIZ_BANG        ;WHIZ_BANG is a subroutine
CALL       [BX]             ;Perform subroutine with
                            ;  address at [BX]
CALL       EAX              ;Subroutine address in EAX
```

Description: Execution of the instruction (CALL) causes the following to happen:

- Offset address of next instruction is pushed on the stack

- If procedure being called is declared as FAR, segment address of next instruction is pushed on the stack

- Offset address of the procedure being called is loaded in IP

- If procedure being called is declared as FAR, the segment address of the procedure being called is loaded in CS

Execution then continues at the newly loaded CS:IP address until a RET instruction is encountered.

CBW: Convert Byte to Word

Category: Arithmetic instructions

Flags affected: None

Coding example:

```
CBW
```

Description: CBW converts the byte value in AL to a word value in AX by extending the high-order bit value of AL through all bits of AH.

CDQ: Convert Doubleword to Quadword

Category: Arithmetic instructions

Flags affected: None

Coding example:

```
CDQ
```

Description: CDQ converts the doubleword value in EAX to a quadword value in EDX:EAX by extending the high-order bit value of EAX through all bits of EDX.

CLC: Clear Carry Flag

Category: Flag- and processor-control instructions

Flags affected:

11	1Ø	F	E	D	C	B	A	9	8	7	6	5	4	3	2	1	Ø
VM	R		NT	IOPL		OF	DF	IF	TF	SF	ZF		AF		PF		CF
																	X

Coding example:

```
CLC
```

Description: CLC clears the carry flag of the flags register by setting the flag to 0.

CLD: Clear Direction Flag

Category: Flag- and processor-control instructions

Flags affected:

11	1Ø	F	E	D	C	B	A	9	8	7	6	5	4	3	2	1	Ø
VM	R		NT	IOPL		OF	DF	IF	TF	SF	ZF		AF		PF		CF
							X										

Coding example:

    CLD

Description: CLD clears the direction flag of the flags register by setting the flag to 0.

CLI: Clear Interrupt Flag

Category: Flag- and processor-control instructions

Flags affected:

11	1Ø	F	E	D	C	B	A	9	8	7	6	5	4	3	2	1	Ø
VM	R		NT	IOPL		OF	DF	IF	TF	SF	ZF		AF		PF		CF
								X									

Coding example:

    CLI

Description: CLI clears the interrupt flag of the flags register by setting the flag to 0. While the flag is cleared, no maskable interrupts are recognized by the CPU.

CLTS: Clear Task Switched Flag

Category: Flag- and processor-control instructions

Flags affected: None in flags register—affects machine status word

Coding example:

    CLTS

Description: CLTS clears the task switched flag of the machine status register. This instruction is for use in operating system software only and is not used in applications software.

CMC: Complement Carry Flag

Category: Flag- and processor-control instructions

Flags affected:

11	1Ø	F	E	D	C	B	A	9	8	7	6	5	4	3	2	1	Ø
VM	R			NT	IOPL		OF	DF	IF	TF	SF	ZF		AF		PF		CF
																		X

Coding example:

```
CMC
```

Description: CMC switches the carry flag of the flags register to the opposite of the flag's current setting.

CMP: Compare

Category: Arithmetic instructions

Flags affected:

11	1Ø	F	E	D	C	B	A	9	8	7	6	5	4	3	2	1	Ø
VM	R			NT	IOPL		OF	DF	IF	TF	SF	ZF		AF		PF		CF
						X				X	X			X		X		X

Coding examples:

```
CMP       AX,BX           ;
CMP       AX,TEMP         ;TEMP must be a word
CMP       SUM,EBX         ;SUM must be a doubleword
CMP       CL,3            ;Compare to constant
CMP       AX,TEMP[BX]     ;Indirect address example
```

Description: CMP is considered an arithmetic instruction because the source operand is subtracted from the destination operand. The result, however, is used for setting the flags—it is not stored anywhere. Subsequent testing of the flags can be used for program control.

CMPSB: Compare Strings, Byte-for-Byte

Category: String-manipulation instructions

Flags affected:

11	1Ø	F	E	D	C	B	A	9	8	7	6	5	4	3	2	1	Ø
VM	R			NT	IOPL	OF	DF	IF	TF	SF	ZF		AF		PF		CF
						X				X	X		X		X		X

Coding examples:

```
CMPSB              ;Compare strings
REPE CMPSB         ;Repeat a comparison loop
```

Description: This instruction compares strings, byte-for-byte. DI and SI change in an increment or decrement of 1, depending on the setting of the direction flag. Usually, this instruction is used with the REPE, REPNE, REPNZ, or REPZ instructions to repeat the comparison for a maximum of CX number of bytes. This instruction affects only the flags; no changes are made to the operands.

CMPSW: Compare Strings, Word-for-Word

Category: String-manipulation instructions

Flags affected:

11	1Ø	F	E	D	C	B	A	9	8	7	6	5	4	3	2	1	Ø
VM	R			NT	IOPL	OF	DF	IF	TF	SF	ZF		AF		PF		CF
						X				X	X		X		X		X

Coding examples:

```
CMPSW              ;Compare strings
REPE CMPSW         ;Repeat a comparison loop
```

Description: This instruction compares strings, word-for-word. DI and SI change in increments or decrements of 2, depending on the setting of the direction flag. Usually, this instruction is used with REPE, REPNE, REPNZ, or REPZ instructions to repeat the comparison for a maximum of CX number of words. This instruction affects only the flags; no changes are made to the operands.

CMPSD: Compare Strings, Doubleword-for-Doubleword

Category: String-manipulation instructions

Flags affected:

11	1Ø	F	E	D	C	B	A	9	8	7	6	5	4	3	2	1	Ø
VM	R		NT		IOPL	OF	DF	IF	TF	SF	ZF		AF		PF		CF
						X				X	X		X		X		X

Coding examples:

```
CMPSD            ;Compare strings
REPE CMPSD       ;Repeat a comparison loop
```

Description: This instruction compares strings, doubleword-for-doubleword. EDI and ESI change in increments or decrements of 4, depending on the setting of the direction flag. Usually, this instruction is used with REPE, REPNE, REPNZ, or REPZ instructions to repeat the comparison for a maximum of ECX number of words. This instruction affects only the flags; no changes are made to the operands.

CWD: Convert Word to Doubleword

Category: Arithmetic instructions

Flags affected: None

Coding example:

```
CWD
```

Description: CWD converts the word value in AX to a doubleword value in DX:AX by extending the high-order bit value of AX through all bits of DX.

CWDE: Convert Word to Doubleword

Category: Arithmetic instructions

Flags affected: None

Coding example:

```
CWDE
```

Description: CWDE converts the word value in AX to a doubleword value in EAX by extending the high-order bit value of AX through the remaining bits of EAX.

DAA: Decimal Adjust for Addition

Category: Arithmetic instructions

Flags affected:

11	1Ø	F	E	D	C	B	A	9	8	7	6	5	4	3	2	1	Ø
VM	R		NT	IOPL		OF	DF	IF	TF	SF	ZF		AF		PF		CF
										X	X		X		X		X

Coding example:

    DAA

Description: DAA corrects the result (AL) of a previous binary-coded decimal (BCD) addition operation.

DAS: Decimal Adjust for Subtraction

Category: Arithmetic instructions

Flags affected:

11	1Ø	F	E	D	C	B	A	9	8	7	6	5	4	3	2	1	Ø
VM	R		NT	IOPL		OF	DF	IF	TF	SF	ZF		AF		PF		CF
										X	X		X		X		X

Coding example:

    DAS

Description: DAS corrects the result (AL) of a previous binary-coded decimal (BCD) subtraction operation.

DEC: Decrement

Category: Arithmetic instructions

Flags affected:

11	10	F	E	D	C	B	A	9	8	7	6	5	4	3	2	1	0
VM	R		NT	IOPL		OF	DF	IF	TF	SF	ZF		AF		PF		CF
						X				X	X		X		X		

Coding examples:

```
DEC     AX
DEC     ECX
DEC     SUM
DEC     BL
DEC     TEMP[SI]
```

Description: DEC changes the contents of the operand in decrements of 1. The operand is assumed to be an unsigned binary value.

DIV: Divide

Category: Arithmetic instructions

Flags affected:

11	10	F	E	D	C	B	A	9	8	7	6	5	4	3	2	1	0
VM	R		NT	IOPL		OF	DF	IF	TF	SF	ZF		AF		PF		CF
						?				?	?		?		?		?

Coding examples:

```
DIV     BX              ;AX=DX:AX/BX
DIV     WORD_TEMP       ;AX=DX:AX/WORD_TEMP
DIV     BYTE_SUM        ;AL=AX/BYTE_SUM
DIV     DWORD_SUM       ;EAX=EDX:EAX/DWORD_SUM
DIV     WORD_TBL[BX]    ;Indirect address example
```

Description: If the operand is a byte value, DIV divides the contents of AX by the contents of the operand and stores the result in AL and the remainder in

AH. If the operand is a word value, DIV divides the contents of DX:AX by the contents of the operand and stores the result in AX and the remainder in DX. If the operand is a doubleword value, DIV divides the contents of EDX:EAX by the contents of the operand and stores the result in EAX and the remainder in EDX. This instruction treats numbers as unsigned binary values.

ENTER: Make Stack Frame for Procedure Parameters

Category: Flag- and processor-control instructions

Flags affected: None

Coding examples:

```
ENTER       PPTR,3
ENTER       DS:BX,Ø
```

Description: ENTER modifies the stack appropriately for entry to a high-level language procedure. The first operand specifies the number of bytes of storage to be allocated on the stack; the second operand specifies the nesting level of the routine. The effects of this instruction are undone by the LEAVE instruction.

ESC: Escape

Category: Flag- and processor-control instructions

Flags affected: None

Coding examples:

```
ESC         6,TEMP
ESC         15,CL
```

Description: This instruction provides a means for coprocessors, such as the 80387, to access data in the 80386 data stream. When this instruction is encountered, it causes the 80386 to place the operand on the data bus and perform an NOP internally.

HLT: Halt

Category: Flag- and processor-control instructions

Flags affected: None

Coding example:

```
HLT
```

Description: HLT causes the 80386 to stop execution and leave the CS:IP registers pointing to the instruction following the HLT. This halt condition is terminated only after receipt of an interrupt or activation of the RESET line.

IDIV: Integer Divide

Category: Arithmetic instructions

Flags affected:

11	10	F	E	D	C	B	A	9	8	7	6	5	4	3	2	1	0
VM	R		NT	IOPL		OF	DF	IF	TF	SF	ZF		AF		PF		CF
						?				?	?		?		?		?

Coding examples:

```
IDIV      BX              ;AX=DX:AX/BX
IDIV      WORD_TEMP       ;AX=DX:AX/WORD_TEMP
IDIV      BYTE_SUM        ;AL=AX/BYTE_SUM
IDIV      DWORD_SUM       ;EAX=EDX:EAX/DWORD_SUM
IDIV      WORD_TBL[BX]    ;Indirect address example
```

Description: If the operand is a byte value, IDIV divides the contents of AX by the contents of the operand and stores the result in AL and the remainder in AH. If the operand is a word value, IDIV divides the contents of DX:AX by the contents of the operand and stores the result in AX and the remainder in DX. If the operand is a doubleword value, IDIV divides the contents of EDX:EAX by the contents of the operand and stores the result in EAX and the remainder in EDX. This instruction treats numbers as signed binary values.

IMUL: Integer Multiply

Category: Arithmetic instructions

Flags affected:

11	10	F	E	D	C	B	A	9	8	7	6	5	4	3	2	1	0
VM	R		NT	IOPL		OF	DF	IF	TF	SF	ZF		AF		PF		CF
						X				?	?		?		?		X

Coding examples:

```
IMUL      BX                    ;DX:AX=AX*BX
IMUL      WORD_TEMP             ;DX:AX=AX*WORD_TEMP
IMUL      BYTE_SUM             ;AX=AL*BYTE_SUM
IMUL      WORD_TBL[BX]          ;Indirect address example
IMUL      ECX,DWORD_TEMP,10     ;ECX=DWORD_TEMP*10
```

Description: The results of this operation depend on the number of operands specified.

If only one operand is given, it is multiplied by either AL, AX, or EAX. If the operand is a byte value, IMUL multiplies the contents of AL by the contents of the operand and stores the result in AX. If the operand is a word value, IMUL multiplies the contents of AX by the contents of the operand and stores the result in DX:AX.

If two operands are given, IMUL multiplies the first operand by the second one and stores the result in the first operand. Both operands must agree in size.

If three operands are given and the third operand is an immediate value, IMUL multiplies the second operand by the third one and stores the result in the first operand.

This instruction treats numbers as signed binary values.

IN: Input from Port

Category: Data-transfer instructions

Flags affected: None

Coding examples:

```
IN        AL,64h
IN        AX,DX
IN        EAX,DX
```

Description: IN loads a byte, word, or doubleword to AL, AX, or EAX, respectively, from the specified hardware I/O port address. A port number below 256 may be specified as a constant or as a variable in the DX register. A port number above 255, however, *must* be specified in the DX register.

INC: Increment

Category: Arithmetic instructions

Flags affected:

11	1Ø	F	E	D	C	B	A	9	8	7	6	5	4	3	2	1	Ø
VM	R		NT	IOPL		OF	DF	IF	TF	SF	ZF		AF		PF		CF
						X				X	X		X		X		

Coding examples:

```
INC     AX
INC     SUM
INC     CL
INC     EDI
INC     TEMP[SI]
```

Description: INC changes the contents of the operand in increments of 1. The operand is assumed to be an unsigned binary value.

INS: Input String from Port

Category: Data-transfer instructions

Flags affected: None

Coding examples:

```
INS     CX,DX       ;Load word
INS     BL,DX       ;Load byte
INS     EAX,DX      ;Load doubleword
```

Description: INS loads a byte, word, or doubleword from the specified hardware I/O port address (indicated by the value in DX) to the destination operand. The size of the destination operand determines whether a byte, word, or doubleword is transferred. If the destination operand is an offset address, that address is relative to the ES register. No segment override is possible.

INSB: Input String Byte from Port

Category: Data-transfer instructions

Flags affected: None

Coding example:

    INSB

Description: INSB loads a byte from the hardware I/O port address specified in DX to the address specified by ES:[DI]. The port number may range from 0 to 65,535. After the transfer, DI changes in an increment or decrement of 1, depending on the setting of the direction flag.

INSD: Input String Doubleword from Port

Category: Data-transfer instructions

Flags affected: None

Coding example:

    INSD

Description: INSD loads a word from the hardware I/O port address specified in DX to the address specified by ES:[EDI]. After the transfer, EDI changes in increments or decrements of 4, depending on the setting of the direction flag.

INSW: Input String Word from Port

Category: Data-transfer instructions

Flags affected: None

Coding example:

    INSW

Description: INSW loads a word from the hardware I/O port address specified in DX to the address specified by ES:[DI]. The port number may range from 0 to 65,535. After the transfer, DI changes in increments or decrements of 2, depending on the setting of the direction flag.

INT: Software Interrupt

Category: Control-transfer instructions

Flags affected:

11	1Ø	F	E	D	C	B	A	9	8	7	6	5	4	3	2	1	Ø
VM	R		NT	IOPL		OF	DF	IF	TF	SF	ZF		AF		PF		CF
								X	X								

Coding examples:

```
INT        1Øh
INT        13h
```

Description: INT initiates a software interrupt of the 80386 CPU. The instruction initiates the following functions:

- Pushes the flags on the stack

- Clears the TF and IF flags

- Pushes the value of CS on the stack

- Loads CS with the segment address of the interrupt being invoked. This address is found at the calculated address in the interrupt vector table.

- Pushes the value of IP on the stack

- Loads IP with the offset address of the interrupt being invoked. This address is found at the calculated address in the interrupt vector table.

Execution then continues at the newly loaded CS:IP address until an IRET instruction is encountered.

INTO: Interrupt on Overflow

Category: Control-transfer instructions

Flags affected: None

Coding example:

```
INTO
```

Description: If the overflow flag (OF) is set, an interrupt 4 is executed and control proceeds as though an INT 4 had been issued. Be aware that, in this case, the flags register is affected as described for the INT instruction.

IRET: Return from Interrupt

Category: Control-transfer instructions

Flags affected:

11	1Ø	F	E	D	C	B	A	9	8	7	6	5	4	3	2	1	Ø
VM	R		NT	IOPL		OF	DF	IF	TF	SF	ZF		AF		PF		CF
X	X	X	X	X	X	X	X	X	X	X	X	X	X	X	X	X	X

Coding example:

```
IRET
```

Description: IRET causes termination of an interrupt procedure and, by popping the values of IP, CS, and the flags register from the stack, returns control to the point at which the interrupt occurred.

JA: Jump if Above

Category: Control-transfer instructions

Flags affected: None

Coding example:

```
JA         NEXT_STEP
```

Description: JA causes program execution to branch to the operand address if both the carry and zero flags are clear. This instruction is functionally the same as JNBE.

JAE: Jump if Above or Equal

Category: Control-transfer instructions

Flags affected: None

Coding example:

```
JAE        NEXT_STEP
```

Description: JAE causes program execution to branch to the operand address if the carry flag is clear. This instruction is functionally the same as JNB or JNC.

JB: Jump if Below

Category: Control-transfer instructions

Flags affected: None

Coding example:

```
JB         NEXT_STEP
```

Description: JB causes program execution to branch to the operand address if the carry flag is set. This instruction is functionally the same as JC or JNAE.

JBE: Jump if Below or Equal

Category: Control-transfer instructions

Flags affected: None

Coding example:

```
JBE         NEXT_STEP
```

Description: JBE causes program execution to branch to the operand address if either the carry or zero flag is set. This instruction is functionally the same as JNA.

JC: Jump on Carry

Category: Control-transfer instructions

Flags affected: None

Coding example:

```
JC          NEXT_STEP
```

Description: JC causes program execution to branch to the operand address if the carry flag is set. This instruction is functionally the same as JB or JNAE.

JCXZ: Jump if CX=0

Category: Control-transfer instructions

Flags affected: None

Coding example:

```
JCXZ        SKIP_LOOP
```

Description: JCXZ causes program execution to branch to the operand address if the value of CX is zero.

JE: Jump if Equal

Category: Control-transfer instructions

Flags affected: None

Coding example:

```
JE          NEXT_STEP
```

Description: JE causes program execution to branch to the operand address if the zero flag is set. This instruction is functionally the same as JZ.

JECXZ: Jump if ECX=0

Category: Control-transfer instructions

Flags affected: None

Coding example:

```
JECXZ     SKIP_LOOP
```

Description: JECXZ causes program execution to branch to the operand address if the value of ECX is zero.

JG: Jump if Greater

Category: Control-transfer instructions

Flags affected: None

Coding example:

```
JG    NEXT_STEP
```

Description: JG causes program execution to branch to the operand address if the sign flag equals the overflow flag or the zero flag is clear. This instruction is functionally the same as JNLE.

JGE: Jump if Greater or Equal

Category: Control-transfer instructions

Flags affected: None

Coding example:

```
JGE       NEXT_STEP
```

Description: JGE causes program execution to branch to the operand address if the sign flag equals the overflow flag. This instruction is functionally the same as JNL.

JL: Jump if Less Than

Category: Control-transfer instructions

Flags affected: None

Coding example:

```
JL    NEXT_STEP
```

Description: JL causes program execution to branch to the operand address if the sign flag does not equal the overflow flag. This instruction is functionally the same as JNGE.

JLE: Jump if Less Than or Equal

Category: Control-transfer instructions

Flags affected: None

Coding example:

```
JLE        NEXT_STEP
```

Description: JLE causes program execution to branch to the operand address if the sign flag does not equal the overflow flag or the zero flag is set. This instruction is functionally the same as JNG.

JMP: Jump

Category: Control-transfer instructions

Flags affected: None

Coding examples:

```
JMP        EXIT_CODE
JMP        [BX]            ;Jump to address at [BX]
JMP        AX              ;Jump to address in AX
```

Description: JMP causes program execution to begin at the designated operand address. JMP affects the CS and IP registers as necessary to cause this unconditional branch.

JNA: Jump if Not Above

Category: Control-transfer instructions

Flags affected: None

Coding example:

```
JNA        NEXT_STEP
```

Description: JNA causes program execution to branch to the operand address if either the carry or zero flag is set. This instruction is functionally the same as JBE.

JNAE: Jump if Not Above or Equal

Category: Control-transfer instructions

Flags affected: None

Coding example:

```
JNAE      NEXT_STEP
```

Description: JNAE causes program execution to branch to the operand address if the carry flag is set. This instruction is functionally the same as JB or JC.

JNB: Jump if Not Below

Category: Control-transfer instructions

Flags affected: None

Coding example:

```
JNB       NEXT_STEP
```

Description: JNB causes program execution to branch to the operand address if the carry flag is clear. This instruction is functionally the same as JAE or JNC.

JNBE: Jump if Not Below or Equal

Category: Control-transfer instructions

Flags affected: None

Coding example:

```
JNBE      NEXT_STEP
```

Description: JNBE causes program execution to branch to the operand address if both the carry and zero flags are clear. This instruction is functionally the same as JA.

JNC: Jump on No Carry

Category: Control-transfer instructions

Flags affected: None

Coding example:

```
JNC       NEXT_STEP
```

Description: JNC causes program execution to branch to the operand address if the carry flag is clear. This instruction is functionally the same as JAE or JNB.

JNE: Jump if Not Equal

Category: Control-transfer instructions

Flags affected: None

Coding example:

```
JNE       NEXT STEP
```

Description: JNE causes program execution to branch to the operand address if the zero flag is clear. This instruction is functionally the same as JNZ.

JNG: Jump if Not Greater Than

Category: Control-transfer instructions

Flags affected: None

Coding example:

```
JNG       NEXT_STEP
```

Description: JNG causes program execution to branch to the operand address if the sign flag does not equal the overflow flag or the zero flag is set. This instruction is functionally the same as JLE.

JNGE: Jump if Not Greater Than or Equal

Category: Control-transfer instructions

Flags affected: None

Coding example:

```
JNGE      NEXT_STEP
```

Description: JNGE causes program execution to branch to the operand address if the sign flag does not equal the overflow flag. This instruction is functionally the same as JL.

JNL: Jump if Not Less Than

Category: Control-transfer instructions

Flags affected: None

Coding example:

```
JNL        NEXT_STEP
```

Description: JNL causes program execution to branch to the operand address if the sign flag equals the overflow flag. This instruction is functionally the same as JGE.

JNLE: Jump if Not Less Than or Equal

Category: Control-transfer instructions

Flags affected: None

Coding example:

```
JNLE       NEXT_STEP
```

Description: JNLE causes program execution to branch to the operand address if the sign flag equals the overflow flag or the zero flag is clear. This instruction is functionally the same as JG.

JNO: Jump on No Overflow

Category: Control-transfer instructions

Flags affected: None

Coding example:

```
JNO        NEXT_STEP
```

Description: JNO causes program execution to branch to the operand address if the overflow flag is clear.

JNP: Jump on No Parity

Category: Control-transfer instructions

Flags affected: None

Coding example:

```
JNP        NEXT_STEP
```

Description: JNP causes program execution to branch to the operand address if the parity flag is clear. This instruction is functionally the same as JPO.

JNS: Jump on Not Sign

Category: Control -transfer instructions

Flags affected: None

Coding example:

```
JNS          NEXT_STEP
```

Description: JNS causes program execution to branch to the operand address if the sign flag is clear.

JNZ: Jump on Not Zero

Category: Control-transfer instructions

Flags affected: None

Coding example:

```
JNZ          NEXT_STEP
```

Description: JNZ causes program execution to branch to the operand address if the zero flag is clear. This instruction is functionally the same as JNE.

JO: Jump on Overflow

Category: Control-transfer instructions

Flags affected: None

Coding example:

```
JO    EXT_STEP
```

Description: JO causes program execution to branch to the operand address if the overflow flag is set.

JP: Jump on Parity

Category: Control-transfer instructions

Flags affected: None

Coding example:

```
JP    NEXT_STEP
```

Description: JP causes program execution to branch to the operand address if the parity flag is set. This instruction is functionally the same as JPE.

JPE: Jump on Parity Even

Category: Control-transfer instructions

Flags affected: None

Coding example:

```
JPE        NEXT_STEP
```

Description: JPE causes program execution to branch to the operand address if the parity flag is set. This instruction is functionally the same as JP.

JPO: Jump on Parity Odd

Category: Control-transfer instructions

Flags affected: None

Coding example:

```
JPO        NEXT_STEP
```

Description: JPO causes program execution to branch to the operand address if the parity flag is clear. This instruction is functionally the same as JNP.

JS: Jump on Sign

Category: Control-transfer instructions

Flags affected: None

Coding example:

```
JS    NEXT_STEP
```

Description: JS causes program execution to branch to the operand address if the sign flag is set.

JZ: Jump on Zero

Category: Control-transfer instructions

Flags affected: None

Coding example:

```
JZ    NEXT_STEP
```

Description: JZ causes program execution to branch to the operand address if the zero flag is set. This instruction is functionally the same as JE.

LAHF: Load AH Register with Flags

Category: Data-transfer instructions

Flags affected: None

Coding example:

```
LAHF
```

Description: LAHF copies the low-order byte of the flags register to AH. After execution of this instruction, bits 7, 6, 4, 2, and 1 of AH are equal to SF, ZF, AF, PF, and CF, respectively.

LAR: Load Access-Rights Byte

Category: Data-transfer instructions

Flags affected:

11	1Ø	F	E	D	C	B	A	9	8	7	6	5	4	3	2	1	Ø
VM	R		NT	IOPL		OF	DF	IF	TF	SF	ZF		AF		PF		CF
											X						

Coding example:

```
LAR       AX,SELECT
```

Description: Based on the selection in the second operand, the high byte of the destination register is overwritten by the value of the access-rights byte, and the low byte is zeroed. The loading is done only if the descriptor is visible at the current privilege level and at the selector RPL. The zero flag is set if the loading operation is successful.

LDS: Load DS Register

Category: Data-transfer instructions

Flags affected: None

Coding example:

```
LDS        SI,SOURCE_BUFFER
```

Description: LDS performs two distinct operations: it loads DS with the segment address of the source operand, and then loads the destination operand with the offset address of the source operand.

LEA: Load Effective Address

Category: Data-transfer instructions

Flags affected: None

Coding examples:

```
LEA        AX,MESSAGE_1
LEA        EBX,SOURCE_BLOCK
```

Description: LEA transfers the offset address of the source operand to the destination operand. The destination operand must be a general word or doubleword register.

LEAVE: High-Level Procedure Exit

Category: Flag- and processor-control instructions

Flags affected: None

Coding example:

```
LEAVE
```

Description: LEAVE undoes the changes performed by the ENTER instruction. You use LEAVE for exiting high-level language subroutines.

LES: Load ES Register

Category: Data-transfer instructions

Flags affected: None

Coding example:

```
LES        DI,DEST_BUFFER
```

Description: LES performs two distinct operations: it loads ES with the segment address of the source operand, and then loads the destination operand with the offset address of the source operand.

LFS: Load FS Register

Category: Data-transfer instructions

Flags affected: None

Coding example:

```
LFS        DI,DEST_BUFFER
```

Description: LFS performs two distinct operations: it loads FS with the segment address of the source operand, and then loads the destination operand with the offset address of the source operand.

LGDT: Load Global Descriptor Table Register

Category: Data-transfer instructions

Flags affected: None

Coding example:

```
LGDT       TEMP[BX]
```

Description: LGDT loads the six bytes associated with the global descriptor table from the memory address specified in the operand. This instruction is for use in protected-mode operating system software and is not used in applications software.

LGS: Load GS Register

Category: Data-transfer instructions

Flags affected: None

Coding example:

```
LGS        DI,DEST_BUFFER
```

Description: LGS performs two distinct operations: it loads GS with the segment address of the source operand, and then loads the destination operand with the offset address of the source operand.

LIDT: Load Interrupt Descriptor Table Register

Category: Data-transfer instructions

Flags affected: None

Coding example:

```
LIDT       TEMP[BX]
```

Description: LIDT loads the six bytes associated with the interrupt descriptor table from the memory address specified in the operand. This instruction is for use in protected-mode operating system software and is not used in applications software.

LLDT: Load Local Descriptor Table Register

Category: Data-transfer instructions

Flags affected: None

Coding example:

```
LLDT       AX
```

Description: Based on the selector specified in the operand, LLDT transfers the valid global descriptor table entry to the local descriptor table. This instruction is for use in protected-mode operating system software and is not used in applications software.

LMSW: Load Machine Status Word

Category: Data-transfer instructions

Flags affected: None

Coding example:

```
LMSW       AX
```

Description: LMSW copies the value of the operand to the machine status word. This instruction is for use in operating system software only and is not used in applications software.

LOCK: Lock Bus

Category: Flag- and processor-control instructions

Flags affected: None

Coding example:

```
LOCK XLAT
```

Description: LOCK prohibits interference from any other coprocessors during the execution of the next instruction. This instruction is a prefix that must be used with other operations.

LODSB: Load a Byte from String into AL

Category: String-manipulation instructions

Flags affected: None

Coding example:

```
LODSB
```

Description: This instruction loads AL with the contents of the address pointed to by SI. SI then changes in an increment or decrement of 1, depending on the setting of the direction flag.

LODSD: Load a Doubleword from String into EAX

Category: String-manipulation instructions

Flags affected: None

Coding example:

```
LODSD
```

Description: This instruction loads EAX with the contents of the address pointed to by ESI. ESI then changes in increments or decrements of 4, depending on the setting of the direction flag.

LODSW: Load a Word from String into AX

Category: String-manipulation instructions

Flags affected: None

Coding example:

```
LODSW
```

Description: This instruction loads AX with the contents of the address pointed to by SI. SI then changes in increments or decrements of 2, depending on the setting of the direction flag.

LOOP: Loop

Category: Control-transfer instructions

Flags affected: None

Coding example:

```
LOOP       PRINT_LOOP
```

Description: Based on the contents of CX, program execution branches to the address of the destination operand. If CX does not equal 0, CX changes in a decrement of 1, and the branch occurs. If CX is 0, no decrement or branching occurs, and execution proceeds to the next instruction.

LOOPE: Loop While Equal

Category: Control-transfer instructions

Flags affected: None

Coding example:

```
LOOPE  TEST_LOOP
```

Description: Based on the contents of CX and the zero flag, program execution branches to the address of the destination operand. If CX does not equal 0 and the zero flag is set, CX changes in a decrement of 1, and the branch occurs. If CX is 0 or the zero flag is clear, no decrement or branching occurs, and execution proceeds to the next instruction. This instruction is functionally equivalent to LOOPZ.

LOOPNE: Loop While Not Equal

Category: Control-transfer instructions

Flags affected: None

Coding example:

```
LOOPNE TEST_LOOP
```

Description: Based on the contents of CX and the zero flag, program execution branches to the address of the destination operand. If CX does not equal 0 and the zero flag is clear, CX changes in a decrement of 1, and the branch occurs. If CX is 0 or the zero flag is set, no decrement or branching occurs, and execution proceeds to the next instruction. This instruction is functionally equivalent to LOOPNZ.

LOOPNZ: Loop While Not Zero

Category: Control-transfer instructions

Flags affected: None

Coding example:

```
LOOPNZ TEST_LOOP
```

Description: Based on the contents of CX and the zero flag, program execution branches to the address of the destination operand. If CX does not equal 0 and the zero flag is clear, CX changes in a decrement of 1, and the branch occurs. If CX is 0 or the zero flag is set, no decrement or branching occurs, and execution proceeds to the next instruction. This instruction is functionally equivalent to LOOPNE.

LOOPZ: Loop While Zero

Category: Control-transfer instructions

Flags affected: None

Coding example:

```
LOOPZ  TEST_LOOP
```

Description: Based on the contents of CX and the zero flag, program execution branches to the address of the destination operand. If CX does not equal 0 and the zero flag is set, CX changes in a decrement of 1, and the branch occurs. If CX is 0 or the zero flag is clear, no decrement or branching occurs, and execution proceeds to the next instruction. This instruction is functionally equivalent to LOOPE.

LSL: Load Segment Limit

Category: Data-transfer instructions

Flags affected:

11	10	F	E	D	C	B	A	9	8	7	6	5	4	3	2	1	0
VM	R		NT	IOPL		OF	DF	IF	TF	SF	ZF		AF		PF		CF
											X						

Coding example:

```
LSL       AX,SELECTOR
```

Description: Based on the selector specified in the source operand, LSL loads the descriptor's limit field into the target operand (register). The descriptor denoted by the selector must be visible. If the loading is successful, the zero flag is set; otherwise, it is cleared.

LSS: Load SS Register

Category: Data-transfer instructions

Flags affected: None

Coding example:

```
LSS       DI,DEST_BUFFER
```

Description: LSS performs two distinct operations: it loads SS with the segment address of the source operand, and then loads the destination operand with the offset address of the source operand.

LTR: Load Task Register

Category: Data-transfer instructions

Flags affected: None

Coding examples:

```
LTR       DX
LTR       TEMP[BX]
```

Description: LTR loads the task register from the value of the source operand. This instruction is for use in operating system software only and is not used in applications software.

MOV: Move

Category: Data-transfer instructions

Flags affected: None

Coding examples:

```
MOV      AX,BX           ;AX=BX
MOV      EAX,TEMP        ;EAX=TEMP (doubleword)
MOV      SUM,BX          ;SUM=BX (SUM is a word)
MOV      CL,57           ;CL=57
MOV      DECIMAL,1Ø      ;DECIMAL=1Ø
MOV      AX,TEMP[BX]     ;Indirect address example
```

Description: MOV copies the contents of the source operand to the destination operand. When the source operand is not an immediate value, both operands must agree in length. If the source or destination operand is a doubleword register, the other register can be a special register, such as CR0, CR2, CR3, DR0, DR1, DR2, DR3, DR6, DR7, TR6, or TR7.

MOVSB: Move String, Byte-by-Byte

Category: String-manipulation instructions

Flags affected: None

Coding examples:

```
MOVSB
REP MOVSB       ;Repeat a move loop
```

Description: This instruction moves strings, byte-by-byte. The values of SI and DI change in an increment or decrement of 1, depending on the setting of the direction flag. Usually, this instruction is used with the REP instruction to repeat the move for a maximum of CX bytes.

MOVSD: Move String, Doubleword-by-Doubleword

Category: String-manipulation instructions

Flags affected: None

Coding examples:

```
MOVSD
REP MOVSD       ;Repeat a move loop
```

Description: This instruction moves strings, doubleword-by-doubleword. The values of ESI and EDI change in increments or decrements of 4, depending on the setting of the direction flag. Usually, this instruction is used with the REP instruction to repeat the move for a maximum of ECX words.

MOVSW: Move String, Word-by-Word

Category: String-manipulation instructions

Flags affected: None

Coding examples:

```
MOVSW
REP MOVSW        ;Repeat a move loop
```

Description: This instruction moves strings, word-by-word. The values of SI and DI change in increments or decrements of 2, depending on the setting of the direction flag. Usually, this instruction is used with the REP instruction to repeat the move for a maximum of CX words.

MOVSX: Move with Sign Extended

Category: Data-transfer instructions

Flags affected: None

Coding examples:

```
MOVSX       EAX,BX      ;EAX=BX
MOVSX       EAX,TEMP    ;EAX=TEMP (TEMP is a word)
MOVSX       CX,AL       ;CX=AL
```

Description: MOVSX moves the source operand to the destination operand and extends the high-order bit to the balance of the bits in the destination operand. The source operand must be smaller than the destination operand.

MOVZX: Move with Zero Extended

Category: Data-transfer instructions

Flags affected: None

Coding examples:

```
MOVZX       EAX,BX      ;EAX=BX
MOVZX       EAX,TEMP    ;EAX=TEMP (TEMP is a word)
MOVZX       CX,AL       ;CX=AL
```

Description: MOVZX moves the source operand to the destination operand and clears the remaining bits in the destination operand. The source operand must be smaller than the destination operand.

MUL: Multiply

Category: Arithmetic instructions

Flags affected:

11	1Ø	F	E	D	C	B	A	9	8	7	6	5	4	3	2	1	Ø
VM	R		NT	IOPL		OF	DF	IF	TF	SF	ZF		AF		PF		CF
						X				?	?		?		?		X

Coding examples:

```
MUL        BX              ;DX:AX=AX*BX
MUL        ECX             ;EDX:EAX=EAX*ECX
MUL        WORD_TEMP       ;DX:AX=AX*WORD_TEMP
MUL        BYTE_SUM        ;AX=AL*BYTE_SUM
MUL        WORD_TBL[BX]    ;Indirect address example
```

Description: If the operand is a byte value, MUL multiplies the contents of AL by the contents of the operand and stores the result in AX. If the operand is a word value, MUL multiplies the contents of AX by the contents of the operand and stores the result in DX:AX. If the operand is a doubleword value, MUL multiplies the contents of EAX by the contents of the operand and stores the result in EDX:EAX. This instruction treats numbers as unsigned binary values.

NEG: Negate

Category: Arithmetic instructions

Flags affected:

11	1Ø	F	E	D	C	B	A	9	8	7	6	5	4	3	2	1	Ø
VM	R		NT	IOPL		OF	DF	IF	TF	SF	ZF		AF		PF		CF
						X				X	X		X		X		X

Coding examples:

```
NEG     TEMP
NEG     CL
NEG     EAX
```

Description: NEG calculates the two's complement of the destination operand and stores the result in the destination operand. This calculation is effectively the same as subtracting the destination operand from 0.

NOP: No Operation

Category: Flag- and processor-control instructions

Flags affected: None

Coding example:

```
NOP
```

Description: NOP does nothing but take space and time. It causes the CPU to do nothing.

NOT: Logical NOT on Bits

Category: Bit-manipulation instructions

Flags affected: None

Coding examples:

```
NOT     CL
NOT     BYTE_SUM        ;Use byte value
NOT     WORD_SUM        ;Use word value
NOT     DWORD_SUM       ;Use doubleword value
NOT     AX
NOT     EBX
```

Description: NOT inverts the bits that make up the destination operand (0 becomes 1, and 1 becomes 0) and stores them in the destination operand.

OR: Logical OR on Bits

Category: Bit-manipulation instructions

Flags affected:

11	10	F	E	D	C	B	A	9	8	7	6	5	4	3	2	1	0
VM	R		NT	IOPL		OF	DF	IF	TF	SF	ZF		AF		PF		CF
						X				X	X		?		X		X

Coding examples:

```
OR    AL,BL
OR    EAX,ØFFFFh
OR    DX,TEMP
OR    AX,CX
```

Description: OR performs a logical OR of the operands and stores the result in the destination operand. Each bit of the resultant byte or word is set to 1 if either or both of the corresponding bits of each operand are set to 1.

OUT: Output to Port

Category: Data-transfer instructions

Flags affected: None

Coding examples:

```
OUT       64h,AL
OUT       DX,AX
OUT       DX,EAX
```

Description: OUT sends a byte (AL), word (AX), or doubleword (EAX) to the specified hardware I/O port address. A port number below 256 may be specified as a constant or as a variable in the DX register. A port number above 255, however, *must* be specified in the DX register.

OUTS: Output String to Port

Category: Data-transfer instructions

Flags affected: None

Coding examples:

```
OUTS      DX,CX       ;Output word
OUTS      DX,BL       ;Output byte
```

Description: OUTS sends a byte or a word (length is specified by the size of the source operand) to the hardware I/O port address specified in DX.

OUTSB: Output String Byte to Port

Category: Data-transfer instructions

Flags affected: None

Coding example:

    OUTSB

Description: OUTSB sends a byte from the address specified by DS:[SI] to the hardware I/O port address specified in DX. After the transfer, DI changes in an increment or decrement of 1, depending on the setting of the direction flag.

OUTSD: Output String Doubleword to Port

Category: Data-transfer instructions

Flags affected: None

Coding example:

    OUTSD

Description: OUTSD sends a word from the address specified by DS:[ESI] to the hardware I/O port address specified in DX. After the transfer, DI changes in increments or decrements of 4, depending on the setting of the direction flag.

OUTSW: Output String Word to Port

Category: Data-transfer instructions

Flags affected: None

Coding example:

    OUTSW

Description: OUTSW sends a word from the address specified by DS:[SI] to the hardware I/O port address specified in DX. After the transfer, DI changes in increments or decrements of 2, depending on the setting of the direction flag.

POP: Remove Data from Stack

Category: Data-transfer instructions

Flags affected: None

Coding examples:

```
POP     AX
POP     DS
POP     GS
POP     HOLD_REG
```

Description: POP removes a word or a doubleword (depending on the size of the operand) from the stack and places that word or doubleword in the desired destination operand.

POPA: Pop All General Registers

Category: Data-transfer instructions

Flags affected: None

Coding example:

```
POPA
```

Description: POPA removes and loads the general-purpose registers from the stack in this order: DI, SI, BP, SP, BX, DX, CX, AX. The SP register is discarded when it is popped.

POPAD: Pop All General Doubleword Registers

Category: Data-transfer instructions

Flags affected: None

Coding example:

```
POPAD
```

Description: POPAD removes and loads the general-purpose registers from the stack in this order: EDI, ESI, EBP, ESP, EBX, EDX, ECX, EAX. The ESP register is discarded when it is popped.

POPF: Remove Flags from Stack

Category: Data-transfer instructions

Flags affected:

11	1Ø	F	E	D	C	B	A	9	8	7	6	5	4	3	2	1	Ø
VM	R		NT	IOPL		OF	DF	IF	TF	SF	ZF		AF		PF		CF
		X	X	X	X	X	X	X	X	X	X	X	X	X	X	X	X

Coding example:

```
POPF
```

Description: POPF removes a word from the stack and places the word in the flags register.

POPFD: Remove Extended Flags from Stack

Category: Data-transfer instructions

Flags affected:

11	1Ø	F	E	D	C	B	A	9	8	7	6	5	4	3	2	1	Ø
VM	R		NT	IOPL		OF	DF	IF	TF	SF	ZF		AF		PF		CF
X	X	X	X	X	X	X	X	X	X	X	X	X	X	X	X	X	X

Coding example:

```
POPFD
```

Description: POPFD removes a doubleword from the stack and places that doubleword in the extended flags register.

PUSH: Place Data on Stack

Category: Data-transfer instructions

Flags affected: None

Coding examples:

```
PUSH     AX
PUSH     EBX
PUSH     DS
PUSH     HOLD_REG
```

Description: PUSH places a copy of the value of the operand on the stack.

PUSHA: Push All General Registers

Category: Data-transfer instructions

Flags affected: None

Coding example:

```
PUSHA
```

Description: This instruction pushes the general-purpose registers on the stack in this order: AX, CX, DX, BX, SP, BP, SI, DI. The SP value pushed is the value existing before this instruction is executed.

PUSHAD: Push All General Doubleword Registers

Category: Data-transfer instructions

Flags affected: None

Coding example:

```
PUSHAD
```

Description: This instruction pushes the general-purpose doubleword registers on the stack in this order: EAX, ECX, EDX, EBX, ESP, EBP, ESI, EDI. The ESP value pushed is the value existing before this instruction is executed.

PUSHF: Place Flags on Stack

Category: Data-transfer instructions

Flags affected: None

Coding example:

```
PUSHF
```

Description: PUSHF places a copy of the flags register on the stack.

PUSHFD: Place Extended Flags on Stack

Category: Data-transfer instructions

Flags affected: None

Coding example:

```
PUSHFD
```

Description: PUSHFD places a copy of the extended flags register on the stack.

RCL: Rotate Left through Carry

Category: Bit-manipulation instructions

Flags affected:

11	10	F	E	D	C	B	A	9	8	7	6	5	4	3	2	1	0
VM	R		NT	IOPL		OF	DF	IF	TF	SF	ZF		AF		PF		CF
						X											X

Coding examples:

```
RCL        AX,1
RCL        BL,3
RCL        EDX,16
RCL        TEMP,CL
```

Description: RCL rotates all bits in the destination operand to the left by the number of places specified in the source operand. The rotation is done through the carry flag in an order that rotates the most significant bit of the destination operand to the carry flag, and the carry flag to the least significant bit of the destination operand.

RCR: Rotate Right through Carry

Category: Bit-manipulation instructions

Flags affected:

11	10	F	E	D	C	B	A	9	8	7	6	5	4	3	2	1	0
VM	R		NT	IOPL		OF	DF	IF	TF	SF	ZF		AF		PF		CF
						X											X

Coding examples:

```
RCR       AX,1
RCR       BL,3
RCR       EDX,16
RCR       TEMP,CL
```

Description: RCR rotates all bits in the destination operand to the right by the number of places specified in the source operand. The rotation is done through the carry flag in an order that rotates the least significant bit of the destination operand to the carry flag, and the carry flag to the most significant bit of the destination operand.

REP: Repeat

Category: String-manipulation instructions

Flags affected: None

Coding example:

```
REP MOVSB
```

Description: REP causes string-manipulation instructions to be repeated the number of iterations specified in CX (if working with byte or word operands) or ECX (if working with doubleword operands).

REPE: Repeat if Equal

Category: String-manipulation instructions

Flags affected: None

Coding example:

```
REPE CMPSW
```

Description: REPE causes string-manipulation instructions to be repeated the number of iterations specified in CX (if working with byte or word operands) or ECX (if working with doubleword operands). When used with CMPSB, CMPSW, SCASB, or SCASW, this instruction repeats only while the zero flag is set. This instruction is functionally equivalent to REPZ.

REPNE: Repeat if Not Equal

Category: String-manipulation instructions

Flags affected: None

Coding example:

```
REPNE CMPSW
```

Description: REPNE causes string-manipulation instructions to be repeated the number of iterations specified in CX (if working with byte or word operands) or ECX (if working with doubleword operands). When used with CMPSB, CMPSW, SCASB, or SCASW, this instruction repeats only while the zero flag is clear. This instruction is functionally equivalent to REPNZ.

REPNZ: Repeat if Not Zero

Category: String-manipulation instructions

Flags affected: None

Coding example:

```
REPNZ CMPSW
```

Description: REPNZ causes string-manipulation instructions to be repeated the number of iterations specified in CX (if working with byte or word operands) or ECX (if working with doubleword operands). When used with CMPSB, CMPSW, SCASB, or SCASW, this instruction repeats only while the zero flag is clear. This instruction is functionally equivalent to REPNE.

REPZ: Repeat if Zero

Category: String-manipulation instructions

Flags affected: None

Coding example:

```
REPZ CMPSW
```

Description: REPZ causes string-manipulation instructions to be repeated the number of iterations specified in CX (if working with byte or word operands) or ECX (if working with doubleword operands). When used with CMPSB, CMPSW, SCASB, or SCASW, this instruction repeats only while the zero flag is set. This instruction is functionally equivalent to REPE.

RET: Return from Subroutine

Category: Control-transfer instructions

Flags affected: None

Coding examples:

```
RET
RET        2
```

Description: By popping IP from the stack, RET transfers program control back to the point at which a CALL was issued. If the CALL was to a FAR procedure, both CS:IP are popped from the stack.

If the RET has a specified return value (2, in the coding example), the stack is adjusted by that many bytes. In the coding example, a word is discarded from the stack after either IP or CS:IP is popped.

ROL: Rotate Left

Category: Bit-manipulation instructions

Flags affected:

11	1Ø	F	E	D	C	B	A	9	8	7	6	5	4	3	2	1	Ø
VM	R			NT	IOPL	OF	DF	IF	TF	SF	ZF		AF		PF		CF
						X											X

Coding examples:

```
ROL        AX,1
ROL        BL,3
ROL        DX,16
ROL        TEMP,CL
```

Description: ROL rotates all bits in the destination operand to the left by the number of places specified in the source operand.

ROR: Rotate Right

Category: Bit-manipulation instructions

Flags affected:

11	10	F	E	D	C	B	A	9	8	7	6	5	4	3	2	1	0
VM	R		NT	IOPL		OF	DF	IF	TF	SF	ZF		AF		PF		CF
						X											X

Coding examples:

```
ROR        AX,1
ROR        BL,3
ROR        DX,16
ROR        TEMP,CL
```

Description: ROR rotates all bits in the destination operand to the right by the number of places specified in the source operand.

SAHF: Store AH into Flag Register

Category: Data-transfer instructions

Flags affected:

11	10	F	E	D	C	B	A	9	8	7	6	5	4	3	2	1	0
VM	R		NT	IOPL		OF	DF	IF	TF	SF	ZF		AF		PF		CF
										X	X	X	X	X	X	X	X

Coding example:

```
SAHF
```

Description: SAHF copies the contents of AH into the low-order byte of the flags register. After execution of this instruction, SF, ZF, AF, PF, and CF are equal to bits 7, 6, 4, 2, and 1 of AH, respectively.

SAL: Arithmetic Shift Left

Category: Bit-manipulation instructions

Flags affected:

11	1Ø	F	E	D	C	B	A	9	8	7	6	5	4	3	2	1	Ø
VM	R		NT	IOPL		OF	DF	IF	TF	SF	ZF		AF		PF		CF
						X				X	X		?		X		X

Coding examples:

```
SAL     AX,1
SAL     BL,3
SAL     DX,16
SAL     TEMP,CL
```

Description: SAL shifts all bits in the destination operand to the left by the number of places specified in the source operand. High-order bits are lost, and low-order bits are cleared.

SAR: Arithmetic Shift Right

Category: Bit-manipulation instructions

Flags affected:

11	1Ø	F	E	D	C	B	A	9	8	7	6	5	4	3	2	1	Ø
VM	R		NT	IOPL		OF	DF	IF	TF	SF	ZF		AF		PF		CF
						X				X	X		?		X		X

Coding examples:

```
SAR     AX,1
SAR     BL,3
SAR     DX,16
SAR     TEMP,CL
```

Description: SAR shifts all bits in the destination operand to the right by the number of places specified in the source operand. Low-order bits are lost, and high-order bits are set equal to the existing high-order bit.

SBB: Subtract with Carry

Category: Arithmetic instructions

Flags affected:

11	10	F	E	D	C	B	A	9	8	7	6	5	4	3	2	1	0
VM	R		NT	IOPL		OF	DF	IF	TF	SF	ZF		AF		PF		CF
						X				X	X		X		X		X

Coding examples:

```
SBB        AX,BX          ;AX=AX-AX-CF
SBB        AX,TEMP        ;AX=AX-TEMP-CF
SBB        SUM,EBX        ;SUM=SUM-EBX-CF
SBB        CL,10          ;CL=CL-10-CF
SBB        AX,TEMP[BX]    ;Indirect address example
```

Description: SBB subtracts the contents of the source operand from (and stores the result in) the destination operand. If the carry flag is set, the result changes in a decrement of 1. In this instruction, the values being added are assumed to be binary.

SCASB: Scan String for Byte

Category: String-manipulation instructions

Flags affected:

11	10	F	E	D	C	B	A	9	8	7	6	5	4	3	2	1	0
VM	R		NT	IOPL		OF	DF	IF	TF	SF	ZF		AF		PF		CF
						X				X	X		X		X		X

Coding examples:

```
SCASB
REPNZ SCASB      ;Repeat a scan loop
```

Description: This instruction subtracts the destination operand string byte (pointed to by DI) from the value of AL. The result is not stored, but the flags are updated. Then the value of DI changes in an increment or decrement of 1, depending on the setting of the direction flag. Usually, this instruction is used with the REPE, REPNE, REPNZ, or REPZ instructions to repeat the scan for a maximum of CX bytes or until a match or difference is found.

SCASD: Scan String for Doubleword

Category: String-manipulation instructions

Flags affected:

11	1Ø	F	E	D	C	B	A	9	8	7	6	5	4	3	2	1	Ø
VM	R		NT	IOPL		OF	DF	IF	TF	SF	ZF		AF		PF		CF
						X				X	X		X		X		X

Coding examples:

```
SCASD
REPNZ SCASD     ;Repeat a scan loop
```

Description: This instruction subtracts the destination operand string word (pointed to by EDI) from the value of EAX. The result is not stored, but the flags are updated. Then the value of EDI changes in increments or decrements of 4, depending on the setting of the direction flag. Usually, this instruction is used with the REPE, REPNE, REPNZ, or REPZ instructions to repeat the scan for a maximum of CX bytes or until a match or difference is found.

SCASW: Scan String for Word

Category: String-manipulation instructions

Flags affected:

11	1Ø	F	E	D	C	B	A	9	8	7	6	5	4	3	2	1	Ø
VM	R		NT	IOPL		OF	DF	IF	TF	SF	ZF		AF		PF		CF
						X				X	X		X		X		X

Coding examples:

```
SCASW
REPNZ SCASW     ;Repeat a scan loop
```

Description: This instruction subtracts the destination operand string word (pointed to by DI) from the value of AX. The result is not stored, but the flags are updated. Then the value of DI changes in increments or decrements of 2, depending on the setting of the direction flag. Usually, this instruction is used with the REPE, REPNE, REPNZ, or REPZ instructions to repeat the scan for a maximum of CX bytes or until a match or difference is found.

SETA: Set Byte if Above

Category: Data-transfer instructions

Flags affected: None

Coding example:

```
SETA    CL
```

Description: SETA stores a 1 in the operand if the carry and zero flags both are clear. If this condition is not met, a 0 is stored in the operand. The operand must be a byte-length register or memory location. This instruction is functionally the same as SETNBE.

SETAE: Set Byte if Above or Equal

Category: Data-transfer instructions

Flags affected: None

Coding example:

```
SETAE   CL
```

Description: SETAE stores a 1 in the operand if the carry flag is clear. If this condition is not met, a 0 is stored in the operand. The operand must be a byte-length register or memory location. This instruction is functionally the same as SETNB or SETNC.

SETB: Set Byte if Below

Category: Data-transfer instructions

Flags affected: None

Coding example:

```
SETB    CL
```

Description: SETB stores a 1 in the operand if the carry flag is set. If this condition is not met, a 0 is stored in the operand. The operand must be a byte-length register or memory location. This instruction is functionally the same as SETC or SETNAE.

SETBE: Set Byte if Below or Equal

Category: Data-transfer instructions

Flags affected: None

Coding example:

```
SETBE   CL
```

Description: SETBE stores a 1 in the operand if either the carry or zero flag is set. If this condition is not met, a 0 is stored in the operand. The operand must be a byte-length register or memory location. This instruction is functionally the same as SETNA.

SETC: Set Byte on Carry

Category: Data-transfer instructions

Flags affected: None

Coding example:

```
SETC    CL
```

Description: SETC stores a 1 in the operand if the carry flag is set. If this condition is not met, a 0 is stored in the operand. The operand must be a byte-length register or memory location. This instruction is functionally the same as SETB or SETNAE.

SETE: Set Byte if Equal

Category: Data-transfer instructions

Flags affected: None

Coding example:

```
SETE    CL
```

Description: SETE stores a 1 in the operand if the zero flag is set. If this condition is not met, a 0 is stored in the operand. The operand must be a byte-length register or memory location. This instruction is functionally the same as SETZ.

SETG: Set Byte if Greater

Category: Data-transfer instructions

Flags affected: None

Coding example:

```
SETG    CL
```

Description: SETG stores a 1 in the operand if the sign flag equals the overflow flag or the zero flag is clear. If neither condition is not met, a 0 is stored in the operand. The operand must be a byte-length register or memory location. This instruction is functionally the same as SETNLE.

SETGE: Set Byte if Greater or Equal

Category: Data-transfer instructions

Flags affected: None

Coding example:

```
SETGE   CL
```

Description: SETGE stores a 1 in the operand if the sign flag equals the overflow flag. If this condition is not met, a 0 is stored in the operand. The operand must be a byte-length register or memory location. This instruction is functionally the same as SETNL.

SETL: Set Byte if Less Than

Category: Data-transfer instructions

Flags affected: None

Coding example:

```
SETL    CL
```

Description: SETL stores a 1 in the operand if the sign flag does not equal the overflow flag. If this condition is not met, a 0 is stored in the operand. The operand must be a byte-length register or memory location. This instruction is functionally the same as SETNGE.

SETLE: Set Byte if Less Than or Equal

Category: Data-transfer instructions

Flags affected: None

Coding example:

```
SETLE   CL
```

Description: SETLE stores a 1 in the operand if the sign flag does not equal the overflow flag or the zero flag is set. If neither condition is not met, a 0 is stored in the operand. The operand must be a byte-length register or memory location. This instruction is functionally the same as SETNG.

SETNA: Set Byte if Not Above

Category: Data-transfer instructions

Flags affected: None

Coding example:

```
SETNA   CL
```

Description: SETNA stores a 1 in the operand if either the carry or zero flag is set. If either condition is not met, a 0 is stored in the operand. The operand must be a byte-length register or memory location. This instruction is functionally the same as SETBE.

SETNAE: Set Byte if Not Above or Equal

Category: Data-transfer instructions

Flags affected: None

Coding example:

```
SETNAE CL
```

Description: SETNAE stores a 1 in the operand if the carry flag is set. If this condition is not met, a 0 is stored in the operand. The operand must be a byte-length register or memory location. This instruction is functionally the same as SETB or SETC.

SETNB: Set Byte if Not Below

Category: Data-transfer instructions

Flags affected: None

Coding example:

```
SETNB  CL
```

Description: SETNB stores a 1 in the operand if the carry flag is clear. If this condition is not met, a 0 is stored in the operand. The operand must be a byte-length register or memory location. This instruction is functionally the same as SETAE or SETNC.

SETNBE: Set Byte if Not Below or Equal

Category: Data-transfer instructions

Flags affected: None

Coding example:

```
SETNBE CL
```

Description: SETNBE stores a 1 in the operand if both the carry and zero flags are clear. If this condition is not met, a 0 is stored in the operand. The operand must be a byte-length register or memory location. This instruction is functionally the same as SETA.

SETNC: Set Byte on No Carry

Category: Data-transfer instructions

Flags affected: None

Coding example:

```
SETNC  CL
```

Description: SETNC stores a 1 in the operand if the carry flag is clear. If this condition is not met, a 0 is stored in the operand. The operand must be a byte-length register or memory location. This instruction is functionally the same as SETAE or SETNB.

SETNE: Set Byte if Not Equal

Category: Data-transfer instructions

Flags affected: None

Coding example:

```
SETNE  CL
```

Description: SETNE stores a 1 in the operand if the zero flag is clear. If this condition is not met, a 0 is stored in the operand. The operand must be a byte-length register or memory location. This instruction is functionally the same as SETNZ.

SETNG: Set Byte if Not Greater Than

Category: Data-transfer instructions

Flags affected: None

Coding example:

```
SETNG   CL
```

Description: SETNG stores a 1 in the operand if the sign flag does not equal the overflow flag or the zero flag is set. If either condition is not met, a 0 is stored in the operand. The operand must be a byte-length register or memory location. This instruction is functionally the same as SETLE.

SETNGE: Set Byte if Not Greater Than or Equal

Category: Data-transfer instructions

Flags affected: None

Coding example:

```
SETNGE CL
```

Description: SETNGE stores a 1 in the operand if the sign flag does not equal the overflow flag. If this condition is not met, a 0 is stored in the operand. The operand must be a byte-length register or memory location. This instruction is functionally the same as SETL.

SETNL: Set Byte if Not Less Than

Category: Data-transfer instructions

Flags affected: None

Coding example:

```
SETNL   CL
```

Description: SETNL stores a 1 in the operand if the sign flag equals the overflow flag. If this condition is not met, a 0 is stored in the operand. The operand must be a byte-length register or memory location. This instruction is functionally the same as SETGE.

SETNLE: Set Byte if Not Less Than or Equal

Category: Data-transfer instructions

Flags affected: None

Coding example:

```
SETNLE CL
```

Description: SETNLE stores a 1 in the operand if the sign flag equals the overflow flag or the zero flag is clear. If either condition is not met, a 0 is stored in the operand. The operand must be a byte-length register or memory location. This instruction is functionally the same as SETG.

SETNO: Set Byte on No Overflow

Category: Data-transfer instructions

Flags affected: None

Coding example:

```
SETNO  CL
```

Description: SETNO stores a 1 in the operand if the overflow flag is clear. If this condition is not met, a 0 is stored in the operand. The operand must be a byte-length register or memory location.

SETNP: Set Byte on No Parity

Category: Data-transfer instructions

Flags affected: None

Coding example:

```
SETNP  CL
```

Description: SETNP stores a 1 in the operand if the parity flag is clear. If this condition is not met, a 0 is stored in the operand. The operand must be a byte-length register or memory location. This instruction is functionally the same as SETPO.

SETNS: Set Byte on Not Sign

Category: Data-transfer instructions

Flags affected: None

Coding example:

```
SETNS   CL
```

Description: SETNS stores a 1 in the operand if the sign flag is clear. If this condition is not met, a 0 is stored in the operand. The operand must be a byte-length register or memory location.

SETNZ: Set Byte if Not Zero

Category: Data-transfer instructions

Flags affected: None

Coding example:

```
SETNZ   CL
```

Description: SETNZ stores a 1 in the operand if the zero flag is clear. If this condition is not met, a 0 is stored in the operand. The operand must be a byte-length register or memory location. This instruction is functionally the same as SETNE.

SETO: Set Byte on Overflow

Category: Data-transfer instructions

Flags affected: None

Coding example:

```
SETO    CL
```

Description: SETO stores a 1 in the operand if the overflow flag is set. If this condition is not met, a 0 is stored in the operand. The operand must be a byte-length register or memory location.

SETP: Set Byte on Parity

Category: Data-transfer instructions

Flags affected: None

Coding example:

```
SETP      CL
```

Description: SETP stores a 1 in the operand if the parity flag is set. If this condition is not met, a 0 is stored in the operand. The operand must be a byte-length register or memory location. This instruction is functionally the same as SETPE.

SETPE: Set Byte on Parity Even

Category: Data-transfer instructions

Flags affected: None

Coding example:

```
SETPE     CL
```

Description: SETPE stores a 1 in the operand if the parity flag is set. If this condition is not met, a 0 is stored in the operand. The operand must be a byte-length register or memory location. This instruction is functionally the same as SETP.

SETPO: Set Byte on Parity Odd

Category: Data-transfer instructions

Flags affected: None

Coding example:

```
SETPO     CL
```

Description: SETPO stores a 1 in the operand if the parity flag is clear. If this condition is not met, a 0 is stored in the operand. The operand must be a byte-length register or memory location. This instruction is functionally the same as SETNP.

SETS: Set Byte on Sign

Category: Data-transfer instructions

Flags affected: None

Coding example:

```
SETS      CL
```

Description: SETS stores a 1 in the operand if the sign flag is set. If this condition is not met, a 0 is stored in the operand. The operand must be a byte-length register or memory location.

SETZ: Set Byte if Zero

Category: Data-transfer instructions

Flags affected: None

Coding example:

```
SETZ        CL
```

Description: SETZ stores a 1 in the operand if the zero flag is set. If this condition is not met, a 0 is stored in the operand. The operand must be a byte-length register or memory location. This instruction is functionally the same as SETE.

SGDT: Store Global Descriptor Table Register

Category: Data-transfer instructions

Flags affected: None

Coding example:

```
SGDT        TEMP[BX]
```

Description: SGDT transfers the six bytes of the global descriptor table to the memory address specified in the operand. This instruction is for use in protected-mode operating system software and is not used in applications software.

SHL: Shift Left

Category: Bit-manipulation instructions

Flags affected:

11	1Ø	F	E	D	C	B	A	9	8	7	6	5	4	3	2	1	Ø
VM	R		NT	IOPL		OF	DF	IF	TF	SF	ZF		AF		PF		CF
						X				X	X		?		X		X

Coding examples:

```
SHL      AX,1
SHL      BL,3
SHL      DX,16
SHL      TEMP,CL
```

Description: SHL shifts all bits in the destination operand to the left by the number of places specified in the source operand. High-order bits are lost, and low-order bits are cleared.

SHLD: Shift Left, Double Precision

Category: Bit-manipulation instructions

Flags affected:

11	10	F	E	D	C	B	A	9	8	7	6	5	4	3	2	1	0
VM	R		NT	IOPL		OF	DF	IF	TF	SF	ZF		AF		PF		CF
						?				X	X		?		X		X

Coding examples:

```
SHLD     AX,BX,4
SHLD     DWORD_TEMP,EAX,16
```

Description: SHLD shifts all bits in the first operand to the left by the number of places specified in the third operand. High-order bits are lost, and low-order bits are copied from the second operand, starting with the second operand's low-order bit. The result is stored in the first operand.

SHR: Shift Right

Category: Bit-manipulation instructions

Flags affected:

11	10	F	E	D	C	B	A	9	8	7	6	5	4	3	2	1	0
VM	R		NT	IOPL		OF	DF	IF	TF	SF	ZF		AF		PF		CF
						X				X	X		?		X		X

Coding examples:

```
SHR     AX,1
SHR     BL,3
SHR     DX,16
SHR     TEMP,CL
```

Description: SHR shifts all bits in the destination operand right by the number of places specified in the source operand. Low-order bits are lost, and high-order bits are cleared.

SHRD: Shift Right, Double Precision

Category: Bit-manipulation instructions

Flags affected:

11	1Ø	F	E	D	C	B	A	9	8	7	6	5	4	3	2	1	Ø
VM	R			NT	IOPL	OF	DF	IF	TF	SF	ZF		AF		PF		CF
						?				X	X		?		X		X

Coding examples:

```
SHRD    AX,BX,4
SHRD    DWORD_TEMP,EAX,16
```

Description: SHRD shifts all bits in the first operand to the right by the number of places specified in the third operand. Low-order bits are lost, and high-order bits are copied from the second operand, starting with the second operand's high-order bit. The result is stored in the first operand.

SIDT: Store Interrupt Descriptor Table Register

Category: Data-transfer instructions

Flags affected: None

Coding example:

```
SIDT    TEMP[BX]
```

Description: SIDT transfers the six bytes of the interrupt descriptor table to the memory address specified in the operand. This instruction is for use in protected-mode operating system software and is not used in applications software.

SLDT: Store Local Descriptor Table Register

Category: Data-transfer instructions

Flags affected: None

Coding examples:

```
SLDT        AX
SLDT        LDT_TEMP
```

Description: SLDT copies the contents of the local descriptor table to the two bytes of the operand. This instruction is for use in protected-mode operating system software and is not used in applications software.

SMSW: Store Machine Status Word

Category: Data-transfer instructions

Flags affected: None

Coding examples:

```
SMSW        AX
SMSW        MSW_TEMP
```

Description: SMSW copies the value of machine status word to the operand. This instruction is for use in operating system software only and is not used in applications software.

STC: Set Carry Flag

Category: Flag- and processor-control instructions

Flags affected:

11	1Ø	F	E	D	C	B	A	9	8	7	6	5	4	3	2	1	Ø
VM	R		NT	IOPL		OF	DF	IF	TF	SF	ZF		AF		PF		CF
																	X

Coding example:

    STC

Description: STC sets the carry flag, regardless of its present condition.

STD: Set Direction Flag

Category: Flag- and processor-control instructions

Flags affected:

11	1Ø	F	E	D	C	B	A	9	8	7	6	5	4	3	2	1	Ø
VM	R		NT	IOPL		OF	DF	IF	TF	SF	ZF		AF		PF		CF
							X										

Coding example:

    STD

Description: STD sets the direction flag, regardless of its present condition. The setting of this flag has an effect on the string instructions.

STI: Set Interrupt Flag

Category: Flag- and processor-control instructions

Flags affected:

11	1Ø	F	E	D	C	B	A	9	8	7	6	5	4	3	2	1	Ø
VM	R		NT	IOPL		OF	DF	IF	TF	SF	ZF		AF		PF		CF
								X									

Coding example:

    STI

Description: STI sets the interrupt flag, regardless of its present condition. While this flag is set, the 80386 CPU responds to maskable interrupts.

STOSB: Store Byte in AL at String

Category: String-manipulation instructions

Flags affected: None

Coding example:

```
STOSB
```

Description: This instruction copies the contents of AL to the byte address pointed to by DI. DI then changes in an increment or decrement of 1, depending on the setting of the direction flag.

STOSD: Store Doubleword in EAX at String

Category: String-manipulation instructions

Flags affected: None

Coding example:

```
STOSD
```

Description: This instruction copies the contents of EAX to the word address pointed to by EDI. DI then changes in increments or decrements of 4, depending on the setting of the direction flag.

STOSW: Store Word in AX at String

Category: String-manipulation instructions

Flags affected: None

Coding example:

```
STOSW
```

Description: This instruction copies the contents of AX to the word address pointed to by DI. DI then changes in increments or decrements of 2, depending on the setting of the direction flag.

STR: Store Task Register

Category: Data-transfer instructions

Flags affected: None

Coding examples:

```
STR        AX
STR        MSW_TEMP
```

Description: STR copies the value of the task register to the operand. This instruction is for use in operating system software only and is not used in applications software.

SUB: Subtract

Category: Arithmetic instructions

Flags affected:

11	1Ø	F	E	D	C	B	A	9	8	7	6	5	4	3	2	1	Ø
VM	R		NT	IOPL		OF	DF	IF	TF	SF	ZF		AF		PF		CF
						X				X	X		X		X		X

Coding examples:

```
SUB        AX,BX            ;AX=AX-AX
SUB        AX,TEMP          ;AX=AX-TEMP
SUB        SUM,EBX          ;SUM=SUM-EBX
SUB        CL,1Ø            ;CL=CL-1Ø
SUB        AX,TEMP[BX]      ;Indirect address example
```

Description: SUB subtracts the contents of the source operand from (and stores the result in) the destination operand. In this instruction, the values being added are assumed to be binary.

TEST: Test Bits

Category: Bit-manipulation instructions

Flags affected:

11	1Ø	F	E	D	C	B	A	9	8	7	6	5	4	3	2	1	Ø
VM	R		NT	IOPL		OF	DF	IF	TF	SF	ZF		AF		PF		CF
						X				X	X		?		X		X

Coding examples:

```
TEST        AX,BX          ;
TEST        AX,TEMP        ;TEMP must be a word
TEST        SUM,EBX        ;SUM must be a doubleword
TEST        CL,ØØØØ1111b    ;
TEST        AX,TEMP[BX]    ;Indirect address example
```

Description: TEST performs a logical AND of the operands, but the result is not stored. Only the flags are affected. Each bit of the resultant byte or word is set to 1, only if the corresponding bit of each operand is set to 1.

VERR: Verify a Segment for Reading

Category: Flag- and processor-control instructions

Flags affected:

11	1Ø	F	E	D	C	B	A	9	8	7	6	5	4	3	2	1	Ø
VM	R		NT	IOPL		OF	DF	IF	TF	SF	ZF		AF		PF		CF
											X						

Coding examples:

```
VERR        TEMP
VERR        AX
```

Description: VERR determines whether the selector specified in the operand is visible at the current privilege level and is readable. The zero flag is set if the selector is accessible.

VERW: Verify a Segment for Writing

Category: Flag- and processor-control instructions

Flags affected:

11	1Ø	F	E	D	C	B	A	9	8	7	6	5	4	3	2	1	Ø
VM	R		NT	IOPL		OF	DF	IF	TF	SF	ZF		AF		PF		CF
											X						

Coding examples:

```
VERW    TEMP
VERW    AX
```

Description: VERW determines whether the selector specified in the operand is visible at the current privilege level and is writable. The zero flag is set if the selector is accessible.

WAIT: Wait

Category: Flag- and processor-control instructions

Flags affected: None

Coding example:

```
WAIT
```

Description: WAIT causes the 80386 CPU to wait for an external interrupt on the TEST line before continuing.

XCHG: Exchange

Category: Data-transfer instructions

Flags affected: None

Coding examples:

```
XCHG    AX,BX               ;Swap AX with BX
XCHG    EAX,DWORD_TEMP      ;Swap EAX with DWORD_TEMP
XCHG    CL,CH               ;Swap CL with CH
XCHG    AX,TEMP             ;Swap AX with TEMP
```

Description: SCHG swaps the contents of the source and destination operands. The length of both operands must agree.

XLAT: Translate

Category: Data-transfer instructions

Flags affected: None

Coding example:

```
XLAT
```

Description: Assuming that the offset address of a 256-byte translation table is contained in BX, this instruction uses the value in AL as a zero-based offset into the table, and subsequently loads AL with the byte value at that calculated offset. This instruction is helpful for translation tables.

XOR: Logical Exclusive-Or on Bits

Category: Bit-manipulation instructions

Flags affected:

11	1∅	F	E	D	C	B	A	9	8	7	6	5	4	3	2	1	∅
VM	R		NT	IOPL		OF	DF	IF	TF	SF	ZF		AF		PF		CF
						X				X	X		?		X		X

Coding examples:

```
XOR        AX,BX            ;
XOR        EAX,TEMP         ;TEMP must be a doubleword
XOR        SUM,BX           ;SUM must be a word
XOR        CL,∅∅∅∅1111b     ;
XOR        AX,TEMP[BX]      ;Indirect address example
```

Description: XOR performs a logical XOR of the operands and stores the result in the destination operand. Each bit of the resultant byte or word is set to 1, only if the corresponding bits of each operand contain opposite values.

Instruction Set
for the Intel 8087

Intel calls the 8087 a "numeric processor extension," because, to all intents and purposes, the 8087 appears transparent to programmers. The instruction and register sets of the 8086/8088 simply seem to be expanded.

No special assembler directives are needed to use the 8087 mnemonic instructions with the Microsoft Macro Assembler. The assembler's default instruction set allows proper translation of the 8086/8088 and 8087 source code. You may, however, want to study Chapter 6 to learn about assembler options. Pay particular attention to the /R option.

This section does not explain all the intricacies of using the 8087 properly or efficiently. The section is designed as a quick reference for programmers who want to use the 8087 instruction extensions. For a more in-depth look at the 8087, several books available on the market may be of interest.

Before you begin looking at the register and instruction sets of the 8087, you must realize that the 8087 works on the principle of a floating stack (similar to that of the 8086/8088) in which virtually all operations are performed.

The 8087 Registers

The 8087 uses eight internal stack registers, each of which is 80 bits wide. These stack registers are numbered 0 through 7, with most operations able to address these registers directly as ST, ST(1), ST(2), ST(3), and so on, through ST(7).

The 8087 Status Word

The 8087 uses a status word to describe the current condition of the 8087. Table 8087.1 depicts this 16-bit word.

Table 8087.1
Usage of the 8087 Status Word

Bit(s)	Code	Use
0	IE	Invalid operation exception
1	DE	Denormalized operand exception
2	ZE	Zerodivide exception
3	OE	Overflow exception
4	UE	Underflow exception
5	PE	Precision exception
6		
7	IR	Interrupt request
8	C0	Condition code 0
9	C1	Condition code 1
10	C2	Condition code 2
11 – 13	ST	Stack-top pointer
14	C3	Condition code 3
15	B	Busy signal

This status word cannot be examined directly. It must be transferred by specific 8087 instructions to memory, where it can be analyzed by 8086/8088 instructions.

The 8087 Control Word

The 8087 uses a control word for program control of the 8087 operations. This 16-bit word is detailed in table 8087.2.

Table 8087.2
Usage of the 8087 Control Word

Bit(s)	Code	Use
0	IM	Invalid operation exception mask
1	DM	Denormalized operand exception mask
2	ZM	Zerodivide exception mask
3	OM	Overflow exception mask
4	UM	Underflow exception mask
5	PM	Precision exception mask
6		Reserved
7	IEM	Interrupt enable mask
		0 = Interrupts enabled
		1 = Interrupts disabled

Table 8087.2—cont.

Bit(s)	Code	Use
8 – 9	PC	Precision control
		00 = 24 bits
		01 = (Reserved)
		10 = 53 bits
		11 = 64 bits
10 – 11	RC	Rounding control
		00 = Round to nearest or even
		01 = Round down
		10 = Round up
		11 = Truncate
12	IC	Infinity control
		0 = Projective
		1 = Affine
13 – 15		Reserved

This word can be constructed in the main memory and then directed to the 8087 by specific 8087 instructions.

Instruction Set Groupings

The 8087 extends, by 77 instructions, the instruction set of the 8086/8088. This section details only those 77 new instructions, which are grouped according to the purpose of the instruction. The six general classifications of instructions are

Data transfer
Arithmetic
Comparisons
Transcendental
Constant
Processor control

Table 8087.3 shows the individual instructions that make up these categories.

Table 8087.3
Instruction Set Groupings for the 8087

Instruction	Meaning
Data Transfer	
FBLD	BCD load
FBSTP	BCD store and pop
FILD	Integer load
FIST	Integer store
FISTP	Integer store and pop
FLD	Load real
FST	Store real
FSTP	Store real and pop
FXCH	Exchange registers
Arithmetic	
FABS	Absolute value
FADD	Add real
FADDP	Add real and pop
FCHS	Change sign
FDIV	Divide real
FDIVP	Divide real and pop
FDIVR	Divide real reversed
FDIVRP	Divide real reversed and pop
FIADD	Integer add
FIDIV	Integer divide
FIDIVR	Integer divide reversed
FIMUL	Integer multiply
FISUB	Integer subtract
FISUBR	Integer subtract reversed
FMUL	Multiply real
FMULP	Multiply real and pop
FPREM	Partial remainder
FRNDINT	Round to integer
FSCALE	Scale
FSQRT	Square root
FSUB	Subtract real
FSUBP	Subtract real and pop
FSUBR	Subtract real reversed
FSUBRP	Subtract real reversed and pop
FXTRACT	Extract exponent and significand

Table 8087.3—cont.

Instruction	Meaning
Comparisons	
FCOM	Compare real
FCOMP	Compare real and pop
FCOMPP	Compare real and pop twice
FICOM	Integer compare
FICOMP	Integer compare and pop
FTST	Test
FXAM	Examine
Transcendental	
F2XM1	$2^x - 1$
FPATAN	Partial arctangent
FPTAN	Partial tangent
FYL2X	$Y*\log_2 X$
FYL2XP1	$Y*\log_2(X+1)$
Constant	
FLD1	Load 1.0
FLDL2E	Load $\log_2 e$
FLDL2T	Load $\log_2 10$
FLDLG2	Load $\log_{10} 2$
FLDLN2	Load $\log_e 2$
FLDPI	Load pi
FLDZ	Load 0.0
Processor Control	
FCLEX	Clear exceptions with WAIT
FDECSTP	Decrement stack pointer
FDISI	Disable interrupts with WAIT
FENI	Enable interrupts with WAIT
FFREE	Free register
FINCSTP	Increment stack pointer
FINIT	Initialize processor with WAIT
FLDCW	Load control word
FLDENV	Load environment
FNCLEX	Clear exceptions
FNDISI	Disable interrupts
FNENI	Enable interrupts
FNINIT	Initialize processor

Table 8087.3—cont.

Instruction	Meaning
FNOP	No operation
FNSAVE	Save state
FNSTCW	Store control word
FNSTENV	Store environment
FNSTSW	Store status word
FRSTOR	Restore state
FSAVE	Save state with WAIT
FSTCW	Store control word with WAIT
FSTENV	Store environment with WAIT
FSTSW	Store status word with WAIT
FWAIT	CPU wait

Detailed Instruction Information

The balance of this section is designed as a reference to the 8087 instruction set. Each instruction is described in detail and in an organized manner. The following information is listed for each instruction:

- *Instruction name.* This name is based upon the standard mnemonic code designed by Intel.

- *Instruction category.* The general classification for the instruction

- *Status affected.* The majority of the instructions change the status word in one way or another. The individual bits affected in the status word are listed in the following format:

F	E	D	C	B	A	9	8	7	6	5	4	3	2	1	Ø
B	C3	--	ST	--	C2	C1	CØ	IR		PE	UE	OE	ZE	DE	IE
										X	X	X		X	X

In this format, an X indicates that the bit is changed.

- *Coding examples.* A line or two to show how the instruction is used

- *Description.* A narrative description of the instruction

The instructions are arranged in ascending alphabetical order.

F2XM1: 2^x-1

Category: Transcendental instruction

Status affected:

F	E	D	C	B	A	9	8	7	6	5	4	3	2	1	Ø
B	C3	--	ST	--		C2	C1	CØ	IR		PE	UE	OE	ZE	DE	IE
											X	X				

Coding example:

    F2XM1

Description: Calculates $Y=2^x$-1, where X is the top stack element (ST). The result (Y) replaces X as the top stack element (ST). This instruction performs no validation checking of the input value. The program ensures that $0<=X<=0.5$.

FABS: Absolute Value

Category: Arithmetic instruction

Status affected:

F	E	D	C	B	A	9	8	7	6	5	4	3	2	1	Ø
B	C3	--	ST	--		C2	C1	CØ	IR		PE	UE	OE	ZE	DE	IE
																X

Coding example:

    FABS

Description: Changes the top stack element (ST) to its absolute value

FADD: Add Real

Category: Arithmetic instruction

Status affected:

F	E	D	C	B	A	9	8	7	6	5	4	3	2	1	Ø
B	C3	--	ST	--		C2	C1	CØ	IR		PE	UE	OE	ZE	DE	IE
										X	X	X		X	X

Coding examples:

```
FADD        TEMP            ; ST=ST+TEMP
FADD        TEMP,ST(3)      ; TEMP=TEMP+ST(3)
```

Description: Adds two numbers together and stores them at the destination operand. If no destination operand is given (only one operand is specified), ST is assumed to be the destination.

FADDP: Add Real and Pop

Category: Arithmetic instruction

Status affected:

F	E	D	C	B	A	9	8	7	6	5	4	3	2	1	Ø
B	C3	--	ST	--		C2	C1	CØ	IR		PE	UE	OE	ZE	DE	IE
										X	X	X		X	X

Coding examples:

```
FADDP       TEMP            ; ST=ST+TEMP
FADDP       TEMP,ST(3)      ; TEMP=TEMP+ST(3)
```

Description: Adds two numbers together, stores them at the destination operand, and pops the stack. If no destination operand is given (only one operand is specified), ST is assumed to be the destination.

FBLD: BCD Load

Category: Data-transfer instruction

Status affected:

F	E	D	C	B	A	9	8	7	6	5	4	3	2	1	Ø
B	C3	--	ST	--		C2	C1	CØ	IR		PE	UE	OE	ZE	DE	IE
																X

Coding example:

```
FBLD       TEMP
```

Description: Converts the BCD number at the operand address to a temporary real and pushes on the stack

FBSTP: BCD Store and Pop

Category: Data-transfer instruction

Status affected:

F	E	D	C	B	A	9	8	7	6	5	4	3	2	1	Ø
B	C3	--	ST	--		C2	C1	CØ	IR		PE	UE	OE	ZE	DE	IE
																X

Coding example:

```
FBSTP      TEMP
```

Description: Converts the top stack element (ST) to a BCD integer, stores it at the operand address, and pops the stack

FCHS: Change Sign

Category: Arithmetic instruction

Status affected:

F	E	D	C	B	A	9	8	7	6	5	4	3	2	1	Ø
B	C3	--	ST	--		C2	C1	CØ	IR		PE	UE	OE	ZE	DE	IE
																X

Coding example:

```
FCHS
```

Description: Changes the sign of the top stack element (ST)

FCLEX: Clear Exceptions with WAIT

Category: Processor-control instruction

Status affected:

F	E	D	C	B	A	9	8	7	6	5	4	3	2	1	Ø
B	C3	--	ST	--		C2	C1	CØ	IR		PE	UE	OE	ZE	DE	IE
X								X		X	X	X	X	X	X

Coding example:

```
FCLEX
```

Description: Clears the exception flags, interrupt request, and busy flags of the 8087 status word. This instruction is preceded by a CPU wait prefix. See also FNCLEX.

FCOM: Compare Real

Category: Comparison instruction

Status affected:

F	E	D	C	B	A	9	8	7	6	5	4	3	2	1	Ø
B	C3	--	ST	--		C2	C1	CØ	IR		PE	UE	OE	ZE	DE	IE
	X				X		X							X	X

Coding examples:

```
FCOM                 ;Compare ST to ST(1)
FCOM        ST(4)    ;Compare ST to ST(4)
FCOM        TEMP     ;Compare ST to memory
```

Description: The top stack element (ST) is compared to either the second stack element (ST(1)) or another specified operand. Condition codes are affected accordingly.

FCOMP: Compare Real and Pop

Category: Comparison instruction

Status affected:

F	E	D	C	B	A	9	8	7	6	5	4	3	2	1	Ø
B	C3	--	ST	--		C2	C1	CØ	IR		PE	UE	OE	ZE	DE	IE
	X				X		X								X	X

Coding examples:

```
FCOMP                   ;Compare ST to ST(1)
FCOMP       ST(4)       ;Compare ST to ST(4)
FCOMP       TEMP        ;Compare ST to memory
```

Description: The top stack element (ST) is compared to either the second stack element (ST(1)) or another specified operand; the stack then is popped. Condition codes are affected accordingly.

FCOMPP: Compare Real and Pop Twice

Category: Comparison instruction

Status affected:

F	E	D	C	B	A	9	8	7	6	5	4	3	2	1	Ø
B	C3	--	ST	--		C2	C1	CØ	IR		PE	UE	OE	ZE	DE	IE
	X				X		X								X	X

Coding example:

```
FCOMPP      ;Compare ST to ST(1)
```

Description: The top stack element (ST) is compared to the second stack element (ST(1)) and the stack is popped twice. Condition codes are affected accordingly.

FDECSTP: Decrement Stack Pointer

Category: Processor-control instruction

Status affected:

F	E	D	C	B	A	9	8	7	6	5	4	3	2	1	Ø
B	C3	--	ST	--		C2	C1	CØ	IR		PE	UE	OE	ZE	DE	IE
		X	X	X												

Coding example:

```
FDECSTP
```

Description: Decrements the stack pointer of the 8087 status word

FDISI: Disable Interrupts with WAIT

Category: Processor-control instruction

Status affected: None

Coding example:

```
FDISI
```

Description: Sets the interrupt enable mask of the 8087 control word, thus preventing the 8087 from initiating an interrupt. This instruction is preceded by a CPU wait prefix. See also FNDISI.

FDIV: Divide Real

Category: Arithmetic instruction

Status affected:

F	E	D	C	B	A	9	8	7	6	5	4	3	2	1	Ø
B	C3	--	ST	--		C2	C1	CØ	IR		PE	UE	OE	ZE	DE	IE
											X	X	X	X	X	X

Coding examples:

```
FDIV      TEMP              ;ST=TEMP/ST
FDIV      TEMP,ST(3)        ;TEMP=ST(3)/TEMP
```

Description: Divides the destination by the source operand, and stores the result at the destination operand. If no destination operand is given (only one operand is specified), ST is assumed to be the destination.

FDIVP: Divide Real and Pop

Category: Arithmetic instruction

Status affected:

F	E	D	C	B	A	9	8	7	6	5	4	3	2	1	Ø
B	C3	--	ST	--		C2	C1	CØ	IR		PE	UE	OE	ZE	DE	IE
											X	X	X	X	X	X

Coding examples:

```
FDIVP     TEMP              ;ST=TEMP/ST
FDIVP     TEMP,ST(3)        ;TEMP=ST(3)/TEMP
```

Description: Divides the destination by the source operand, stores the result at the destination operand, and pops the stack. If no destination operand is given (only one operand is specified), ST is assumed to be the destination.

FDIVR: Divide Real Reversed

Category: Arithmetic instruction

Status affected:

F	E	D	C	B	A	9	8	7	6	5	4	3	2	1	Ø
B	C3	--	ST	--		C2	C1	CØ	IR		PE	UE	OE	ZE	DE	IE
											X	X	X	X	X	X

Coding examples:

```
FDIVR     TEMP              ;ST=ST/TEMP
FDIVR     TEMP,ST(3)        ;TEMP=TEMP/ST(3)
```

Description: Divides the source by the destination operand, and stores the result at the destination operand. If no destination operand is given (only one operand is specified), ST is assumed to be the destination.

FDIVRP: Divide Real Reversed and Pop

Category: Arithmetic instruction

Status affected:

F	E	D	C	B	A	9	8	7	6	5	4	3	2	1	Ø
B	C3	--	ST	--		C2	C1	CØ	IR		PE	UE	OE	ZE	DE	IE
										X	X	X	X	X	X

Coding examples:

```
FDIVRP      TEMP              ; ST=ST/TEMP
FDIVRP      TEMP,ST(3)        ; TEMP=TEMP/ST(3)
```

Description: Divides the source by the destination operand, stores the result at the destination operand, and pops the stack. If no destination operand is given (only one operand is specified), ST is assumed to be the destination.

FENI: Enable Interrupts with WAIT

Category: Processor-control instruction

Status affected: None

Coding example:

```
FENI
```

Description: Clears the interrupt enable mask of the 8087 control word, thus allowing the 8087 to initiate interrupts. This instruction is preceded by a CPU wait prefix. See also FNENI.

FFREE: Free Register

Category: Processor-control instruction

Status affected: None

Coding example:

```
FFREE      ST(3)
```

Description: Changes the tag for the specified stack register to indicate that the stack register is empty

FIADD: Integer Add

Category: Arithmetic instruction

Status affected:

F	E	D	C	B	A	9	8	7	6	5	4	3	2	1	Ø
B	C3	--	ST	--		C2	C1	CØ	IR		PE	UE	OE	ZE	DE	IE
											X		X		X	X

Coding examples:

```
FIADD      TEMP              ;ST=ST+TEMP
FIADD      TEMP,ST(3)        ;TEMP=TEMP+ST(3)
```

Description: Adds two numbers together as integers and stores them at the destination operand. If no destination operand is given (only one operand is specified), ST is assumed to be the destination.

FICOM: Integer Compare

Category: Comparison instruction

Status affected:

F	E	D	C	B	A	9	8	7	6	5	4	3	2	1	Ø
B	C3	--	ST	--		C2	C1	CØ	IR		PE	UE	OE	ZE	DE	IE
	X			X		X									X	X

Coding example:

```
FICOM      TEMP_INT          ;Compare memory to ST
```

Description: Converts the operand (assumed to be an integer) to a temporary real and compares it to the top stack element (ST). Condition codes are set accordingly.

FICOMP: Integer Compare and Pop

Category: Comparison instruction

Status affected:

F	E	D	C	B	A	9	8	7	6	5	4	3	2	1	Ø
B	C3	--	ST	--		C2	C1	CØ	IR		PE	UE	OE	ZE	DE	IE
	X				X		X								X	X

Coding example:

```
FICOMP     TEMP_INT        ;Compare memory to ST
```

Description: Converts the operand (assumed to be an integer) to a temporary real, compares it to the top stack element (ST), and then pops the stack. Condition codes are set accordingly.

FIDIV: Integer Divide

Category: Arithmetic instruction

Status affected:

F	E	D	C	B	A	9	8	7	6	5	4	3	2	1	Ø
B	C3	--	ST	--		C2	C1	CØ	IR		PE	UE	OE	ZE	DE	IE
											X	X	X	X	X	X

Coding examples:

```
FIDIV      TEMP            ;ST=TEMP/ST
FIDIV      TEMP,ST(3)      ;TEMP=ST(3)/TEMP
```

Description: Divides the destination by the source operand, as integers, and stores the result at the destination operand. If no destination operand is given (only one operand is specified), ST is assumed to be the destination.

FIDIVR: Integer Divide Reversed

Category: Arithmetic instruction

Status affected:

F	E	D	C	B	A	9	8	7	6	5	4	3	2	1	Ø
B	C3	--	ST	--		C2	C1	CØ	IR		PE	UE	OE	ZE	DE	IE
											X	X	X	X	X	X

Coding examples:

```
FIDIVR    TEMP          ;ST=ST/TEMP
FIDIVR    TEMP,ST(3)    ;TEMP=TEMP/ST(3)
```

Description: Divides the destination by the source operand, as integers, and stores the result at the destination operand. If no destination operand is given (only one operand is specified), ST is assumed to be the destination.

FILD: Integer Load

Category: Data-transfer instruction

Status affected:

F	E	D	C	B	A	9	8	7	6	5	4	3	2	1	Ø
B	C3	--	ST	--		C2	C1	CØ	IR		PE	UE	OE	ZE	DE	IE
																X

Coding example:

```
FILD      TEMP
```

Description: Converts the binary integer number at the operand address to a temporary real, and pushes it on the stack.

FIMUL: Integer Multiply

Category: Arithmetic instruction

Status affected:

F	E	D	C	B	A	9	8	7	6	5	4	3	2	1	Ø
B	C3	--	ST	--	C2	C1	CØ	IR		PE	UE	OE	ZE	DE	IE
										X		X		X	X

Coding examples:

```
FIMUL      TEMP              ;ST=ST*TEMP
FIMUL      TEMP,ST(3)        ;TEMP=TEMP*ST(3)
```

Description: Multiplies the source by the destination operand, as integers, and stores the result at the destination operand. If no destination operand is given (only one operand is specified), ST is assumed to be the destination.

FINCSTP: Increment Stack Pointer

Category: Processor-control instruction

Status affected:

F	E	D	C	B	A	9	8	7	6	5	4	3	2	1	Ø
B	C3	--	ST	--	C2	C1	CØ	IR		PE	UE	OE	ZE	DE	IE
		X	X	X											

Coding example:

```
FINCSTP
```

Description: Increments the stack pointer of the 8087 status word

FINIT: Initialize Processor with WAIT

Category: Processor-control instruction

Status affected: None

Coding example:

```
FINIT
```

Description: Initializes the 8087. This action is functionally equivalent to performing a hardware RESET. This instruction is preceded by a CPU wait prefix. See also FNINIT.

FIST: Integer Store

Category: Data-transfer instruction

Status affected:

F	E	D	C	B	A	9	8	7	6	5	4	3	2	1	Ø
B	C3	--	ST	--		C2	C1	CØ	IR		PE	UE	OE	ZE	DE	IE
										X					X

Coding example:

```
FIST        TEMP
```

Description: Rounds the top stack element (ST) to a binary integer number, and stores it at the operand address

FISTP: Integer Store and Pop

Category: Data-transfer instruction

Status affected:

F	E	D	C	B	A	9	8	7	6	5	4	3	2	1	Ø
B	C3	--	ST	--		C2	C1	CØ	IR		PE	UE	OE	ZE	DE	IE
										X					X

Coding example:

```
FIST        TEMP
```

Description: Rounds the top stack element (ST) to a binary integer number, stores it at the operand address, and pops ST from the stack.

FISUB: Integer Subtract

Category: Arithmetic instruction

Status affected:

F	E	D	C	B	A	9	8	7	6	5	4	3	2	1	Ø
B	C3	--	ST	--		C2	C1	CØ	IR		PE	UE	OE	ZE	DE	IE
											X		X		X	X

Coding examples:

```
FISUB      TEMP            ;ST=ST-TEMP
FISUB      TEMP,ST(3)      ;TEMP=TEMP-ST(3)
```

Description: Subtracts the source from the destination operand, as integers, and stores the result at the destination operand. If no destination operand is given (only one operand is specified), ST is assumed to be the destination.

FISUBR: Integer Subtract Reversed

Category: Arithmetic instruction

Status affected:

F	E	D	C	B	A	9	8	7	6	5	4	3	2	1	Ø
B	C3	--	ST	--		C2	C1	CØ	IR		PE	UE	OE	ZE	DE	IE
											X		X		X	X

Coding examples:

```
FISUBR     TEMP            ;ST=TEMP-ST
FISUBR     TEMP,ST(3)      ;TEMP=ST(3)-TEMP
```

Description: Subtracts the destination from the source operand, as integers, and stores the result at the destination operand. If no destination operand is given (only one operand is specified), ST is assumed to be the destination.

FLD: Load Real

Category: Data-transfer instruction

Status affected:

F	E	D	C	B	A	9	8	7	6	5	4	3	2	1	Ø
B	C3	--	ST	--		C2	C1	CØ	IR		PE	UE	OE	ZE	DE	IE
															X	X

Coding examples:

```
FLD     ST(3)
FLD     TEMP
```

Description: Pushes the value of the source operand on the stack

FLD1: Load 1.0

Category: Constant instruction

Status affected:

F	E	D	C	B	A	9	8	7	6	5	4	3	2	1	Ø
B	C3	--	ST	--		C2	C1	CØ	IR		PE	UE	OE	ZE	DE	IE
															X

Coding example:

```
FLD1
```

Description: Pushes the value +1.0 on the stack. This value becomes ST.

FLDCW: Load Control Word

Category: Processor-control instruction

Status affected: None

Coding example:

```
FLDCW     MEM_CW          ;Transfer control word
```

Description: Loads the 8087 control word with the word value pointed to by the source operand

FLDENV: Load Environment

Category: Processor-control instruction

Status affected:

F	E	D	C	B	A	9	8	7	6	5	4	3	2	1	Ø
B	C3	--	ST	--		C2	C1	CØ	IR		PE	UE	OE	ZE	DE	IE
X	X	X	X	X	X	X	X	X	X	X	X	X	X	X	X

Coding example:

```
FLDENV    SAVE_AREA
```

Description: Restores all environment variables of the 8087 from the 14-word memory location specified by the operand

FLDL2E: Load $\log_2 e$

Category: Constant instruction

Status affected:

F	E	D	C	B	A	9	8	7	6	5	4	3	2	1	Ø
B	C3	--	ST	--		C2	C1	CØ	IR		PE	UE	OE	ZE	DE	IE
															X

Coding example:

```
FLDL2E
```

Description: Pushes the value of $\log_2 e$ on the stack. This value becomes ST.

FLDL2T: Load $\log_2 10$

Category: Constant instruction

Status affected:

F	E	D	C	B	A	9	8	7	6	5	4	3	2	1	Ø
B	C3	--	ST	--		C2	C1	CØ	IR		PE	UE	OE	ZE	DE	IE
															X

Coding example:

    FLDL2T

Description: Pushes the value of $LOG_2 10$ on the stack. This value becomes ST.

FLDLG2: Load $\log_{10} 2$

Category: Constant instruction

Status affected:

F	E	D	C	B	A	9	8	7	6	5	4	3	2	1	Ø
B	C3	--	ST	--		C2	C1	CØ	IR		PE	UE	OE	ZE	DE	IE
															X

Coding example:

    FLDLG2

Description: Pushes the value of $LOG_{10} 2$ on the stack. This value becomes ST.

FLDLN2: Load $\log_e 2$

Category: Constant instruction

Status affected:

F	E	D	C	B	A	9	8	7	6	5	4	3	2	1	Ø
B	C3	--	ST	--		C2	C1	CØ	IR		PE	UE	OE	ZE	DE	IE
															X

Coding example:

    FLDLN2

Description: Pushes the value of LOG$_e$2 on the stack. This value becomes ST.

FLDPI: Load Pi

Category: Constant instruction

Status affected:

F	E	D	C	B	A	9	8	7	6	5	4	3	2	1	Ø
B	C3	--	ST	--		C2	C1	CØ	IR		PE	UE	OE	ZE	DE	IE
																X

Coding example:

    FLDPI

Description: Pushes the value of pi on the stack. This value becomes ST.

FLDZ: Load 0.0

Category: Constant instruction

Status affected:

F	E	D	C	B	A	9	8	7	6	5	4	3	2	1	Ø
B	C3	--	ST	--		C2	C1	CØ	IR		PE	UE	OE	ZE	DE	IE
																X

Coding example:

    FLDZ

Description: Pushes the value 0.0 on the stack. This value becomes ST.

FMUL: Multiply Real

Category: Arithmetic instruction

Status affected:

F	E	D	C	B	A	9	8	7	6	5	4	3	2	1	Ø
B	C3	--	ST	--		C2	C1	CØ	IR		PE	UE	OE	ZE	DE	IE
										X	X	X		X	X

Coding examples:

```
FMUL       TEMP              ;ST=ST*TEMP
FMUL       TEMP,ST(3)        ;TEMP=TEMP*ST(3)
```

Description: Multiplies the source by the destination operand, and stores the result at the destination operand. If no destination operand is given (only one operand is specified), ST is assumed to be the destination.

FMULP: Multiply Real and Pop

Category: Arithmetic instruction

Status affected:

F	E	D	C	B	A	9	8	7	6	5	4	3	2	1	Ø
B	C3	--	ST	--		C2	C1	CØ	IR		PE	UE	OE	ZE	DE	IE
										X	X	X		X	X

Coding examples:

```
FMULP      TEMP              ;ST=ST*TEMP
FMULP      TEMP,ST(3)        ;TEMP=TEMP*ST(3)
```

Description: Multiplies the source by the destination operand, stores the result at the destination operand, and pops the stack. If no destination operand is given (only one operand is specified), ST is assumed to be the destination.

FNCLEX: Clear Exceptions

Category: Processor-control instruction

Status affected:

F	E	D	C	B	A	9	8	7	6	5	4	3	2	1	Ø
B	C3	--	ST	--	C2	C1	CØ	IR		PE	UE	OE	ZE	DE	IE
X								X		X	X	X	X	X	X

Coding example:

```
FNCLEX
```

Description: Clears the exception flags, interrupt request, and busy flags of the 8087 status word. This instruction is not preceded by a CPU wait prefix. See also FCLEX.

FNDISI: Disable Interrupts

Category: Processor-control instruction

Status affected: None

Coding example:

```
FNDISI
```

Description: Sets the interrupt enable mask of the 8087 control word, thus preventing the 8087 from initiating an interrupt. This instruction is not preceded by a CPU wait prefix. See also FDISI.

FNENI: Enable Interrupts

Category: Processor-control instruction

Status affected: None

Coding example:

```
FNENI
```

Description: Clears the interrupt enable mask of the 8087 control word, thus allowing the 8087 to initiate interrupts. This instruction is not preceded by a CPU wait prefix. See also FENI.

FNINIT: Initialize Processor

Category: Processor-control instruction

Status affected: None

Coding example:

```
FNINIT
```

Description: Initializes the 8087. This action is functionally equivalent to performing a hardware RESET. This instruction is not preceded by a CPU wait prefix. See also FINIT.

FNOP: No Operation

Category: Processor-control instruction

Status affected: None

Coding example:

```
FNOP
```

Description: Does nothing but take time and space—the 8087 performs no operation.

FNSAVE: Save State

Category: Processor-control instruction

Status affected: None

Coding example:

```
FNSAVE     SAVE_AREA
```

Description: Saves, at the memory location specified by the operand, all registers and environment variables of the 8087. This save requires 94 words of memory. After the save, the 8087 is initialized as though the FINIT or FNINIT instructions had been issued. This instruction (FNSAVE) is not preceded by a CPU wait prefix. See also FSAVE.

FNSTCW: Store Control Word

Category: Processor-control instruction

Status affected: None

Coding example:

```
FNSTCW    MEM_CW     ;Transfer control word
```

Description: Copies the 8087 control word to the word value pointed to by the source operand. This instruction is not preceded by a CPU wait prefix. See also FSTCW.

FNSTENV: Store Environment

Category: Processor-control instruction

Status affected: None

Coding example:

```
FNSTENV   SAVE_AREA
```

Description: Saves, at the memory location specified by the operand, all environment variables of the 8087. This save requires 14 words of memory. After the save, this instruction sets the exception masks of the 8087 control word. This instruction is not preceded by a CPU wait prefix. See also FSTENV.

FNSTSW: Store Status Word

Category: Processor-control instruction

Status affected: None

Coding example:

```
FNSTSW    MEM_SW     ;Transfer status word
```

Description: Copies the 8087 status word to the word value pointed to by the source operand. This instruction is not preceded by a CPU wait prefix. See also FSTSW.

FPATAN: Partial Arctangent

Category: Transcendental instruction

Status affected:

F	E	D	C	B	A	9	8	7	6	5	4	3	2	1	Ø
B	C3	--	ST	--	C2	C1	CØ	IR		PE	UE	OE	ZE	DE	IE
										X	X				

Coding example:

```
FPATAN
```

Description: Computes Θ=ARCTAN(Y/X), where X is the top stack element (ST) and Y is the second stack element (ST(1)). Both stack elements are popped, and the result (0) is pushed on the stack and becomes ST. This instruction performs no validation checking of the input value. The program ensures that 0<Y<X<∞.

FPREM: Partial Remainder

Category: Arithmetic instruction

Status affected:

F	E	D	C	B	A	9	8	7	6	5	4	3	2	1	Ø
B	C3	--	ST	--		C2	C1	CØ	IR		PE	UE	OE	ZE	DE	IE
	X					X	X				X			X	X

Coding example:

```
FPREM
```

Description: Calculates the modulo of the two top stack elements. By successively subtracting ST(1) from ST, an exact remainder is calculated and remains in ST.

FPTAN: Partial Tangent

Category: Transcendental instruction

Status affected:

F	E	D	C	B	A	9	8	7	6	5	4	3	2	1	Ø
B	C3	--	ST	--		C2	C1	CØ	IR		PE	UE	OE	ZE	DE	IE
											X					X

Coding example:

```
FPTAN
```

Description: Computes Y/X=TAN(Θ), where Θ is the top stack element (ST). The top stack element is replaced by the computed Y, and the computed X is pushed on the stack. Thus, at the end of this operation, ST(1)=Y and ST=X. This instruction performs no validation checking of the input value. The program ensures that $0<=\Theta<=\pi4$.

FRNDINT: Round to Integer

Category: Arithmetic instruction

Status affected:

F	E	D	C	B	A	9	8	7	6	5	4	3	2	1	Ø
B	C3	--	ST	--		C2	C1	CØ	IR		PE	UE	OE	ZE	DE	IE
											X					X

Coding example:

```
FRNDINT
```

Description: Rounds the number in the top stack element (ST) to an integer

FRSTOR: Restore State

Category: Processor-control instruction

Status affected:

F	E	D	C	B	A	9	8	7	6	5	4	3	2	1	Ø
B	C3	--	ST	--		C2	C1	CØ	IR		PE	UE	OE	ZE	DE	IE
X	X	X	X	X	X	X	X	X	X	X	X	X	X	X	X

Coding example:

```
FRSTOR     SAVE_AREA
```

Description: Restores all registers and environment variables of the 8087 from the 94-word memory location specified by the operand

FSAVE: Save State with WAIT

Category: Processor-control instruction

Status affected: None

Coding example:

```
FSAVE      SAVE_AREA
```

Description: Saves, at the memory location specified by the operand, all registers and environment variables of the 8087. This save requires 94 words of memory. After the save, the 8087 is initialized as though the FINIT or FNINIT instructions had been issued. This instruction (FSAVE) is preceded by a CPU wait prefix. See also FNSAVE.

FSCALE: Scale

Category: Arithmetic instruction

Status affected:

F	E	D	C	B	A	9	8	7	6	5	4	3	2	1	Ø
B	C3	--	ST	--	C2	C1	CØ	IR		PE	UE	OE	ZE	DE	IE
											X	X			X

Coding example:

```
FSCALE
```

Description: Calculates $X = X*2^Y$, where X is the value of the top stack element (ST), and Y is the value of the second stack element (ST(1))

FSQRT: Square Root

Category: Arithmetic instruction

Status affected:

F	E	D	C	B	A	9	8	7	6	5	4	3	2	1	Ø
B	C3	--	ST	--	C2	C1	CØ	IR		PE	UE	OE	ZE	DE	IE
										X				X	X

Coding example:

```
FSQRT
```

Description: Calculates the square root of the top stack element (ST) and stores it as the new ST. The old ST is lost.

FST: Store Real

Category: Data-transfer instruction

Status affected:

F	E	D	C	B	A	9	8	7	6	5	4	3	2	1	Ø
B	C3	--	ST	--	C2	C1	CØ	IR		PE	UE	OE	ZE	DE	IE
										X	X	X			X

Coding examples:

```
FST        ST(3)
FST        TEMP
```

Description: Copies the value of the top stack element (ST) to the operand or operand address

FSTCW: Store Control Word with WAIT

Category: Processor-control instruction

Status affected: None

Coding example:

```
FSTCW      MEM_CW      ;Transfer control word
```

Description: Copies the 8087 control word to the word value pointed to by the source operand. This instruction is preceded by a CPU wait prefix. See also FNSTCW.

FSTENV: Store Environment with WAIT

Category: Processor-control instruction

Status affected: None

Coding example:

```
FSTENV    SAVE_AREA
```

Description: Saves, at the memory location specified by the operand, all environment variables of the 8087. This save requires 14 words of memory. After the save, this instruction sets the exception masks of the 8087 control word. This instruction is preceded by a CPU wait prefix. See also FNSTENV.

FSTP: Store Real and Pop

Category: Data-transfer instruction

Status affected:

F	E	D	C	B	A	9	8	7	6	5	4	3	2	1	Ø
B	C3	--	ST	--	C2	C1	CØ	IR		PE	UE	OE	ZE	DE	IE
										X	X	X			X

Coding examples:

```
FSTP      ST(3)
FSTP      TEMP
```

Description: Copies the value of the top stack element (ST) to the operand or operand address, and pops the stack

FSTSW: Store Status Word with WAIT

Category: Processor-control instruction

Status affected: None

Coding example:

```
FSTSW     MEM_SW      ;Transfer status word
```

Description: Copies the 8087 status word to the word value pointed to by the source operand. This instruction is preceded by a CPU wait prefix. See also FNSTSW.

FSUB: Subtract Real

Category: Arithmetic instruction

Status affected:

F	E	D	C	B	A	9	8	7	6	5	4	3	2	1	Ø
B	C3	--	ST	--		C2	C1	CØ	IR		PE	UE	OE	ZE	DE	IE
											X	X	X		X	X

Coding examples:

```
FSUB        TEMP              ;ST=ST-TEMP
FSUB        TEMP,ST(3)        ;TEMP=TEMP-ST(3)
```

Description: Subtracts the source from the destination operand, and stores the result at the destination operand. If no destination operand is given (only one operand is specified), ST is assumed to be the destination.

FSUBP: Subtract Real and Pop

Category: Arithmetic instruction

Status affected:

F	E	D	C	B	A	9	8	7	6	5	4	3	2	1	Ø
B	C3	--	ST	--		C2	C1	CØ	IR		PE	UE	OE	ZE	DE	IE
											X	X	X		X	X

Coding examples:

```
FSUBP       TEMP              ;ST=ST-TEMP
FSUBP       TEMP,ST(3)        ;TEMP=TEMP-ST(3)
```

Description: Subtracts the source from the destination operand, stores the result at the destination operand, and pops the stack. If no destination operand is given (only one operand is specified), ST is assumed to be the destination.

FSUBR: Subtract Real Reversed

Category: Arithmetic instruction

Status affected:

F	E	D	C	B	A	9	8	7	6	5	4	3	2	1	Ø
B	C3	--	ST	--		C2	C1	CØ	IR		PE	UE	OE	ZE	DE	IE
											X	X	X		X	X

Coding examples:

```
FSUBR       TEMP            ;ST=TEMP-ST
FSUBR       TEMP,ST(3)      ;TEMP=ST(3)-TEMP
```

Description: Subtracts the destination from the source operand and stores the result at the destination operand. If no destination operand is given (only one operand is specified), ST is assumed to be the destination.

FSUBRP: Subtract Real Reversed and Pop

Category: Arithmetic instruction

Status affected:

F	E	D	C	B	A	9	8	7	6	5	4	3	2	1	Ø
B	C3	--	ST	--		C2	C1	CØ	IR		PE	UE	OE	ZE	DE	IE
											X	X	X		X	X

Coding examples:

```
FSUBRP      TEMP            ;ST=TEMP-ST
FSUBRP      TEMP,ST(3)      ;TEMP=ST(3)-TEMP
```

Description: Subtracts the destination from the source operand, stores the result at the destination operand, and pops the stack. If no destination operand is given (only one operand is specified), ST is assumed to be the destination.

FTST: Test

Category: Comparison instruction

Status affected:

F	E	D	C	B	A	9	8	7	6	5	4	3	2	1	Ø
B	C3	--	ST	--	C2	C1	CØ	IR		PE	UE	OE	ZE	DE	IE
	X				X		X							X	X

Coding example:

FTST

Description: Compares the top stack element (ST) to zero and sets the condition codes accordingly

FWAIT: CPU Wait

Category: Processor-control instruction

Status affected: None

Coding example:

FWAIT

Description: Effectively the same as the 8086/8088 WAIT command. This instruction permits the synchronization of the 8086/8088 and the 8087. It causes the 8086/8088 to suspend operation until reception of a signal which indicates that the 8087 has completed the last operation.

FXAM: Examine

Category: Comparison instruction

Status affected:

F	E	D	C	B	A	9	8	7	6	5	4	3	2	1	Ø
B	C3	--	ST	--	C2	C1	CØ	IR		PE	UE	OE	ZE	DE	IE
	X				X	X	X								

Coding example:

FXAM

Description: Examines the top stack element (ST) and reports (in the condition codes) the condition, or attributes, of the value.

FXCH: Exchange Registers

Category: Data-transfer instruction

Status affected:

F	E	D	C	B	A	9	8	7	6	5	4	3	2	1	Ø
B	C3	--	ST	--		C2	C1	CØ	IR		PE	UE	OE	ZE	DE	IE
																X

Coding examples:

```
FXCH      ST(3)
FXCH      TEMP
```

Description: Switches the value of the top stack element (ST) with that of the operand

FXTRACT: Extract Exponent and Significand

Category: Arithmetic instruction

Status affected:

F	E	D	C	B	A	9	8	7	6	5	4	3	2	1	Ø
B	C3	--	ST	--		C2	C1	CØ	IR		PE	UE	OE	ZE	DE	IE
																X

Coding example:

```
FXTRACT
```

Description: Removes the top stack element (ST) and converts it to two numbers—the exponent and significand of the original number. The exponent is pushed on the stack, followed by the significand, which results in ST=significand and ST(1)=exponent.

FYL2X: $Y*\log_2 X$

Category: Transcendental instruction

Status affected:

F	E	D	C	B	A	9	8	7	6	5	4	3	2	1	Ø
B	C3	--	ST	--		C2	C1	CØ	IR		PE	UE	OE	ZE	DE	IE
											X					

Coding example:

```
FYL2X
```

Description: Calculates $Z = Y * LOG_2 X$, where X is the top stack element (ST) and Y is the second stack element (ST(1)). Both stack elements are popped, and the result (Z) is pushed on the stack and becomes the new ST. This instruction performs no validation checking of the input value. The program ensures that $0 < X < \infty$ and $-\infty < Y < +\infty$.

FYL2XP1: $Y * \log_2(X+1)$

Category: Transcendental instruction

Status affected:

F	E	D	C	B	A	9	8	7	6	5	4	3	2	1	Ø
B	C3	--	ST	--		C2	C1	CØ	IR		PE	UE	OE	ZE	DE	IE
											X					

Coding example:

```
FYL2XP1
```

Description: Calculates $Z = Y * LOG_2(X=1)$, where X is the top stack element (ST) and Y is the second stack element (ST(1)). Both stack elements are popped, and the result (Z) is pushed on the stack and becomes the new ST. This instruction performs no validation checking of the input value. The program ensures that $0 < |X| < (1 - (\sqrt{2}/2))$ and $-\infty < Y < +\infty$.

Instruction Set
for the Intel 80287

As with the 8087, Intel calls the 80287 a "numeric processor extension" because, to all intents and purposes, the 80287 appears transparent to programmers. The instruction and register sets of the 80286 simply seem to have been expanded.

A descendent of the 8087, the 80287 is similar in function to the 8087. Most instructions that work on the 8087 also work correctly on the 80287. Changes to the instruction set include the deletion of several processor-control instructions (FDISI, FENI, FNDISI, and FNENI) and the addition of a new processor-control instruction (FSETPM). Because of the limited number of changes to the 8087 instruction set, and because the 8087 instructions will work on the 80287, this section contains general information about the 80287 and details the new processor-control instruction (FSETPM). (Refer to the section on the 8087 for other instructions that apply to the 80287.)

To use the 80287 mnemonic instructions with the Microsoft Macro Assembler, you need no special assembler directives. The assembler's default instruction set allows for the proper translation of 80286 and 80287 source code. You may want to study Chapter 6, however, to learn about assembler options. Pay particular attention to the /R option.

This section, which does not explain all the intricacies of using the 80287 properly or efficiently, is designed as quick reference material for programmers who want to use the 80287 instruction extensions. For those who want an in-depth look at the 80287, other books are available.

Before you begin looking at the register and instruction sets of the 80287, you should realize that the 80287 works on the principle of a floating stack (similar to the 80286), in which virtually all operations are performed.

The 80287 Registers

Each of the eight internal stack registers (numbered 0 through 7) used by the 80287 is 80 bits wide. Most operations are able to address these registers directly as ST, ST(1), ST(2), ST(3), etc., through ST(7).

The 80287 Status Word

The 80287 uses a status word to describe the current condition of the 80287. This 16-bit word is shown in table 80287.1.

Table 80287.1
Using the 80287 Status Word

Bit(s)	Code	Use
0	IE	Invalid operation exception
1	DE	Denormalized operand exception
2	ZE	Zerodivide exception
3	OE	Overflow exception
4	UE	Underflow exception
5	PE	Precision exception
6		Reserved
7	ES	Error summary status
8	C0	Condition code 0
9	C1	Condition code 1
10	C2	Condition code 2
11 – 13	ST	Stack top pointer
14	C3	Condition code 3
15	B	Busy signal

This status word cannot be examined directly. Specific 80287 instructions must be used for transferring the status word to memory, where it can be analyzed by 80286 instructions.

The 80287 Control Word

The 80287 uses a control word to allow program control of the operations of the 80287. This 16-bit word is detailed in table 80287.2.

Table 80287.2
Using the 80287 Control Word

Bit(s)	Code	Use
0	IM	Invalid operation exception mask
1	DM	Denormalized operand exception mask
2	ZM	Zerodivide exception mask
3	OM	Overflow exception mask
4	UM	Underflow exception mask
5	PM	Precision exception mask

Table 80287.2—cont.

Bit(s)	Code	Use
6		Reserved
7		Reserved
8 – 9	PC	Precision control
		00 = 24 bits
		01 = (Reserved)
		10 = 53 bits
		11 = 64 bits
10 – 11	RC	Rounding control
		00 = Round to nearest or even
		01 = Round down
		10 = Round up
		11 = Truncate
12	IC	Infinity control
		0 = Projective
		1 = Affine
13		Reserved
14		Reserved
15		Reserved

This word can be constructed in main memory and then directed to the 80287 by specific 80287 instructions.

Instruction Set Information

The 80287 extends (by 74 instructions) the instruction set of the 80286. Not all of these instructions will be examined here, however. (Refer to the section on the 8087 for the instructions used by both the 8087 and the 80287.)

Several 8087 instructions (FDISI, FENI, FNDISI, and FNENI) have no counterpart in the instruction set of the 80287. Although programs for the 80287 should avoid these instructions, using them will not cause problems on the 80287—the 80287 will treat these instructions as "NOP" values, and no operation will occur.

Only one additional instruction particular to the 80287 (FSETPM) is detailed here. This instruction, which falls under the category of processor control, is used to set protected mode for the 80287.

FSETPM: Set Protected Mode

Category: Processor-control instruction

Status affected: None

Coding example:

```
FSETPM
```

Description: Causes the 80287 to operate in protected mode. Normally, the operation mode is of no concern to programmers of applications software.

A

ASCII Character Set

ASCII Value	Character	Control Character	ASCII Value	Character	Control Character
000	(null)	NUL	016	►	DLE
001	☺	SOH	017	◄	DC1
002	●	STX	018	↕	DC2
003	♥	ETX	019	‼	DC3
004	♦	EOT	020	¶	DC4
005	♣	ENQ	021	§	NAK
006	♠	ACK	022	▬	SYN
007	(beep)	BEL	023	↨	ETB
008	■	BS	024	↑	CAN
009	(tab)	HT	025	↓	EM
010	(line feed)	LF	026	→	SUB
011	(home)	VT	027	←	ESC
012	(form feed)	FF	028	(cursor right)	FS
013	(carriage return)	CR	029	(cursor left)	GS
014	♪♪	SO	030	(cursor up)	RS
015	☼	SI	031	(cursor down)	US

ASCII Value	Character	ASCII Value	Character
032	(space)	069	E
033	!	070	F
034	''	071	G
035	#	072	H
036	$	073	I
037	%	074	J
038	&	075	K
039	'	076	L
040	(	077	M
041	)	078	N
042	*	079	O
043	+	080	P
044	,	081	Q
045	-	082	R
046	.	083	S
047	/	084	T
048	0	085	U
049	1	086	V
050	2	087	W
051	3	088	X
052	4	089	Y
053	5	030	Z
054	6	091	[
055	7	092	\
056	8	093	]
057	9	094	∧
058	:	095	—
059	;	096	'
060	<	097	a
061	=	098	b
062	>	099	c
063	?	100	d
064	@	101	e
065	A	102	f
066	B	103	g
067	C	104	h
068	D	105	i

ASCII Value	Character	ASCII Value	Character
106	j	143	Å
107	k	144	É
108	l	145	æ
109	m	146	Æ
110	n	147	ô
111	o	148	ö
112	p	149	ò
113	q	150	û
114	r	151	ù
115	s	152	ÿ
116	t	153	Ö
117	u	154	Ü
118	v	155	¢
119	w	156	£
120	x	157	¥
121	y	158	Pt
122	z	159	ƒ
123	{	160	á
124	|	161	í
125	}	162	ó
126	~	163	ú
127	⌂	164	ñ
128	Ç	165	Ñ
129	ü	166	ª
130	é	167	º
131	â	168	¿
132	ä	169	⌐
133	à	170	¬
134	å	171	½
135	ç	172	¼
136	ê	173	¡
137	ë	174	«
138	è	175	»
139	ï	176	░
140	î	177	▒
141	ì	178	▓
142	Ä	179	│

ASCII Value	Character		ASCII Value	Character
180	┤		218	┌
181	╡		219	█
182	╢		220	▄
183	╖		221	▌
184	╕		222	▐
185	╣		223	▀
186	║		224	α
187	╗		225	β
188	╝		226	Γ
189	╜		227	π
190	╛		228	Σ
191	┐		229	σ
192	└		230	μ
193	┴		231	τ
194	┬		232	Φ
195	├		233	Θ
196	─		234	Ω
197	┼		235	δ
198	╞		236	∞
199	╟		237	$\emptyset$
200	╚		238	ϵ
201	╔		239	$\cap$
202	╩		240	$\equiv$
203	╦		241	$\pm$
204	╠		242	$\geq$
205	═		243	$\leq$
206	╬		244	$\lceil$
207	╧		245	$\rfloor$
208	╨		246	$\div$
209	╤		247	$\approx$
210	╥		248	$\circ$
211	╙		249	$\bullet$
212	╘		250	$\cdot$
213	╒		251	$\sqrt{}$
214	╓		252	n
215	╫		253	^{2}
216	╪		254	■
217	┘		255	(blank 'FF')

B

The Disk Base Table

The disk base table is a set of parameters that controls the operation of a disk drive. Most of these parameters help directly govern the drive controller.

The location of the disk base table can be determined from the vector at interrupt 1Eh. This vector points to the RAM address where the table begins. In the early days of DOS (Version 1.0), the disk base table was contained in ROM. Now, this table is constructed and vectored when you load DOS so that system changes in DOS can be reflected in the disk operation.

Table B.1 details the makeup of the disk base table. The values in this table will differ according to the needs of your particular version of DOS or the disk drives you use in your computer.

Table B.1
The Disk Base Table for Controlling Disk Drives

Byte	Meaning
0	Step rate/head unload time in milliseconds
1	Head load time, DMA mode in milliseconds
2	Motor turn-off delay in clock ticks
3	Bytes/sector code
	0 = 128 bytes/sector
	1 = 256 bytes/sector
	2 = 512 bytes/sector
	3 = 1024 bytes/sector
4	Sectors per track
5	Inter-sector gap length for read/write operations
6	Data length (if sector length not specified)
7	Inter-sector gap length for formatting
8	Initial data value for newly formatted sectors
9	Head settle time in milliseconds
10	Motor start-up time in 1/8 second increments

Occasionally, you must change the contents of this table to perform certain BIOS operations, especially if you format 360K floppy disks on an IBM Personal Computer AT or compatible. (For additional information, refer to Chapter 12.)

C

Keyboard Interpretation Tables

This appendix contains two tables that will be useful when you interface to the keyboard, either through BIOS or directly through the hardware port.

BIOS Keyboard Codes

Table C.1 shows the scan code/ASCII value combinations that are returned through the BIOS keyboard services. The keyboard controller does not return the scan codes directly. Instead, BIOS translates (into the codes shown in this table) the codes it gives to the keyboard controller.

Table C.1
BIOS Keyboard Codes

Scan Code		ASCII Value		
Decimal	*Hex*	*Decimal*	*Hex*	*Keystroke*
0	00	0	00	Break
1	01	27	1B	Esc
2	02	49	31	1
		33	21	!
3	03	50	32	2
		64	40	@
		0	00	Ctrl-@
4	04	51	33	3
		35	23	#
5	05	52	34	4
		36	24	$
6	06	53	35	5
		37	25	%

Table C.1—cont.

Scan Code		ASCII Value		Keystroke
Decimal	Hex	Decimal	Hex	
7	07	54	36	6
		94	5E	^
		30	1E	Ctrl-^
8	08	55	37	7
		38	26	&
9	09	56	38	8
		42	2A	* (shift-8)
10	0A	57	39	9
		40	28	(
11	0B	48	30	0
		41	29	)
12	0C	45	2D	-
		95	5F	_
		31	1F	Ctrl-_
13	0D	61	3D	=
		43	2B	+
14	0E	8	08	backspace
		127	7F	Ctrl-backspace
15	0F	9	09	tab
		0	00	back tab
16	10	113	71	q
		81	51	Q
		0	00	Alt-Q
		17	11	Ctrl-Q
17	11	119	77	w
		87	57	W
		0	00	Alt-W
		23	17	Ctrl-W
18	12	101	65	e
		69	45	E
		0	00	Alt-E
		5	05	Ctrl-E

Table C.1—cont.

Scan Code		ASCII Value		
Decimal	Hex	Decimal	Hex	Keystroke
19	13	114	72	r
		82	52	R
		0	00	Alt-R
		18	12	Ctrl-R
20	14	116	74	t
		84	54	T
		0	00	Alt-T
		20	14	Ctrl-T
21	15	121	79	y
		89	59	Y
		0	00	Alt-Y
		25	19	Ctrl-Y
22	16	117	75	u
		85	55	U
		0	00	Alt-U
		21	15	Ctrl-U
23	17	105	69	i
		73	49	I
		0	00	Alt-I
		9	09	Ctrl-I
24	18	111	6F	o
		79	4F	O
		0	00	Alt-O
		15	0F	Ctrl-O
25	19	112	70	p
		80	50	P
		0	00	Alt-P
		16	10	Ctrl-P
26	1A	91	5B	[
		123	7B	{
		27	1B	Ctrl-[
27	1B	93	5D	]
		125	7D	}
		29	1D	Ctrl-]

Table C.1—cont.

| Scan Code | | ASCII Value | | |
Decimal	Hex	Decimal	Hex	Keystroke
28	1C	13	0D	Return
30	1E	97	61	a
		65	41	A
		0	00	Alt-A
		1	01	Ctrl-A
31	1F	115	73	s
		83	53	S
		0	00	Alt-S
		19	13	Ctrl-S
32	20	100	64	d
		68	44	D
		0	00	Alt-D
		4	04	Ctrl-D
33	21	102	66	f
		70	46	F
		0	00	Alt-F
		6	06	Ctrl-F
34	22	103	67	g
		71	47	G
		0	00	Alt-G
		7	47	Ctrl-G
35	23	104	68	h
		72	48	H
		0	00	Alt-H
		8	08	Ctrl-H
36	24	106	6A	j
		74	4A	J
		0	00	Alt-J
		10	0A	Ctrl-J
37	25	107	6B	k
		75	4B	K
		0	00	Alt-K
		11	0B	Ctrl-K

Table C.1—cont.

Scan Code		ASCII Value		
Decimal	Hex	Decimal	Hex	Keystroke
38	26	108	6C	l
		76	4C	L
		0	00	Alt-L
		12	0C	Ctrl-L
39	27	59	3B	;
		58	3A	:
40	28	39	27	'
		34	22	"
41	29	96	60	` (accent grave)
		126	7E	~
43	2B	92	5C	\
		124	7C	|
		28	1C	Ctrl-\
44	2C	122	7A	z
		90	5A	Z
		0	00	Alt-Z
		26	1A	Ctrl-Z
45	2D	120	78	x
		88	58	X
		0	00	Alt-X
		24	18	Ctrl-X
46	2E	99	63	c
		67	43	C
		0	00	Alt-C
		3	03	Ctrl-C
47	2F	118	76	v
		86	56	V
		0	00	Alt-V
		22	16	Ctrl-V
48	30	98	62	b
		66	42	B
		0	00	Alt-B
		2	02	Ctrl-B

Table C.1—cont.

Scan Code		ASCII Value		
Decimal	Hex	Decimal	Hex	Keystroke
49	31	110	6E	n
		78	4E	N
		0	00	Alt-N
		14	0E	Ctrl-N
50	32	109	6D	m
		77	4D	M
		0	00	Alt-M
		13	0D	Ctrl-M
51	33	44	2C	,
		60	3C	<
52	34	46	2E	.
		62	3E	>
53	35	47	2F	/
		63	3F	?
55	37	42	2A	* (next to keypad)
		0	00	Alt-Pause
56	38	0	00	Alt-Break
57	39	32	20	space
58	3A	0	00	Caps Lock
59	3B	0	00	F1
60	3C	0	00	F2
61	3D	0	00	F3
62	3E	0	00	F4
63	3F	0	00	F5
64	40	0	00	F6
65	41	0	00	F7
66	42	0	00	F8
67	43	0	00	F9
68	44	0	00	F10

Table C.1—cont.

Scan Code		ASCII Value		
Decimal	Hex	Decimal	Hex	Keystroke
69	45	0	00	Num Lock
70	46	0	00	Scroll Lock
71	47	0	00	Home
		55	37	7 (keypad)
72	48	0	00	up-arrow
		56	38	8 (keypad)
73	49	0	00	PgUp
		57	39	9 (keypad)
74	4A	45	2D	- (next to keypad)
75	4B	0	00	left-arrow
		52	34	4 (keypad)
76	4C	0	00	center key on keypad
		53	35	5 (keypad)
77	4D	0	00	right-arrow
		54	36	6 (keypad)
78	4E	43	2B	+ (next to keypad)
79	4F	0	00	End
		49	31	1 (keypad)
80	50	0	00	down-arrow
		50	32	2 (keypad)
81	51	0	00	PgDn
		51	33	3 (keypad)
82	52	0	00	Ins
		48	30	0 (keypad)
83	53	0	00	Del
		46	2E	. (keypad)
84	54	0	00	shift-F1
85	55	0	00	shift-F2
86	56	0	00	shift-F3

Table C.1—cont.

Scan Code		ASCII Value		
Decimal	Hex	Decimal	Hex	Keystroke
87	57	0	00	shift-F4
88	58	0	00	shift-F5
89	59	0	00	shift-F6
90	5A	0	00	shift-F7
91	5B	0	00	shift-F8
92	5C	0	00	shift-F9
93	5D	0	00	shift-F10
94	5E	0	00	Ctrl-F1
95	5F	0	00	Ctrl-F2
96	60	0	00	Ctrl-F3
97	61	0	00	Ctrl-F4
98	62	0	00	Ctrl-F5
99	63	0	00	Ctrl-F6
100	64	0	00	Ctrl-F7
101	65	0	00	Ctrl-F8
102	66	0	00	Ctrl-F9
103	67	0	00	Ctrl-F10
104	68	0	00	Alt-F1
105	69	0	00	Alt-F2
106	6A	0	00	Alt-F3
107	6B	0	00	Alt-F4
108	6C	0	00	Alt-F5
109	6D	0	00	Alt-F6
110	6E	0	00	Alt-F7

Table C.1—cont.

Scan Code		ASCII Value		
Decimal	Hex	Decimal	Hex	Keystroke
111	6F	0	00	Alt-F8
112	70	0	00	Alt-F9
113	71	0	00	Alt-F10
114	72	0	00	Ctrl-PrtSc
115	73	0	00	Ctrl-left arrow
116	74	0	00	Ctrl-right arrow
117	75	0	00	Ctrl-End
118	76	0	00	Ctrl-PgDn
119	77	0	00	Ctrl-Home
120	78	0	00	Alt-1 (keyboard)
121	79	0	00	Alt-2 (keyboard)
122	7A	0	00	Alt-3 (keyboard)
123	7B	0	00	Alt-4 (keyboard)
124	7C	0	00	Alt-5 (keyboard)
125	7D	0	00	Alt-6 (keyboard)
126	7E	0	00	Alt-7 (keyboard)
127	7F	0	00	Alt-8 (keyboard)
128	80	0	00	Alt-9 (keyboard)
129	81	0	00	Alt-0 (keyboard)
130	82	0	00	Alt-- (keyboard)
131	83	0	00	Alt-= (keyboard)
132	84	0	00	Ctrl-PgUp

Keyboard Controller Codes

Table C.2 shows the key codes returned when you access the keyboard controller through hardware port 60h. Notice that this table is a good deal shorter than table C.1. The keyboard controller does no translation on the Shift, Ctrl, and Alt keys. Each key is given a specific position value, which BIOS translates into the appropriate scan code/ASCII value combination.

Table C.2
Keyboard Controller Codes

Key Code Decimal	Hex	Key
1	01	Esc
2	02	1
3	03	2
4	04	3
5	05	4
6	06	5
7	07	6
8	08	7
9	09	8
10	0A	9
11	0B	0
12	0C	-
13	0D	=
14	0E	backspace
15	0F	tab
16	10	q
17	11	w
18	12	e
19	13	r
20	14	t

Table C.2—cont.

Key Code Decimal	Hex	Key
21	15	y
22	16	u
23	17	i
24	18	o
25	19	p
26	1A	[
27	1B	]
28	1C	Enter
29	1D	Ctrl
29/69	1D/45	Pause
30	1E	a
31	1F	s
32	20	d
33	21	f
34	22	g
35	23	h
36	24	j
37	25	k
38	26	l
39	27	;
40	28	'
41	29	` (accent grave)
42	2A	left shift
42/52	2A/34	PrtSc (enhanced keyboard)
42/71	2A/47	Home (middle, enhanced keyboard)

Table C.2—cont.

Key Code Decimal	Hex	Key
42/72	2A/48	up-arrow (middle, enhanced keyboard)
42/73	2A/49	PgUp (middle, enhanced keyboard)
42/75	2A/4B	left-arrow (middle, enhanced keyboard)
42/77	2A/4D	right-arrow (middle, enhanced keyboard)
42/79	2A/4F	End (middle, enhanced keyboard)
42/80	2A/50	down-arrow (middle, enhanced keyboard)
42/81	2A/51	PgDn (middle, enhanced keyboard)
42/82	2A/52	Insert (middle, enhanced keyboard)
42/83	2A/53	Del (middle, enhanced keyboard)
43	2B	\
44	2C	z
45	2D	x
46	2E	c
47	2F	v
48	30	b
49	31	n
50	32	m
51	33	,
52	34	.
53	35	/

Table C.2—cont.

Key Code Decimal	Hex	Key
54	36	right shift
55	37	* (next to keypad)
56	38	Alt
57	39	space
58	3A	Caps Lock
59	3B	F1
60	3C	F2
61	3D	F3
62	3E	F4
63	3F	F5
64	40	F6
65	41	F7
66	42	F8
67	43	F9
68	44	F10
69	45	Num Lock
70	46	Scroll Lock
71	47	Home (keypad)
72	48	up-arrow (keypad)
73	49	PgUp (keypad)
74	4A	- (next to keypad)
75	4B	left-arrow (keypad)
76	4C	5 (keypad)
77	4D	right-arrow (keypad)
78	4E	+ (next to keypad)
79	4F	End (keypad)

Table C.2—cont.

| Key Code | | Key |
Decimal	Hex	
80	50	down-arrow (keypad)
81	51	PgDn (keypad)
82	52	Ins (keypad)
83	53	Del (keypad)
84	54	[currently unused]
85	55	[currently unused]
86	56	[currently unused]
87	57	F11
88	58	F12

Some keys, especially on the enhanced 101-key keyboard, return double values. These values are shown with a slash between the two numbers and are placed in the order designated by the first number of the pair.

Each key is designated by the unshifted value shown on the keycap.

Glossary

Align type. An assembly language directive specifying how the start of the segment is to be aligned in memory. The align type is specified on the same line as the segment name. See also *BYTE, PAGE, PARA,* and *WORD*.

ALU. Arithmetic/Logic Unit, the portion of the CPU that performs arithmetic functions on data. The ALU controls the settings of the bits in the flags register.

ASCII. American Standard Code for Information Interchange.

ASCIIZ. An ASCII string that is terminated with a nul character (value of 0). ASCIIZ is used extensively in DOS interrupt services.

Assembler. The software program that translates (assembles) assembly language mnemonics into machine language for direct execution by the computer.

Assembly language. The pseudo-English language, called *source code*, that is written and hopefully readable by humans. Assembly language is not directly executable by a computer.

Assembly. The process of code conversion performed by an assembler. Assembly language source code is translated into machine language through this process.

AT. A segment combine type used generally to prepare a template to be used for accessing fixed location data. In the format *AT XXXX* (where *XXXX* is a memory address), *AT* signifies that addresses and offsets are to be calculated relative to the specified memory address. See also *Combine type, COMMON, MEMORY, PUBLIC,* and *STACK*.

Auxiliary carry flag. The bit in the flag register that indicates whether the previous decimal operation resulted in a carry out of or borrow into the four low-order bits of the byte.

AX. A general-purpose data register.

Base register. A register containing an address that is used as a base in indirect addressing methods. The base register is usually the BP or BX register.

Binary. A numbering system based on 2s. The only valid digits in a binary system are 0 and 1. See also *Bit*.

Bit. Binary digit, the smallest unit of storage on a computer. Each bit can have a value of 0 or 1, indicating the absence or presence of an electrical signal. See also *Binary*.

BP. The base pointer register.

BX. A general-purpose data register.

Byte. A basic unit of data storage and manipulation. A byte is equivalent to 8 bits and can contain a value ranging from 0 through 255.

BYTE. A segment align type that directs the assembler to place the segment at the next available byte after completing the preceding segment. See also *Align type*, *PAGE*, *PARA*, and *WORD*.

CALL. An assembly language instruction telling the assembler to perform the subroutine.

Carry flag. The bit in the flag register that indicates whether the previous operation resulted in a carry out of or borrow into the high-order bit of the resulting byte or word.

CGA. Color Graphics Adapter.

Class type. An assembler directive indicating how individual segments are to be grouped when linked. Segments having the same class type are loaded contiguously in memory before another class type is begun. The class type is specified on the same line as the segment name and is enclosed by single quotation marks.

Combine type. An optional assembler directive that defines how segments with the same name will be combined.

COMMON. A segment combine type. It causes individual segments of the same name and of the COMMON combine type to begin at a common memory address. All COMMON segments with the same name begin at the same point, with the resulting segment equal in length to the longest individual segment. All addresses and offsets in the resulting segment are relative to a single segment register. See also *AT*, *Combine type*, *MEMORY*, *PUBLIC*, and *STACK*.

CPU. The microprocessor (central processing unit) responsible for operations within the computer. These operations generally include system timing, logical processing, and logical operations.

CS. The code segment register.

CX. A general-purpose data register, usually used for counting functions.

DASD. Direct access storage device. The term is used extensively in the IBM Personal Computer AT BIOS listings.

DI. The destination index register.

Direction flag. The bit in the flag register that indicates whether string operations should increment (DF clear) or decrement (DF set) the index registers.

Displacement. An offset from a specified base point.

DMA. Direct memory access; a method of data transfer involving direct access of the RAM buffer area through specialized circuitry. DMA frees the CPU for other operations and results in a more efficient use of computer resources.

DOS. Disk Operating System.

DS. The data segment register.

DTA. A memory area (disk transfer area) used with FCB file operations for the transfer of information to and from the floppy disk. See also Chapter 13, service 21/1A.

DX. A general-purpose data register.

EGA. Enhanced Graphics Adapter.

ENDP. An assembler directive indicating the end of a procedure. See also *PROC*.

EQU. An assembly language directive (equate). See also *Equate*.

Equate. The full-word form of the assembly language instruction EQU. Equate assigns a value to a mnemonic label that is later substituted for other occurrences of the label during program assembly. See also *EQU*.

ES. The extra segment register.

FAR. A procedure that pushes the full return address (effectively the contents of CS:IP) on the stack. FAR is assumed to be in a code segment different from the current segment.

FCB. File Control Block.

Flag. An indicator used to control or signal other software or hardware functions.

Function. A self-contained coding segment designed to do a specific task. A function is sometimes referred to as a procedure or subroutine.

Graphics. A video presentation consisting mostly of pictures and figures instead of letters and numbers. See also *Text*.

Group. A collection of segments that fit within a 64K segment of RAM. At link time, LINK.EXE uses segment group classifications to determine how segments are combined.

Hexadecimal. A numbering system based on 16 elements. Digits are numbered 0 through F, as follows: 0, 1, 2, 3, 4, 5, 6, 7, 8, 9, A, B, C, D, E, F.

HGA. Hercules Graphics Adapter.

Index register. A register assumed to contain an address for use in indirect addressing modes. Usually, the index register consists of the SI (source index) or DI (destination index) registers.

Instruction Set. The group of mnemonic directions used to control a processor.

Interrupt flag. The bit in the flag register that indicates whether the CPU should handle maskable interrupts. If this flag is set, interrupts are handled. If it is clear, interrupts are ignored.

IP. The instruction pointer register.

LIB.EXE. The library management software distributed by Microsoft and IBM with their assemblers.

Library. A collection of object code modules saved in a single file. The assembler searches this file during the linking process to resolve external references in the main programs.

Linking. The process of resolving external references and address references in object code, resulting in machine language instructions that are directly executable by the computer.

Machine language. The series of binary digits that a microprocessor executes to perform individual tasks. People seldom (if ever) program in machine language. Instead, they program in assembly language, and an assembler translates their instructions into machine language.

MDA. Monochrome Display Adapter.

Memory map. An organized method of depicting the use of an area of computer memory.

MEMORY. A segment combine type that results in all segments with the same name being joined into one segment when linked. All addresses and offsets in the resulting segment relate to a single segment register. See also *AT*, *Combine type*, *COMMON*, *PUBLIC*, and *STACK*.

Monochrome. A single color.

NEAR. An assembly language directive that indicates the type of procedure you are creating. Issued on the same line as the PROC directive, NEAR controls how you call and return from the procedure.

Object code. A "halfway step" between source code and executable machine language. Object code consists mostly of machine language, but is not directly executable by the computer. It must first be linked in order to resolve external references and address references.

Offset. A distance from a given paragraph boundary in memory. The offset is usually given as a number of bytes.

Overflow flag. The bit in the flag register that indicates whether the signed result of the preceding operation can be represented in the result byte or word.

PAGE. A segment align type that directs the assembler, after it completes the preceding segment, to place the segment at the next available hexadecimal address ending in 00. See also *Align type*, *BYTE*, *PARA*, and *WORD*.

PARA. A segment align type that directs the assembler, after it completes the preceding segment, to place the segment at the next available hexadecimal address ending in 0. See also *Align type*, *BYTE*, *PAGE*, and *WORD*.

Parity flag. The bit in the flag register that indicates whether the low-order 8 bits of the result contain an even number (PF set) or odd number (PF clear) of bits equal to 1.

PROC. An assembly language directive indicating the start of a procedure. See also *ENDP*.

Procedure. A self-contained coding segment designed to do a specific task, sometimes referred to as a subroutine.

Pseudo-Op. A type of operation code that is not a direction to the microprocessor, but a command for the assembler or linker to follow when producing the executable file.

PSP. Program Segment Prefix.

PUBLIC. A segment combine type that results in all segments with the same name being joined into one segment when linked. All addresses and offsets in the resulting segment relate to a single segment register. See also *AT*, *Combine type*, *COMMON*, *MEMORY*, and *STACK*.

RAM. Random-Access Memory.

Register. The data-holding areas, usually 16 bits in length, used by the processor in performing operations.

ROM. Read-Only Memory.

Run-time system. A system manager that oversees proper operation of the language during program execution.

Segment. A particular area of memory, 64K in size.

Segment offset. The value to be added to the result of 16 times the segment value, thereby producing an absolute memory address.

Segment register. Any of the CPU registers designed to contain a segment address. They include the CS, DS, ES, and SS registers.

SI. The source index register.

Sign flag. The bit in the flag register that is set equal to the high-order bit of the result of the last operation.

Source code. The assembly language instructions, written by humans, that an assembler translates into object code.

SP. The stack pointer register.

SS. The stack segment register.

Stack. An area of memory set aside for the temporary storage of values in a computing environment. The stack operates in a LIFO fashion. In an 8088-based environment, only whole words (16 bits) can be pushed on and popped from the stack.

STACK. A segment combine type resulting in all segments with this combine type being joined to form one segment when linked. All addresses and offsets in the resulting segment are relative to the stack segment register. The SP register is initialized to the ending address of the segment. This combine type normally is used to define the stack area for a program. See also *AT*, *Combine type*, *COMMON*, *MEMORY*, and *PUBLIC*.

Subroutine. A self-contained coding segment designed to do a specific task, sometimes referred to as a procedure.

Text. A video presentation scheme consisting mostly of letters and numbers. See also *Graphics*.

Trap flag. The bit in the flag register that indicates a single-step instruction execution mode. If the trap flag is set, a single-step interrupt occurs. The flag then is cleared after the assembler executes the next instruction.

WAIT. An assembly language instruction (wait).

WORD. A segment align type that directs the assembler, after it completes the preceding segment, to place the segment at the next available even address. If the preceding segment ends on an odd address, WORD effectively is equivalent to BYTE. See also *Align type*, *BYTE*, *PAGE*, and *PARA*.

Zero flag. The bit in the flag register that indicates whether the result of the preceding operation is zero. If the result is zero, the flag is set. If the result is not zero, the flag is clear.

Index

C

E

H

I

J

K

More Computer Knowledge from Que

SELECT QUE BOOKS TO INCREASE
YOUR PERSONAL COMPUTER PRODUCTIVITY

C Programming Guide, 2nd Edition

by Jack Purdum, Ph.D.

To accommodate current revisions of the C language, Que has published a second edition of the *C Programming Guide*. This tutorial book expands and updates your knowledge of the applications introduced in the first edition. The second edition of the *C Programming Guide* gives numerous examples and illustrations to help you learn how to program in C. You won't want to miss the second edition of this best-selling C programming tutorial.

Turbo Pascal For BASIC Programmers

by Paul Garrison

If you write programs in BASIC, this book will help you advance to Pascal, a compiled programming language. *Turbo Pascal for BASIC Programmers* concentrates on a number of useful programs, comparing BASIC versions with their Pascal equivalents and thus familiarizing you with "structured programming." Additional features of this book include an appendix that explains some of the differences among the dialects of BASIC used by different computers, a comprehensive program library, and a glossary of computer terms and abbreviations for Pascal phrases.

C Programmer's Library

by Jack Purdum, Ph.D., Tim Leslie, and Alan Stegemoller

If you write programs in C, this book can save you hours of programming time and can help you write more efficient code. Techniques presented include a terminal installer, terminal handler, several sorting routines, and the ISAM functions. The book discusses design considerations in writing programs, and offers programming tips to help you take full advantage of the power of C. Use this book to improve your skills as a C programmer and gain highly useful additions to your C library.

Turbo Pascal Program Library

by Tom Rugg and Phil Feldman

This long-overdue tutorial satisfies the needs of Pascal users who are developing programs by the hit-or-miss method. Containing over 100 subprograms (procedures and functions), *Turbo Pascal Program Library* gives you more time to concentrate on your main program. This book will help you improve your techniques and increase your speed in writing programs in Pascal. Subprograms saved on disk can be incorporated into your main program easily by using a block move in edit mode or by using Turbo Pascal's compiler directive.

ORDER FROM QUE TODAY

Item	Title	Price	Quantity	Extension
188	C Programming Guide, 2nd Edition	$19.95		
45	C Programmer's Library	21.95		
184	Turbo Pascal for BASIC Programmers	18.95		
35	Turbo Pascal Program Library	19.95		

Book Subtotal	
Shipping & Handling ($2.50 per item)	
Indiana Residents Add 5% Sales Tax	
GRAND TOTAL	

Method of Payment:

☐ Check ☐ VISA ☐ MasterCard ☐ American Express

Card Number _____ Exp. Date _____

Cardholder's Name _____

Ship to _____

Address _____

City _____ State _____ ZIP _____

If you can't wait, call **1-800-428-5331** and order TODAY.

All prices subject to change without notice.

FOLD HERE

- -

Que Corporation
P.O. Box 90
Carmel, IN 46032

REGISTRATION CARD

Register your copy of *Using Assembly Language* and receive information about Que's newest products. Complete this registration card and return it to Que Corporation, P.O. Box 90, Carmel, IN 46032.

Name _____ Phone _____

Company _____ Title _____

Address _____

City _____ ST _____ ZIP _____

Please check the appropriate answers:

Where did you buy *Using Assembly Language*?
- ☐ Bookstore (name: _____)
- ☐ Computer store (name: _____)
- ☐ Catalog (name: _____)
- ☐ Direct from Que
- ☐ Other: (_____)

How many computer books do you buy a year?
- ☐ 1 or less   ☐ 6-10
- ☐ 2-5   ☐ More than 10

How many Que books do you own?
- ☐ 1   ☐ 6-10
- ☐ 2-5   ☐ More than 10

How long have you been programming?
- ☐ Less than 6 months   ☐ 1 to 3 years
- ☐ 6 months to 1 year   ☐ Over 3 years

Do you program in:
- ☐ C?   ☐ BASIC?
                      ☐ Pascal?
- ☐ Other? (_____)

What kind of assembler do you use?
_____

What kind of compiler do you use?
_____

What influenced your purchase of this book?
(More than one answer is OK.)
- ☐ Personal recommendation
- ☐ Advertisement   ☐ Price
- ☐ In-store display   ☐ Que catalog
                         ☐ Que postcard
                         ☐ Que's reputation
- ☐ Other: (_____)

How would you rate the overall content of *Using Assembly Language*?
- ☐ Very good   ☐ Not useful
- ☐ Good   ☐ Poor

How would you rate the *debugging chapter*?
- ☐ Very good   ☐ Not useful
- ☐ Good   ☐ Poor

How would you rate the chapters on *BIOS and DOS interrupts*?
- ☐ Very good   ☐ Not useful
- ☐ Good   ☐ Poor

What do you like *best* about *Using Assembly Language*?

What do you like *least* about *Using Assembly Language*?

Why did you buy *Using Assembly Language*?

How do you use this book?

What other Que products do you own?

What other software do you own?

Please feel free to list any other comments you may have about *Using Assembly Language*.

_____

_____

_____

_____

_____

_____

_____

FOLD HERE

_____

_____

_____

_____

Que Corporation
P.O. Box 90
Carmel, IN 46032